Baptism of Desire and Christian Salvation

Baptism of Desire and Christian Salvation

Anthony R. Lusvardi, SJ

The Catholic University of America Press
Washington, D.C.

Vidimus et approbamus ad normam
Statutorum Pontifcii Athenaei S. Anselmi.

Moderator: Prof. A. Grillo
Censor: R. D. M. Monfrinotti
Censor: R. P. S. Geiger, OSB
Romae, die 1 decembris 2021

NIHIL OBSTAT:
R. P. Bernhard A. Eckerstorfer, OSB
Rector Magnificus
Pontificii Athenaei S. Anselmi
Romae, die 5 septembris 2023

The paper used in this publication meets the minimum
requirements of American National Standards for
Information Science—Permanence of Paper for Printed
Library Materials, ANSI Z39.48-1992.
∞

Cataloging-in-Publication Data is available
at the Library of Congress
ISBN: 978-0-8132-3798-5
eISBN: 978-0-8132-3799-2

For Mom and Dad,
who gave me the gift of Baptism

Contents

Acknowledgments   ix

Introduction   1

Chapter One. Patristic Precursors   8

From the Apostles to the Apologists / 9

Controversy and Creativity in North Africa / 29

Cappadocian Skepticism / 42

Chapter Two. The Birth of the Doctrine   63

Ambrose of Milan and Valentinian's Salvation / 65

Augustinian Ambiguities / 77

The Late Patristic Period / 97

The Patristic Doctrine Summarized / 106

Chapter Three. The Medieval Crucible   110

Baptism in Flux: From the Fall of Rome to the Rise of
Scholasticism / 112

The Scholastic Debate / 121

Thomas Replies / 160

The Denouement of the Medieval Debate / 183

Chapter Four. The Crosscurrents of Early
Modernity   189
Theology Discovers America / 190
Cajetan's Gambit / 209
The Council of Trent / 214
Life after Trent / 230

Chapter Five. The Long Nineteenth Century   253
Revolution and Reaction / 254
Twentieth Century Turmoil / 279
The Rahnerian Turn and Vatican II / 303

Conclusion. Water, Blood, and Desire   331

Bibliography   363

Index   389

Acknowledgments

This book has been a long time in the making and has seen several incarnations. It first took shape as my S.T.L. *tesina* and then doctoral dissertation at the Pontifical Atheneum of St. Anselm in Rome; so thanks must go to the faculty, administration, and support staff at Sant'Anselmo for offering a thorough and stimulating program in sacramental theology. I was helped, in particular, by several advisors along the way: Giulio Meiattini, OSB, during the licentiate; Gregory Gresko, OSB, as I formulated my proposal; and Andrea Grillo, who accompanied the writing of the doctorate with encouragement, enthusiasm, and wisdom.

I could never have finished the project without the platoon of supporters who helped me with various aspects of preparing the text: Francesca Dore corrected the Italian of the first version; Tom Carroll, SJ, proofread the English chapters; and Sara Boehk performed the complicated and frustrating process of converting the text from Roman dissertation style into English legibility. Stephen Wolfe, SJ, was notably generous helping me when I was unsure of Latin and Greek translations. The clear advice of John Martino at Catholic University of America Press helped me cut down the text to the argument's heart. Vincent Strand, SJ, my readers Matteo Monfrinotti and Stefan Geiger, OSB, and the anonymous peer reviewers for CUAP also offered helpful insights that shaped the final text. Brian Dunkle, SJ, got me started on my research years ago by casually mentioning Marcia Colish's book on baptism, though I doubt he remembers doing so. And I'm thankful to Mark Lewis, SJ, and Giuseppe De Luccio, SJ, for helping with the necessary permissions from the Gregorian University for publication. Despite the best efforts of this diverse and generous band, I'm sure some mistakes still remain, and those are my responsibility alone.

Many more helped indirectly—what a stellar cast of teachers I had at Wilshire Park, St. Anthony High School, Notre Dame, Loyola, and Boston College. For Mom and Dad, I just don't have words. If I can't name everyone here, know that I am grateful and pray for you, nonetheless. I must, however, mention my superiors in the Society of Jesus and my companions—in Jogues House, the Collegio Bellarmino, and the Gregorian community—who showed so much care for me as a scholar, as a Jesuit, and as a person. Thanks for supporting me in this endeavor even if at times I was a most imperfect subject and brother. For the great calling to the Society of Jesus and for my mission, of which this book represents some small fruit, I am grateful, above all else, to the Lord.

Baptism of Desire and Christian Salvation

Introduction

What must we do to be saved?

In the Acts of the Apostles, when the guilt-ridden residents of Jerusalem pose this question to the Apostle Peter, he answers them, "Repent, and be baptized, every one of you" (Acts 2:38). For centuries, the rite of baptism has always figured into the Church's answer to this question; the necessity of baptism for salvation is among the most ancient and the most consistently affirmed of Christian doctrines. Baptism may not always have been sufficient for salvation—one also had to persevere in Christian fidelity—but it was a necessary threshold across which one had to pass to enter the kingdom of God, reflecting Christ's own passage through death to the resurrection.

The early Church's affirmation of the necessity of this rite occurred without hesitation or embarrassment, but the first Christians also confronted hard cases—paradigmatically, catechumens dying unexpectedly—that caused them to think that baptism's salvific reach must extend a bit further than the font. In the case of martyrs, it was relatively easy to see how this could happen; those who shed their blood for Christ could clearly be said "to be baptized with the baptism with which [Jesus was] baptized" (Mk 10:39). Baptism meant participation in the Lord's sacrificial death, and martyrs did exactly that. In other cases, the solution was not so obvious. This study addresses those hard cases and the doctrine that emerged from reflection on them—baptism of desire.

In brief, baptism of desire is the doctrine that someone who desires to be baptized but is prevented from reaching the sacrament by circumstances outside of his or her control will nonetheless receive the benefits of the sacrament, the most important of which is entry into eternal life. Today this seems straightforward enough, a matter of elementary fairness, but the doctrine provokes a host of questions. Does one have to request the sacrament explicitly? How much does one have to desire baptism to be saved? And if the benefits of baptism can be obtained without the sacrament, does that mean that baptism was not *really* necessary to begin with? If not, why bother with the rite at all? And if the rite can be left out, why not other things as well—the creed professed in baptism, for example? What about babies who die without baptism or in the womb?

The attention given to these questions has shifted over time. A major concern of twentieth-century and contemporary theologians has been the salvation of non-Christians, and baptism of desire has figured into discussions of this topic. Yet when one delves into the specifics of what such contemporary theologians have to say about baptism of desire, one discovers something curious. While they often acknowledge the doctrine as absolutely essential if any non-Christian is to be saved, recent theologians tend to brush past it with a minimum of attention. When I first began research on this topic, one professor I approached expressed skepticism. "Baptism of desire sounds a little old-fashioned, doesn't it?" he said. This attitude itself prompts what turns out to be an equally interesting, and perhaps even more fundamental, question: Why would this be the case? In other words, what changed between the Acts of the Apostles and today that made baptism of desire—and, when we get down to it, baptism—fall out of favor as a way of addressing salvation in "hard cases"?

To answer this question, we must embark on a rather extensive historical survey. This journey, however, will reward its length because, by focusing on issues on the margins of our theological understanding, we will see how theologians, pastors, and everyday Christians were forced to stretch their minds and their faith in search of answers. Some of those answers will turn out to be more creative than plausible, though even these sometimes reveal deeper truths; others will satisfy whole generations, but only because they reduce a larger problem to one of its parts, ignoring the real issues. Because this survey deals with a question somewhat on the margins of recent theology, it will call into question the categories often used to approach the issue of salvation. It will be, at least a little, disruptive.

Not all of the conventional narratives about the development of theology will stand up to scrutiny; moments thought to be decisive—the Age of Discovery, for example—will turn out to be rather ambiguous. Neglected periods, figures, and evidence will prove pivotal—a gravestone in Gaul, the School of Laon, an obscure passage from Cajetan. In the end, however, this study aims to do more than disrupt. It aims to offer an approach to salvation—especially to the hard cases—that is of practical benefit to theologians, pastors, missionaries, and Catholics in general.

I began this research with an intuition that the concept of baptism of desire offered something that other approaches left out. How many homilies have we heard that treat salvation as a reward for good behavior? And how much of the Christian faith does such moralism omit? *Baptism* of desire, on the other hand, maintains at least some connection to the Church's sacramental life; emphasizing *desire* also implies something important about the human will, freedom, and our ability to love. Of course, I was not yet sure exactly what it implied. Still, it seemed to me that, if what the Church had to say about salvation did not involve those two elements in a substantial way, then the Church probably did not have all that much worth saying. Why bother with *any* of the religious paraphernalia of Catholicism if what salvation really boiled down to was good behavior? As I read more deeply across historical periods and probed different styles of doing theology, this intuition grew. I now believe that a mature theology of baptism of desire provides the best approach to the hard cases of salvation. This is not because baptism of desire is guaranteed to give us the results we want or to provide the quickest formula to soothe our anxieties. It is the best approach because it is most grounded in revelation, theology, and the Church's sacramental practice; it leaves out the least and cuts the fewest corners.

This is, I admit, a rather bold claim since the general drift of theology over the past two centuries may be said to have been in a different direction. The burden falls on me to explain why this is the case. Our historical survey, therefore, aims to do two things: to identify and analyze the different expressions of the doctrine of baptism of desire that have appeared in Catholic theology, with a view to arriving at the strongest possible expression of the doctrine; and to explain how we got where we are. Patristic and medieval writers give radically different explanations of the doctrine than those which we find in the late twentieth century. The Fathers who first articulated the doctrine—Ambrose and Augustine—focused on the concrete cases of a catechumen dying before baptism and the Good Thief (Lk 23:40–43). The entry on baptism of desire by Gregory Baum in the great modern theological encyclopedia *Sacramentum Mundi*, on the other hand, defines the term as "the vast action of God to save and sanctify men outside the visible boundaries of the Church" and mentions the Anglican Archbishop John A.T. Robinson but neither Latin Father.[1] Neither catechumens nor biblical precedents figure into Baum's explanation. Ambrose and Augustine would have scratched their heads.

So, how did we get from Ambrose to Baum? To answer this question, we must start even before Ambrose, examining beliefs about the afterlife when Christianity entered history and how and why early Christians believed that a rite could be salvific (chapter one). We will also look at a few early "dead ends" proposed to deal with hard cases. We will perceive inklings of the doctrine as well as reasons it proved difficult to articulate. In chapter two, we will turn to Ambrose and Augustine, who put into place the essential elements for future development of the idea: the centrality of desire, its limits, the problem of original sin, the uniqueness of the rite, and the building blocks of scholastic sacramental theology. These provided the tools for understanding baptism of desire as a corollary to the necessity of baptism, rather than an exception to the rule.

The Middle Ages put the doctrine to the test, subjecting it to scrutiny and lively debate (chapter three). The outcome was a consensus in favor of baptism of desire accompanied by the theological loose ends that resulted from trying to squeeze Ambrose's idea into scholastic categories. Before plunging into the details of the scholastic debate, we will also examine the practice of the rite itself and how the social, political, and religious changes of the much-neglected early Middle Ages affected the way baptism was practiced. No chapter on medieval theology would be complete without an ample discussion of Thomas Aquinas, and we will chart the subtle

---

1. Gregory Baum, "Baptism of Desire," in *Sacramentum Mundi: An Encyclopedia of Theology*, vol. 1, ed. Karl Rahner, Juan Alfaro, Alberto Bellini (London: Burns & Oates, 1968), 145–46. Even the modern *Catechism* shows the effects of scholarly neglect; none of the references cited in the *Catechism*'s treatment of the doctrine actually refer to baptism of desire. *Catechism of the Catholic Church* (Vatican City: Libreria Editrice Vaticana, 1993), http://www.vatican.va/archive/ccc/index_it.htm, 1257–61.

evolution of the Angelic Doctor's treatment of the doctrine. Thomas will also provide us with a solid basis for tackling the concepts of necessity and implicit desire.

If the drama of our first three chapters is debate over whether baptism of desire is a legitimate concept at all, the narrative in the second half of the work becomes more complex and indirect. We will examine but eventually have to reject the popular hypothesis that the discovery of the Americas at the end of the fifteenth century produced a revolution in Catholic thinking about salvation (chapter four). We will also see baptism of desire find magisterial expression in the decrees of the Council of Trent and note a skirmish on the Council's sidelines over Cajetan's proposal to expand the concept to include infants and unborn children. After Trent, we will witness baptism of desire recede into the intricacies of baroque scholasticism.

When we reach the nineteenth century, subtle tendencies noted in the previous chapters will begin to take on a life of their own (chapter five). Scholastic intellectualism will merge with Enlightenment disdain for religious ritual as theology struggles to come to terms with what the collapse of Christendom means for salvation. In the twentieth century, Christianity's diminished cultural status produced such wildly different reactions as Leonard Feeney's insistence on the impossibility of salvation outside of the Church and Karl Rahner's Anonymous Christianity. Baptism of desire would be invoked at cardinal moments in the debates around these proposals, but often enough the concept came to involve neither baptism nor desire. I believe these omissions represent a real failure, one which goes a long way to explaining why, today, Catholic theology seems so ambivalent on such key questions as salvation and the purpose of the sacraments.

Our historical journey, therefore, will not end in a particularly satisfying place, but our conversation with the various interlocutors we meet along the way—from Ambrose to Rahner—will, I believe, provide us with the elements necessary for revivifying the doctrine, for resolving some of the loose ends left over from the Middle Ages, and for providing a credible way of responding to questions that remain perennially hard, such as the quality of desire necessary for salvation and the fate of non-Christians and infants dying before baptism. While I call into question certain aspects of sacramental theology, such as the *sacramentum/res* distinction, I hope to indicate a direction that respects the irreducibility of all that happens in the rite. I am aiming for a theology that is sober but well-grounded, one which avoids both inventing alternatives to the sacrament and a double predestination that excludes some from salvation in principle. In hard cases, we cannot have absolute certainty about who is saved and who is not, but it would be a mistake—a false kind of humility—to be silent about salvation in the absence of certainty. Doing so effectively removes salvation as a motive for concrete action. A rigorous theology of baptism of desire is, I hope, capable of providing grounds to guide the Church's practical decision-making so that her salvific mission is not paralyzed by anxiety and ambivalence.

As I have waded through the evidence from different centuries, I have, as much as possible, tried to avoid fitting it to a predetermined answer. I do not think we have arrived at the end point of history or of theology, and I do not see any reason to suppose that our own age is less subject to blind spots than any other moment in Christian history, so the story I tell is not of the inevitable march of progress toward an enlightened present. Nor have I found there to be any particular "golden age" of baptism of desire to which I think we must return. The Middle Ages were the high point of discussion in terms of the energy of the debate, but medieval thinkers also left us with a few doctrinal ruts from which we must escape. I have tried to be critical of both ancient and modern thinkers and to give a fair hearing even to positions that have been rightly set aside by the tradition. Because of the diversity of sources we will encounter, I have avoided rigid methodological constraints but have tried, as much as possible, to approach thinkers within their historical context, trying to avoid such dismissive generalities as "he was a man of his times" so as to engage with the words and arguments of earlier thinkers. Where I think this study adds something methodologically significant is its emphasis on the *lex orandi*. It treats baptism as central to the question of salvation. Other studies that cover some of the same territory I do—from Louis Capéran's groundbreaking *Le problème du salut des infidèles* to the more recent studies of Francis Sullivan and Bernard Sesboüé on the doctrine *extra ecclesiam nulla salus*—have largely left the sacraments to the side.[2]

2. Louis Capéran, *Le problème du salut des infidèles*, 2 vols. (Toulouse: Grand Séminaire, 1934); Francis A. Sullivan, *Salvation Outside the Church? Tracing the History of the Catholic Response*

Over the course of the following pages, I hope to show why this is the case—and why it should not be the case. Instead, I propose that baptism should be at the heart of our search for responses to hard questions about salvation today, just as it was for early Christians.

The answers that the rite provides may not be as easy and clear-cut as some would like because the sacrament itself holds together various tensions and ambiguities, the same tensions and ambiguities, however, that result from God becoming incarnate in one man and the salvation of every human person depending on that man. Baptism speaks the language of symbol and ritual action, and it demands, I believe, action from us; it points to a salvation that is participation before it is doctrine. Because of the breadth of sources used, I am sure that specialists in the various fields I touch upon may find room to quarrel; others may legitimately lament important figures I have had to leave out. For reasons of length, I have only included the most essential of original language quotations. I have tried to ground the "big picture" I am sketching in a way that does not depend exclusively on any single figure and thus does not suffer too much from my own inevitable limitations. I have limited myself to Catholic theology to avoid turning what is already a complex question into an unworkable one. I hope that even readers who disagree with some of my conclusions will find that the concept of baptism of desire deserves renewed attention, that the relationship of ritual to salvation is worth raising, and that shaking up the usual categories with which we approach the questions involved here can freshen theological waters that have grown stagnant. The waters of baptism wash away our sins; a mature theology of baptism of desire at least should dissolve too-easy answers.

(New York: Paulist Press, 1992); Bernard Sesboüé, *"Fuori Dalla Chiesa Nessuna Salvezza": Storia di una formula e problemi di interpretazione* (Cinisello Balsamo: Edizioni San Paolo, 2009).

Chapter One

Patristic Precursors

Baptism of desire as a distinct doctrine finds its first articulation in a funeral oration given after the death of the Roman emperor Valentinian II by Ambrose of Milan in 392. Why, then, begin this study some four centuries earlier with sources that are often fragmentary and ambiguous? In fact, this ambiguity itself is an important piece of evidence, for in it we can perceive both an early instinct for something like baptism of desire and reasons the doctrine would be, for many, difficult to accept. Baptism of desire is the corollary of the still more fundamental Christian belief in the necessity of baptism for salvation, emblematically expressed in John 3:5: "unless one is born of water and the Spirit, he cannot enter the kingdom of God." This conviction was so deeply rooted that, as Everett Ferguson concludes at the end of his encyclopedic *Baptism in the Early Church*, "The main variation among mainstream Christian authors was in how strongly different individuals affirmed the necessity of baptism for salvation."[1]

Nonetheless, even early on, this necessity created certain "hard cases," those who had been unable to receive the sacrament but about whom

---

1. Everett Ferguson, *Baptism in the Early Church: History, Theology, and Liturgy in the First Five Centuries* (Grand Rapids, MI: Eerdmans, 2009), 854.

ancient Christians felt that something more needed to be said or done. Catechumens who died unexpectedly and ancestors who lived before the preaching of the apostles were the most obvious such cases. We will see in Christianity's first four centuries several ways in which early believers grappled with these problems, none of which was to prove satisfactory. Yet such dead ends are valuable for at least three reasons. First, they help us to appreciate the mindset in which Christianity took root—the assumptions behind the early preaching of the Gospel. Second, they show why baptism of desire remains a necessary doctrine. In more recent centuries, many theologians have preferred other ways of addressing hard cases. A careful examination of the patristic period reveals that support for these alternatives is shakier than is claimed, often because they do not take into account the importance the early Church placed on the baptismal rite. And, third, the theological building blocks for baptism of desire emerge in surprising places, salvaged, for example, from the detritus of North Africa's contentious third century debates over rebaptism.

We will begin, however, even before the writing of the New Testament—with the practice of baptism that Paul and the evangelists presuppose and the ancient vision of the afterlife that gave the concept of "salvation" its force. Only by appreciating humanity's universal need for a savior can the issues at stake in this study come into focus.

From the Apostles to the Apologists

Baptism predates the writing of the New Testament. Christians were baptizing and reflecting on baptism before Paul dictated his first epistle or Mark compiled his Gospel, and their experience shaped the composition of scripture. Today, when seeking to ground a theological argument in the most authoritative strata of tradition, we naturally turn first to the Bible, but the first generation of Christians did not yet have a New Testament to cite. Instead, in his most heated moments of theological combat, Paul appeals to his readers' experience of baptism as authoritative—just as today we might appeal to Paul.[2] The Gospels were also shaped by baptism, with the Synoptics placing the baptism of Jesus—despite its potential for theological embarrassment—prominently at the beginning

---

2. E.g., 1 Cor 1:13; Gal 3:26–28; Eph 4:4–6; Rom 6:3–5.

of his ministry, a narrative structure that would have reflected every believer's experience of entry into the Christian way of life.[3] The evangelists,
moreover, were determined to assert the uniqueness of the Christian rite
and its superiority to that of John. The power of Christian baptism, as
opposed to all other rites that preceded it, came from its relationship to
the death and resurrection of Jesus. Jesus himself describes his death as a
baptism (Mk 10:38, Lk 12:50), and Paul makes this theology explicit (Rom
6:3–5, Col 2:12). Baptism is salvific because it is a participation in the Paschal Mystery, uniting one with Christ's death and resurrection in such a
way that these events become the cardinal experience of one's own life.
What was at stake for ancient Christians, then, was not the fulfillment of
an ecclesial precept, but the nature of salvation as participation in the saving action of Jesus. Faith, sacrament, and the salvific experience of Christ
were a single reality, and separating them would have been like unweav-
ing one's baptismal gown, leaving a handful of thread but no garment.

Understanding baptism as participation in the death and resurrection
of Jesus makes sense of the New Testament's assertions of the sacrament's
necessity for salvation. Every stage of the historical development of the
doctrine of baptism of desire took place in the shadow of John 3:5 and
Mark 16:16, "He who believes and is baptized will be saved; but he who
does not believe will be condemned."[4] Other passages likewise assert or
imply the necessity of baptism for salvation, including Matthew's account
of the Great Commissioning (Mt 28:19), Titus 3:5, and the Pentecost dialogue between Peter and the residents of Jerusalem in which the Apostle commands his listeners, "Repent and be baptized, every one of you"
(Acts 2:38). Patristic writers saw the connection between baptism and the
story of Noah and the Flood drawn by 1 Peter 3:20–21 as a reaffirmation of

3. Charles Bobertz applies this insight to the whole of Mark's Gospel, in *The Gospel of Mark: A Liturgical Reading* (Grand Rapids, MI: Baker Academic, 2016), Ebook. John also puts baptism up front (Jn 1:6–8, 19–34).

4. Reading Mk 16:16 as privileging faith over baptism, as does Sesboüé, is unpersuasive because it imposes an anachronistic distinction between faith and ritual—a post-Reformation dichotomy—on something early Christians experienced as a unity. Sesboüé, *"Fuori dalla Chiesa Nessuna Salvezza,"* 21. As Mary Healy puts it, "Belief alone is not enough; it must be expressed and ratified with baptism," in *The Gospel of Mark* (Grand Rapids, MI: Baker Academic, 2008), 333. Michael F. Hull makes the same point about the theology of Paul—"Baptism is *the* ultimate act of faith in the gospel"—in *Baptism on Account of the Dead (1 Cor 15:29)* (Atlanta: Society of Biblical Literature, 2005), 233.

the ritual's necessity for salvation.[5] However, the more forceful verses from John and Mark feature most prominently in patristic and medieval discussion because their wording is decidedly exclusivist, not only asserting baptism's necessity but also negating the possibility of salvation without it.

The afterlife before Christianity

The ritual of baptism, in other words, was an intrinsic part of the first Christians' understanding of salvation. To enter the mindset of the first century recipients of the Gospel, we must also recall that, for them, salvation was *news*. That is, even the possibility of a favorable postmortem existence—let alone a glorious resurrection—could by no means be taken for granted. The different understandings of death present in the Old Testament provide little reason for hope in the life to come; Simcha Paull Raphael describes the vision of the netherworld, Sheol, that emerges from the oldest layer of Hebrew scriptures as "a bleak and forlorn subterranean realm."[6] Jewish belief in the resurrection emerged after the Babylonian exile, particularly in the Maccabean period, but without producing any consensus on key questions such as who would rise. The vision of Sheol as an inevitable realm of lifeless existence—a kind of universal limbo—continued to have adherents within Judaism into the second century after Christ. Nor was pessimism about the afterlife limited to Judaism. While Egyptians and Zoroastrians maintained the possibility of survival after death, the peoples of Canaan and Mesopotamia generally conceived of post-mortem existence in bleak terms.[7] Greco-Roman thought about the afterlife was also marked by diffidence and anxiety: Epicureans denied life after death; the Stoic, Seneca, expressed uncertainty; Platonists achieved a certain optimism about death's

5. On the parallels between 1 Pt 3:21, Mk 16:16, and Ti 3:5, see John H. Elliott, *1 Peter: A New Translation with Introduction and Commentary*, The Anchor Bible 37B (New York: Doubleday, 2000), 674.

6. Simcha Paull Raphael, *Jewish Views of the Afterlife* (Lanham, MD: Rowman & Littlefield, 2019), 43. Neil Gillman emphasizes the isolated character of Sheol, from which there was no return, in "Death and Afterlife, Judaic Doctrines of," in *The Encyclopaedia of Judaism*, ed. Jacob Neusner, Alan J. Avery-Peck, and William Scott Green (Leiden: Brill, 2000), 198.

7. In Mesopotamian soteriology, "There is no such thing as 'salvation' and the only 'alternative' to humdrum death is a heroic death, in war." Jon Davies, *Death, Burial and Rebirth in the Religions of Antiquity* (London: Routledge, 1999), 53. Even in the sunnier cosmologies of Egypt and Zoroaster, a blessed existence after death was hardly a given, as the Egyptians' elaborate burial practices demonstrate. Davies, 28–34, 43.

liberating potential but only by treating the body as a prison.[8] Popular belief conceived of Hades along the lines of gloomy Sheol—even those who hoped to be reunited with lost relatives still regarded such an existence as shadowy at best. When ancient religions did hold out hope for immortality, those who achieved it were strikingly few: Elijah and Enoch in the Hebrew scriptures, Herakles and Dionysus in Greco-Roman mythology.[9] The prospect of immortality present in such worldviews—the Isles of the Blessed for Homeric heroes—amounted to little more than the fame one might achieve in battle.[10] In short, the ancients thought eternal happiness an improbable wish.

The problems death posed were twofold. At the time of Christ, the idea of rewards and punishments in the underworld had begun to develop among Jews, though without any great clarity. Eventually, rabbinic Judaism would come to distinguish between Sheol, the undifferentiated realm of the dead, and Gehenna, a place of punishment for the wicked.[11] The distinction between Sheol and Gehenna brings into relief the two related problems addressed by the Christian announcement of salvation: the universal reality of death and the punishment individuals deserve due to their sins. At the time of Christ even the most "optimistic" responses to these problems were based mostly on philosophical speculation and would not have carried the conviction of the Christian claim that one had returned from the dead to reveal salvation. This claim was not made in a vacuum. The premise required for the Christian proclamation to be received as good news is that we are in need of salvation in the first place, that we will be—indeed already are—lost without such intervention. This presupposition helps to explain why ancient and modern theologians often have such different attitudes toward the suggestion that any specifically Christian means might be required for salvation. Thus, Bernard Sesboüé is troubled by the use of Noah's ark as an analogy for salvation in 1 Peter because the story implies that the number of those saved will be few relative to those who perish. But as Biblical scholar Donald Senior

---

8. Davies, 129–40.

9. Davies, 163.

10. Davies, 51. The importance Romans placed on funeral monuments reflects the suspicion that one's memory among the living was the only real hope of life after death. Davies, 140.

11. Raphael, *Jewish Views of the Afterlife*, 67–73, 111.

points out, that is precisely the author's point.[12] Nothing about the religious environment into which Christianity was first preached would have made such a conclusion implausible.

Yet even if those who first heard the Gospel did not begin with a prior assumption that all, most, or any people would be saved, they could not have failed to see that what the necessity of baptism for salvation implies for the unbaptized is not particularly positive. The question of just how negative such results might be is one for which we should reserve judgment; the neutrality of Sheol does not necessarily imply the punishments of Gehenna. Still, early Christians certainly had relatives and friends who were not baptized, and the prospect of being separated from them in the afterlife must have given them pause. Even if we assume that the extended catechumenate was a later development, situations analogous to the unexpected death of Valentinian would almost certainly have arisen in the apostolic era. Whether such cases had any impact on the composition of those texts that would become touchstones in discussions of baptism of desire, such as the Good Thief of Luke 23:39–43, is impossible to know. However, a mostly ignored text—one of the New Testament's strangest—likely reflects one early Christian community's attempt to grapple with just such "hard cases."

Baptizing the Dead

1 Corinthians 15:29. Paul's first letter to the Corinthians is addressed to a fractured and confused community, in which social and theological divisions had led to moral scandals and sacrilege. The Corinthians' bad behavior, however, is our spiritual gain because Paul's response to it includes some of the New Testament's most memorable passages on themes as fundamental as love and the resurrection. Indeed, one of the most serious of the Corinthian errors—the denial of the resurrection of the dead—prompted the apostle to compose an impassioned defense of this belief. In the midst of Paul's affirmation of the resurrection of Christ and of his followers, we also find one of the New Testament's most puzzling verses.

12. Sesboüé, *"Fuori Dalla Chiesa Nessuna Salvezza,"* 19–20, 40. Donald P. Senior, "1 Peter," in *1 Peter, Jude and 2 Peter*, ed. Daniel J. Harrington, Sacra Pagina Series 15 (Collegeville, MN: Liturgical Press, 2003), 104.

Continuing a line of argument that begins with the rhetorical question, "How can some of you say there is no resurrection of the dead?" (15:12), Paul goes on to ask, "Otherwise, what do people mean by being baptized on behalf of the dead? If the dead are not raised at all, why are people baptized on their behalf?" (15:29).

The verse refers to a practice known to the Corinthians but opaque to all later commentators. Some have counted as many as two hundred different interpretations of the passage. Joseph Fitzmyer narrows these to six; of these, he, with the majority of commentators, considers some kind of vicarious baptismal ritual the most plausible.[13] No other scripture passage sheds light on what the practice entailed, and commentators are nearly unanimous in noting that Paul does not endorse the practice but mentions it to support his more urgent argument that the dead will truly be raised; his rhetorical questions merely point out the incoherence of the Corinthians' actions. Whatever the Corinthian practice, it never became widespread and seems not to have persisted into the second century.

Persuasively defending the majority view, N.H. Taylor considers it likely that vicarious baptism for the dead was a local innovation conceived of as a way of procuring salvation for either the Corinthian Christians' deceased relatives or adherents to Christianity who died before initiation.[14] Taylor points out that the problem of relatives who died before the arrival of the apostles would have been particularly acute among the first generation of Christians. While in the Gospels Jesus demands a loyalty greater than that shown to kin (Matt 10:35, Luke 12:53, 14:26), the

13. Joseph A. Fitzmyer, *First Corinthians*, The Anchor Yale Bible 32 (New Haven, CT: Yale University Press, 2008), 577–81. Other contenders include: (2) "the dead" refers to those about to die; (3) "for the sake of" (Greek *hyper*) should be translated "because of," i.e., because of other Christians who have since passed on; (4) the reference is to baptism over the graves of the dead; (5) baptism here refers to martyrdom; (6) the term "baptism" is being used metaphorically in the sense of "drowning" to refer to Paul's great effort, meaning something like working himself to death on behalf of the Gospel. These alternate explanations continue to have serious defenders, e.g., Hull, *Baptism on Account of the Dead*; Joel R. White, "'Baptized on Account of the Dead': The Meaning of 1 Corinthians 15:29 in its Context," *Journal of Biblical Literature* 116, no. 3 (1997): 487–99.

14. Nicholas H. Taylor, "Baptism for the Dead (1 Cor 15:29)?" *Neotestamentica* 36, no. 1/2 (2002): 116–17. Jeffrey A. Trumbower considers deceased catechumens to be the ritual's most likely beneficiaries in *Rescue for the Dead: The Posthumous Salvation of Non-Christians in Early Christianity* (New York: Oxford University Press, 2001), 36. Franco Manzi concurs in *Prima lettera ai Corinzi: Introduzione, traduzione e commento* (Cinisello Balsamo: Edizioni San Paolo, 2013), 228.

prospect of separation from family members in the afterlife might have been painful enough to motivate the Corinthians' adventurous theology. Lack of evidence makes definite conclusions about the beneficiaries of such a ritual impossible, but in either instance we are dealing with the sort of cases that would fuel the theology of baptism of desire. What is most noteworthy in the passage is where the Corinthians thought to look for a solution to these hard cases—in a ritual extension of baptism.

The fundamental objection to the possibility that the Corinthians practiced some kind of vicarious baptism is not its historical implausibility but the theological problems such a practice would have posed. George Montague asks if Paul would really have taken a neutral stance toward a practice that so "smack[s] ... of magic."[15] Still, Paul's Corinthian correspondence makes clear that the community was hardly immune to theological bone-headedness. Without knowing precisely what such a ritual involved, we can only speculate about the problems it created. If practiced on behalf of a non-Christian ancestor, it would have left no room for a free profession of faith because the dead can exercise no right of refusal. The sense that such a ritual is in some way coercive lies at the heart of objections to the contemporary Mormon practice of "baptizing" the dead.[16] Even in the case of a catechumen, the "Corinthian solution" makes the actions of those performing the vicarious baptism more decisive than the will of the intended beneficiary. Moreover, Paul understands baptism as dying with Christ in order to rise to life in Christ (Rom 6:3–5). It is hard to see how this theology of baptism could apply to the vicarious baptism of the dead, who, if already dead, could no longer die with Christ. The practice also weakens the Incarnational logic which makes the present world the crucible in which salvation is worked out.

Shepherd of Hermas. While the Corinthian practice was abandoned, the idea of baptizing the dead recurred from time to time on Christianity's margins. Jumping slightly forward in history, we find different versions of posthumous baptism in the pseudepigraphal literature. The *Apocalypse of Peter*, the *Epistle of the Apostles*, the *Gospel of Nicodemus*, and the *Apocalypse of Paul*, dating from between the mid-second and sixth centuries, contain

---

15. George T. Montague, *First Corinthians* (Grand Rapids, MI: Baker Academic, 2011), 275.
16. Trumbower, *Rescue for the Dead*, 4–6.

stories associated with baptisms performed in the underworld.[17] These
stories involve the baptism of the righteous who died before the coming
of Christ and are made possible, Ferguson wryly notes, by the convenient
presence of the Acherusian lake in the pagan geography of Hades. In some
cases, it is Jesus who baptizes; in others, the apostles; and, in the *Apocalypse
of Paul*, the Archangel Michael is tasked with administering the sacrament. Such stories carry little theological weight, though they reinforce
just how strongly the necessity of ritual baptism was felt in the ancient
world. A more significant work in which we find a similar scenario played
out is *Shepherd of Hermas*. This text, from the middle of the second century,
enjoyed enormous prestige and influence before falling rather suddenly
into obscurity in the fourth century.[18] *Shepherd* is complex and repetitive,
characterized by lengthy—and, at times, tortured—allegories. Despite its
difficulty, the text provides us with rare insight into the eschatology, morality, and sacramental theology of early second century Roman Christianity.

Hermas's vision is apocalyptic; the work's central preoccupation is
preparing oneself for salvation in the face of a sinful world, overcoming
both diabolical powers and one's own evil desires. The work's first-person
narrator, Hermas, is identified as a liberated slave who receives four visions from a woman—sometimes young, sometimes old—who person-
ifies the Church. Later, he is visited by a supernatural "shepherd" tasked
with watching over him. The first passage relevant to baptism occurs in
the narrative's initial visions; Hermas witnesses a stone tower, identified
with the Church, in the process of being built—upon water. When he
asks about this implausible feat of architecture, the old woman tells him,
"It is because your life has been, and will be, saved through water."[19] The

17. Ferguson, *Baptism in the Early Church*, 225–28. Vicarious baptisms practiced by followers of Marcion were condemned by the Third Council of Carthage in 397. Giuseppe Barbaglio,
La Prima Lettera ai Corinzi (Bologna: Dehoniane Bologna, 2005), 832.

18. See Maria Beatrice Durante Mangoni's introduction in Hermas, *Il Pastore*, ed. and
trans. Maria Beatrice Durante Mangoni (Bologna: Dehoniane Bologna, 2003), 20–22. The
work was cited by Jerome, Origen, and many others. Irenaeus seems to have regarded *Shepherd*
as sacred scripture. Joseph T. Lienhard, *The Bible, the Church, and Authority: The Canon of the
Christian Bible in History and Theology*, A Michael Glazier Book (Collegeville, MN: Liturgical
Press, 1995), 27, 40. Jonathon Lookadoo provides a summary of key issues surrounding the text
and a helpful synopsis of the work itself in *The Shepherd of Hermas: A Literary, Historical, and
Theological Handbook* (London: T&T Clark, 2021).

19. Hermas, "The Pastor," trans. F. Crombie, in *Fathers of the Second Century*, The Ante-
Nicene Fathers 2 (Grand Rapids, MI: Eerdmans, 1986), Vision 3.2–3, pp. 13–14.

stones of the tower fit perfectly together, but Hermas also observes various scattered stones. Some are ill-fitting or cracked, some on fire, others far away, and still others near the water's edge. These last, we are told, "wished to be rolled down, and to enter the water." The old woman goes on to interpret these stones as those who "have heard the word and wish to be baptized in the name of the Lord; but when the chastity demanded by the truth comes into their recollection, they draw back."[20] Thus, Hermas identifies a less than salvific desire, an attraction to Christ that turns out to be inadequate because it is unable to motivate the moral and spiritual conversion baptism requires.

When he eventually meets the Shepherd, Hermas directly addresses the question of the necessity of baptism: "I heard, sir, some teachers maintain that there is no other repentance than that which takes place, when we descended into the water and received the remission of our former sins." To this, the angelic Shepherd replies, "That was sound doctrine which you heard; for that is really the case."[21] A scene from the work's final section of extended allegories reinforces the necessity of baptism even for those not guilty of personal sin. The image of the stone tower returns, and Hermas insists that one must receive the name of Christ and be clothed in the virtues to enter the kingdom of God.[22] Stones ascending "out of the pit" into the tower then prompt the Shepherd to explain that the apostles, upon their death, continued their mission among the dead, baptizing the righteous who had died before Christ. Hermas, in other words, seems to have developed a baptismal variation of the "harrowing of hell." Carolyn Osiek notes the similarity between this passage and the practice in 1 Corinthians 15:29.[23] The episode also makes it clear that righteousness apart from baptism is not sufficient for salvation; some

---

20. "The Pastor," Vision 3.7, p. 15.

21. "The Pastor," Commandment 4.3, p. 22. Lars Hartman argues in "Obligatory Baptism—but Why? On Baptism in the *Didache* and in the *Shepherd* of Hermas," *Svensk exegetisk årsbok* 59 (1994), 127–43, that in the *Shepherd* (and in the *Didache*) baptism is integrated into the process of conversion, defining the boundary between the old life of sin and the new life of the Christian. Because the text assumes baptism to be well-established, the sin of baptized believers is the more troubling problem for Hermas. Mark Grundeken, *Community Building in the Shepherd of Hermas: A Critical Study of Some Key Aspects* (Leiden: Brill, 2015), 128–40.

22. Hermas, "The Pastor," Similitude 9.12–13, pp. 47–48. Hermas identifies the reception of the name of Christ with baptism. "The Pastor," Similitude 9.16, p. 49.

23. Carolyn Osiek, *Shepherd of Hermas: A Commentary* (Minneapolis: Fortress Press, 1999), 238.

people "slept in righteousness and in great purity, but only they had not this [baptismal] seal." This fits with a distinction made by the Shepherd earlier between "heathen and sinners," both of whom "shall be burnt as wood," though for different reasons, sinners "because they sinned and did not repent" and heathen "because they knew not Him who created them."[24] For Hermas, separation from eternal salvation is inevitable without entering into the name of Christ through the waters of baptism.

In both 1 Corinthians and *Shepherd of Hermas*, then, we can perceive in embryonic form the theological problems that would drive later debate over baptism of desire. Hermas provides mid-second century confirmation of the earlier biblical affirmations of the necessity of baptism for salvation. The responses we find to "hard cases" of the sacrament's absence involve some version of posthumous baptism, either by proxy or in the netherworld. While such solutions would not withstand later theological scrutiny, it is noteworthy that the first Christian instinct seems to have been somehow to expand the reach of the ritual, rather than positing exceptions to its necessity. In the mindset of the earliest Christians, the rite of baptism was intrinsic to salvation.

The Second-Century Apologists

The Didache. Aside from *Shepherd of Hermas*, second century Christian texts contain few references bearing directly upon baptism of desire. This is not to say that these texts ignored baptism. The earliest non-Biblical Christian text, the *Didache*, which dates from the end of the first or the beginning of the second century, contains a brief instruction on the celebration of baptism.[25] The text suggests that baptism is to be administered after the catechumen has been given Christian moral instruction and has prepared for the ritual with two days of fasting but says little about the theology of the sacrament. The text's "surprisingly punctilious" discussion of the kind of water to be used in baptism reflects the concern that the rite be performed correctly.[26] At the same time, the flexibility it allows—granting the legitimacy of baptism performed by pouring water

---

24. Hermas, "The Pastor," Similitude 4, p. 33.

25. *The Didache: Text, Translation, Analysis, and Commentary*, ed. and trans. Aaron Milavec, A Michael Glazier Book (Collegeville, MN: Liturgical Press, 2003), 7:1–7:4, pp. 18–21.

26. Hartman, "Obligatory Baptism—but Why?" 129.

over the head in the absence of sufficient water for immersion—shows some willingness to adapt the ritual to exceptional circumstances arising in Christian missionary life.[27] Still, the *Didache*'s presupposition is that the rite must be performed and that its reception marks a clear separation from one's former life. Its pejorative language about the unbaptized suggests pronounced skepticism toward the possibility of salvation for those outside the Christian fold.[28]

Justin Martyr. The most important apologist of the post-apostolic generation, Justin Martyr (ca. 100–165), is sometimes held up as representing a more inclusive stance. In contrast to the unambiguously negative view of non-Christian religions found in Tatian, Hermias, and Tertullian, Justin's work is presented as the anticipation of Karl Rahner's twentieth century theory of the Anonymous Christian whereby one can be "justified without Christian faith."[29] Josep Vives classifies Justin's concept of salvation as "existential," in contrast to the "objective" tendency of Tertullian and others.[30] Instead of the objective confession of Christ, Vives argues, what mattered to Justin was the orientation of one's existence toward the Good and the Absolute. If such an interpretation is correct, Justin could be considered a proponent not of baptism of desire as understood by Ambrose, but of the most expansive late-twentieth-century versions of the theory. In fact, if such an interpretation were true, there would have been little need for early Christians to have posited either the posthumous baptisms we have just examined or baptism of desire.

---

27. Willy Rordorf, "Baptism according to the *Didache*," in *The* Didache *in Modern Research*, ed. Jonathan A. Draper (Leiden: Brill, 1996), 218–20.

28. *Didache*, 9:5, pp. 22–23. Hartman, "Obligatory Baptism—but Why?" 131.

29. This is the assumption of Sullivan, *Salvation Outside the Church?* 15; Sesboüé, *"Fuori Dalla Chiesa Nessuna Salvezza,"* 33, 295; and Richard H. Drummond, "Christian Theology and the History of Religions," *Journal of Ecumenical Studies* 12, no. 3 (1975): 399–400. These authors make the mistake of beginning with a twentieth-century paradigm rather than taking Justin on his own terms. In contrast, scholars basing their conclusions on an examination of Justin's work in context reject classifying him as an "inclusivist," that is, as affirming the reality of Christian revelation but holding that salvation can be attained in other religious traditions as well. See Graham Keith, "Justin Martyr and Religious Exclusivism," *Tyndale Bulletin* 43, no. 1 (1992): 69; Shawn C. Smith, "Was Justin Martyr an Inclusivist?" *Stone-Campbell Journal* 10 (2007): 194; and Adam Sparks, "Was Justin Martyr a Proto-Inclusivist?" *Journal of Ecumenical Studies* 43, no. 4 (2008): 495–96.

30. Josep Vives, "Los Padres de la Iglesia ante las religiones no cristianas," *Estudios Eclesiásticos* 79 (1995): 294–96.

Those attributing a proto-Rahnerian stance to Justin point to several features of his work. Like all the Fathers, Justin takes for granted that Old Testament prophets, such as Moses, are saved. He also has positive words to say about Socrates and Plato. He emphasizes man's natural capacity for reason, and reason's capacity to apprehend God's will; because this capacity is not limited to Christians, it would seem to provide a pathway to salvation even for those ignorant of revelation. Such arguments invariably cite a striking passage within Justin's *First Apology*, in which the apologist uses language that seems, on the surface, reminiscent of Rahner:

> We have been taught that Christ was First-begotten of God [the Father] and we have indicated above that He is the Word of whom all mankind partakes. Those who lived by reason are Christians, even though they have been considered atheists: such as, among the Greeks, Socrates, Heraclitus, and others like them; and among the foreigners, Abraham, Elias, Ananias, Azarias, Misael, and many others whose deeds or names we now forbear to enumerate, for we think it would be too long. So, also, they who lived before Christ and did not live by reason were useless men, enemies of Christ, and murderers of those who did live by reason. But those who have lived reasonably, and still do, are Christians, and are fearless and untroubled.[31]

Unfortunately, a look at the broader context provided by Justin's *First Apology* and other extant works reveals that his words carry a meaning quite different from that of Rahner's Anonymous Christianity—so different, in fact, as to be fundamentally incompatible with the later theory.

Justin's *First Apology*, written around 150, is addressed to the emperor Antoninus Pius and argues that Christians are being unjustly persecuted by the pagan authorities. Throughout the work Justin addresses charges made against Christians by drawing parallels with Greco-Roman culture in order to demonstrate that Christians are being unfairly targeted. Christians reject the pagan gods and are therefore accused of atheism; but, Justin counters, Socrates and other philosophers also rejected the

31. Justin Martyr, "The First Apology," in *Saint Justin Martyr*, ed. and trans. Thomas B. Falls (New York: Christian Heritage, 1948), 46, pp. 83–84.

pagan gods, and therefore it is unfair to persecute only Christians.[32] Justin is unsparing in his condemnation of the pagan pantheon, repeatedly identifying Greco-Roman religious practices with the work of demons; the virtue of the philosophers, then, is not their positive teaching—which Justin judges to be full of contradictions—but their rejection of pagan religion.[33]

Pursuing the same strategy, Justin at times even employs the pagan gods themselves. Answering objections to the belief that the Son of God was born of a woman, Justin argues, "we propose nothing new or different from that which you say about the so-called sons of Jupiter."[34] Justin intends no real praise of Jupiter, whom he shortly goes on to call "a parricide and the son of a parricide [...] seized by a lust of evil and shameful pleasures" whose actions are the work of "wicked demons." From the fact that Justin draws parallels between Christian beliefs and those of other religions, therefore, it does not follow that he equates salvific value to such points of commonality. Instead, the only conclusion he wishes to draw is that it is unfair to punish Christians for beliefs that pagans also hold. In fact, he says that often those pagan practices that most closely resemble their Christian counterparts are demonic tricks, the resemblance due not to a common root in the logos but to the demons' attempt to obscure the truth; in particular, he mentions pagan sprinkling rites intended to ape baptism.[35]

Christian belief in the judgment of the wicked seems to have been a particularly contentious point and arises repeatedly in Justin's works. In the *First Apology*, he draws a parallel to Plato's belief in post-mortem punishment, while noting an important difference between the Christian teaching and that of Plato: Plato taught that the wicked would be tormented for one thousand years while Christianity holds that hell is

32. "The First Apology," 5–6, pp. 37–38.
33. "The First Apology," 5, p. 38; 20, p. 55. See Justin's treatment of the Greek philosophers in his "Dialogue with Trypho," in *Saint Justin Martyr*, 1–2, pp. 148–50. In this work, Justin pleads with Trypho, a Jew, to embrace Christianity for the sake of his salvation. "Dialogue with Trypho," 8, p. 160; 141–42, pp. 364–66. Justin relies more heavily on scripture and more explicitly affirms the superiority of the prophets to the philosophers. "Dialogue with Trypho," 48, p. 221; 7, p. 159.
34. Justin Martyr, "The First Apology," 21, pp. 56–57.
35. "The First Apology," 62, p. 101.

eternal.[36] In fact, the question of judgment provides the immediate context for the above citation from the *First Apology* and reveals further difficulties for a Rahnerian interpretation. For when Justin refers to Socrates as a "Christian," it is to refute a specific objection raised against the new religion: the charge that because Christian revelation happened at a particular, relatively recent historical moment, "all men before the time of Christ were not accountable for their actions."[37] The criticism comes up elsewhere in the *First Apology*; in response, Justin argues that, because all men have been endowed with reason, "no man has an excuse if he does evil."[38] In other words, his argument is intended to deny the possibility that the wicked will escape punishment by pleading invincible ignorance. When Justin elsewhere discusses salvation history and allows that "a few" of the Jews were saved before Christ, he also claims, "All the Gentiles were desolate of the true God."[39] His positive words about Socrates and Heraclitus raise the possibility that Justin acknowledged a few exceptions to this general desolation; perhaps the absoluteness of his wording was intended for rhetorical effect—though here another problem arises. For while such figures were not ethnic Jews, Justin believed that they had been recipients of the prophetic message contained in the Old Testament. What is good in Plato, Justin claims, the philosopher pilfered from Moses:

> Moses is more ancient than all the Greek authors, and everything the philosophers and poets said in speaking about the immortality of the soul, or retribution after death, or speculation on celestial matters, or other similar doctrines, they took from the Prophets as the source of information, and from them they have been able to understand and explain these matters. Thus, the seeds of truth seem to be among all men, but that they did not grasp their exact meaning is evident from the fact that they contradict themselves.[40]

Given Justin's assumptions, therefore, such good Greeks do not provide an example of anyone saved through reason alone.

---

36. "The First Apology," 8, pp. 40–41; see also, 18–20, pp. 52–56.
37. "The First Apology," 46, p. 83.
38. "The First Apology," 28, pp. 64–65.
39. "The First Apology," 53, p. 91.
40. "The First Apology," 44, p. 81. Also see, 49, p. 97; 54, p. 92.

This context is key to understanding how Justin uses the image of "the seeds of the truth," which some have taken to argue for a greater appreciation of non-Christian religions.[41] Justin draws precisely the opposite conclusion: "The truths which men in all lands have rightly spoken belong to us Christians" because "our teachings are more noble than all human teaching."[42] Christianity, in other words, provides the standard by which the truths found outside it must be evaluated. This allows Justin to deliver a sweepingly negative assessment of pagan mythology and religious practices, while maintaining that Plato, the Stoics, and other Greeks "spoke very well" insofar as they rejected those practices.[43] If we probe a bit deeper, we can perceive that Justin's purpose is not really to praise Plato; the account of his own rejection of Platonism in the *Dialogue with Trypho* presupposes the philosophy's inadequacy and the necessity of Christian conversion for salvation.[44] When Justin does emphasize the continuities between Platonism and Christianity, it is to reassure pagans that they are not losing what was good in their previous beliefs by becoming Christian. He concludes his *Second Apology* by making it clear that the seeds of the truth cannot substitute for the truth itself: "the seed of something and its imitation, given in proportion to one's capacity, is one thing, but the thing itself, which is shared and imitated according to His grace, is quite another."[45] One cannot make apple pie from apple seeds.

This context indicates that when Justin refers to "those who have lived reasonably" as "Christians" he is not making a soteriological claim. As Keith puts it, Justin "was no exception to the exclusivism of mainline Christians of his period."[46] Nonetheless, Justin did believe in the salvation of the Old Testament recipients of revelation and, related to this,

41. E.g., Drummond, "Christian Theology and the History of Religions," 397, 403–4; Vimal Tirimanna, "*Logos*: A Bridge-Builder for Interreligious Dialogue?" *Studies in Interreligious Dialogue* 19, no. 2 (2009): 211.

42. Justin Martyr, "The Second Apology of Justin to the Roman Senate in Behalf of the Christians," in *Saint Justin Martyr*, 13, pp. 133–34; 10, pp. 129–30.

43. "The Second Apology," 13, p. 133. Justin's treatment of the Stoics is a case in point; he considers their beliefs about the future of the world a "disgraceful doctrine," but praises them for opposing idolatry. "The Second Apology," 7–8, pp. 126–28.

44. Justin Martyr, "Dialogue with Trypho," 1–8, pp. 148–60.

45. Justin Martyr, "The Second Apology," 13, p. 134.

46. Keith, "Justin Martyr and Religious Exclusivism," 80. He goes on, "His achievement lay in arguing not only that Christianity fulfilled all that was good in Greek philosophy but that it was also much superior to that philosophy."

saw baptism present in symbolic form in God's pre-Christian revelation.[47] Here Justin is again representative of the patristic consensus; in
the minds of the Fathers, even the salvation of those living in the centuries before the Incarnation is not divorced from the sacrament of cleansing and rebirth. Justin is equally clear, however, that the rites of the Old
Testament, including Jewish washing rituals, no longer have any salvific
value.[48] Justin never explains why this should be the case, leading Keith
to conclude, "Justin has not satisfactorily sorted out the relationship between the law and the gospel." More precisely, Justin does not answer the
question, "Why should obeying the Mosaic Law be sufficient at one stage
of Jewish history and not at another?"[49]

One reason some scholars may have been inclined to a proto-Rahnerian reading of Justin despite the incompatibility of this reading with his
overarching theological claims is the modern tendency to overlook the
importance of the sacraments in the early Christian worldview. Drummond, for example, begins with the principle "that the judgments of God
relate primarily to the ethical quality of humans' deeds," thereby mar-
ginalizing sacramental considerations.[50] Like his contemporary Hermas,
however, Justin cites John 3:5 to affirm the necessity of baptism for salvation.[51] Justin contrasts the rebirth experienced in baptism with one's
natural birth; breaking free from that first life is necessary so that "we
do not continue as children of necessity and ignorance." Here Justin's
emphasis is on the choice one makes to be regenerated. Absent such
a choice, he seems to view humanity's trajectory as inevitably negative:
"The whole human race could be said to be under a curse."[52] While this
falls short of a theology of original sin, Justin's language suggests that

---

47. Justin Martyr, "Dialogue with Trypho," 86, pp. 285–86. Tallying up a slew of Old Testament events involving water or wood Justin concludes that Christ, crucified on the wood of
the cross, "raised us up" "by sanctifying us by water."

48. Justin tolerated the continued observance of certain aspects of the Mosaic Law among
Jews who converted to Christianity but was firm that on their own these no longer saved.
"Dialogue with Trypho," 47, pp. 218–19. Ferguson addresses Justin's treatment of Jewish ritual
washings within the early Christian polemic on the inferiority of Jewish purification rites in
Baptism in the Early Church, 266–75.

49. Keith, "Justin Martyr and Religious Exclusivism," 66.

50. Drummond, "Christian Theology and the History of Religions," 394.

51. Justin Martyr, "The First Apology," 61, pp. 99–100.

52. Justin Martyr, "Dialogue with Trypho," 95, p. 298.

analogous concepts play a similar role in his thinking. His emphasis on demons, for example, leads him to speak of man's enslavement, from which baptism is the means of liberation.[53] Justin's baptismal theology cannot, however, be reduced to liberation from demonic enslavement. In line with common patristic usage, he uses the term "illumination" to refer to baptism, suggesting that through the washing "they who learn these things become illuminated intellectually."[54] The manner in which liturgy was celebrated in Justin's time no doubt contributed to his sense of baptism as enlightenment. Post-baptismal mystagogy and participation in the Eucharist meant that neophytes would have experienced the world in a new light. For Justin, participation in the sacraments, especially the Eucharist, meant sharing in a reality that could not be accessed in other religions or philosophies, "the whole Logos, namely the Logos of body and soul."[55] Justin, in short, holds to the uniqueness of both Christianity and its sacraments. Nothing in his theology provides a way around the necessity of baptism for salvation.

Irenaeus. The most important apologist and theologian of the latter half of the second century, Irenaeus (bishop of Lyons ca. 180–202), demonstrates broad theological continuity with Justin on the questions under consideration. In his most significant work, *Against Heresies*, however, Irenaeus is not concerned with defending Christians from Roman persecution, but with asserting the intellectual coherence of orthodoxy against the diverse currents of Gnosticism that had sprung up on the margins of the Church. Gnosticism's most distinguishing features are its rejection of the material world as irremediably corrupt and the pursuit of salvation through hidden knowledge (*gnosis*) to attain a purely spiritual existence.[56] In Irenaeus's work, therefore, we find a defense of the doctrines of creation, the Incarnation, the resurrection of the body, and sacramental

---

53. Sparks, "Was Justin Martyr a Proto-Inclusivist?" 501.

54. Justin Martyr, "The First Apology," 61, p. 100.

55. "The First Apology," 66, p. 105; Justin Martyr, "The Second Apology," 10, p. 129.

56. Irenaeus, *Against Heresies*, ed. Alexander Roberts and James Donaldson, trans. Alexander Roberts and W.H. Rambaut, in Nicene and Post-Nicene Fathers 5 and 9 (Edinburgh: T&T Clark, 1868–1969), vol. 5, 1.6.1–4, pp. 24–27. The Gnostics' indifference to the material world, according to Irenaeus, led them to ritual and moral indifference; they participated in pagan rites without scruple because they regarded these as not really mattering.

baptism. The ritual of water and spirit is necessary, Irenaeus says, because man is both body and soul; baptism, faith, and salvation make up a single unified reality, so that rejection of the sacrament is "a renunciation of the whole faith."[57] Participation in this reality is, for Irenaeus, the only path to salvation. While he recognizes the presence of divine precepts in the heart of man, like Justin, Irenaeus does not regard such natural moral knowledge as an effective path to salvation. In fact, he notes that, if nature alone provided sufficient means for salvation, the Incarnation would have been superfluous.[58]

Irenaeus's sense of the unity of baptism and faith undergirds one of his greatest contributions to patristic theology, his articulation of the concept of the *regula fidei*, the rule of faith. The *regula fidei*, the norm of belief by which to measure the Christian search for truth, allowed one to judge the coherence of scriptural interpretations and was even the criteria for deciding which writings were to be included in the canon.[59] The content of the rule of faith was expressed in the structure of the Christian sacraments, especially baptism. Jeremy Driscoll notes, "In the patristic period the relation between liturgy and theology was much tighter than it is today, functioning at first almost unconsciously, very naturally."[60] Thus, Irenaeus speaks of Christian faith not just as propositions to be believed, but as something received in baptism, an experience of new life involving both body and soul.[61] And it is above all this experience of "salvation accomplished by the Father through the Son and in the Holy Spirit" that provides the fundamental norm for determining which beliefs are compatible with Christianity.[62] Indeed, in light of what we have seen thus far—and what we will observe throughout the patristic period—it should

57. *Against Heresies*, vol. 5, 1.21.1, p. 81; cf. 3.17.2, p. 334; cf. 1.21.4, p. 83.

58. *Against Heresies*, vol. 5, 2.29.1, pp. 228–29; 3.20.1–3, pp. 347–50; 5.2.3, vol. 9 p. 60. Like Justin, he holds that such natural precepts mean that no one may dispute the justice of sinners' punishment. *Against Heresies*, vol. 5, 4.15.1–2, pp. 419–21. Thus, the vast majority of those who lived before Christ were justly condemned. *Against Heresies*, vol. 5, 4.27.4, p. 469–71.

59. Vittorino Grossi, "*Regula Fidei*," in *Nuovo dizionario patristico e di antichità cristiane*, vol. 3, ed. Angelo Di Berardino (Genova: Marietti 1820, 2008), 4491; Lienhard, *The Bible, the Church, and Authority*, 40–41, 50–52, 96–100.

60. Jeremy Driscoll, "Uncovering the Dynamic *Lex Orandi—Lex Credendi* in the Baptismal Theology of Irenaeus," *Pro Ecclesia* 12, no. 2 (2003): 214.

61. Irenaeus, *On the Apostolic Preaching*, trans. John Behr (Crestwood, NY: St. Vladimir's Seminary Press, 1997), 2–3, 6–7, pp. 40–44.

62. Driscoll, "Baptismal Theology of Irenaeus," 219. "It is God who is acting in baptism,

be apparent that understanding faith-baptism-salvation as a unity is by no means unique to Irenaeus. Modern thought tends to conceive of faith in terms of an intellectual belief or a psychological state; for the early Church, belief was integrated into the sacramental-liturgical encounter.

The irreducibility of the sacrament is perceptible in Irenaeus's treatment of a scriptural passage which would play an important, if not entirely felicitous, role in medieval debates on baptism of desire, the account of the conversion of the centurion Cornelius in Acts 10.[63] The outpouring of the spirit in the story—and the speaking in tongues that results—is meant to authorize the baptism of the Gentiles, according to Irenaeus, not to replace the rite. Indeed, Peter uses the event in precisely this way, asking, "Can anyone forbid water for baptizing these people who have received the Holy Spirit" (Acts 10:47)? Similarly, when Irenaeus turns to the story of the Ethiopian eunuch, he treats the man's previous righteous way of life and knowledge of God as preparation for baptism in Christ, the one thing he still lacks.[64]

On the question of the salvation of the righteous of Israel before the coming of Jesus, Irenaeus's discussion is more developed than what we find in Justin and opens the door to a salvific role for desire. Irenaeus holds to the patristic consensus that such Old Testament figures as Adam, Abraham, Moses, and the prophets will rise to eternal life.[65] Goaded on by Marcion's rejection of the Old Testament, Irenaeus insists that God's providence extends to all times. But instead of diminishing the necessity of the New Testament requirements for salvation, Irenaeus projects these elements back into the Old Testament. He sees Christ present in a direct and physical way in God's interactions with the patriarchs: speaking and eating with Abraham; directing the construction of the ark; punishing

---

accomplishing the salvation of the one baptized. This is part of the sacramental experience of Irenaeus and of every orthodox Christian." Driscoll, 216–17.

63. Irenaeus, *Against Heresies*, vol. 5, 3.12.15, pp. 313–14.

64. *Against Heresies*, vol. 5, 4.23.2, pp. 456–57. The second- and third-century Pseudo-Clementine literature reflects a similar line of thought: "If you are righteous, being baptized is the only thing lacking for salvation," says one source. Ferguson, *Baptism in the Early Church*, 255–56. Another, however, depicts Peter reassuring Clement's apparently unbaptized mother, who had just survived a shipwreck: "If you had died, the deep itself would have become for you a baptism for the salvation of your soul on account of your self-control." Ferguson, 258. While such writings are intriguing, controversy over their dating and provenance and their theological idiosyncrasy limit their relevance for our study.

65. Irenaeus, *Against Heresies*, vol. 5, 4.22, pp. 453–55; cf. 3.23, pp. 362–69.

Sodom; appearing to Jacob; speaking to Moses from the bush.[66] Irenaeus
even emphasizes Christ's visibility in these encounters, so that they function in a manner similar to the sacraments; though unique events instead
of repeatable rituals, they connect those participating in them with the
salvific events of the New Testament. The degree of specific knowledge
of Christ which Irenaeus attributes to the figures of the Old Testament
is not substantially less than that required in post-apostolic times. When
Irenaeus affirms that Abraham's faith "and ours are one and the same,"
it is because "he believed in things future, as if they were already accomplished."[67] Irenaeus attributes to the patriarch a knowledge of the
Incarnation not less than that of Simeon who encounters the infant Jesus
in the opening chapters of Luke's Gospel.[68] This revelation prompts in
Abraham a desire to embrace Christ akin to Simeon's; this desire for
Christ made the precepts of the Old Testament salvific and explains why
they are no longer so afterwards.[69] We will see this insight developed
more fully in the medieval period by the masters of Laon.

Irenaeus's treatment of desire, though arising only occasionally in
Against Heresies, is sophisticated enough to merit our attention. He regards "the prophecy of future things" as an essential part of God's revelation to the Jews because it was necessary to provoke in them the desire
for Christ that salvation requires.[70] This argument implies a limitation
on how far a saving desire can potentially extend: One cannot form a
significant desire without at least some knowledge of its object. Irenaeus
elsewhere discusses an imperfect knowledge of God, which does not appear to have been sufficient for salvation; some Gentiles, he notes, were
"moved, though but slightly," acting in accord with God's providence
insofar as they observed moral discipline.[71] This faint acquaintance allowed them to avoid some errors and to acknowledge God as maker of
the universe. The passage, however, forms part of a larger discussion of

66. *Against Heresies*, vol. 5, 4.10.1, pp. 403–4.

67. *Against Heresies*, vol. 5, 4.21.1, pp. 451.

68. *Against Heresies*, vol. 5, 4.7.1, p. 394. Salvation is available "from the beginning" to those
who "have both feared and loved God, and practiced justice and piety toward their neighbours,
and have earnestly desired to see Christ, and to hear his voice." *Against Heresies*, vol. 5, 4.22.2,
pp. 454–55.

69. *Against Heresies*, vol. 5, 4.16, pp. 421–25.

70. *Against Heresies*, vol. 5, 4.16.1, pp. 421–22; 4.11.1, pp. 405–6.

71. *Against Heresies*, vol. 5, 3.15.1, pp. 320–21.

heresies and false philosophies that arrive only at partial truths. Such faint-hearted Gentiles, he concludes, "always have the excuse of searching [after truth] (for they are blind), but never succeed in finding it."[72] He likens their beliefs to miry water in contrast to the "limpid fountain which issues from the body of Christ."[73] Irenaeus may not entirely close the door on the possibility of Gentiles before the time of Christ being saved through desire, but he seems to regard it as remote.[74] There can be no doubt of Irenaeus's conviction that that the spread of the Church made salvation available to a vastly wider swath of humanity than had previously been the case.

Controversy and creativity in North Africa

Before turning to the two theological heavyweights of the third century North African Church—Tertullian and Cyprian of Carthage—it is worth signaling the existence of another body of evidence which provides insights into early Christian attitudes toward baptism: Christian funerary inscriptions. In recent decades such inscriptions have figured into debates over the origins of infant baptism; for our purposes, they provide further evidence of the widespread conviction of the necessity of baptism for salvation not just among bishops and apologists but also among everyday Christians. When it came to the question of when to baptize the children of Christian parents, this conviction had to be weighed against the difficult and uncertain prospects of repentance for any sins committed after baptism. That baptism could be administered to infants does not seem to have been in question, but the circumstances under which it should be was an object of prolonged dispute. Without entering into the particulars of that debate, we can glean a few insights from the research involved in it. For example, Ferguson lists a striking number of third- and

72. *Against Heresies*, vol. 5, 3.24.2, pp. 370–71. Nor is belief in God alone sufficient for salvation. *Against Heresies*, vol. 5, 1.22.1, pp. 84–85; cf. Irenaeus, *On the Apostolic Preaching*, 1, p. 40.

73. Irenaeus, *Against Heresies*, vol. 5, 3.24.1, pp.369–70.

74. Like Justin, Irenaeus considered idolatry to be an absolute obstacle to salvation, arguing that Paul had to labor more for the conversion of the Gentiles because they did not have the scriptures to prepare them to reject idolatry and to embrace Christ. *Against Heresies*, vol. 5, 4.24.2, pp. 458–59. His repeated deployment of the Biblical citation "many are called, but few are chosen" (Mt 22:14) makes it clear that Irenaeus believes hell to be far from empty. *Against Heresies*, vol. 5, 4.15.2, pp. 420–21; 4.27.4, pp. 469–71.

fourth-century inscriptions providing evidence of what we would call emergency baptisms: inscriptions that record one having been "made a believer" (*fidelis facta*) a very short time before death.[75] His list includes inscriptions for both small children and adults, often accompanied by brief, poignant expressions of grief and faith. A small number of inscriptions seem to imply that the deceased was a catechumen (or a "hearer"), a fact deemed significant enough to record and consonant with belief in baptism of desire, if short of decisive evidence.

Tertullian

A work which no study of baptism in the early Church can overlook is Tertullian's *De baptismo*, Christianity's first treatise of sacramental theology. Controversial and prolific, Tertullian was born in Carthage around the year 160, converted to Christianity sometime before 197, and probably died around 220. We have only the scarcest evidence of his life after 213, when, apparently repelled by the laxity of the Roman clergy, he seems to have abandoned Catholicism for a rigorous sect known as Montanism. Despite his relationship with the heretical sect, his early writings were considered authoritative by Cyprian and other defenders of orthodoxy.[76]

De baptismo (ca. 200–206) was written to catechize those being formed in the faith; in it, Tertullian is particularly concerned to counter the teaching of a Gnostic sect opposed to water baptism.[77] The first section of the treatise is, therefore, an encomium on water and the appropriateness of its use in the ritual; in a broader sense, it can be seen as a defense of sacramentality in general, of the necessity of a rite that touches both body and spirit. The second section of the work addresses particular

75. Everett Ferguson, "Inscriptions and the Origin of Infant Baptism," *The Journal of Theological Studies* 30, no. 1 (1979): 41–43.

76. J. Leal, "Tertulliano," in *Letteratura Patristica*, ed. Angelo Di Bernardino, Giorgio Fedalto, and Manlio Simonetti (Cinisello Balsamo: Edizioni San Paolo, 2007), 1157; Pietro Podolak, *Introduzione a Tertulliano* (Brescia: Morcelliana, 2006), 11.

77. Tertullian, "Concerning Baptism," in *Tertullian's Treatises, Concerning Prayer, Concerning Baptism*, trans. Alexander Souter, Leopold Classic Library (London: Society for Promoting Christian Knowledge, 1919), 1–9, pp. 46–58. On the beliefs of this "Cainite" sect and why they so irked Tertullian, see Robin M. Jensen, "'With Pomp, Apparatus, Novelty, and Avarice': Alternative Baptismal Practices in Roman Africa," in *Studia Patristica*, vol. 45, ed. J. Baun, A. Cameron, M. Edwards, and M. Vinzent (Leuven: Peeters, 2010), 77–83.

theological problems raised with respect to baptism; some of these problems touch on salvation in the Old Testament and the question of when the apostles were baptized. The final section addresses practical questions about the administration of the sacrament, such as its proper minister and when and on whom it should be conferred.

Tertullian is clear from the first words of the treatise that baptism aims at the forgiveness of sins and the attainment of eternal life. He treats the necessity of baptism for salvation as settled doctrine and is clear about the consequences of its omission; though he cautions against prematurely baptizing someone not ready to live up to the commitment the sacrament involves, he also warns that if someone is in danger of death and one does not confer baptism "he will be guilty of ruining a human being."[78] He addresses certain cases that might seem to cast into doubt baptism's necessity, though he calls these objections "reckless questionings on the part of some."[79] One difficulty which his reflections on water partially resolve is the salvation of those prophetic figures who lived before Christ. The numerous places in which water plays a decisive role in the Old Testament served to "build up the religion of baptism," though none of these instances was the equivalent of baptism.[80] His reflection on how figures such as Abraham could be saved is not as developed as that of Irenaeus, though Tertullian is quick to refute "those criminals" who, citing Abraham, claim that "Baptism is not necessary to those for whom faith is enough."[81] While the faith of Abraham was salvific in the past, now it "has no efficacy"; it has been amplified by the Lord's passion and resurrection and sealed with baptism. Tertullian attributes less explicit knowledge of Christ to Abraham than Irenaeus does, though both see the efficacy of Old Testament faith coming from its fulfillment in the New.

More complex for Tertullian is an objection that had apparently been raised about the apostles' baptism—or lack thereof. He acknowledges that the New Testament contains an account only of Paul's baptism and

---

78. Tertullian, "Concerning Baptism," 17, p. 67.

79. "Concerning Baptism," 12, p. 61.

80. "Concerning Baptism," 10, p. 58. His judgment on the value of pagan rituals that bear a superficial resemblance to baptism is similar to Justin's; though such rituals demonstrate the symbolic power of water, they are false imitations "furnished by God's enemy." "Concerning Baptism," 5, p. 52.

81. "Concerning Baptism," 13, pp. 63–64.

considers several possibilities regarding the other apostles' baptismal status. The most probable is that the apostles were baptized by John; this
claim, however, only partially resolves the problem. Tertullian had already
argued that the preparatory baptism of John expressed human repentance
without yet embodying salvific participation in the Paschal Mystery.[82]
Here he argues that Jesus' words to Peter at the Last Supper—"He that
hath washed once, hath no need to do so again" (Jn 13:10)—express the
Lord's judgment that the previous baptism of the apostles had become
sufficient.[83] Jesus takes this unusual step of retroactively Christianizing
the baptism of John because he wants to demonstrate that there is only
one baptism. Tertullian dismisses proposals identifying the apostles' baptism with other episodes from the Gospels involving water—for example,
that they were baptized when sprinkled with water from the boat—as
fanciful. Still, the fact that Tertullian was aware of multiple interpretations, even if farfetched, shows that the problem raised enough concern
to have generated considerable discussion. He concludes by noting that
the apostles are a special case because of their "inseparable association
with the Lord," which should make us cautious about drawing general
conclusions from their example.

De baptismo acknowledges one important precedent for baptism of
desire, the martyr's baptism of blood "which makes real even a baptism
that has not been received, and restores one that has been lost," a reference to the forgiveness of post-baptismal sin.[84] His treatment of the
theme of conversion in another treatise written around the time of De
baptismo also shows the considerable thought he gave to desire and its
relation to salvation. In De paenitentia, he argues that the object of penitence is true conversion, which allows one to attain salvation. But a purely
emotional repugnance at one's sins is not enough if repentance is not also
guided by reason, which comes from God, and grounded in the firm resolve of the will.[85] The treatise emphasizes the dispositions necessary be-

82. "Concerning Baptism," 11, pp. 60–61.
83. "Concerning Baptism," 12, pp. 61–63.
84. "Concerning Baptism," 16, p. 66. Tertullian identifies these two types of baptism with
the water and blood flowing from Christ's crucified side.
85. Tertullian, "On Repentance," trans. S. Thelwall, in *Latin Christianity: Its Founder, Tertullian*, ed. Alexander Roberts, James Donaldson, and A. Cleveland Coxe, *The Ante-Nicene
Fathers* 3 (Grand Rapids, MI: Eerdmans, 1989), 1–3, pp. 657–59.

fore receiving baptism so that one does not fall back into perdition. Here again, Tertullian describes John's baptism of repentance as preparatory, removing those obstacles which hinder the arrival of the Holy Spirit, who brings salvation. Tertullian sees a similar dynamic playing out in the lives of Christians; in the case of the Christian sacrament, however, conversion and repentance are the preparation for baptism. Tertullian seems especially concerned with those who put off baptism in order to delay conversion, making the period before baptism "a holiday-time for sinning." At the same time, he is aware that an overhasty reception of the sacrament may lead one to take it for granted; instead, he attributes a salutary effect to the desire for the sacrament. Nurturing such a desire predisposes one to receive baptism as a true gift: "it is becoming that learners *desire* baptism, but do not hastily *receive* it: for he who desires it, honours it; he who hastily receives it, disdains it."[86]

Tertullian does not address the specific case of catechumens who die before baptism, but he may leave the door open to the possibility of their salvation if they are in the process of sincere conversion: "Not that I deny that the divine benefit—the putting away of sins, I mean—is in every way sure to such as are on the point of entering the (baptismal) water; but what we have to labour for is that it may be granted us to attain that blessing."[87] Still, he cautions against presumption: "the penitent does not yet merit—so far as merit we can—his liberation." Those who have delayed baptism to prolong their sinfulness show that formal enrollment as a catechumen is no guarantee of salvation: "Let no one, then, flatter himself on the ground of being assigned to the 'recruit-classes' of learners, as if on that account he [would] have a license even now to sin."

We can reasonably conclude that, for such lazy catechumens, Tertullian saw little chance of salvation if they were caught off guard by death. For a catechumen cultivating the penitential spirit Tertullian praises, however, the story might be different. In another section of *De paenitentia*, Tertullian indirectly puts into place one of the premises that might allow for baptism of desire; in underlining the importance of the

---

86. "On Repentance," 4, pp. 661–62.

87. "On Repentance," 6, p. 661. He also denies the efficacy of baptism as practiced by heretics, indicating definite limits to any notion of implicit desire. Tertullian, "Concerning Baptism," 15, p. 65.

will, he argues that, if one decides to sin but is impeded from accomplishing the act by some external difficulty, one is nonetheless guilty by reason of having willed the sin.[88] Applying the same line of reasoning to a happier circumstance—i.e., having the will to be baptized—would provide grounds for believing that a sincere catechumen impeded by outside forces from receiving the sacrament might still benefit from it. We must remember that Tertullian's concern is not to elaborate a theology of baptism of desire, and we would be going beyond the evidence to attribute Ambrose's beliefs to him. Nonetheless, many of the elements Ambrose would eventually use to articulate his doctrine are already present in the great Carthaginian otherwise known for his rigor.

Cyprian and Opponents

The bishop of Carthage from 248 until his beheading in 258, Cyprian exercised an enormous influence over the North African Church in his own day and enjoyed even greater prestige after his martyrdom. His episcopacy was marked by conflict. He fled Carthage and directed his see from hiding during the Decian persecution in 250. When he was able to return to the city the following year, he was faced with the problem of reconciling those Christians who had apostatized during the persecution, as well as schisms caused by North Africa's abundant sects. Debates over whether or not those baptized by heretics should be rebaptized produced further divisions, putting Cyprian at odds with Pope Stephen of Rome. Before their conflict could be resolved, both Stephen and Cyprian were executed during Emperor Valerian's renewed persecution. While Cyprian's position—he followed Tertullian's hard line against the validity of heretics' baptisms—was later refuted by Augustine, the arguments the controversy occasioned give us insights into the ways third century Christians approached difficult cases. Before turning to Cyprian's writings on baptism, along with a treatise from an anonymous opponent, it is time to introduce another controversial issue we will find often intersecting with—and sometimes confusing—the question of baptism of desire, namely the teaching that there is no salvation outside the Church. For

---

88. Tertullian, "On Repentance," 3, p. 659. Irenaeus makes a similar argument in *Against Heresies*, vol. 5, 2.32.1, pp. 242–243.

with no other patristic figure is the saying *extra ecclesiam nulla salus* so closely associated as with Cyprian of Carthage.[89]

Extra ecclesiam nulla salus. Unlike baptism of desire, the doctrine *extra ecclesiam nulla salus* has been the subject of much scholarly attention in recent decades, and it is not hard to see why. As noted in the introduction, a considerable amount of the late twentieth century's theological energy has gone into articulating expansive understandings of salvation that would include non-Catholics, non-Christians, and even, in some cases, atheists. The twentieth century magisterium has sounded distinct notes of "salvation optimism" that create a certain dissonance with the more ancient doctrine. Such dissonance poses a serious challenge to theologians who wish both to be faithful to the Church's tradition and to affirm more expansive understandings of salvation. Among the most important recent attempts to resolve this problem is Francis Sullivan's *Salvation Outside the Church?*[90] Sullivan argues for the legitimacy of the late twentieth century shift in understanding *extra ecclesiam nulla salus* by claiming that the saying's original intent was more limited than the understanding it took on in the post-Augustinian Church. With respect to Cyprian, Sullivan argues that his use of the phrase was meant to apply only to those Christians guilty of dividing the Church through heresy and schism; in other words, the saying was a warning against leaving the Church or refusing to do the penance necessary to return to it from a state of schism.[91] The argument is appealing because it presents the theological developments of the twentieth century as the rediscovery of a more pristine teaching. This meaning was obscured, in Sullivan's narrative, by the Constantinian Church, in which the saying *extra ecclesiam nulla salus* was transformed into a weapon used against the Empire's Jewish and pagan minorities.[92]

---

89. The first recorded use of the saying, however, is in Origen. Sesboüé, *"Fuori dalla Chiesa nessuna salvezza,"* 40–42.

90. Sesboüé largely follows Sullivan. Though authors such as Ralph Martin and Matthew Ramage have challenged Sullivan's reading of Vatican II as one-sided, they largely accept his historical analysis. Matthew Ramage, *"Extra Ecclesiam Nulla Salus* and the Substance of Catholic Doctrine: Towards a Realization of Benedict XVI's 'Hermeneutic of Reform,'" *Nova et Vetera* 14, no. 1 (2016): 321–23.

91. Sullivan, *Salvation Outside the Church?* 20–24; Sesboüé, *"Fuori dalla Chiesa nessuna salvezza,"* 42–45, 207.

92. Sullivan, *Salvation Outside the Church?* 26–27.

The evidence we have already seen in this study, however, should give us serious pause before accepting this argument; second century Christians—such as Justin and Hermas—clearly foresaw eternal loss for Jews and pagans, who represented the overwhelming majority of the population at the time.

In fact, examining the question of baptism of desire reveals a major fault in the approach taken by Sullivan, for his focus on the dictum *extra ecclesiam nulla salus* largely bypasses the role of the sacraments in salvation. His claim that the teaching's original meaning applied only to those considering leaving the Church—or resisting the penitence necessary for re-entry—ignores the more ancient belief that baptism is necessary for salvation. While the two teachings might on the surface seem to be restating the same thing, their implications are slightly different. The necessity of baptism for salvation, strictly speaking, does not address the problem of those who are baptized but then leave the Church. Thus, *extra ecclesiam nulla salus* makes a somewhat broader claim than the statement that baptism is necessary for salvation. To affirm that there is no salvation outside of the Church excludes two groups from salvation—those who have never entered the Church (the unbaptized) and those who have entered but chosen to leave. At first glance, the distinction might seem esoteric; the Church Fathers were, after all, adamant that one had to live out one's baptismal commitment if one were to receive the sacrament's eternal benefits. Remembering this distinction will become important in our study, however, because the reasons these two categories of people are excluded from salvation are different. Those who leave the Church voluntarily commit a personal sin, heresy or schism, which, according to Cyprian, thwarts God's will for its unity. Sullivan is correct to note that Cyprian's *On the Unity of the Church* is a condemnation of heresy and does not really address the eternal destiny of non-Christians.[93] However,

93. Even if this were Cyprian's only work, the claim that his theology leaves room for the salvation of non-Christians would be a stretch. The necessity of incorporation into the Church for salvation is the presupposition upon which his arguments rest. For example, Cyprian invokes Noah's ark: "If whoever was outside the ark of Noe was able to escape, he too who is outside the Church escapes." Cyprian, "The Unity of the Catholic Church," in *Saint Cyprian: Treatises*, trans. Roy J. Deferrari (Washington, DC: The Catholic University of America Press, 1981), 6, p. 100. It is surely not lost on Cyprian that those who never entered the ark are just as drowned as those who jump overboard. Likewise, his insistence that "there is no other house for believers except the one Church." "The Unity of the Catholic Church," 8, p. 103. When,

Cyprian's view of the destination of non-Christians becomes apparent in his discussion of baptism.

In a letter addressed to his fellow bishop Fidus, the Carthaginian rejects his colleague's proposal that the baptism of infants should be delayed until the eighth day after birth.[94] In doing so, he clearly equates the omission of baptism with the loss of salvation. He adds that baptizing infants is a matter of justice: The Church baptizes penitent sinners and "how much more should an infant not be prohibited, who recently born, has not sinned at all, except that, born carnally according to Adam, he has contracted the contagion of the first death."[95] Here Cyprian anticipates the doctrine of original sin, most often associated with Augustine. The principle that Adam's sin affects all mankind seems to have been accepted widely enough for Cyprian to use it here as a premise of his argument.

By passing over the role of baptism in salvation, Sullivan overlooks essential evidence as to how Cyprian understood the *extra ecclesiam* formulation. For Cyprian's argument against his heretical opponents is not only that they are committing a grievous sin by dividing the Church; it is that the means of salvation are not present outside the Church. Like Tertullian before him, Cyprian argues that baptisms performed by heretics are not real baptisms. He develops this position at length in a 255 letter to Magnus addressing the efficacy of such baptisms. His argument again turns on the oneness of the Church; from this he argues that "the Church alone has the life-giving water and the power of baptizing and

---

emphasizing the necessity of perseverance, he states, "Confession [of Christ] is the beginning of glory," he does not imply that one can achieve glory without such a beginning. "The Unity of the Catholic Church," 21, p. 116.

94. Cyprian, "Letter 64," in *Saint Cyprian: Letters (1–81)*, trans. Rose Bernard Donna (Washington, DC: The Catholic University of America Press, 1981), 216–19. Though Cyprian's presuppositions about baptism's necessity are the same as Tertullian's, he arrives at a different conclusion on the prudential question of whether, absent the danger of death, infants should normally be baptized. Then again, Fidus's arguments were spectacularly bad. The rite of baptism at the time included the bishop kissing the foot of the newly baptized, and Fidus complained "that the foot of the infant in the first days after his birth is not clean, that each one of us shudders at the thought of kissing it." "Letter 64," 4, p. 218.

95. "Letter 64," 5, p. 219. The letter closes with the image of infants pleading for the sacrament: "immediately at the very beginning of their birth, wailing and weeping, they can do nothing but plead." The phrasing might suggest a kind of pre-verbal desire on the part of the infants, though the letter's overall argument makes it clear that Cyprian did not consider such desire salvific. More likely he is simply exercising a bit of poetic license on the newborns' behalf.

of cleansing men."[96] Cyprian also claims that it is necessary to assemble in the Church in order to "escape from the destruction of the world."[97] Some of Cyprian's writings have an apocalyptic flare, and he might have had in mind either this world's final destruction or the mortality to which all living things are subject. Either way, what is most important for our purposes is to note that, whether one conceives of it in terms of original sin or the destruction to which creation naturally tends, Cyprian understands humanity to face an existential problem prior to all individual sins. The remedy to this problem is the rebirth of baptism, and without that remedy one remains lost. On this point, Cyprian and his opponents seem to have been largely in agreement; third century debates over whether to rebaptize heretics were heated and divisive because all sides understood the stakes to be nothing less than salvation.

Baptism, rebaptism, and inadvertent omission. When Cyprian says there is no salvation outside of the Church, then, he means precisely that. Perhaps, therefore, it is surprising to find a few passages in his writings that leave room for baptism of desire, even if he cannot be said to endorse a concept not yet articulated. Still these passages were substantial enough to have drawn Augustine's attention. They can be found in the above-mentioned letter to Magnus and a letter to Bishop Jubaian in which Cyprian lays out the theological case for his position against the validity of heretics' baptisms. In the former letter, in addition to the question of baptisms performed by those separated from the Church, Cyprian addresses another question posed to him by Magnus about the effects of "sprinkling" baptism, which seems to have been conferred in cases where sickness made the normal practice of immersion impossible. The fact that the question was controversial shows the importance attributed to the correct ritual. Nonetheless, Cyprian considers those "sprinkled" to have been completely baptized provided the rite is done "with full and complete faith" on the part of both recipient and administrator.[98] The dispute may seem arcane today—when immersion is the exception rather than the rule—but it is significant because it demonstrates Cyprian's willingness to show a certain

---

96. Cyprian, "Letter 69," in *Saint Cyprian: Letters (1–81)*, 3, p. 246.
97. "Letter 69," 4, p. 247.
98. "Letter 69," 12, p. 253.

flexibility with regard to what was considered a less than ideal modality of the rite.

Such flexibility becomes even more significant when we examine a comment made at the end of Cyprian's letter to Jubaian. The main thrust of the letter is that, because those outside the Church do not possess the true faith, and one cannot give what one does not possess, heretics and schismatics cannot baptize. Baptism is necessary for salvation because from it "begin all origin of faith and the salutary entrance to the hope of eternal life."[99] Here Cyprian connects the teaching "there is no salvation outside of the Church" with John 3:5, again demonstrating that he understood the former statement to apply to non-Christians as well as apostates.[100] Given Cyprian's unflinching position on both the necessity of the Church for salvation and the invalidity of baptisms conferred outside it, his answer to a final objection at the letter's end is surprising:

> But someone says: 'What, therefore, will become of those who, in the past, coming to the Church from heresy were admitted without baptism?' The Lord is powerful in His mercy to grant indulgence and not to separate from the gifts of His Church those who, admitted to the Church through simplicity, are dead.[101]

Cyprian adds, however, that such errors should not be allowed to continue. How he reconciles his answer with John 3:5 remains unexplained. The group he mentions had at least attempted baptism as heretics, and eventually they ended up professing the true faith, so the elements necessary for salvation were present, if not in the right order. Since he is most interested in inculcating what he regards as the correct practice for the future, Cyprian does not elaborate on the point. Though the Ambrosian concept of baptism of desire would be able to account for the salvation of the unusual category of believers Cyprian mentions, the passage cannot represent the foundation for a doctrine of baptism of desire because it is based upon Cyprian's false premise of the invalidity of the original baptisms.

99. Cyprian, "Letter 73," in *Saint Cyprian: Letters (1–81)*, 12, p. 275.

100. "Letter 73," 21, p. 282. Cyprian refers to the Jews having received "the most ancient baptism of the law and of Moses" but is quick to note that this "baptism" is not salvific unless baptism "in the Name of Jesus Christ" is added to it. "Letter 73," 17, p. 279.

101. "Letter 73," 23, p. 283.

A more solid precedent for baptism of desire, also mentioned in the letter, is baptism of blood. We have already seen expressions of the widespread belief that martyrdom constituted a type of baptism and even resulted in the forgiveness of sins committed after baptism, a belief never seriously challenged even by those who would eventually take the hardest line against baptism of desire. Cyprian's letter to Jubaian gives clear expression to the doctrine; if a catechumen "should be seized and killed for the confession of the Name" before being baptized, his salvation is assured because such catechumens "are not deprived of the Sacrament of baptism, nay rather, they are baptized with the most glorious and greatest baptism of blood."[102] What is noteworthy here is that Cyprian does not present martyrdom as an alternative to baptism but as a variation of the same reality. The two modalities of baptism are inextricably linked by participation in Christ's passion and death: Martyrdom is implicit in baptism. The scenario Cyprian outlines—catechumens seized and put to death—was an existential reality in the Carthage of his day. As we approach the question of baptism of desire, therefore, we would do well to keep in mind that its most important precedent—baptism of blood—cannot really be considered a work-around to the necessity of baptism. The sacrament is the "easier" alternative. Finally, as an exemplar of baptism of blood, Cyprian mentions the Good Thief of Luke 23:40–43; as we will see, later commentators would object to this classification—on the grounds that the thief is put to death not for his faith, but for his crimes—leading Augustine and others to posit a third category of baptism.

On Rebaptism. Perhaps the nearest approximation of belief in baptism of desire prior to Ambrose can be found in an anonymous treatise *On Rebaptism* written by a North African bishop in opposition to Cyprian.[103] While the anonymous author's conclusion would eventually win acceptance—in fact, the author presents his opinion as the Church's tradition and accuses Cyprian's side of being the innovators—his reasoning is idiosyncratic. The author begins with a history of baptism, referring to

---

102. "Letter 73," 22, pp. 282–83. Cyprian's rigor with regard to the teaching *extra ecclesiam nulla salus*, however, comes out in the passage, for he insists that even martyrdom is of no benefit to heretics.

103. Ferguson, *Baptism in the Early Church*, 385–86.

the baptisms of Moses and John, which he considers superseded by the baptism of the Holy Spirit.[104] Referring to John 3:5, he affirms that only the baptism of the Holy Spirit is sufficient for salvation. Since "outside the Church there is no Holy Spirit," his reasoning thus far would seem to lead him to the same conclusion as Cyprian.[105] Here, however, he breaks from Cyprian because he associates the bestowal of the Holy Spirit with the laying on of the bishop's hands; the way to reconcile those baptized outside of the Church, then, is not to rebaptize them with water but for hands to be imposed upon them. Biblical precedent, he argues, supports his view, for the apostles were baptized prior to the arrival of the Holy Spirit on Pentecost and were not rebaptized. Indeed, the New Testament records all of the necessary elements for a fruitful baptism, but it also shows those elements arriving in a jumbled order. In the case of Cornelius, for example, the Holy Spirit arrives before baptism in the name of Jesus.[106]

Most importantly for us, the author seems to leave room for someone who professed true faith in Jesus but died before baptism to receive salvation. He has in mind catechumens who have "taken up the name of Christ" but who die without baptism in water.[107] Though he brings up martyrdom later on in the paragraph, he does not specify that the catechumens mentioned above must be martyrs. On the other hand, he unambiguously insists on the necessity of the correct Christian confession, for "this assuredly ought not to be taken too liberally, as if it could be stretched to such a point as that any heretic can confess the name of Christ who notwithstanding denies Christ Himself." Furthermore, while insisting on the necessity of baptism in the Holy Spirit, which he associates with the laying on of hands, he also considers the case in which an orthodox believer is baptized with water in the name of Jesus but dies before the arrival of a bishop to lay on hands, a situation that seems to have been relatively common.[108] Though the treatise does not neatly bind

104. "A Treatise on Re-Baptism by an Anonymous Writer," in *Fathers of the Third Century: Hippolytus, Cyprian, Caius, Novatian, Appendix*, ed. Alexander Roberts, James Donaldson, and A. Cleveland Coxe, The Ante-Nicene Fathers 5 (Grand Rapids, MI: Eerdmans: 1986), 2–3, p. 668.

105. "A Treatise on Re-Baptism," 10, p. 673.

106. "A Treatise on Re-Baptism," 4–5, pp. 669–70.

107. "A Treatise on Re-Baptism," 11, p. 673.

108. "A Treatise on Re-Baptism," 5, p. 669.

up its different lines of reasoning, the author's position seems to be that a full and complete baptism—in the name of the Father, Son, and Holy Spirit—is necessary for salvation, but that in the event of deficiency in one aspect of this baptism the trajectory toward its fulfillment is sufficient. Such a trajectory requires the absence of heresy or other obstacles subject to the will of the person involved. In the case of a catechumen who dies before baptism, the treatise appears to hold that this trajectory toward salvation is present in the sincere confession of faith in Christ. Thus, despite their hard line against the possibility of salvation outside of the Church, in both Cyprian's work and *On Rebaptism*, we find baptism of desire distinctly foreshadowed.

Cappadocian skepticism

If the tentative preamble to baptism of desire found in the work of Tertullian and Cyprian cuts against the rigorous stereotypes of the North African Church, perhaps equally surprising will be the ways in which one of the most important sources of baptismal theology in Eastern Christianity—Gregory Nazianzen's pair of baptismal homilies—seems to abruptly close the door on the idea. Today the current of theology with which Gregory is associated, encompassing Origen and the Cappadocians, has drawn interest for its perceived congeniality to the possibility of universal salvation.[109] In fact, the Nazianzen's treatment of baptism—as well as that of other contemporary figures such as Cyril of Jerusalem and Basil the Great—indicates that the universalism some have sought in the Eastern Church of the third and fourth centuries was less pronounced than current discussion suggests. Nonetheless, the concept of *apokatastasis* and the possibility of universal salvation it seems to open in the theology of Origen and Gregory of Nyssa merits a brief digression. Like the Corinthians' vicarious baptisms, Origenist universalism was to be—with good reason—a theological path not taken; nonetheless, the

---

109. For example, see, John R. Sachs, "Apocatastasis in Patristic Theology," *Theological Studies* 54 (1993): 617–40; and David Bentley Hart, *That All Shall Be Saved: Heaven, Hell, and Universal Salvation* (New Haven, CT: Yale University Press, 2019). The contradictions between universalism and Christian belief are extensively explored by Michael J. McClymond in *The Devil's Redemption: A New History and Interpretation of Christian Universalism* (Grand Rapids, MI: Baker Academic, 2018).

wide-ranging and creative speculation it engendered foreshadowed ideas that remain relevant to our theme.

The apokatastasis*: From Plato to Gregory of Nyssa*

The theory of the *apokatastasis* posits that all of creation—in some versions, even the devil—will be restored to eternal blessedness after a period of postmortem purification. While it eventually appeared in Christian theology, the *apokatastasis* arose from Platonism. We have already seen an allusion to the doctrine's origins in Justin Martyr's *First Apology*; Justin contrasts Christianity's belief in the eternity of hell with Plato's teaching that the torment of the wicked would last for a thousand years.[110] Plato envisions rewards and punishments meted out in hundred-, thousand-, and ten-thousand-year cycles, with a wicked person's transgressions normally punished ten times over, i.e., once every hundred years for a thousand-year cycle. For Plato, the key moment of decision for a soul comes at the end of this cycle of purification when it must choose what sort of being—animal or human—into which it will be reincarnated. While such a decision is freely made and is influenced by the soul's previous preparation in this life (philosophers, it is no surprise, make better choices), it is made by a disembodied (and potentially non-human!) soul and thus runs contrary to the logic of the Incarnation. Justin's observation is instructive because when the *apokatastasis* begins to appear in Christianity half a century or so after his death, it is only within those theological currents most heavily indebted to Platonism, most notably in the thought of Origen.[111]

---

110. Justin Martyr, "The First Apology," 8, pp. 40–41; Plato, *Republic*, trans. G.M.A. Grube, rev. C.D.C. Reeve, in *Complete Works*, ed. John M. Cooper (Indianapolis: Hackett Publishing Co., 1997), bk. 10, 614b–621d, pp. 1218–223; *Phaedrus*, trans. Alexander Nehamas and Paul Woodruff, in *Complete Works*, 248c–249c, pp. 526–28. The transgressions of some evil-doers, particularly tyrants, are so wicked as to require further, perhaps perpetual, punishment. *Republic*, bk. 10, 615a–e, pp. 1218–219. David Syme Russell points to the influence of Zoroastrian eschatology on the Hellenism of Syria and Egypt, in *Between the Testaments* (Philadelphia: Fortress Press, 1975), 20–24. Even a writer as sympathetic to *apokatastasis* as John R. Sachs perhaps inadvertently concedes the doctrine's non-Christian genesis by listing precedents in Persian, Gnostic, and Platonic thought before admitting, "Turning to the Scriptures, we find that the language about final restoration is notably scarce," in "Current Eschatology: Universal Salvation and the Problem of Hell," *Theological Studies* 52 (1991): 227–28.

111. Themes related to the *apokatastasis* are also present in the work of Clement of Alexandria,

Origen. Origen (c. 183–253) was a product of Alexandria's third century neo-Platonic milieu, though in the latter part of his career he found himself in conflict with the city's bishop and relocated to Caesarea in Palestine. He underwent torture during the Decian persecution but refused to apostatize, dying of his injuries shortly after being released from imprisonment. Despite such heroism, Origen remains a controversial figure because some of the positions he entertained, especially his speculation on the *apokatastasis*, fall outside of Christian orthodoxy.[112] While an exhaustive analysis of Origen's eschatology is impossible here, John Behr's recent translation of Origen's most philosophical work *On First Principles* makes a valuable contribution to understanding Origen by highlighting the different strata of thought present in the work.[113] In some places, Origen is transmitting what he regards to be the *regula fidei* announced by the apostles and passed on in ecclesial preaching; in others, he addresses questions that he considers open. In these later cases, his thought is speculative, at times wildly so. An intellectual's intellectual, Origen relishes test-driving ideas to see where they might lead. Origen scholar Henri Crouzel compares him to "a professor of philosophy who tries to present to his students different doctrines with all their implications and in all their force even if he personally holds yet another view" or remains undecided.[114]

As an intellectual exercise, there is much to admire in this approach, though it resulted in contradictions within Origen's work and led to misunderstandings and disputes both within and after his lifetime. When it comes to eschatology, at times Origen faithfully reports the rule of faith;

---

likely an influence on Origen. Based on his emphasis on purifying—as opposed to punishing— fire, Brian E. Daley concludes that Clement may suggest the possibility of universal salvation "with great caution," in *The Hope of the Early Church: A Handbook of Patristic Eschatology* (Grand Rapids, MI: Baker Academic, 2010), 47. Trumbower cautions that "Clement does not speak of an inevitable universal salvation" but "clearly presupposes that some might reject the offer," in *Rescue for the Dead*, 99–100.

112. It remains a matter of debate whether the condemnations of Origen by the Synod of Constantinople (543) and the Second Council of Constantinople (553) should be understood as directed at Origen himself or at his sixth-century followers. See *Enchiridion symbolorum definitionum et declarationum de rebus fidei et morum*, ed. Heinrich Denzinger and Peter Hünermann, Latin-English 43rd ed. (San Francisco: Ignatius Press, 2012), 403–11, 421–38.

113. Origen, *On First Principles*, ed. and trans. John Behr, 2 vols. (Oxford: Oxford University Press, 2017).

114. Henri Crouzel, *Origen: The Life and Thought of the First Great Theologian*, trans. A.S. Worrall (San Francisco: Harper & Row, 1989), 166.

at others he uses Platonic categories to imagine the *apokatastasis*. Origen seems sympathetic to the Platonic vision of a cosmos renewed and all creatures saved, though he is equally aware that this is not the message of the apostolic preaching. *On First Principles*, therefore, involves an exploration of whether Christian revelation can be reconciled with Origen's universalistic instinct. Thus, in its opening paragraphs we find an affirmation of the Christian belief in the eternity of both heaven and hell; a few lines later, however, Origen asserts that what existed before the beginning of the world and what will happen after its end is unclear—indicating the space he considers open for speculation.[115] The possibility of universal salvation Origen entertains depends on purgation after death and some kind of reincarnation.[116] As later belief in purgatory attests, the existence of purifying fire does not necessarily imply universal salvation; that *some* punishment is temporary and purifying does not mean that *all* punishment is of this type. In his discussion of eternal fire, for example, Origen identifies the fire that tortures sinners as something self-produced, inherent in the nature of sin itself.[117] This is quite different from fire sent by God to purify. His discussion of the outer darkness seems to countenance the possibility that some will make themselves "alien to every glimmer of reason or understanding" and, after the general resurrection, will rise to blackened bodies.[118] Thus, while universal salvation is one of the outcomes Origen considered emerging from the *apokatastasis*, it is not the only scenario he puts into play.

Despite discussing hypotheticals that at times resemble science fiction, Origen shows a sincere concern for adhering to the rule of faith.[119]

---

115. Origen, *On First Principles*, vol. 1, Pr. 5, 7, pp. 17–19; he similarly shifts in 1.6.1, pp. 104–5, noting that what came before was an exposition of dogma and what comes after is "discussion."

116. *On First Principles*, vol. 1, 1.6.3–1.64, pp. 114–17; 2.3.7, pp. 174–77; vol. 2, 2.9.8, pp. 250–51; 3.5.3, pp. 426–29; 3.6.3, p. 445; 3.6.6, pp. 448–51. Origen may not have in mind so much the reincarnation of individuals into this world as the entire cosmos being formed anew, perhaps repeatedly. Origen's language of "return" and the cyclical vision he at times adopts creates the possibility of repeated falls as well as repeated rebirths.

117. *On First Principles*, vol. 2, 2.10.4–2.10.5, pp. 260–63.

118. *On First Principles*, vol. 2, 2.10.8, pp. 266–67.

119. Origen vehemently denied teaching the salvation of the devils, though some of his writings on the *apokatastasis* could give such an impression. Daley, *The Hope of the Early Church*, 58–59. Also noting that Origen writes of the devil's salvation as something not even a lunatic could believe, Crouzel hesitates to attribute universalism to Origen, "for if there are texts pointing in that direction, too many others exist on the other side." Crouzel, *Origen*, 262–63, 265.

And he, like other patristic figures we have seen, identifies the necessity of baptism within that rule's content.[120] His use of the principle "there is no salvation outside of the Church" slightly predates that of Cyprian, and he is quite clear that salvation is inseparable from faith in Christ. "Would you like to know that no one possesses eternal life except the one who believes in Christ?" he writes. "Then hear the voice of the Savior himself making it very plain in the Gospels, 'And this is eternal life, that they may know you, the only true God, and Jesus Christ whom you have sent.'"[121]

Understanding belief in Christ to be constitutive of the eternal life promised in the Gospels sheds light on what Origen says about the "baptism of fire" to take place in the afterlife. Origen mentions a posthumous baptism in a river of fire. This "baptism of fire," however, is not a substitute for the sacrament but a final cleansing of post-baptismal sin: "whoever does not have the sign of earlier baptisms, him Christ will not baptize in the fiery bath."[122] Origen indicates that the good works and sins of Jews and pagans will affect their existence in the afterlife, but he considers their future to be categorically different than that of Christians.[123] Like Cyprian, when he speaks of martyrdom, Origen presents the baptism of blood not as an alternative to the sacrament but its fulfillment. Martyrdom must be a baptism, he insists, because "it is impossible to receive forgiveness of sins apart from baptism."[124] In fact, Origen heaps scorn on those who would eliminate the explicitly religious and sacramental elements of religion. In his day, for example, some had called into question the necessity of prayer; Origen attributes these "most impious doctrines" to the devil and goes on: "The ones who defend this opinion are those who do away with perceptible things entirely and practice neither

---

120. Origen, *Commentary on the Epistle to the Romans, Books 1–5*, trans. Thomas P. Scheck, The Fathers of the Church 103 (Washington, DC: The Catholic University of America Press, 2001), 2.7.3, p. 123.

121. *Commentary on the Epistle to the Romans*, 2.7.4, p. 124.

122. Origen, *Homilies on Luke*, 24.2, quoted in Ferguson, *Baptism in the Early Church*, 409.

123. Origen, *Commentary on the Epistle to the Romans*, 2.7.4–2.7.5, pp. 124–25.

124. Origen, "An Exhortation to Martyrdom," in *Origen: An Exhortation to Martyrdom, Prayer and Selected Works*, ed. and trans. Rowan A. Greer (New York: Paulist Press, 1979), 30, p. 61. Crouzel makes the crucial point that Origen saw martyrdom as the supreme baptism: "It would scarcely be in accordance with Origen's outlook to represent the baptism of blood as a kind of substitute for the baptism of water […] that would be somehow to subordinate the mystery to the image." Crouzel, *Origen*, 224.

baptism nor the eucharist, explaining the Scriptures with sophisms."[125]

Despite its breadth and creativity, little in Origen's work directly suggests baptism of desire. He clearly includes the necessity of baptism for salvation in the rule of faith; his notion of purifying fire seems to apply only to the baptized and thus would not save those who have not received the sacrament; and his speculation on the *apokatastasis* is too enmeshed in Platonic concepts of reincarnation to represent a viable Christian doctrine. Nevertheless, Origen's eschatological speculation did attract interest—both positive and negative—in the centuries after his death. The most significant patristic theologian to take up his ideas on the *apokatastasis* was the youngest of the Cappadocians, Gregory of Nyssa (c. 335–94).

Nyssa. Gregory's treatment of the doctrine in *On the Soul and the Resurrection* is more credible than Origen's because it sheds some of the latter's more outlandish conjectures, such as reincarnation, the pre-existence of souls, and an endlessly repeated cycle of ages.[126] The key Biblical text for Gregory's *apokatastasis* is 1 Corinthians 15:28 which envisions a final stage of fulfillment that ends with God as "all in all." The text, part of Paul's defense of the resurrection of the dead, comes immediately before his reference to the Corinthians' baptism of the dead. Gregory reads the passage as indicating a final stage of salvation, arriving after the general resurrection. The decisive mechanism providing the basis for universal salvation is again purifying fire in the ages to come. The souls of the wicked, Gregory argues, will experience being drawn to God as "a state of torture" akin to a refiner's fire; such purgation will be proportionate to the evil in one's soul, with the greatest of sinners undergoing purgation "commensurate with an entire age."[127] At the end of the work he portrays the purification that must happen after the resurrection as occurring so that "some day after long courses of ages" the soul "will get back again that universal form which God stamped upon us at the beginning."[128]

125. Origen, "On Prayer," in *Origen: An Exhortation to Martyrdom, Prayer and Selected Works*, 5.1, pp. 90–91.

126. Gregory of Nyssa, "On the Soul and the Resurrection," in *Gregory of Nyssa: Dogmatic Treatises, Etc.*, ed. Philip Schaff and Henry Wace, trans. W. Moore, Nicene and Post-Nicene Fathers of the Christian Church, 2nd ser., vol. 5 (Grand Rapids, MI: Eerdmans, 1988), 455–58.

127. "On the Soul and the Resurrection," 451.

128. "On the Soul and the Resurrection," 468. Crouzel points out that Gregory relies on

Though employing Biblical imagery, Gregory's reasoning throughout the treatise is fundamentally Platonic, with his notion of the purified soul mirroring the spiritualized ideal of a Platonic philosopher and the general resurrection only an intermediate event. Indeed, Mario Baghos notes the "lack of Christ-centered eschatological reflection" in the work.[129] Despite its sophistication, therefore, the work does not manage to resolve the fundamental problems with the *apokatastasis*. The salvation of the individual is detached from the Incarnation, and, while Gregory insists on the importance of free will and criticizes deterministic views of existence, his own views cannot escape the deterministic trap.[130] In his scenario, the religious and moral choices one makes in this life provide a short-cut to achieving blessedness, but they do not change one's ultimate destination. In the end, like a cosmic Don Corleone, God makes man an offer he can't refuse.

Despite the marked tendency toward universalism present in Gregory's work, Baghos suggests that his position may not be clear-cut. I have already highlighted a few cases in which scholars have tended to read modern sensibilities back into the Fathers' writing—does the Nyssen provide yet another example of this tendency? A look at Gregory's writings on baptism complicates the picture even if it does not, it seems to me, change the final verdict. Baghos argues that the philosophical speculation found in *On the Soul and the Resurrection* should not be read apart from Gregory's *Catechetical Oration*, which provides a fuller Christian "metanarrative" in which to evaluate the former work.[131] Indeed, this systematic presentation of the Christian faith explicitly affirms the necessity of baptism: "without the laver of regeneration it is impossible for the man to be in the resurrection."[132] He adds that everyone will rise again in the sense

---

the dominant axiom of Origen's cosmology, that "the end is like the beginning." Crouzel, *Origen*, 205.

129. Mario Baghos, "Reconsidering *Apokatastasis* in St Gregory of Nyssa's *On the Soul and Resurrection* and the *Catechetical Oration*," *Phronema* 27, no. 2 (2012): 135.

130. Gregory of Nyssa, "On the Soul and the Resurrection," 456–57. To get around the problem of determinism, Baghos argues that Gregory's *apokatastasis* amounts essentially to a second chance to make the choice with which Christ presents us in this life, in "Reconsidering *Apokatastasis*," 151.

131. Baghos, 126.

132. Gregory of Nyssa, "The Great Catechism," in *Gregory of Nyssa: Dogmatic Treatises, Etc.*, 35, p. 504. Elsewhere, Gregory warns that death can overtake one at any age and that one must

of being given a new body, but that does not mean that all will enjoy "a blessed and divine condition," for "there is a wide interval between those who have been purified, and those who still need purification." There is nothing particularly Christological in the purification Gregory envisions, however, which he describes as "freedom from passion." And this, he does allow, will be possible for the unbaptized after the resurrection, though by the far less pleasant means of fire, rather than water. Gregory, then, seems to envision a wider scope for the posthumous baptism of fire than does Origen. Whereas the earlier thinker saw such purification as a supplement to the sacrament, Gregory seems to allow that it might replace it.

Thus, on the one hand, Gregory's treatment of the necessity of baptism implies a distinction between believers and non-believers. On the other, he seems to think that the sins of the unbaptized can be purified in a future post-resurrection world.[133] Does this mean that this distinction is overcome and that the benefit of sacramental baptism is temporal—albeit lasting for ages—rather than everlasting? In fact, Gregory's treatment of another "hard case" adds yet more complexity. In the brief essay *On Infants' Early Deaths*, Gregory takes up the question of the fate of infants who die shortly after birth; baptism does not figure much in the discussion, which is driven more by reasoning based on natural phenomena than revelation.[134] That we are dealing with unbaptized infants is probably assumed.[135] Gregory finds the question difficult, however, not because the infants are unbaptized but because their brief lives provide

---

not risk dying unbaptized. Everett Ferguson, "Exhortations to Baptism in the Cappadocians," in *Studia Patristica*, vol. 32, ed. Elizabeth A. Livingstone (Leuven: Peeters, 1997), 122.

133. For Gregory of Nyssa, the necessity of Christ for salvation rules out alternative pathways in other religions: "It is, in fact, impossible for persons to reach the same goal unless they travel by the same ways." "The Great Catechism," 35, p. 502. He does not believe that salvation can be attained merely by following our natural instincts, since we are born into death and have no means of escaping this "labyrinth" on our own. "The Great Catechism," 33–35, pp. 501–3. Gregory affirms the necessity of baptism on the grounds that sharing in Christ's Incarnation and saving actions—and not merely following his teachings—is necessary for salvation. It is unclear how these aspects of the sacrament would be present in a posthumous baptism of fire.

134. Tellingly, Gregory of Nyssa turns first to Plato for an answer, in "On Infants' Early Deaths," in *Gregory of Nyssa: Dogmatic Treatises, Etc.*, 373. The philosopher, however, offers little help, brushing off the fate of short-lived infants as not worth recounting. Plato, *Republic*, 615c, p. 1218.

135. Gregory of Nyssa mentions those who expire immediately after birth and those "exposed or suffocated" by their parents. "On Infants' Early Deaths," 374.

no basis for either punishment or reward. Such infants could not have meaningfully willed either good or evil.

Interestingly, Gregory does not seem to regard his notion of the *apokatastasis* as contributing to the problem's answer. Purifying fire, after all, is only of value for cleansing evil, not for providing something that is missing. The most serious problem for Gregory is that the infants never developed the capacity for exercising virtue. In the next chapter we will examine Augustine's position that unbaptized infants are in hell, which would later prompt the objection: How could God punish someone who has done nothing wrong? For Gregory, the objection goes the opposite way. He wonders: How could God reward someone who has done nothing right? The problem is a serious one for Gregory because he conceives of punishments and rewards in the afterlife not as coming from an outside source, but as being in some way intrinsic to one's character.[136] Just as evil produces its own internal fire, loving God and neighbor with purity is itself a reward. The mere absence of sin, therefore, is not the same thing as blessedness.[137] So while Gregory is adamant that infants are not punished, he envisions them enjoying only the blessings commensurate with their low capacity for virtue. This provides an important insight into Gregory's conception of the afterlife, one perhaps capable of reconciling some of the tensions in his thought. For when God is "all in all" in the *apokatastasis*, this does not mean that God will be equally in all.[138] God will be in all according to the capacity of each, but Gregory does not believe that everyone's capacity is equal. Gregory's thought, in other words, allows for some differentiation in people's eternal destinies even after the fires of purgation have died down. Egalitarianism may seem desirable in today's mindset, but ancient thinkers were more likely to see hierarchy and differentiation as a positive part of God's plan.[139] Gregory realizes that his answer does not paint a particularly rosy picture of the infants'

---

136. "On Infants' Early Deaths," 376.

137. "On Infants' Early Deaths," 377.

138. "On Infants' Early Deaths," 378.

139. As an argument from the end of the work attests: "some portion of the blessedness of the virtuous will consist in this; in contemplating side by side with their own felicity the perdition of the reprobate [...] not indeed as rejoicing over the torments of those sufferers, but as then most completely realizing the extent of the well-earned rewards of virtue." "On Infants' Early Deaths," 381.

future; in fact, the line of reasoning he pursues—based on the development of virtue—would not seem to provide much comfort for baptized infants who die prematurely either. Much of the latter part of the work is dedicated to the argument that, if God allows the infants' death, it must be to prevent some greater evil.[140]

The treatise introduces one further complication, the fate of Judas, for whom the Gospel implies that no amount of purification is likely to be enough (Matt 26:24). As Gregory puts it, "on account of the depth of the ingrained evil, the chastisement in the way of purgation will be extended into infinity."[141] It may be that certain sinners have become so warped as to lack the capacity for blessedness, just as a stone lacks the capacity for feeling; such a line of thinking would preserve the principle that, in the *apokatastasis*, all will experience blessedness according to their capacity and still leave intact Christian belief in the eternity of hell. It may be that Gregory never worked out answers to all of the questions his speculation raises or that some of his opinions changed over time. In the end, not all of the problems with the *apokatastasis* can be resolved because its core innovation—salvation achieved in a future world—is fundamentally Platonic and cannot be reconciled with the *regula fidei* centered on the Incarnation. While the eschatology of Origen and Gregory is rich and creative, it can most generously be understood as a first draft of the doctrine of purgatory. Future articulations of that doctrine would insist that the purification the saved undergo after death is the ratification of their decision for Christ in this life. As a way of addressing the difficult cases of those dying without baptism, however, theology would have to look elsewhere.

---

140. "On Infants' Early Deaths," 378–81. It is worth comparing Gregory's position to the conclusions drawn by Jane Baun about the bleak fate of unbaptized infants in ancient and medieval Byzantium, in "The Fate of Babies Dying Before Baptism in Byzantium," in *The Church and Childhood*, ed. Diana Wood, Studies in Church History 31 (Oxford: Blackwell, 1994), 115–25. Even without the influence of Augustine's formulation of the doctrine of original sin, the imperative to baptize infants—and the dread of them dying unbaptized—was as strong in the East as in the West. Baun concludes that infants' deaths were seen as a kind of spiritual annihilation, as if the child had not been allowed to gain existence to begin with: "Our unbaptized deceased infants do not fail to enter the kingdom because they bear a guilt burden of inherited sin […] but because, I would argue, their unbaptized state means they have no identity at all, whether moral, personal, or spiritual." Baun, 121.

141. Gregory of Nyssa, "On Infants' Early Deaths," 378.

The Catechetical Mainstream

Cyril of Jerusalem. Because the eschatology of Origen and Gregory of
Nyssa never represented the mainstream of Christian theology, we need
to look elsewhere to get a sense of the aspects of baptismal theology
Eastern Christians of the period generally considered essential to the rule
of faith.[142] Here the *Catechetical Lectures* of Cyril of Jerusalem (bishop
from 350–87) are particularly valuable because they represent a distilla-
tion of the beliefs the bishop considered necessary for those entering the
Church. The lectures urge the catechumens to whom they are addressed
to receive the sacrament and to do so with the commitment to live out
its promises. Both of these dimensions, Cyril maintains, are necessary for
salvation.

Cyril equates the reception of baptism with becoming a believer, placing heavy emphasis on the transition catechumens undergo in the sacrament.[143] His references to pre-baptismal exorcisms indicate that these
were an important part of preparation for the rite.[144] Though his insistence on sin as the product of an individual's free will precludes a theology of original sin as such, Cyril's insistence on the necessity of baptism
is unwavering: "nor will a man who acts virtuously, but does not receive
the seal by water, enter into the kingdom of heaven. This may appear a
bold saying, but it is not mine, for it was Jesus who pronounced it."[145]
Like Irenaeus, Cyril holds that both the corporeal and spiritual aspects of
baptism are necessary for salvation because man is both a corporeal and
spiritual being.[146] He considers baptism of blood another side of the same

142. "After [the Second Council of Constantinople in] 553, in fact, Origenism—especially
Origenist eschatology—was generally considered heretical in both the Eastern and Western
Churches." Daley, *The Hope of the Early Church*, 190.

143. "You are being given a new name you did not possess. Instead of catechumen, you
will now be called a Believer." Cyril of Jerusalem, "Lenten Lectures (*Catecheses*)," in *The Works
of Saint Cyril of Jerusalem*, vol. 1, trans. Leo P. McCauley and Anthony A. Stephenson, The
Fathers of the Church (Washington, DC: The Catholic University of America Press, 1969),
Catechesis 1.4, p. 93. The "candidates for Enlightenment" are described as being in the outer
court of a palace. "Lenten Lectures," Prologue 1, pp. 69–70.

144. "[T]he soul cannot be purified without exorcisms." "Lenten Lectures," Protocatechesis 9, p. 77.

145. "Lenten Lectures," Catechesis 3.4, p. 110. For sin and free will, see, Catechesis 2.1–4,
pp. 96–98.

146. Alexis J. Doval sees Cyril's insistence on the physical aspect of the sacrament as rooted

reality. Baptism in water and in blood both involve body and soul; both include a profession of faith; and both originate in the Passion of Jesus:

> If a man does not receive baptism he does not attain salvation, ex-
> cepting only the martyrs, who, even without the water, receive the
> kingdom. For the Savior who redeemed the world by the Cross,
> when His side was pierced, poured forth blood and water, that in
> time of peace men might be baptized in water, but in time of per-
> secution in their own blood. For the Savior could call martyrdom
> a baptism, saying: 'Can you drink the cup of which I drink or be
> baptized with the baptism with which I am baptized?'[147]

Also like Irenaeus, Cyril offers the story of Cornelius as proof of baptism's necessity; despite his upright life and extraordinary spiritual gifts, the centurion still required the sacrament.[148] All of this does not appear to leave much room for baptism of desire, even in the case of catechumens. Granted, Cyril's emphasis in the *Catechetical Lectures* is on the myriad impure reasons catechumens have for delaying conversion rather than on those who die unexpectedly, and he clearly affirms God's universal salvific will. But Cyril acknowledges that, although God throws open the doors of salvation to everyone, not everyone heeds his call.[149]

Basil. Equally firm in asserting the necessity of baptism is Basil the Great, elder brother of Gregory of Nyssa, friend of Gregory Nazianzen and bishop of Caesarea in Cappadocia (370–79). Basil's *Protreptic on Holy Baptism* strikes many of the same notes as Cyril's exhortation. He warns against excuses and delays intended to prolong the pursuit of worldly pleasures. This context again means that Basil is not addressing the hard-est cases—sincere catechumens dying unexpectedly—but the reasoning he employs would seem to preclude exceptions to the rule promulgated by John 3:5. "The one who is not baptized is not illuminated. And without illumination the eye cannot see its proper objects and the soul cannot contemplate God," he says, adding, "Not to know God is the death of the

---

in his emphasis on the Incarnation, in *Cyril of Jerusalem, Mystagogue: The Authorship of the Myst-agogic Catecheses* (Washington, DC: The Catholic University of America Press, 2001), 171–76.

147. Cyril of Jerusalem, "Lenten Lectures," Catechesis 3.10, pp. 114–15.

148. "Lenten Lectures," Catechesis 3.4, p. 110.

149. "Lenten Lectures," Catechesis 3.2, p. 109.

soul."[150] Again, the reason for the sacrament's necessity is not original sin per se, but the recognition of human existence as fatally—and inevitably—flawed, in need of illumination in order to experience divine life. Drawing upon the imagery of Exodus, Basil compares the sacrament to rescue from the angel of death—a force to which all people are subject regardless of personal culpability.[151] In a slightly different context he adds the argument that the absence of vice is not the same thing as having virtue, a principle that if generally applied would indicate that the mere absence of sin—in infants, for example—is no guarantee of salvation.[152]

This assumption undergirds his unique treatment of the conversion of Cornelius in another source. The righteous centurion comes up in Basil's discussion of the parable of the laborers in the vineyard, in which a day's wage is paid to every worker regardless of how many hours each works (Matt 20:1–16). Cornelius, Basil notes, used his natural gifts justly for many years but arrived only late at "perfection."[153] Nevertheless, he is sure that Cornelius's delayed conversion will not be held against him: The delay was not his fault, and his God-fearing life expressed the desire to reach perfection when the opportunity presented itself. Basil seems to believe that God would provide the same opportunity to anyone else in the same position, though he in no way indicates that it would involve anything other than what Cornelius received, knowledge of God through baptism. The point that until his baptism Cornelius fell short of perfection is treated as uncontroversial. Thus, though the example shows that Basil considered pre-baptismal righteousness to have real value, he does not consider what that value would be in the absence of the sacrament. In fact, when he directly addresses the question of what would happen to catechumens if they were to die before baptism, it is to warn dramatically that no amount of groaning or repentance will save them in the afterlife.[154] Moreover, Daley notes that, despite being influenced by Origen in

150. Basil, "Protreptic on Holy Baptism," in *Baptism: Ancient Liturgies and Patristic Texts*, trans. Thomas Halton, ed. André Hamman (New York: Alba House, 1967), 1, p. 76.

151. "Protreptic on Holy Baptism," 4, p. 81.

152. "Protreptic on Holy Baptism," 5, p. 83.

153. Basil, "Regole Brevi," in *Opere Ascetiche di Basilio di Cesarea*, ed. Umberto Neri, trans. Maria Benedetta Artioli (Turin: Unione Tipografico-Editrice Torinese, 1980), q. 224, pp. 448–49.

154. Basil, "Protreptic on Holy Baptism," 8, p. 86–87: "Unhappy me, not to have washed away my stains [...] I am tormented for eternity for a temporary enjoyment of my sins."

his youth, Basil firmly rejected the idea of universal salvation or of hell's fires ever being quenched, regarding such ideas as demonic tricks.[155] All of this suggests that the atmosphere of fourth century Christianity in the east was generally unfavorable to baptism of desire.

Gregory Nazianzen's Baptismal Sermons

Baptismal instructions, such as those of Cyril and Basil, are of theological importance because, as Claudio Moreschini points out, they put into words the faith being passed on in the sacrament.[156] As a guide for determining what the Fathers understood the essentials of the *regula fidei* to be—and consequently what ordinary Christians believed—they are particularly valuable sources. The sense of responsibility bishops felt to hand on only the most authoritative teachings on such occasions would have been strong. This was particularly the case, Moreschini argues, in Gregory Nazianzen's baptismal orations, the final example of the genre we will examine in this chapter. Known in the East as "the Theologian," the bishop of Nazianzus, like the other Cappadocians, lived through the height of the Arian controversy and is known for his contribution to Trinitarian theology. Given the divisions wrought by this and other heresies, it is no surprise that Gregory's baptismal theology emphasizes the importance of entering into "perfection" with a faith unmarred by error.[157] His pair of baptismal sermons was, therefore, composed with particular care. These sermons are of interest for the theme of baptism of desire because they list multiple types of baptism about a decade before Ambrose delivered *De obitu Valentiniani.* Gregory will surprise us, however, because a careful examination of his arguments shows that he should be classed among baptism of desire's early skeptics rather than its heralds.

155. Daley, *The Hope of the Early Church,* 81.

156. Claudio Moreschini, "Il battesimo come fondamento dell'istruzione del cristiano in Gregorio Nazianzeno," in *Sacerdozio battesimale e formazione teologica nella catechesi e nella testimonianza di vita dei padri,* ed. Sergio Felici, Biblioteca di scienze religiose 99 (Rome: Libreria Ateneo Salesiano, 1992), 73–74, 78. Cyril instructs his listeners not to treat his catechetical lectures as if they were just ordinary sermons, in "Lenten Lectures," Protocatechesis, 11, pp. 78–79.

157. Moreschini, "Il battesimo come fondamento," 79–81.

Oration 39. Gregory's "Oration on the Holy Lights" was delivered for
the feast of the Epiphany in 381 and considers baptism within salvation
history, specifically with regard to the Son's Incarnation and his baptism
by John. Baptism is described as illumination and as the culmination of
a process of purification for which the catechumens have already been
preparing.[158] It is also treated as initiation into the Church's worship;
tellingly, Gregory describes heaven in terms of worship: "There, where is
the dwelling of all the Blissful, is nothing else than this, the hymns and
praises of God, sung by all who are counted worthy of that City."[159] This
conception of heaven helps to explain why participation in the liturgy
was understood to be intrinsically related to salvation, not a mere external
prerequisite.

Gregory's sermon is perhaps most noteworthy for its articulation of
five different types of baptism.[160] The first two, of Moses and of John
the Baptist, are pre-Christian, and Gregory considers them partial. He
identifies the baptism of Moses with the crossing of the Red Sea and the
cloud guiding the Israelites. It is unclear what salvific power Gregory
attaches to these signs, since he regards them as a prefiguration of the
sacrament, just as manna prefigures the Eucharist. The baptism of John,
he argues, was superior to that of Moses because it involved not only
water but also repentance. However, it lacked the Spirit which makes
the third type of baptism—that of Jesus—perfect. It is clear, then, that
the two pre-Christian baptisms derive their value from their relationship
to the perfect baptism of Jesus. Gregory does not suggest that they retain any salvific value in the present; they seem to refer to quite singular
moments in salvation history.[161] The final two types of baptism Gregory

158. Gregory Nazianzen, "Oration 39: Oration on the Holy Lights," in *S. Cyril of Jerusalem,
S. Gregory Nazianzen*, ed. Philip Schaff and Henry Wace, trans. Charles Gordon Browne and
James Edward Swallow, Nicene and Post-Nicene Fathers of the Christian Church, 2nd ser.,
vol. 7 (Grand Rapids, MI: Eerdmans, 1989), 9–10, pp. 354–55.

159. "Oration 39," 11, p. 355. The phrasing calls to mind Bobertz's observation about the New
Testament concept of salvation: "Justification or salvation (the Greek word sōzō in Mark) was
not some personal existential reality or spiritual awareness, as it is so often thought to be today,
but quite literally a place at the sacred ritual meal." Bobertz, *The Gospel of Mark*, loc. 416 of 8173.
Gregory Nazianzen returns to the theme of the worship into which the catechumens are about
to enter as a foretaste of their experience of heaven near the end of "Oration 40," in *S. Cyril of
Jerusalem, S. Gregory Nazianzen*, 46, p. 377.

160. Gregory Nazianzen, "Oration 39," 17, p. 358.

161. As for Gentile religions, the sermon begins with a lengthy critique of pagan rituals,

lists are baptism by blood, "far more august" than the others because it cannot be spoiled by post-baptismal sin, and baptism "of tears." The baptism of tears, however, is nothing other than penitence for post-baptismal sin and is thus not comparable to baptism of desire. Though he considers post-baptismal penance more laborious and uncertain than baptism, Gregory dedicates a significant amount of space in the sermon to refuting the teachings of Novatus, who denied any possibility of a second repentance.[162] Gregory's digression ends with a final reference to "baptism with fire," by which he means post-mortem purification. Gregory does not call this a sixth type of baptism, and the context indicates that he regards it as an extension of the baptism of tears. In other words, it is improbable that he regarded the "baptism of fire" as an alternative path to salvation for those who leave this life without the sacrament.[163] When we turn to the homily Gregory delivered the next day, in which he expands upon the same themes, this conclusion will become inescapable.

Oration 40. That sermon, the "Oration on Holy Baptism," is both catechetical and hortatory, with some sections dedicated to explaining the rite and the Trinitarian faith it expresses and others aimed at persuading catechumens not to delay their reception of the sacrament. The oration begins with a reflection on the way light has been used in salvation history, concluding that the illumination of baptism is unique because it contains the "great and marvelous sacrament of our salvation" through which we participate in the Paschal Mystery.[164] However, the key parts of the sermon for our theme come in its long, impassioned central

which Gregory regards as ungodly even if they share some superficial similarities with baptism. "Oration 39," 3–8, pp. 352–54.

162. "Oration 39," 18–19, pp. 358–59.

163. And he has also already drawn a sharp distinction "between the faithful and the unbeliever" marked by baptism. "Oration 39," 15, p. 358. D.F. Winslow's attempt to soften Gregory's rigor with respect to the necessity of baptism is unsuccessful because he fails to recognize that the baptism of tears does not replace the sacrament, nor do the Old Testament precedents retain their validity in the present day. D.F. Winslow, "Orthodox Baptism—A Problem for Gregory of Nazianzus," in *Studia Patristica*, vol. 14, ed. Elizabeth A. Livingstone (Berlin: Akademie, 1976), 371–74. The passages he cites from Orations 32 and 33 apply to different contexts. Winslow is successful in showing that Gregory does not possess a magical view of the sacrament, i.e., that its reception does not equate to automatic entrance into heaven but depends also on the life one lives after baptism.

164. Gregory Nazianzen, "Oration 40," 6, p. 361; 9, p. 362.

argument against delaying baptism. The fundamental reason Gregory offers is that dying without the sacrament means the loss of eternal life; at
one point he warns rather ominously of the many "unexpected mischanc-
es" in which one could perish: earthquakes, shipwrecks, animal attacks,
sickness, choking on food, storms, accidents, poisonings.[165] Some of these
might be the negligent catechumen's fault—Gregory mentions perishing
at the end of a drinking bout—but what is notable for our purposes is
that most are due to circumstances beyond the individual's control. Circumstances seem not to matter to Gregory. What matters is simply the
fact of dying unbaptized; the same belief is evident in the story of his own
baptism, recounted in the eulogy given upon his father's death. While
traveling from Alexandria to Greece as a young man, Gregory recalls, his
ship was overcome by a violent storm: "While all were afraid of a common death, I was in greater fear of spiritual death. Unfortunately, I was in
danger of departing from life unbaptized, and I yearned for the spiritual
water amid the waters of death."[166] Gregory attributes his survival to the
prayers of his parents, who had been warned in a dream of the danger he
faced. He was baptized after returning safely to shore.

The incident shows that, although Gregory speaks of the sacrament
as the fulfillment of our highest desires, he does not seem to have put any
stock in the salvific power of those desires alone.[167] In his "Oration on
Holy Baptism" he explains why with a devastatingly simple argument: If
you desire something, it means you do not have it.

> But then, you say, is not God merciful, and since He knows our
> thoughts and searches out our desires, will He not take the desire
> of Baptism instead of Baptism? You are speaking in riddles, if what
> you mean is that because of God's mercy the unenlightened is en-
> lightened in His sight; and he is within the kingdom who merely
> desires to attain to it, but refrains from doing that which pertains
> to the kingdom.[168]

---

165. "Oration 40," 14, p. 364.

166. Gregory Nazianzen, "Oration 18: On the Death of his Father," in *S. Cyril of Jerusalem,
S. Gregory Nazianzen*, 31, pp. 144–45.

167. "Illumination is the satisfying of desire to those who long for [...] the Greatest Thing."
Gregory Nazianzen, "Oration 39," 8, p. 354.

168. Gregory Nazianzen, "Oration 40," 22, p. 367.

Later he adds that we would not judge a man who merely desired someone else's murder guilty of the crime. And, he goes on, if desire for a thing is the same as the thing itself, then those who desire heavenly glory should be content with that desire even if they never arrive at the glory.[169] While he regards the reality of the sacrament as something no subjective consideration can replace, Gregory does acknowledge that the circumstances and motives that might prevent a person from receiving baptism vary. He distinguishes three classes of the unbaptized: the truly wicked who hold the sacrament in contempt; the lazy or greedy who procrastinate; and those who remain unbaptized due to "some perfectly involuntary circumstance." Gregory believes that punishments will differ depending on these motivating factors, with the first category of the wicked punished the most severely, the second less so, and the third "neither glorified nor punished by the righteous Judge [...] For not everyone who is not bad enough to be punished is good enough to be honoured; just as not everyone who is not good enough to be honoured is bad enough to be punished." Gregory specifically lists infants as belonging to this third category of individuals. Later on, he advocates infant baptism in danger of death, "For it is better that they should be unconsciously sanctified than that they should depart unsealed and uninitiated."[170]

Gregory, then, seems to hold to the absolute necessity of the sacrament for salvation, while foreseeing a neutral state of existence for those who, while not guilty of personal sin, die unbaptized. Though he does not use the word, the concept is strikingly similar to what would later be called "limbo."[171] His conclusion is also similar to Gregory of Nyssa's discussion of the question of children who die in infancy, though the Nyssen's reasoning is based on the children's capacity for virtue and the Nazianzen's on the reception of baptism. Thus, the bishop of Nazianzus urges catechumens involved in worldly affairs to proceed to the baptismal font, even if such dealings are likely to involve them in moral imperfection. Though elsewhere he emphasizes the preferability of avoiding sin to facing cleansing fire in the afterlife, in this case the equation changes:

169. "Oration 40," 23, pp. 367–68.

170. "Oration 40," 28, p. 370. In happier circumstances he considers it better to wait until children are around three years old, when they can consciously participate in the ritual.

171. Ferguson attributes similar reasoning to Theodoret of Cyrus and to *Questions to the Governor of Antioch*, attributed to Athanasius. Ferguson, *Baptism in the Early Church*, 459, 718.

It is better both to attain the good and to keep the purification. But if it be impossible to do both it is surely better to be a little stained with your public affairs than to fall altogether short of grace; just as I think it is better to undergo a slight punishment from father or master than to be put out of doors; and to be a little beamed upon than to be left in total darkness [...] Wherefore do not overmuch dread the purification.[172]

The instruction *not* to dread postmortem purification only makes sense given the categorical difference between those who have been buried with Christ in baptism and those who have not.[173]

Gregory expands upon his understanding of purifying fire later in the oration, drawing a distinction between fire that purifies and fire that punishes. The first is kindled by Christ's coming upon the earth and burns away evil habits. Gregory contrasts this fire with another: "I know also a fire which is not cleansing, but avenging."[174] This is the fire God sent upon Sodom as a precursor of "that which is prepared for the Devil and his Angels." This is "the unquenchable fire which is ranged with the worm that dieth not but is eternal for the wicked." Gregory acknowledges another viewpoint, noting that "some may prefer even in this place to take a more merciful view of this fire, worthily of Him That chastises." Both Daley and Sachs cite this digression as evidence of Gregory's sympathy for an Origenist position that would see all fire as purgative and the punishments of hell melting away after the *apokatastasis*.[175] At most, however, it suggests that Gregory knew of such a position—and that some of those he was addressing were familiar with it as well—but that it was not *his* position. He immediately goes on, "And as I know of two kinds of fire, so

---

172. Gregory Nazianzen, "Oration 40," 19, p. 366.

173. In another work Gregory Nazianzen treats immersion in the Paschal Mystery as the single factor allowing what is glorious and divine in man to escape the fate of what is earthly and mortal. Gregory Nazianzen, "Oration 7: Panegyric on his Brother S. Caesarius," in *S. Cyril of Jerusalem, S. Gregory Nazianzen*, 22–23, p. 237. His treatment of his younger brother Caesarius's conversion manifests the same beliefs about the absolute necessity of baptism outlined above. "Oration 7," 15, p. 234.

174. Gregory Nazianzen, "Oration 40," 36, p. 373.

175. Sachs, "Apocatastasis in Patristic Theology," 360; Daley, *The Hope of the Early Church*, 84. Gregory elsewhere acknowledges the justice of punishment, which is "a fate to be desired for the wicked, who are worthy of the fire yonder." "Oration 7," 22, p. 237. The Origenist interpretation, moreover, requires us to ignore Gregory's insistence on the necessity of baptism.

also do I of light."[176] Thus, in no way does Gregory abandon what he has just said about the two types of fire, nor is the digression meant to signal that Gregory parts with Basil and the theological mainstream on the eternity of heaven and hell. In fact, perhaps Gregory's most significant contribution to our investigation is the way he so starkly expresses the fundamental problem driving it. Baptism is necessary for entry into the kingdom of heaven. Gregory takes this principle to mean exactly what it says—not that those without baptism will be punished for that fact but neither that the rule admits of exceptions. No matter the circumstances, not being baptized means not being saved.

At the end of this chapter, perhaps this conclusion will surprise us less than it might have at the beginning. Evidence from Christianity's first four centuries underscores with striking consistency the irreducibility of the rite of baptism in *defining* Christian faith in salvation. Before it was a doctrinal principle or Church regulation, the necessity of baptism was part of early Christians' experience of salvation. The presupposition that made the proclamation of the Gospel meaningful to the ancient world was mankind's universal need for a savior, the fact that we are born into a trajectory that leads inevitably to death. Baptism was the turning point at which believers broke free of this trajectory by participating in the death of Jesus and receiving his new life. The assertion of the necessity of baptism for salvation was, for early Christians, the natural expression of what both baptism and salvation meant. Even "optimistic" thinkers such as Justin Martyr were not exceptions to this rule. In those instances in which early Christians reveal an instinct to widen the prospect of salvation to accommodate hard cases, the rite remained central to their thinking—from the posthumous baptisms of the Corinthians and Hermas to the "rebaptisms of desire" of Cyprian. These early ventures at solutions to hard cases, however, did not stand up to theological scrutiny or pass the test of time. Likewise, the posthumous cleansing fire discussed in the third and fourth centuries would prove, at most, a supplement to baptism, not its replacement. At the end of the fourth century, in fact, Gregory Nazianzen seemed to preemptively close the door on the possibility of

176. Gregory Nazianzen, "Oration 40," 37, p. 373.

baptism of desire with the judgment that if you desired something, it meant you did not have it.

Gregory's verdict, however, would not be the last word. On the other side of the Roman Empire, another bishop was about to confront a hard case in the most extreme of circumstances: Speaking over the body of a catechumen—the Roman emperor, no less—murdered before his baptism, Ambrose of Milan would give a very different response.

Chapter Two

The Birth of the Doctrine

Late in May of 392, a messenger from Vienne in Gaul, where the Western Roman emperor Valentinian II had been temporarily residing, intercepted the party of Ambrose, bishop of Milan, with alarming news shortly after it had crossed the Alps.[1] The emperor, who had urgently summoned Ambrose only days before, had been found dead in his chambers, strangled with his own handkerchief. Suspicion immediately fell upon the commander of Roman forces in Gaul, Arbogast, who, backed by his own troops and supported by the local population, had treated Valentinian virtually as his prisoner. In fact, Valentinian had summoned Ambrose hoping that the diplomatically astute bishop would be able to mediate the dispute between the two men. Arbogast denied the murder, claiming that Valentinian had died by suicide, and Ambrose returned immediately to Milan, the imperial capital, where the dead emperor's sisters

---

1. Thomas A. Kelly provides a succinct summary of the political background of *De obitu Valentiniani* in *Santcti Ambrosii Liber de Consolatione Valentiniani: A Text with a Translation, Introduction and Commentary* (Washington, DC: The Catholic University of America Press, 1940), 16–41. Two modern biographies of Ambrose paint quite different pictures of the bishop: Cesare Pasini, *Ambrogio di Milano: Azione e pensiero di un vescovo* (Cinisello Balsamo: Edizioni San Paolo, 1997); Neil B. McLynn, *Ambrose of Milan: Church and Court in a Christian Capital* (Berkeley: University of California Press, 1994), Kindle.

awaited his body. When it arrived, they would have to wait another two months before the Eastern emperor Theodosius, to whom all the Western factions looked for legitimacy, granted permission for a formal burial. It fell to Ambrose to preside at a ceremony taut with political tension. With Arbogast denying the murder but supporting his own claimant to the imperial throne, Theodosius's ultimate reaction to events in the West uncertain, and what was left of the imperial family hunkered down in Milan, Ambrose's city braced for civil war.

As if the political—and personal—stakes were not high enough, Ambrose faced a theological conundrum. Valentinian had, in fact, summoned the bishop with two urgent requests: He hoped that Ambrose might resolve his conflict with Arbogast, and he desired to be baptized. Delay in baptism was common at the time; at the age of thirty-four Ambrose himself was famously still a catechumen when elected Milan's bishop by acclamation in 374 and was baptized a week before his ordination. Throughout his episcopacy Ambrose had to contend with the Empire's religious divisions, and relations between bishop and emperor had seen their ups and downs. During the early years of Valentinian's reign, the religious policy of the teenage emperor, which seems to have been guided by his Arian mother Justina, provoked repeated clashes with Ambrose. Since Justina's death in 388, however, Valentinian—just twenty-one years old when he died—had proven himself both orthodox and devout. Yet, despite Valentinian's request, Ambrose had not arrived in time to baptize him, and the absence of the sacrament weighed heavily on the minds of the emperor's pious sisters. Ambrose rose to the occasion, crafting a masterpiece of classical rhetoric and Biblical imagery, fusing personal emotion with a carefully constructed theological argument that Valentinian would be saved. The baptismal grace Valentinian sought, Ambrose said, would come in virtue of his desire for the sacrament. In *De obitu Valentiniani*, baptism of desire was born.

The doctrine's birth was not creation *ex nihilo*. As we have already seen, rough precursors of the theory had begun gestating in the writings of Cyprian and his opponents in North Africa's third century baptismal controversies. Ambrose did not refer to these precedents in *De obitu Valentiniani*, but they would be taken up by another Ambrosian catechumen destined to exercise a more lasting influence on Western thought than

Valentinian. A few years after Valentinian's burial, though apparently independently of his one-time catechist, Augustine of Hippo, embroiled in another North African baptismal controversy, would construct a remarkably similar argument for baptism of desire based on his exegesis of the story of the Good Thief in Luke 23. The birth of the Augustinian version of the doctrine, however, faced a complicated labor. Augustine appears to have had second thoughts about his early interpretation of the Good Thief's salvation, and his later writings would provide the most important lines of attack for subsequent opponents of baptism of desire. The scarce data we have from later in the patristic age is no more conclusive than the evidence we saw in chapter one. So, while it is too much to argue that baptism of desire represented the patristic consensus, thanks to the two great Latin doctors we will examine in this chapter, we can legitimately consider the theory a patristic doctrine, if a contested one.

Because the contexts in which they developed their parallel theologies were so different, our approach to Ambrose and Augustine must also be different. We will first examine Ambrose's baptismal theology and then take a detailed look at *De obitu Valentiniani*. Ambrose argues that Valentinian's desire for baptism made him turn more fervently to the Lord in prayer and bases his confidence on the Lord's promise to answer the prayer of those in need. Augustine's version of the doctrine, on the other hand, is based on the example of the Good Thief. The main difficulty of this chapter will be coming to grips with what seems to be Augustine's skeptical stance toward baptism of desire later in his career. We will need to identify the broader theological considerations raised in the bishop of Hippo's polemics first with Donatists, then with Pelagians, and then examine how these come into tension in the issue of baptism of desire. A brief survey of the late patristic period will turn up a supporter of baptism of desire in Theodore of Mopsuestia and an opponent in Gennadius of Massilia.

Ambrose of Milan and Valentinian's Salvation

To appreciate the significance of Ambrose's assertions in *De obitu Valentiniani*, we must understand the work's theological presuppositions. Perhaps the first fact to note about Ambrose's presumptions is how thoroughly

mainstream they were. Ambrose has been criticized for a lack of theological originality—though the theological dexterity shown in *De obitu Valentiniani* should call into question such global judgments.[2] Nonetheless,
as even scholars sympathetic to Ambrose recognize, he was more pastor
than speculative theologian. His lack of ecclesiastical formation before his
election as bishop—he had risen through the civil service to become Milan's governor—required Ambrose to devote significant time early in his
career to bringing his theological reading up-to-date, and his involvement
in imperial diplomacy also took its toll on his time and energy. Ambrose
himself may have regarded the charge that he was no innovator as a com-
pliment, for, like most of his contemporaries, he placed greater value on
fidelity to the rule of faith than on personal inventiveness; his skirmishes
with Arianism demonstrate the importance he placed on orthodoxy. Since
baptism of desire was a bold position to stake out in the late fourth century, the fact that it comes from such a staunchly orthodox authority adds
to its theological weight.

Theological Presuppositions

Baptism. The most important of the theological presuppositions driving
Ambrose's argument in *De obitu Valentiniani*—one which by now should
not surprise us—is the necessity of baptism for salvation. If Valentinian's
sisters had not believed baptism to be necessary for salvation, Ambrose
would have had no need to address the issue in his sermon. Not only did
this belief represent the common faith of the Christian people, Ambrose
himself forcefully affirms it. In an early exegetical work, *On Abraham*,
Ambrose resembles Gregory Nazianzen in his absolute affirmation of
the necessity of baptism: "none has ascended to the Kingdom of Heav-
en," he asserts, "save through the Sacrament of Baptism."[3] Furthermore,
according to Ambrose, the Lord exempts no one from the injunction

---

2. W.G. Rusch, "Baptism of Desire in Ambrose and Augustine," in *Studia patristica*, vol. 15,
ed. Elizabeth A. Livingstone (Berlin: Akademie, 1984), 378. See also Pasini, *Ambrogio di Milano*,
30–31.

3. Ambrose, *On Abraham*, trans. Theodosia Tomkinson (Etna, CA: Center for Tradition-
alist Orthodox Studies, 2000), 2.11.79, p. 97. On the work's dating, perhaps around 382–83, see
Ambrose, *Opera Omnia di Sant'Ambrogio*, vol. 2, bk. 2, *Opere esegetiche II/II*, trans. Franco Gori
(Rome: Città Nuova, 1984), 9–10.

of John 3:5, "not the infant, not one hindered by any necessity."[4] Like
Gregory, Ambrose leaves the door open to a limbo-like state of existence
for those without personal sin: "but although they may have a hidden
immunity to punishments, I know not whether they have the honour of
the Kingdom."

Here Ambrose might seem to contradict the position he would eventually take in *De obitu Valentiniani*, though the context of his affirmations
complicates matters. In *On Abraham*, he is discussing circumcision, baptism's Old Testament precursor. Treating circumcision as a proto-baptism
is common enough among patristic authors and already shows a willingness to stretch the understanding of what constitutes baptism to include
Old Testament signs. It does not, however, afford salvific value to Jewish
rituals in the present day. Since Ambrose saw circumcision's purifying
value as coming from its reference to baptism and the Paschal Mystery,
the implicit power in its foreshadowing necessarily expired when the reality appeared. Put in another way, circumcision is not salvific unless it
points toward baptism. With respect to "one hindered by any necessity,"
Ambrose may have changed his mind when confronted with the concrete
circumstances of Valentinian's death. On the other hand, when we examine the phrasing the eulogy employs, we will see that Ambrose does not
claim that Valentinian is an exception to this injunction but that he has
received baptism in a different way.[5]

Sin. In Ambrose's theology, baptism is necessary for two reasons: to wash
away sin and to impart life-giving faith. He believes that all people need
baptism for both of these reasons, differentiating him from Cyril of Jerusalem, who maintained that those who had never committed a personal
sin required baptism only for the second reason. Ambrose's thinking more

4. Ambrose, *On Abraham*, 2.11.84, p. 100. "Vitique nullum excepit, non infantem, non aliqua praeeuentum necessitate: habeant tamen illam opertam poenarum inmunitatem, nescio an
habeant regni honorem," *Opere esegetiche II/II*, 248.

5. Cf. Ambrose, *Opera Omnia di Sant'Ambrogio*, vol. 9, *Opere esegetiche VIII/I: Commento
al Salmo CXVIII (Lettere I–XI)*, trans. Luigi F. Pizzolato (Roma: Città Nuova, 1987), 3.14–18,
pp. 134–41. Here, in language similar to Gregory Nazianzen's, Ambrose declares that there is
not only one form of baptism ("Non unum est baptisma"). To sacramental baptism, he adds
baptism of blood and a posthumous baptism by purifying fire. Like Origen, he does not regard
purifying fire as a substitute for sacramental baptism because he speaks of those who undergo
it as being baptized in both water *and* fire.

closely aligns with the doctrine of original sin that Augustine would articulate. Ambrose sees all humanity as unavoidably tarnished by sin, though
he does not arrive at this understanding through an account of genea-
logical descent but simply by noting sin's ubiquitous effects. The human
tendency toward sin, he observes, is present from the very beginning of
our lives. This is the reason the Mosaic Law prescribed circumcision in
infancy: "just as sin begins in infancy, so circumcision is performed in
infancy. No age should be devoid of tutelage, because none is devoid of
guilt."[6] The reality of sin, in other words, is active within us from the first
moment of our lives.

Ambrose makes the same point in his mystagogical work *The Sacraments*. "No man is without sin," he claims, though before we have been
enlightened by the light of Christ, one of sin's effects is to blind us to our
own neediness.[7] The proof of this claim is our universal subjugation to
death, the consequence of sin. Referring to Genesis 3:19—"you are dust,
and to dust you shall return"—Ambrose describes death as God's just
sentence upon humanity.[8] Because baptism is a kind of death, it satisfies
this sentence, though it also requires those who undergo it to rise to a
different kind of life. Ambrose places significant emphasis on the period
of conversion and penitence in preparation for Christian initiation in a
shorter mystagogical work, *The Mysteries*. The bishop begins with an allusion to a previous series of daily sermons on moral conduct that the newly baptized had received as catechumens; the purpose of these sermons
was to prepare them for the life they would live as Christians.[9] The heavy
demands of Christian moral integrity explain why, even given the necessity of baptism for salvation, reception of the sacrament in Ambrose's day
was often delayed until well into adulthood.

6. Ambrose, *On Abraham*, 2.11.81, p. 98.

7. Ambrose, *The Sacraments*, in *Theological and Dogmatic Works*, trans. Roy J. Deferrari, The
Fathers of the Church 44 (Washington, DC: The Catholic University of America Press, 1963),
3.2.13–14, pp. 294–95.

8. *The Sacraments*, 2.6.19, pp. 285–86. Ambrose is consistent on this point in other works;
our existence is inevitably tainted by sin and without God's intervention humanity tends toward a kind of moral entropy; see *Commento al Salmo CXVIII* (*Lettere I–XI*), 3.12–13, 3.18,
pp. 134–37, 140–41; "Letter 25," in *Saint Ambrose: Letters*, trans. Mary Melchior Beyenka, Fathers
of the Church 26 (Washington, DC: The Catholic University of America Press, 1967), 132–33.

9. Ambrose, *The Mysteries*, in *Theological and Dogmatic Works*, 1.1, p. 5. See also, *The Sacraments*, 3.2.12, p. 294.

Faith. Having been cleansed of sin in baptism, one was freed to receive the Church's faith. "Faith," as Ambrose uses the term, is itself a part of the sacramental reality, not merely an intellectual belief or an affective stance. *On Abraham* ties the reception of faith to penitence and the sacrament: "unless ye weep for your sins, unless ye receive the Grace of Baptism, the Faith of the Church [...] [is] not given to you."[10] This way of conceiving of faith as intrinsic to baptism is reflected in Ambrose's insistence on the *disciplina arcani*, withholding explanation of the sacraments until after their reception. In his first sermon to the newly baptized in *The Sacraments*, Ambrose notes that the content of his mystagogy "should not have been presented to you before" because "in the Christian man faith is first."[11] This patristic understanding of faith as something received in the sacraments may seem strange to modern readers accustomed to identifying faith with assent to a particular set of beliefs. It becomes less so if we think of faith as our response to an encounter with Christ, an encounter that occurs in the sacraments.[12] The conviction that Christ is uniquely accessible in the sacraments reinforces the patristic consensus that baptism is necessary for salvation; a personal presence is not reducible to more fundamental principles and, therefore, not subject to substitution. On the other hand, once we assume the validity of baptism of desire, the *disciplina arcani*—the practice of explaining the details of the rite only to the initiated—has important implications for how we evaluate what kind of desire is necessary for salvation. Because some aspects of catechesis

10. Ambrose, *On Abraham*, 1.9.87, p. 42.

11. Ambrose, *The Sacraments*, 1.1.1, p. 269. He also uses Christ's healing of the deaf and mute man (Mk 7:31–37) to explains the *disciplina arcani*. The encounter with Jesus—in this case including the physical elements of saliva and touch—creates the conditions necessary for the deaf man to hear. Ambrose, *The Mysteries*, 1.2–4, pp. 5–6.

12. In his exegesis of David's penitential prayer—in response to which he imagines the Lord revealing a prefiguration of baptism—Ambrose describes the sacraments in terms of a face-to-face encounter with the Lord, in *De apologia prophetae David ad Theodosium Augustum*, in *Opera Omnia di Sant'Ambrogio*, vol. 5, *Opere esegetiche V: De apologia prophetae David ad Theodosium Augustum, Apologia David Altera*, trans. Filippo Lucidi (Rome: Città Nuova, 1981), 12.58, pp. 116–19: "*Ecce enim ueritatem dilexisti*: non per speculum, non in aenigmate, sed faciem ad faciem te mihi, Christe, demonstras, in tuis teneo sacramentis. Haec sunt tuae uera sacramenta sapientiae, quibus mentis occulta mundantur." Perhaps the most lapidary expression of patristic sacramental theology is found in Leo the Great's claim that after the Ascension, "What was to be seen of our Redeemer has passed over into the Sacraments." Leo I, *Pope Leo I: Sermons*, trans. Jane Patricia Freeland, Fathers of the Church 93 (Washington, DC: The Catholic University of America Press, 1996), 74.2, p. 326.

were held back until the mystagogy following initiation, the practice of Ambrose's church assumes that in order to receive baptism, one's intellectual grasp of the faith need not be complete. Since a catechumen who died before baptism would not have had the benefit of all of the knowledge of fully-initiated Christian, Ambrose could not have regarded incomplete catechesis as an insurmountable obstacle to baptism of desire.[13]

The Doctrine of De obitu Valentiniani

With this background in mind, we can turn directly to *De obitu Valentiniani*. Like any eulogy, a good part of the funeral oration is taken up with praise of the deceased; we need not be excessively concerned with the historical accuracy of Ambrose's assessment of Valentinian's character, though the (no doubt somewhat idealized) portrait of the young emperor is valuable from a theological perspective because of the insights it gives us into the characteristics Ambrose considered necessary for baptism of desire. Ambrose praises Valentinian's asceticism, chastity, sense of justice, piety, and courage; while these virtues are laudable in themselves, Ambrose sees their true value as signs of the emperor's sincere pursuit of penance. Valentinian, in Ambrose's telling, does not seem to have had a particularly sinful past; Ambrose refers generically to the Biblical "sins of my youth" from which Valentinian turned rather quickly. Ambrose faults him for a fleeting interest in the Roman circus and for briefly allowing hunting and sports to distract from the affairs of state, errors he corrected in decisive fashion.[14] Nonetheless, Ambrose emphasizes the specifically penitential character of Valentinian's pursuit of virtue—using phrases like "the heavy yoke of amendment" and "rigor of amendment" and referring to a "timely confession" and "speedy amendment."[15] Highlighting Valentinian's penitential spirit allows Ambrose to align the emperor's life with the extensive pre-baptismal penance catechumens underwent and

13. Because he understood the sacrament as imparting faith, Ambrose was not so sanguine about heretical beliefs. He insisted on accurate Trinitarian belief, for "the baptism of unbelievers does not heal, does not cleanse, but pollutes." Ambrose, *The Mysteries*, 5.23, p. 13; cf. 5.28, p. 15.

14. Ambrose, *On Emperor Valentinian*, in *Funeral Orations by Saint Gregory Nazianzen and Saint Ambrose*, trans. Roy J. Deferrari, The Fathers of the Church 22 (Washington, DC: The Catholic University of America Press, 1988), 14–15, pp. 272–73. Valentinian "ordered all the beasts to be slain" so that hunting would never again become a distraction.

15. *On Emperor Valentinian*, 9–12, pp. 270–71.

Ambrose's mystagogical works so emphasize. Penance signaled that the catechumen was not just formally enrolled but was sincerely preparing for baptism and all of its obligations.

In itself even Valentinian's virtuous lifestyle was not sufficient for salvation, Ambrose knows, because salvation is not the achievement of human virtue. No one is capable of redeeming himself, and no amount of penance can equal the grace of baptism.[16] Toward the end of the oration Ambrose addresses Valentinian's lack of baptism head on, and his response emphasizes the emperor's desire for the sacrament. Speaking directly to Valentinian's sisters, he says,

> But I hear that you grieve because he did not receive the sacrament of baptism. Tell me: what else is in your power other than the desire, the request? But he even had this desire for a long time, that, when he should come into Italy, he would be initiated, and recently he signified a desire to be baptized by me, and for this reason above all others he thought that I ought to be summoned. Has he not, then, the grace which he desired; has he not the grace which he requested?[17]

Here Ambrose pulls together a number of arguments running through the discourse up to this point, making it clear that Valentinian's lack of baptism had been the speech's core theological problem all along. While narrating the account of his death, in fact, Ambrose had repeatedly mentioned Valentinian's requests for baptismal instruction.[18] At one point in this narrative Ambrose had launched into what might seem at first glance to be an incongruous digression: a reflection on poverty based on the

16. *On Emperor Valentinian*, 48, p. 286. In *The Mysteries*, Ambrose makes reference to catechumens being marked with the sign of the cross and argues that in itself neither this sign nor the belief it implies is sufficient for salvation: "even a catechumen believes in the cross of the Lord Jesus, with which he, too, is signed, but unless he be baptized [...] he cannot receive remission of sins nor drink in the benefit of spiritual grace." *The Mysteries*, 20, p. 12. If enrollment in the catechumenate were itself sufficient for salvation, the preparatory rite would be more important than baptism.

17. *On Emperor Valentinian*, 51, pp. 287–88. "Sed audio uos dolere, quod non acceperit sacramenta baptismatis. Dicite mihi: Quid aliud in nobis est nisi uoluntas, nisi petitio? Atqui etiam dudum hoc uoti habuit, ut, antequam in Italiam uenisset, initiaretur, et proxime baptizari se a me uelle significauit, et ideo prae ceteris causis me acciendum putauit. Non habit ergo gratiam, quam desierauit, non habet, quam poposcit?" *Opera Omnia di Sant'Ambrogio*, vol. 18, *Discorsi e Lettere I: Le Orazioni Funebri,* ed. Gabriele Banterle (Rome Città Nuova, 1985), p. 192.

18. *On Emperor Valentinian*, 23, 25, 30, pp. 276–79.

beatitude "Blessed are the poor in spirit."[19] Ambrose's point has to do with the fervor of Valentinian's prayer. The poor must beg for what they do not have—in Valentinian's case the grace of baptism. By showing the emperor to be in the position of an impoverished supplicant, Ambrose reassures his listeners that the Lord, who looks mercifully on the cry of the poor, will indeed grant him his desire. In the previous chapter we noted Gregory Nazianzen's concise argument against baptism of desire—that those who desire something do not possess it. Ambrose turns that argument on its head based on God's willingness to answer the prayers of the poor.

Two elements are crucial in Ambrose's thinking: desire (*uoluntas*) and request (*petitio*). These elements—desire and request—are repeated in the key paragraph quoted above. Both elements carry theological weight. Throughout the eulogy Ambrose is at pains to demonstrate the sincerity and passion of Valentinian's desire for baptism. When the sermon reaches its rhetorical crescendo, for example, he compares Valentinian to an infant yearning to suck milk at the breasts of the Church.[20] The care with which Ambrose emphasizes Valentinian's sincere, consistent, and powerful desire indicates that he believes that not all desires are equal and that he likely regards some desires—fleeting or lukewarm—as insufficient for salvation. Like a skilled defense attorney, he is also demonstrating that the circumstances which prevented Valentinian's baptism—his murder by Arbogast—were beyond his control.[21] To this, Ambrose adds the element of petition. Valentinian's explicit request reinforces the sincerity of his desire, but it also shows that this desire went beyond a subjective disposition. Indeed, Ambrose speaks of Valentinian as having made two types of request for baptism—one directed to him as bishop and the other to God in prayer. His emphasis on the role of petitionary prayer echoes his description of Valentinian's "poverty." He goes so far as to compare Valentinian's prayer to that of Christ, because his argument hinges on the

---

19. *On Emperor Valentinian*, 30–33, pp. 279–80.

20. *On Emperor Valentinian*, 75, p. 296.

21. Ambrose clearly regarded Arbogast's version of events—that Valentinian committed suicide—as false. As for the young man's decision to leave Milan and travel north, Ambrose frames this as the selfless fulfillment of his duties as emperor, even comparing Valentinian's willingness to face death for others to Christ's self-sacrifice. *On Emperor Valentinian*, 22, 35, pp. 275–76, 281.

belief that God answers his faithful's prayers.[22] The emphasis Ambrose places on Valentinian's request for baptism sheds further light on the quality of desire he regards as necessary; while the desire may not require perfect knowledge of Christian doctrine, it does seem to have to be clear enough to prompt a concrete request.

In addition to Valentinian's own prayer, Ambrose mentions other intercessions offered on the deceased's behalf. These prayers come from Valentinian's dead brother Gratian, about whose salvation Ambrose seems assured, as well as from the bishop himself, who declares, "I also assume the role of intercessor for him for whom I anticipate reward!"[23] The final words of the sermon are addressed directly to God in a moving plea for Valentinian's resurrection.[24] Ambrose urges his listeners to offer their prayers for Valentinian too. While he never suggests that such intercessory prayer could act as a substitute for Valentinian's own desire, it expresses the Church's participation in and assent to Valentinian's request. The rite of baptism, after all, involves the Christian assembly, and, as Ambrose describes it, baptism of desire remains an ecclesial event.[25] In a way, Ambrose sees the desires of God, the Church, and Valentinian aligning.

God's way of answering Valentinian's prayer is also worth noting. God does not make an exception to the rule of the necessity of baptism, but

22. *On Emperor Valentinian*, 32–34, pp. 280–81. Ambrose places a high value on the power of intercessory prayer because he sees the Holy Spirit as already at work guiding our prayer—provided it is directed at the right object. See, for example, Ambrose, "Letter 53," in *Saint Ambrose: Letters*, 284–85. He makes much of the Lord's reply to the leper's request for healing in Lk 5:12–16. *Commento al Salmo CXVIII* (*Lettere I–XI*), 3.29, pp. 152–55. The story demonstrates, according to Ambrose, that the Lord wills that all be purified in the true faith.

23. Ambrose, *On Emperor Valentinian*, 54–56, pp. 288–89.

24. *On Emperor Valentinian*, 81, p. 299.

25. Here it is appropriate to take note of Ambrose's exegesis of the Good Thief pericope. Ambrose does not address the sacramental problem the Good Thief's salvation seems to raise, i.e., how he could be saved without baptism. Ambrose's repeated references to baptism in his commentary on the passage—noting that we participate in the crucifixion through baptism—suggest that the problem did not occur to him. Ambrose, *Opera Omnia di Sant'Ambrogio*, vol. 12, *Opere esegetiche IX/II: Expositionis Evangelii Secundum Lucam*, trans. Giovanni Coppa (Rome: Città Nuova Editrice, 1978), 10.123–4, pp. 480–81. While Ambrose does not use the passage to support the doctrine articulated in *De obitu Valentiniani*, his exegesis places a similarly strong emphasis on the role of desire and petitionary prayer. Ambrose depicts the Thief, like Valentinian, as an example of the spirit of conversion manifesting itself in prayer. *Expositionis Evangelii Secundum Lucam*, 10.121, pp. 478–79. And he describes Christ's response to the Thief's petition as an example of his "sacerdotal intercession." *Expositionis Evangelii Secundum Lucam*, 10.129, pp. 486–87.

instead Valentinian receives baptism from Christ himself: "He baptized you, because the ministry of men was lacking you."[26] Ambrose does not, however, describe a posthumous baptism such as we saw in *Shepherd of Hermas*. Instead, the precedents he cites to justify his claim are the Old Testament prophets and martyred catechumens.[27] He takes Valentinian's longing for baptismal grace to be on par with the prophetic insight granted to Moses and David and no less the work of God's Spirit. Then, addressing Valentinian's mourners, he adds that, if they are disturbed that the mysteries had not been solemnly celebrated, they should remember that "not even the martyrs are crowned if they are catechumens, for they are not crowned if they are not initiated." Nonetheless, no one doubts that the martyrs are saved. Ambrose's language raises certain interpretive questions, such as what exactly he means when he says the martyrs are not crowned—is he referring to a part of the ritual of initiation that takes place after baptism (i.e., an anointing)? Or to some element of the funeral rites which were not celebrated in Valentinian's case? On the fundamental question of Valentinian's salvation, however, the parallel he establishes between the martyrs' baptism of blood and Valentinian's baptism of "piety and desire" is clear enough. Again, Ambrose's phrasing suggests not an exception to the necessity of baptism but another modality through which the mystery is received, one no less real than that solemnly conferred in the ritual.

Beyond Valentinian? Ambrose's subtlety is worthy of a doctor of the Church. He is well aware of the doctrinal stakes involved in the argument he advances and is careful to show its consistency with the *regula fidei*. He painstakingly avoids proposing an alternative to baptism, and the circumstances of Valentinian's death make his case straightforward. Valentinian's request for the sacrament was explicit, and his actions were consistent with the intention to live a Christian life. He was prevented by circumstances entirely outside of his control. The prayers of the Church echo Valentinian's own desire with equal clarity. In succeeding centuries,

26. Ambrose, *On Emperor Valentinian*, 75, p. 296.
27. *On Emperor Valentinian*, 52–53, p. 288. "Aut si, quia sollemniter non sunt celebrata mysteria, hoc mouet, ergo nec martyres, si catechumeni fuerint, coronantur; non enim coronantur, si non initiantur. Quodsi suo abluuntur sanguine, et hunc sua pietas abluit et uoluntas," *De obitu Valentiniani* in *Le Orazioni Funebri*, p. 194.

as Ambrose's doctrine gained acceptance, another question would arise: could someone be saved if his desire were not as explicit as Valentinian's? Ambrose was certainly aware that the theological argument he was advancing had implications beyond the salvation of Valentinian; he seems to have been confident of the salvation of a catechumen with analogous intentions who died through unexpected illness.[28] On the question of implicit desire, however, the evidence is ambiguous. Ambrose clearly does not see such desire present in non-Christian religions. While deeply versed in and appreciative of the cultural achievements of pagan civilization,[29] Ambrose saw no salvific value in paganism. In fact, he bases his case for the sincerity of Valentinian's faith partially on the emperor's unflinching rejection of paganism: The day before he died, Valentinian refused a petition from the Roman Senate to restore state subsidies to pagan temples.[30] In Ambrose's eyes this decision, while incurring the displeasure of some of Rome's most powerful aristocrats, reflected Valentinian's overriding concern for salvation. Ambrose imagines the emperor saying, "Let Mother Rome demand whatever else she may desire. I owe love to a parent, but still more I owe obedience to the Author of salvation."[31] Pagan religion, for Ambrose, is an obstacle to salvation because it prevents the wholehearted identification with Christ that baptism requires.

A stronger case for implicit desire might be made based on Ambrose's use of Old Testament precedents. Ambrose treats such narratives as the crossing of the Red Sea, the Flood, and the miracles of Elijah as forms of baptism.[32] He is absolutely clear, however, that such signs are inferior to the reality itself; as noted above, these forms derive their power from the reality—baptism—to which they point. When they cease to point toward that reality, they too become obstacles to salvation, even if they still bear some resemblance to baptism:

---

28. *On Emperor Valentinian*, 52, p. 288.

29. His opponents criticized Ambrose for using too many images from pagan literature. McLynn, *Ambrose of Milan*, 113, loc. 2270 of 11158.

30. Ambrose, *On Emperor Valentinian*, 19–20, 52, pp. 274–75, 288.

31. *On Emperor Valentinian*, 20, p. 275.

32. Ambrose, *The Sacraments*, 2.1–4, 1–13, pp. 279–83.

The Apostle proclaims many kinds of baptism, but *one baptism*.
Why? There are the baptisms of the Gentiles, but they are not
baptism. They are baths, but they cannot be baptisms. The flesh is
bathed; fault is not washed away; rather, in that bath fault is contracted. There were baptisms among the Jews, some superfluous,
others in figure. And the figure itself was of benefit to us, since it is
an indication of the truth.[33]

The salient distinction between Jewish and Gentile "baptisms" here seems
to be that the Hebrew figures point toward Christ while the pagan baths
do not. Discussing the healing at the pool of Bethsaida (John 5:1–18), a
New Testament precursor of baptism, Ambrose affirms that one who does
not believe in Jesus' Incarnation cannot be saved.[34] At the beginning of
the story, the paralyzed man does not know that Jesus, the mediator between God and men, had already come. Still, Ambrose notes, he hoped
for his coming. His, then, was an imperfect faith, though it becomes sufficient for healing—which Ambrose equates with salvation—when Christ
appears: "so he deserved to come to good health, because he believed in
Him coming. Yet he would have been better and more perfect if he had
believed that He had already come whom he hoped would come." We
see, then, that implicit faith in Christ has real value—enough value, in
this case, to prompt Christ's intervention. Still, even though Ambrose
treats the story within his mystagogy of baptism, it is not clear that we
can draw any conclusions from it with respect to baptism of desire in the
present day. The paralytic's hope is based on the specific revelation of the
Old Testament; the fact that his healing happens before the Resurrection
means that the story is at most suggestive of the dynamics of eternal
salvation.

If there is room for implicit desire in Ambrose's theology, it is narrow.

---

33. *The Sacraments*, 2.1.2, pp. 279–80.

34. *The Sacraments*, 2.2.7, p. 281. "*Hominem*, inquit, *non habeo*. Hoc est: *quia per hominem
mors et per hominem resurrectio*, non poterat descendere, non poterat saluari, qui non credebat,
quod dominus noster Iesus Christus carnem suscepisset ex urgine. Hic autem qui opperiebatur
mediatorem dei et hominum, hominem Iesum, expectans eum, de quo dictum est: *et mittet
dominus hominem, qui saluos faciet eos*, dicebat: *Hominem non habeo*, et ideo ad sanitatem mer-
uit peruenire, quia credebat in aduenientem. Melior tamen et perfectior fuisset, si credidisset
iam uenisse, quem sperabat esse uenturum." "De Sacramentis" in *Opere dogmatiche III*, trans.
G. Banterle (Rome: Città Nuova Editrice, 1996) 60. Cf. Ambrose, *On Abraham*, 2.11.80, p. 97:
pagan philosophy lacks a connection to the Paschal Mystery, which is "the only salvation."

Salvific desire is incompatible with the errors of paganism and heresy, and the emphasis Ambrose places on petitionary prayer in the case of Valentinian makes it seem that for one's desire for salvation to be effective it must be at least concrete enough to form the content of a prayer. Ambrose's emphasis on other aspects of Valentinian's desire—his summoning of the bishop for baptism, the reform of his life, and his loyalty to Christ—make it seem as if anything less might have cast his salvation into doubt. The rhetorical question he poses in response to Valentinian's sisters' concern, however, suggests the most important limit to the concept Ambrose is developing: "what else is in your power other than the desire, the request?" In other words, if what *is* in our power—our own will—prevents our baptism, then one's desire will not be salvific. On the other hand, the nature of the baptismal ritual as it was celebrated in Ambrose's day, the salvation of Old Testament figures with incomplete knowledge of the Messiah, and Valentinian's own neediness all demonstrate that Ambrose did not equate baptism of desire with theological perfection. In the end, the circumstances in which he proposed the doctrine—the genre of the funeral oration—precluded him from working out its ambiguities and implications. A somewhat more systematic approach to baptism of desire would come not long after Ambrose delivered *De obitu Valentiniani* from the great Milanese bishop's most famous catechumen, Augustine, who would articulate a version of the same idea with greater precision—though shakier conviction.

Augustinian Ambiguities

For Augustine (354–430)—convert, bishop, and the greatest theologian of the first millennium—the question of baptism of desire arose as a side issue of scriptural interpretation within more pressing controversies over Donatism and, later, Pelagianism. Augustine's final position on baptism of desire is neither entirely clear nor entirely consistent. The same qualities that make him such a great theologian—his capaciousness intellect and restless desire for truth—make Augustine difficult to buttonhole. Often enough he is working out his theology as he goes—all the while rethinking previous opinions. Marcia Colish wryly observes that, although Augustine was the privileged authority in medieval debates over baptism of desire, his writings were sufficiently ambiguous to be cited by all sides, often resulting in a debate of "Augustine against Augustine."[35] Nonetheless, even if he himself expressed doubts about the theory, a concept of baptism of desire to complement Ambrose's teaching is clearly present in Augustine's writings.

Augustine vs. Donatists

The Donatist controversy was, in a sense, the final act of the drama that began in Cyprian's time with the controversy over rebaptism.[36] Donatism arose in the aftermath of the Diocletian persecution of 303–4, when the followers of the Carthaginian bishop Donatus came to consider themselves the only legitimate heirs to Cyprian and the martyrs of the North African Church. They achieved religious dominance in Roman North Africa during the fourth century, though by the time Augustine became bishop of Hippo in 395 their influence was on the wane. With Aurelius, the Catholic bishop of Carthage, Augustine made a determined effort to bring the schism to an end. His *De Baptismo contra Donatistas* is the product of this effort. While the division had sociological and political dimensions, the principal theological issue dividing Donatists and Catholics was baptism. Donatists maintained that baptism depended on the worthiness of the minister conferring it and, therefore, could not exist outside the Church. Augustine's *De Baptismo*, on the other hand, argues that those baptized in heretical sects should not be rebaptized when entering into Catholic communion.

Sacramental principles. The work is a watershed in sacramental theology. It establishes the principle that the sacrament is conferred (*ex opere operato*) even by an unworthy minister with the argument that it is really Christ acting through the rite, using human ministers as instruments of his grace. It also introduces the distinction, which would become a mainstay of Catholic theology, between a sacrament's validity and its

---

35. Marcia L. Colish, *Faith, Fiction & Force in Medieval Baptismal Debates* (Washington, DC: The Catholic University of America Press, 2014), 3.

36. See Pamela Bright, "Donatist Bishops," in *Augustine through the Ages*, ed. Allan D. Fitzgerald (Grand Rapids, MI: Eerdmans, 2009), 281–84; Robert A. Markus, "Donatus, Donatism," in Fitzgerald, *Augustine through the Ages*, 284–87.

fruitfulness. This distinction allows Augustine to argue that those baptized outside of the Catholic Church are *validly* baptized—that their souls are objectively changed—but that the sin of schism prevents the sacrament from becoming *fruitful*—from producing its full effect—unless and until they are reconciled to the Church.[37] Augustine compares the indelible mark received in baptism to the tattoos that identified soldiers as members of a Roman legion; soldiers retain their tattoos even if they desert their post. Nonetheless, Augustine, no less than Cyprian, held that those who died outside the Catholic Church were lost even if baptized; in effect, the difference between the two bishops was the process by which they required heretics to be reconciled. Much of *De Baptismo* is a detailed response to Cyprian in which Augustine attempts to correct the Carthaginian's oversights while still preserving his authority. Cyprian's urgent concern for Church unity, Augustine claims, caused him to overlook the theological distinction that made rebaptism unnecessary. The subtle openings to baptism of desire we noted in Cyprian's letters do not escape Augustine's attention; in fact, the particular version of the doctrine he develops owes more to his disagreements with Cyprian than to his agreement with Ambrose.[38]

Before turning to the passages in *De Baptismo* that directly address baptism of desire, it is worth noting the implications of Augustine's treatment of baptism administered by heretics or schismatics for his conception of the sacraments more generally. The distinction Augustine makes between a sacrament's validity and its fruitfulness strikes a delicate balance between objectivity and subjectivity in the sacramental encounter. Holding both of these dimensions together is necessary to preserve a sense of the sacraments as relational and participatory. Vittorino Grossi points to Augustine's Christological emphasis as the decisive feature of

37. Augustine, *Baptism*, in *The Donatist Controversy I*, trans. Maureen Tilley and Boniface Ramsey (Hyde Park, NY: New City Press, 2019), 1.4,5, p. 396.

38. While *De obitu Valentiniani* predates *De Baptismo* by around eight years, the evidence available does not allow us to know whether Augustine was familiar with the eulogy. "It is clear that Augustine did not hear Ambrose deliver the sermon, for by 388 Augustine had returned to Africa [...] However, he may have read a copy of it. Valentinian's death would have been a matter of interest in the western empire. Nevertheless, a direct link between Ambrose and Augustine on this matter cannot be demonstrated. In spite of this fact, Augustine's indebtedness to Ambrose for his explanation of baptism of desire cannot be excluded." Rusch, "Baptism of Desire in Ambrose and Augustine," 376–77.

his sacramental theology; his answer to the Donatists rests on the conviction that it is Christ acting in baptism.[39] This puts the accent on the objectivity of the sacraments, which is necessary if our participation in them is to be more than the product of our own imagination; participation in Christ's death and resurrection can be salvific only because the Paschal Mystery was a real event. But the nature of participation requires that our response to that event be personal, including all that is truly our own, our subjectivity, our will, even our bodies. Augustine is very much attuned to the relational dynamics present in the sacraments and the danger of falling either into solipsism (if their objective dimension is lost) or magic (if no subjective response is required). The fundamental drama of his sacramental theology is his attempt to do justice to both dimensions.

Doing so is most difficult—though, perhaps, most interesting—in limit cases, from which Augustine does not back away in *De Baptismo*. So, for example, he holds that it would be a sin to receive baptism from schismatics. But what if someone desiring baptism in the Catholic Church found himself in danger of death with only schismatics around? Under such circumstances, Augustine says, one could be baptized "while guarding Catholic peace in his soul" and should even be praised for demonstrating faith in the power of the sacrament.[40] Slightly different is the case of those who receive baptism from Donatists out of ignorance, a scenario likely to have been common in the North Africa of Augustine's day. Such people would still be wounded by sin and punished, though less so than those rejecting Catholicism outright.[41] These distinctions give us insight into Augustine's conception of the will's power and its limits. An objectively right will can overcome certain deficiencies in circumstances. However, it seems that doing so requires a conscious effort; the mere absence of malice is not the same as willing the good. This is consistent with Augustine's argument in *The City of God* that the will exists only when we use it.[42] We see the same line of thought in Augustine's treatment

39. Vittorino Grossi, *I sacramenti nei Padri della Chiesa: l'iter semiologico, storico, teologico* (Rome: Istituto Patristico Augustinianum, 2009), 87–88.

40. Augustine, *Baptism*, 1.2,3, p. 394.

41. *Baptism*, 1.5,6, p. 398. Later Augustine compares heresy to avarice, suggesting an objective moral fault. *Baptism*, 4.4,6, pp. 468–69. Like other moral failures, one's degree of willfulness and knowledge can affect one's subjective culpability. *Baptism*, 4.16,23, pp. 487–88.

42. Augustine, *The City of God (1–10)*, trans. William Babcock (Hyde Park, NY: New City

of liturgical defects. Apparently, the prayers priests of his day said when consecrating the baptismal waters often left much to be desired.

> For the prayers of many [over the water] are corrected on a daily basis [...], and many things are found in them that are contrary to Catholic belief. If it were to be shown that some people were baptized when those prayers were said over the water, will they be ordered to be baptized anew? Why not? Because the intention of the one praying more than makes up for the defect of the prayer, and because those particular gospel words, without which baptism cannot be consecrated, have such power that, thanks to them, whatever is said in the defective prayer that is contrary to the rule of faith is canceled out.[43]

Though the example reinforces the importance of right intention, we cannot draw conclusions about baptism of desire from it because it presupposes that the essential parts of the rite were present. In fact, it is the objective power of this fixed part of the ritual that, for Augustine, counterbalances defects in priestly ad-libbing.

The Good Thief. The more difficult question of the absence of the rite comes up in the commentary on Cyprian's work that fills *De Baptismo*'s central chapters, though as an aside. In fact, Augustine raises the issue to insist that it does not directly pertain to his dispute with the Donatists. Cyprian had affirmed that a Catholic catechumen martyred before baptism would enter the kingdom of heaven. Augustine points out that this universally accepted position does not help answer the question of what happens when heretics administer baptism. It does, however, provide Augustine with the opportunity to show how the distinctions he is developing apply in a variety of non-standard cases, as well as to correct an apparently minor point of Cyprian's exegesis. Augustine insists that both the objective sacrament of baptism and the correct subjective response of the believer—conversion to the true faith—are necessary for salvation. "Just as a good catechumen needs baptism in order to enter the kingdom of heaven," he says, "so a bad person who has been baptized [needs] a true

---

Press, 2012), 5.10, p. 156. In the same passage Augustine discusses necessity, something that happens when we do not will it, using death as his prime example.

43. Augustine, *Baptism*, 6.25,47, p. 556.

conversion." Sometimes, however, these two do not coincide, as when a heretic receives baptism. In such a case, Augustine says he would prefer a "Catholic catechumen on fire with divine charity" to a baptized heretic or, for that matter, a baptized but morally rotten Catholic. He takes for granted that the catechumen, like Cornelius in Acts 10, will receive baptism. If the righteous centurion had not done so, Augustine says, he would have been "guilty of contempt for this great sacrament."[44] Thus far the discussion does not imply anything one way or another for a catechumen who, like Valentinian, dies before baptism.

But Augustine's digression is not yet finished; Cyprian's discussion of baptism of blood needs correction.[45] Cyprian had given as an example the Good Thief (Luke 23:40–43), to whom Jesus promised paradise despite his lack of baptism. Augustine argues that the Thief cannot be considered a martyr since he was crucified for his crimes, not for having professed faith in Christ. We have, then, a case not of a martyr's blood supplying baptism, but of something else. Celebrating the sacrament was impossible in the Thief's extreme circumstances, Augustine says, so "faith and conversion of heart" must have taken the place of martyrdom. He adds a reference to Romans 10:10: "Faith comes from the heart for righteousness, but confession is made with the mouth for salvation." This verse, which we will see in later debates over baptism of desire, asserts two conditions for salvation that Augustine believes the Thief fulfilled: conversion of heart, that is, the correct disposition of the will, and an outward profession of faith, as demonstrated by his words to the Lord. In Augustine's thinking, conversion of heart and the confession of faith naturally lead to the sacrament of faith, baptism. Therefore, he says, the Thief's baptism is completed invisibly. Here he also adds a condition that would become the *sine qua non* of baptism of desire: This invisible baptism can happen only because the Thief was prevented by necessity (*articulus necessitatis*) from receiving the sacrament; he did not choose to forgo it out of "contempt for religion" (*contemptus religionis*). It is worth noting that Augustine's language suggests the fulfillment or filling up (*implere, impletur*) of baptism rather than a substitution, as many translations suggest.[46]

44. *Baptism*, 4.21,28, pp. 492–93.
45. *Baptism*, 4.22,29, p. 494.
46. "Sed tunc impletur invisibiliter, cum ministerium Baptismi non contemptus religionis,

The absence of "contempt for religion" will become a key condition for baptism of desire—universally affirmed by the doctrine's medieval proponents—and Augustine goes to great lengths to emphasize the concept. By "contempt for religion," he means any attitude that would cause one to regard the sacrament as unnecessary. He considers this a particularly strong danger for those who have achieved—or believe they have achieved—an advanced level of spiritual understanding or moral progress. He cites the Lord's baptism by John to rebuke those who think the ritual superfluous.[47] No matter how impressive one's virtues, these can never equal the grace of the sacrament. He returns to the example of Cornelius to show that even the extraordinary gift of the Holy Spirit did not render baptism superfluous. Like "contempt for religion," *articulus necessitatis* would also become a key phrase in the scholastic theology of baptism of desire. "*Articulus*" derives from the term for a joint or knuckle and can refer to a critical moment in time, a turning point.[48] As such, it suggests a critical event that changes one's course of action, in this case preventing one from carrying through one's intention to receive baptism.

Augustine next launches into another digression—within what is already a digression from his argument with the Donatists—by raising the question of infant baptism.[49] He does so because his insistence that salvation requires both baptism and conversion might seem to call into question the salvation of baptized infants, who are not yet capable of the "belief in the heart" or "confession of faith" alluded to in Romans 10:10. The examples Augustine has already mentioned, however, demonstrate that baptism's subjective and objective dimensions—conversion and the

sed articulus necessitatis excludit." Augustine, *De Baptismo Contra Donatistas*, in *Polemica con i Donatisti*, trans. Antonio Lombardi (Rome: Città Nuova, 1998), 4.22.29, p. 432.

47. Augustine repeats this interpretation in his sermons on John: "there were many people who were going to scorn baptism on the grounds that they were endowed with greater grace than they saw in some of the faithful [...] To prevent such presumption from hurling those who were inordinately conscious of the merits of their justice down to their doom, the Lord chose to be baptized." Augustine, "Homily 13," in *Homilies on the Gospel of John 1–40*, ed. Allan D. Fitzgerald, trans. Edmund Hill (Hyde Park, NY: New City Press, 2009), 6, pp. 247–48. He is quite insistent that catechumens still carry "the load of their own iniquity [...] until the moment they come to baptism." "Homily 13," 7, p. 248. Cf. the discussion of John 3:5 in "Homily 11," 1, p. 210.

48. Charlton T. Lewis and Charles Short, *A Latin Dictionary* (Oxford: Clarendon Press, 1879), Perseus Digital Library, http://www.perseus.tufts.edu/hopper/text?doc=Perseus%3Atext%3A1999.04.0059%3Aentry%3Darticulus.

49. Augustine, *Baptism*, 4.23,30–24,31, pp. 495–96.

sacrament—can, depending on the circumstances, come in a different order. Baptized infants, it is to be hoped, will begin to confess the faith as they become capable. In the event that one of these two dimensions is lacking, Augustine argues that "the beneficence of the Almighty" can bring salvation to completion. This can only happen in the case of necessity—that is, if the deficiency is not in the person's will either to receive baptism or to confess Christ. In the case of the Thief, the ritual was lacking; in the case of baptized infants, conscious faith is lacking; yet, in both cases, the tradition of the Church testifies to the salvation of those in question.[50]

Because Augustine lays out the principles of baptism of desire in the context of his exegesis of the Good Thief, its relevance for contemporary cases such as Valentinian's requires examination. Ambrose's doctrine seems readily applicable to cases similar to Valentinian's, but the circumstances of the Good Thief's conversion and death were singular. Does Augustine's treatment of his case imply a more general theory of baptism of desire? As far as *De Baptismo* is concerned, the evidence seems to say yes. After his discussion of the salvation of baptized infants, Augustine summarizes his conclusions as succinct general principles, suggesting a wider application.[51] His admonition that an individual's defect of will would prevent the completion of baptism is also expressed in general terms. Moreover, Augustine's treatment of the Good Thief in another work from roughly the same period is substantially the same, if somewhat less involved.[52]

Within *De Baptismo*, Augustine also applies the reasoning from his treatment of the Good Thief to his discussion of Cyprian's letter to

50. "Et sicut in / illo latrone quod ex Baptismi sacramento defuerat complevit Omnipotentis benignitas, quia non superbia vel contemptu, sed necessitate defuerat: sic in infantibus qui baptizati moriuntur, eadem gratia Omnipotentis implere credenda est, quod non ex impia voluntate, sed ex aetatis indigentia, nec corde credere ad iustitiam possunt, nec ore confiteri ad salutem. Ideo cum alii pro eis respondent, ut impleatur erga eos celebratio Sacramenti, valet utique ad eorum consecrationem, quia ipsi respondere non possunt. At si pro eo qui respondere potest alius respondeat, non itidem valet." Augustine. "*De Baptismo Contra Donatistas*," in *Polemica con i Donatisti*, 4.24,31, pp. 434–36.

51. *Baptism*, 4.25,32, p. 497.

52. Augustine, *Eighty-Three Different Questions*, trans. David L. Mosher, The Fathers of the Church 70 (Washington, DC: The Catholic University of America Press, 1982), q. 62, pp. 124–27.

Jubaian (Letter 73).[53] This is the letter in which Cyprian opened a door to baptism of desire by granting that those who had mistakenly omitted rebaptism could still receive pardon. Augustine is here working with hypotheticals since, unlike Cyprian, he would have recognized the original baptisms as still valid. He attributes to Cyprian the view that, in this case, the bond of unity made up for what was lacking ritually. Augustine's conception of the bond of unity, or charity, is not detached from the sacraments; he uses the term to refer specifically to ecclesial communion. Augustine identifies the bond of charity as Cyprian's overriding concern in order to smooth over the differences he has with the martyred bishop's position on baptism. Since, as we shall see, at certain points in history, baptism of desire will be referred to as the "baptism of charity," it is worth noting here how the term applies in its earliest usage. In the context of Cyprian's letter, "charity" fulfills the same function as conversion of heart in Augustine's treatment of the Good Thief; we might define it as the individual's will to ecclesial communion. The concept cannot be understood as either exemplary ethical conduct or humanistic good will because it is directed specifically toward Catholic communion.[54] Indeed, in the example discussed by Cyprian, the individuals in question had already been admitted to sacramental communion. Thus, in Augustine's thinking the desire necessary for baptism of desire would seem to be identified with the desire for Christian communion.

Augustine vs. Pelagians

Augustine's treatment of the Good Thief in *De Baptismo* was to provide the template for the development of the doctrine of baptism of desire in future centuries, yet the bishop of Hippo's influence would extend over the debate in other ways as well. His articulation of the doctrine of original sin and the necessity of baptism to expunge it raises issues any credible doctrine of baptism of desire must confront. Augustine worked out this aspect of his teaching in the context of his conflict with the monk Pelagius and his allies. Unlike Donatism, Pelagianism seems not to have

53. Augustine, *Baptism*, 2.13,18, p. 438.
54. Consider that Augustine insists that martyrdom does heretics no good because outside the Church even a martyr lacks charity. Augustine, *Baptism*, 4.17,24, p. 488.

been a well-organized movement, making the identification of precise Pelagian doctrines difficult.[55] In broad terms, "Pelagianism" tended toward an overly optimistic evaluation of the human will and its capacity to achieve perfection without the intervention of God's grace. Taken to an extreme, such a tendency casts into doubt the necessity of the sacraments for salvation.

Original Sin. Augustine completed *De Baptismo* around 401. By 411 he had turned his attention to Pelagianism with the publication of *De peccatorum meritis et remissione, et de baptismo parvulorum*. Augustine's anti-Pelagian writing would continue throughout the rest of his career, though this initial work lays out its essential principles. It also addresses head on what is arguably the most difficult issue raised by the doctrine of original sin and the necessity of baptism for salvation, the fate of unbaptized infants. Augustine is sometimes cast as a villain in discussions of this problem because he so clearly concluded that such innocents could not be saved. But, while I hope eventually to suggest how baptism of desire might allow for modification of the Augustinian position, this caricature is unjust. The great theologian did not *want* unbaptized infants to go to hell and sought evidence that might lead him to other conclusions.[56] Moreover, our investigation thus far suggests that Augustine's position expressed what was already the theological consensus.[57] It was not cruelty, then, but Augustine's integrity as a theologian, his refusal to distort the evidence supplied by revelation to produce desired results, that led to his uncomfortable conclusions. In *De peccatorum meritis et remissione*, he repeatedly returns to the verse: "O the depth of the riches and wisdom and knowledge of God! How unsearchable are his judgments and how inscrutable his ways!" (Rom 11:33). While lesser theologians might take God's mysteriousness as a license simply to follow their own preferences, when it came to the most troubling cases, Augustine recognized that

55. See Mathijs Lamberigts, "Pelagius and Pelagians," in *The Oxford Handbook of Early Christian Studies*, ed. Susan Ashbrook Harvey and David G. Hunter (New York: Oxford University Press, 2008), 258–78.

56. William Harmless, "Baptism," in Fitzgerald, *Augustine through the Ages*, 90.

57. Pope Siricius, writing in 385 to the bishop Tarragona, takes as a given that an infant departing this world without baptism "loses both his life and the kingdom." *Enchiridion symbolorum*, 184.

intellectual humility requires the theologian to remain obedient to the rule of faith especially when it is most difficult to do so.

From Augustine's perspective, the fundamental principle at stake in the Pelagian controversy is whether the mission of Christ is necessary at all. Do we *need* a savior? As I pointed out in the first chapter, the ancient world's presupposition that death means irrevocable loss made the Gospel both "good" and "news." Likewise, all humanity needs a savior because we are all sinners. If we do not start out lost, we need neither salvation nor savior.[58] If "salvation" is the default setting for human existence, the concept is misnamed and Christ's redemption is superfluous. Augustine makes this point in different ways, both as it buttresses his general understanding of original sin and as it applies specifically to the case of infants.[59] Here Augustine ends up at odds not just with Pelagius but also with those such as Cyril of Jerusalem whose theology does not include original sin. Both figures agree that baptism is necessary for salvation, even for infants; for Cyril, however, this is because even those without sin do not possess perfect grace. Augustine, on the other hand, argues that it is because no person is truly without sin. In fact, the belief that babies can be saved without baptism seems not to have been held even by the Pelagians. Instead, the Pelagian position at which Augustine takes aim is that unbaptized infants exist in a middle state, gaining eternal life but not the kingdom of heaven.[60] Augustine insists that these terms are syn-

58. Before Adam's fall, Augustine argues, humanity had no need of a mediator. *The Augustine Catechism: The Enchiridion on Faith, Hope, and Charity*, ed. Boniface Ramsey, trans. Bruce Harbert (Hyde Park, NY: New City Press, 1999), 108, p. 130.

59. "Who then would dare to claim that little ones can attain eternal salvation without this rebirth, as if Christ did not die for them? After all, *Christ died for sinners* (Rom 5:6). But, if they are not held by any bond of sinfulness stemming from their origin, how did Christ, who died for sinners, die for these infants who obviously had done nothing sinful in their own lives? If they are not afflicted by the disease of original sin, why do those caring for them bring them out of a holy fear to Christ the physician, that is, to receive the sacrament of eternal salvation? [...] The physician [...] is not needed by those who are in good health, but by those who are sick, and he has come, not to call the righteous, but sinners." Augustine, *The Punishment and Forgiveness of Sins and the Baptism of Little Ones*, in *Answer to the Pelagians I*, ed. John E. Rotelle, trans. Roland J. Teske (Hyde Park, NY: New City Press, 2018), 1.18,23–19,24, pp. 46–47.

60. *Punishment and Forgiveness of Sins*, 2.21,30, p. 49; 1.28,55, p. 64: "They would have them to be in eternal life as if by the merit of their innocence, but not with Christ in his kingdom, since they were not baptized." The Pelagian position distinguishes "eternal life" from the "kingdom of heaven" and then posits that John 3:5 excludes the unbaptized only from the latter. *Punishment and Forgiveness of Sins*, 1.30,58, pp. 66–67.

onymous and that revelation admits no middle ground when it comes to being with Christ or against him. Within this context, the characteristic that sets Augustine's position apart is his decisive rejection of any kind of limbo-like middle state, an idea considered at least plausible by such orthodox thinkers as Gregory Nazianzen and Ambrose. Even here, however, the distance between Augustine and his Pelagian opponents may not be as great as it first appears, for Augustine repeatedly insists that the punishment infants receive because of original sin will be "the mildest condemnation of all."[61] Augustine held fast to this position throughout his career; though he allows for differing levels of reward and punishment in the afterlife—and considers various ways God might mitigate the sufferings of those in hell—the fundamental punishment of being separated from the kingdom of heaven is by its nature not subject to mitigation.[62] In a sermon dedicated to the topic, he argues that the middle place Pelagians propose is not neutral but, in fact, a punishment.[63] This argument lays the groundwork for the theory of limbo proposed by the School of Laon in the Middle Ages.

Here it is worth making clear that the Christian practice of baptizing infants did not arise in response to the Augustinian doctrine of original sin; rather, Augustine articulated this doctrine to explain something inherent to Christian practice. The Pelagians implicitly conceded the necessity of baptism for salvation by continuing to baptize their own infants.[64] The Church's practice, Augustine therefore insisted, requires us to believe

61. *Punishment and Forgiveness of Sins*, 1.16,21, p. 44.

62. Augustine, *Augustine Catechism*, 111–113, pp. 132–34.

63. Augustine, "Sermo 294," in *Discorsi V*, trans. Marcella Recchia (Rome: Città Nuova, 1986), 6, p. 287. Augustine's logic raises questions about the actual suffering involved in this punishment. Someone who does not know what he is lacking may suffer an objective deficiency without feeling any subjective distress.

64. Augustine, *Punishment and Forgiveness of Sins*, 2.25,41, p. 104. Augustine argues that the *lex orandi* supports his position in other ways, such as the fact that only the baptized can receive the Eucharist, which he identifies with eternal life. *The Punishment and Forgiveness of Sins*, 1.20,26, pp. 47–48. He notes the Carthaginian custom of referring to baptism as "salvation" and the Eucharist as "life." *Punishment and Forgiveness of Sins*, 1.24,34, p. 53; cf. "Sermo 294," 8–10, pp. 288–93, 20, pp. 306–9. This usage gives a sense of how, in Augustine's sacramental theology, the ritual is identified with the reality it represents. Innocent I, writing to the Synod of Milevum in 417, also argues that to deny the necessity of baptism for the salvation of children is the equivalent of professing that "the sacred cleansing of rebirth does no good." *Enchiridion symbolorum*, 219.

in the doctrine of original sin. Augustine's contribution, then, is to root the already established necessity of baptism for salvation not just in a few scriptural proof texts but in the fundamental logic of the Christian narrative, in Christ's coming to save sinners. In itself, the theology Augustine developed during the Pelagian debates does not block the path to baptism of desire that he opened in the Donatist controversies, though it does add two important considerations that highlight the narrowness of the path.

Implications. The first of these is the gratuitousness of salvation. Augustine makes it clear that no one can claim salvation on the basis of personal virtue. The bishop of Hippo thoroughly absorbed the lesson God so painfully imparts to Job from the whirlwind: No man ever has grounds to question God's justice. Understanding why some are saved and others are not is beyond our human capacity because, as a matter of justice, no one would be saved.[65] The salvation of even a single human being is beyond human logic. Augustine returns to the example of the Good Thief to show that it is not to the most virtuous that salvation is promised but to the most unremarkable of sinners who turns to Christ.[66] Sometimes criminals are saved through baptism, while virtuous people who die unbaptized are not. Others looked to Platonic concepts such as reincarnation to resolve the difficulty, positing that the disparity between people's fates can be explained by their behavior in a previous existence. Augustine rejects this view as unbiblical and as creating more problems than it solves.[67] He does not attempt to draw any implications for baptism of desire from these observations, but it remains essential to note that, if the Good Thief is taken as the paradigmatic case for the doctrine, then baptism of desire cannot mean that a morally exemplary life substitutes for the sacraments.

With regard to infants, Augustine's insistence on realism is relentless. He recognizes as an evident fact that infants do suffer the punishment for sin: They are subject to sickness, weakness, ignorance, and untimely

---

65. Augustine, *Punishment and Forgiveness of Sins*, 1.21,29–30, pp. 49–50.

66. *Punishment and Forgiveness of Sins*, 1.22,31, p. 51.

67. *Punishment and Forgiveness of Sins*, 1.22,32–33, pp. 51–52. Augustine does, however, allow that *some* post-mortem punishment is purgatorial. Augustine, *The City of God (11–22)*, trans. William Babcock (Hyde Park, NY: New City Press, 2013), 21.13, pp. 467–68.

death.[68] These are the punishments of sin, yet Augustine rejects the suggestion that they are guilty of any personal sin.[69] If infants did not already share in the culpability of original sin, then, it would be unjust to subject them to these punishments. Here Augustine's treatment of the ignorance into which we are born is noteworthy. Like other patristic thinkers, Augustine sees ignorance as a punishment; the fact that children are ignorant of the moral law and must be taught over time to obey it is evidence that we come into the world already wounded by sin. Related to this consideration is the key stumbling block to applying the doctrine of baptism of desire to infants: their inability to formulate, let alone express, a desire similar to that of the Good Thief on Golgotha. Augustine's pastoral experience as bishop of Hippo peeks through in several references he makes to babies crying in protest at their baptism, and we might imagine that the great doctor of the Latin Church had been splashed abundantly at the font.[70] While such cries do not carry any moral weight—Augustine does not imagine them an obstacle to the sacrament's validity—his point is that we have no grounds for attributing desire for baptism to the infants themselves. Augustine's view of childhood is unsentimental but hard to dispute. Children are capable of bald-faced selfishness, which even seems to be their natural state until they are taught otherwise.[71] Little in the behavior of children generally suggests the desire for conversion or Christ-like self-sacrifice. Augustine maintains that baptized infants participate in the faith of the Church by emphasizing the objectivity of the sacrament. We might wish that infants could desire baptism, but Augustine insists on a theology grounded in reality, and the plain fact is that, on their own, they do not.

"Augustine vs. Augustine"

None of the considerations Augustine raises in his discussion of infant baptism—original sin, the gratuitousness of salvation, the inability of

68. Augustine, *Punishment and Forgiveness of Sins*, 1.35,66–37,69, pp. 71–74; see also, 1.25,36, pp. 53–54.
69. *Punishment and Forgiveness of Sins*, 1.17,22, p. 45.
70. *Punishment and Forgiveness of Sins*, 1.25,36, p. 54.
71. *Punishment and Forgiveness of Sins*, 1.35,65, p. 71. See also Augustine, *The City of God* (*11–22*), 21.16, p. 471.

infants to express a desire for baptism—automatically rules out the possibility of baptism of desire for adults. Like Augustine's formulations in *De Baptismo*, these considerations only suggest limits within which that doctrine can be conceived. Augustine's battle against Pelagianism had, however, made him particularly sensitive to any suggestion that the grace of the sacraments is superfluous or optional. The theological terrain on which he found himself fighting seems to have caused Augustine to rethink some of the evidence he had used to support his position in *De Baptismo*, though whether he reversed that position entirely is less clear. Specifically, in several of his later works, Augustine hesitates over his first interpretation of the Good Thief's salvation. We turn now to these specific hesitations, as well as to a few more general considerations of Augustine's sense of the sacraments, desire, and salvation.[72]

The Good Thief revisited. Two of Augustine's works from 419–21 revisit his interpretation of the Good Thief. The pericope comes up in his commentary on the book of Leviticus, where Augustine addresses the necessity of religious ritual.[73] His main concern in the passage, which deals with the Old Testament priesthood, is to assert that sanctification is always the result of the action of the Holy Spirit; in other words, he rejects a superstitious understanding of religious ritual in which holiness is manufactured independently of God's action. Religious rituals can produce a visible effect without resulting in invisible sanctification, as in the case of Simon the Magician (Acts 8). Augustine also allows that the Holy Spirit can bring about invisible sanctification without a visible rite, though he adds with the same breath that this does not diminish the importance of divinely established rituals. Indeed, the examples he cites—Moses and John the Baptist—received the Spirit's invisible action precisely in order to establish such rituals. The same cannot be said of the Good Thief. Augustine mentions his example, again adding that one can in no way be saved if he holds the sacraments in contempt. To buttress

72. Anthony Dupont and Matthew A. Gaumer give an overview of the literature dedicated to the question of Augustine's theological evolution in "*Gratia Dei, Gratia Sacramenti*: Grace in Augustine of Hippo's Anti-Donatist Writing," *Ephemerides Theologicae Lovanienses* 86, no. 4 (2010): 307–29.

73. Augustine, *Questioni sull'Ettateuco: Questioni sul Levitico*, 3.84, http://www.augustinus .it/italiano/questioni_ettateuco/index2.htm.

the point, he mentions Cornelius, baptized even after having been enlightened by the Holy Spirit.

In another contemporary work, Augustine reveals his reason for hesi-
tating when drawing conclusions from the Good Thief's salvation: Some
Pelagians had indeed cited the case to call into question the necessity of
baptism.[74] His opponent in this work, *On the Nature and Origin of the
Soul*, was a recent convert from Donatism named Vincent Victor. Vincent had developed his own idiosyncratic theory of the soul's origin on
which to base the salvation of infants. Vincent—as Augustine understood him—believed the soul to emanate directly from God, even sharing
in his essence, incurring the guilt of sin only upon contact with the flesh.
Augustine points out that, if Vincent's theory were true, contact with the
flesh would be an undeserved—and therefore unjust—punishment; thus,
he doubles down on the claim that we must bear the guilt of original sin
from the first moment of our existence.[75] Vincent seems to have hypoth-
esized other ways in which unbaptized infants could achieve salvation,
for example, by mention in the Eucharistic liturgy, a novelty Augustine
regarded as obviously contrary to the rule of faith.[76] In this context, Augustine emphasizes the uncertainties involved in the Good Thief's case
to show that the episode does not provide sufficient evidence to overturn
the Church's constant teaching on the necessity of baptism for salvation.
He also cites the anti-Pelagian canons of the recently concluded synod
of Carthage to affirm that original sin makes baptism necessary for all.[77]

In response to Vincent's misuse of Luke 23:39–43, Augustine emphasizes the uncertainty of all the proposed resolutions to the passage's
difficulties. He recalls Cyprian's interpretation of the Thief's death as
martyrdom; though he had previously rejected this interpretation, here
he eloquently emphasizes its plausibility by contrasting the faith of the
Thief with the cowardice of the apostles, who would nonetheless one day
be martyrs.[78] By warming to Cyprian's interpretation, however, Augus-

---

74. Augustine, *The Nature and Origin of the Soul*, in *Answer to the Pelagians I*, 1.11, pp. 462–63.

75. *The Nature and Origin of the Soul*, 2.13, p. 488. Augustine maintains that the available
evidence does not allow us fully to resolve the question of how the soul originates. *The Nature
and Origin of the Soul*, 4.16, p. 525.

76. *The Nature and Origin of the Soul*, 1.13, p. 464; 2.15, p. 490.

77. *The Nature and Origin of the Soul*, 1.34, p. 477; cf. *Enchiridion symbolorum*, 222–30.

78. Augustine, *The Nature and Origin of the Soul*, 1.11, pp. 462–63. For baptism of blood see
also, Augustine, *The City of God (11–22)*, 13.7–8, pp. 73–74.

tine ends up implicitly stretching the definition of martyrdom in this instance into something like a baptism of desire. In other words, the Thief's
profession of faith turns his death into a martyrdom though he did not
choose to die for Christ at his original sentencing. Could a profession of
faith do the same thing if one's death was not violent? Augustine mentions
other theories as well: that the Thief was somehow baptized with the water
flowing from Christ's pierced side or that he had been baptized prior to
his execution.[79] His argument is not that one of these theories is definitely
correct but that the evidence the Good Thief provides is insufficient to
draw conclusions for present practice. Augustine seems troubled by the
notion of promising salvation in cases where it is not really certain. He
is motivated, in other words, by a sense of justice toward those to whom
the Gospel is announced, like a doctor duty-bound to convey the news of
a cancer diagnosis even if a patient would rather hear that his problem is
indigestion. The pessimism of which Augustine is sometimes accused is
the result of alertness to the injustice of anesthetizing falsehoods.

Indeed, it is the certainty of his earlier interpretation of the Good
Thief pericope in *De Baptismo* that Augustine seems most intent on correcting in his *Retractationes*, the reflections on his life's work published
shortly before his death in 430. He mentions the Good Thief twice, first
in connection with his answers to *Eighty-Three Different Questions* and
then when commenting on *De Baptismo*. In the first instance, he notes
that other authorities had taken the same position as he had but admits,
"I do not know by what proof it can be adequately demonstrated that
the thief was not baptized."[80] His works addressed to Vincent Victor, he
says, better represent the uncertain state of the question. Critiquing *De
Baptismo*, he corrects himself for the same reason: "In the fourth book,
when I said that suffering could take the place of baptism, the example of
the thief that I offered was not quite apropos, because it is uncertain that
he was not baptized."[81] It is interesting that here Augustine remembers
that he considered the Thief's *suffering* to have been salvific, though in *De*

79. Augustine considered the latter more plausible. *The Nature and Origin of the Soul*, 3.12,
p. 505. Ephraim the Syrian seems to have spoken of the Thief as baptized by the water flowing
from Christ's side. *Luca*, ed. Arthur A. Just Jr., Sara Petri, and Giovanna Taponecco, La Bibbia
Commentata Dai Padri, Nuovo Testamento 3 (Rome: Città Nuova, 2006), 514.

80. Augustine, *Revisions*, ed. Roland Teske, trans. Boniface Ramsey (Hyde Park, NY: New
City Press, 2010), 1.26 (25), p. 105.

81. Augustine, *Revisions*, 2.18 (45), p. 126.

Baptismo his emphasis falls on the Good Thief's "faith and conversion of heart." In fact, Augustine had opened the question precisely in order to challenge Cyprian's interpretation of the Thief as martyr.

Conclusions. While providing ammunition for opponents of baptism of desire in the Middle Ages, Augustine's doubts in *Retractationes* do not amount to a complete refutation of the possibility of baptism of desire. The hesitations Augustine felt nonetheless underline the uncertainty the doctrine inevitably involves. Augustine's caution against promising salvation without clear warrant from the *regula fidei* is the key to making sense of his ambivalence; he knows it would be reckless to preach any path to salvation beyond baptism and the commitment it entails. Nonetheless, young Augustine was more theologically nimble than old Augustine gives him credit for: Understood robustly, the caution that baptism of desire cannot occur if it is the result of contempt for religion protects the doctrine from reckless interpretations.

Here, at the risk belaboring the point, it is worth repeating: For Augustine and his contemporaries, salvation was a sacramental question. One could not consider hard cases apart from the logic of the ritual around which the life of the Church revolved. In this respect, Augustine is in continuity with Paul, who, as we saw in the previous chapter, appeals to the sacramental experience of the earliest Christians to resolve doctrinal disputes. William Harmless rightly calls attention to the intensity of Augustine's own experience of baptism in 387; reception of the sacrament produced tears and amazement, transforming the disquiet of his youth into peace.[82] Augustine understood baptism as the moment of salvation because that is how he and others in the early Church experienced the sacrament. Even if infant baptism was widely practiced at the time, the experience of adult converts played a significant enough role in shaping Christian consciousness that the temptation to treat baptism as a mere formality would have seemed implausible both theologically and existentially.

This does not mean that Augustine or the other Fathers were unaware

---

82. The *disciplina arcani* likely explains why Augustine did not concentrate more on the particulars of the rite. Harmless, "Baptism," 84–85; cf., Augustine, *Confessions*, trans. Henry Chadwick (Oxford: Oxford University Press, 1992), 9.6.14, p. 164.

of or insensitive to the plight of those who, through no personal fault, were unable to receive the sacrament. Augustine strenuously insists that unbaptized infants are not excluded from paradise because they have failed to observe a precept and that they remain immune from any punishment beyond that due to original sin.[83] But more fundamental than following rules, for the Fathers, is participation in the Paschal Mystery.[84] Augustine is aware of the large number of people who are not baptized because they do not know the Gospel, but he indicates that even his opponents would regard their salvation as absurd.[85] His insistence on the necessity of the Church for salvation was not, therefore, premised on a lack of geographical awareness. Though he considered the possibility of an undiscovered continent on the opposite side of the globe to be improbable, Augustine was fascinated by the vast size and diversity of the world and its peoples.[86] He may not have known how many unevangelized people there were or where they lived, but he knew that such peoples existed. Nor should we forget that, in the period we have studied thus far, Christians remained a minority of the Empire's population.[87] Augustine was aware of arguments for universal salvation and recognized God's universal salvific will, arguing that we should never despair of anyone's conversion, whether inside or outside the Church.[88] But he does not equate salvation with anything less than conversion to Christ.

Even here, however, there is some room to play Augustine against Augustine. Prior to the coming of Christ, the rites revealed in the Old Testament were sufficient for salvation because of their relationship to the fullness of revelation in Christ. Augustine allows that God could also

---

83. Augustine, *The City of God (11–22)*, 16.27, p. 218; cf. Augustine, *Augustine Catechism*, 93–99, pp. 116–23.

84. Augustine identifies "participation in the light of God" as the only source of true happiness. *The City of God (1–10)*, 10.1, p. 304. Context makes it clear that he sees this mystical participation happening through the Christian liturgy.

85. Augustine, *The Nature and Origin of the Soul*, 2.21, pp. 294–95.

86. Augustine, *The City of God (11–22)*, 16.9, p. 197.

87. On Christianity's rate of growth see, Rodney Stark, *The Rise of Christianity* (San Francisco: Harper Collins, 1997), 4–13.

88. Augustine, *The City of God (11–22)*, 21.1, p. 448; 21.17–18, pp. 472–73; *Baptism*, 4.14,21, p. 484. He takes 1 Tm 2:4 to indicate that no group is excluded a priori from salvation and emphasizes prayer for the conversion of unbelievers. Augustine, *Augustine Catechism*, 104, p. 127; 112, p. 132.

have revealed salvific prophecies outside of Israel.[89] While only Israel can be considered the people of God, he says, those "in other nations," such as Job, belonged to the heavenly city of God. While the number of such people could not have been great—"a few other persons, here and there, who were found worthy of divine grace by the most hidden and most just judgment of God"—they do raise the possibility of temporal and geographical obstacles to salvation being at least exceptionally overcome.[90] Augustine, however, adds several formidable caveats. First, the content of salvific revelation is always Christ, even in the veiled forms of the Old Testament; so acknowledging God's action beyond the borders of Israel does not imply any salvific value for religious diversity in general. Augustine's critique of paganism in the first ten books of *The City of God* is withering. Second, because the religious rites of the Old Testament reach their fulfillment in the New, they no longer exercise any salvific function; it is, therefore, unlikely that parallel prophetic figures would continue to exist outside of Israel after the fullness of revelation. Third, the forces of evil and deception are active in the world, so attributing non-Christian religious phenomena to God always carries the risk of being ensnared in diabolical error. Fourth, Augustine recognizes that preparatory sanctification can be partial, not adding up to salvation; hearing the word of God can be a step toward conversion while the journey remains incomplete.[91] Finally, and most importantly for our theme, Augustine raises a problem that has to do with the nature of desire.

For Augustine, desire is a function of the human will and can direct us to or away from God.[92] The theory of baptism of desire outlined in *De Baptismo* depends on the conviction that one's will can have a positive effect on one's eternal state even when external circumstances prevent one's desire from being fulfilled. But while Christ provides the only true fulfillment of human desires, it is evident that not all people desire association with Christ.[93] In fact, in order to desire something we need

---

89. Augustine, *The City of God (11–22)*, 18.47, pp. 333–34.

90. Augustine, *The City of God (1–10)*, 3.1, pp. 71–72.

91. Augustine, "Sermo 294," 19, pp. 304–7.

92. Augustine, *The City of God (11–22)*, 14.6–7, pp. 105–7.

93. *The City of God (11–22)*, 18.48, p. 335. God *is* the reward promised in heaven, so, if God is to fulfill our desires, then God must be the object of our desire. *The City of God (11–22)*, 22.30, pp. 551–54.

some knowledge of that object; while not perfect, such knowledge must be at least clear enough to distinguish that object from others, especially those that are opposed to it.[94] If we are to slake our thirst, we must be able to distinguish water from sand, though we do not need to know the chemical formula H_2O. The ritual of baptism presents a real choice to receive the sacrament or not, a choice that requires channeling and clarifying our desires. The rituals of the Old Testament, which stood in for the Christian sacraments, were also capable of focusing the will, requiring a decision to participate in them. Perhaps the most difficult obstacle to extending the concept of baptism of desire beyond catechumens who have explicitly requested the sacrament is the problem of how one's desire could be directed toward the right object. This problem is particularly acute when speaking of the unevangelized. No process of conversion is of benefit if one is converted to something other than Christ.

Whatever one makes of Augustine's final position on baptism of desire, at a minimum, he sets the terms for the idea's future development, both by articulating the doctrine in a relatively systematic way in *De Baptismo* and by bringing the difficulties it must face to the surface in a way no previous thinker had. From *contemptus religionis* and *articulus necessitatis* to *ex opere operato* and original sin, future conversation would take place in the language of Hippo's great rhetorician.

The Late Patristic Period

Chrysostom. Any debate we find over baptism of desire after Augustine pales in comparison with the debate that took place within Augustine himself. The considerations that weighed on the bishop of Hippo can also be found in his contemporaries. John Chrysostom (ca. 349–407) affirms

---

94. Augustine puts this well in his letter to Proba on prayer: "[H]ow could it be put into words when what is desired is unknown? On the one hand, if it were entirely unknown, it would not be desired; on the other, if it were seen, it would not be desired or sought with groanings." Augustine, "Letter 130," in *Saint Augustine Letters II (83–130)*, trans. Wilfrid Parsons, The Fathers of the Church 18 (Washington, DC: The Catholic University of America Press, 1967), 399. The letter calls to mind Ambrose's emphasis on Valentinian's "poverty" when Augustine tells Proba that she must make herself desolate. In other words, for both thinkers, a sense of our own neediness—of not yet having the object we desire—imbues prayer with salutary longing. "Letter 130," 380–81, 399. For both, as well, prayer directed toward the proper object is evidence of the Spirit already working within us. "Letter 130," 398.

the necessity of baptism for salvation and, in line with the other fourth
century eastern theologians we have examined, makes no exception for
catechumens who die prematurely.[95] Indeed, in a homily on John 3:5,
Chrysostom goes out of his way to emphasize the necessity of water for
baptism, arguing that, like the matter of creation itself, water is simply a
given; the story of Cornelius, he adds, reinforces this point.[96] A reference
to the parable of Lazarus (Luke 16:19–31), likewise, drives home the message that the afterlife affords no second chance to alter decisions made in
the present.[97] While he does not articulate a full-fledged doctrine of original sin, Chrysostom argues that entrance into the kingdom of heaven is
impossible because without baptism one still "bears the garment of death,
of the curse, of destruction."[98] De Roten notes that Chrysostom does not
seem concerned to address the question of infants dying without baptism,
speculating that the Constantinopolitan bishop may not have thought
them to be lost.[99] When examined in context, however, the sermons de
Roten cites, in which Chrysostom offers consolation to mothers who

95. Philippe de Roten, *Baptême et mystagogie enquête sur l'initiation chrétienne selon S. Jean Chrysostome* (Münster: Aschendorf, 2005), 11–12.

96. John Chrysostom, "Homily 25," in *Commentary on Saint John the Apostle and Evangelist: Homilies 1–47*, trans. Thomas Aquinas Goggin (Washington, DC: The Catholic University of America Press, 2000), 246–47. "The catechumen is a stranger to the believer [...] if it should happen—and may it not!—that, death coming upon us unexpectedly, we depart from here uninitiated, even if we have earthly blessings without number, nothing else will welcome us than hell." "Homily 25," 248–49. In the *Fathers of the Church* edition, the English translator qualifies this statement with a footnote claiming that Chrysostom meant only those putting off baptism and "did not include in their number, of course, those who remained unbaptized through invincible ignorance." The footnote illustrates the tendency to read modern concepts back into the Fathers; "invincible ignorance" is not a patristic concept and there is not a shred of evidence in Chrysostom's words to support the footnote's interpretation.

97. "Homily 25," 249–50.

98. "Homily 25," 243.

99. De Roten, *Baptême et mystagogie enquête sur l'initiation chrétienne selon S. Jean Chrysostome*, 13. Cf., John Chrysostom, "On Thessalonians Homily 6," "On Colossians Homily 8," in *Saint Chrysostom: Homilies on Galatians, Ephesians, Philippians, Colossians, Thessalonians, Timothy, Titus, and Philemon*, ed. Philip Schaff, Nicene and Post-Nicene Fathers 13 (Grand Rapids, MI: Eerdmans, 1988), 348–52, 298; "On First Corinthians Homily 12," in *Saint Chrysostom: Homilies on First and Second Corinthians*, ed. Philip Schaff, Nicene and Post-Nicene Fathers 12 (Grand Rapids, MI: Eerdmans, 1989), 71. In "On Acts of the Apostles Homily 21," Chrysostom speaks of children being saved in virtue of their parents' actions and includes an admonishment to parents not to be "negligent" in bringing them to the font, in *Saint Chrysostom: Homilies on the Acts of the Apostles and the Epistle to the Romans*, ed. Philip Schaff, Nicene and Post-Nicene Fathers 11 (Grand Rapids, MI: Eerdmans, 1989), 140.

have lost children, suggest that he is speaking to parents of the baptized. Chrysostom does not, in other words, show evidence of having staked out a notably more inclusive position regarding salvation than was the norm at the turn of the fifth century. Likewise, though Daley suggests that Jerome (ca. 347–419) entertained the possibility that all Christians might in the end be saved, such speculation did not extend to the unbaptized.[100] Harmless notes that Jerome never responded to Augustine's plea for guidance as to the fate of unbaptized babies.[101]

Theodore of Mopsuestia. On the other side of the ledger, Theodore of Mopsuestia (ca. 350–428), without any of the late Augustine's scruples, treats the Good Thief as a straightforward case of an individual saved without baptism. In his commentary on 1 Timothy, Theodore rebukes those who undergo the ritual while still trying to avoid living a Christian life.[102] Some people do this by delaying baptism until their deathbed in order to persist in a dissolute lifestyle for as long as possible; others fail to live a life of grace after being baptized as infants. Against such abuses of the sacrament, Theodore points to two scriptural passages, which highlight the importance of one's intention (*propositum*) if the sacrament is to lead to salvation: Simon the Magician was baptized, but with self-serving motives that prevented the sacrament from enlightening him; in contrast, the Good Thief, in virtue of his good intention, entered paradise without baptism. Theodore is quick to add that he does not wish to denigrate the sacrament with such examples, but to warn those who incur God's judgment by misusing it. Baptism does not work because of the nature of water, he adds; instead, the faith of its recipients "is accustomed to draw" (*adtrahere solet*) God's perfect generosity into the sacrament.

---

100. Daley, *The Hope of the Early Church*, 103–4. Maximus of Turin (d. 423), who held a similar position, framed the issue in sacramental terms: "the water of baptism puts out the fire of Gehenna." Daley, 126. Jerome strongly affirmed the necessity of the Church for salvation. Sesboüé, *"Fuori dalla Chiesa nessuna salvezza,"* 47. For Jerome, the Good Thief shows that it is never too late for conversion. Jerome, "Letter 57," in *Select Letters of St. Jerome*, trans. F.A. Wright, Loeb Classical Library 262 (Cambridge, MA: Harvard University Press, 1991), 2, p. 341.

101. Harmless, "Baptism," 90. Jerome's emphasis on the responsibility of parents for their children's baptism suggests that his beliefs did not substantially differ from Augustine's. Jerome, "Letter 57," 6, p. 355.

102. Theodore of Mopsuestia, "In Ep. Ad Timotheum I," in *In Epistolas B. Pauli Commentarii*, edited by H.B. Swete, vol. 2, *I. Thessalonians–Philemon, Appendices, Indices* (Cambridge: Cambridge University Press, 1882), 3.2, pp. 107–8.

Theodore emphasizes the intention of the recipient of baptism because, as the Good Thief shows, when this intention is present, God can bring to completion the gifts the sacrament conveys.

Theodore does not attempt a more systematic formulation of this insight. His phrasing suggests that God's generosity normally works (*solet*) through the sacrament and that salvation without baptism by water, therefore, would be exceptional. He does not say whether such exceptional circumstances might extend beyond the case of the Good Thief, though his reasoning in this passage would seem to make room for salvation in a case such as that of Valentinian. Theodore's reasoning, like Ambrose's, also implies real limits to how far baptism of desire's reach extends. Having the right intention cannot be taken for granted; the main point of the passage, after all, is that even some who receive the sacrament lack the proper faith. Furthermore, there can be little doubt that the faith which makes the sacrament fruitful is Christian; preaching on baptism elsewhere, Theodore condemns pagan and Jewish practices that bear an outward resemblance to the Christian sacraments as the work of Satan.[103] Moreover, Theodore sees baptism as necessary for salvation because, until we are liberated by it and born again, we remain slaves of the devil, not even fully aware of the harm incurred by Adam's sin.[104] Theodore's sacramental theology is deeply eschatological, and he sees the purpose of the sacraments fulfilled in eternal life, so much so that some commentators have accused him of reducing the sacraments to mere symbols of future events. Frederick McLeod defends Theodore from such a charge by pointing out that, for the bishop of Mopsuestia, the effects of the sacraments begin in this world, even if they reach fulfillment in the life to come. To put it more precisely, Theodore understands baptism as providing us with the potential for eternal life, a potential which we do not possess in virtue of our natural birth.[105] The seed baptism plants is real, though we must have the right intention for it to bear eternal fruit.

Theodore's emphasis on intention suggests that he understands it as

103. Theodore of Mopsuestia, "Baptismal Homily II," in Edward Yarnold, *The Awe-Inspiring Rites of Initiation: The Origins of the R.C.I.A.* (Edinburgh: T&T Clark, 1994), 2.10, p. 174.

104. "Baptismal Homily II," 2.1–6, pp. 168–71.

105. Frederick G. McLeod, "The Christological Ramifications of Theodore of Mopsuestia's Understanding of Baptism and the Eucharist," *Journal of Early Christian Studies* 10, no. 1 (2002): 37–75. See Theodore of Mopsuestia, "Baptismal Homily III," in Yarnold, *The Awe-Inspiring Rites of Initiation*, 3.10, p. 186.

part of the reality of baptism. In exceptional circumstances—such as that of the Good Thief—this intention seems to render that reality partially present. God, of course, must bring this partial presence to perfection, but in Theodore's mind the same thing happens even in the case of one who receives the sacrament; in all circumstances the seed of baptism reaches its perfection in eternal life. Unfortunately for the theology of baptism of desire, the hints Theodore left on the subject were themselves never to grow beyond the seminal stage. In contrast to the golden-tongued but contentious John Chrysostom—with whom he was educated in Antioch—Theodore was to pass a tranquil life in the sleepy see of Mopsuestia but encounter controversy after death. His theology became associated with Nestorianism, leading to his condemnation by the Second Council of Constantinople in 553. Consequently, his work survived only in fragments and translations and was unknown during medieval debates over baptism of desire.[106] His brief but suggestive comments on the Good Thief are still valuable, however, because they demonstrate that the arguments advanced by Ambrose in *De obitu Valentiniani* and by Augustine in *De Baptismo* were compatible with the thought of other patristic writers.

Augustinian consensus. This observation is important because there is little record of discussion about baptism of desire over the next several centuries. If any general theological trend relevant to our study can be discerned in the chaotic age marked by the disintegration of the Roman Empire, it is an increased emphasis on the urgency of infant baptism, driven by Augustine's anti-Pelagian theology. As Ferguson puts it, "Once original sin was established as the basic framework for thinking, then it was natural for it to become the principal reason for infant baptism."[107] We have already seen that the longstanding belief in baptism's necessity for salvation was shared even by those, such as Cyril of Jerusalem, who did not hold a doctrine of original sin. Augustine's theology, however, clarified the stakes involved. Thus, we find in this era a plethora of figures, from Peter Chrysologus to Leo the Great to Fulgentius of Ruspe, affirming in stark terms the necessity of baptism for the salvation of children.[108] The considerations involved in the decision of when to baptize

106. Colish, *Faith, Fiction & Force*, 24.

107. Ferguson, *Baptism in the Early Church*, 816.

108. An inscription in the baptistry of St. John Lateran, dating from the pontificate of

may not have changed since Tertullian voiced skepticism about baptizing too early—one still had to weigh the risk of a premature death against the possibility of falling into post-baptismal sin—but the post-Augustinian discussion seems to have shifted the emotional heft of those considerations. Other factors—which we will address in the following chapter—were also at play, such as the emergence of uniformly Christian societies and changing penitential practices. The Augustinian consensus did not, of course, mean that hard cases had become easy; Peter Cramer points out that Gregory the Great, writing on the guilt of unbaptized children in 599, though apparently troubled by Augustine's conclusions, continued to back them.[109]

Gennadius. The gravity and forcefulness with which the necessity of baptism is affirmed in this period might lead one to believe that Ambrose's assertions in *De obitu Valentiniani* had been forgotten or rejected. In some cases, they had. Gennadius of Massilia (d. ca. 496) categorically rules out the possibility of salvation even in the specific case of a catechumen dying "in good works."[110] Martyrdom is the only exception, and Gennadius goes on to describe, point by point, how the martyr's testimony fulfills the essential actions of the ritual. A partial sacrament is not, for Gennadius, sufficient for salvation. At a minimum, Gennadius's work demonstrates that Ambrose's teaching in *De obitu Valentiniani* did not achieve universal approval in the century after it was delivered. Gennadius does not treat the question as controversial—he straightforwardly asserts his position as the Church's belief—and does not provide any supporting argumentation. The opinion of this obscure priest, however, took on an outsized

---

Sixtus III (432–40), affirms "the blessed life does not receive those born only once." Quoted in Ferguson, *Baptism in the Early Church*, 769. Peter Chrysologus emphasizes a Christian's responsibility for bringing those hindered by age, ignorance, vice, or poverty to the font. Ferguson, 758. Leo I says, "No one is clean from stain, not even an infant." Leo I, *Sermons*, 21.2, p. 77. John J. Gavigan, in "Fulgentius of Ruspe on Baptism," *Traditio* 5 (1947): 316–19, notes that Fulgentius argues from original sin to the necessity of baptism, whereas Augustine had necessarily argued in the other direction. Fulgentius neither endorses nor explicitly excludes baptism of desire.

109. Peter Cramer, *Baptism and Change in the Early Middle Ages, c. 200 – c. 1150* (Cambridge: Cambridge University Press, 2002), 132–33.

110. "Baptizatis tantum iter esse salutis credimus. Nullum catechumenum, quamvis in bonis operibus defunctum, vitam aeternam habere credimus, excepto martyrio, ubi tota baptismi sacramenta complentur." Gennadius, *Liber de ecclesiasticis dogmatibus*, PL 58:997.

importance during the Middle Ages because his *Liber de ecclesiasticis dog-matibus* was mistakenly attributed to Augustine.[111]

"Little Theudosius." Gennadius's opinion, however, was not universal. Circumstances similar to those of Valentinian's death underlie a remarkable piece of archeological evidence from the same time period that allows us to consider the words not of a bishop or theologian, but of the anonymous parents of "little Theudosius"—a child whose fifth century gravestone was found in southern Gaul. Theudosius died too soon for his biography to contain anything more than mention of his innocence.

> Worthy child, circled round by the rampart of the cross, innocent, undarkened by the filth of sin, little Theudosius, whose parents in purity of mind intended to bury him in the holy baptismal font, was snatched away by shameless death; yet the ruler of high Olympus will give rest to any member lying beneath the noble sign of the cross, and the child will be heir to Christ.[112]

We cannot expect an epitaph to expostulate a delicate doctrinal position in the same way as a sermon or a treatise, but the inscription encapsulates the kernel of Ambrose's argument in *De obitu Valentiniani*. Theudosius's parents seem to have been aware of the necessity of baptism for salvation because, although his innocence is stipulated, they feel the need to mention their intention to immerse him in the font. They emphasize the purity of their intention (*pura mente*) and that they were prevented from realizing it by circumstances beyond their control—Theudosius was seized (*rapuit*) by death. We probably should not read much into their mention of "Olympus" beyond a poetic reference to God; it is clear that they see the cross as the sign of salvation and expect the child to be called to eternal life by Christ. While it is impossible to speculate on how they

111. Colish, *Faith, Fiction & Force*, 24–25, 33, 88. Others attributed it to Isidore of Seville. Salvatore Pricoco, "Gennadio di Marsiglia," in *Nuovo dizionario patristico e di antichità cristiane*, vol. 2, ed. Angelo Di Bernardino (Genova: Marietti 1820, 2007), 2076.

112. "Insignem genitum crucis munimine septum / Insontem, nulla peccati sorde fucatum, / Theodosium paruum, quem pura mente parentes / Optabant sacro fonte baptismate tingui / Improba mors rapuit: sed summi rector Olympi / Praestabit requiem membris uit nobile signum / Praefixum est crucis, Xpique uocabitur heres." "*Epitaphe* de Theudosius," in *Le baptême des enfants dans la tradition de l'église*, ed. J.C. Didier (Tournai: Desclée, 1959), 125. The English translation is from Cramer, *Baptism and Change*, 131.

may or may not have conceived of original sin and its effects, it is clear
that they believed that something more than Theudosius's innocence was
required for salvation, something supplied by their wish for his baptism.
This wish finds concrete expression in the burial of their child under the
sign of the cross. Such a symbolic expression, along with the words of the
inscription themselves, parallel Ambrose's heartfelt prayer for the Lord
to receive Valentinian at the end of his funeral oration.

The inscription does not say how old Theudosius was when he died,
though he was apparently too young to have committed personal sin—or
to have approached the font on his own, for it is his parents' wish (*optabant*) to have him baptized that is mentioned. In fact, a bold theological
move has just occurred, even if Theudosius's parents probably did not
realize it. For, as we shall see, even after baptism of desire gained acceptance, the theological majority—with a few exceptions—did not see the
doctrine as helpful when considering the fate of infants; as Augustine had
glumly concluded, infants cannot formulate their own desires. Theudosius's parents, however, applied the Ambrosian logic of baptism of desire
to their child's situation, with their own desire taking the place of the
catechumen's. We have no way of knowing the theological sophistication of Theodosius's parents or their religious influences, but perhaps this
does not matter, because they have tapped into something deeper. The
reasoning of the inscription does not rely on the constructs of systematic
theology but on the symbols of the rite—the sign of the cross and immersion in water. And in the rite, parents bring their children to the font
for baptism, and the Church baptizes them. In other words, according to
the practice of the Church, parents' desire is sufficient for the sacrament.
If such a desire is valid under normal circumstances, why would it not
be sufficient for Theudosius? While such an argument does not emerge
from the usual theological sources, the Gallic gravestone is our earliest
indication that the logic of baptism of desire might be able to account for
the salvation of infants.

Damascene. In the east, one final figure, the Syrian monk John Damascene (d. 749), bears mentioning for several reasons. Living at the very
end of the patristic era and more a compiler than an original theologian,
John's three part *The Fount of Knowledge* is often considered a kind of

Summa theologiae of the age. Aquinas, in fact, cites the Damascene on the question of baptism, demonstrating his enduring authority.[113] John also wrote within a unique social milieu: Damascus had fallen under Muslim rule in 634. In addition to recapitulating orthodox Christian thought on baptism and salvation, the Damascene is credited with making the philosophical distinction between God's antecedent and consequent will, explaining that, though God wills all to be saved (antecedent will), as a consequence of sin he wills our just punishment (consequent will).[114] In some cases this punishment prompts conversion, though this depends on the individual's free response to it.

The relatively long section on baptism in John's *An Exact Exposition of the Orthodox Faith* repeats essential themes: Baptism leads to the remission of sin and eternal life; it can be received only once; it involves the twofold purification of water and spirit because man is a composite of body and soul; it requires a new way of living.[115] Adding to Gregory Nazianzen's list, John counts eight different types of baptism, though the larger number is more a question of classification than of substantive theological differences. Whereas Gregory had counted one Old Testament "baptism of Moses," the Damascene lists the flood, the parting of the Red Sea, and the ablutions of the Law as distinct types. This is followed by John's baptism and then Jesus's. By undergoing John's baptism, the Damascene reasons, Jesus transforms it into the salvific baptism we receive. Like Gregory, he includes the baptism of tears (post-baptismal repentance) and baptism by the blood of martyrdom.[116] Finally, he adds: "An eighth, which is the last, is not saving, but, while being destructive of evil, since evil and sin no longer hold sway, it chastises endlessly."[117] In

113. Thomas Aquinas, *Summa theologica*, vol. 2, trans. Fathers of the English Dominican Province (New York: Benziger Brothers, 1947), 3.66.11, obj. 3.

114. John Damascene, *An Exact Exposition of the Orthodox Faith*, in *Saint John of Damascus Writings*, trans. Frederic H. Chase Jr., Fathers of the Church 37 (Washington, DC: The Catholic University of America Press, 1958), 2.29, pp. 260–63.

115. *An Exact Exposition of the Orthodox Faith*, 4.9, pp. 343–48.

116. Isidore of Seville (c. 560–636) also speaks of three types of baptism, water, blood, and tears, in *De Ecclesiasticis officiis*, ed. Christopher M. Lawson (Turnhout: Brepols, 1989), 2.25(24).3 CCL 113, 102–3, lines 22–36. Some identified the latter with baptism of desire. Colish, *Faith, Fiction & Force*, 243. However, Isidore's language recalls that of Gregory Nazianzen, emphasizing the laborious and penitential character of this third type of baptism, making identification with the Ambrosian concept improbable.

117. John Damascene, *An Exact Exposition of the Orthodox Faith*, 4.9, p. 347–48.

other words, John refers to the fire of eternal punishment as a "baptism." This idiosyncratic classification is somewhat infelicitous since the waters of baptism are usually spoken of as quenching hell's fires. Nonetheless, nothing about John's exposition suggests a change in the substance of mainstream patristic soteriology or baptismal theology.

No version of baptism on John's list can be identified with baptism of desire, and his dependence on Gregory Nazianzen argues against attributing such a belief to him. A comment at the end of the section—almost an afterthought—suggests a slight opening to a broader sense of the sacrament; John the Baptist he says, "was baptized when he placed his hand upon the divine head of the Lord." Such an action clearly differs from the standard rite, so much so that the Damascene feels the need to allay doubt by adding, "He was also baptized in his own blood." Drawing conclusions for the present from this example is probably going too far, and we can add that even if John Damascene were willing to stretch the definition of baptism to account for other hard cases, he did not see salvation extending beyond Christianity. Faith is necessary for salvation, he says when addressing the possibility of someone being baptized fraudulently, and "he who does not believe in accordance with the tradition of the Catholic Church [...] is without faith."[118] John lived in an atmosphere of religious diversity—possibly even working directly for Syria's Muslim rulers—but this did not lessen his sense of Christianity's necessity for salvation.[119]

The Patristic Doctrine Summarized

While baptism of desire is sometimes referred to as a medieval doctrine—and its systematic vetting would only really begin in the twelfth century—it originates in the patristic era. To be sure, the idea likely never enjoyed universal—or perhaps even majority—support at any time in that epoch. Perhaps this should not surprise us. The doctrine of the necessity of baptism and, even more importantly, the rite of baptism belong to the most ancient core of the Christian proclamation. Christianity's first

---

118. *An Exact Exposition of the Orthodox Faith*, 4.10, p. 348.

119. In his catalogue of heresies, John Damascene specifically notes that Mohammed forbids his followers to be baptized. *On Heresies*, in *Saint John of Damascus Writings*, 101, p. 159.

eight centuries show remarkable stability in the fundamental conviction that baptism is necessary for salvation, a belief that persisted whether Christianity was a persecuted religion or the official one, whether it was in the minority or in the majority. The evidence does not support the notion of an inclusivist primitive Church turning towards exclusivism in a post-Constantinian or post-Augustinian era. Instead, it points to a powerful sense of the irreducibility of the ritual, a sense so obvious as not really to require articulation. Thus, Paul appeals to the Corinthians' experience of baptism to support belief in the resurrection, and Gennadius of Massilia affirms the efficacy of martyrdom by showing that it mirrors the baptismal rite. Even the Pelagians baptized their children to assure them entrance into the kingdom of heaven.

At the same time, for some early Christians, this profound belief in the salvific power of baptism seems to have been compatible with a more extensive sense of the rite's reach, whether this included a baptismal ritual for the dead, as the Corinthians seem to have practiced, or the apostles baptizing in the afterlife, as Hermas imagined. The suspicion that in certain hard cases baptism's saving effects could somehow be extended is present, if vaguely, throughout the era. Both Cyprian of Carthage and one of his anonymous opponents hint at something like baptism of desire in exceptional circumstances. And such exceptional circumstances—the classic case of a catechumen's death—prompted the first full-throated articulation of the doctrine from Ambrose of Milan. Ambrose bases his theory not on any alternative to baptism but on desire for the sacrament itself. Joined eventually by Augustine and Theodore of Mopsuestia, Ambrose indicates that, if the desire for baptism is present but death intervenes unexpectedly, God can bring that desire to fulfillment. In Ambrose's thinking, this phenomenon is intertwined with God's ability to answer our prayers and thus requires a desire at least clear enough to formulate a prayer of petition. It seems not, however, to require perfect knowledge of Christian doctrine. Ambrose takes for granted enough knowledge to request the sacrament, as well as the absence of any non-Christian religious loyalties that would impede such a request. When the sacrament is neglected because of a defect in the individual's will—a lack of conversion to Christ—Ambrose implies, nothing can supply what is missing. For Ambrose, the neediness that provokes desire is part of what makes baptism of desire work. Thirst for salvation prompts our prayer, which the Lord himself desires to answer. By wanting baptism, our desire aligns with the Lord's will.

Augustine expresses Ambrose's insights more systematically with the condition that the sacrament must not have been omitted because of *contemptus religionis* but must be the result of *articulus necessitatis*. These key conditions would be accepted in the medieval debate as the presuppositions that make the doctrine credible. Augustine set the stage for future discussion of baptism of desire in other ways as well. The force with which he defended the doctrine of original sin tended to lead later thinkers to treat this as the chief obstacle to salvation removed by baptism. Furthermore, Augustine's sacramental theology—the principle *ex opere operato*, the distinction between validity and fruitfulness, hints of what would become the *sacramentum* and *res sacramenti* distinction—provided the framework for medieval discussion. And Augustine's *De Baptismo* ensured that the Good Thief would become the preferred medieval exemplar of baptism of desire. By throwing Cornelius, who was baptized, into the mix of biblical precedents, Augustine also contributed an element of confusion destined to dog later debates. Most patristic thinkers seem to have agreed that the example of Cornelius reinforced the necessity of baptism.

Historical circumstances meant that Ambrose's theory was never fully debated within the patristic era—if one doesn't count Augustine's second thoughts. After all, excluding circumstances such as the funeral of Valentinian, the occasions on which one might have preached about baptism of desire were limited. An essential feature of the patristic version of the doctrine is that it does not suggest a pathway to salvation that could in any way be in competition with the sacrament. Indeed, this observation provides a criterion for evaluating future articulations of the doctrine, for if a theory were to suggest such an alternative pathway, it would have to be considered a contradiction to the patristic doctrine and not its development. This is not to say that the patristic theory does not invite further systematic questioning. Ambrose hints at a relationship between baptism of desire and the prefiguration of baptism in the Old Testament, for example, but does not fully flesh this out.

It is, then, possible to speak of a patristic doctrine of baptism of desire.

Even though Ambrose, Augustine, and Theodore of Mopsuestia each seem to have developed the concept independently, their words on the subject are broadly compatible, indeed complementary. Each of these three shows a remarkable sensitivity to the fundamental theological issues involved, the testimony of scripture, and the dynamics of the Church's baptismal practice, even if they leave some questions unresolved. The true test of the doctrine, however, would come several centuries in the future, when baptism of desire would be rediscovered, given a name, and put through the theological crucible—where it would be opposed, supported, mangled somewhat by all parties, and, eventually, established in the Catholic theological consensus.

Chapter Three

The Medieval Crucible

The story of baptism of desire is rife with paradoxes. In the previous chapter, we saw Ambrose show Valentinian's "poverty" leading to his salvation. In this chapter, which takes us from the fall of Rome to the doorstep of the Renaissance, we will find still more paradoxes. The diversity of figures and circumstances found in these eight hundred years is intimidating, and it would be tempting to pass over the more obscure swaths of time, skipping directly from Augustine to Thomas, allowing him alone to represent "the medievals." But doing so would miss the key turning points in our story. Previous studies of related topics such as the doctrine *extra ecclesiam nulla salus* have tended to overlook the ritual dimension of the question—a striking omission since, as we have already seen, in Christianity's early centuries participation in the rite of baptism was seen to be the heart of the matter. In the Middle Ages, we will begin to understand the paradoxical way in which the ritual got lost. In post-Augustinian Christendom, infant baptism almost entirely eclipsed adult baptism, a development driven by belief in the absolute necessity of the rite. But the dominance of baptism *quamprimum*—as soon as possible—eventually led to minimalism in the way the rite was practiced. In societies of the baptized, it became possible to take the sacrament for granted, even to see it as a kind of formality; this, in turn, distorted the way salvation itself was understood. Instead of participation in the action of Christ, heaven became an external reward bestowed for obedience to divine law.

The first part of this chapter will focus, then, on the underappreciated question of changing sacramental practice, even if this happened mostly in the early Middle Ages, when baptism of desire had disappeared from view. It is another irony that, after this long dormancy, interest in the doctrine would reawaken at a time—roughly the eleventh century—when universal infant baptism had made those to whom the doctrine would most clearly apply—adult catechumens—rarer than at any time in Christianity's first millennium. Interest in the question had to do with the rise of the scholastic method and the delight the scholastics took in hard cases, no matter how theoretical. Thus, while Ambrose addressed baptism of desire only because he was forced to do so by the death of Valentinian, Thomas pondered what would happen to an imaginary boy raised by wolves in the forest. Eventually the scholastic debate would lead theology from early medieval skepticism toward baptism of desire to a thirteenth century consensus in favor of the doctrine. This general agreement seems to have led to a decline of interest in the topic thereafter. The turning point in the history of the doctrine—and the period of most vigorous debate—occurred in the school of Laon at the beginning of the twelfth century and continued through the writing of Peter Lombard. With Peter and other prominent figures such as Bernard of Clairvaux and Hugh of St. Victor approving of the idea, discussion shifted from the legitimacy of the doctrine to the theological conundrums it raises. We see this shift reflected in the theology of Thomas Aquinas, which we will trace from his *Commentary* on Peter's *Sentences* to the *Summa theologiae*. Thomas comes closest to fitting the patristic sense of the sacrament as participation in the Incarnation within a scholastic framework, providing both a robust sense of baptism's necessity and a plausible starting point for understanding implicit desire. Even in Thomas's account, however, certain issues, such as the relationship of baptism of desire to sacramental character, remain thorny. As discussion petered out in the fourteenth century, such conundrums remained unresolved.

Baptism in Flux: From the Fall of Rome
to the Rise of Scholasticism

The early Middle Ages, roughly the late fifth to the eleventh century, are sometimes referred to as the Dark Ages, an unnecessarily pejorative label that nonetheless accurately suggests the relative lack of historical sources from the period and the consequent difficulty studying it. Nothing in the theological record indicates that baptism of desire was much discussed during the early Middle Ages and only one theologian—the Venerable Bede—has left us with an original, if oblique, contribution to the subject. Nonetheless, changes that the practice of baptism underwent in the period are crucial for understanding theological shifts that would happen much later. Here we are dealing with almost imperceptible changes, like ocean currents altering a ship's direction while its captain studies the stars and wind. In this first section, therefore, we will seek to identify trends that cut across the centuries rather than to proceed in a purely chronological progression.

From adults to infants. It is a central contention of this study that the way baptism was celebrated eventually led to changing attitudes toward the sacraments and their necessity. Changes in the felt significance of the rite, however, were not always reflected in theology—at least not right away—because the theological principle of the necessity of baptism inherited from the patristic era was so unambiguous. In fact, Christendom's insistent embrace of this principle led to the very practices that made baptism eventually *feel* less significant. Augustine was the great master of the early Middle Ages, and his emphasis on the necessity of baptism for the salvation of infants combined with pre-modernity's heartrendingly high infant mortality rate resulted in an urgent push to see that every child was baptized as quickly as possible. Speed meant a rite shorn down to its necessities. With the rite thus reduced, it eventually became possible, at the level of imagination and attitude, to perceive the sacrament as a mere formality in a way that would have been unthinkable to those undergoing "the awe-inspiring rites" of Ambrose, Augustine, and Theodore.[1]

---

1. Yarnold suggests that this patristic phrase could just as faithfully be translated as "spine-chilling rites," in *The Awe-Inspiring Rites of Initiation*, ix.

Augustine's emphasis on original sin permeates the theology of the era.[2] Consequently—and in contrast to the practice Augustine himself grew up with—infant baptism increasingly came to be seen as desirable, eventually becoming the norm. Under Charlemagne, Frankish law mandated the baptism of infants within a year of their birth, and later medieval kingdoms adopted the law of *quamprimum*.[3] This led to a shift in ritual practice perceptible in the liturgical books of the period. Our oldest sacramentary, the *Gelasianum Vetus*, contains instructions for an extended process of initiation based on the patristic catechumenate running through Lent and culminating in baptism on Holy Saturday.[4] While the prayers in the sacramentary seem mostly to refer to adults, the instructions that accompany them make reference to infants as well.[5] Even more significant, the *Gelasianum* includes a second set of instructions for an abbreviated baptismal rite; the label for these instructions suggests that they were originally intended for the baptism of sick catechumens though the abbreviated rite likely became the norm for most baptisms, especially of infants.[6] Historians of the liturgy note that medieval copyists tended to preserve older liturgical forms even if they were no longer commonly in use, making it likely that instructions for full rites of adult initiation remained in liturgical books even after they had fallen out of practice.[7]

2. The canons of the Synod of Orange (529) are representative. Lewis Ayres and Thomas Humphries, "Augustine and the West to AD 650," in *The Oxford Handbook of Sacramental Theology* (Oxford: Oxford University Press, 2015), 163; cf. *Enchiridion symbolorum*, 371–72.

3. Richard Fletcher, *The Conversion of Europe: From Paganism to Christianity, 371–1386 AD* (London: Fontana Press, 1998), 215; Cramer, *Baptism and Change*, 125.

4. *Sacramentarium Gelasianum*, ed. Leo Cunibert Mohlberg, Leo Eizenhöffer, and Peter Siffrin (Rome: Casa Editrice Herder, 1960), 193–452, pp. 32–74. The oldest extant manuscript of the *Gelasianum*, based on an earlier Roman prototype, was copied near Paris around AD 750. Cyrille Vogel, *Medieval Liturgy: An Introduction to the Sources*, trans. William G. Storey and Niels K. Rasmussen (Washington, DC: Pastoral Press, 1986), 65. Thus it likely reflects seventh century Roman baptismal practices. Bryan D. Spinks, *Early and Medieval Rituals and Theologies of Baptism* (Farnham: Ashgate, 2006), 110–11.

5. *Sacramentarium Gelasianum*, 311, p. 48; 419–24, pp. 67–68.

6. *Sacramentarium Gelasianum*, 595–616, pp. 92–97.

7. Michael S. Driscoll, "The Conversion of the Nations," in *The Oxford History of Christian Worship*, ed. Geoffrey Wainwright and Karen B. Westerfield Tucker (New York: Oxford University Press, 2006), 183–85. Another important baptismal instruction from the era the *Ordo Romanus XI* includes directions for an extended period of infant initiation, with the scrutinies carried out over the course of several weeks; Driscoll suggests that these rites could be completed in just two sessions, a process of reduction reflected in later ritual books. See also, Joseph H. Lynch, *Godparents and Kinship in Early Medieval Europe* (Princeton, NJ: Princeton

Nonetheless, churchmen of the time seemed to perceive something of value in these more extensive rites and perhaps even felt a certain unease over what had been lost. For example, Amalarius of Metz (ca. 775–ca. 850) inherited the patristic sense of the importance of pre-baptismal catechesis and justified its omission in the case of infants by arguing that the pre-baptismal exorcism took its place.[8] Describing the "disintegration" of the process of Christian initiation in the medieval era, Nathan Mitchell observes that the tendency toward a minimalistic—and in the Late Middle Ages, less tactile—celebration of the rites necessarily led to a "loss of the heuristic power of the symbol," by which he means the symbolic resonances and felt power of the event.[9] Clearly, when baptism immediately follows natural birth, the sense of the sacrament as an existential turning point—the end of a life in the flesh and the beginning of a new life in the Spirit—is obscured. It is not coincidental that the early Middle Ages also witnessed a long process of shifting penitential disciplines, so that moral conversion came to be less strongly associated with baptism and more with penance.[10] George Williams argues persuasively that systematic theologians and historians of dogma in the past century tended to neglect the effect of the medieval Church's sacramental life on theologians such as Anselm of Canterbury (c. 1033–1109). As he puts it:

> Anselm belongs to the group who responded theologically to the attenuation of baptism and accentuation of the eucharist. Baptism, from having been the unique sacrament of incorporation in the

University Press, 1986), 293. For the *Ordo Romanus XI*, see *Les Ordines Romani du Haut Moyen Age II*, ed. Michel Andrieu, vol. 2, *Les Texts (Ordines I–XIII)* (Louvain: Spicilegium Sacrum Lovaniense, 1971), 365–447, and the convenient summary of Spinks, *Early and Medieval Rituals and Theologies of Baptism*, 114–15.

8. Susan A. Keefe, *Water and the Word: Baptism and the Education of the Clergy in the Carolingian Empire*, vol. 1, *A Study of Texts and Manuscripts* (Notre Dame, IN: University of Notre Dame Press, 2002), 118.

9. Nathan Mitchell, "Christian Initiation: Decline and Dismemberment," *Worship* 48, no. 8 (1974): 477.

10. On penance, see Rob Meens, *Penance in Medieval Europe 600–1200* (Cambridge: Cambridge University Press, 2014). Lynch emphasizes that one of the primary functions of the ancient catechumenate was to scrutinize the sincerity of would-be converts and to test their readiness for a life of Christian discipline. Lynch, *Godparents and Kinship in Early Medieval Europe*, 85, 88–91. Churchmen of the early Middle Ages showed some concern that infant baptism obscured the moral imperatives implicit in baptism; in response, Pseudo-Dionysius argued that growing up in a Christian environment would naturally lead children to live as Christians. Lynch, 138–39.

body of Christ in the ancient Church, was in Anselm demoted to serving as the ablutionary preparation therefor [sic], or at best was regarded as a contingent *incorporatio imperfecta* to be followed by eucharistic *incorporatio perfecta*.[11]

References to baptism as it came to be commonly practiced later in the medieval era provide evidence that speed had become the norm, with most baptisms taking place within twenty-four hours of birth.[12] This often gave the service an *ad hoc* quality, leading to confusion and disputes—even scuffles—over naming, the drafting of godparents from whomever happened to be nearby, and the inadvertent exclusion of family members from the ceremony. Yet, haste did not mean that baptism was felt to be unimportant; other aspects of the ceremony, such as fine materials used for baptismal garments and processions accompanying the newly baptized child home, often left a lasting impression on participants.[13] The religious presuppositions of the time meant that the increasing ritual minimalism did not immediately diminish the importance attributed to baptism; only once such assumptions began to fall away would the diminished sacrament be vulnerable to being perceived as mere formality.

Political interference. A similar dynamic can be seen in another trend originating in the early Middle Ages: Baptism came to assume a political function, which at times eclipsed its religious meaning. While in the popular imagination the conversion of Constantine marks the triumph of Christianity and the demise of paganism, the historical record is quite different. As Augustine's polemic against Christianity's detractors in the first ten books of *The City of God* demonstrates, paganism was hardly a spent force even within the borders of the disintegrating Western Empire; it likely persisted in Europe's rural areas long after the Empire's fall. Meanwhile, the diverse peoples who would shape the future face

---

11. George Hunston Williams, "The Sacramental Presuppositions of Anselm's *Cur Deus Homo*," *Church History* 26, no. 3 (1957): 267.

12. William S. Deller, "The First Rite of Passage: Baptism in Medieval Memory," *Journal of Family History* 36, no. 1 (2011): 4–5. Deller's novel study examines references to baptism in legal testimony for a sense of how the ceremony was described by the general population. He notes that, with the norm of hasty baptisms taken for granted, the theological reasons for speed no longer needed to be mentioned.

13. Deller, "The First Rite of Passage," 9.

of Europe—Franks, Saxons, Angles, Vikings, Slavs—remained almost entirely unevangelized. This meant that the early medieval period was one of intense missionary activity, and adult baptisms continued to play an important role in European Christianity. Unlike the evangelization of the Apostolic Age, however, political factors heavily influenced these later missionary efforts, even shaping the way baptism was practiced. While ostensibly favoring the celebration of the sacrament, in the long run political influence tended to confuse baptism's theological significance. Charlemagne, who ruled over a Frankish empire covering much of France, Germany, and Northern Italy from 768 to 814, is a key figure for understanding these dynamics. Frankish kings had at least nominally professed Christianity since the conversion of Clovis at the beginning of the sixth century.[14] Because religious affiliations often influenced one's political loyalties, Frankish rulers from then on had an interest in seeing their subjects baptized; this was particularly the case in Charlemagne's vast and ethnically diverse empire. Charlemagne saw himself as possessing a divine mission for the spiritual well-being of his subjects and seems to have genuinely believed in the importance of baptism. Troubled by the haphazard way in which the sacrament was celebrated, he sent a circular letter to the archbishops of his empire in 812 inquiring how the sacrament was administered within their jurisdiction. The fact that the emperor felt the need for such an inquiry is also evidence of decay in the quality of ritual observance.

Even if we grant that Charlemagne was moved by religious feeling to send the circular letter of 812, the motives behind his baptismal policies more generally are unlikely to have been pure.[15] Attempting to bind together the peoples of his realm, at times Charlemagne ordered the forced baptism of conquered tribes. To his credit, when faced with opposition to the practice from his leading court theologian, Alcuin of York (d. 804), the emperor appears to have softened his policy.[16] Alcuin and other theologians

14. Fletcher, *The Conversion of Europe*, 106.

15. G.C.J. Byer points out that Charlemagne was 70 when he sent the inquiry, an age when one's thoughts naturally turn from this life to the next. Glenn C.J. Byer, *Charlemagne and Baptism: A Study of Responses to the Circular Letter of 811/812* (Lanham, MD: International Scholars Publications, 1999), 23–26.

16. Fletcher, *The Conversion of Europe*, 221–22; Cramer, *Baptism and Change*, 185–86. For the theological debate over forced baptisms, see Colish, *Faith, Fiction & Force*, 227–310.

and bishops raised theological objections to forced baptisms—which, if involuntary, could hardly profit their recipients for salvation—but Charlemagne was not the only civil ruler to order the practice. To kings and princes, baptism's salvific value often mattered less than its political and social effects. As Susan Keefe succinctly puts it, "The Franks perceived baptism as a realignment of allegiances."[17] In a "society of the baptized," the sacrament meant social belonging, alongside whatever implications it held for eternal life; it distinguished citizens of Charlemagne's realm from the pagan tribes across its borders.[18] Consequently, Carolingian baptismal policies also accelerated the turn toward ritual minimalism; the patristic catechumenate was simply incompatible with the mass baptisms of conquered peoples. Even when force was not used, Carolingian policies hardly favored sincere conversion; accounts of the Frankish mission to the Danes include reports of individuals returning repeatedly to the font motivated by material gain, such as acquiring a new white garment every year.[19] Thus, even for adults, baptism's significance as a moral rebirth diminished. In the Carolingian state's appropriation of baptism, we see the same dynamic at play as in *quamprimum* baptisms: Belief in the sacrament's importance led to the diminishment of the rite, with problematic long-term consequences. In this case, conflating baptism with citizenship would make the sacrament easier to take for granted in predominantly Christian societies, opening the door to the perception of the rite as a social formality, the ecclesial equivalent of a social security card.

We should not, however, imagine that such a shift happened right away. The evidence overwhelming indicates that baptism was in no way thought to be superfluous when it came to salvation. Richard Fletcher's monumental study of the era concludes with an insightful caution against imposing a modern religious paradigm—centered on the individual's interior experience, epitomized by William James—on the religious experience of people in the Middle Ages. Even a minimalistic baptism might not have been experienced as a *pro forma* event by an eighth century Frank or Saxon. The importance of religious ritual was felt instinctually: "there was nothing 'mere' for early medieval men and women about the

17. Keefe, *Water and the Word*, 1:3.
18. Driscoll, "The Conversion of the Nations," 182–83.
19. Fletcher, *The Conversion of Europe*, 224–25.

acceptance of a rite."[20] We perceived a similar sense of the importance of religious ritual, for example, in the posthumous baptisms of ancient Corinth.

In the second half of the first millennium, in fact, northern Europe was as much mission territory as the Mediterranean had been in the first, and converts within it inevitably faced the same dilemmas. For many, anxiety about separation from one's pagan ancestors in the afterlife proved a genuine obstacle to conversion.[21] This did not lead to a relaxation of preaching the necessity of Christianity for salvation. Pope Nicholas I, replying to a long series of questions put to him by the convert Kahn Boris of Bulgaria, wrote that it was not licit even to pray for parents who died unbelievers.[22] Certain legends from the time suggest that, if there were a solution to such problems, it would somehow have to involve baptism. A biography of St. Patrick composed by the seventh century Irish bishop Tírechán includes, among accounts of the saint's frenetic baptismal activity, the story of Patrick coming upon the grave of a swineherd dead a hundred years, striking the grave with his staff to raise the man to life, and baptizing him. Then Patrick allowed the man, thus christened, to return to the grave and a greatly improved afterlife.[23]

We have, then, little reason to suppose that baptism of desire was much considered in the era. No evidence suggests that Ambrose's *De obitu Valentiniani* was widely known; with the catechumenate abbreviated or eliminated, situations similar to that of Valentinian would have become less common. And the strong emphasis on the deadly shadow cast over infants by original sin probably made the intellectual climate of the early Middle Ages unfavorable for baptism of desire. Keefe's study of the

---

20. Fletcher, 515. This matches Andrea Grillo's analysis of the "classical" stance toward liturgy, in which the self-evident importance of the rite needs no explanation, in *Introduzione alla teologia liturgica: Approccio teorico alla liturgia e ai sacramenti cristiani* (Padua: Edizioni Messaggero Padova, 2011), 86–87.

21. Fletcher, *The Conversion of Europe*, 239.

22. Nicholas I, *Epistola XCVII: Responsa Nicolai ad Consulta Bulgarorum*, PL119:1011.

23. Tirechani, *Tirechani collectanea de sancto Patricio*, trans. Ludwig Bieler (Royal Irish Academy, 2011), https://www.confessio.ie/more/tirechan_english#, 40–41. Baun reports a similar story—a deceased infant brought back to life just long enough to undergo baptism—first found in the seventh century collection of Abbot Anastasios of Sinai and repeated in collections five and six centuries later. Baun, "The Fate of Babies Dying Before Baptism in Byzantium," 115–16.

baptismal treatises produced to educate the clergy in response to Charlemagne's circular letter begins with the popular Carolingian saying: "Take
away the water, it is not baptism. Take away the word, it is not baptism."[24]
Even if such a rule admitted exceptions, it reinforces the impression of a
climate unfavorable to baptism of desire. Colish points to a reference to
the "baptism of tears" in one of these texts as evidence to the contrary.[25]
In fact, the phrase appears in several texts, all of which copy Isidore of
Seville's *De Ecclesiasticis officiis*, which in turn draws on the five types of
baptism in Gregory Nazianzen's Oration 39. None of these instructions
give any indication that "baptism of tears" is to be understood as anything
other than the post-baptismal repentance Gregory originally intended.[26]
Some of the Carolingian scribes may not even have had a particularly
clear idea of what the phrase meant to begin with. The anonymous author
of one text, perhaps finding Isidore's formula unnecessarily confusing,
simply reduces the modes of baptism from three to two, keeping water
and blood but dropping baptism of tears.[27] Perhaps we should not be
surprised if these Carolingian treatises make no real contribution to our
understanding of baptism of desire; they were intended to improve the
knowledge of the poorly educated Frankish clergy rather than to explore
limit cases pushing the boundaries of theology. Perhaps the formula pre-
disposed later medieval theologians to think about the modes of baptism
as a triad, even if the precise identity of the third mode changed.

Bede.   One of few direct contributions to the theology of baptism of desire to emerge from the era comes from the Venerable Bede (672–735),
writing slightly before the Carolingian reforms and from the remote—
but intensely scholarly—atmosphere of the British monasteries of the

24. Keefe, *Water and the Word*, 1:1.

25. Colish, *Faith, Fiction & Force*, 26–27. Colish refers to Text 8 in Keefe's study, *Water and the Word: Baptism and the Education of the Clergy in the Carolingian Empire*, vol. 2, *Editions of the Texts*, 226–37.

26. The discussion of the forgiveness of post-baptismal sins later in the treatise bolsters the likelihood that the author of Text 8 understood the baptism of tears to be post-baptismal penance. Keefe, *Water and the Word*, 2:230, Text 8, 5.4–5. This discussion is followed by an affir-mation of the necessity of baptism for salvation drawing on John 3:5. Several texts, including those of Amalarius of Metz and Theodulf of Orléans, suggest that catechumens remain in their sins until baptism. Keefe, 1:118–19. Cf. Texts 4, 8, and 21.

27. "Duobus, id es aut per aquam aut per sanguinem." Keefe, 2:617, Text 57.

period. Bede's commentary on the Gospel of Luke shows him to be alert
to the problem of the Good Thief's baptism. Drawing on Romans 6:3,
Bede fits both of the thieves into the category of the baptized.[28] However, though they both share the Lord's crucifixion, only the Good Thief's
death is accompanied by a profession of faith. Bede argues that although
the Thief's hands and legs were bound, he still managed, with what freedom remained to him, to fulfill the conditions for salvation laid down
in Romans 10:10, belief in the heart and confession with the lips.[29] This
confession of faith, according to Bede, made the Good Thief a martyr.
Bede is well aware that the Good Thief was not sentenced to death for
professing faith in Christ, but he does not think that it is his executioners'
intention that counts. Several features are noteworthy in Bede's treatment, which shows an incisive understanding of both scripture and sacrament. To begin with, Bede identifies baptism with participation in the
death of Christ; thus, both thieves fit into the category of the baptized.
For such participation to be salvific, however, it must involve the sincere
profession of faith in Christ. If there is a pastoral target of his message,
it is not the unbaptized but, rather, nominal Christians failing to live out
their baptismal faith with sincerity. Finally, Bede's analysis of the Thief,
like Ambrose's eulogy of Valentinian, makes reference to his use of freedom: His faith was expressed in the only way that was possible for him,
given circumstances that—literally—bound him.

The venerable English monk does not, then, directly address the
question of baptism of desire, but by using the key baptismal text from
Romans to analyze the story of the Good Thief, he offers a more intellectually congenial home for the concept than anything else found in the
period. The thieves' crucifixion on Golgotha made their particular case
unique, but it nonetheless provides at least one example of a baptism that
participates in the death of Christ without water. And the Good Thief's
prayer—which, Bede notes, the Lord answered more abundantly than
anyone could have expected—shows desire playing a role in his salvation.
Granted, Bede's classification of the Good Thief as a martyr does not
imply any third type of baptism beyond that of blood; on the other hand,

---

28. Bede, *In Lucae Evangelium Expositio*, ed. D. Hurst (Turnhout: Brepols, 1960), 23.43
CCL 120, 406, lines 1707–1711.

29. *In Lucae Evangelium Expositio*, 23.40–42.1683–1687, p. 405.

Bede expands the category of martyrdom by discounting the relevance of the executioner's motives. In the end, the Thief's desire made his participation in the death of Christ salvific.

The Scholastics Debate

Marcia Colish's survey of medieval baptismal debates identifies renewed interest in baptism of desire with the production of collections of ecclesial canons at the turn of the twelfth century to support reforms initiated by Pope Gregory VII. Among those who compiled such collections, she identifies Bonizo of Sutri as skeptical of baptism of desire, Ivo of Chartres as a proponent, and Gratian as giving "with one hand and [taking away] with the other."[30] In reality, because these works are compilations of more ancient authorities, it is difficult to know to what degree their compilers appreciated the conflicts within their sources and how they thought best to resolve them. In the case of Bonizo, Colish believes him to dismiss baptism of desire because, although he quotes from Augustine's treatment of the Good Thief in *De Baptismo*, his *Liber de vita christiana* (1089) gives the final word to Gennadius—thinking him to be Augustine—who denies that even a catechumen who dies without baptism can be saved.[31] Ivo of Chartres (1096–1116), on the other hand, begins with Gennadius (disguised, again, as Augustine) and follows with *De Baptismo*, though he streamlines Augustine's argument—eliminating, for example, the ambiguous references to Cornelius—making the case for baptism of desire more straightforward than in the original.[32] Still, while strategic editing may color how we approach the question, none of these early canonical compilers offers any new reasons to prefer the pro-baptism of desire Augustine over the anti-baptism of desire Augustine/Gennadius or vice versa. The most that can be said about these early canonists is that, by placing conflicting passages in close proximity, they forced later theologians to confront the issue.

In fact, baptism of desire was precisely the sort of question theologians of the next two centuries could dive into with relish. The same

---

30. Colish, *Faith, Fiction & Force*, 27–33.

31. Bonizo of Sutri, *Liber de Vita Christiana*, ed. Ernst Perels (Berlin: Weidmannsche Buchhandlung, 1930), Preambula 3, pp. 2–5; 1.33, pp. 28–29.

32. Ivo of Chartres, *Panormia*, PL 161:1068–1069.

impulses prompting canonists such as Bonizo and Ivo to bring order
to the mass of patristic authorities, papal letters, decrees, and conciliar
rulings that had accumulated over the course of Christianity's first millennium pushed theologians to develop new methods for resolving the
apparent contradictions within these sources.[33] Other factors, such as the
eucharistic heresy of Berengar of Tours in the eleventh century and the
anti-sacramentalism of the Waldensian movement in the twelfth spurred
the development of systematic sacramental theology. As Colish puts it,
"In the first half of the twelfth century, there was a felt need, for the first
time in the history of the western Christian tradition, for an organized,
systematic, general theology of the sacraments."[34] The rise of cathedral
schools and then universities changed *where* theology was done and in
so doing changed *how* it was done as well. Whereas patristic sacramental
theology developed within the celebration of the ritual itself—often in
the form of homilies—and monastic theology is largely an extension of
lectio divina, the type of theology that developed in the schools of the
High Middle Ages is marked by a shift away from exegesis and mystagogy and toward precise definitions and general principles honed through
academic debate.[35]

Baptism of desire was an appealing test case for this new style of
theology—scholasticism—because it involved conflicting evidence and
pushed the limits of accepted theological principles. The rise of scholasticism also coincided with the consolidation of Christendom, a European society thoroughly permeated by Christianity; whereas the early
Middle Ages were characterized by intense missionary activity across the
continent, by the eleventh century even Scandinavia had been largely
evangelized. True, paganism persisted in the Baltic region, with Lithua-
nia officially adopting Christianity only in 1385, but such distant events
do not seem to have greatly shaped the theological consciousness of the

33. As James A. Brundage points out, this impulse can be perceived in the original title
of Gratian's *Decretum*, "*Concorida discordantium canonum*," a "harmony of conflicting canons."
James A. Brundage, *Medieval Canon Law* (London: Routledge, 1995), 47. The methods devel-
oped by canonists for harmonizing disparate texts were later adopted by theologians. Philipp
W. Rosemann, *Peter Lombard* (New York: Oxford University Press, 2004), loc. 330–36 of 3521,
Kindle.

34. Marcia L. Colish, *Peter Lombard* (Leiden: Brill, 1994), 2:516.

35. Spinks, *Early and Medieval Rituals and Theologies of Baptism*, 135; Meens, *Penance in
Medieval Europe*, 190–91, 209.

schoolmen of France, Italy, and England.[36] As noted above, by this time infant baptism had almost entirely eclipsed adult baptism in practice, so discussion of baptism of desire was largely theoretical. For most of the participants in the discussion, an adult catechumen of any sort would have been exotic.

While this milieu allowed baptism of desire to move into the theological spotlight, it also limited the discussion of the idea in certain ways. Artur Michael Landgraf notes that those early scholastics who defended the possibility of receiving the grace of baptism without the sacrament struggled to explain the necessity of the rite and ended up falling back, at least implicitly, upon insistence on the "necessity of precept"—a scholastic distinction to which we will return. Here, it suffices to describe the "necessity of precept" as the view that the sacrament is necessary simply because God's law has made it so.[37] Since baptism of desire came to the scholastic consciousness through the work of canonists, it is not surprising that theologians would use a legal framework to make sense of it. Such an explanation was perhaps more satisfying at a time when the felt need for religious ritual was strong enough to take for granted, though in retrospect it seems rather thin. The consequences of such thinking can be seen in the scholastics' divergence from their patristic forebears on the question of pre-baptismal penance; since baptism had the effect of a full pardon, it seemed unnecessarily stringent to insist on doing penance for sins that would soon be cancelled out anyway.[38] Patristic consciousness, evolving out of experience with the complexities and challenges of adult conversions, saw the sacrament not as a legal declaration, but as the pivotal point of a life transformation, a conversion not limited to a single instant. In the Middle Ages, the "momentary effulgence of baptism" became detached from the moral life.[39] Mitchell describes this process as the "cerebralization" of Christian initiation—exemplified by theology's move from the pulpit to the academy—which fed into a ritual minimalism.[40] In short, a weakness of the age was that the "depression

---

36. Fletcher, *The Conversion of Europe*, 507.

37. Artur M. Landgraf, *Dogmengeschichte der Frühscholastik*, part 3, vol. 1, *Die Lehre von den Sakramenten* (Regensburg: Verlag Friedrich Pustet, 1954), 238–40.

38. Colish, *Faith, Fiction & Force*, 154, 157–58.

39. Cramer, *Baptism and Change*, 206.

40. Mitchell, "Christian Initiation: Decline and Dismemberment," 477.

and routinization of baptism" tended to reduce the sacrament to a legal formality, even if an indispensable one.[41]

Another more general issue that we should address before plunging into the specifics of the scholastic debates is the effect of limited pre-modern geographical knowledge on soteriology. We have already seen that twentieth century scholars, such as Francis Sullivan, sought to neutralize the force of the principle *extra ecclesiam nulla salus* by arguing that those who used it were misled by the erroneous assumption that the entire world had been evangelized. Therefore—so the argument goes—they conceived of the failure to enter the Church as a moral fault that deserved punishment, when it was merely the result of invincible ignorance. In the previous two chapters we saw that the evidence from the patristic period emphatically does not support this interpretation. In medieval Christendom, on the other hand, we do find some evidence to support Sullivan's contention. For example, Hugh of St. Victor (1096–1141), conceiving of the necessity of baptism as a legal obligation, argues that anyone unaware of the precept's institution was no more bound by it than those living before Christ, a situation that might have occurred in the brief period between the Great Commissioning and the evangelization carried out by the apostles. But then he goes on:

> Now if anyone wishes to be stubborn and contends that some of this kind still live in unknown regions and in remote seats of the world, who perhaps have not heard the divine mandate of receiving the sacrament of baptism, I affirm either there is no such person or, should there be someone, if his sin had not prevented, he could have heard and known and was obligated without delay, especially when the Scripture clearly proclaims: 'Their sound hath gone forth unto all the earth: and their words unto the ends of the world,' (Psal. 18,5). If then their sound has gone forth unto all the earth, in all the earth either they have been heard and their contemners are condemned or they have not been heard according to their sin, and being ignorant they are ignored and are not saved.[42]

---

41. Williams, "The Sacramental Presuppositions of Anselm's *Cur Deus Homo*," 251.

42. Hugh of St. Victor, *On the Sacraments of the Christian Faith*, ed. J. Saint-George, trans. Roy J. Deferrari (Cambridge, MA: The Mediaeval Academy of America, 1951), 2.6.5, p. 292.

Hugh's error about the existence of those to whom the Gospel had not been proclaimed is rather dramatic; in fact, he seems not to take the issue particularly seriously. The question then arises, if the existence of the Americas were to have been revealed to Hugh, would his answer have changed? Perhaps. On the other hand, if we dig a bit deeper into his response, we see that for Hugh a more fundamental problem than lack of information is human sinfulness, which prevents us even from searching for what is necessary for salvation. In other words, while the successful evangelization of Europe made it possible for some Christians living in Western Europe in the High Middle Ages to believe that, as a practical matter, the whole world had been evangelized, this was not the decisive factor in their soteriology. The problem of failing to obey the precept to be baptized paled in comparison to the problem of original sin. Furthermore, theologians of the early Middle Ages, when the existence of large numbers of unbaptized peoples was evident, seem to have been notably more restrictive in their soteriology than the scholastics. Nor did all later thinkers share Hugh's misunderstandings. Aquinas, for example, would have been aware not only of pagans in northern Europe but also of Mongols and Tartars.[43] Innocent IV (1243–1254) had sent ambassadors to the Mongols, hoping to expose them to Christianity, and Mongol ambassadors were present at the Council of Lyon in 1274. And, of course, Marco Polo set out on his journey at around the same time, returning to Europe in 1295.

Whatever opening to the possibility of salvation for the unbaptized we find in high scholasticism may ironically have been due to the unconscious shift in perspectives created by a society of the baptized. Because baptism followed so closely after birth, the world of most medieval Christians was one in which practically everyone began life saved unless and until they ran afoul of the moral law. We will explore this issue in greater depth in the following chapters, but for now it is enough to point out that twenty-first century maps would not have fundamentally changed medieval soteriology.

---

43. Jean-Pierre Torrell, "Saint Thomas et les non-chrétiens," *Revue thomiste* 106, no. 1/2 (2006): 19–20.

The School of Laon

Direct theological debate on the question of baptism of desire seems to have begun in the cathedral school of Laon, a center of learning since the ninth century that rose to particular prominence around the turn of the twelfth century under the guidance of the masters Anselm (d. 1117) and his brother Ralph (d. 1131/3). Historian Beryl Smalley attributes "the first concerted effort toward theological systematization" to the masters of Laon, and the school exercised an enormous influence on the development of scholastic theology over the course of the next century.[44] While the sentence collections of Laon do not bear the organizational mark of high scholasticism, they show that the members of the school sought consistency when answering questions about baptism and sacramental theology in general. A number of these collections have survived in manuscripts, though these have produced no shortage of scholarly disagreement. The school was controversial even in its own day, with its most famous pupil, Peter Abelard, ridiculing Anselm as stodgy and superficial. Fortunately, we need not enter into technical discussions about the authorship, dating, and provenance of manuscripts in order to demonstrate that the debate within Anselm's school on the question of baptism of desire was—*pace*, Abelard—lively and intelligent.

Anselm. In the *Sententie divine pagine*, Anselm arrives at baptism after a discussion of original sin and the "remedies" for it available in the natural and written law. Strikingly, desire is the key concept around which the discussion turns. Anselm's understanding of original sin and its pervasiveness is as extensive as that of Augustine, and he treats the necessity of baptism for salvation a given.[45] Like numerous writers before him, Anselm sees a parallel between circumcision and baptism, with the former

---

44. David A. Salomon, *An Introduction to the* 'Glossa Ordinaria' *as Medieval Hypertext* (Cardiff: University of Wales Press, 2012), 33–34. Marcia L. Colish provides a useful overview of areas of scholarly dispute, such as just how systematic Anselm's approach really was, in "Another Look at the School of Laon," *Archives d'histoire doctrinale et littéraire du Moyen Age* 53 (1986): 7–22.

45. Anselm of Laon, *Sententie divine pagine*, in *Anselms von Laon Systematische Sentenzen*, ed. Franz Bliemetzrieder (Münster: Aschendorffscehn Verlagsbuchhandlung, 1919), 95c, p. 38. Although some can be saved without receiving communion or confirmation, "absque baptismo nullus." *Sententie divine pagine*, 97a, p. 43.

functioning as a remedy before the institution of the sacrament. He posits similar remedies in the natural law, the precepts of which—for example, forbidding murder—are accessible through reason. Anselm acknowledges that we do not read about the institution of natural law remedies for original sin in scripture, as we do about the institution of circumcision; nonetheless, these included religious services and sacrifices, such as the offering of Abel.[46] Despite the divine institution of these remedies, they are only preparatory—"the sign and figure of the new law"—which, like the baptism of John, prefigure the salvation to come, but do not themselves justify.[47] In fact, part of the pedagogical value of the precepts of both the natural and written laws was that they manifested their own inadequacies, thus increasing humanity's desire for the coming savior.[48]

More clearly than any theologian we have seen thus far, Anselm emphasizes desire as the link connecting those who lived before Christ to salvation. Like his more famous namesake Anselm of Canterbury, Anselm of Laon is concerned with the question of why God chose to work out salvation in the way he did, why God became man. Since God was in no way bound to save man through the Incarnation, Anselm's answer turns on the fittingness of this path of redemption. The theme of desire runs through the discussion, and—although Anselm does not make the connection explicit—puts figures such as Abel in the same position vis-à-vis the Incarnation as Valentinian vis-à-vis baptism. As we noted earlier, Ambrose's use of the Old Testament prophets as a precedent for his conclusions in *De obitu Valentiniani* shows that he seems to have been thinking along similar lines. Anselm fleshes out the theme of Old Testament desire further still. In fact, he concludes his long discussion on the fittingness of the Incarnation with a reference to Abel's desire, followed immediately by reference to the institution of the sacraments and a detailed discussion of baptism.[49]

This discussion includes a number of tricky issues, such as ministers who garble the baptismal formula, and, near the end, the question of

46. *Sententie divine pagine*, 94d, p. 36. On the importance of institution, see 97a, p. 43.

47. *Sententie divine pagine*, 95a, p. 37. John's baptism is bound to penance, Anselm says, but not to the remission of sins. *Sententie divine pagine*, 97b, p. 43.

48. *Sententie divine pagine*, 95b, p. 37. Anselm's treatment of circumcision highlights its inadequacy compared to baptism. *Sententie divine pagine*, 95d, p. 38.

49. *Sententie divine pagine*, 96d, p. 42.

believers dying without the sacrament. Here Anselm is responsible for one of the key theological turns in the debate on baptism of desire—and in sacramental theology. He places the question within the framework of the distinction between the *sacramentum* and the *res sacramenti*, between the visible rite and the invisible reality conferred in the rite. Some distinction along these lines was already implicit in the position Augustine took against rebaptism, when he argued that it was possible to receive the sacrament validly without receiving its spiritual benefits. Ronald F. King traces the development of this framework to the mid-eleventh century eucharistic controversies provoked by Berengar of Tours.[50] Though the precise vocabulary used remained fluid for some time, the opponents of Berengar—Lanfranc, Guitmond of Aversa, and Alger of Liège—began to adopt the terminology of *sacramentum*, *res sacramenti*, and *sacramentum et res*. Their intention was not to create a dualistic view of the sacraments, but to assert that the Eucharist—*sacramentum et res*—was more than a mere visible sign. Nonetheless, the terminology is not without its difficulties, even at the most basic level of translation: Translate *res* as "thing," and it seems one is transacting in commodities; translate it as "reality," and *sacramentum* seems unreal, like a stage prop. Used clumsily it might seem to justify ritual minimalism. Why fuss over externals when what really matters is getting the *res*? It fits rather uneasily with the emphasis of twentieth century liturgical theologians who reacted against such minimalism by emphasizing the meaning inherent in the ritual action itself. We should thus treat this particular scholastic toolset with care; Ambrose did not employ it when eulogizing Valentinian; so baptism of desire does not necessarily depend upon the formulation. Nonetheless, we should also appreciate Anselm's insight in deploying the distinction at the dawn of the scholastic age.[51]

After having dealt with a number of difficult questions involving baptism, Anselm uses this framework to identify four categories of men.[52] Those who have both the *sacramentum* and the *res sacramenti* are saved. Those who have neither, such as pagans, are damned. Babies, he says, can

50. Ronald F. King, "The Origin and Evolution of a Sacramental Formula: *Sacramentum tantum, res et sacramentum, res tantum*," *The Thomist* 31, no. 1 (1967): 21–82.

51. King, 32–33.

52. Anselm of Laon, *Sententie divine pagine*, 98ab, p. 46.

have the *sacramentum* but not the *res*, which he here identifies with their own faith ("*fidem propriam*"); nonetheless, they are saved. Anselm's usage here is perhaps surprising; the classical examples of those receiving the sacrament without the *res*—from which the distinction arose—tend to be negative, such as those baptized insincerely or with a heretical intention. This alerts us to the difficulty inherent in establishing a general theological framework for the sacraments—of defining its terms in a way that does justice to the reality of the sacraments. It is also noteworthy that Anselm seems to be using the *res*—personal faith—not as something received in the sacrament but as a condition that would normally accompany its reception. This becomes apparent when he turns to the final possibility his categories allow—namely, someone who has the *res* without the sacrament. As an example, he mentions Cornelius. Of those who fall into this category, he says, some are saved and others not, depending on why they were not baptized. If baptism is lacking because of critical necessity (*articulus necessitatis*) and not contempt for religion (*contempus religionis*), salvation is possible.

Anselm's terminology shows that he is drawing from Augustine's *De Baptismo*, and yet he does not cite the obvious Biblical example—the Good Thief—to support his position, mentioning instead Cornelius, a supporting character in Augustine's exegesis whose value is limited by the fact that he was rather promptly baptized. The reason for Anselm's choice, however, soon becomes clear. He next mentions Augustine's *Retractationes*, in which the elderly bishop of Hippo backed off his earlier assumption that the Thief was unbaptized, and Anselm, here at least, appears to have deferred to his authority's judgment. The effect, as far as the text of the *Sententie divine pagine* is concerned, is to leave the question open. Because Cornelius was baptized, if this were the only work we had from Anselm's school, we might put him with Bonizo of Sutri and Gratian in the "interested but undecided" category with regard to baptism of desire. In another collection, however, Landgraf finds an argument from Anselm that shows the master of Laon to be on the pro-baptism of desire team. The *Retractationes*, Anselm says, only retract the example, but not the general argument, just as the withdrawal of a single witness in a court case does not necessarily mean the end of the trial.[53] Anselm's

---

53. Landgraf, *Die Lehre von den Sakramenten*, 1:220.

argument would be repeated by proponents of baptism of desire, most notably Peter Lombard, to blunt the authority of the anti-baptism of desire Augustine.[54]

In the *Liber Pancrisis*, in fact, Anselm directly addresses the salvation of a catechumen dying without baptism, and his answer is more confidently affirmative. The book is unflinching in its insistence on the necessity of baptism and takes the same line we saw in the *Sententie divine pagine* regarding the effectiveness of pre-Christian rites such as circumcision and the baptism of John. These did not confer the forgiveness of sins but were given as preparation and instruction for Christian baptism.[55] Here Anselm brings up Cornelius to reinforce baptism's necessity. Even though the righteous centurion had the Spirit before baptism and spoke in tongues, Anselm says, he did not yet have the forgiveness of sins.[56] His is an example of the promise of baptism implicit in the preparatory actions of the Holy Spirit. But what of catechumens who die before being baptized in water? Anselm answers that if they are impeded by necessity, they are saved and can even be said to be baptized. Not so, however, if their own negligence prevented baptism.[57] The distinction between necessity and negligence is essentially the same as that between necessity and contempt in the *Sententie divine pagine*. By adding that such catechumens can be said to be baptized, Anselm implies that he, like Ambrose, conceives of their salvation as via another mode of baptism, rather than as an exception to the rule.

Anselm also includes in his discussion the question of children who die before baptism. His answer applies clearly to adults who are being catechized, but he acknowledges that children who are incapable of knowledge are also thus incapable of negligence.[58] He does not, however, depart from the Augustinian conclusion that such children are damned;

54. Peter Lombard, *The Sentences*, bk 4, *On the Doctrine of Signs*, trans. Giulio Silano (Toronto: Pontifical Institute of Mediaeval Studies, 2010), 4.4.3, p. 22.

55. Anselm of Laon, *Liber pancrisis*, in *Psychologie et Morale aux XIIᵉ et XIIIᵉ siècles*, ed. Odon Lottin, vol. 5, *Problèmes d'histoire littéraire: L'école d'Anselme de Laon et de Guillaume de Champeaux* (Gembloux: J. Duculot, 1959), 52, p. 49.

56. *Liber pancrisis*, 51.9–11, p. 48.

57. *Liber pancrisis*, 58.1–4, p. 54.

58. *Liber pancrisis*, 58.4–11, p. 54. In another sentence, which Lottin judges to be probably Anselm's, he distinguishes between culpable ignorance due to pride or neglect and inculpable ignorance that is simply the result of human limitations. "Sentences d'authenticité probable,"

the negligence of their parents, he says, hinders them. After all, they, like everyone else, bear the guilt of original sin, which in itself demands damnation.[59] Though Anselm maintains the generally accepted hard line, the question arose with enough frequency in the school of Laon to suggest some unease with the answer. The apparent dissonance between the idea of guilt passed on through human generation and Ezekiel's dictum that "the son shall not suffer for the iniquity of the father" (Ez. 18:20) is repeatedly raised in the sections under discussion. Anselm reasons that the saying applies only after baptism.[60] The *sacramentum/res* distinction as Anselm has defined it reinforces this answer since infants do not have the *res* of personal faith. Still, the fact that Anselm discusses children who die before baptism in response to a question about catechumens suggests that he sensed some relevance of the one case to the other and the need for coherence in the way theologians dealt with both hard cases.

William of Champeaux and others. In fact, another master associated with the school of Laon, William of Champeaux (d. 1121), offered a significant nuance to the Augustinian doctrine that was to exercise immense influence among the scholastics and beyond. William observes that Augustine held that the punishment of those dying only in the guilt of original sin would be the mildest possible. He raises the possibility, without offering certainty on the question, that this punishment is only the deprivation of the vision of God, the "shadows."[61] While we saw similar ideas among patristic writers—Gregory of Nazianzen's "neither punishment nor reward"—William's formulation, though tentative, is significant because it attempts to fit this insight within a more systematic approach to salvation. Perhaps even more significant is the genealogy of William's statement,

---

in Lottin, *Problèmes d'histoire littéraire*, 141, p. 109. For the case of the mentally ill see Anselm of Laon, *Liber pancrisis*, 58, p. 54.

59. Anselm of Laon, "Sentences d'authenticité probable," 108, p. 87; cf. Anselm of Laon, *Liber pancrisis*, 57, p. 53. Anselm's treatment of the negligence of parents would seem to leave open still one more scenario—namely, that the parents sincerely desire for their child to be baptized but are prevented by necessity rather than negligence. Cédric Giraud addresses the relevance of the parents' faith to their infants, in *Per verba magistri: Anselme de Laon et son école au XIIe siècle* (Turnhout: Brepols, 2010), 281–85.

60. Anselm of Laon, *Sententie divine pagine*, 94c, p. 35.

61. "Quidam autem dicunt quod eorum pene tantum sunt tenebre et quod Dei uisione non fruuntur," William of Champeaux, *Sentences*, in Lottin, *Problèmes d'histoire littéraire*, 269, p. 216.

for his reasoning does not draw on Gregory, dubious Platonism, or colorful popular legends. Instead, it arises from the theology of the tradition's
most authoritative guardian of soteriological rigor, Augustine. In other
words, while not yet giving the idea a name, William ventures a hypothesis of limbo on Augustinian grounds.

The energy with which such questions must have been discussed in
Laon can be inferred from the variety of positions taken in its unattributable sentences. Among these we find an affirmation of the position
taken by Anselm in the *Liber pancrisis* that, while no one can be saved
without the sacrament, if an adult asked for baptism but was prevented
from receiving it by necessity and not out of contempt for religion, the
Lord would not fail him.[62] Along the same lines, another opinion claims
that those who have faith—the *res sacramenti*—and want the sacrament
but are prevented by death from receiving it are saved, adding that John
3:5 should be understood to include the qualifier "unless prevented by
critical necessity."[63] In the same text we also find an attempt to apply
the logic of baptism of desire to children who die on the way to church,
in virtue of the faith of their parents, though this is countered by the
authority of Augustine.[64] Thus, although at this early stage we see that
the masters of Laon seek consistency in their treatment of the cases of
adults and children, the child's lack of an independent will creates an
insuperable obstacle.

While we can perceive a general attraction to the idea of baptism of
desire within the school of Laon, enough opposition existed to suggest lively discussion. For example, one author claims that only martyrs are saved
apart from the font since martyrdom is another type of baptism; even if
someone's life and behavior should seem like that of an angel, he insists,

---

62. School of Laon, "Recueils systematiques," in Lottin, *Problèmes d'histoire littéraire*,
521.199–204, pp. 337–38. Infants, however, could not be saved without the sacrament.

63. School of Laon, "Sententiae Atrebatenses," in Lottin, *Problèmes d'histoire littéraire*,
532.12.29–36, p. 428.

64. "Sententiae Atrebatenses," 532.12.37–43, pp. 428–29: "De paruulis queritur qui neut-
rum habent, si in uia moriantur dum a parentibus ad ecclesiam ducuntur, si saluantur. Dicunt
quidam quod in fide parentum saluantur, si sine aliqua negligentia parentum ad ecclesiam
ducantur. Quidam uero dicunt quod dampnatur, quia Augustinus dicit de his: si etiam in man-
ibus sacerdotis moriantur, dampnantur. Unde etia iudicio Ecclesie extra atria ponuntur." This
last sentence seems to refer to the practice of burying unbaptized persons outside of church
grounds, an important indicator of the beliefs at the time.

no one can be saved without baptism. As for the Good Thief, his case is no precedent because the precept enjoining baptism came into effect only after the Resurrection.[65]

Yes or No? Abelard vs. Bernard and Hugh

Abelard. Destined to overshadow the school of Laon, if only because of his superior talent for self-promotion, Peter Abelard—a one-time student of Anselm who set himself up as a rival lecturer in 1112 before moving on to the brighter lights of Paris—proved an important catalyst for the development of the scholastic theology of baptism of desire. Abelard (1079–1142) was a master of scholastic *disputatio* with a knack for finding himself in conflicts of all sorts; his treatise *Sic et Non* was something like a textbook for medieval debaters, laying out a series of 158 questions on which authorities seem "not only at variance with each other, but truly opposite."[66] Abelard's prologue indicates that even though some ancient authorities are frankly in error—Origen's opinions are often heretical, he says—apparent contradictions can frequently be resolved by careful linguistic or logical analysis. His purpose in the book is not to resolve these questions himself but to provoke students to sharpen their intellectual skills through debate and thereby to arrive at a more profound knowledge of the truth. Midway through the work he addresses the proposition, "No one can be saved without baptism by water ... or one can be," and lays out the conflicting evidence for and against baptism of desire as skillfully as any medieval thinker we shall see. It is perhaps no surprise that the century and a half that followed was to see the liveliest debate in the doctrine's history.

Most of the evidence Abelard presents is familiar to us. He begins with authorities who support the uncompromising proposition "No one can be saved without baptism by water," starting with John 3:5.[67] He adds Ambrose in *The Mysteries*, the anti-Pelagian Augustine, and Prosper of Aquitaine. Something of a rejoinder follows, with Biblical references to salvation through martyrdom (Matt. 10:32, 16:25) supported by Augustine,

---

65. School of Laon, "Sentences," in Lottin, *Problèmes d'histoire littéraire*, 367, p. 274.
66. Peter Abelard, *Yes and No*, trans. Priscilla Throop (Charlotte, VT: MedievalMS, 2008), 11.
67. *Yes and No*, 106.1–10, pp. 246–48.

Fulgentius, and Gennadius. The picture thus nuanced, Abelard drops the Good Thief into the mix with generous quotations from Augustine's *De Baptismo* positing salvation through "faith and conversion of heart," when the sacrament is lacking due to necessity rather than contempt.[68] But Abelard knows that where Augustine zigs he also zags, and his *Retractationes* follow along with an uncompromising statement on the fate of unbaptized infants from *On Nature and Grace*. Then another pivot: a line from Jerome claiming that Cornelius was cleansed by the spirit while still a pagan and one from Ambrosiaster making a similar point.[69] These are followed by the key paragraphs from *De obitu Valentiniani*. To Ambrose, Abelard adds a legend from the *Life of Saint Gregory* in which the pope prays the emperor Trajan—for the medievals, the model of a just pagan ruler—out of the pains of hell, though apparently not into heaven. Instead, in a clear step toward the full-fledged doctrine of limbo, Trajan "avoids physical fire and enjoys those very mild pains of small children."[70] The question concludes with a series of more skeptical quotations, which do not necessarily negate the notion of baptism of desire but certainly suggest that its scope is limited.[71] Jerome insists that Jews, Gentiles, and heretics are lost and should not be mourned, and Augustine and Fulgentius repeat that unbaptized infants have no path to salvation. A final, eccentric word goes to Pope Siricius, who seems to allow baptism in wine in the event of grave necessity.

Sic et Non leaves the question of Abelard's own position on baptism of desire unsettled; it is intended, after all, to stir debate. Indications in his other works do not entirely resolve the question, either. The most decisive piece of evidence that he took a negative view of the theory is a

---

68. *Yes and No*, 106.11–19, pp. 248–51. Also included is a similar passage from Augustine's letter to Seleuciana (*Epist.* 265).

69. *Yes and No*, 106.20–21, p. 251. Jerome's point has to do not with salvation, but with the relative unimportance of ecclesiastical office. Ambrosiaster's passage (attributed to Ambrose) argues that sacramental effects should not be a source of human pride because God is their cause. Ambrosiaster, *In Epistulas ad Corinthios,* ed. Heinrich Joseph Vogels, CSEL 81 (Vienna: Hoelder-Pichler-Tempsky, 1968), 3.6, p. 34. Though their logic is compatible with baptism of desire, neither passage is particularly decisive.

70. Peter Abelard, *Yes and No*, 106.26, pp. 252–53. Abelard follows William of Champeaux, positing the absence of "the spectacular and beautiful things of divine knowledge" without external punishment as the only penalty for unbaptized children; see 158, pp. 413–14.

71. Peter Abelard, *Yes and No*, 106.27–31, pp. 253–54.

reference to *De obitu Valentiniani* in a letter to his lover Heloise. Moved by an over-ardent desire to comfort Valentinian's sisters, Abelard says, Ambrose promised "certain miracles which are contrary to the faith." He adds that Ambrose "ventured to promise [Valentinian] salvation because he died a catechumen; this can be seen to differ widely from the Catholic faith and the truth of the Gospel."[72] Ambrose gets better treatment in *Theologia Christiana*, where Abelard juxtaposes *De obitu Valentiniani* with Gennadius's *Liber de ecclesiasticis dogmatibus*.[73] Without engaging either work's substance, he states that Ambrose is more greatly to be admired. Here, however, Abelard has drafted Ambrose into a battle—the salvation of pre-Christian philosophers—which the Milanese was not fighting. Abelard's main concern is to defend the legitimacy of using pagan literature in Christian theology, and the question of those who die without the sacraments comes up as a side issue. Abelard repeats the story of Trajan's commuted sentence in response to Pope Gregory's prayers, though the story does not necessarily prove anything about salvation, since it only involves a reduction in the severity of Trajan's punishment.[74] Having mentioned these two examples of mercy shown to pagans living after the promulgation of the Gospel, Abelard asks rhetorically how God could deny his indulgence to those upright philosophers whose work prefigured the coming of Christ. As Colish observes, the rhetorical questions mimic those posed by Ambrose in *De obitu Valentiniani*.[75] Abelard may have believed that the salvation of the humanistic pagans he so much admired had been possible in antiquity but was no longer so in the present, or he may simply have changed his mind between his letter to Heloise and *Theologia Christiana*.

72. Peter Abelard, "Letter 7," in *The Letter Collection of Peter Abelard and Heloise*, ed. David Luscombe, trans. Betty Radice and rev. David Luscombe (Oxford: Oxford University Press, 2013), 50, p. 349.

73. Peter Abelard, *Theologia Christiana*, in *Petri Abaelardi Opera Theologica II*, ed. E.M. Buytaert, CCCM 12 (Turnhout: Brepols, 1969), 2.112–15, pp. 182–84.

74. This legend was popular throughout the Middle Ages and was taken seriously by a scattering of other theologians. The earliest version, by a monk of Whitby writing ca. 704–14, describes Trajan as being baptized by St. Gregory's tears. Marcia L. Colish, "The Virtuous Pagan: Dante and the Christian Tradition," in *The Fathers and Beyond: Church Fathers between Ancient and Medieval Thought* (Aldershot: Ashgate, 2008), 4–5. In the Whitby monk's account, the Lord makes it clear that the event is a one-time grace and will not be repeated. In his dialogues, Gregory himself states that the damned cannot be helped by prayers. Colish, 7, 20–21.

75. Colish, *Faith, Fiction & Force*, 37–38.

Colish argues that Abelard's tendency to yoke baptism of desire with "troublesome fellow travelers" limited the influence his opinions had among contemporaries, though it seems to me that his inconsistencies and idiosyncrasies likely hindered him even more.[76] Abelard's sympathy for pre-Christian philosophers was hardly the most controversial opinion interwoven with his theology of baptism of desire. His doctrine of original sin was to provoke the ire of William of St. Thierry (d. 1148) and Bernard of Clairvaux (1090–1153) and was one of the propositions condemned by the Council of Sens in 1140.[77] In brief, Abelard's general definition of sin requires the consent of the individual's will; his emphasis on the interior nature of sin is so strong that he does not regard deeds themselves as sinful. This emphasis on an individual's interior disposition might favor baptism of desire, since for Abelard the moral value of an act does not depend on its completion but on the state of one's will.[78] However, it also put Abelard in a difficult position with regard to the doctrine of original sin. Scholars are generally agreed that Abelard uses Augustinian terminology, while changing its meaning.[79] He agrees with Augustine that original sin exists and that it is shared by all.[80] Employing scholastic linguistic analysis, however, Abelard notes the range of meanings "sin" is given in scripture; sometimes it refers to the offense, sometimes to the punishment.[81] While Augustine insists that everyone inherits the

76. Colish, 35.

77. Abelard recanted the condemned thesis, "That we do not get guilt from Adam, but only punishment." Paul C. Kemeny, "Peter Abelard: An Examination of His Doctrine of Original Sin," *Journal of Religious History* 16, no. 4 (1991): 374–86. See also Constant J. Mews, "The Council of Sens (1141): Abelard, Bernard, and the Fear of Social Upheaval," *Speculum* 77, no. 2 (2002): 344; Wim Verbaal, "The Council of Sens Reconsidered: Masters, Monks, or Judges?" *Church History* 74, no. 3 (2005): 490; A. Victor Murray, *Abelard & St Bernard: A Study in Twelfth Century 'Modernism'* (Manchester: Manchester University Press, 1967).

78. "Whenever [Abelard] devotes his attention to the sacraments of the Church, he attempts to effect an interiorization in their meaning that is consistent with his radical interiorization of the meaning of sin and the benefits received from the event of Christ's incarnation and death." Richard E. Weingart, "Peter Abailard's Contribution to Medieval Sacramentology," *Recherches de théologie ancienne et médiévale* 34 (1967): 177.

79. For a concise summary and ample bibliography, see Cartwright, introduction to Peter Abelard, *Commentary on the Epistle to the Romans*, trans. Steven R. Cartwright, Fathers of the Church Mediaeval Continuation 12 (Washington, DC: The Catholic University of America Press, 2011), 51–55.

80. Kemeny, "Peter Abelard," 375–77.

81. Peter Abelard, *Commentary on the Epistle to the Romans*, 2.164–65, pp. 215–17.

guilt of Adam's sin, this is impossible for Abelard because guilt exists only where there has been interior consent. Guilt cannot be passed on from generation to generation, which means that infants must enter life guiltless; only the *punishment* of Adam's sin is passed on to them. If, at first glance, Abelard seems to be moderating the perceived harshness of the Augustinian doctrine, deeper reflection shows that he has arrived at something much darker.

Whereas Augustine's notion of original sin means that all are guilty and, therefore, justly punished, Abelard's entails that unbaptized children are guiltless but punished anyway.[82] Abelard's attenuated view of the suffering endured by children in the afterlife perhaps arose in response to this injustice, though it does not really resolve the problem.[83] Abelard believes such children's punishment to be nothing more than the neutrality of limbo, but he still regards it as punishment, which means that there is no way to escape the conclusion that God punishes the innocent for others' sins. Unwilling to modify his definition of sin, Abelard ends up appealing to predestination and an argument reminiscent of Gregory of Nyssa: God must have foreseen that those infants who die prematurely would otherwise have turned to evil when they grew up, so their death is really a mercy.

In his *Commentary on the Epistle to the Romans*, we find Abelard's most original treatment of baptism of desire enmeshed in his theology of original sin and predestination. In a section that emphasizes the inadequacy of "bodily observances," such as sacrifices and circumcision, without spiritual justification, he cites a number of Biblical examples of those made righteous before baptism—Abraham, perhaps Cornelius, Jeremiah, and John the Baptist.[84] He takes it for granted that circumcision once held the place of baptism, a less sophisticated treatment of the issue than that of Anselm. In any case, John the Baptist and Jeremiah were both sanctified in the womb. Still, this does not make baptism unnecessary. Even in the case of someone sanctified beforehand, Abelard says,

82. Other medieval theologians, such as Bonaventure, recognized the problem with Abelard's position. Christopher Beiting, "The Idea of Limbo in Alexander of Hales and Bonaventure," *Franciscan Studies* 75 (1999): 28–29. Thomas Aquinas makes the same point in *On Evil*, ed. Brian Davies, trans. Richard Regan (New York: Oxford University Press, 2003), 5.1, ad 2, p. 235.

83. Peter Abelard, *Commentary on the Epistle to the Romans*, 2.169–70, pp. 221–23.

84. *Commentary on the Epistle to the Romans*, 2.111, p. 161; 2.119, p. 169.

baptism is required in the same way that all the precepts of the moral law are required.[85] Those people made righteous by faith before baptism must still approach the sacrament because their punishment has not yet been remitted. For Abelard, the situation of such people is analogous to those who are predestined to eternal life but fall into mortal sin, such as David. God is sure to keep the predestined alive until whatever remains necessary for their salvation is revealed to them. In the end, Abelard is more interested in working out the paradoxes involved in predestination than in the reasons for the necessity of the sacrament.[86]

Nonetheless, like a catalyst that speeds a reaction without becoming a part of the final product, this most colorful of the scholastics can at least be credited with thrusting the issue of baptism of desire firmly into the spotlight. Abelard's erudition is impressive, and, as Colish points out, by reintroducing Ambrose into the medieval debate he gave proponents of baptism of desire a way to move beyond the trench warfare of Augustine vs. Augustine.[87] If, as in other areas of his life, Abelard was more skilled in provoking controversy than resolving it, even this was a contribution. Abelard's greatest contribution to the acceptance of the doctrine within the theological tradition was, perhaps, the inadequacy of his own position.

Bernard's response. One of the key texts in the scholastic debate over baptism of desire, in fact, is believed to be a response to Abelard—Bernard of Clairvaux's Letter 77 to Hugh of St. Victor, written around 1125. Hugh had asked Bernard to refute an unnamed "inventor of new assertions and asserter of inventions," whom scholars generally identify as Abelard.[88] What we know of Abelard's position from Bernard's account is thirdhand at best since Hugh's original letter does not survive. The two clashed on other occasions as well, with Bernard less than scrupulous

---

85. *Commentary on the Epistle to the Romans*, 2.119–21, pp. 169–71.

86. His treatment of Paul's baptismal theology in Rom 6:3–5 is also rather perfunctory. *Commentary on the Epistle to the Romans*, 2.176–78, pp. 229–30. Weingart judges that, although he maintains that baptism is necessary for infants' salvation, Abelard's doctrine of original sin means that the sacrament has "depreciated in value." Weingart, "Peter Abailard's Contribution to Medieval Sacramentology," 168.

87. Colish, *Faith, Fiction & Force*, 35.

88. Bernard of Clairvaux, *Letter 77 to Master Hugh of Saint Victor*, trans. Hugh Feiss, in Sommerfeldt, *Bernardus Magister*, 2.7, p. 365. Cf., Colish, 38–39; Hugh Feiss, "*Bernardus Scholasticus*: The Correspondence of Bernard of Clairvaux and Hugh of Saint Victor on Baptism," in *Bernardus Magister*, 351.

in accurately depicting Abelard's opinions.[89] Hugh had requested Bernard's opinion of four theses, the first three of which touch upon our theme. The first proposition might well have been that of Gennadius; it asserts, on the basis of John 3:5, that no one can be saved without the sacrament or martyrdom, even "if it should happen that someone desired baptism with true faith and a contrite heart" but died before receiving it.[90] Bernard's response suggests that he is thinking not so much about a catechumen as about a very particular historical circumstance: He seems to be responding to the idea that the obligation to be baptized—and the resulting damnation of anyone who died unbaptized—took effect at the time of Christ's conversation with Nicodemus. At that point the remedies of the Old Law would no longer have been effective, but Christian baptism was not yet available, creating a kind of donut hole in the plan of salvation. Anyone who died during that time period would have had no escape from condemnation.

While this particular historical scenario may seem far-fetched, it demonstrates the degree to which the effectiveness of the sacraments had come to be seen in legal terms. Bernard's response is framed in terms of obedience to the law, though he finds the idea of being damned because of a technicality "unduly rigorous and harsh." The first part of his argument turns on the principle that no one can be punished for failure to obey an unpromulgated law. Baptism is not a part of the natural law, he says, so knowledge of it depends upon the proclamation of the Gospel.[91] This principle would eventually have important implications, for example, for the salvation of those living in the Americas prior to 1492. Bernard concludes that it is not reasonable to imagine that the old means of salvation—circumcision for the Jews and sacrifices for the Gentiles—would have immediately been invalidated after the resurrection.[92] Only "when there could be no excuse for him to be ignorant of that precept" would an unbaptized person be liable for disobeying Christ's command to be

---

89. The conflict between Bernard and Abelard is often portrayed as a turning point in intellectual history, with the Abbot of Clairvaux representing the monastic tradition's resistance to the theology of the schools; in this particular letter, however, Bernard employs the scholastic method—"logical, speculative, impersonal, and argumentative"—with crisp skill. Feiss, "Bernardus Scholasticus," 359.

90. Bernard of Clairvaux, *Letter 77*, 1.1, p. 361.

91. *Letter 77*, 1.2, pp. 361–62.

92. *Letter 77*, 2.6, pp. 364–65.

baptized. This means, Bernard concludes, that for a while "the old sacraments continued to be valid for infants and those who did not have the
use of reason."

To be sure, not all ignorance is blameless, particularly once the Gospel
had been publicly preached. "Neglect of knowledge, laziness in learning, or shame of asking" are no excuses for ignorance of religious obligations.[93] Bernard's response to the third thesis, in fact, is a refutation of the
proposition that "there can be no sin of ignorance."[94] Bernard insists that
we most certainly can sin through ignorance. Still, we have in Bernard
the first clear use of the concept of "invincible ignorance" applied to our
theme, and its introduction is a direct result of the legal framework in
which Bernard situates the problem. This framework has its drawbacks;
for example, it might give the impression that baptism's role in salvation is more test of obedience than participation in divine mystery. The
relationship of the rites of the Old Law to the sacraments of the New,
consequently, comes to seem rather arbitrary. Bernard's response to the
second thesis touches indirectly on this problem. He denies that those
who were saved before Christ had, through a prophetic gift, knowledge
of the Christian mysteries equal to that of those who came after Christ.[95]
This would mean, Bernard objects, that the Gospel added nothing to revelation. Pointing to simple people who possess a profound faith, Bernard
holds that perfect knowledge is not necessary for salvation, but he leaves
no doubt that the closer one is to Christ, whether in knowledge or otherwise, the closer one is to salvation.[96] The scriptural passages he quotes in
this context suggest that those with a genuine but partial understanding
of the Gospel will necessarily seek a more perfect fulfillment.[97] Not to
do so or to maintain beliefs or attitudes that stand in the way of such
fulfillment entails culpable ignorance. Thus, the desire for more perfect
religious knowledge is the key factor distinguishing guiltless ignorance
from an ignorance that leads to condemnation.[98]

93. *Letter 77*, 1.3, pp. 262–63.
94. *Letter 77*, 4.16–17, pp. 373–74.
95. *Letter 77*, 3.11, pp. 369–70.
96. *Letter 77*, 3.15, p. 372.
97. *Letter 77*, 3.14, p. 372. E.g., Lk 10:24.
98. The desire of the Gentiles to know the true God plays a key role in the account of salvation history in Bernard's sermon on the Canticle of Canticles. Marek Chojnacki, *Il battesimo*

Turning from ignorance back to the main question of the necessity of baptism, another problem arises from Bernard's initial response. Bernard acknowledges the objection that even those innocent of contempt for the sacrament are still guilty of original sin. Original sin alone is sufficient grounds for damnation, but Bernard points out that remedies existed for it before the institution of baptism—circumcision and, for the Gentiles, "faith and sacrifices."[99] Strictly speaking, then, Bernard's argument is not that it is unfair for pagans to be damned because of original sin, but that it is wrong to conclude that the Lord "laid a trap of public damnation for all those throughout the world who did not know about" his conversation with Nicodemus.[100] Bernard regards the law of baptism by his own day to have been universally promulgated: "This state of affairs lasted until the era of baptism, when one replacement left all the others obsolete."[101] The present era offers no excuse to omit baptism. Still, the effectiveness Bernard attributes to pre-Christian means of salvation is noteworthy; he even draws the conclusion that, for Gentile children who died prematurely, "the faith of their parents was the sole, but sufficient remedy." While Bernard affirms the medieval consensus about the grim fate of unbaptized infants, this position would seem to provide grounds to argue that the effectiveness of baptism of desire could extend to the children of faithful parents who die in circumstances that make baptism impossible. An implicit premise of Bernard's argument is that the promulgation of the Gospel could not have made salvation generally more difficult; so, if, for example, a stillborn son of Noah could have been saved under the old dispensation, it hardly seems plausible that he would be damned under the new. In the sixteenth century, Cajetan would seize upon precisely this inconsistency to propose that baptism of desire might extend to infants and unborn children.

What, then, of the classic case of a Christian catechumen dying unexpectedly? According to Bernard, Ambrose in *De obitu Valentiniani* and

---

e l'eucaristia: fonti rituali della vita Cristiana secondo San Bernardo di Chiaravalle (Rome: Pontificia Università Gregoriana, 2002), 87.

99. Bernard of Clairvaux, *Letter 77*, 1.4, p. 363. Refusing baptism adds a second fault to original sin. *Letter 77*, 2.6, p. 365.

100. *Letter 77*, 4.16, p. 373.

101. *Letter 77*, 1.4, p. 363.

Augustine in *De Baptismo* gave the definitive word on the subject.[102] For Bernard, the key to salvation is faith. This principle applies equally to the baptism of blood; without faith, martyrdom is simply being killed. Bernard concludes, "if martyrdom obtains its prerogative only by the merit of faith, so that it is safely and singularly accepted in place of baptism, I do not see why faith itself cannot with equal cause and without martyrdom be just as great in God's eyes." The qualifiers expressed by Augustine are repeated by Bernard: One cannot be saved if one disdains baptism, but only if one is prevented by "untimely death or some other insuperable force." Since the true faith includes baptism, anyone refusing the sacrament would, by definition, not possess it. Bernard puts his explanation in terms of legal obedience: "True and full faith complies with all the commandments; this particular commandment [to be baptized] is the foremost of them all." Bernard seems to have in mind some kind of request for baptism, though he does not think it necessary for such a request to be public or even particularly formal. Instead, he speaks about turning to Jesus in prayer in the moment of death. In support, he cites New Testament passages in which the intention to commit a sin is treated as morally equivalent to the sin itself, arguing that the same principle applies to positive intentions as well.[103]

Hugh. Bernard's letter, important in its own right, is important also for its influence on the recipient, Hugh of St. Victor. In 1133 Master Hugh became head of the school founded by William of Champeaux at the monastery of St. Victor in Paris. Regarded as among the most learned men of his age by contemporaries,[104] Hugh's masterpiece *De Sacramentis* (composed about 1134) foreshadows the systematic *summae* that were to characterize scholasticism's heyday though it retains much of the narrative and allusive flavor of patristic and monastic theology. Michael Girolimon calls the work a "watershed in the history of Christian sacramental theology."[105] There is something of *The City of God* in Hugh's project—a

---

102. *Letter 77*, 2.7–8, pp. 365–67. He accepts Anselm's interpretation of Augustine's *Retractationes*.

103. 1 Jn 3:15; Mt 5:28.

104. Mews, "The Council of Sens (1141)," 349.

105. Michael T. Girolimon, "Hugh of St Victor's *De sacramentis Christianae fidei*: The Sacraments of Salvation," *Journal of Religious History* 18, no. 2 (1994): 127.

retelling of the history of salvation—though the thread tying Hugh's account together is not the give and take between the City of God and the City of Man, but "the general sacramental nature of created reality."[106] This unifying concept gives the work its systematic character. That said, on the surface Hugh's use of the term "sacrament" seems as undisciplined Augustine's: He uses the word to refer to everything from holy water to vestments, from the words of the Bible to creation itself. Faith is called a sacrament. The term's range, in fact, is so broad that Hugh refers not only to secular sacraments but to the sacraments of the devil.[107] Girolimon offers a helpful schema to understand the internal logic of Hugh's complex use of the term.[108] De Sacramentis divides history into the same three dispensations which we saw in Bernard: the eras of the natural law, of the written law, and of grace. Within each of these dispensations, there are three types of sacraments: the preparatory, the beneficial, and those essential to salvation. Hugh's use applies to any "empirical representation and/or indicator of a metaphysical reality," which could include material objects, actions, or words, so the "sacraments" within any of these categories could be subject to further classification.

On the specific question of "whether after the precept of baptism was given anyone could be saved without actually receiving the sacrament," Hugh closely follows Bernard.[109] His preceding answers to questions dealing with the time of the sacrament's institution and with the baptism of John show that he also conceived of baptism's necessity primarily in terms of obedience to divine law.[110] He points out that John 3:5 does not contain an explicit exception clause for martyrdom, yet no one doubts the efficacy of baptism of blood.[111] Like Bernard, Hugh understands a martyr's confession of faith to be salvific, so it is easy for him to attribute salvation to someone who professes the same faith but dies of unexpected

106. Thomas D. McGonigle, "The Significance of Albert the Great's View of Sacrament within Medieval Sacramental Theology," *The Thomist* 44, no. 4 (1980): 569.

107. Hugh of St. Victor, *On the Sacraments of the Christian Faith*, 1.10.9, p. 180; 1.8.11, pp. 148–49.

108. Girolimon, "Hugh of St Victor's *De sacramentis Christianae fidei*," 128–29. McGonigle's discussion of Hugh's concept of sacrament is also helpful. McGonigle, "Significance of Albert the Great's View," 569–72.

109. Hugh of St. Victor, *On the Sacraments of the Christian Faith*, 2.6.7, pp. 293–95.

110. *On the Sacraments of the Christian Faith*, 2.6.4–6, pp. 290–92.

111. *On the Sacraments of the Christian Faith*, 2.6.7, p. 293.

natural or accidental causes. He cites Augustine in *De Baptismo*—not mentioning Ambrose—and deals with the *Retractationes* in the same way as did Anselm and Bernard. He is thus able to conclude that "to be baptized can be in the will, even when it is not in possibility."

Hugh ends his treatment of this question with a reference back to his earlier chapters on the sacraments in general. In other words, he attempts to situate baptism of desire within his overall understanding of the sacraments and his sacramental understanding of the world. Returning to Girolimon's schema, we see that baptism fits within the essential sacraments of the time of grace; along with the Eucharist, it is the sacrament "in which salvation principally is established and received."[112] Hugh claims that three things (which he also refers to as sacraments) have always been necessary for salvation: faith, the sacraments of faith, and good works. Here the limitations of Hugh's vocabulary become apparent, for we have sacraments within sacraments, though context makes clear that the "sacraments of faith" he mentions correspond to liturgical sacraments. On the other hand, Hugh's overlapping layers of sacraments do help to convey the sense in which, for him, these are all part of a unified salvific reality. Indeed, faith, sacraments, and good works "so cling together that they cannot have the effect of salvation if they are not simultaneous." Such unity gives us one key for understanding how Hugh thinks about baptism of desire. For a "faith" that refused either the liturgical sacraments or right action with regard to neighbors would not be salvific. Prior to sanctification Hugh seems to have in mind a kind of proto-faith at work, through which one recognizes the truth of Christianity, at least to some degree. Such "provisional faith" provides the basis for one to make a choice to obey the Lord's commandments, but it lacks merit until joined to action—action that includes the reception of baptism. However, if only external circumstances prevent one from carrying out one's intended actions, these still exist "in true will and desire."

What more can be said of the quality of the faith that makes baptism of desire possible? Hugh's treatment of faith, which immediately follows the question of the three necessary "sacraments," begins with the classic New Testament definition, "the substance of things to be hoped

<hr/>

112. *On the Sacraments of the Christian Faith*, 1.9.7–8, pp. 164–65.

for" (Heb. 11:1).[113] For him this means that faith is the subsistence in our hearts of things to be hoped for but not yet present in act. Faith is a kind of symbolic presence, a presence which points beyond itself. For Hugh, faith involves both a cognitive and an affective element, since understanding something without believing it is not faith. Such belief also requires a certain constancy, and here we can perceive why provisional faith is not always salvific. We can also begin to see that, although Hugh passionately defends the possibility of baptism of desire, his sense of the faith that it requires is formidable. In terms of cognitive certitude, faith is not the same thing as knowledge, but it is more than mere conjecture. Hugh explains, "when there is still doubt, there is no faith." An important guide for understanding Hugh's sense of what separates salvific faith from, say, curiosity or wistfulness, is his observation near the beginning of the discussion that "faith is defined not in that which is but that which does."[114] Faith requires enough firmness of intention to act in obedience to the Lord. In the relationship of faith to action, we can perceive how the liturgical sacraments quite practically aid salvation by allowing believers to express their faith in a concrete act.

Just as faith requires enough investment of the will to lead to action, so too it requires enough cognitive content to correctly guide action.[115] Hugh remarks that "even infidels do not live without faith"— they believe in and hope for certain things—but they cannot be considered "faithful" because they do not hope for the right things.[116] In other words, Hugh regards erroneous belief—as opposed to incomplete belief—as detrimental to salvation. In terms of the minimum positive content required for faith, two principal things are required: belief that God is Creator and belief that God is Savior.[117] These necessarily require the believer to recognize himself as created and in need of redemption.[118] Though belief in the Creator alone is inadequate, in the case of those living before Christ,

113. *On the Sacraments of the Christian Faith*, 1.10.2–3, pp. 165–69.

114. *On the Sacraments of the Christian Faith*, 1.10.2, p. 166.

115. *On the Sacraments of the Christian Faith*, 1.10.3, p. 169–70: "there must always be some cognition with faith, which should direct faith itself through intention."

116. *On the Sacraments of the Christian Faith*, 1.10.5, pp. 171–72. Thus non-Christian "sacraments" do not sanctify but pollute, 1.10.9, p. 180.

117. *On the Sacraments of the Christian Faith*, 1.10.5, p. 172.

118. *On the Sacraments of the Christian Faith*, 1.10.8, p. 179.

belief in the coming savior was sufficient.[119] Hugh is here developing an idea of implicit faith. Central to his understanding of the concept is the distinction between simple believers and those to whom salvation had been revealed in explicit detail; he seems to believe that some such "more perfect believers" existed throughout history. Thus, he attributes explicit knowledge of Christianity to the prophets. Hugh has no doubt that simple believers are "saved in their simplicity" and that their belief may take the form of trust in more perfect believers.[120] John Marenbon helpfully summarizes Hugh's understanding of implicit faith—which was largely followed by later scholastics, including Peter Lombard and Thomas—thus:

> According to Hugh, then, people can be said to have faith in what is affirmed by a proposition p, without holding or even contemplating p, if they accept a general proposition, of which p is an instantiation, and they also place their trust in other people who actually believe that p.[121]

Marenbon's formulation should be slightly amended to take into account Hugh's sense of the harm done by incorrect belief. For a general principle to imply salvific faith, it is not enough that p be one of its possible instantiations but that it leads eventually to p and not in the wrong direction. When Hugh, Bernard, and other medieval thinkers speak of Gentile sacrifices as sacraments, they have in mind figures like Melchizedek and Noah—not those who sacrificed to Zeus, Baal, or Ishtar.

The question of implicit faith is crucial for a contemporary theology of baptism of desire, and we will take it up again when we turn to Aquinas. Another issue that will repeatedly arise is the principle that God is not bound by the sacraments, which we find articulated by Hugh. Since this principle sometimes takes on an exaggerated role today, it is important to understand its original context. We can perceive its antecedents in

---

119. "[In the beginning, the simple] believed that the Redeemer would come in the flesh and would die in the same flesh, would arise and ascend, even if they manifestly did not know certain other things which were hidden in those times." *On the Sacraments of the Christian Faith*, 1.10.7, p. 178. "Therefore, true faith rests in two: Creator and Redeemer. One does not suffice for you without the other." *On the Sacraments of the Christian Faith*, 1.10.8, p. 179.

120. *On the Sacraments of the Christian Faith*, 1.10.6, pp. 173–74.

121. John Marenbon, *Pagans and Philosophers* (Princeton, NJ: Princeton University Press, 2015), 169.

the importance placed on the institution of the sacraments by thinkers like Anselm and Hugh, who are concerned to avoid a magical understanding of Christian rites—one which sees their power coming from manipulating the forces in earthly elements independently of God's will.[122] The plausibility of baptism of desire depends upon something like this principle and the intuition that, if a sincere catechumen dies on the way to the font and is not saved, the very purpose of baptism seems to have been thwarted by a technicality or an accident. Nonetheless, Hugh does not regard the principle as diminishing the necessity of the sacraments for salvation. As Girolimon's careful analysis of Hugh's sacramental hierarchy makes clear, it would be a mistake to read his expansive use of the term "sacrament" as diluting the importance of the liturgical sacraments. These do not exhaust God's action in the world—which includes miracles, sacramentals, prayer, and the working of the natural order—but they stand at its center and give shape and direction to those other "sacraments" that are merely preparatory or beneficial. The motion of the sun does not exhaust the movement of the solar system, but the movement of all the other bodies in the system cannot be fully understood apart from their relation to the sun. The liturgical sacraments form the gravitational center of Hugh's sacramental universe.

When Hugh introduces the principle that God's power is not limited by the sacraments, therefore, he pairs it with a corresponding principle to account for their necessity. Necessity, he argues, means different things if applied to God or man.

> The institution of the sacraments, therefore, in so far as pertains to God the author, is of dispensation but, in so far as pertains to obedient man, is of necessity, since it is within God's power to save man without these but it is not within man's power to attain to salvation without these. For God could have saved man, even if he had not instituted these, but man could not by any means be saved if he contemned these.[123]

Hugh believes, then that, as far as human efforts are concerned, man cannot be saved without baptism. Yet, he cites John the Baptist and Jeremiah

122. Anselm of Laon, *Sententie divine pagine*, 97a, p. 43.
123. Hugh of St. Victor, *On the Sacraments of the Christian Faith*, 1.9.5, pp. 160–61.

as examples of those justified in the womb by God's extra-baptismal power. However, these examples in particular do not imply a salvific plan detached from baptism since they are involved, directly or indirectly, in the institution of baptism. Hugh sees the general dispensation by which God has chosen to work out our salvation as defined by the sacraments; as we will see in Thomas, the necessity of the sacraments for salvation parallels the necessity of the Incarnation. Hugh's understanding of baptism of desire fits within this sense of baptism's necessity. Anyone acting as if baptism were not necessary would show contempt for God's work; those seeking baptism but prevented from receiving it by an untimely death, on the other hand, manifest their faith in the sacrament's necessity. In sanctifying such people, God is not, therefore, contradicting what he has revealed but acting consistently with his own dispensation.

The Long Reign of the Sentences

As Colish points out, Hugh's inclusion of baptism of desire in *De Sacramentis* ensured a wide hearing for the arguments he and Bernard worked out. Both Hugh and Bernard argued at length and with considerable passion in the doctrine's favor, demonstrating that it must have been a live issue in the middle of the twelfth century. Colish's research into other thinkers from the 1140s and 1150s reinforces this point; while it is obvious that Hugh and Bernard set the direction of discussion, the considerable energy and creativity surrounding the topic produced differences in how the evidence was analyzed. The anonymous author of the *Summa sententiarum* follows Hugh, but with greater emphasis on the *sacramentum/res sacramenti* distinction.[124] The canonist Roland of Bologna bases his argument on the principle that a law only becomes binding once it has been promulgated; he also considers scenarios other than the unexpected death of a catechumen that might make ritual baptism impossible, such as imprisonment by infidels.[125] The Englishmen Robert of Melun and Cardinal Robert Pullen also weigh in on the side of baptism of desire,

---

124. Colish, *Faith, Fiction & Force*, 44.

125. Colish, 43–46. Roland's hypothetical cases show that baptism of desire need not be limited to the case of *unexpected* death, but it seems to me that death remains the decisive factor. If Roland's prisoners were ransomed, presumably they would seek out the sacrament.

both emphasizing the efficaciousness of faith based on Romans 10:10.[126]
The followers of Gilbert of Poitiers attribute support for the doctrine to
their master; unlike most medieval theologians, they make no attempt to
claim Augustine for their side, acknowledging him as an opponent but
attributing his opposition to a misreading of Cyprian.[127]

Opposition. We should not imagine, however, that twelfth century support for baptism of desire was universal. The anonymous author of the
Sententiae divinitatis breaks with the other Porretans to argue that past
exceptions to the now universal necessity of baptism for salvation—such
as the Good Thief—are unique and no longer relevant in present circumstances. In fact, now that the age of martyrdom has passed, even baptism
of blood no longer provides a guide for present practice.[128] In an aside
to his account of the death of Valentinian in his *Chronicle of the Two
Cities*—a kind of update of Augustine's *The City of God*—the German
bishop and historian Otto of Freising rejects baptism of desire.[129] He allows that God, who is omnipotent, can save by means other than baptism
"on His own express testimony," but he does not believe that such extraordinary cases provide the basis for a general rule. Otto does not seem
to know Ambrose's text directly—he refers to it as a letter—but only
through quotations in other works.[130] He reads these as exclamations
of grief rather than a cogent theological position. His main theological
concern is with what can actually be deduced from the principle that God
is not bound by the sacraments; essentially, he argues that, on its own, this
principle cannot be used to make positive claims about salvation. God
may not be bound by revelation, but our understanding of God's work is.
While Otto acknowledges that the proponents of baptism of desire are
moved by pity, he points out the inconsistency of holding that adults can
be saved without baptism but infants cannot. Like Augustine, he returns
to Romans 11:33 and the inscrutability of God's ways.

---

126. Colish, 45–47.
127. Colish, 47–49.
128. Colish, 52.
129. Colish, 54. Otto of Freising, *The Two Cities: A Chronicle of Universal History to the Year 1146 A.D.*, trans. Charles Christopher Mierow (New York: Columbia University Press, 2002), 4.18, p. 299.
130. See Mierow's footnote in Otto of Freising, *The Two Cities*, p. 299.

Similar misgivings are voiced by the master of a school, located perhaps in Flanders or the Rhine Valley, writing between 1145–1160 and known only as Simon.[131] Master Simon's treatment of the sacraments shows a thinker who is both independent and precise. On the question of baptism, he identifies the sacrament's institution with Christ's conversation with Nicodemus and addresses the previously little discussed question of whether one can baptize oneself (one cannot).[132] His use of the *sacramentum/res* framework shows that accepting this distinction does not necessarily imply an affirmation of baptism of desire. He also employs the word "character"—a term that will become important in the later scholastic debate—to describe the effects of baptism but offers no definition. In fact, he does not seem to consider the word a technical term; he associates it with the mark of Christ the king, indicating to whom the baptizand now belongs. This sense of the importance of belonging to the true God contributes to Simon's insistence on the correct baptismal formula.

Simon signals his skepticism toward baptism of desire early in the treatise when he indicates that there are two ways in which one can be baptized, in water or in blood.[133] He is familiar with the debate on the subject, however, and cites the evidence for the idea from Augustine's *De Baptismo*.[134] He allows that Cornelius seems to have possessed faith working through charity. He repeats the standard qualifiers for baptism of desire—that it is not attained by those demonstrating *contemptus religionis* but only by those impeded by *articulus necessitatis*. And he is aware of the principle that God's power is not limited by the sacrament—but therein lies the heart of his objection. If the unknown judgments of God are held back from our knowing, Simon reasons, we cannot legitimately make affirmations beyond what God chooses to reveal. The clearest evidence on the question is John 3:5, articulated by Christ, and the Church has no right to expand the definition of the faithful beyond what was indicated by the Savior. Simon, to be sure, is not trying to limit salvation;

131. Simon, *Maître Simon et son groupe De sacramentis*, ed. Henri Weisweiler (Louvain: Spicilegium Sacrum Lovaniense, 1937), ccxiv.

132. Simon, *Tractatus Magistri Simonis de sacramentis*, in *Maître Simon et son groupe*, 3–6.

133. *Tractatus Magistri Simonis de sacramentis*, 3. A second, more compact treatise attributed to Simon, the *Tractatus de septem sacramentis ecclesie*, omits the issue entirely.

134. *Tractatus Magistri Simonis de sacramentis*, 9–10.

he fully acknowledges God's power to save using exceptional means, but he believes that offering a definitive judgment in cases going beyond Christ's words would require special revelation from God. He adds that a singular privilege does not make a general law.

In support of his caution, Simon refers to the Church's practice, which, he says, runs contrary to baptism of desire because unbaptized people are not afforded the prayers of the baptized nor are they buried in holy ground. Indeed, given the skepticism toward the concept that seems to have characterized the early Middle Ages, Simon may well have been expressing the popular Christian sentiment. Neither Otto nor Simon are absolutists in the objections they raise about baptism of desire: Simon's tone is markedly different from that of Gennadius or even, for that matter, Gregory Nazianzen. Their objections might be blunted if one's theology of baptism of desire were to hew closely to the logic of the sacrament and be modest in making claims beyond what is authorized by revelation.

Peter Lombard. After this flurry of objections in the mid-twelfth century, opinion shifted decisively in favor of baptism of desire and discussion turned to untangling the theological knots created once the doctrine had been accepted. In bringing this shift about, a second letter from Bernard of Clairvaux addressed to the monks of St. Victor played a pivotal role, though this letter did not mention baptism of desire at all. Instead, it recommended to the Abbey of St. Victor a young student who had been staying with Bernard in Rheims, asking the community to feed and lodge him during his stay in Paris. Like Ambrose, the student hailed from northern Italy and became known to the world as Peter Lombard (ca. 1096–1160). Before becoming archbishop of Paris, Peter composed a theological course, the *Sentences*, that was to become Christendom's standard theological "textbook" for the next several centuries. The *Sentences* are a systematic compendium of Christian theology and give a more coherent shape to the diverse voices from the tradition than does, say, Abelard's *Sic et Non*. They do not, however, eliminate this diversity entirely and thus leave room for future generations of commentators to weigh in with opinions, objections, and clarifications.

Peter arrived in Paris just as Hugh of St. Victor was completing *De Sacramentis*, a work that was to be one of the principal sources for the

Sentences.[135] On the question of baptism of desire, Peter reaches the same affirmative conclusion as did Hugh. His approach, though, is less personal and passionate, as his goal is to show how this conclusion fits within the system of scholastic theology. The fourth book of the *Sentences* addresses the sacraments specifically, and it is here that we find Peter's discussion of baptism of desire. This discussion is part of a larger conceptual structure at the core of which is the *sacramentum*/*res* distinction. Peter introduces this terminology three chapters before baptism of desire, positing that some people receive the *res et sacramentum*, others only the *sacramentum*, and still others only the *res*.[136] Both children who are washed of original sin and adults who approach the sacrament with sincere faith receive the *sacramentum et res*.[137] Peter identifies the baptismal *res* with the cleansing of sins. We can note how the content of the *res* changed between Anselm of Laon and Peter, from the faith necessary to receive the sacrament to the forgiveness granted by the sacrament. But even if faith is no longer the *res*, Peter still thinks it necessary to receive the *res*: "remission is not even given in baptism to children without someone else's faith, since they are unable to have their own."[138] Adults who approach falsely fall into Peter's second category, receiving the *sacramentum* without forgiveness.[139] This leaves the third possibility, which required the most involved discussion. It is telling that Peter introduces baptism of desire not with a specific example—from either history or the Bible—but with reference to the remaining square on his conceptual grid: "There are others, as we said earlier, who receive the thing and not the sacrament."[140]

In this third category are, first, the martyrs, whose suffering takes the place of baptism. Peter then inserts Augustine's analysis of the Good Thief from *De Baptismo* into his text; this rejects Cyprian's classification of the thief as a martyr, leading to the conclusion that "not only suffering, but also faith and contrition confer remission, where the sacrament is not held in contempt."[141] He adds Ambrose's support to the claim that

135. Rosemann, *Peter Lombard*, loc. 390, 477, 496 of 3521.
136. Peter Lombard, *The Sentences*, 4.4.1.1, p. 18.
137. *The Sentences*, 4.4.1.2, pp. 18–19.
138. *The Sentences*, 4.4.2.3, p. 19.
139. *The Sentences*, 4.4.2, pp. 19–20.
140. *The Sentences*, 4.4.4.1, p. 21.
141. *The Sentences*, 4.4.4.2–3, pp. 21–22.

"some are justified and saved without baptism," though surprisingly he quotes only one brief line from *De obitu Valentiniani*.[142] Next he turns to the question of how to interpret John 3:5, determining that the warning applies only to "those who can be baptized, but contemptuously fail to do so." He takes this to be the equivalent of saying that regeneration can be brought about not only through baptism "but also through penance and blood."[143] As for those authorities who explicitly deny baptism of desire, he misattributes quotations from Fulgentius and Gennadius to Augustine, who he says addresses the issue more fully in the works already cited.[144] This was an effective—if thoroughly misleading—way to clear the field of opponents and gave those who used Lombard's *Sentences* as their theological sourcebook an inaccurate picture of the support baptism of desire had received in the tradition. Students of the *Sentences* would have had no way of knowing that the position that would carry the day from the twelfth century onward had most likely been held by a minority of theologians for most of Christianity's first millennium.

Peter continues with Augustine, using the distinction between visible rites and invisible sanctification from the latter's commentary on Leviticus to bolster his broader objective of demonstrating the viability of the *sacramentum/res* framework.[145] Here he throws in the problematic case of Cornelius, considered in his schema to have been sanctified invisibly before receiving the sacrament, which was nonetheless not "adjudged to be superfluous." He concludes the chapter with a reaffirmation of the traditional Augustinian teaching on the effectiveness and necessity of baptism for children. Unbaptized children will be damned, for "the faith of the Church is not sufficient for children without the sacrament."[146] Here, infant baptism comes at the end of the section, but it is evident that when writing about baptism Peter had been thinking primarily of infants; we see this in his discussion of the ceremony. Such a presupposition, based

---

142. *The Sentences*, 4.4.4.5, p. 22.

143. *The Sentences*, 4.4.4.6–7, p. 23. He cites Heb 6:2, which speaks of baptisms in the plural but does not adopt such language himself, instead speaking of those saved without baptism. Since the question of how to celebrate the rite of baptism properly was intensely discussed in the theological treatises of the day, Peter may have been concerned not to lend inadvertent support to mistaken liturgical practices, baptisms celebrated "otherwise than in water."

144. *The Sentences*, 4.4.4.9–10, pp. 23–24.

145. *The Sentences*, 4.4.4.11, p. 24.

146. *The Sentences*, 4.4.4.12–13, pp. 24–25.

on the era's longstanding practices, was probably hard to avoid. One of its indirect consequences, however, was that, when combined with his explanation of baptism of desire, it makes adult baptism difficult for Peter to explain.

In his next chapter, he turns to this problem. If adults already come to the sacrament with faith and can be justified prior to it, then what good is baptism? We can see how the line of thought on baptism of desire from Bernard to Peter has created a new class of individuals that did not exist in patristic theology: the justified who still need baptism. The works we examined from the patristic era—whether from Gregory Nazianzen, Cyril of Jerusalem, or Ambrose—do not speak of anyone reborn before baptism. It is noteworthy, in fact, that the Fathers—from Irenaeus on— speak of faith as something received in baptism. Such a dynamic is implicit in the rite itself, in which a catechumen asks to receive faith from God's Church. In the *Sentences*, Peter speaks of faith being received when discussing infant baptism, but in his discussion of adults, faith becomes the condition allowing the *res* to be given. Part of this shift in meaning may simply be that Peter is using the term "faith" in a more limited way, to refer to belief and assent, whereas the patristic writers identified it more broadly with the whole experience of conversion and salvation.

We will return to this shifting understanding of faith when treating modern thought. Here, however, we can simply point out that this particular difficulty points to a larger limitation of the scholastic project: The rich symbols of the liturgy are dynamic and irreducible, so any attempt to define the *res* of baptism apart from the rite itself will be guilty of a certain reductivism. This is the "cerebralization" for which Mitchell faults scholastic sacramental theology.[147] And he is hardly alone. Cramer also sees an intellectualization of the sacraments in the *Sentences*, so that sacramental doctrines "arrogate to themselves the efficacy of sacrament." He wonders "whether there was not some slippage between the language 'of' sacrament, and language 'about' sacrament, in such a way that the force of the sacrament came to lie in the priest's discussion of it rather than only in the doing of it."[148] Such slippage became possible when, as Arthur Yates puts it, "an abstract 'grace' replaced the concrete 'event'

147. Mitchell, "Christian Initiation: Decline and Dismemberment," 477.
148. Cramer, *Baptism and Change*, 260.

as the theological focus of the sacrament."[149] Drawing on the work of Orthodox theologian Alexander Schmemann, Yates argues that the scholastics tended to transform the sacraments into "mere obligations without meaning," a weakness we have already begun to perceive in the legal language medieval sacramental theology came to employ.[150] A loss of meaning becomes apparent when we compare Peter Lombard's definition of the *res*—the remission of guilt—to St. Paul's description of baptism as participation in the death and resurrection of Jesus (Rom 6:3–5). Paul's theology is both broader and more figurative than scholastic categories allow. The paschal imagery of baptism does not fit in the Lombard's *res*, nor, by definition, does the sacrament's corporeal dimension.

To be sure, Peter knows that a reductive approach to the sacraments is mistaken if it leads to the conclusion that baptism is optional, and his next three chapters address this difficulty. What does one gain by being baptized if one is already justified by faith? Peter's first response makes use of scholastic penitential categories: Someone justified before baptism is absolved of eternal punishment, but it remains for him to make temporal satisfaction for his sins.[151] The sacrament, on the other hand, eliminates both guilt and temporal satisfaction. Additionally, the virtues associated with regeneration are increased in water baptism, and the "incentive to sin is also further weakened." Peter quotes Matthew 25:29—"to every one who has will more be given"—though the verse is included more as scriptural ornamentation than as genuine theological grounding. Indeed, while Peter's answer fits within his conceptual categories, it has little basis in sacramental practice. And he ignores the question of why, if God is not bound by the sacraments, he does not include the remission of temporal punishments along with justification when one receives baptism of desire. Repeating the argument that the sacrament offers a discount on temporal punishment in the next chapter, Peter runs into another problem: Sacramental baptism does not eliminate the most obvious punishment of sin, bodily death. Theologians had raised this issue before, but it is a particular problem for Peter since he had only just argued that the

149. Arthur S. Yates, *Why Baptize Infants? A Study of the Biblical, Traditional and Theological Evidence* (Norwich: The Canterbury Press, 1993), 119.

150. Alexander Schmemann, *Of Water & the Spirit: A Liturgical Study of Baptism* (Crestwood, NY: St. Vladimir's Seminary Press, 1974), 58–60.

151. Peter Lombard, *The Sentences*, 4.4.5, pp. 25–26.

distinctive virtue of water baptism is its washing away of temporal punishments. In any case, God leaves death in place, he says, so that we have
to struggle in life, for only through struggle can we "conquer."[152]

Peter's final chapter on the question is perhaps his most subtle. He
sees that his affirmation of pre-baptismal justification has come into conflict with his definition of a sacrament, which includes efficaciousness; he
had previously argued that "the sacraments were not instituted only for
the sake of signifying, but also to sanctify."[153] This is why, taking a more
restrictive view than did Hugh, he rejects using the term "sacrament"
for the observances of the Old Testament; these were signs of things to
come, Peter insists, but did not confer the sacred realities they signified.[154]
When someone receives baptism after having been justified, baptism is
still the sign and cause of justification, Peter argues; in this case, the effect simply precedes the cause.[155] Peter does not dwell on the question of
cause and effect, though both the possibilities and the difficulties of pursuing this line of thinking are intriguing. Baptism, understood as a goal,
can already begin to bring about changes in the behavior of a convert, for
example, so there is undoubtedly some sense in which its efficaciousness
begins before it is received. On the other hand, it is not clear how the unrepeatable change brought by baptism, later identified with the baptismal
character, fits within the dynamics he describes.

To Peter's answer to the question of what an already justified person
gains from baptism, we can add a section from his treatment of the sacraments in general where he discusses why the Lord instituted sacraments
in the first place. He gives three reasons: to facilitate humility, to offer
instruction, and to require exercise.[156] The sacraments promote humility
because of the material elements they employ. Man's nature is higher than
these elements, Peter says, so it is humbling for him to have to depend on
such things for salvation, to have to stoop to seek God in the lowlier strata of creation. Secondly, our instruction in spiritual realities depends upon
the use of visible elements because our ability to perceive such realities
directly was damaged by original sin. And finally, Peter says, when our

152. *The Sentences*, 4.4.6.2, p. 26.
153. *The Sentences*, 4.1.4.2, p. 4.
154. *The Sentences*, 4.1.4.3, pp. 4–5.
155. *The Sentences*, 4.4.7.1, pp. 26–27.
156. *The Sentences*, 4.1.5.1–4, pp. 5–6.

time and energy are occupied with the exercise of the sacraments, we are less likely to become involved in "vain and harmful activities." Peter concludes the chapter by invoking the principle that God is not bound by the sacraments, though placed in this context the dictum actually buttresses the necessity of the sacraments; God did not need to institute the sacraments to give grace, yet these were the means he chose.[157] Peter does not repeat the corresponding principle we saw in Hugh's *De Sacramentis*— that we are bound to the sacraments even if God is not—because this is already implied by the sacraments' divine institution. His focus on the sacraments' institution reminds us of what for him is the unavoidable reason for their necessity—God's command.

These observations indicate that, even though the favorable treatment of baptism of desire in the Lombard's *Sentences* was the key moment in its twelfth century transformation from marginal hypothesis to mainstream doctrine, this support came at a cost. Not all of the arguments Peter offers to defend baptism of desire rest on stone foundations. Even ignoring the Lombard's factual mistakes—his misattribution of quotations to Augustine—Master Simon probably would not have found his concerns adequately addressed in the *Sentences*. Peter's grasping for answers as to what is gained by water baptism if one is justified beforehand reveals scholastic theology's tendency to get lost in juridical categories; as Schmemann observes, such categories make liturgical rites seem arbitrary. Unlike patristic thinkers, Peter does not root the institution of the sacraments in the Incarnation, so the Pauline theology of participation fades out of his theological vision. The corporeal dimension of the sacraments is reduced from a profound response to embodied existence to a moralistic lesson in humility. We should note, however, that nothing in Peter's treatment of baptism of desire implies that Christianity is any less necessary for salvation than it had been for Hugh or Augustine. Christian faith remains the presupposition of both water baptism and baptism of desire.[158]

---

157. *The Sentences*, 4.1.5.4, p. 6. Peter tucks the principle into his defense of baptism of desire, though he does not make much of it. *The Sentences*, 4.4.4.10, p. 24. He makes a similar, though not identical, point in his discussion of inept confessors; God is not bound by their mistaken judgments in administering penance. *The Sentences*, 4.18.6.3, p. 111.

158. In fact, Peter thinks that the observances of the Old Law not only lose their power with the death of Christ but become obstacles to salvation. *The Sentences*, 4.3.8, p.17.

Other thinkers. The limitations of the *Sentences'* sacramental theology were not the result of Peter's own idiosyncrasies, but reflect the intellectual trends of his day. Thus, they proved no obstacle to the acceptance of his views on baptism of desire by his contemporaries. The Lombard's successors in the chair of theology at the cathedral school of Paris, Peter Comestor and Peter of Poitiers, agreed that baptism of desire is possible in the case of grave necessity (sudden death, as Peter of Poitiers explains it) for those with faith, contrition, and the absence of contempt of religion.[159] Peter the Chanter illustrates this last condition with the hypothetical cases of two identical converts who die before baptism: one who had the opportunity to be baptized and passed it up; the other who had no such opportunity. Only the latter will be saved, he says. Alan of Lille, writing shortly before the turn of the thirteenth century, introduced the triad "*fluminis, flaminis et sanguinis,*" which became a commonly used formula for speaking of the different modes of baptism.[160] Alan's circumstances made him particularly keen to insist on ritual baptism. Preaching in the south of France between 1180–1200, he came into direct contact with the Cathar heresy, which emphasized interior contrition alone as the basis of salvation and denied the efficacy of baptism.[161] Alan insists upon the scriptural mandate to baptize and prefers to speak of those baptized in *flaminis,* through the action of the Spirit, rather than of those saved without baptism, as had Peter Lombard.

Theological opinion in the first half of the thirteenth century seems to have been unanimous, or nearly so, in favor of the possibility of baptism of desire. The doctrine also gained a decisive vote of confidence from the papal magisterium around this time. The massive collection of papal decrees published by Gregory IX in 1234 includes a response from the Apostolic See to a query from the bishop of Cremona about the bizarre case of a priest who had not been baptized.[162] Since baptism is the foundation

---

159. Colish, *Faith, Fiction & Force,* 60–64. To those expressing favorable opinions toward baptism of desire in this period, Colish adds Bandinus, Gandulph of Bologna, Prepositinus of Cremona, and Radulphus Ardens. Colish, 57–71.

160. Alan of Lille, *De fide catholica contra haereticos sui temporis,* PL 210:348. See Colish, *Faith, Fiction & Force,* 70–71; baptism of "water, blood, and repentance" also appears. Colish, 62–63.

161. Alan of Lille, *De fide catholica,* PL 201:349–51.

162. The original text attributes the letter to Innocent III (1198–1216); a marginal correction

of all the other sacraments, the "priest" would not have been validly ordained either. The letter offers no explanation as to how the situation came about, but apparently it was discovered too late and the man died before he could be baptized, prompting the bishop of Cremona to inquire whether it would be licit to offer prayers for his soul. The bishop testifies that the priest had "persevered in the faith of Holy Mother Church and in the confession of Christ's name." Without hesitation, the pope declares the unfortunate presbyter to have been freed of original sin—an indication of what was understood to be the essential effect of baptism in this period—and now to enjoy the heavenly fatherland. He encourages "prayers and sacrifices" for him.

The exchange confirms Master Simon's observation that, by not according them the prayers of the baptized, the *lex orandi* implied that those who were not baptized were not saved. But it also makes clear that this general rule does not apply in the sort of exceptional cases addressed by baptism of desire; the pope's reply, in fact, mandates a liturgical practice consonant with the doctrine. The reply distills the late twelfth century conception of baptism of desire: Augustine and Ambrose are cited as providing the patristic authority for the proposition that "Baptism is administered invisibly when it is impeded, not by the contempt of religion, but by the barrier of necessity." The papal decree does not enter into the more fraught systematic questions that characterized the era, such as the relationship between the *sacramentum* and the *res*, the definition of the *res*, the relationship of sacrament to law, and of Old Law to New. Moreover, the strange circumstance the decree addresses would seem to argue against a broad application. Still, the priest's case—baptism omitted through a misunderstanding—is strikingly similar to the one that prompted Cyprian a millennium before to reassure Jubian that the "Lord is powerful in his mercy to grant indulgence."[163] That patristic instinct now had papal validation.

in the 1584 edition attributes it to Innocent II (1130–1143). Gregory IX, *Decretales* (Rome: In Aedibus Populi Romani, 1584), 3.43.1–2, pp. 991–92; *Enchiridion symbolorum*, 741.

163. Cyprian, "Letter 73," 23, p. 283.

Thomas Replies

Inclusion in Peter Lombard's *Sentences* meant that baptism of desire was on the potential agenda of any theologian commenting on the work in subsequent centuries. Following the example of the Franciscan Alexander of Hales, master at the University of Paris from 1220–1245, theologians adopted the *Sentences* as the standard basis for their lectures; so, far more commentaries were written on the work than we could possibly examine.[164] As Colish's survey of the thirteenth century makes clear, baptism of desire gained widespread support, but such acceptance did not always indicate agreement among authors on the many secondary problems the doctrine raised. Colish argues, for example, that Alexander of Hales and William of Auxerre (d. 1231) take different paths on the question of whether the three modes of baptism identified by Alan of Lille—*fluminis, flaminis, sanguinis*—can be considered equal. William argues that only *fluminis* (in water) is properly baptism and that the others are called so only metaphorically, while Alexander argues for their equality.[165] Alexander's case is undercut, however, by the issue of baptismal character: Both theologians agree that such character is only imparted by sacramental baptism. The concept of "character," implicit in Augustine's argument against the repeatability of baptism, refers to the permanent effect of the sacrament, which is distinct from the baptismal grace that can be lost through sin.[166] Only toward the beginning of the thirteenth century, however, did theologians begin to explore the implications of the concept in a systematic way. The question of how character fits with baptism of desire was to prove among the most vexing of the period, one which, as we shall see shortly, not even Aquinas was able to resolve satisfactorily.

A number of other ideas which we saw germinate in the twelfth century came to fruition in this period of high scholasticism. Alexander, along with Bonaventure (1221–1274) and Albert the Great (1200–1280),

---

164. Philipp W. Rosemann, *The Story of a Great Medieval Book Peter Lombard's* Sentences (Toronto: University of Toronto Press, 2007), loc. 953 of 5593, Kindle.

165. Colish, *Faith, Fiction & Force*, 71–77. Of thirteenth-century thinkers prior to or contemporary with Aquinas, Colish also discusses Bonaventure, Richard of Mediavilla, William of Ware, and Albert the Great. Colish, 77–82.

166. Roger W. Nutt, *General Principles of Sacramental Theology* (Washington, DC: The Catholic University of America Press, 2017), 153–55.

were instrumental in molding the insight of William of Champeaux—
that unbaptized infants experience the deprivation of the beatific vision
without any additional suffering—into a full-fledged theology of limbo.[167] Aquinas would take their theories to another level by positing that
such a state of existence could even involve a kind of happiness, if not the
highest happiness.[168] While all of these authors favor baptism of desire,
they also agree that because of infants' undeveloped mental state they
are incapable of the use of the will that makes desire possible. Related to
the question of limbo and the fate of unbaptized infants is the question
of what happens to virtuous pagans in the afterlife; as Dante's *Divine
Comedy* demonstrates, a dignified but joyless limbo was seen by many as
the most likely destiny of admirable pagans who lacked explicit Christian
faith.[169]

While today he stands out as the giant of the age, Thomas Aquinas
(1225–1274) was not so pivotal in bringing baptism of desire into the Catholic mainstream as were Bernard, Hugh, and Peter Lombard. Thomas
seems to regard the question as largely settled. Compared to Abelard's
Sic et Non, the objections raised by Thomas to the proposition that "a man
can obtain salvation without the sacrament of Baptism" seem almost perfunctory.[170] Thomas's great genius was organizational: He managed to pull
together the fruits of two centuries of scholastic debate, his own reading
of Aristotle and his commentators—Christian, Islamic, and Jewish—and
numerous personal insights into an overarching vision of existence that
begins and ends with God. The particular contribution of Aquinas to the

167. A 1201 letter of Innocent III had in the meantime confirmed the proposition that
the "punishment of original sin is the deprivation of the vision of God, but the punishment of
actual sin is the torment of eternal hell." *Enchiridion symbolorum*, 780.

168. Beiting, "The Idea of Limbo in Alexander of Hales and Bonaventure," 3–56; Chris-
topher Beiting, "The Idea of Limbo in Thomas Aquinas," *The Thomist* 62, no. 2 (1998): 240.
Aquinas develops his theology of limbo most fully when discussing original sin in qq. 4–5 of
De Malo.

169. Beiting finds Dante's vision of limbo closest to the neutrality of Bonaventure, though
the intellectual attainment of its denizens suggests a certain debt to Aquinas, "The Idea of
Limbo in Alexander of Hales and Bonaventure," 55; cf. Dante Alighieri, *Inferno*, trans. Robert
Hollander and Jean Hollander (New York: Doubleday, 2000), 4.25–38, pp. 60–63. The Floren-
tine also adds a great swarm of aimless souls outside of limbo, who lived with neither praise
nor disgrace and find no home even in hell. *Inferno*, 3.36, 62, pp. 44–47. In our age of religious
indifferentism, perhaps this image is the *Comedy*'s most haunting and most prophetic.

170. Thomas Aquinas, *ST*, 3.68.2.

doctrine of baptism of desire, then, is to show how the idea fits within
the overall system of Christian theology. This Thomistic systematization
allows us to address the question: Once the basic idea of Ambrose and
Augustine is accepted, what are its broader implications? Since baptism of
desire is a limit case, it can also function as a kind of theological stress test
of the sort engineers might run on a protype in order to identify weak-
nesses in the machinery. And, indeed, despite the intricacy of Thomas's
machinery and his engineering skill, we will identify a few points where
the engine rattles.

The Commentary on the Sentences

Thomas's first brush with the doctrine of baptism of desire comes in his
Commentary on the Sentences, written to earn the degree of master while
lecturing at the University of Paris from 1552 to 1556—the equivalent of
his doctoral dissertation. His treatment of this issue is a bit more wander-
ing than in the *Summa theologiae*. He builds upon the *sacramentum* and
res distinction utilized by Peter, but he is also alert to the risk that always
shadows such a distinction of reducing the visible rite to something optional or decorative. So, while he acknowledges that the term "sacrament"
is sometimes used generically to include, for example, the ceremonies
of the Old Law, he insists that Christian sacraments cause what they
signify.[171] This allows him to follow Peter in drawing a sharp distinction
between the Old Testament "sacraments," which merely point toward future graces, and the Christian sacraments, in which there exists a "hidden
divine power" that sanctifies.[172] He sees an unacceptable reductionism in
the formulations employed by other scholastic theologians whose focus
on sacraments as signs obscures their role as causes; Bernard's comparison
of the sacraments to a bishop's crozier or ring is misleading, according to
Thomas, because, while ring and crozier symbolize episcopal authority,
they do not cause it.[173]

171. Thomas Aquinas, *Commentary on the Sentences, Book IV, Distinctions 1–21*, trans. Beth
Mortensen, vol. 7 of *Latin-English Opera Omnia* (Green Bay, WI: Aquinas Institute, 2018),
4.1.1.1, rep. quaest. 1, p. 10; 4.1.1.1, rep. quaest. 3, ad 5, p. 13.
172. *Commentary on the Sentences*, 4.1.1.1, rep. quaest. 4, p. 13.
173. *Commentary on the Sentences*, 4.1.1.5, quaest. obj. 1, p. 25, rep. quaest. 1, ad 1, p. 32. Bernard's example appears to have irritated Thomas, for he criticizes it again. *ST*, 3.62.1.

Necessity. Thomas dedicates the second article on the sacraments in his *Commentary* to the question of their necessity; he makes reference to the reasons given in the *Sentences* for the institution of sacraments—humiliation, instruction, and exercise—though he does not structure his answer around Peter's response. He also quotes Augustine to the effect that every religion has need of external signs.[174] One senses, however, that Aquinas thinks that to describe the sacraments as "necessary" requires something more. They are necessary, after all, not just to provide a unifying activity for the institutional Church, but for the salvation of individuals.[175] Aquinas returns repeatedly to Hugh of St. Victor's description of the sacraments as medicine for the wound of sin; for medicine to be healing, it must be appropriate—or "proportionate," to use Thomas's word—to the disease. As far as the corporeal dimension of the sacraments, this puts Thomas closer to the sense of the Fathers—that sacraments contain both material and spiritual elements because man is a composite of both body and soul—than to Peter's moralistic claim that the material elements are meant to instill humility. The totality of human nature has been harmed by sin, so a correct course of treatment must include the body as well as the soul.[176]

Aquinas, then, sees the need to go beyond Peter's analysis of necessity. One of his most important contributions to the discussion of baptism of desire is making explicit the different senses in which we use the term "necessity." The necessity of the sacraments for salvation is not absolute, in the sense that it is necessary for God to exist, Aquinas says; rather the necessity of the sacraments is of a second type, "the necessity that comes from supposing the end."[177] The nature of reality does not demand that I turn on my computer, but if my goal is write a document with Microsoft Word, it is necessary for me to do so. This second category of necessity itself admits of different degrees. Aquinas gives two examples to show the difference: Eating is necessary to sustain human life, and a horse is

---

174. Augustine, *Contra Faustum*, 19.11; Thomas Aquinas, *Commentary on the Sentences*, 4.1.1.2, quest. 1, p. 15.

175. The obstacle to heaven was removed for humanity in general by Christ's passion, but individuals must participate in the passion for Christ's action to become effective in their particular case. Thomas Aquinas, *Commentary on the Sentences*, 4.4.2.2, rep. quaest 6, p. 183; cf. *Summa contra Gentiles*, https://isidore.co/aquinas/ContraGentiles4.htm#56, 4.56.1; *ST*, 3.49.1, ad 4.

176. Thomas Aquinas, *Commentary on the Sentences*, 4.1.1.2, p. 15.

177. *Commentary on the Sentences*, 4.1.1.2, resp. quaest. 1, p. 18.

necessary for a journey. The first is more necessary than the second; the horse is necessary in the way the sacraments are necessary, as a fitting means. Here we could press Aquinas's examples further; for the necessity of a horse is rather different for a journey from Rome to Milan than from Rome to Vladivostok. Omitting what is "fitting" could mean anything from causing inconvenience to making something practically impossible. By treating the sacraments as necessary in the sense of fitting, however, Aquinas at least opens the door for baptism of desire. Beyond this, how we understand baptism's necessity will depend on a range of other circumstances. A horse is necessary even for the journey from Rome to Milan because inconvenience and discomfort would likely deter most people from making such a journey by foot unless they were in good physical condition and unusually determined. Reaching the shores of the Pacific from Rome without transportation, however, would not only require extraordinary determination and strength but also improbably favorable circumstances, like friendly Russian border guards and a mild Siberian winter. At a minimum, Thomas's example suggests that the absence of a necessary means is likely to deter most people from seeking an otherwise desirable end; it might also imply that the end is unlikely to be achieved without the occurrence of other generally improbable circumstances. Among the sacraments, Thomas acknowledges that "necessity" admits a range of meaning, but he insists repeatedly that baptism is the most necessary of the sacraments.[178]

This background on necessity puts into context Thomas's use of the principle that God is not bound by the sacraments. This principle shields baptism of desire from one potential objection, though not a particularly strong one; not even Gennadius would have claimed that it was impossible for an omnipotent being to arrange some other means of salvation. In fact, when Aquinas deploys the maxim, he demonstrates an awareness of the second principle with which it is paired in Hugh's De Sacramentis: God's power may not be limited by the sacraments, but ours is. Responding to the ancient controversy over whether the apostles were baptized

---

178. *Commentary on the Sentences*, 4.3.1.3, quaest. 3, p. 138; 4.4.3.3, rep. quaest. 1, ad 2, p. 201. According to Thomas, this strong sense of baptism's necessity is the reason it employs such a common element as water and why anyone can administer an emergency baptism. The degree to which baptism is necessary for salvation is even higher in the case of children, who "cannot be rescued any other way." *Commentary on the Sentences*, 4.5.2.1, resp. quaest. 1, p. 224.

with the baptism of Christ or only that of John, Thomas allows that even if theirs was a special case, this would not set a precedent relevant to current practice. For "if Christ, who had the power of forgiving sins and who did not bind his own power to the sacraments, wanted to sanctify them without baptism by way of a certain privilege, such a privilege would not have been handed down to the succession."[179] In another place, Thomas invokes the principle in answer to the question of whether angels can baptize.[180] His answer is no: "baptism is an act of the Church Militant. But angels are not members of the Church Militant." The sacraments flow from the Incarnation and thus are not congruent with the purely spiritual nature of angels. But he adds, "God did not bind his own power in the sacraments [...] hence he, who gave this power to men, could give it to angels as well." Here we are clearly dealing with a theoretical exercise, one which demonstrates the limited practical utility of the principle that God has not limited his power to the sacraments. God could save someone baptized in the name of Bilbo, Frodo, and Samwise Gamgee, but under no circumstances are we authorized to baptize in such a way or to promise salvation to those so "baptized." Such a rite, in fact, would be decidedly unfitting—incongruent with what God has revealed about himself and about salvation. The importance of the notion of congruence for Aquinas can be seen in his treatment of the Incarnation, an event which was not absolutely necessary but clearly represents the will of God. Thomas explains the Incarnation in terms of its fittingness; in this case, fittingness represents a strong version of necessity.[181]

Baptism. These reflections on the necessity of the sacraments set the stage for Aquinas's explicit treatment of baptism of desire in the *Commentary*. In fact, Aquinas does even more stage-setting; he uses the Lombard's defense of the possibility of baptism of desire as the occasion for a detailed treatment of the sacrament's effects. He presupposes the distinction between the *res sacramenti* (the effect) and the *sacramentum* (the washing). Though one should receive both together, he says, some people, because of their insincerity, receive only the physical washing; other

179. *Commentary on the Sentences*, 4.2.2.4, ad 3, p. 112. In any case, he thinks it more probable that the apostles were baptized with the baptism of Christ.

180. *Commentary on the Sentences*, 4.5.2.3, quaest. 1–3, pp. 233–34.

181. Thomas Aquinas, *Commentary on the Sentences*, 3.1.1.2; cf. Thomas Aquinas, *ST*, 3.1.1–2.

adults are able to receive the effect without the *sacramentum*, or baptism of desire.[182] The effects of the sacrament, however, are various; they include baptismal character (Question 1) and both the removal of evil and the conferral of good (Question 2).

Baptism of desire comes up in Thomas's third question, which deals with baptism's recipients. He divides this question into three articles. The first defends the possibility and advisability of infant baptism; Aquinas acknowledges that today the only way for infants to be cleansed of original sin is through baptism.[183] Thomas's overarching concern in the article is to show that infants receive both the sacrament and its effects, even if they are, in some sense, a special case. So he argues that infants receive the "habit" of faith, a potential for faith that is put into act when they reach the age of reason. The second article deals with those who, because of their insincerity, receive the *sacramentum* but not the sacrament's effects. Without entering into all of the details of the discussion, it is noteworthy that Aquinas distinguishes two effects of the sacrament: the imposition of baptismal character and salvific grace. The baptismal character is imposed so long as the recipient intends to receive the sacrament, but the grace of the sacrament—which includes the forgiveness of sins—also requires "faith and contrition" from the recipient.[184] While these dispositions require more of the recipient, they do not imply that one needs a perfect will to benefit from baptism. On the contrary, it is precisely the grace of the sacrament that restores and fulfills all that is lacking in the recipient.[185] When Aquinas refers to faith and contrition in the context of baptism of desire, then, he is using the dispositions necessary for the fruitful reception of the sacrament as his basis. The article also contains an illuminating reference to another key concept: "contempt" for the sacrament. This happens, Thomas says, not only in the obvious case of one who neglects to receive baptism but also of someone who "views it as unimportant, not considering it to be efficacious for salvation."[186]

Thomas frames his discussion of baptism of desire in a slightly different way in his *Commentary* than Peter does in the original *Sentences*, a

182. *Commentary on the Sentences*, 4.4, p. 151.
183. *Commentary on the Sentences*, 4.3.1, rep. quaest. 1–2, pp. 189–90.
184. *Commentary on the Sentences*, rep. quaest. 1, p. 194.
185. *Commentary on the Sentences*, 4.3.2, quest. 1, p. 192.
186. *Commentary on the Sentences*, 4.3.2, rep. quaest. 2, ad 5, p. 196.

shift that will become more pronounced in the *Summa theologiae*. While still using Peter's category of those receiving the *res* without the *sacramentum*, he begins the article dealing with this issue by asking whether there are multiple modes of baptism. Perhaps this decision reflects the popularity achieved by Alan of Lille's triad *fluminis, flaminis, sanguinis* by Aquinas's time. In any case, Thomas finds justification for this categorization deep in the tradition, noting that John Damascene also speaks of several types of baptism. Thomas seems to prefer the term baptism of repentance (*poenitentiae*) to Alan's *flaminis*, though it is obvious that, unlike patristic authors, he is using the term to refer to baptism of desire rather than to post-baptismal penance.[187] Of course, the Damascene was not dealing with the same issue as Peter or Thomas, which Thomas acknowledges later in the article. Here he slightly walks back his initial response by claiming that only baptism in water is baptism "properly speaking"; the other examples are called "baptisms" because they are ordered to the sacrament. These include the pre-Christian precursors of the sacrament, such as the Flood and the baptism of John. The relationship of the former to the sacrament is the weakest, since it is only a sign of baptism; John's baptism, however, is a "cause" of Christian baptism because it played a role in its institution. Baptism of blood and repentance, on the other hand, are related to baptism "according to [their] proportion to the same effect."[188] Later in the paragraph Aquinas hedges slightly by specifying that he is speaking of their "principal effect." Like Peter, Thomas will, with some difficulty, attempt to articulate differences between the modes of baptism. The relationship of these two secondary modes of baptism to the sacrament, however, is essential; suffering itself is not salvific but only becomes so when it conforms one to the passion of Christ, represented sacramentally in baptism.[189] Likewise the baptism of repentance is not "simply and absolutely" sufficient for salvation but is so only under certain conditions: *articulus necessitatis*, the absence of contempt, the intention to receive baptism in water.[190]

187. *Commentary on the Sentences*, 4.4.3.3, quaest. 1, p. 198.

188. *Commentary on the Sentences*, 4.4.3.3, rep. quaest. 1, pp. 200–201.

189. *Commentary on the Sentences*, 4.4.3.3, rep. quaest. 3, pp. 202–3. Aquinas consistently holds that baptism receives its efficacy from the passion of Christ.

190. *Commentary on the Sentences*, 4.4.3.3, rep. quaest. 2, p. 201; 4.4.3.3, rep. quest 1, ad 1, p. 201: "baptismus sanguinis et poenitentiae non valent ad regenerationem nisi ei qui habet

While the intention to receive baptism in water gives the other two modes of baptism the same force of regeneration, there are differences between them. Aquinas seems to accept Peter's contention that baptism of desire does not fully remit the temporal punishment of sin, though he does not make much of this in the *Commentary*. Perhaps because of his adamant insistence that one can only attain baptism of desire if intending to receive the sacrament, Aquinas seems less worried than Peter to explain why one should go ahead with the sacrament. But the question remains a tricky one. Thomas accepts the interpretation of the story of Cornelius he inherited via the *Sentences* in which the righteous centurion receives the *res* of baptism before the sacrament, but his treatment of the story shows the difficulty of defining what exactly Cornelius received. He indicates that Cornelius was able to receive the first fruits of the Spirit because he had the "habitual intention" to receive baptism, though he also acknowledges the incongruity of Cornelius not yet being admitted to "the acts of the faithful" until after visible baptism.[191] He also argues—calling to mind his fundamental concept of a sacrament as an efficacious sign—that the baptisms of blood and desire do not signify.[192] With regard to martyrdom this seems a contestable position, since the very word derives from bearing witness; the weakness of this distinction is exacerbated later in the article when Aquinas repeats Gennadius's description of the ways martyrdom corresponds to the baptismal ceremony.[193] He selectively omits Gennadius's denial that unbaptized catechumens can be saved.

Character. The raw material Aquinas has inherited from the tradition contains two slightly different ways of conceiving of baptism of desire—as salvation without baptism (the conception of the *Sentences*) or as an alternative mode of baptism (as Alan of Lille's formulation suggests). Both

---

baptismum aquae in proposito, scilicet quando articulus necessitatis non contemptus religionis sacramentum escludit, ut in littera dicitur, et sic quodammodo agunt in vi baptismi acquae."

191. *Commentary on the Sentences*, 4.3.1.1, quaest. 4 obj. 1, p. 119, and rep. quaest. 4, ad 1, p. 124. Aquinas further distinguishes Cornelius's "habitual intention" from the "actual intention" of those who know explicitly about baptism.

192. *Commentary on the Sentences*, 4.4.3.3, rep. quaest. 1, ad 3, p. 201.

193. *Commentary on the Sentences*, 4.4.3.3, rep. quaest. 4, p. 203. He misidentifies Gennadius as Augustine.

impulses are present in Aquinas' *Commentary*, and tension emerges when the Angelic Doctor turns to the question of baptismal character. Aquinas agrees that baptism confers a character and that this character—or at least the desire for it—is necessary for salvation.[194] He is clear, however, that neither baptism of desire nor baptism of blood confers character.[195] In fact, Aquinas's way of speaking here treats the baptismal character as if it were simply a synonym for the sacrament rather than an effect produced by the sacrament. When he introduces the question of character, he tries to have it both ways, defining it as "the effect that is the sacrament-and-reality in baptism." This is apparently distinct from the "ultimate effect of baptism," which is the *res* alone.[196] He takes as generally accepted among theologians that the baptismal character is a seal imprinted on those who receive it, distinguishing them from non-believers and configuring them to Christ, making them like him and therefore signs of him.[197] We can understand, perhaps, why Aquinas would consider baptism of desire insufficient to imprint such a character, but, as noted above, martyrdom seems a distinguishing and configuring sign with indelible effects. Aquinas weakens his case further when he notes that the visible sacrament provides the sign of character; this is no different, he says, than when a crown and scepter are given to a king or a crozier to a bishop.[198] Yet he had criticized Bernard's use of the very same examples as inadequate to describe the way in which sacraments are signs.

Some light can be shed on Thomas's sense of baptismal character by the other sacraments that produce an indelible seal: confirmation and, especially, orders. For Thomas goes on to define character as a power, in the sense of a ministerial office; character is a sign through which one can participate in divine operations.[199] With regard to baptism, he has in mind

---

194. *Commentary on the Sentences*, 4.2.2.4, pp. 110–11.

195. *Commentary on the Sentences*, 4.4.1.4, rep. quaest. 3, ad 1–2, p. 170.

196. *Commentary on the Sentences*, 4.4.4, p. 152. Elsewhere he explains: "In the sacrament of baptism there are three things. There is something that is only a sacrament, like the water that flows externally and flows away, and does not remain; and something that is a sacrament-and-reality, and this remains forever, namely, the character; and something that is only a reality, which sometimes remains and sometimes passes away, namely grace." *Commentary on the Sentences*, 4.3.1.1, rep. quaest.1, ad 1, p. 120.

197. *Commentary on the Sentences*, 4.4.1.1, p. 154.

198. *Commentary on the Sentences*, 4.4.1.2, rep. quaest. 1, ad 1–2, p. 160.

199. *Commentary on the Sentences*, 4.4.1.1, p. 156.

participation in the sacramental life of the Church. This makes the character "a disposition to grace" because it facilitates the reception of grace
through the sacraments.[200] There is, then, a certain fittingness in Thomas's
insistence that initiation into the sacramental system should come only
through sacramental baptism, though there is also a problem: As Thomas
recognizes, the Church's earthly action is in continuity with its heavenly
life.[201] Presumably those sanctified through baptism of desire will participate in this heavenly worship. Does this mean that they will receive the
character necessary to do so in the afterlife? Or that character only really
matters as far as visible, earthly participation is concerned? If so, is speaking of a spiritual seal and a configuration of the soul really the best way
to conceptualize character? And if character is a disposition to grace, as
Thomas says, then those who receive baptism of desire would seem to be
getting a grace which they are not disposed to receive. When it comes to
baptism of desire and character, therefore, we can hear a certain clanging
in the machinery of the Thomistic system.

The Summa theologiae

A full understanding of Thomas's conception of baptism of desire, however, requires us to move beyond his *Commentary on the Sentences* to the
Summa theologiae, which is both more mature and more thoroughly his
own. Here Thomas is free of Peter's structure, and his treatment of baptism of desire likely reflects the theological developments of the intervening years; because Aquinas does not seem as pressed to defend the
possibility of baptism of desire, his treatment of the subject in the *Summa*
is both more streamlined and more thoroughly integrated into the rest
of his theology than in the *Commentary*. In fact, baptism of desire becomes the basis for other arguments Aquinas makes, for example, about
the possibility of spiritual communion.[202] A careful reading reveals that
Aquinas's thought has also undergone certain changes in emphasis. In the
Summa, Aquinas becomes more insistent on the necessity of baptism for
salvation—like the necessity of a horse for a long and arduous journey.

200. *Commentary on the Sentences*, 4.4.1.1, ad 5, p. 157; 4.4.1.2, rep. quaest. 1, p. 159.
201. *Commentary on the Sentences*, 4.4.1.3, rep. quaest. 4, ad 2, p. 166.
202. Thomas Aquinas, *ST*, 3.73.3.

He also seems to have shifted somewhat in the direction of Alan of Lille and away from Peter Lombard, treating baptism of desire as a mode of baptism rather than as an alternative to it, though some ambiguity still remains. Cornelius appears again in the *Summa* to play the same problematic role as he had in Peter's *Sentences*, and the question of sacramental character remains thorny. The *Summa* also gives us the best insight into Aquinas's understanding of implicit desire, perhaps the concept of most interest to theologians concerned with the salvation of non-Christians.

Exception or partial participation? The subtle changes from the *Commentary* to the *Summa* allow Thomas to address the fundamental difficulty raised by baptism of desire—how to reconcile the doctrine with the necessity of baptism for salvation—in a more coherent and defensible way. As both baptism of desire skeptics (e.g., Master Simon) and supporters (e.g., Hugh of St. Victor) recognize, only God can carve out exceptions to a rule of divine origin.[203] God may not be limited to the means of salvation he has revealed, but human beings risk culpable arrogance if they presume pathways beyond—or worse, in contradiction to—revelation. And Aquinas clearly holds that the requirement for baptism applies universally.[204] His way of dealing with the difficulty posed by cases like that of Valentinian or the salvation of Old Testament figures in the *Summa* is to include their salvation in the reality of baptism, rather than to claim the existence of alternatives. Water is one means by which this reality can be attained, though martyrdom and desire also conform one to the sanctification the sacrament confers. But these other modes of baptism require a relationship with the sacrament. Thus, in defending the appropriateness of the *fluminis, sanguinis, flaminis* triad, Aquinas answers the objection that this creates three different baptisms by stating that the "other two Baptism are included in the Baptism of Water."[205]

When Aquinas says that *sanguinis* or *flaminis* "takes the place of Baptism," the Latin verb he uses (*supplet*) has the connotation of "filling

203. Thomas makes this same point about the specific material elements necessary for the sacraments. *ST*, 3.60.6.

204. *ST*, 3.68.1.

205. *ST*, 3.66.11; see ad 1. At times, Thomas's language could be construed to imply that baptism of desire is a substitute for, rather than mode of, baptism; this is due mostly to using "baptism" to mean "baptism in water."

up" or "completing," which better conveys the more integral relationship among the three modes that the overall context of Aquinas's answer favors. The unity between these three modes means that the sacrament must always be present at least in desire:

> The sacrament of Baptism may be wanting in two ways. First both in reality and in desire; as is the case with those who neither are baptized, nor wished to be baptized: which clearly indicates contempt of the sacrament, in regard to those who have the use of the free-will. Consequently those to whom Baptism is wanting thus, cannot obtain salvation [...] Secondly, the sacrament of Baptism may be wanting to anyone in reality but not in desire: for instance, when a man wishes to be baptized, but by some ill-chance he is forestalled by death before receiving Baptism. And such a man can obtain salvation without being actually baptized, on account of his desire for Baptism.[206]

Thomas, in other words, thinks of the sacrament as being partially present in the will of those who receive baptism of desire, rather than entirely absent.

Aquinas's instinct to define "baptism of desire" as intrinsically related to both the sacrament and martyrdom—rather than a pious way of speaking about any non-sacramental means of salvation—seems to me to be the strongest position theologically, the one best able to withstand the criticism of Master Simon or the doubts of the late Augustine. It allows us to understand baptism of desire as a corollary to the rule laid down in John 3:5, rather than—as critics might charge—an exception invented by theologians unhappy with the implications of the revealed teaching. Though his mode of expression is different, Thomas's underlying sensibility is surprisingly close to what we observed among the Fathers. In *De obitu Valentiniani*, after all, Ambrose speaks of Valentinian receiving the baptism he desired, not having a rule waived. Thomas might reply to Gregory Nazianzen that desiring something means its partial, but not total, absence.

Necessity continued. On firmer ground with regard to how to conceptualize baptism of desire, Aquinas becomes more insistent about the

206. *ST,* 3.68.2.

necessity of baptism in the *Summa* than he was in the *Commentary*. This is especially clear when we compare the necessity of baptism with that of the Incarnation. Part III of the *Summa*, which includes the sacraments, begins with a question on the fittingness of the Incarnation. In the second article Thomas defends the proposition that the Incarnation was necessary for man's salvation.[207] He repeats his analysis of the multiple levels of necessity, though he simplifies what he said in the *Commentary*, omitting absolute necessity. He uses the same examples to indicate that something can be necessary in two ways: if an end cannot be attained without it (food for life) or if an end can better be attained with it (a horse for a journey). Like the sacraments, the Incarnation is necessary in the second way, for "God of His omnipotent power could have restored human nature in many other ways." The congruence between the necessity of the Incarnation and the necessity of the sacraments illuminates a perhaps under-appreciated aspect of Aquinas's sacramental theology: the degree to which he, like Ambrose and the other Fathers, saw the sacraments as an extension of the Incarnation in which we encounter Christ.[208] This Christological foundation can easily be obscured by the profusion of philosophical and canonical language in Aquinas's work— the Aristotelian categories, the limit cases, the distinctions and precisions—but it is present in the structure of the *Summa*, developed by the Angelic Doctor because he had come to find Peter Lombard's framework inadequate.[209] Aquinas's treatment of the Incarnation in Part III of the *Summa* flows directly into his treatment of the sacraments—which in turn would have flowed into his treatment of eternal life, had he been able to finish the work. The strong connection between the Incarnation and the sacraments—including the necessity of both—will be important

207. *ST*, 3.1.2. Later Aquinas introduces yet another relevant distinction by distinguishing necessity of constraint, which is "brought about by an external agent," from natural necessity, which "results from natural principles." *ST*, 3.14.2. The *articulus necessitatis* that prevents one from being baptized despite one's own desire is caused by external forces, if not necessarily by an agent.

208. Liam G. Walsh points out that for Aquinas the particularity of the sacraments is rooted in the particularity of Christ. Liam G. Walsh, "Sacraments," in *The Theology of Thomas Aquinas*, ed. Rik van Nieuwenhove and Joseph Wawrykow (Notre Dame, IN: University of Notre Dame Press, 2005), 337, 356–57. See also Thomas Aquinas, *Summa contra Gentiles*, 4.56.7, 4.56.2.

209. Aquinas considered the *Summa*'s organization "its most important pedagogical innovation." Eleonore Stump, *Aquinas* (London: Routledge, 2003), 10.

to keep in mind when we turn to more recent theology, for it suggests that a theology that diminishes the necessity of the sacraments will tend toward a weak sense of the Incarnation's necessity as well. When Thomas dedicates a question to the necessity of the sacraments in general, his argument centers on the necessity of a means of salvation appropriate to the incarnate nature of human beings.[210]

When we turn to the specific question of the necessity of baptism, we can perceive a significant development when Thomas compares the necessity of the different sacraments to each other. Addressing the question of whether all the sacraments are necessary for salvation, Thomas reprises the familiar distinction between the two types of necessity—"simple necessity of end" (food for life) and necessity of convenience or fittingness (a horse for a journey). After what was said about the Incarnation, we would expect to find all of the sacraments in the second category, but Thomas surprises us:

> In the first way, three sacraments are necessary for salvation. Two of them are necessary to the individual; Baptism, simply and absolutely; Penance, in the case of mortal sin committed after Baptism; while the sacrament of Order is necessary to the Church [...] But in the second way the other sacraments are necessary.[211]

What is extraordinary is to find baptism "simply and absolutely" in the "food for life" category of necessity. Since Thomas had already established that the Incarnation is necessary only in the "horse for a journey" way, a superficial reading could leave one with the impression that baptism is more necessary for salvation than the Incarnation. A better way of understanding Thomas's classification, however, assumes that by the time he reaches baptism he is taking certain presuppositions for granted; God

210. Thomas Aquinas, *ST,* 3.61; cf. *Summa contra Gentiles,* 56.1. On the question of why the general cause of salvation—Christ's passion—must be applied to individuals in a personal way, see the fine articles of Thomas P. Harmon, "The Sacramental Consummation of the Moral Life According to St. Thomas Aquinas," *New Blackfriars* 91, no. 1034 (2010): 465–80; and Franklin T. Harkins, "The Early Aquinas on the Question of Universal Salvation, or How a Knight May Choose Not to Ride His Horse," *New Blackfriars* 95, no. 1056 (2014): 209–17. Participation is the key for Aquinas, Harkins points out, because a universal cause without a particular application would leave a person "neither an active participant in the process nor therefore truly human. Consequently, universal salvation would not be *human* salvation in any real sense." Harkins, 217.

211. Thomas Aquinas, *ST,* 3.65.4.

could, after all, have created a world in which not even food was necessary for human life. By the time we arrive at the sacraments, the Incarnation has already been incorporated into Thomas's background assumptions; given these, he is able to assert that baptism is necessary for salvation in the strong sense. We might fill in his formulation with something like, "*Given Christian revelation*, three sacraments are necessary in the first way ..." We return to our earlier observation that even the two categories of necessity Thomas distinguishes admit a great deal of gradation: the *Summa* places baptism closer to the "practically inconceivable without" end of the spectrum than the "will save time and effort" end—the journey is to Vladivostok, not Milan.

Aquinas's firmer stance on the necessity of baptism for salvation goes hand-in-hand with the position that baptism of desire is not salvation *without* baptism but another mode of baptism. This conclusion is reinforced by the contrast between the necessity of baptism for infants and for adults. For infants, the sacrament is absolutely necessary because they have no possibility of receiving baptism through desire.[212] Aquinas is no less insistent than Augustine on the issue. In another work Aquinas was presented with the hypothetical case of a child born in a waterless desert. Could the child be saved through his mother's faith? Thomas's answer is unambiguous: "Clearly, then, the boy who dies in the desert without being baptized does not achieve salvation."[213] This reply provides decisive evidence that Aquinas does not believe that any desire with which we are born—say, the natural inclination of the will to the good—is sufficient for salvation.

---

212. *ST,* 3.67.3. On this basis, Aquinas argues that baptism should never be deferred for children but can be for adults. *ST,* 3.68.3.

213. Thomas Aquinas, *Thomas Aquinas's Quodlibetal Questions*, trans. Turner Nevitt and Brian Davies (New York: Oxford University Press, 2020), Apple Books, quodlibet 6, q. 3, a. 1: "there are three kinds of baptism: by water, by the spirit, and by blood. The latter two have the force of baptism by water, so long as one intends to receive such a baptism, and is only kept from doing so by necessity, and not by contempt for religion. Now, children who are not yet able to use their reason clearly cannot be moved by faith and love, nor can they intend to receive baptism." However, the Holy Innocents prove that infants can be saved by baptism of blood. In the *Commentary on the Sentences*, Aquinas had argued that a man attempting to baptize himself—because he was living among Jews unwilling to baptize him—would still be saved if he died, not because the "baptism" was valid—it was not—but through baptism of desire. *Commentary on the Sentences*, 4.5.2.1, rep. quaes. 3., ad 2, p. 226.

Baptism of desire vs. baptism. The absolute necessity of sacramental baptism for the salvation of infants is one way in which, for Thomas, water baptism is superior to baptism of desire.[214] By continuing to follow Peter Lombard, Aquinas ends up admitting other ways in which baptism *flaminis* falls short of the sacrament, even for adults. He argues that the spiritual effects of baptism are more fully present when the reality is received sacramentally, a principle he also applies to "spiritual communion."[215] In the case of baptism, this means a fuller remission of sins—presumably less time in purgatory—and an increase in grace and virtues. This is a weak point for Thomas, just as it was for Peter. He has no real basis from scripture, tradition, or the logic of the sacrament itself to support such claims. He and Peter have been worked into a theological corner by Cornelius and the theory that baptism of desire can somehow happen *before* reception of the sacrament. Thomas still must insist that the sacrament produces some spiritual effect, because otherwise the rite of baptism would cease to fit within his definition of a sacrament as an *efficacious* sign. As we have seen, he criticizes Bernard on precisely this point; baptism must be more than an *ex post facto* sign. Moreover, if Thomas's answer held, it would turn out that those who desire baptism do not really obtain what they desired, as Ambrose had said of Valentinian, because presumably they desire all of the sacrament's effects, not a reduced version.

As we saw in the *Commentary*, another difference between baptism of desire and the sacrament, according to Thomas, is the character, the quality that makes baptism unrepeatable but is not received in baptism of desire. Thomas's concept of baptismal character is somewhat more clearly expressed in the *Summa*, though this clarity brings into relief the difficulty the issue poses. Thomas begins his discussion of sacramental character by noting the twofold purpose for which the sacraments were instituted: as a remedy against sin and to perfect the soul through divine worship.[216]

---

214. Colish is wrong to conclude that Thomas aims to "equalize the nature and extent of [baptism of desire's] gifts with those of the other forms of baptism" in either the *Commentary* or the *Summa*. Colish, *Faith, Fiction & Force*, 83. She also misreads his treatment of baptismal character by assuming that because one is conformed to the passion of Christ in baptism *sanguinis* or *flaminis* this translates into the reception of the baptismal character.

215. Thomas Aquinas, *ST*, 3.86.4, ad 2; 3.80.1, ad 3.

216. *ST*, 3.63.1.

Character has to do with the second of these; it gives the soul the "instrumental power" to participate in the life of Christian worship, either the passive power to receive grace or the active power to dispense it.[217] This receptivity to grace seems to be the particular quality of the baptismal character, which opens the door to the reception of all the other sacraments. Those without the baptismal character, then, seem limited in their capacity to receive further graces. Moreover, though the sacraments pertain to the worship of Christ on earth, Thomas insists that the mark of sacramental character remains with the soul in the afterlife.[218] According to the logic of Aquinas's argument, those baptized only with desire (or blood) lack this glory in the afterlife. We have already seen Aquinas suggest temporal advantages of water baptism, the ability to participate in the Church's life on earth and a shortened purgatory. His theology of character suggests an eternal benefit as well.

Implicit desire. The final issue that must loom large in any contemporary account of baptism of desire is the question of implicit desire. Most contemporary authors dealing with the issue recognize that some idea of implicit desire is necessary to link baptism of desire to the salvation of non-Christians.[219] Like Hugh of St. Victor, Thomas uses the language of implicit desire; his concept of implicit desire is both precise and robust. To understand how Thomas uses the idea, we might begin with the way he addresses another problem in medieval sacramental theology that occasionally arises on the periphery of debate over baptism of desire: Why is the Eucharist less necessary for salvation than baptism? The biblical language on the necessity of these sacraments is nearly identical (compare Jn 3:5 to Jn 6:53), but the Church has consistently held that those dying after baptism but before receiving communion can be saved. Thomas

---

217. *ST*, 3.63.2. This suggests that Aquinas conceives of baptism of desire as achieving only the first of the sacrament's purposes, the (partial) remission of sins. What is left out, however, is hardly trivial since participation in Christian worship is participation in the action of Christ. As M. Dauphinais puts it, "character provides the basic identity of the Christian." Michael Dauphinais, "Christ and the Metaphysics of Baptism in the *Summa theologiae* and the *Commentary on John*," in *Rediscovering Aquinas and the Sacraments*, ed. Matthew Levering and Michael Dauphinais (Chicago: Hillenbrand Books, 2009), loc. 597 of 3969, Kindle.

218. Thomas Aquinas, *ST*, 3.63.5, ad 3.

219. For example, Jennifer Hart Weed, "Thomas Aquinas and the Baptism of Desire," *Res Philosophica* 96, no. 1 (2019): 77–78.

answers that the desire for the Eucharist is implicit in the reception of baptism: "by Baptism a man is ordained to the Eucharist; and therefore from the fact of children being baptized, they are destined by the Church to the Eucharist; and just as they believe through the Church's faith, so they desire the Eucharist through the Church's intention." On the other hand, "they are not disposed for Baptism by any previous sacrament."[220] This response does not diminish the necessity of the Eucharist in itself, allowing us to see communion with the Lord as essential to the meaning of salvation. Instead, it relies on the notion of desire, or "being ordered toward something in intention," to use Thomas's somewhat clunky language. For this desire to be salvific, the individual need not say aloud, "I desire to receive the Eucharist," nor even formulate the sentence mentally. Desire for the Eucharist is implicit in an action already taken, being baptized. The nature of baptism fully and properly understood implies reception of the Eucharist, so by receiving the first, one necessarily intends the second. The same would not hold, however, if one misunderstood the meaning of baptism in such a way as to refuse the reception of the Eucharist.[221] In other words, it is possible for erroneous beliefs or disordered desires to undercut a potentially salvific implicit desire. We also should note that simply having a generic desire is not enough to generate an effective implicit desire. While saying "I desire baptism" implies "I desire Eucharist," saying "I desire to participate in a ritual" could equally well imply sacrificing prisoners to the Aztec gods. Implicit error is just as possible as implicit faith, and "if anything false is signified in outward worship, this worship will be pernicious."[222] The possibility of false worship makes increasing the generality of one's desires less, not more, likely to lead to salvation.

For Thomas, then, an implicit desire is something that, while itself not articulated, is necessarily implied by an explicit action or desire (or

220. Thomas Aquinas, *ST*, 3.73.3. He also says that baptism is necessary to start the spiritual life, while the Eucharist is its consummation.

221. Such a refusal would amount to contempt for the sacrament, as Thomas's treatment of confirmation makes clear: "all sacraments are in some way necessary for salvation: but some, so that there is no salvation without them; some as conducing to the perfection of salvation; and thus it is that Confirmation is necessary for salvation: although salvation is possible without it, provided it be not omitted out of contempt." *ST*, 3.72.1, ad 3.

222. *ST*, 2-2.93.1. See also, 2-2.92–94.

some combination of these). Put another way, an "implicit desire" is the same thing as an only partially explicit desire; there is no such thing as an *entirely* implicit desire. This is consistent with Aquinas's general understanding of how the human will works. In order for our amorphous inclinations to be directed toward specific actions we need at least enough knowledge to form an object of intention or desire.[223] Our desires might in various ways be poorly understood, but they still must have some object. Here we might observe that the very concreteness of the sacraments aids human salvation because it helps us to direct our desires into real action. Thomas's way of understanding implicit desire suggests confidence in salvific desire among determined but not-yet-fully-catechized catechumens.[224] In the absence of any anti-sacramental heresies, someone who died unexpectedly with a sincere faith in Christ might ordinarily be expected to receive baptism of desire, even if he had not yet read John 3:5. He need not, like Valentinian, have made an appointment for the sacrament with his bishop.

But what of those without explicit knowledge of Christ? For Aquinas, knowledge of Christ seems to be intrinsic to salvation. Thus, he states, "belief of some kind in the mystery of Christ's Incarnation was necessary at all times and for all persons." Still, he adds, "this belief differed according to differences of times and persons."[225] Like Hugh of St. Victor, Thomas recognizes that certain individuals throughout history have been given greater knowledge of the specifics of the Christian mysteries, either through revelation or preaching, and that simple people are not bound to explicit knowledge of, for example, the whole content of scripture.[226] Belief before the Incarnation was necessarily less complete than it is among those who have received the Gospel, though Aquinas seems to think that revelation allowed many of those saved before Christianity to have some intuition of the Christian mysteries, such as John the Baptist's knowledge of the Passion. When he deals with the "sacraments" of the Old

223. On the dynamic relationship between intellect and will, see Stump, *Aquinas*, 277–78.

224. As Matthew Levering puts it, "desire for the sacrament of baptism belongs to right faith itself." Matthew Levering, *Paul in the Summa theologiae* (Washington, DC: The Catholic University of America Press, 2014), 98.

225. Thomas Aquinas, *ST*, 2-2.2.7. Belief in Christ implies faith in the Trinity, according to Thomas, and Trinitarian faith is implied in the act of baptism. *ST*, 2-2.2.8.

226. *ST*, 2-2.2.5–6.

Law and those that preceded it—such as the sacrifices of Melchizedek or Job—Thomas states that these were not endowed with the power to cause sanctifying grace, but that they nonetheless allowed men to profess their faith in Christ's (still future) Passion.[227] In the case of these rites, what is implicit—desire for the coming of the Messiah—is more salvific than the actions themselves. The centrality of desire, in turn, makes it possible for us to use baptism of desire as the paradigm for understanding salvation even in a pre-Christian context.[228] It also allows us to see why Aquinas believes that Old Testament rites would no longer be salvific after the coming of Christ. The legal terminology of the scholastics can sometimes make the shift from the Old to the New Covenant seem like a contract's arbitrary expiration date—a problem in Bernard's letter to Hugh—but Thomas allows us to see a consistent, underlying logic. The old rites derived their salvific power only because they implied the new. Now that the new rites are available, if the old are practiced in their place, this can only be because they are being improperly understood. In other words, if practiced as an alternative to the new rites, the old rites negate what they were meant to imply in the first place. Moreover, the Eucharist is implied more directly in baptism than in the sacrifices of the Jerusalem Temple; the more explicitly Christian a rite, the less prone it is to erroneous interpretations.

What of cases even more remote from Christian revelation than those mentioned in the Old Testament? Aquinas seems to think that some sort of contact with explicit revelation is always necessary for salvation. Several times he cites Hebrews 11:6 to the effect that for salvation one must believe that God "exists and that he rewards those who seek him." But he notes that the verse lays down a necessary but not sufficient condition for salvation.[229] One's understanding of God's reward, for Aquinas, must also involve belief in Christ. In the most remote possibility for salvation he discusses—Gentiles who have not received any special revelation—Aquinas says salvation would be possible if they had come to believe that

227. *ST*, 3.62.6; 3.61.3.

228. Michael Dauphinais and Matthew Levering emphasize the longing of the prophets (Mt 13:17) in Aquinas's account of salvation history, in *Knowing the Love of Christ* (Notre Dame, IN: University of Notre Dame Press, 2002), 106–7.

229. Thomas Aquinas, *ST*, 2-2.2.8, ad 1.

God would deliver mankind through a mediator.[230] Since he had earlier argued that reason alone is insufficient to attain salvation, however, it is hard to see how one could come to have correct, if incomplete, faith in a mediator without some contact with revelation.[231] The "common and confused knowledge of God which is found in practically all men" is insufficient for salvation.[232]

We can gain further context for what Aquinas says in the *Summa* about the necessity of (some) explicit Christian faith by turning to *De veritate*, where he makes the argument at somewhat greater length. The contours of the argument are already familiar. What must be explicitly believed varies according to the era in which one lives and one's station in life; teachers are required by their position to affirm more than do simple believers, whose faith in the Church allows many doctrinal specifics to remain implicit.[233] Still, faith cannot be entirely unformed; it cannot, in other words, be entirely passive but must be capable of correctly directing our actions.[234] Because heavenly glory is higher than any natural good, natural reason alone is not capable of directing our actions toward beatitude.[235] Aquinas tackles two limit cases to flesh out his thinking. The first is that of Gentile believers saved before Christ; since Gentiles were not recipients of the Mosaic revelation, they all fit within the category of "simple believers."[236] So, explicit knowledge of the Trinity, for example, was not necessary for them—though it is today, even for common believers. Instead, "it was enough for them to have implicit faith in the Redeemer, either as part of their belief in the faith of the law

---

230. *ST*, 2-2.2.7, ad 3. "Aquinas's elaborate discussions of implicit faith can be taken as confirming this point: it is clear in these discussions that the object of faith always includes some specifically Christian content." J.A. DiNoia, "Implicit Faith, General Revelation and the State of Non-Christians," *The Thomist* 47, no. 2 (1983): 229.

231. Thomas Aquinas, *ST*, 2-2.2.3; 1-2.109.6; cf. 1-2.5.5.

232. Thomas Aquinas, *Summa contra Gentiles 3:I*, trans. Vernon J. Bourke (Notre Dame, IN: University of Notre Dame Press, 1975), 38.1–2, pp. 125–26. Here, too, he makes the point that generic knowledge is more prone to error. *Summa contra Gentiles 3:I*, 38.6, pp. 126–27. On the contrast between the knowledge of faith and natural knowledge, see *Summa contra Gentiles 3:I*, 40, pp. 130–32.

233. Thomas Aquinas, *Quaestiones disputatae de veritate*, trans. Robert W. Mulligan, James V. McGlynn, and Robert W. Schmidt, ed. J. Kenny (1952–1954), https://isidore.co/aquinas/QDdeVer.htm, 14.11.

234. *Quaestiones disputatae de veritate*, 14.6.

235. *Quaestiones disputatae de veritate*, 14.10.

236. *Quaestiones disputatae de veritate*, 14.11, ad 5.

and the prophets, or as part of their belief in divine providence itself."
Here Thomas seems to have in mind both those Gentiles who had some
contact with the Hebrew people and those who arrived at faith through
other means; he considers it probable that many Gentiles received special
revelation, such as through the Sibylline oracles. We see here too that
Aquinas understands Hebrews 11:6 in the strong sense of requiring faith
in Christ, if only as the future savior. Again, one's explicit beliefs cannot
imply error if they are to be salvific.[237]

The second even more extreme case Aquinas addresses is that of a
theoretical boy raised by wolves in the wilderness. Aquinas raises the
objection that, if explicit faith is necessary, this means that the boy will
inevitably be damned, which he regards as an untenable conclusion. He
does not, however, back off the claim that "everyone is bound to believe
something explicitly." Instead, his solution is to point out that providence
could devise a way to reveal the truths of the faith to the boy either by
sending a preacher—as happened to Cornelius—or through a special interior illumination, such as that received by the prophets and apostles.[238]
Aquinas seems to imagine this happening only in the rare case of someone like Cornelius, who lives virtuously according to natural reason; he
adds the principle that, even though faith is not within our own power
to obtain, if we do all within our power to follow the teaching of natural
reason, "God will not withhold from us that which we need."[239]

What is perhaps surprising to modern readers is that even in such
an extreme scenario Aquinas does not simply waive the requirement
of explicit Christian faith altogether. Such a solution would be tenable
only if Aquinas saw the problem as primarily juridical in nature. But,
though he often uses the canonical language that had become a staple of
medieval theological discourse, Thomas does not lose sight of the more
fundamental ideas which this language describes. He understands that
eliminating certain "rules" is not a matter of dispensing with formalities but of changing the nature of salvation. For Thomas, neither faith in
Jesus Christ nor the sacraments are formalities. Having enough correct

---

237. *Quaestiones disputatae de veritate*, 14.10, ad 10.
238. *Quaestiones disputatae de veritate*, 14.11, obj. and ad 1; for perspective on interior illuminations, see 18.4.
239. *Quaestiones disputatae de veritate*, 14.11, ad 2.

knowledge of Christ to form an active desire to participate in his saving action—which we do through the sacraments—defines salvation. One could have a somewhat happy afterlife without this—God could shower an unbeliever with an eternity of champagne breakfasts—but that existence would not be the salvation proclaimed by the Gospel.

Not losing sight of this fundamental insight will be crucial as we move into the centuries that follow, as a profusion of "Thomists" seek to understand the implications of baptism of desire in light of the challenges of Early Modernity. Thomas's ability to penetrate to what is most deeply at stake theologically will make the Angelic Doctor worth returning to when we consider how best to formulate the doctrine of baptism of desire in our own day. The shift from Peter Lombard's understanding of the doctrine as an exception to the law of baptism to the idea, more strongly present in the *Summa*, that desire can provide a partial participation in the sacrament is as important as it is easy to miss. Thomas's sophisticated treatment of necessity and implicit faith still provides the most solid starting point from which to address these complex issues. At the same time, when it comes to the problems baptism of desire raises, the question of why Thomas's treatment of sacramental character becomes so uncharacteristically awkward will also require our attention. As the centuries progress we will see the same concepts found in the *Summa* deployed by other theologians, but few will be able to match Thomas's cogency and insight.

The Denouement of the Medieval Debate

Colish notes waning theological interest in baptism of desire as the thirteenth century drew to a close, no doubt largely due to the success the doctrine had come to enjoy.[240] As noted above, within the span of Aquinas's career we can perceive a shift from concern with whether baptism of desire is possible to the doctrine's broader implications for theology. This shift is perceptible in the writings of other theologians of the time. Peter of Tarentaise (1225–1276), a Dominican elected pope two years after Aquinas's death, addressed the issue in his own commentary on the *Sentences* (written shortly after that of Thomas, around 1257–1259). His

240. Colish, *Faith, Fiction & Force*, 87.

preface to Book IV, Distinction 4 rehashes the standard arguments in favor of the doctrine, making use of the *res/sacramentum* framework and drawing heavily on Augustine's *De Baptismo*.[241] Ambrose is invoked both in the preface and in a later article to emphasize that baptism of desire is sufficient for salvation—so long, of course, as the sacrament is omitted only because of *articulus necessitatis* and not *contemptus religionis*.[242] The primary difficulty the future pope wrestles with, however, is how to reconcile the doctrine of Peter Lombard's *Sentences* with the necessity of baptism. His approach differs slightly from that of previous thinkers, including the Lombard and Thomas. Peter of Tarentaise frames the issue in terms of whether those already justified are still required to be baptized. He believes that the answer must be affirmative; Cornelius, after all, went on to be baptized. But if one posits that someone has already received the *res* of baptism, then the sacrament seems to have lost its primary purpose. Peter of Tarentaise seems to accept the Lombard's contention that baptism *flaminis* does not revoke the full punishment of sin, but his main answer takes a different line. Baptism has two effects, he says. For the individual, it remits sin. The obligation imposed by precept, however, reflects baptism's second effect of distinguishing the people of God from those outside the Church. He seems to concede that in a case like Cornelius's the waters of baptism do not wash away sin (though they may eliminate some residual punishment), but that the value of baptism as a public sign remains. His is not an entirely satisfactory answer, since it seems to create two baptisms, each at fifty-percent strength. In Peter's account, Christ's command to baptize—the precept—remains an ordinance useful for Church order, but the sacrament's connection to salvation becomes purely negative; by failing to observe the precept, one risks losing the salvation already granted. In fact, his answer reflects the tendency of legal categories to obscure what happens in the ritual itself; the language and symbolism of the baptismal liturgy would ring false if the rite did not involve dying and rising to new life. Peter puts his finger on a problem, but his solution is inadequate.

---

241. Peter of Tarentaise, *In IV Librum Sententiarum Commentaria*, vol. 4, ed. J.-B. de Marinis (Toulouse: Arnaldum Colomerium, 1651; repr. Ridgewood, NJ: Gregg Press, 1964), 4, preface, pp. 39–42; cf. Colish, *Faith, Fiction & Force*, 85–87.

242. Peter of Tarentaise, *Sententiarum Commentaria*, 4.2.2–3, pp. 49–50.

Scotus. Dissatisfaction with this aspect of the theology of baptism of desire is also perceptible in the limited treatment the topic received from the final towering figure of medieval theology, the Oxford master John Duns Scotus (1266–1308). Colish claims that Scotus eliminates baptism of desire, insisting on the necessity of the ritual except in the case of martyrdom.[243] This is not quite correct. In his *Ordinatio*—lectures following the usual pattern of commentary on the *Sentences*—Scotus poses the question Peter of Tarentaise had asked, whether those already justified are bound to receive baptism.[244] Here he mentions baptism *flaminis*, though he sees no need to defend the concept.[245] Instead, the possibility of receiving the *res* of baptism before the sacrament is simply the premise of the question. Scotus does not deny the premise, even if he does not seem overly enthusiastic about it. His argument is that the possibility of receiving the *res* without the sacrament does not make the command laid down in John 3:5 less binding. This precept was universally promulgated, he says, and universal precepts oblige unless an exception is included in their promulgation.[246]

This answer is not quite the same thing as a denial of the possibility of salvation in a case like Valentinian's. Instead, Scotus's argument deals with the weight of obligation on the living. Responding to the observation that baptism of blood can take the place of the font, he says that it does so only because the martyr dies; sacramental obligations bind only in this life.[247] In fact, someone who suffered but did not die for the faith—perhaps escaping after torture—would not receive a complete baptism *sanguinis* and would still be obligated to seek the sacrament. Like Thomas, Scotus recognizes the problem with performing a baptism that no longer conveys the

243. Colish, *Faith, Fiction & Force*, 79–80.

244. John Duns Scotus, *Opera Omnia*, ed. B. Hechich et al., vol. 11, *Ordinatio IV, dist. 1–7* (Vatican City: Typis Vaticanis, 2008), dist. 4, pars 3, q. unica, n. 120, p. 261.

245. In a parallel passage in another version of his lectures compiled from student notes, Scotus includes both adults and children. John Duns Scotus, *Reportata Parisiensia IV*, in *Opera Omnia, editio minor,* vol. 2, bk. 2, *Opera Theologica*, ed. Giovanni Lauriola (Alberobello: Editrice AGA, 1999), dist. 4, q. 6, n. 85, p. 1304. This does not imply an extension of the concept of baptism of desire to infants, but is prompted by cases like Jeremiah or John the Baptist who receive grace in the womb. He argues that such individuals are still obligated to be baptized once born. Baptism *flaminis* is also mentioned in Scotus's discussion of baptisms carried out by an unworthy minister. *Ordinatio IV*, dist 5. q 2. n. 43, 50, pp. 291, 293.

246. John Duns Scotus, *Ordinatio IV*, dist. 4, pars 3. q. unica, n. 126–27, p. 262.

247. *Ordinatio IV*, dist 4, pars 3, q. unica, n. 134, p. 265.

res; he raises the objections that receiving baptism "in vain" does injury to the sacrament by making it a false sign. His answer to these objections is a bit muddled; in the end, it amounts to the assertion that the sacrament still confers grace in such circumstances, though it is only an increase in grace rather than justification.[248] One senses here that Scotus is not interested in devoting more time to the issue of baptism *flaminis* because it seems to have little practical relevance. If one is alive, one is obligated to be baptized to attain salvation. If one receives the grace of justification while still unbaptized but neglects the sacrament, one forfeits salvation. Scotus does not deny the possibility of baptism *flaminis*, but, since one's obligations remain unaltered, his way of treating the idea significantly devalues it. The salvation of those who receive *flaminis* is still conditional upon reception of the sacrament. The same critique could not be made in a case like that of Valentinian when, as with martyrs, death frees one of earthly obligations.

Scotus's terse treatment of baptism of desire reveals the limits of the medieval theology of the concept. The notion of a pre-baptismal baptism of desire cannot quite be reconciled with the *lex orandi*—that is, with the logic expressed in the celebration of the sacrament—which is why Peter Lombard, Thomas, and Peter of Tarentaise struggle to explain what good the sacrament serves in such circumstances. Scotus's abbreviated treatment of the concept could be thought of as a dour verdict: Since baptism *flaminis* requires that one still be baptized anyway, then perhaps it is not worth spilling much ink on the topic.

At the close of this chapter, it is worth reflecting on how this particular conundrum was made possible by the developments we observed in the early Middle Ages: the diminishment of the baptismal ritual as an existential turning point; the social milieu of Christendom making it possible to take baptism for granted; and the abstract and forensic style of scholastic theology. Scotus's question would have been incomprehensible in the mystagogy of the Fathers. His answer relies entirely on the notion of legal obligation.

As we will see more fully in the next chapter, Scotus's emphasis on obligation would prove of more enduring consequence to the theology of baptism of desire than anything in his direct treatment of the subject. We

---

248. John Duns Scotus, *Reportata Parisiensia IV*, dist 4. q. 6. n. 98–99, p. 1306.

need not enter into a technical discussion of the Subtle Doctor's thought to note the tendency toward ethical voluntarism in his work.[249] That is, Scotus concludes from God's absolute omnipotence that for something to be right or wrong it is enough for God simply to declare it to be so. This way of thinking predisposes Scotus to be satisfied with reliance on precept as such. The same ethical tendency is even more pronounced in the work of Scotus's fellow Franciscan, William of Ockham (1288–1347). Ockham's commentary on the *Sentences* makes only passing reference to baptism *flaminis*, confirming Colish's observation of waning theological interest in the topic.[250] As with Scotus, scholars disagree over the precise degree of Ockham's ethical voluntarism, but for us it is enough to observe that an Ockhamist way of thinking makes it easier to see baptism's necessity simply as a matter of sacramental legislation.

As the golden age of scholasticism came to a close, the theology of baptism of desire had arrived at an equilibrium that was stable on the surface but hid certain fault lines. The three centuries from Anselm of Laon to William of Ockham were a period of remarkable theological development. While baptism of desire seems not to have been much considered —if at all—during the early Middle Ages and had aroused considerable theological passion around the time of Abelard and Bernard, by the late medieval period, it seemed clear to most theologians that the desire for baptism could, under limited circumstances, be salvific for adults. Thomas and, to lesser extent, Hugh of St. Victor provided a way to conceive of the theory most in line with its patristic roots, as a partial participation in the sacrament through the will. This contrasted with other thinkers, from Bernard to Scotus, who considered the doctrine purely in terms of legal obligation. How explicit one's desire for baptism had to be and how the effects of baptism of desire differed from the sacrament remained

249. For an introduction to this question, see Richard Cross, *Duns Scotus* (New York: Oxford University Press, 1999), 83–100.

250. William of Ockham, *Opera Theologica*, ed. Rega Wood, Gedeon Gál, and Romualdo Green, vol. 7, *Quaestiones in Librum Quartum Sententiarum* (St. Bonaventure, NY: The Franciscan Institute of St. Bonaventure University, 1984), quaestio 5, p. 53; quaestio 10, p. 216. On Ockham's voluntarism, see Marilyn McCord Adams, "Ockham on Will, Nature, and Morality," and Peter King, "Ockham's Ethical Theory," in *The Cambridge Companion to Ockham*, ed. Paul Vincent Spade (New York: Cambridge University Press, 1999), 245–72, 227–44.

unsettled questions. Compared to the Fathers, the scholastic approach of Peter Lombard and others relied less on the liturgical act itself and more on secondary categories such as the *res sacramenti*. Such categories tended to reduce baptism to a delivery vehicle for an abstract *res*. It is doubtful, however, that such abstraction appeared problematic at the time. The importance of the rite was felt so deeply from the top to the bottom of medieval society that newborns were customarily rushed to the font within hours of their birth. In such a society, baptism of desire, like a boy raised by wolves in the forest, remained a largely theoretical discussion. In the coming centuries, that—and much else in Christendom—was about to change.

Chapter Four

The Crosscurrents of
Early Modernity

In 1347, a few months after the death of William of Ockham, the bacterium *Yersinia pestis* arrived via rat fleas in the port of Messina, Sicily. In the years that followed, between a third and half of Europe's population was wiped out and the continent's intellectual life was dealt a devastating setback. On the question of baptism of desire, theologians of the century or so after the Black Death followed Ockham's lead, aware of the idea—still referred to mostly as *baptismus flaminis*—but not much interested in exploring it. In 1442, the Council of Florence, without addressing baptism of desire, pronounced one of the magisterium's strongest affirmations of the necessity of the Church for salvation.[1] This emphasis on membership in the Church—with baptism taken for granted and the Great Western Schism (1378–1417) a recent memory—reflected the concerns of an almost uniformly Christian society in which heresy or schism were perceived as greater practical threats to salvation than the omission of the rite. But change was brewing. When the bishops of East and West met in Florence for their ultimately unsuccessful attempt at reconciliation, the

---

1. *Enchiridion symbolorum*, 1351.

Renaissance, with its rediscovery—and idealization—of antiquity, was blossoming in the same city. By the end of the century, Portuguese and Spanish explorers would redraw the map of the known world, adding new nations and continents. And early in the following century, the Reformation would add new colors to Europe's religious map as well.

As theologians confronted these new landscapes, baptism of desire enjoyed its own sort of renaissance. The doctrine was recognized as relevant to discussions about the salvation of those pagans—now much admired—living before Christ as well as those living in an analogous situation in the New World. Perhaps surprisingly, however, the discoveries of the fifteenth century did not fundamentally change the way either missionaries or theologians thought about salvation. Instead, they prompted thinkers such as Francisco de Vitoria to apply concepts developed in previous centuries, such as baptism of desire, with greater precision. Vitoria and others quickly recognized that individuals living in the newly discovered territories would not be punished for their ignorance of Christianity, but that such ignorance did not excuse them from other sins, eliminate original sin, or make them participants in the Paschal Mystery. And the era's boldest theological suggestion had nothing to do with the New World, but with the age-old problem of infants dying without baptism.

Baptism of desire also received a warm reception at the era's greatest ecclesiastical event, the Council of Trent. Trent's precise words on the topic might be considered the zenith in the fortunes of Ambrose's doctrine, but, in this case, fortune proved fleeting. Almost as soon as baptism of desire had received its Tridentine affirmation, it disappeared into the labyrinth of post-Tridentine scholasticism. Baroque scholasticism focused, instead, on the minimum of faith necessary for salvation, producing ever more abstruse distinctions but few lasting results. Included in these modern developments was the Jansenist controversy—an arid landscape for baptism of desire but one which would have important future reverberations.

Theology Discovers America

Historians looking for a convenient date to signal the transition from the medieval to the modern world often pick 1492. Columbus's landing on Hispaniola changed the way people imagined the planet on which they lived. It put Europeans in touch with profoundly different cultures, with both creative and tragic results. It forever reshaped geopolitics. Sixteenth century exploration also corresponded with a Catholic missionary endeavor of unmatched energy and scope.[2] It is natural enough, then, that we begin this chapter with these discoveries. The evidence, however, will compel us to break with what has come to be the conventional narrative about theology and the Age of Discovery. The theologians of the era did not find the doctrines bequeathed to them by the tradition to be inadequate, and the exploration of the globe provoked no grand rethinking of medieval soteriology. Instead, theologians applied their medieval tools to the new circumstances, using them with greater precision but producing no revolution.

New World—Old Problems

Twentieth century theologians routinely pointed to the discovery of the Americas and the exploration of Asia and Africa by Spanish, Portuguese, and Dutch sailors as a turning point in Christian attitudes toward salvation. For Catholic theologians inclined to a more "inclusivist" view, this is a particularly attractive position since it provides a relatively benign way to claim continuity with a tradition that, as we have seen, emphatically maintained that there is no salvation outside of the Church. In this interpretation, medieval thinkers had been hampered by their uncritical assumption that "the world was practically co-extensive with Christendom."[3] The shattering of this assumption by the discovery of unevangelized continents forced a rethinking of Christianity's claims about salvation; confronted with a new set of geographical facts, theologians made "progress" toward a less exclusivist soteriology. The claims of the past could be set aside—or, better, "reinterpreted"—without casting into doubt the authority of Catholic doctrine. As Francis Sullivan puts it, the discovery of America presented a "new problem" for soteriology.[4]

2. Contemporary Protestants, by contrast, tended to hold negative opinions about sending missionaries overseas due to the movement's emphasis on predestination. Ronnie Po-Chia Hsia, "Theological Developments in the Non-European World, 1500–1800," in *The Oxford Handbook of Early Modern Theology, 1600–1800*, ed. Ulrich L. Lehner, Richard A. Muller, and A.G. Roeber (New York: Oxford University Press, 2016), 13.

3. Sullivan, *Salvation Outside the Church?* 69.

4. Sullivan, 71.

As we have already begun to see, the facts do not quite fit this story. Baptism was considered to be necessary for salvation whether Christians were in the minority or majority, whether the unevangelized were thought to be many or few. Sullivan's "new problem" might be expressed thus:

> A man is born upon the bank along the Indus, with no one there to speak, or read, or write of Christ, and all that he desires, everything he does, is good. As far as human reason can discern, he is sinless in his deeds and in his words. He dies unbaptized, dies outside the faith. Wherein lies the justice that condemns him? Wherein lies his fault if he does not believe?[5]

These words, however, are those of Dante Alighieri (d. 1321), and the problem he raises does not change if one replaces the Indus with the Mississippi. In 1492, Columbus listed the conversion of unevangelized peoples first among the reasons for embarking on his voyages.[6] This is not to say that the discoveries of the late fifteenth century did not provoke theological reflection and development. They did, as we will see. But that development did not add fundamentally new elements to the theology of salvation. Neither theologians nor missionaries thought that Christian doctrine on the necessity of the sacraments for salvation had developed on the basis of false premises.

Secular historians have sometimes been more clear-headed than theologians in their assessment of the effect of early modernity's discoveries. Philosopher John Marenbon, for example, sums up the overall effect of the age with sobriety:

> The Middle Ages in Western Europe are frequently associated with narrowness and religious bigotry, and the Renaissance and seventeenth century with the beginnings of the Enlightenment. It would be natural, therefore, to expect that attitudes to pagans would progress from medieval severity, according to which pagans lacked know-

5. Dante Alighieri, *Paradiso*, trans. Robert Hollander and Jean Hollander (New York: Doubleday, 2007), 19.70–78, p. 465. Dante's answer echoes God's answer to Job from the whirlwind and Paul's words in Rom 9:20: "But who are you, a man, to answer back to God?" The way we see the problem "from a thousand miles away" (v. 80) is not the way God sees it. Dante does, interestingly, hint at a kind of baptism of desire operative before Christianity. *Paradiso*, 20.127–29, p. 490.

6. Samuel E. Morison, *Admiral of the Ocean Sea: A Life of Christopher Columbus* (Boston: Northeastern University Press, 1983), 153–54.

ledge and virtue and were heading for eternal punishment, to Early
Modern toleration, in which pagan goodness, wisdom and salvation were widely accepted. But there was no such progression. No
sixteenth- or seventeenth-century writer pleaded the pagan case
more fervently than Abelard in the twelfth century. No early medieval ascetic (nor even Augustine himself) so willingly accepted the
wickedness of pagans as many seventeenth-century Protestants and
Jansenists.[7]

Marenbon equally rejects a general progression in the opposite direction, toward greater stringency. Sixteenth century discoveries may have
changed the relative numbers of those thought to be pagans, but it did
not change the theological principles involved in the question of salvation. "Such unchangingness is remarkable," Marenbon concludes, "because according to almost every historical account, the three centuries
involved were a time of epochal change, […] and the most emblematic
event of the new era, Columbus's voyages, had a direct bearing on the
Problem of Paganism." To anticipate somewhat—if the discovery of the
Americas caused any shift in the direction of Christian soteriology, this
shift came centuries later and was the result of the way these unevangelized continents came to be used in Enlightenment polemics. It was not
based on new data gained from the discovery itself.

To arrive at an accurate, if less black-and-white, understanding of
the theology of this era—and the way in which it employed the doctrine
of baptism of desire—we need both to avoid exaggerating medieval ignorance and to appreciate the diversity of forces shaping early modern
theology. It is true, for example, that both patristic and medieval writers
tended to overestimate the extent of the Gospel's spread throughout the
world.[8] But this misperception was never decisive because the real ob-

---

7. Marenbon, *Pagans and Philosophers*, 304. Alberto Frigo agrees that early modern thinkers
worked out their reaction to the "renewal of pagan antiquity" and the discovery of America
within the conceptual framework developed by medieval scholastic theologians. "The debate
on the virtues and salvation of the pagans was certainly transformed, but this transformation
mainly consisted in readjustments of old positions, or in a more systematic use of hypotheses
fleetingly presented by previous authors." Alberto Frigo, introduction to Inexcusabiles: *Salvation and the Virtues of the Pagans in the Early Modern Period*, ed. Alberto Frigo (Cham: Springer,
2020), 5.

8. Some used the words of Ps 19:4, quoted by Paul in Rom 10:18, to the effect that God's
words "have gone out to all the earth" to support the belief that no one could claim ignorance

stacle to salvation, as they saw it, was not ignorance but original sin. The universal difficulty of finding any way to salvation for unbaptized children reinforces this conclusion. Some medieval thinkers even acknowledged— if in convoluted ways—the possibility of the occasional virtuous pagan emerging from the Muslim world. Dante, for example, puts Saladin along- side Homer, Caesar, and Socrates in limbo.[9] Moreover, medieval misper- ceptions also worked in the other direction, at times supporting a more expansive view of salvation. Christian scholars tended to exaggerate the putative virtues of those pagans they admired to justify squeezing them into heaven. We saw this in the medieval legend of Trajan's conversion. The paradigmatic recipient of such hagiography was Aristotle. Idealization of the ancients reached a crescendo with the humanism of the 1400s. In 1499, for example, the Thomist Lambertus de Monte published the tract *De salvatione Aristotelis* arguing explicitly for the philosopher's salvation.[10] One of the reasons the seventeenth century Jansenist, Antoine Arnauld, whom we will meet at the end of this chapter, was dismissive of the salva- tion of pagan philosophers was precisely because his historical perceptions were more "modern." By his day, historical criticism had shown that the "Aristotle of faith" existed only in the minds of his Christian admirers.[11]

Of course, any difficulty we might have understanding earlier genera- tions of Christians results not only from their beliefs, but also from ours. It is worth pausing briefly to consider some of the diverging presupposi- tions that make the fifteenth century such foreign territory. For example,

---

of the Gospel as an excuse for unbelief. John Major, who we will encounter shortly, was trou- bled by the fact that these verses no longer seemed to have been fulfilled, though that disap- pointment stems less from soteriological considerations than from the fact that words used to praise God's grandeur were no longer so apt. These verses were woven into a web of often apoc- alyptic prophecy that also needed reinterpretation. Jacques Lafaye, *Quetzalcóatl and Guadalupe: The Formation of Mexican National Consciousness, 1531–1813*, trans. Benjamin Keen (Chicago: University of Chicago Press, 1976), 184.

9. Dante Alighieri, *Inferno*, 4.129, p. 69.

10. Marenbon, *Pagans and Philosophers*, 281–82. On the humanist "cult of the philoso- phers and pagan literati," see also S. Harent, "Infidèles (Salut des)," in *Dictionnaire du Théologie Catholique*, vol. 7, bk. 2, ed. A. Vacant, E. Mangenot, and E. Amann (Paris: Letouzey et Ané, 1923), 1749.

11. Craig Martin contrasts the scholastic view in which, quoting David Lindberg, "by the sixteenth century Aristotle had taken on the appearance of a Christian saint" with the opinion, "hardly controversial" today, that the Stagirite's philosophy is "incompatible with Christianity." Craig Martin, *Subverting Aristotle: Religion, History, and Philosophy in Early Modern Science* (Baltimore: Johns Hopkins University Press, 2014), 1, 4.

the reality of personal sin weighed more heavily on the consciousness of medieval and early modern Christians than it does, by and large, on Christians today.[12] The likelihood of great numbers of people living free of mortal sin anywhere in the world would not have seemed particularly high to any early modern thinker. Moreover, reports from explorers and missionaries in the New World included stories of such atrocities as cannibalism and human sacrifice. Adults facing punishment only for original sin, therefore, would have been few and far between. We should also consider that one's membership in a larger social group—family, community, and society—may have played a larger role in earlier generations' sense of identity than it does in our individualistic era. Cramer's analysis of the meaning of infant baptism in the Middle Ages is worth recalling here; he points out that the practice came to express the "feeling that the destiny of the child and that of his parents, or of the community into which he has been born, are one and the same."[13] That one's identity is shaped by social relationships even before one starts to make personal decisions makes infant baptism plausible. Our own inclination, therefore, might be to think it unfair to punish (but not reward?) someone who is simply following the beliefs and customs of the society in which he grew up. But someone from a pre-modern or non-Western culture might retort by asking, "After taking away one's upbringing, what of the individual is left?" Indeed, if most modern Westerners are inclined to an individualistic self-understanding, isn't this because we too are the products of a quite particular culture? All of this is to say that if one's personal identity is at least in part a reflection of one's social identity, the idea that social factors would play a strong role in salvation seems less surprising. This may explain why medieval and early modern writers generally reject the idea of a class of people incapable *in principle* of salvation, but they do not seem surprised if, as a practical matter, individuals in some groups are more likely to find salvation than others. Nothing in Christianity demands that the saved be evenly distributed historically or geographically.

Of course, Christianity offers potential rescue even from a sinful environment, and this possibility drove the missionaries of the sixteenth

12. It has become a commonplace to note the erosion of a "sense of sin" in the contemporary West; for example, John Paul II, Post-Synodal Apostolic Exhortation *Reconciliatio et Paenitentia* (December 2, 1984), 18.

13. Cramer, *Baptism and Change*, 133.

century. Here, too, we should perhaps reflect that, while in a work such as this it is natural to focus on the theological response to the discovery of new continents, early modern Catholics might have claimed that their primary response was not intellectual but missionary. Here they were self-consciously following the example of the apostolic Church, which also faced unevangelized continents. The presuppositions we have examined, including a strong belief in the necessity of baptism, motivated and sustained the missionary efforts of the sixteenth century just as they had those of the early Church. The reaction of missionaries to the people, cultures, and religious practices they encountered was varied—from repulsion and pity to admiration and compassion—and no doubt depended as much on the personality and outlook of each missionary as on the inhabitants of the mission territories. But it is worth noting that sixteenth century missionaries did not find anything they regarded as an obvious substitute for baptism in the non-Christian societies they encountered. This response held even for those who were strongly sympathetic to the peoples they encountered and cannot be chalked up to cultural prejudice.

The first theologians. The key theological change that occurred after 1492 was not the shift from a more to a less restrictive soteriology (or vice versa), but the application to the inhabitants of the New World of concepts originally developed with regard to the pagans of antiquity.[14] In other words, the scope, but not the fundamental nature, of the problem changed.[15] Very quickly European theologians seemed to accept that those who had not been exposed to either the Old or New Testaments were not at fault for their ignorance and would be held to "pre-Christian

14. Idealization of the ancients also transferred to other cultural contexts, as is shown by Jesuit missionary Matteo Ricci's attitude toward Chinese culture. Ricci (1552–1610) used the classical texts of Confucianism as an apologetic tool and expressed hope for the salvation of the ancient Chinese sages who adhered to them, while regarding contemporary Chinese intellectuals as atheists. As Marenbon puts it, Ricci "does, indeed, want to argue for the real salvation of many Chinese people, but only the ancient ones." Marenbon, *Pagans and Philosophers*, see footnote 33, p. 288; cf. 258–62.

15. Ilaria Morali posits a subtle shift in the way the question of salvation was framed, from a focus on individuals to peoples, in "*Gratia* ed *infidelitas*: nella Teologia di Francisco de Toledo e Francisco Suarez al tempo delle grandi missioni gesuitiche," *Studia missionalia* 55 (2006): 100. Even this somewhat overstates the case; when early moderns spoke of salvation among non-Christians, they too had in mind exceptional individuals, not, for example, the whole Aztec nation.

standards," whatever those were. The obvious conclusion of theologians evaluating the state of those who had died before the arrival of missionaries was that those exercising natural virtue would end up in limbo. This was the opinion of Baptistus of Mantua, the first theologian to address the question, writing within a decade of Columbus's first voyage.[16] His view was seconded by Abbot Johann Trithemius (1462–1516), responding to a query from Emperor Maximillian. Maximillian asked whether those who grew up in the recently discovered territories might have been saved through good works and the practice of whatever religion they happened to believe in. Trithemius insisted that Christian faith was necessary for salvation, though, if sinless in other ways, those who died without it would not suffer any punishment beyond the deprivation of the beatific vision.[17] Aquinas's theory of limbo, we should recall, described a happy state of existence—not the highest happiness, to be sure, but one without the suffering we experience on earth. Claude Seyssel (1458–1520), Archbishop of Turin, addressed the issue in some detail, allowing for the possibility of special revelation in extraordinary cases, and endorsing the idea of limbo for those who lived decently but knew nothing of the Gospel.[18] Baptism of desire does not seem to have played a significant role in these first assessments, though a more thorough examination of the work of these early writers could reveal otherwise.

The missionaries. Few churchmen were more sympathetic to the plight of the American Indians than the Dominican Bartolomé de Las Casas (1484–1576), later to become bishop of Chiapas. The fiery Las Casas became known as the "Defender and Apostle to the Indians" for denouncing atrocities committed against indigenous peoples in scathing terms, most famously in his *A Short Account of the Destruction of the Indies*, addressed to Philip II and published in 1552. Las Casas arrived in Hispaniola in 1502 and on his first return to Spain in 1515 denounced the

---

16. Marenbon, *Pagans and Philosophers*, 286.

17. Capéran, *Le problème du salut des infidèles*, vol. 1, *Essai historique*, 220–22; Marenbon, *Pagans and Philosophers*, 286–87.

18. Seyssel's work does not fit into the modern narrative of theological "progress" and is largely passed over today. Nonetheless, it continued to exercise influence into the following century in such works as Francesco Collius's 1622 *De Animabus Paganorum*. Capéran, *Le problème du salut des infidèles*, 1:222–25, 286–93; Marenbon, *Pagans and Philosophers*, 287.

brutality he had seen there to King Ferdinand. Making the outrages even more deplorable, for Las Casas, was the fact that the inhuman conduct of the conquistadores had impeded the work of evangelization, resulting in "the enormous loss of life as well as the infinite number of human souls despatched to Hell."[19] The Dominican describes the people of the Indies with warmth and repeatedly expresses his outrage that such brutality has resulted in many of them "having gone to their deaths with no knowledge of God and without the benefit of the Sacraments."[20]

The greatest of the sixteenth century missionaries—indeed, the patron saint of missionaries—the Jesuit Francis Xavier (1506–1552) likewise insisted on the necessity of baptism for salvation, even when doing so damaged his own missionary interests. A 1552 letter, written to his confreres in Europe, describes Xavier's experience in Japan, the hardships and dangers of the journey, the successes and failures of the mission, and local religious beliefs. Christian teaching on hell proved a point of contention; the Buddhist sects Xavier encountered believed in a hell from which souls could be freed by the penances and prayers of the Buddhist monks, the bonzes.[21] In Yamaguchi, where Xavier found faithful and enthusiastic converts, the absence of a comparable Christian remedy for deceased ancestors troubled the new Christians whom Xavier had taught that "no one can be saved if he does not adore God and believe in Jesus Christ."[22] From this the Japanese Christians drew the conclusion that any relatives who had died before the preaching of the Gospel were in hell. Though moved by the distress of his friends, Xavier concurred, adding that they should be diligent to avoid the fate of their ancestors. Xavier's biographer Georg Schurhammer argues that the incident could not have represented the saint's real views.[23] He points to references in Xavier's correspondence

19. Bartolomé de Las Casas, *A Short Account of the Destruction of the Indies*, trans. Nigel Griffin (Penguin Classics, 2004), loc. 764 of 2613, p. 6, Kindle. We need not enter here into controversies that continue to surround the complex missionary, his motives, and his legacy, though Las Casas continues to have critics, defenders, and those who would enlist his name in the service of modern causes.

20. *A Short Account of the Destruction of the Indies*, loc. 703, p. 13; cf. loc. 876, p. 26; loc. 1351, p. 64; loc. 2181, p. 126.

21. Francis Xavier, *The Letters and Instructions of Francis Xavier*, trans. and ed. M. Joseph Costelloe (St. Louis: The Institute of Jesuit Sources, 1992), 96.7–8, 20–23, pp. 328–29, 334–35.

22. Xavier, *Letters and Instructions*, 96.48–49, p. 341; 96.14, p. 332.

23. Georg Schurhammer, *Francis Xavier*, vol. 4, trans. M. Joseph Costelloe (Rome: The Jesuit Historical Institute, 1982), 235–36; see note 101.

to "the law of nature written in the heart of every man by the Creator through which all can be saved." Both this phrasing and the belief it expresses, however, are Schurhammer's, not Xavier's. Xavier did believe that God had placed the natural law into the hearts of all men, but—like Thomas Aquinas before him and the Council of Trent shortly after—he denied that following that law alone was sufficient for salvation. When he mentioned the natural law, Xavier was responding to the charge that it was unjust for God to punish people for violating moral laws that had not been explicitly revealed to them. The premise of the objection, then, is that non-Christians are punished for their sins. Xavier's response was that the moral law is known to everyone, so no one can plead invincible ignorance for violating the Ten Commandments. The pagans' punishment was, therefore, just.[24] In fact, Xavier drew almost exactly the opposite conclusion from the one Schurhammer suggests.

Aquinas and other medieval thinkers had argued that, if one did everything in one's power to obey the dictates of the natural law, God would provide the missing element of explicit faith through a preacher, angel, or interior illumination. Xavier did not see any evidence that this had happened before his arrival.[25] And, he indicates, the Japanese religion presented additional obstacles to salvation, particularly by failing to recognize God as creator.[26] The letter does include an intriguing reference to a learned convert to Christianity who had previously abandoned the teaching of the bonzes and "always adored the one who created the world."[27] Xavier does not explore the implications of this man's readiness for the Gospel, but there is no reason to think he would have seen it as a challenge to the medieval conventional wisdom. In the end, after all, Providence had sent the man a preacher, no less than Francis Xavier. Other Japanese Christians echoed Xavier's insistence on the necessity of Christian faith for salvation; in a contemporary account of the martyrdom of the Jesuit Paul Miki, crucified in Nagasaki in 1597, the Japanese saint declares, "I tell you plainly there is no way to be saved except the

24. Xavier, *Letters and Instructions*, 96.23–25, p. 335.

25. Xavier, *Letters and Instructions*, 96.35, p. 338: "I made great efforts in Japan to find out if they had ever received tidings about God and about Christ. From their writings and from what was said by the people, I discovered that they had never received tidings about God."

26. *Letters and Instructions*, 96.7, p. 328; 96.18–19, pp. 333–34.

27. *Letters and Instructions*, 96.44, p. 340.

Christian way [...] I do gladly pardon the Emperor and all who have sought my death. I beg them to seek baptism and be Christians themselves."[28]

Schurhammer's attempt to harmonize Xavier's beliefs with those of twentieth century thinkers such as Karl Rahner and Edward Schillebeeckx comes out of his desire to defend the saint from the accusation of holding "harsh and merciless" views. Here, however, a better approach is that suggested by historian Brad Gregory whose book on the martyrs of early modernity—both Protestant and Catholic—suggests that in order to learn from history we must seek to understand the people of earlier ages on their own terms, rather than squeezing them into our categories. He writes, "Fundamentally, my approach seeks simply to answer the question 'What did it [in this case, martyrdom] mean to them?'"[29] He points out that, for early modern Christians,

> hell was no "ideological construct," but a terrifying prospect for souls stained by sin, a danger magnified by thoughtless indifference. Quite correctly, they knew that if hell is real, then trying to disbelieve it away is folly [...] A relaxed attitude toward behavior would have been unconscionably negligent, "humane" moderation a monstrous inhumanity.[30]

While I believe that a robust theology of baptism of desire provides a more satisfying answer to the question the Christians of Yamaguchi posed to Xavier than what he offered in 1552, to condemn him or his words as "harsh and merciless" is anachronistic and presumptuous. Xavier's answer to the question of the salvation of non-believers was not a lecture delivered in a European classroom; it was a life of hardship, danger, and sacrifice poured out for the salvation of people who looked and lived and thought very differently than himself. Within a year of sending his letter on the Japanese missions to his companions in Europe, Xavier would die trying to reach China, sick and alone, on the island of Shangchuan. Such self-sacrifice is not the mark of a "harsh and merciless" outlook.

---

28. The account is included in the Office of Readings for St. Paul Miki and Companions (Feb. 6). *The Liturgy of the Hours*, vol. 3 (New York: Catholic Book Publishing, 1975), 1367–1368.

29. Brad S. Gregory, *Salvation at Stake: Christian Martyrdom in Early Modern Europe* (Cambridge, MA: Harvard University Press, 1999), 15.

30. Gregory, *Salvation at Stake*, 14.

Schurhammer is right, then, to defend Xavier, but trying to "modernize" his views is not the way to do so. Still, we should not forget that after his conversation with the Christians of Yamaguchi—"my friends, so loved and cherished"—Xavier himself felt a pang of sadness on their behalf. This seems to me to indicate some level of disquiet with the answer he was able to give, just as the Corinthians' first century practice of "baptizing the dead" pointed to a problem they were not quite able to solve.

Francisco de Vitoria and the School of Salamanca

One effect of the discovery of the New World was a sharpening of theological concepts. When speculating about philosophers who lived centuries ago, theologians could afford a certain amount of imprecision; when one needed to make decisions affecting whole nations in the present, greater clarity was necessary. No theologians contributed more to this process than the Spanish Dominicans of the University of Salamanca. There, a revival of Thomism coincided with a remarkably honest assessment of the moral and theological problems raised by the Spanish conquest of the New World. Originating with Francisco de Vitoria (1483–1546)—a brilliant legal theorist as well as theologian—the "School of Salamanca" would also influence Franciscan and Jesuit theologians of the following centuries. Today Vitoria's statue stands outside the United Nations building in New York with the inscription "*Fundador del derecho de gentes*" because of his role as one of the fathers of international law. Like his confrere Las Casas, Vitoria proved sympathetic to the rights of indigenous Americans. Salamanca also boasted such notable theologians as Melchor Cano (1509–1560) and Domingo de Soto (1494–1560), whose influence extended well into the following century.[31] The 1549 edition of Soto's *De natura et gratia* adds a somewhat novel argument in favor of baptism of desire based on the Church's liturgical practice—namely, that

31. On the necessity of the sacraments, see Dionisio Borobio, *Sacramentos en general: Bautismo y Confirmación en la Escuela de Salamanca: Fco. Vitoria, Melchor Cano, Domingo Soto* (Salamanca: Publicaciones Universidad Pontificia, 2007), 37–45 (Cano); 228–31 (Soto); see also Domingo de Soto, *De natura et gratia* (Paris: Apud Ioannem Foucher, 1549), 2.12, pp. 147–48. In an earlier edition of *De natura et gratia*, Soto had entertained the possibility that natural reason alone could bring one to salvation, though he rejected that idea upon more careful consideration. Sullivan, *Salvation Outside the Church?* 75–76.

the existence of the catechumenate implies the possibility of baptism of desire because it would not have been legitimate to delay an adult's baptism if doing so would have put him at risk of damnation. In other respects, Soto largely follows Vitoria's analysis.

John Major. Before our examination of Vitoria's work, however, his teacher at the University of Paris, Scottish-born philosopher and theologian, John Major (1469–1550), deserves mention. Major's work addressed many of the issues Vitoria would take up—such as sovereignty over newly discovered territory—though without the Spaniard's precision. Maurice Beuchot detects a combination of realism and nominalism in Major's work and notes its strong jurisprudential orientation.[32] Reasoning based on legal principles is evident in Major's treatment of the necessity of the sacraments.[33] His vision revolves around the idea—developed by medieval thinkers such as Bernard and Hugh—that divine law can be divided into different periods; he seems to regard sacraments as having always been necessary for salvation, with the particular form of those sacraments determined by positive divine legislation. Hence, Major is keen to determine the timing of the promulgation of the sacraments of the natural law, of circumcision, and of baptism; their institution determined when such rituals became obligatory. Unfortunately, this legal framework does not allow Major to perceive—as had Anselm of Laon—a relationship based on desire between earlier rites and the Christian sacraments. Major's work is significant, however, because he discusses the implication of this medieval legal framework for the recently discovered "islands" where the Gospel had not yet been proclaimed. Even more importantly, he seems to have been the first thinker to perceive the relevance of baptism of desire for those living on such "islands." Since the New Law had not yet been promulgated in such places, their inhabitants would not have been

32. Maurice Beuchot, "El primer planteamiento teológico-jurídico sobre la conquista de América: JOHN MAIR," *Ciencia Tomista*, 103, no. 2 (1976): 213–30. Beuchot judges the combination not entirely successful. In general, determining what Major thought with any confidence is difficult; we lack critical texts for his massive work—written in a notoriously "barbarous" Latin—and the scholarly literature discussing it is limited. David C. Fink, "John Mair's Doctrine of Justification within the Context of the Early 16th Century," in *A Companion to the Theology of John Mair*, ed. John T. Slotemaker and Jeffrey C. Witt (Leiden: Brill, 2015), 15, 225. See also Marenbon, *Pagans and Philosophers*, 287.

33. John Major, *Quartus sententiarum* (Paris: Poncet le Preux, 1509), 4.3.1, folio 18–20.

obligated by the precept commanding baptism. Major considers various ways those on unevangelized islands might have found remedy against original sin; if there were any Jews living there, for example, the law of circumcision might still apply to them. If such islanders had received no revelation but, nonetheless, did all that was possible (*si faciant quod in eis est*), Major speculated, God would give them an illumination and the baptism *flaminis*.[34] He thinks this was likely the reward of the Athenian philosophers who acted according to right reason. It does not seem that Major thought such baptisms *flaminis* would have been terribly common. Citing Mark—"he who does not believe will be condemned" (Mark 16:14)—he insists on the necessity of supernatural illumination.

De Indis. Francisco de Vitoria developed many of Major's ideas with greater precision and clarity. News of Columbus's discoveries would have reached the little town of Vitoria when Francisco was about nine years old, and extensive study of the various issues raised by those discoveries engaged him from the earliest days of his career.[35] Vitoria soon took up the cause of his confrere Las Casas, defending the rights of the new continent's original inhabitants. But where the bishop of Chiapas thundered with righteous indignation against the gruesome violence inflicted upon the native peoples, Vitoria approached the problem point by point with nuance and lawyerly resolve. We see this method in his 1530s lectures published as *De Indis*. Vitoria allows that the Spanish had legitimate rights in the New World: to travel, to trade, to defend themselves, and to "preach and declare the Gospel."[36] However, he says, the actual conduct of the conquistadores often amounted to little more than robbery, and the legal arguments offered to deny the Indians' ownership of the lands they inhabited were specious.[37]

Today, Vitoria's work draws attention mostly for its contribution to the theories of just war, international law, and human rights, but *De Indis*

34. *Quartus sententiarum*, 4.3.1, folio 20, quinta propositio.

35. James Brown Scott, *The Spanish Origin of International Law: Francisco de Vitoria and his Law of Nations* (Oxford: Clarendon Press, 1934), 77–78.

36. Francisco de Vitoria, *De Indis*, trans. John Pawley Bate, in Scott, *The Spanish Origin of International Law*, 3.9.396, p. xli. Vitoria is wary of war even when justified, for even a just war might hinder conversions, and evangelization is always his top priority. *De Indis*, 3.12.400, p. xliii. He staunchly opposes coercion in the proclamation of the Gospel. *De Indis*, 3.11.398, p. xlii.

37. *De Indis*, 2.7.360, p. xxv.

also reveals a consistent concern with baptism.[38] The work's first words are Matthew's Great Commission to make disciples and baptize all nations. Vitoria's lead-in to the issue of the Spanish conquest is the question of whether the children of unbelievers can be baptized against the will of their parents.[39] Vitoria's theology of baptism is largely what we would expect from a convinced Thomist. In his lectures on the sacraments, he acknowledges that baptism is threefold (*flaminis, sanguinis, et aquae*).[40] He says little about baptism *flaminis*, however, instead including a list of patristic and medieval references. He adds that only water baptism is a sacrament with matter and form; since baptism of desire is not a sacrament, it does not confer grace *ex opere operato*. In the *Summa sacramentorum*, Vitoria does not explore whether the concept might be relevant in the context of the New World.

When, in *De Indis*, Vitoria does mention baptism in the context of the New World, his language suggests a line of thought not far from that of Xavier: "it is through no fault of theirs that these aborigines have for many centuries been outside the pale of salvation, in that they have been born in sin and void of baptism and the use of reason whereby to seek out the things needful for salvation."[41] Vitoria's phrasing indicates that he doubted the Indians had, in fact, sought or desired salvation. Still, he does not consider them to have been at fault for that omission. This passage forms part of a larger argument refuting the claim that the Indians were never the true owners of their lands. Certain thinkers had claimed that unbelievers cannot own property.[42] Nothing in natural or human law, Vitoria says, supports this view. The laws of Europe recognize the property

38. The contribution of the *lex orandi* to Catholic thought on Indian rights has been underappreciated. As Michael Stogre puts it, "the Catholic Church's teaching on baptism was significant because it implied that the Indians were true members of the human race." Michael Stogre, *That the World May Believe: The Development of Papal Social Thought on Aboriginal Rights* (Sherbrooke: Éditions Paulines, 1992), 81.

39. Vitoria spends little time on the question in *De Indis*, though he devotes greater attention to it elsewhere. Scotus had defended the legitimacy of baptisms conducted against the will of non-Christian parents, but Vitoria sides with Thomas in rejecting such a practice. Francisco de Vitoria, *Summa sacramentorum Ecclesiae* (Rome: Apud Iulium Accoltum, in platea Peregrini, 1567), 26, p. 30.

40. Francisco de Vitoria, *Summa sacramentorum Ecclesiae*, 23, pp. 27–28.

41. *De Indis*, 1.23.334, p. xiii. In this particular passage he is addressing the spurious argument that the Indians' lack of belief demonstrates their lack of reason.

42. *De Indis*, 1.7.322–23, pp. viii–ix.

rights of Jews and Muslims; the violation of these rights is robbery. The argument against Indian property rights is based on a sleight of hand, Vitoria says; the law allows for the seizure of property as a punishment for certain crimes, including heresy, which at the time was considered a civil as well as a spiritual offence. But the American Indians could not have been guilty of heresy because they were never Christians to begin with. In fact, they cannot be guilty of any crime of unbelief because the ignorance into which they were born was not their fault.

One might ask, if the Indians' ignorance of the Gospel excuses them from civil penalties, how could Vitoria have considered it just that they be punished with the eternal penalty of hell? Here we must appreciate the precision of Vitoria's analysis. Vitoria recognizes that the law of the Gospel imposes certain obligations on all of humanity, among these explicit belief in Christ and baptism. To fail to observe these or other Gospel precepts is to be guilty of the sin of unbelief. We should clarify here that, when speaking of "unbelief" as a sin, we are using the term in a technical sense; it does not indicate the mere absence of belief but, rather, the culpable failure to adhere to the obligations religious truth implies. If one is ignorant of those obligations through no fault of one's own—as were the Indians of the New World prior to the arrival of missionaries—then one is also free of any guilt for failing to observe such precepts. One cannot, then, legitimately be punished in this life or the next for the sin of unbelief. But not all ignorance is inculpable; when the Gospel is proclaimed, Vitoria believes, one is bound to hear it. We have already seen several authors point out that laziness, fear, or the pursuit of worldly goods—obstacles arising from one's character and will—do not excuse from the obligation to pursue religious truth. Inculpable ignorance only results when the Gospel has not been proclaimed or, in the legal terminology of the era, promulgated. Vitoria's notion of promulgation is objective; once the Gospel has been adequately announced, one is bound by the content of that proclamation. Here, however, Vitoria raises another consideration further mitigating any guilt the Indians might incur. He is painfully aware of the circumstances of the Gospel's promulgation in the Spanish territories. The brutality of many conquistadors—the "many scandals and cruel crimes and acts of impiety"—have seriously impeded the work of faithful missionaries. Because of the inadequacy of the promulgation, many Indians remained in a state of invincible ignorance even decades after the arrival of Europeans.[43]

Here, though, we reach the limit of what invincible ignorance can excuse. Invincible ignorance excuses the guilt and, therefore, eliminates the punishment of one particular sin, unbelief. But it does nothing *more* than this.[44] It does not excuse or offer pardon for any other sins. A Christian who faultlessly observes religious precepts but commits murder and adultery would also be innocent of the sin of unbelief but damned for the other sins. So, too, natives living in ignorance of Christianity will not be punished for unbelief, but they remain guilty of all the other sins to which humanity seems so stubbornly inclined. Moreover, our particular sins are evidence of an even more fundamental guilt—that of original sin. And invincible ignorance leaves the problem of original sin entirely unmitigated. For all these reasons, Vitoria writes in response to an author who had used the Indians' alleged unbelief as an excuse for making war on them:

> [A]fter our Lord's passion the Jews in India or in Spain were invincibly ignorant of His passion [...] And it is certain that the Jews who were away from Judaea, whether they were in sin or not, had invincible ignorance about baptism and about the faith of Christ. Just as there could at that time be a case of invincible ignorance on this matter, so there may also be nowadays among those who have not had baptism declared to them. But the mistake which the doctors in question make is in thinking that when we postulate invincible ignorance on the subject of baptism or of the Christian faith it follows at once that a person can be saved without baptism or the Christian faith, which, however, does not follow.[45]

Few people can claim to have gone through life free from personal sin. And even if invincibly ignorant Indians somehow managed to avoid sin,

43. "Hence it does not appear that the Christian religion has been preached to them with such sufficient propriety and piety that they are bound to acquiesce in it." *De Indis*, 2.14.372, p. xxx.

44. Thomas M. Osborne, "Unbelief and Sin in Thomas Aquinas and the Thomistic Tradition," *Nova et Vetera* 8, no. 3 (2010): 617–18, shows that Vitoria, reflecting Thomas's teaching, "refuses to make a connection between purely negative unbelief and the salvation of the Native Americans." Benito Méndez Fernández, *El problema de la salvacion de los "infieles" en Francisco de Vitoria* (Rome: Pontificia Universitate Gregoriana, 1993), 58, likewise concludes that Vitoria does not depart from the principles of medieval orthodoxy.

45. Francisco de Vitoria, *De Indis*, 2.9.367–68, p. xxviii.

the mere absence of personal sin does not equate with salvation. Such people would still lack faith and would require an illumination from God "regarding the name of Christ." Vitoria is confident that divine illumination to help virtuous individuals attain explicit faith would be consistent with God's providence, though he also seems to think it would be a rare occurrence; reports from the mission territories gave him no indication that such illuminations had been widespread, if they occurred at all. Thus, we feel in Vitoria the same missionary urgency as in Xavier or Las Casas; each of them understood the peoples in the newly discovered territories to be suffering under the curse of sin and in need of the Savior.

When to baptize converts? Concern for salvation was a primary motivator for Vitoria's defense of Indian legal rights, just as it was for the direct missionary work of Xavier and Las Casas. The same concern undergirds a fascinating but lesser-known document which emerged from the School of Salamanca addressing a related baptismal controversy.[46] This controversy had to do with the question of how much preparation should be required of converts before baptism. Some missionaries—especially Franciscans—required little preparation before performing baptisms, sometimes *en masse*, in the hope that instruction would follow. Dominicans and Augustinians, on the other hand, generally insisted on more instruction prior to baptism. In this controversy, the indomitable Las Casas again raised his voice in protest against what he saw as the laxity of the Franciscans. He complained to Emperor Charles V that the Franciscan practice of baptizing without preparation, catechesis, or discernment resulted in "converts" who lived like pagans, even engaging in pagan religious practices. In 1541, Charles asked Vitoria and the faculty of the University of Salamanca for an opinion. The theologians—including Vitoria, Domingo Soto, Andrés Vega, and the dean of the faculty—acknowledged the reasons behind both sides' positions but came down squarely in favor of an extended period of catechesis. Preparation for the sacrament must include at least instruction in those things necessary for salvation, they argued. This implied not just doctrine but also moral instruction that would facilitate genuine conversion to a Christian way of life. Baptizing

46. The text, with analysis, can be found in Borobio, *Sacramentos en general*, 173–95.

without such instruction, they declared, is "reckless and dangerous."[47] Even more remarkably, the investigation the theologians of Salamanca made into the problems of the New World led them to criticize baptismal practices in Spain. There too, they say, a lack of preparation and discernment resulted in many baptisms and few Christians. They point to the absurd practice of baptizing those who, because they persisted in an unchristian lifestyle, could not be admitted to communion.

Salamanca's response to Charles's inquiry is remarkable because it recognizes problems created by a phenomenon that we took note of in the previous chapter, the slide into ritual minimalism that began in the early Middle Ages. The baptismal ritual in use in early modernity was already a compression of the ancient Church's rites of initiation; yet pressure to baptize *en masse* in the New World had resulted in further compressions and omissions—an even more aggressive minimalism.[48] The weakness of such minimalistic initiation would have been partially masked in Europe, where Catholicism had so thoroughly penetrated society that the ambient culture could be expected to form Christians. This was not the case in the newly discovered territories. The theologians of Salamanca realized that something had gone wrong and that the Church's ritual practice was at the heart of the problem. Turning to their knowledge of the early Church, they recommended the stages of the ancient catechumenate as a model for contemporary practice.[49]

What does Salamanca's response to this New World baptismal debate have to do with baptism of desire? In short, it allows us to point out the unhappy corollary of the *lex orandi—lex credendi*: that ritual distortions can lead to theological and pastoral distortions. Even in the sixteenth century, theologians recognized the subtle effects of certain types of sacramental minimalism. We should keep this ritual background in mind as we observe theologians grasp after doctrinal minimalism—the minimum necessary faith—in post-Tridentine scholasticism. Baptism of desire would likely never have developed as a doctrine if the extended catechumenate of the patristic era had not given Ambrose a first-hand experience of Valentinian's desire for baptism. The opinion authored by

47. Borobio, 190.
48. Borobio, 175.
49. Borobio, 185.

Vitoria, Soto, and their colleagues shows that at least some theologians of early modernity were attentive enough to the implications of liturgical practice to seek pastoral solutions once again in the Church's ancient rites. A similar sensibility was at work in the bold proposal of another of the era's luminaries, Cardinal Cajetan, with regard to an even more intractable theological conundrum.

Cajetan's Gambit

When he was Master General of the Order of Preachers Thomas de Vio (1469–1534)—better known as Cajetan after his birthplace, the Italian city of Gaeta—sent the first Dominican missionaries to the New World.[50] His contribution to our study, however, has nothing to do with the epochal changes that marked early modernity. Rather it was a response to a perennial problem—the fate of unbaptized infants—and arose from carefully probing the medieval tradition. Today, Cajetan is most remembered for his unsuccessful attempt to keep Luther within the Catholic fold while serving as the papal legate to Germany in 1518. His more substantive intellectual contribution, however, was a commentary on Aquinas that helped to secure the Angelic Doctor's canonical status within Catholic theology after the long reign of Peter Lombard's *Sentences*. When Leo XIII appointed a commission to bring an authoritative version of Aquinas's works into print at the beginning of the twentieth century, it included Cajetan's commentary with the text of the *Summa*. And it is in this commentary that Cajetan suggests that baptism of desire might provide a pathway to salvation in the hardest of hard cases, infants and unborn children dying without baptism. In limbo, we have seen, the medieval tradition proposed a benign—or, in the case of Aquinas, genuinely happy—destiny for such children, but it was unanimous in insisting that unbaptized babies had no way of attaining the beatific vision.[51] The

50. J.A. Weisheipl, "Cajetan (Tommaso de Vio)," in *New Catholic Encyclopedia*, vol. 2 (Washington, DC: The Catholic University of America Press, 1967), 1053. For a balanced assessment of Cajetan's work, see Jared Wicks, introduction to *Cajetan Responds: A Reader in Reformation Controversy*, ed. Jared Wicks (Washington, DC: The Catholic University of America Press, 1978).

51. Even limbo did not enjoy unanimous support. The nominalist Gregory of Rimini (d. 1358) earned the unenviable nickname "*tortor infantium*" for maintaining that all those who die unbaptized will be punished with fire. Gedeon Gál, "Gregory of Rimini," in *New Catholic Encyclopedia*,

decrees of the Council of Florence take this theology for granted, asserting that those who die with original sin but no personal sin descend immediately to hell but are not punished in the same way as those guilty of mortal sin.[52]

Cajetan's proposal comes in two places in his commentary on Question 68 of the *Summa*'s third part. In most respects, we should note, Cajetan's thought aligns with that of Thomas; he affirms Thomas's treatment of the necessity of the sacraments in terms of their fittingness and states clearly that no one can be saved without Christ; he affirms sacramental causality against the sacramental occasionalism of Scotus and the Franciscan school; and he too calls the signs of the Old Law "protests" of faith in the Lord's future coming.[53] Cajetan does not bother to offer further commentary on the article in which Thomas affirms the appropriateness of describing three types—"*aquae, sanguinis et flaminis*"—of baptism, an indication of how uncontroversial he considered the doctrine.[54] He too seems to prefer the expression "*in voto*" rather than "*flaminis*," reflecting the more mature thought of Thomas in the *Summa*.

In both of the places where Cajetan sets forth his proposal, he is cautious. It would not be unreasonable to suppose, he writes when first broaching the topic, that, in a case of necessity, a child's parents' desire for his or her baptism would suffice for salvation.[55] He fastens onto an inconsistency in the framework we have seen used by such medieval thinkers as Bernard and Hugh, who thought the means of salvation determined by three different legal regimes, the natural, written, and new laws. He points specifically to Peter Lombard's use of this framework to address the cases of those living before circumcision, Israelite women, and Israelite boys who died before the eighth day.[56] Peter had claimed that under

---

vol. 6 (Washington, DC: The Catholic University of America Press, 1967), 797. Gregory's commentary on the Lombard's *Sentences* is missing the third and fourth books, so we do not know what he made of baptism of desire.

52. *Enchiridion symbolorum*, 1306; 1349; cf. 1314; Joseph Gill, *The Council of Florence* (London: Cambridge University Press, 1959), 326.

53. Cajetan, *In ST*, 3.61.2, pp. 15–16; 3.61.3, p. 17; M.H. Laurent, "La causalité sacramentaire d'après le commentaire de Cajetan sur les *Sentences*," *Revue des sciences philosophiques et théologiques* 20, no. 1 (1931): 77–81.

54. Cajetan, *In ST*, 3.66.11, p. 78.

55. *In ST*, 3.82.1–2, pp. 93–94: "hoc solum non irrationabiliter occurrit dicendum, quod in casu necessitatis ad salutem puerorum sufficere videtur baptismus in voto parentum."

56. Peter Lombard, *The Sentences*, 4.1.8, p. 7.

the pre-Mosaic Gentile law children could be justified by the faith of their parents, as could Israelites dying before circumcision. Surely faith under the old laws was not more powerful than it is among Christians, Cajetan says. It stands to reason, then, that in the case of urgent necessity, the faith of Christian parents would be sufficient for the salvation of a child. He clarifies that he is not asserting the power of faith in competition with the sacrament; he has in mind only cases in which a child's parents desire water baptism but this is impossible.

Cajetan's reasoning thus far relies on the logic of baptism of desire, and the language he uses shows careful attention to the essentials of the doctrine as it had been articulated since the days of Ambrose and Augustine. The substance of his position is similar to that of the fifth century gravestone for young Theudosius we examined at the end of chapter two. Cajetan, however, goes a step further and inadvertently muddies the waters of his argument. Conscious of the fact that sensible signs have always played a role in salvation, he suggests that parents who are unable to baptize a dying infant make the sign of the cross over him, offering the baby to God.[57] While Cajetan never intended such a prayer to be a replacement for baptism, an unsympathetic reading might construe it that way. Indeed, the circumstances in which such a rite would be feasible—when parents had time to pray over their child but no access to water—would be relatively rare.

In a second comment on the subject, however, Cajetan reveals that he is thinking not only of children who die shortly after birth but also of unborn children who die in utero, for whom the rite of baptism is always impossible.[58] Here he adds two arguments specific to the case of unborn children. The first is that it seems reasonable for God to provide some salvific "remedy" to people in all states of life. But because it is physically impossible to baptize a baby who is still in the womb, those who die in utero seem to have no access to salvation. The problem is not that salvation is difficult to achieve—as it might be, for example, for those raised

57. Cajetan, *In ST*, 3.68.11, p. 104: "cum aliqua benedictione prolis seu oblatione ipsius ad Deum, cum invocatione Trinitatis."

58. Cajetan, *In ST*, 3.68.11, p. 104: "Quocirca caute et irreprehensibiliter ageretur, si periclitantibus in utero pueris ob maternam aegritudinem vel partus difficultatem, benedictio in nomine Trinitatis daretur: et causae discussio deinde divino reservaretur tribunali. Quis scit si divina misericordia huiusmodi baptismum in voto parentum acceptet: ubi nulla incuria, sed sola impossibilitas sacramenti executionem excludit?"

in an immoral household—but that salvation for this category of persons is impossible in principle. Cajetan—probably with Jeremiah and John the Baptist in mind—points out that nothing prevents God from conferring special privileges on children in the womb. His second argument is also scriptural: The Holy Innocents demonstrate that infants are able to receive the baptism of blood; yet, their "baptism" was not the result of their own personal, subjective desire. It is reasonable to suppose that the desire of parents could produce the same effect for these infants as did the bodily suffering imposed by King Herod.

Here, again, Cajetan suggests some prayer by which parents offer their unborn child to God and invoke the Trinity. Echoing Thomas's language, he says such children would still be saved by the sacrament of baptism, not "*in re*" but in "*in voto parentum.*" His mention of the Trinity hints at the doctrinal core both he and Thomas consider most foundational for salvation. He suggests that one could not be faulted for offering such a blessing if mother or child became sick during pregnancy or if the mother experienced a difficult birth. The closing lines of his note indicate that he understood his blessing not as an extension of the sacrament's *ex opere operato* authority but as an appeal to God's mercy. In effect, Cajetan is speaking of intercessory prayer, not a rival sacrament. When Ambrose first proposed the doctrine of baptism of desire in the fourth century, he spoke of Valentinian's prayers—united to his own and those of the Christian assembly—in the same way.

A fair reading of Cajetan's proposal, therefore, shows that he is not suggesting an alternative to baptism. The ritual he suggests is no more than an expression of desire, similar to the desire for baptism expressed in the preliminary rites of the catechumenate. Such rites help to form a desire, to give it concreteness and direction, but in themselves are not salvific. Still, one disinclined to read Cajetan's proposal sympathetically (and many were, for it contradicted the long-standing theological consensus) could accuse him of falling into an error any theology of baptism of desire must avoid—namely, of inventing an alternative to the sacrament. This was an easy, if ultimately superficial, charge to level against him because he proposed a ritual, which was visible and concrete. Ironically, many later scholastic authors would be more guilty of attempting to construct a replacement to baptism, though because theirs was a psychological and abstract replacement—a minimal act of faith—the error was harder to see.

In any case, when the third part of Cajetan's commentary was published in Venice in 1523, his proposal caused a stir that continued to reverberate through the Council of Trent, where it was discussed in January 1547.[59] It made it onto a list of dubious propositions submitted by the Council's theologians to the bishops during the drafting of the decree on the sacraments. A majority favored formal condemnation of the idea, though only a few of these spoke up actively against it. Ambrosius Catharinus, who had criticized the proposal in print a decade after the publication of Cajetan's commentary, protested that it introduced a new rite; the bishop of the Canary Islands objected to the idea of baptism taking place in the womb but seemed to allow that a prayer would be pious. A few bishops thought Cajetan's proposal theologically unsound, but were reluctant to condemn it. It did not, after all, touch on any dispute with the Protestants, and Cajetan had not asserted it obstinately. A turning point in the discussion came when Franciscus Romeus and Girolamo Seripando, the Superiors General of the Dominicans and the Augustinians, rose to defend the substance of what Cajetan had said. Romeus pointed out that Cajetan had proposed his remedy only in the case of necessity and that it amounted to a plea for divine mercy. Grasping that Cajetan had sought to remain faithful to the logic of baptism of desire, Seripando—one of the Council's leading figures—delved into the reasons Cajetan had offered for his proposal.

Though a number Council Fathers continued to object, Cajetan's proposition was omitted from subsequent drafts of the decrees. It was a narrow escape. As Umberg points out, the Council elected not to pronounce on the question, so Cajetan's opinion cannot be considered heretical. The strongest points of objection to it seem to have been the uncertainty of the solution Cajetan offered and the inadmissibility of placing another rite on par with baptism. As Cajetan himself knew, he was swimming against a centuries-old theological current. On the other hand, both Cajetan and his defenders, though a minority, enjoyed great prestige as theologians, and the Council, as much as possible, sought to

59. The following is based on the account of J.B. Umberg, "Kajetans Lehre von der Kinderersatztaufe auf dem Trienter Konzil," *Zeitschrift für katholische Theologie* 39, no. 3 (1915): 452–64.

avoid intra-Catholic disputes.[60] Still, it would be hard to claim that Cajetan's baptismal gambit emerged from the sixteenth century as a winner.
In 1570, when the cardinal's commentary on Aquinas was published in
Rome under Pope Pius V—who wanted nothing doubtful to bear his im-
primatur—its paragraphs on baptism of desire were omitted. They reap-
peared in the Leonine edition of 1906. No theologian in the post-conciliar
era rose to Cajetan's defense, and his proposal was largely forgotten. His
attempt to employ baptism of desire to resolve the most troubling problem of Christian soteriology appeared, at least for the time, to have failed.

The Council of Trent

European discoveries in the Americas and Far East raised plenty of questions to occupy sixteenth century theologians, but these questions were
soon thrust into the background by a theological earthquake in the heart
of Christendom—the Protestant Reformation. While the beginning of
the Reformation is conventionally dated to the publication of Martin
Luther's *Ninety-Five Theses* in 1517, the Catholic Church—hampered by
papal incompetence and resistance, conflict between the Holy Roman
Emperor and the King of France, and a jumble of political and logistical
problems—did not manage to convoke a council in response until 1545.[61]
The Council met in the Alpine city of Trent, located in the geographical
and cultural border zone between Italy and Germany, though by the time
the bishops had gathered it was too late to work out any compromise
between the followers of Luther and Calvin and the Church of Rome.
Instead, the Council Fathers set before themselves two interrelated tasks:
clarifying those doctrines thrown into doubt by Protestantism and setting
a course for Church reform. The work of the Council turned out to be
no less fraught than its initial convocation; it unfolded in three periods
under three different popes, from 1545–1549 under Paul III, from 1551–1552
under Julius III, and from 1562–1563 under Pius IV. This included a brief
transfer to Bologna in 1547 because of an outbreak of typhus in Trent.

---

60. Enzo V. Ottolini, "L'istituzione dei sacramenti nella VII sessione del Concilio di Trento," *Rivista Liturgica* 81 (1994): 105, 115.

61. John W. O'Malley, provides an accessible single-volume account of the Council's un-
folding, in *Trent: What Happened at the Council* (Cambridge, MA: Harvard University Press,
2013).

The decrees touching directly on our topic—on original sin, justification, and the sacraments—are the product of the Council's first period and date from 1546–1547. The impact of the Council's teaching on baptism of desire can also be perceived in its 1551 decrees on the Eucharist and reconciliation.

The doctrine of baptism of desire was well-known among the Council Fathers and seems to have been widely accepted. In itself, it was not a point of dispute with Protestantism, but it figured into a broader problem: When it came to salvation, Luther's doctrine of justification by faith alone had made the role of all of the sacraments secondary. It is beyond the scope of this study to examine the baptismal theology of the first generation of Protestants or to ask how accurately the bishops gathered at Trent understood it.[62] In assessing the Council's work, however, we need to keep in mind that Trent aimed neither to present a comprehensive vision of the Catholic faith nor to settle questions disputed by Catholic theologians. The Council Fathers also sought to avoid the technical jargon of scholastic theology as much as possible.[63] This procedure was intended to define the outer limits of Catholic theology only where necessary and to allow theologians to go on discussing whatever remained within those limits, so it would be a mistake to look for a full theology of baptism in Trent's decrees. Nonetheless, the few—extraordinarily precise—words the Council dedicates to baptism of desire carve out clear space for the doctrine within Catholic orthodoxy and indicate certain contours it must maintain to remain there. As we shall see, on this issue, Trent's terseness is deceptive, for its words on baptism of desire are enormously suggestive. In fact, because the Council also blocks off other potential routes for dealing with Christian soteriology's hard cases, Trent indicates that baptism of desire may be the only viable approach to such questions. Trent's words on the subject, though not final, remain the most authoritative we shall encounter in this study.

62. For an overview of Luther's baptismal theology, see Jonathan D. Trigg, *Baptism in the Theology of Martin Luther* (Leiden: Brill, 1994); on the relationship between baptism and salvation, see especially Trigg, 75–79.

63. Hubert Jedin, *A History of the Council of Trent*, trans. Ernest Graf, vol. 2, *The First Sessions at Trent, 1545–47* (Edinburgh: Thomas Nelson and Sons, 1961), 151, 187.

The Decree on Original Sin

The first of the decrees relevant to our subject is that on original sin, approved at Trent's fifth general session on June 17, 1546. The great historian of the Council Hubert Jedin points out that original sin was the first major dogmatic question addressed at Trent; the Council Fathers had decided to forego discussion of the Trinity and creation because these doctrines were not disputed by Protestants.[64] Discussion began on May 25, 1546, and focused first on original sin itself, then on its remedy. Lutherans and Catholics both agreed on the reality of original sin. Setting aside the special case of the Blessed Mother, Trent unambiguously affirmed that all of Adam's descendants bear the guilt of original sin and are thus subject to punishment.[65] In the discussion preceding the decree, several Council Fathers pointed out that, for infants dying without personal sin, this punishment consisted only in the deprivation of the beatific vision. Though this proviso did not make it into the decree itself, it seems to have represented the theological consensus on which it was based.[66]

As discussion progressed, the Council Fathers identified several errors that needed answer. They were concerned that Luther's doctrine of salvation by faith alone made baptism superfluous.[67] And Protestantism was not the only problematic creed circulating; humanist confidence in man's innate powers at times verged on Pelagianism, the extreme opposite of faith alone, but one which made baptism equally superfluous.[68] Trent's theologians also identified as faulty the theory of Dutch

---

64. Jedin, 2:127.

65. The valuable article of Zoltán Alszeghy and Maurizio Flick, "Il Decreto Tridentino sul peccato originale," *Gregorianum* 52, no. 3 (1971): 595–637, identifies the absolute need all men have for Christ's salvation as the dogmatic core of Trent's teaching.

66. *Concilium Tridentinum: Diariorum, Actorum, Epistularum, Tractatuum*, vol. 5, *Concilii Tridentini actorum, pars altera: acta post sessionem tertiam usque ad Concilium Bononiam translatum*, ed. S. Ehses (Freiburg im Breisgau: B. Herder, 1911), 58, pp. 173–75; cf. 63.35, p. 181.

67. Paulus Hörger, "Concilii Tridentini: de necessitate baptismi doctrina in decreto de iustificatione (Sess. VI)," *Antonianum* 17, no. 3 (1942): 195. Ottolini provides context on how different Protestants treated this issue, in "L'istituzione dei sacramenti nella VII sessione del Concilio di Trento," 69.

68. Michael O'Connor, "The Meritorious Human Life of Jesus: Renaissance Humanist Tendencies in the Thomism of Cardinal Cajetan," *New Blackfriars* 81, no. 952 (2000): 288. J. Hardon makes an interesting case that these decrees are a response to a certain kind of Pelagianism implicit in Luther's theology of the Fall. John Hardon, *History and Theology of Grace* (Ypsilanti, MI: Veritas Press, 2002), 14–15.

theologian, Albert Pigge, who claimed that original sin inhered in Adam but not in the rest of mankind.[69] The Anabaptist rejection of infant baptism prompted the Council to reaffirm the legitimacy and necessity of this practice.[70] When it came to the remedy for original sin, the Council Fathers responded with striking unanimity. Variations of the affirmation *remedium est baptismus* appear again and again in the preparatory discussion. Some theologians added a fuller explanation, identifying the remedy for original sin with the merits of the passion of Christ, which were applied to individuals through baptism.[71] Preparatory discussions indicated that the Council Fathers accepted the traditional triad of baptism by water, blood, and *flaminis*, though at that point they did not feel the need to mention it in the text of the decree.[72] The language of the final decree reflects this relatively harmonious discussion:

> If anyone asserts that this sin of Adam [...], which is in all men, proper to each, can be taken away by the powers of human nature or by any remedy other than the merits of the one mediator our Lord Jesus Christ, who reconciled us with God by his blood [...]; or if anyone denies that the same merit of Christ Jesus is applied to adults and children alike through the sacrament of baptism duly administered in the form given by the Church, let him be anathema.[73]

The necessity of Jesus Christ as the only path to salvation is underlined by the addition of Acts 4:12, "For there is no other name under heaven given among men by which we must be saved," and the role of baptism by Galatians 3:27, "as many of you as were baptized into Christ have put on

69. *Concilii Tridentini actorum*, 84.21, p. 212: "Quartus quem Pighius sequi videtur, peccatum originale nihil esse in uno quoque nostrum, sed esse dumtaxat ipsam Adae praevaricationem, quae re vera nobis non insit, sed soli Adae." Pigge still believed that this sin of Adam was imputed to each child at birth. Friedrich Lauchert, "Albert (Pigghe) Pighius," in *The Catholic Encyclopedia* (New York: Encyclopedia Press, 1913), https://en.wikisource.org/wiki/Catholic_Encyclopedia_(1913)/Albert_(Pigghe)_Pighius; cf. Jedin, *A History of the Council of Trent*, 2:145. Alszeghy and Flick provide insightful analysis of Trent's treatment of Pigge in "Il Decreto Tridentino sul peccato originale," 613–15.

70. *Enchiridion symbolorum*, 1514.

71. *Concilii Tridentini actorum*, 64, pp. 182–85.

72. Bishop Benedict De Nobili made the point that baptism includes all three of these. *Concilii Tridentini actorum*, 64.28, p. 183. His point was included in the summary of the discussions, *Concilii Tridentini actorum*, 73.28, p. 195: "Remedium peccati originalis esse baptismum vel aquae vel flammae vel sanguinis."

73. *Enchiridion symbolorum*, 1513.

Christ."The canon rules out salvation based on natural human powers. In fact, any non-Christian path to salvation is ruled out since the merits of Christ are defined as the sole remedy for original sin. The canon implies that these merits must be applied (*applicari*) in some way to individuals for them to receive their benefit; here, however, it does not state explicitly that the *only* way for this to happen is through baptism.

Faith. Does this slight divergence in wording imply a higher degree of necessity for faith in Christ than for baptism? Such an assertion would be claiming too much—as will become apparent when we look at the Council's other canons—but before proceeding to the Council's decree on justification it is worth examining the question, which will come up again. In fact, the question itself creates a false distinction. Separating faith from baptism would have been foreign to the sensibilities of the patristic writers we have studied, for such writers spoke of faith as something received in baptism. In fact, the rite itself suggests as much. We need only think of the opening dialogue in which the catechumen (or godparent) asks the Church for faith.[74] We have seen the term "faith" used in different ways by different scholastic thinkers, emphasizing intellectual, subjective, or voluntaristic dimensions.[75] Helpful insight is offered by Christophe Grellard's analysis of the relationship between will and intellect in the act of belief among late medieval nominalists. In the ancient world, Grellard claims, faith was a juridical and religious phenomenon as much as psychological one; this "social and normative concept of faith" treated it as a norm of life, not just an epistemological concept. Community, authority, and signs—which facilitate social trust—all form an integral part of what is meant by "faith" in this ancient sense.[76] Even into the thirteenth centu-

---

74. For the Tridentine rite, see *De Sacramento Baptismi*, in *Rituale Romanum: Editio Princeps (1614)*, ed. Manlio Sodi and Juan Javier Flores Arcas (Vatican City: Libreria Editrice Vaticana, 2004), 66, p. 21; 121, p. 31.

75. Enzo V. Ottolini points out some of the many ways—both subjective and objective—in which "faith" can be understood, in *Fede e Sacramenti nella VII sessione del Concilio di Trento*, (Rome: Pontificia Università Gregoriana, 1981), 3.

76. Christophe Grellard, *De la certitude volontaire: Débats nominalistes sur la foi à la fin du Moyen Âge* (Paris: Publications de la Sorbonne, 2014), 21–22. P. Fransen makes a similar point, namely, "'Faith' until the time of the Council of Trent covers the universally accepted doctrine and practice of the Roman Church," in "The Sacramental Character at the Council of Trent (Wording en strekking van de canon over het merkteken te Trente)," *Bijdragen* 32, no. 1 (1971): 34.

ry, thinkers spoke of faith as the trust on which social acts are based.[77] We cannot trace the whole evolution of the concept here. But all we really need to see is that, by asking whether faith can be separated from the sacrament, we have already altered what the concept meant to patristic thinkers, and what it means in the baptismal rite itself. In other words, we have reduced "faith" to only one aspect—cognitive or psychological—of the gift catechumens request in baptism.

The Decree on Justification

Signaling the risk of such reductionism is a good lead-in to understanding the overarching intention of the Council's decree on justification. The decree analyzes the "parts" of justification, but it does so in order to show how all of these parts fit together into a coherent whole. Indeed, the interrelatedness of the Council's first three decrees—on original sin, justification, and the sacraments—is fundamental to its teaching. The decree on the sacraments begins, "all true justification either begins through the sacraments or, once begun, increases through them or, when lost, is regained through them."[78] The Council's message is that justification is sacramental; the two decrees are meant to go together. Keeping the overall intention of the Council's work in mind is crucial for appreciating the way it speaks about baptism of desire, because the words that it selects from the tradition are chosen to avoid fragmentation or reductivism. Jedin's description of the Council's deliberations prior to the decree on justification provides helpful insight, for he points out that the novelty of Luther's categories made the work of the Tridentine theologians difficult. The decree on justification proved more difficult to write than that on original sin because "in the past only a very small number of theologians had treated of this matter."[79] This lacuna was not, of course, because Christian theologians had somehow overlooked the question of forgiveness, salvation, and the need for right relationship with God for fifteen hundred years. Rather, they had approached the problem in a different context—namely, that of the sacraments.[80] We have already begun to

77. Grellard, *De la certitude volontaire*, 28–29.
78. *Enchiridion symbolorum*, 1600.
79. Jedin, *A History of the Council of Trent*, 2:172.
80. Jedin, 2:166–67. Jedin points to a single scholastic exception, the nominalist Robert

perceive how the analytical abstraction of the scholastic method stands in a certain tension with the concreteness of the sacraments. The very notion of a symbol—still more, a mystery—suggests a whole that is greater than the sum of its parts and, thus, that is always to some degree resistant to analysis.

Of course, different theological approaches—patristic mystagogy versus scholastic analysis—need not cancel each other out. They can be complementary in the same way that the question, "How will I travel from Rome to Minneapolis?" can be answered either by providing an airline itinerary or by describing the laws of physics that make flight possible. Both approaches address important, but different, aspects of the question. In the leadup to the drafting of the decree on justification, Jedin notes the broad agreement among Council Fathers in favor of a comprehensive understanding of salvation: "It was generally agreed that faith, defined as an assent to revealed truth, does not justify by itself alone but only does so in association with charity—*fides formata caritate et gratia*—the good works that make a man righteous, and the sacraments of Baptism and Penance."[81] This approach stands in some tension with the scholastic tendency to resolve limit cases by identifying a minimum. Ironically, medieval scholasticism's most fiery critic—Luther, with his famous *solae*—is, in this respect, more scholastic than Trent.

Instead of giving a full analysis of the decree on justification or its formation, these general reflections on the Council's understanding of justification as a dynamic, integrated process—holding together grace and free will, faith and sacrament, the Church and the individual—provide the fundamental context necessary to appreciate its words on baptism of desire. The decree on justification contains thirty-three anathemas condemning erroneous propositions in the precise juridical language typical of such canons. But the decree is also the most striking exception to the Council's general method of theological laconicism. The urgent need of Catholic catechists and preachers for a clear explanation with which to respond to Protestant claims overrode the conciliar reluctance to say too much and end up taking sides in disputed questions.[82] The decree's

---

Holcot (1290–1349), who dealt with the question of justification outside of a sacramental framework. Grellard discusses Holcot extensively in *De la certitude volontaire*, 87–109.

81. Jedin, *A History of the Council of Trent*, 2:177.

82. Jedin, 2:310.

canons are preceded by sixteen chapters that lay out the Catholic vision of justification in a positive "narrative" sense; this narrative portion contains a direct reference to baptism of desire, which deserves our careful attention.

After chapters reiterating the Church's teaching on original sin—including the impossibility of salvation by any means available through nature and the necessity that Christ's merits be imparted on individuals for them to be saved[83]—the text turns to the transition (*translatio*) from our state of birth as sons of Adam to that of adoption through Jesus Christ as sons of God:

> After the promulgation of the gospel, this transition cannot take place without the bath of regeneration or the desire for it, as it is written: "Unless one is reborn of water and the Spirit, he cannot enter the kingdom of God."[84]

The inclusion of the phrase "or the desire for it" (*aut eius voto*) clearly indicates that the possibility of baptism of desire was present in the minds of the theologians and bishops at Trent and that they wished for it to be part of the Council's teachings. As discussion during the drafting of the decrees had already suggested, where the Council refers to the necessity of baptism, we should read baptism of desire as being included.

In fact, as in the preparatory sessions for the decree on original sin, baptism of desire does not appear to have caused controversy in the months of debate that went into the decree on justification. The doctrine was mentioned here and there but did not arouse argument. Nonetheless, one can discern some differences in the way certain Council Fathers addressed the issue. On the question of when baptism of desire occurs, some continue to conceive of an event prior to baptism; an early summary of the discussion describes this happening to those with exceptionally ardent faith, citing the common but questionable example of Cornelius.[85] The nature of the discussion, however, tended to suggest that such a concept is problematic.

---

83. "But even though 'Christ died for all' [*2 Cor 5:15*], still not all receive the benefits of his death, but only those to whom the merit of his Passion is imparted." *Enchiridion symbolorum*, 1523.

84. *Enchiridion symbolorum*, 1524: "quae quidem translatio post Evangelium promulgatum sine lavacro regenerationis aut eius voto fieri non potest, sicut scriptum est: 'Nisi quis renatus fuerit ex acqua et Spiritu Sancto, non potest introire in regnum Dei.'"

85. *Concilii Tridentini actorum*, 138, pp. 337–38. Bishop Thomas Campeggi of Feltre had used much the same language in his speech on the matter a few days earlier. *Concilii Tridentini*

Trent's aim, after all, was to describe justification as a complex process; by its nature, a process involves intermediate steps. In the case of someone starting as an unbeliever, these steps lead up to justification in baptism. All agreed that God's grace is a part of every step of this process, but it seemed more logical to many Fathers to speak of the grace that comes before justification as preparatory.[86] Johannes de Salazar, bishop of Lanciano, insists that those actions taken in response to God's call prior to baptism are preparatory and dispose one to justification, but that justification only happens in baptism: "before baptism an unbeliever is not justified."[87] The bishops of Belcastro and Astorga second this view.[88] The intervention of the Archbishop of Corfu shows that these objections need not be taken as negating the possibility of baptism of desire, which could happen at the moment of death if one is prevented from receiving the sacrament.[89] Indeed, because the papal legates had already identified as erroneous the proposition that baptism adds nothing to faith, the logic of Catholic sacramental practice itself made the idea of a pre-baptismal baptism tenuous.[90] The issue did not, however, require the Council to come to an explicit resolution.

Occasional comments shed some light on how the Council Fathers understood the nature of desire required for salvation; the Bishop of Ascoli points to the questions posed to a catechumen in the rite, expressing belief in the articles of faith and the intention to reject sin and live according to the commandments.[91] The concept of grace received in virtue of the desire for a sacrament also appears in the discussion of baptized

actorum, 117.32–36, p. 296. Later on, he compares Cornelius's good works to the catechesis of a catechumen. Concilii Tridentini actorum, 117.1–11, p. 298.

86. Ottolini concludes that the Council did not consider the "votum sacramenti" an anticipation of the effect of the sacrament, but rather an indispensable condition for receiving justification in exceptional cases when the sacrament is not possible. Ottolini, Fede e Sacramenti nella VII sessione del Concilio di Trento, 41.

87. Concilii Tridentini actorum, 123.12, p. 317. Augustine was also invoked to argue that before baptism neither Cornelius nor catechumens had sufficient grace for salvation. Hörger, "Concilii Tridentini," pt. 1, 218.

88. Concilii Tridentini actorum, 127, pp. 321–22. Hörger sees Belcastro as objecting to the reduction of justification to a subjective and psychological process with no objective dimension. Hörger, "Concilii Tridentini," pt. 1, 212–13.

89. Concilii Tridentini actorum, 170.12, p. 411.

90. Concilii Tridentini actorum, 108, p. 282; see error 9: "In baptismate sola fides est, quae reddit hominem iustum, ipso baptismate nihil iuvante."

91. Concilii Tridentini actorum, 115, p. 294.

persons seeking to regain justification through penance. But other issues loomed larger and occupied more time in the Council's deliberations, such as the degree of certainty one can have about one's own justification, the change that occurs in the one who is justified, and the role of free will and predestination in the process. Remarkably, even though baptism of desire was not at the center of its deliberations, an important but subtle theological shift emerged at Trent. In the Council's earlier deliberations on original sin, the language of baptism *flaminis* was in common usage. As the Council's deliberations went on, the term baptism *in voto* seems to have gradually superseded the *flaminis* language. Though *flaminis* did not disappear from the Council's discussions, its decrees speak of baptism *in voto*. This shift was not the result of a deliberate decision, but it mirrors the evolution in Aquinas's thought between his *Commentary* on the *Sentences* and the *Summa theologiae*. Of course, desire was not absent when theologians spoke of baptism *flaminis* or, often enough, combined the language.[92] Dropping the term *flaminis* in favor of speaking simply of baptism *in voto*, however, has the advantage of underscoring what is most central in the doctrine. Though this language is Thomistic, its adoption does not seem to have been the result of any conscious intention to remain faithful to the Angelic Doctor. Rather, as debate on a whole range of issues progressed, brushing the edges of baptism of desire, the *voto* language—and more importantly, the logic it implied—emerged naturally as what was most coherent. Thomas had been moved by the same logic and followed the same path.

If we turn to the specific language of the decree, we can note that the section quoted above from chapter four was not part of its earliest drafts.[93] This does not reflect opposition; if anything, it suggests that it was probably taken for granted.[94] Debate over the decree on justification

---

92. E.g., *Concilii Tridentini actorum*, 120.30–39, p. 308.

93. On these early drafts, see Paulus Hörger, "Concilii Tridentini," *Antonianum* 17, no. 4 (1942): 269–75.

94. Papal theologian Alfonso Salmerón had mentioned the possibility of receiving the grace of justification on the basis of the sacrament *in voto* in his lengthy discourse at the opening of the theologians' congregation on justification on June 23, 1546. *Concilii Tridentini actorum*, 101.6, p. 272. Hörger alludes to murmuring and doubts over the question of baptism *in voto*, which may have had to do with the negative opinions in Augustine and Gennadius. These do not, however, seem to have played a major role in the formation of the decree. Hörger, "Concilii Tridentini," 2:286–87.

was lengthy, complex, and, once, so heated it led to a scuffle. Insertion of the language regarding baptism of desire, by contrast, seems to have fit naturally into the general process of making the decree's language more precise—a task that fell largely to the Augustinian Superior General Girolamo Seripando.[95] During debate on the early drafts, the bishop of Ascoli requested that baptism be referred to specifically as the usual (*regulariter*) means by which original sin is remitted, while the bishop of Castellimaris suggested the phrase "*in re vel in voto*" in a list of proposed refinements.[96] The concept entered explicitly into the draft decree of October 31, 1546, in two places. One of these, later omitted by Seripando, used the phrase "*in proposito et desiderio.*"[97] The third full draft offered for debate on November 5, 1546, bore the shape of the decree eventually approved by the Council, with its explanatory section and canons. The version of the chapter in this third draft remained unchanged in the final decree.

Promulgation. Before turning to the decree on the sacraments, which complements and clarifies the decree on justification, one final aspect of this chapter's wording deserves our attention—namely, the phrase "after the promulgation of the Gospel." The phrase should call to mind the way in which Francisco Vitoria and others had addressed the questions raised by the discovery of unevangelized peoples in the Americas and elsewhere. Promulgation is an objective concept—a law is promulgated when it is publicly announced, not when everyone has personally understood it— but the timeframe of the Gospel's "promulgation" has always been open to different interpretations.[98] Some thinkers believed the Gospel to have been promulgated once and for all within the lifetime of the Apostles.

95. Hörger, "Concilii Tridentini," 2:277–84.

96. *Concilii Tridentini actorum*, 198.15–20, p. 464; 216.24, p. 495.

97. *Concilii Tridentini actorum*, 219.15–16, 34, p. 511. The "propositum" to undergo baptism was seen as one of the preparatory acts, which might be less than fully decisive; it was likely joined with "desiderio" to emphasize the necessity of the intention to go through with the "propositum." Hörger, "Concilii Tridentini," 1:214.

98. Hörger draws upon Vega's contemporary interpretation, in "Concilii Tridentini," 2:289–91. The Tridentine *Catechism* distinguishes between the institution of baptism, identified with the Lord's baptism by John, and the promulgation of the "law of baptism," identified with the Great Commissioning after the resurrection. *Catechism of the Council of Trent*, trans. J. Donovan (New York: Catholic Publishing Society, 1829), 118–19.

Others, such as John Major and Vitoria, understood its promulgation to have occurred at different times in different lands. In the context of the rest of the decree, the phrase seems to be consistent with the theology of Vitoria. However, in keeping with its intention not to take sides in debates among Catholics, Trent leaves the term undefined. André Duval notes that the phrase does not seem to have sparked debate at the Council and suggests that this is the result of an inexplicably still-medieval understanding of the world's population and geography among the Council Fathers.[99] Such a conclusion is implausible. Even though the Council's main focus—the Reformation—was a decidedly European matter, by the mid-sixteenth century the expansion of global Catholic missionary work was a sensation across Christendom.[100] Theologians present at the Council, such as Soto, had worked explicitly on problems involving the new discoveries, and the members of religious orders had confreres prominently engaged in the missions. A more plausible explanation for the lack of discussion on the binding character of the Christian promulgation is that the Fathers of Trent did not perceive the work of theologians such as Vitoria to have been inadequate. They did not call for a new theology in response to the recent discoveries because they believed the current theology to be sound.

The Decree on the Sacraments

The treatment of baptism in the decree on justification set the stage for Trent's expansion on the theme in its first decree on the sacraments, approved a few months later on March 3, 1547. The decree's brief preamble describes it as bringing to completion "the salutary doctrine of justification" promulgated in the Council's previous session. The canons that follow unambiguously vindicate the sacramental nature of Christian salvation. The decree contains thirteen canons on the sacraments in general, followed by fourteen on baptism and three on confirmation. The two canons that most directly concern us are the fourth on the sacraments in general and the fifth on baptism:

99. André Duval, *Des Sacrements au Concile de Trente* (Paris: Cerf, 1985), 15.

100. Even before Trent, Catholic writers spoke of the newly baptized Christians in foreign lands "replacing" those souls lost to the Reformation. Hsia, "Theological Developments in the Non-European World," 12.

Can. 4. If anyone says that the sacraments of the New Law are not necessary for salvation, but that they are superfluous; and that without the sacraments or the desire for them [*sine eis aut eorum voto*] men obtain from God the grace of justification through faith alone (although it is true that not all the sacraments are necessary for each person), let him be anathema.[101]

Can. 5. If anyone says that baptism is optional [*liberum esse*], that is, not necessary for salvation, let him be anathema.[102]

Both canons point to the essential relationship between baptism and salvation; four other canons condemn formulations that fall short of the Church's understanding of this sacramental relationship.[103] Of these, canon 6 of the decree on sacraments in general seems the most relevant to our study, for it repudiates the notion of the sacraments as signs that only signal, but do not cause, the presence of grace. Together these canons stand in deliberate contrast to the proposition that salvation is attained through "faith alone." Godfrey Diekman points out that the decree is not a denial of the necessity of faith—only the "alone" is problematic. Rather it is an affirmation that, to be salvific, faith requires something else.[104] That something must include the sacrament of baptism. More precisely Diekman observes, "Baptism itself is of its nature a *professio fidei*, a profession of that faith of the church which finds essential utterance in the traditional baptismal rite itself."[105] Baptism, we could say, is the primordial form of the Christian profession of faith. Using Grellard's categories we could also say that Trent's decrees seek to preserve the fuller ancient sense of faith—which includes a social dimension—instead of the limited nominalist understanding of the term. The fact that only one of the canons cited above mentions the desire for baptism should not trouble

101. *Enchiridion symbolorum*, 1604. Trent takes a similar line with regard to penance. Reconciliation sometimes happens "through charity" if one possesses "perfect contrition," but "this reconciliation, nevertheless, is not to be ascribed to contrition itself without the desire of the sacrament [*sine sacramenti voto*], a desire that is included in it." *Enchiridion symbolorum*, 1677.

102. *Enchiridion symbolorum*, 1618.

103. *Enchiridion symbolorum*, 1605–8.

104. Godfrey Diekman, "Some Observations on the Teaching of Trent Concerning Baptism," in *Lutherans and Catholics in Dialogue II: One Baptism for the Remission of Sins*, ed. Paul C. Empie and William W. Baum (New York: U.S.A. National Committee of the Lutheran World Federation; Washington, DC: Bishops' Commission for Ecumenical Affairs, 1967), 66.

105. Diekman, 62.

us, for its appearance twice in the Council's decrees indicates that the
necessity of baptism should be understood to include the possibility of
baptism *in voto*. That the Council Fathers did not feel the need to repeat
the *voto* language every time the necessity of baptism is mentioned at
most underscores the fact that baptism of desire should be considered a
corollary of the more fundamental doctrine of the sacrament's necessity.
Ferdinand Cavallera summarizes the amendment process that canon four
(above) underwent, which reflected a desire for clarity rather than substantive differences among the Council Fathers.[106] We have already had
a glimpse of the Council's preparation of this decree because Cajetan's
proposal was discussed at this time.

Evaluation. Having examined each of the key decrees and their composition, we are now in a position to evaluate the profound importance of the
Council of Trent for the doctrine of baptism of desire. Trent unambiguously legitimizes the concept within Catholic theology. The catechism
requested by Trent and approved by Pius V in 1566 for the instruction of
pastors confirms this conclusion and draws practical implications from
the doctrine. While it insists infants be baptized without delay, it warns
against conferring the sacrament on adults without testing their sincerity
and catechizing them. If unforeseen circumstances prevent adults from
being baptized, it says, "their intention of receiving [baptism], and their
repentance for past sins, will avail them to grace and righteousness."[107]
Trent also sets limits within which baptism of desire must be understood.
Its adoption of the *voto* language maintains a role for the sacrament in
any process of salvation; in combination, the decrees on justification and
on the sacraments close the door to any truly non-sacramental path to

106. Ferdinand Cavallera, "Le décret du Concile de Trente sur les sacraments en général
(VIIe session)," *Bulletin de Littérature Ecclésiastique* 6, no. 6 (1914): 423–25. After the canon's
first formulation, the phrase "for salvation" was added to make absolutely clear what was at
stake when the Council spoke of necessity; the addition of the phrase "but superfluous" also
reinforced the sacraments' necessity. Based on the discussion that went into the drafting of the
canon, Ottolini suggests that the phrase "superfluous" indicates *contemptus* for the sacrament,
in *Fede e Sacramenti nella VII sessione del Concilio di Trento*, 29. The most significant addition
in the amendment process was the somewhat ungainly qualifier tacked on to the end of the
canon, specifying that an individual need not receive all seven sacraments to achieve salvation.

107. *Catechism of the Council of Trent*, 124–25, 134. The *Catechism* confirms the "universal and
absolute necessity of baptism," which is to be administered immediately in danger of death.
Catechism of the Council of Trent, 107.

salvation, just as they close the door to any truly non-Christological path. Trent, to be sure, does not grapple directly with the hard cases that have driven this study, though its language reflects the centuries-long discussion of these issues. In my judgment, Trent's decrees leave baptism of desire as the only doctrine left standing to address those hard cases. All paths to salvation run through water, blood, or desire.

One might, however, immediately raise an objection based on a point discussed above. Chapter four of the decree on justification uses a juridical term—promulgation—that could be interpreted as opening the possibility of an entirely non-sacramental path to salvation. One could argue, on the basis of the description of the sacraments as part of the New Law, that salvation could have been achieved in some entirely different way, disconnected from the sacraments, at times and in places where the New Law had not been promulgated. One could say of the time before Jesus and the Apostles, "The rules were simply different back then. Back then, obeying the categorical imperative could have been enough." Some support for such a move can be found among the more legally minded medieval thinkers, though their sense of what exactly was required under the pre-Gospel legal regimes varied. More importantly, however, this way of thinking leaves us with an entirely arbitrary picture of divine legislation. In the end, Trent blocks this road too. Its decrees include canons dealing with the pre-Christian period. The decree on original sin teaches that no "remedy other than the merits of the one mediator our Lord Jesus Christ" can remove the effects of Adam's sin. The decree on justification goes further, claiming that "not only the Gentiles by means of the power of nature but even the Jews by means of the letter of the law of Moses were unable to liberate themselves and to rise" from slavery to sin and death.[108] The decree on the sacraments insists on the inequality of the sacraments of the Old Law with those of the New, though it is studiously vague about defining the difference between the Christian sacraments and their precursors.[109]

This deliberate reticence to define should make us careful not to claim too much as definitive teaching. Trent does not leave us with a formula to describe the relationship between Old and New Testament religion.

---

108. *Enchiridion symbolorum*, 1513, 1521.
109. *Enchiridion symbolorum*, 1602, 1614.

At the same time, if one digs a trench down a hillside, water can only flow in a certain direction. Because the merits of Christ were always and everywhere necessary for salvation, if any rites, practices, or beliefs were salvific before the promulgation of the Gospel, then they had to have been so insofar—and only insofar—as they established a relationship to the Paschal Mystery. This point was made explicitly during the Council's deliberations, most notably by Seripando with respect to the baptism of John.[110] We saw this perspective already in the school of Laon: Pre-Christian rites, whether of the natural law or of the Old Testament, were salvific because they expressed desire for fulfillment in Christianity. In the patristic era this truth was expressed by the Fathers' willingness to see an allegory for baptism at almost every mention of water in the Old Testament. We will have to work out exactly what this means in our conclusion, but for now we can say that the affirmations of the Council of Trent—based on a much longer theological tradition—support the view that all means of salvation before the Gospel drew their power from their orientation toward Christian baptism.

This conclusion lends credibility to the notion of implicit desire, for it is obvious that not everyone who, say, underwent circumcision in the centuries before Christ had a clear idea of baptism in mind. This connection will also give us concrete data with which to scrutinize conceptions of implicit desire, for it is equally clear from the Old Testament that not all religious practices and beliefs point toward the Messiah. For a desire to be salvific, its relation to the Christian sacraments must be more than superficial or generic. An implicit desire for baptism must somehow imply baptism. To be clear, Trent does not make all of these connections explicit. Still, the logic of Trent's decrees, even if they do not fill in all of the details of the sketch, point to a doctrine of baptism of desire rooted in the sacrament in combination with a robust understanding of implicit desire as the most credible path to address the hard cases of salvation.

---

110. *Concilii Tridentini actorum*, 378.16–23, p. 966. Others similarly saw the baptism of Christ fulfilling the baptism of John, cf. *Concilii Tridentini actorum*, 342.7–25, p. 967; 357.8–11, p. 905; 358.23–30, p. 905. The Carmelite General refers to the baptism of Christ as sacrament, that of John as "*dispositio*." *Concilii Tridentini actorum*, 380.34–45, p. 970. Ottolini defines the relationship between the testaments as one of anticipation and fulfillment, in "L'istituzione dei sacramenti nella VII sessione del Concilio di Trento," 112. The Council of Florence had expressed the same perspective. *Enchiridion symbolorum*, 1347.

Life after Trent

The Council of Trent proved something of a triumph for the doctrine proposed more than a millennium before by Ambrose of Milan. Not only did the Council's decrees validate baptism of desire's orthodoxy, but they did so in a way that remained surprisingly close to Ambrose's own sensibilities. In other words, they did so while asserting the more fundamental belief in the necessity of baptism and the sacramental nature of salvation. The Fathers of Trent managed this feat despite the strength of several currents flowing in a different direction—most notably the minimalism that had developed both in scholastic theology and in liturgical practice. Looking over the cliff of Luther's *sola fide*, they articulated a doctrine that defended the comprehensiveness of salvation and pointed toward an approach to hard cases intended to reinforce rather than diminish the centrality of the sacraments. That this approach harmonizes with patristic sensibilities is probably less the result of any conscious effort at *ressourcement* than the consequence of the Council's theological restraint, its decision to avoid disputes among the schools and to say only what was most necessary and fundamental.

But the currents flowing before the Council continued to flow afterwards. Eventually they would carry baptism of desire into the backwaters of theological consciousness, as had the nominalism of the fourteenth century. One of the most important works of twentieth century moral theology, Servais Pinckaers's *The Sources of Christian Ethics*, helps to explain why this was no coincidence. Pinckaers's groundbreaking work argues that the "manualist tradition" that dominated Catholic moral theology from the seventeenth century onward, while ostensibly Thomistic, owed more to the nominalist outlook of William of Ockham than to Thomas. In short, where Aquinas emphasized virtue and the ultimate end of human life, Ockhamist ethics centered on law and obligation.[111] This line of thinking paralleled the moral approach of Immanuel Kant,

---

111. Servais Pinckaers, *The Sources of Christian Ethics*, trans. Mary Thomas Noble (Washington DC: The Catholic University of America Press, 1995), 251. Ockham emphasized God's legislative omnipotence to such a degree that he held that God could command a person to hate him and that such an act would, on the basis of that precept, become good. Pinckaers, 247. E.J. Bauer's overview of the Jesuit scholastic milieu alludes to factors facilitating this trend. Emmanuel J. Bauer, "Francisco Suarez (1548–1617): Scholasticism after Humanism," in

which reinforced the "obligationist" dominance of the nineteenth and early twentieth centuries. Indeed, because moral theologians of the era thought of themselves as Thomists, they seem not to have realized that an alternative even existed.[112] The trend Pinckaers identifies is highly relevant to our study, for it helps to explain how, by the late twentieth century, baptism of desire had effectively disappeared as an approach to the question of salvation. In the moral manuals, sacraments are treated primarily from the point of view of the obligations they impose.[113] We have already seen thinkers such as Francisco de Vitoria discuss obligation as it relates to baptism. Obedience to the Lord's command was one reason baptism was necessary for salvation, though, as Vitoria recognized, it was not the primary one. Freedom from original sin and participation in the Paschal Mystery were more fundamental; indeed, these were the reason baptism was an obligation in the first place. The nominalist approach to morality, however, reversed this emphasis, putting the fulfillment of divine precept first.

Other factors contributed to the marginalization of the sacraments in discussions of salvation. Because commentaries on the *Summa theologiae* came to replace those on the *Sentences* and baptism of desire occupies a less prominent position in the *Summa*, theologians could more easily brush past the doctrine.[114] We saw that Luther's approach to the question of justification led the Council of Trent to treat soteriology in more abstract doctrinal categories. Gregory's study of martyrdom in early modernity argues that the nature of the differences between Catholics and Protestants tended to raise the stakes of correct doctrinal belief; in interconfessional disputes, doctrinal beliefs, not baptism, became the

Philosophers of the Renaissance, ed. Paul Richard Blum (Washington, DC: The Catholic University of America Press, 2010), 236–37.

112. Pinckaers, *The Sources of Christian Ethics*, 5, 250, 253, 278.

113. Pinckaers, 232. Juan Azor's (1535–1603) enormously influential *Institutiones morales* treats the sacraments as part of the moral law. Christoph P. Haar, "A Juridicized Language for the Salvation of Souls: Jesuit Ethics," in *Jesuit Philosophy on the Eve of Modernity*, ed. Cristiano Casalini (Leiden: Brill, 2019), 200–202. A quotation from the forward of Suárez's *De legibus ac Deo legislatore* (1612) captures this view: "for the law is a rule that, if one follows it, leads to eternal salvation, while breaking it leads to its loss." Haar, 204–5.

114. Suárez's comments on the three articles in which Thomas treats baptism of desire, for example, amount to about half a page. Francisco Suárez, *Opera Omnia R. P. Francisci Suárez, s.j.*, vol. 20, *Commentaria ac Disputationes in Tertiam Partem D. Thomae* (Paris: Ludovicum Vivès, 1866), 68.1–3, pp. 404–6.

determining factor in salvation.[115] A comment from Marenbon's introduction to *Pagans and Philosophers* is telling. Setting out the problem of
pagan salvation, he explains, "The obstacle was not in itself lack of baptism, although this reason was often given, simplistically, to explain why
non-Christians were damned."[116] Here Marenbon is reading modern attitudes into patristic and medieval sources, for, as we have seen, ancient
and medieval Christians understood religious ritual to have an irreducible
importance—as is demonstrated by how controversial baptism of desire
remained for more than a millennium. But, just as the necessity of the
sacraments seemed so obvious that it scarcely needed defending for most
of Christian history, at some point—in the centuries to which we are now
turning—those same sacraments came to seem so "simplistic" that even
the best studies breezily brush them aside. The role of the scholasticism
that developed in the baroque period is decisive in explaining this shift,
even if its consequences only became apparent in the nineteenth century.

Of course, not all of the factors that shifted discussion away from the
sacraments originated in this period; some represent the acceleration of
trends beginning in the Middle Ages. For example, even though Trent
clearly intended to bolster the sacraments, some aspects of the Tridentine reforms—an emphasis on liturgical uniformity, for example—tended
to increase ritual minimalism in the centuries that followed. The principle
cuius regio, eius religio adopted at the Peace of Augsburg in 1555—allowing
a territory's prince to determine the religion of its people—reinforced the
subordination of religious practice to political purposes. With these general
trends in the background, it is also important to keep in mind—as Calvin
and the Jansenists demonstrate—that the erosion of a sacramental sense
did not make salvation easier to attain. Nor did abstraction result in greater
theological clarity; this was the era of the *de auxiliis* controversy, a debate
over grace between Dominicans and Jesuits so abstruse and divisive that, in
1607, Pope Paul V told both sides to give it up without resolution.[117]

---

115. Gregory, *Salvation at Stake*, 315–52. M. de Certeau alludes to other factors playing
into the diminishment of traditional rituals, such as the seventeenth and eighteenth centuries'
emphasis on interiority and feeling, religious pedagogy, and, especially in France, the gradual
subordination of religion to a social ethic. Michel de Certeau, *The Writing of History*, trans. Tom
Conley (New York: Columbia University Press, 1988), 128, 130, 148, 160.

116. Marenbon, *Pagans and Philosophers*, 14.

117. Thomas Marschler, "Providence, Predestination, and Grace in Early Modern Catholic
Theology," in Lehner et al., *Oxford Handbook of Early Modern Theology*, 91.

If the era's undercurrents flowed away from baptism of desire, however, that does not mean that the doctrine was unknown or unappreciated in the seventeenth century; a brilliant exception to these trends, Robert Bellarmine (1542–1621), deserves our attention.

Robert Bellarmine

The theologian *par excellence* of Tridentine Catholicism, Jesuit Robert Bellarmine's scholarship earned him a cardinal's hat in his own lifetime and the designation Doctor of the Church after his canonization. His scholarly acumen is on display in his treatise on the sacraments, which provides what is probably the most concise and incisive summary of the doctrine of baptism of desire to appear in several hundred years. The work presents a thorough defense of Catholic theology alongside a meticulous examination of Protestant writings.

Necessity of precept and of means. Early in the treatise Bellarmine shows an awareness of the issues raised by baptism of desire in his discussion of the necessity of the sacraments in general. Adhering, as we would expect, to the teachings of Trent, he makes use of Thomas's analysis of necessity as well as of a more recent distinction developed in scholastic theology between "necessity of precept" and "necessity of means."[118] The language is meant to distinguish between those things that are necessary merely because they have been commanded by positive legislation and those that are necessary in order to achieve a required end. Something necessary only by precept can be more easily dispensed with; if something is a necessary means for achieving an end, however, it is generally impossible to achieve that end without it.[119] If I am traveling to Russia, a visa is neces-

---

118. Robert Bellarmine, *De Sacramentis in genere*, in *Roberti Cardinalis Bellarmini Opera Omnia*, vol. 3, *De Controversiis Christianae Fidei* (Naples: J. Giuliano, 1858), 1.1.22, p. 62. On the terminology's development, see Capéran, *Le problème du salut des infidèles*, 1:266, footnote 1. This particular phrasing is a product of the School of Salamanca, though the idea behind it is present in Thomas (e.g., *ST*, 2-2.2.7–8). Soto and Cano had used expressions such as "necessity of ends" to capture the same idea; Domingo Bañez introduced the phrase "necessity of means." Vega used *"necessitas praecepti"* and *"necessitas simpliciter."* Giovanni Rossi, *L'opinione di Andrea Vega sulla necessità della fede per la giustificazione* (Roma: Scuola Tipografica Pio X, 1942), 23.

119. Francisco Suárez points out that necessity of precept always exists where there is necessity of means. *Commentaria ac Disputationes in Tertiam Partem D. Thomae*, 68.2, p. 404.

sary by precept because it has been commanded by Russian law, though this might be changed by the Russian government or ignored entirely if I bribe the right officials. Some form of transportation, however, will be a necessary means to arrive in Russian territory; not even Vladimir Putin can change that. The distinction was introduced in order to dispel the notion that the sacraments—or the Church—were a kind of legal formality, a conclusion the nominalist emphasis on legal obligation tends to suggest. Bellarmine rightly perceives that mere necessity of precept is inadequate to explain the connection between baptism and salvation. He identifies this error with Protestantism, which treats baptism as helpful but not necessary. The distinction reinforces the limited usefulness of the concept of invincible ignorance; as Bellarmine—in line with Vitoria—observes, baptism is necessary for salvation even if one does not know that it is necessary.[120] Desire can supply baptism; ignorance cannot.

When Bellarmine turns directly to baptism of desire—in a chapter that treats baptism *sanguinis* and *flaminis* together—he demonstrates an incisive historical awareness.[121] First he addresses baptism *sanguinis*, a concept which he claims Protestant theology empties of significance; if faith alone saves, the act of martyrdom cannot bring about the forgiveness of sins. Bellarmine emphasizes the connection between martyrdom and baptism in scripture and uses the *ex opere operato* language of sacramental theology to describe the certainty of martyrdom's salvific effect. He contrasts this with the *ex opere operantis* of baptism *flaminis*, meaning that the effectiveness of baptism of desire depends on the perfection of the subjective state of the person receiving it. Baptism of desire can occur where necessity makes baptism of water impossible, Bellarmine says, but what is required of the individual is greater.[122] Only perfect conversion,

---

120. Bellarmine, *De Sacramentis in genere*, 1.1.22, p. 63; Robert Bellarmine, *De Baptismo et Confirmatione*, in *Roberti Cardinalis Bellarmini Opera Omnia*, vol. 3, *De Controversiis Christianae Fidei* (Naples: J. Giuliano, 1858), 2.1.4, pp. 159–63. Infant baptism, he argues, demonstrates the inadequacy of precept alone to explain baptism's necessity; infants cannot be bound to obey a precept, yet they must be baptized. This indicates that baptism is the necessary means to attain salvation.

121. *De Baptismo et Confirmatione*, 2.1.6, pp. 164–68.

122. *De Baptismo et Confirmatione*, 2.1.6, p. 167: "*Perfecta conversio ac Poenitentia recte Bamptismus flaminis dicitur et Baptismum aquae saltem in necessitate supplet.* Nota, Baptismum flaminis non dici, quamlibet conversionem, sed perfectam, quae includit veram contritionem, et charitatem, et simul etiam desiderium, seu votum Baptismi." In another work, he adopts Gregory Nazianzen's categorization of the people who go without baptism—those who hold the

which includes true contrition, charity, and the desire for baptism, can lead to baptism *flaminis*. Bellarmine demonstrates a command of the patristic sources superior to that found among the Salamancans and other contemporaries. He admits that, among the ancients, belief in baptism of desire was less certain; he mentions the flat denial of salvation for catechumens in the text of Gennadius, which, he realizes, was wrongly attributed to Augustine. He also notes that Bernard's letter on the subject demonstrates that the doctrine had opponents in his day as well. Nonetheless, Bellarmine concludes, the authorities in favor of the doctrine are strong enough to remove any doubt of its validity.[123] Among the evidence he cites is the baptism of the dead in 1 Corinthians 15. He strains a bit to interpret the practice in a way that makes the Corinthians' actions fit within Catholic orthodoxy—their posthumous baptisms served to reduce the penalty of purgatory, he says—but he is almost unique among theologians in perceiving the relevance of this passage for our theme.

Baptism of desire and ecclesiology. Perhaps Bellarmine's greatest contribution to our understanding of baptism of desire is found in his application of the doctrine to ecclesiology. Because of the fracturing of Christianity during the Reformation, the nature of the Church was at the center of Bellarmine's concerns. Catholic theology had to take account of a large number of baptized Christians who had departed from—or, in the second generation, never held—Catholic orthodoxy. In this context, the principle *extra ecclesiam nulla salus* took on more weight than the necessity of baptism per se. But what did it mean to be in the Church? Though salvation was the most important reason to ask this question, theologians of the era also had to be concerned with the obligations and privileges Church membership entailed and questions of civil and ecclesial jurisdiction.[124]

---

sacrament in contempt; those who omit it through negligence; and those who remain unbaptized because of factors beyond their control. Robert Bellarmine, *De amissione gratiae et statu peccati*, in *Roberti Cardinalis Bellarmini Opera Omnia*, vol. 4, bk. 1, *De Controversiis Christianae Fidei* (Naples: J. Giuliano, 1858), 2.6.4, pp. 241–42.

123. He mentions Ez 18:21–22; *De obitu Valentiniani*; Augustine's *De Baptismo*; Bernard's letter to Hugh; Innocent II's letter on the unbaptized priest; the decrees of Trent; and John the Baptist's baptism of repentance. Bellarmine, *De Baptismo et Confirmatione*, 2.1.6, p. 167.

124. Bellarmine's chapter on the non-baptized begins with a verse, "For what have I to do with judging outsiders?" (1 Cor 5:12), that shows his concern with jurisdictional issues. Robert Bellarmine, *De Ecclesia militante*, in *Roberti Cardinalis Bellarmini Opera Omnia*, vol. 2, *De Controversiis Christianae Fidei* (Naples: J. Giuliano, 1857), 3.3, p. 75.

Because of these concerns, Bellarmine emphasizes membership in the
Church as something that can be seen and known, and his definitions
take on a decidedly legal character. It is worth noting that Bellarmine
does not consider formal membership in the Church to be *sufficient* for
salvation because grave sin does not cancel membership in the Church
on earth. He uses the image of body and soul to illustrate how one can
retain membership in the body of the Church while being separated from
her soul by sin. This does not imply the existence of two Churches; just
as a single human being is made up of body and soul, the Church too is
one.[125]

Bellarmine gives three criteria for determining Church membership:
profession of the true faith, sacramental communion, and obedience to
the Church's legitimate pastors. The first criteria means that pagans, Jews,
and heretics are not members of the Church; the second, that neither
are catechumens or those who have been excommunicated; the third excludes schismatics. This second group poses the most interesting dilemma
for Bellarmine, and reveals a difficulty for the *extra ecclesiam* principle.
For, as Bellarmine notes, the doctrine of baptism of desire means that,
under certain circumstances, catechumens can be saved. Bellarmine rejects the imaginative but unwieldy solution of Melchor Cano, who had
posited two Churches, one of Christ and one of Abel, with catechumens
presumably saved because of their membership in the latter. Instead, he
argues that the doctrine of the necessity of the Church for salvation must
be understood in the same way as the doctrine of the necessity of baptism. The principle that there is no salvation outside the Church applies
only to those who are outside the Church both in *re* and *in voto*.[126] In
other words, setting aside the case of non-Catholic Christians, the necessity of the Church for salvation does not make the prospects of salvation for the non-baptized either brighter or darker than the necessity of
baptism itself.

---

125. *De Ecclesia militante*, 3.2, pp. 74–75.
126. *De Ecclesia militante*, 3.3, p. 76: "Respondeo igitur, quod dicitur, extra Ecclesiam ne-
minem salvari, intelligi debere de iis, qui neque re ipsa, nec desiderio sunt de Ecclesia, sicut de
baptismo communiter loquuntur theologi. Quoniam autem catechumeni si non re, saltem voto
sunt in Ecclesia, ideo salvari possunt."

Lost in Baroque Scholasticism

Bellarmine's attention to our question proved something of an exception in the period, in which, as noted above, theologians' focus on baptism of desire became hazier. The tendency toward doctrinal abstraction and the precept-based reasoning described by Pinckaers were prime factors driving this shift. Of course, the hard cases of salvation did not disappear, and it is important to note that, despite some variations in the way theologians discussed these hard cases, their overall picture of salvation remained constant.

How many elect? Avery Dulles points out that even Francisco Suárez (1548–1617), one of the most "optimistic" figures of the age, held that "the number of the reprobate certainly exceeds that of the elect."[127] Suárez was probably the era's most influential theologian, and using his treatment of baptism of desire and related issues as an example saves us the Sisyphean task of wading through the minute differences in all of the epoch's thinkers. The article in which Suárez addresses the question of the relative number of the saved is helpful for identifying certain presuppositions of the period considered so obvious they did not need to be argued.[128] One of these was that humanity is much better off after the coming of Christ than it was before; Suárez says that both knowledge of God and sanctification were rare in the days before Christ. Granting that the indigenous peoples of the Americas or Asia lived before the "promulgation of the Gospel," therefore, did not entail that many—or any—of them

127. Avery Dulles, "The Population of Hell," in *The Church and Society: The Laurence J. McGinley Lectures, 1988–2007* (New York: Fordham University Press, 2008), 391. According to Michael Moriarty, "The Problem of the Pagans and the Number of the Elect," in Frigo, Inexcusabiles, 71, the belief that the elect are a minority was almost universal among Catholic theologians until the nineteenth century. Some, such as the Jansenist Martin de Barcos (1600–1678), argued that the reprobate exceeded the saved even among Christians. Moriarty, 69. Critics of Jansenism were not much more optimistic; Léonard de Marandé explicitly excluded the unbaptized from salvation. Moriarty, 72. Anti-Jansenist Archbishop François Fénelon, while more open to the salvation of pagans, wrote that "among one hundred men there may be barely one who is predestined." François Trémolières, "The Virtue of the Pagans and the Salvation of the Infidels in the Works of Fénelon," in Frigo, Inexcusabiles, 146.

128. Francisco Suárez, *Opera Omnia R. P. Francisci Suárez, s.j.*, vol. 1, *De Deo Uno et Trino* (Paris: Ludovicum Vivès, 1856), 6.3.3–6, pp. 524–25. Suárez also points to the New Testament passages addressing the issue directly (e.g., Mt 7:13–14, 22:14; Lk 13:23–24).

had been saved. Equally important for our study is the prominent role of the sacraments in Suárez's answer. He is unsentimental about the moral lives of Christians—most live badly, he admits—but, of those who die within the Catholic Church, a majority will still be saved because of the abounding power of the sacraments. This easily overlooked point must be taken into consideration when evaluating the theology of the era; for it shows that the felt power of the sacraments was still so obvious as not really to require argument. If issues unconnected to baptism received more attention in theological controversies, we cannot automatically conclude from this that the Christians of the era thought that the rite had become less necessary. Baroque scholasticism, after all, is filled with rivers of ink spilled over technical questions ultimately of secondary concern.

The boy in the woods. When it came to the big picture, the fundamental frame had been set by the Council of Trent and Francisco de Vitoria. Suárez, for example, saw his work as confirming and supporting the Dominican's analysis.[129] Within this framework, however, a number of subpoints became the subject of detailed controversy. Certain questions—the first moral act, the different categories of unbelief, the supernatural origin of faith—received much attention even if they only marginally affected the overall picture of who is saved and who is not. The figure of a boy making his first moral choice provides a good illustration of the sort of discussions that characterized the era. Cano, Soto, Vega, Marcos de Valladares, Bartolomé de Medina, Domingo Bañez, Diego Alvarez, Juan Martínez de Ripalda, Suárez, and others discussed the theoretical example of a boy who, upon reaching the age of reason, orders his life to God with his first moral act; later theologians would cite this discussion as opening a pathway to salvation based on the natural law.[130] The example is based on an aside found in Thomas, intended, at most, as a

129. Morali, "*Gratia ed infidelitas*," 125–26. John P. Doyle seems correct to argue that "for Catholic theologians the question of the evangelization of the Indians was largely settled in the wake of Vitoria," in "Francisco Suárez: On Preaching the Gospel to People Like the American Indians," *Fordham International Law Journal* 15, no. 4 (1991): 884. He points out that—surprisingly, given its volume—Suárez's work contains only one unambiguous reference to American Indians outside of citations of Vitoria.

130. Sullivan, *Salvation Outside the Church?* 61–62; Marenbon, *Pagans and Philosophers*, 289. For an extensive summary of this discussion, see the series of articles by Teofilo Urdanoz, "La necesidad de la fe explícita para salvarse según los teólogos de la Escuela Salmantina," *Ciencia*

thought experiment for exploring the extent of our moral abilities and obligations.[131] In fact, the example comes up in Thomas's discussion of sin and posits the obligation to order our lives correctly. Since the failure to do so is a mortal sin, Thomas's conclusion is that, for anyone still living in original sin, even venial sin is accompanied by the mortal sin of ordering one's life incorrectly.

Suárez hints at the limited value of the example. For even if the boy does all within his powers to follow the natural law, this is not enough for salvation; he still needs supernatural faith from a supernatural source. The scholastic dictum that God will help someone who does all within his power is a pious belief, but whatever "all within oneself" means, it is not the same as the *ex opere operato* power of the sacraments.[132] Suárez mentions the standard medieval supposition that God could send a preacher or an angel to illuminate the boy. Others suggested that the vestiges of a primitive revelation might somehow provide the "supernatural" basis for implicit faith.[133] Jesuit Cardinal Juan De Lugo (1583–1660) developed this idea extensively, suggesting that traces of primeval revelation passed

---

Tomista 59, no. 4 (1940): 398–414; 59, no. 5/6 (1940): 529–53; 60, no. 2 (1941): 109–34; 61, no. 4 (1941): 83–107.

131. Thomas Aquinas, *On Evil*, 5.2, ad 8, p. 239; *Commentary on the Sentences*, 2.2.1.5, ad 7; *ST*, 1-2.89.6. Vitoria understood the example in this way. Fernández, *El problema de la salvacion de los "infieles,"* 56. As Marenbon puts it, in *Pagans and Philosophers*, 176, the example "can hardly be called a theory of Aquinas's about the salvation of pagans." Even if the boy managed to order his life correctly, the example still leaves the question of how he might attain faith unaddressed. Osborne, "Unbelief and Sin," 618. "The difference is not over whether unbelievers can be saved, but the reasons for which unbelievers will be damned." Osborne, 616.

132. Francisco Suárez, *De Fide Theologica*, in *Opera Omnia R.P. Francisci Suárez, s.j.*, vol. 12, *De Virtutibus Theologicis* (Paris: Ludovicum Vivès, 1858), 1.12.2.15, p. 343. Cano earlier and Bañez later would point out the limits of the scholastic principle "facienti quod in se est Deus non denegat gratiam." Urdanoz, "La necesidad de la fe explícita para salvarse," 2:533–34. Strictly speaking, the principle is only valid in the case of someone who has already received and is responding to grace. God has not bound himself to give grace as a reward for obedience to the natural law. Bañez raises the additional point that the boy's first moral act would almost certainly be conditioned by his upbringing. Urdanoz, 3:119. One can fairly wonder what sort of childrearing would produce such a perfect moral ordering and why it is not more commonly adopted.

133. Miguel Medina (1489–1578) raised this possibility, which, however, seems to be inventing revelation to fit a theological system instead of fitting the system to revelation. Capéran, *Le problème du salut des infidèles*, 1:264. More plausible is the suggestion that the echoes of supernatural revelation remain in Judaism and Islam. Juan de la Peña (1513–1565) expressed this idea, though he thought that such revelation would help only those in limited circumstances—certain children—because of the untruth also present in those religions. Urdanoz, "La

down in cultural traditions, even if diluted, could provide access to supernatural faith.[134] The need for belief to have a supernatural origin to
be salvific was in the background of some of the age's more outlandish
theories, including the suggestion that the Apostle Thomas had reached
the Americas after preaching in India or that American Indians were
descendants of the lost tribes of Israel.[135]

Minimum faith. Suárez does not show Bellarmine's understanding of
baptism of desire's history, but his extensive use of the theology of desire in another place, where he discusses the necessity of explicit faith,
deserves our attention. Suárez takes the necessity of supernatural faith
for granted but notes that the doctrine of baptism of desire, as taught by
Thomas and accepted by Trent, means that, in certain circumstances, necessary things can be present either in reality (*re*) or in desire (*voto*). His
reasoning parallels Bellarmine's argument in *De Ecclesia militante* that,
if it is possible to have baptism *in voto*, it is also possible to belong to
the Church *in voto*. Suárez agrees but recognizes that the nature of faith
makes it uniquely difficult to possess *in voto*.[136] The desire to complete
an exterior act such as baptism presupposes an interior act or disposition
(the *votum*); the existence of this interior disposition allows Thomas to
claim that baptism can be present *in voto* when circumstances beyond
one's control make the external part of the act impossible to complete.
However, because faith is an interior act, if it is absent in *re*, then it is
also absent *in voto*. Here Suárez runs up against what Thomas had realized when developing his concept of implicit faith: It must contain at
least some explicit element. An entirely implicit faith is an impossibility.
In good scholastic style, Suárez then sets out to identify the minimum

---

necesidad de la fe explícita para salvarse," 2:544. Marcos de Valladares constructs a (somewhat
implausible) deathbed scenario on similar grounds. Urdanoz, 3:111.

134. Giulio Cardia, *La posizione del De Lugo nella dottrina della universale necessità e possibilità della fede* (Cagliari: F. Tois, 1941), 116–26. The absence of any connection to revelation was
part of the criticism De Lugo leveled against Ripalda. Cardia, 33. De Lugo insists on a minimum of explicit faith in God as a rewarder. Cardia, 60–61. On De Lugo, see also Urdanoz, "La
necesidad de la fe explícita para salvarse," 4:100; Sullivan, *Salvation Outside the Church?* 94–99.

135. Lafaye, *Quetzalcóatl and Guadalupe*, 177–208; Marenbon, *Pagans and Philosophers*, 255. The
more enduring phenomenon Lafaye discusses—the apparition of Our Lady of Guadalupe—better fits the classical theory of special revelation through a preacher, angel, or illumination.

136. Francisco Suárez, *De Fide Theologica*, 1.12.5, p. 335; 1.12.2.11, p. 342.

necessary explicit content for faith to be salvific. His reasoning is extensive and complex, and he considers the time both before and after the
coming of Christ before concluding that explicit belief in God cannot be
supplied by desire but belief in Christ can.[137] The Old Testament, after
all, shows that faith in a coming Messiah was sufficient for salvation at
least at some point in history.

As noted above, applying the *res/votum* distinction to faith in Christ
does not mean that for Suárez the narrow gate has become a superhigh-
way. The people of the newly discovered parts of the world had no revelation akin to that of Abraham to give them supernatural faith even in a
single God, and Suarez's notion of implicit faith would require someone
to convert wholeheartedly to God through faith in God's promises, loving him above all things and hoping for salvation and the forgiveness of
sins.[138] Such perfection is rare enough even with the teachings of Jesus.
Likewise, when Suárez argues in the same article that God provides sufficient grace for salvation, he is not claiming that we should adjust our
estimate of the number of the saved upwards. Rather, he is making the
point that those who are lost are so despite God's abundant grace; in
other words, he is arguing against double-predestination. If we fail to
love God completely, this is not because God did not provide us with the
necessary help.

Suárez's discussion of desire and explicit faith shows that focusing on
doctrinal beliefs instead of the sacrament does not make hard cases easier
to resolve. Nonetheless, attempting to identify an "act of faith" necessary
for salvation was as irresistible to the era's theologians as it was to prove
irresolvable. Casuists even posed the question of how often it was necessary to make an act of faith in one's lifetime.[139] As Capéran observes, despite unanimous agreement that a true act of faith in God is of absolute
necessity, opinion fragmented on the question of what exactly such an act
of faith should contain—the problem of the minimum.[140] The theoretical
examples invented in the controversy give the flavor of the discussion.
Suárez imagines a baptized child who lives such a very short time after

---

137. *De Fide Theologica*, 1.12.1–4, pp. 334–60.
138. *De Fide Theologica*, 1.12.4.13, p. 354.
139. Pinckaers, *The Sources of Christian Ethics*, 288.
140. Capéran, *Le problème du salut des infidèles*, 1:295.

attaining the use of reason that he does not have time to make an act of
faith but has also not committed any mortal sins. In another example,
he asks us to think about a catechumen who is being instructed in the
faith of the Church but has not yet learned about Christ; supposing such
a catechumen were to fall into a coma and be baptized before passing
away, Suárez argues, he would be saved without explicit faith in Christ.[141]
Neither example works because faith in Christ is made explicit in the
baptismal ritual itself. One might also wonder what sort of catechetical
malpractice would lead Suárez's catechumen to desire to belong to the
Church without ever having heard of Jesus. In any case, when presented
with a similar question from the bishop of Quebec in 1703—whether a
missionary should baptize someone who had not yet learned about Jesus—the Holy Office responded in the negative: "A missionary should
not baptize one who does not believe explicitly in the Lord Jesus Christ,
but is bound to instruct him about all those matters that are necessary
<for salvation>, by a necessity of means, in accordance with the capacity
of the one to be baptized."[142] Here, perhaps, the scenario involves a missionary deciding to withhold parts of the faith a catechumen might find
difficult to accept, which would also fail to respect the freedom of the
person being baptized.

Bellarmine seemed to see through the artificiality of such scenarios.
He addresses an objection based on the scenario of a boy raised among
Christians who believes in the truths of faith on the basis of custom, that
is, on a natural, not supernatural basis.[143] But, Bellarmine says, such a
scenario is senseless. If the boy had been baptized—probable if he had
been born among Christians—he would have supernatural faith from
the sacrament. If he had not been baptized but mistakenly believed that
he had—Bellarmine cites Innocent's letter on the unbaptized priest—
he would have baptism of desire. If he had not been baptized and did
not desire baptism, then he did not have supernatural faith. As for the
idea of being raised among Christians but not knowing about baptism,

---

141. Francisco Suárez, *De Fide Theologica*, 1.12.2.9, pp. 341–42; 1.12.4.15–17, pp. 356–57; cf.
Marenbon, *Pagans and Philosophers*, 292.

142. *Enchiridion symbolorum*, 2380–2381.

143. Robert Bellarmine, *De gratia et libero arbitrio*, 6.3, pp. 435–36, in *Roberti Cardinalis
Bellarmini Opera Omnia*, vol. 4, bk. 1.

Bellarmine dismisses such a scenario as frivolous, since baptism is among the most rudimentary aspects of the faith.

Evaluation. These discussions of a minimal "act of faith" show that the baroque scholastics had covertly fallen into the error which Cajetan had been accused of at Trent, that of proposing an alternative rite to baptism. Theologians could never settle on how to perform an act of faith sufficient for salvation because Christianity already had an act of faith both necessary and sufficient—baptism. Baptism professes faith in the Trinity and in the Paschal Mystery, and because it "speaks" in the dynamic and irreducible language of ritual and symbol, propositions will never be able to "say" exactly what it says. The theology of baptism of desire works only because, by its very nature, it resists proposing an alternative to that profession. Such a mistake is easier to recognize when the alternative is another rite (as Cajetan, allegedly, proposed), less so when it is an entirely mental event.

Losing sight of the concreteness of the sacrament in an attempt to define a salvific act of faith in the abstract also lends itself to certain distortions. At times Suárez slips away from Aquinas's robust notion of implicit faith and equates implicit belief with general belief.[144] But belief in generic monotheism does not imply faith in Jesus Christ any more than in Amon-Ra. Suárez seems to be relying on certain unspoken assumptions that preclude such a conclusion. In practical terms, he could probably have afforded a bit of imprecision because, in early seventeenth-century Europe, for both Protestants and Catholics, a generic God still meant the God of Abraham, Isaac, and Jacob. A serious rival only emerged with Enlightenment Deism at the tail end of the century.

Suárez's second flaw—the error of the age—was framing the decisive

---

144. Juan Martínez de Ripalda (1594–1648) went even further by proposing two different species of faith, strict and wide (*fides late*). To evade the problem of Pelagianism, Ripalda posited the elevation of every moral act to the status of supernatural act. Ripalda's views found hardly any support and were subjected to withering critique from De Lugo. Capéran, *Le problème du salut des infidèles*, 1:343–51; Cardia, *La posizione del De Lugo*, 8. It is, indeed, hard to escape the conclusion that Ripalda simply changes terms while preserving the substance of Pelagianism. Ripalda's notion of broad faith was among the slew of rigorist and laxist theses condemned during the Jansenist controversy. *Enchiridion symbolorum*, 2123. For Ripalda's reception in the modern era, see John F. Perry, "Juan Martínez de Ripalda and Karl Rahner's Supernatural Existential," *Theological Studies* 59, no. 3 (1998): 442–56.

question as a search for the minimum. As Capéran puts it, the seventeenth century's key question was, "What is the minimum of truths to
which we must absolutely adhere?"[145] In the end, the question only produced disagreements, and this should not surprise us. Christianity is not
a call to do or to believe the minimum; the search for the lowest theoretical requirement for admission to the kingdom of God can hardly be
reconciled with, say, the Sermon on the Mount. The scholastic minimum,
it is true, always presupposed that the one attaining it had not placed any
obstacle (*obicem*) in the way of grace; given the prevalence of sin, that
"minimum" would still have required extraordinary fidelity. More fundamentally, this way of framing the question points theology in the wrong
direction. Even if it continues to makes use of the *in voto* language, this
direction is deeply at odds with the doctrine of baptism of desire. Arguably the most important precedent for baptism of desire was baptism of
blood, hardly the example to support a minimalistic path to salvation.[146]
Properly understood, baptism of desire does not succumb to minimalism
because the doctrine is framed in terms of desire for a non-minimalistic
end—that is, all that baptism entails. Ambrose did not argue that Valentinian would be saved because he had already attained the minimum,
but because he desired the maximum.

   While later neo-scholastic scholars would sometimes attempt to frame
the theological discussions of the era as progress—Urdanoz speaks of a
"state of perfection" attained at the end of the seventeenth century—the
historical record simply does not support such an interpretation.[147] In
Suárez, we have focused on the more "optimistic" current in the discussion. The defining characteristic of this "optimism" is the position that,
under certain circumstances, some form of implicit faith in Christ could

---

145. Capéran, *Le problème du salut des infidèles*, 1:351. Suárez was also concerned to identify
a concrete minimum so that the theology of desire did not succumb to the problem of infinite
regress, i.e., desiring the desire for the desire for the desire, etc. Suárez, *De Fide Theologica*,
1.12.2.12, p. 343.

146. Mk 10:38–39 connects baptism and martyrdom. Brad Gregory's fascinating study of
martyrdom in early modernity makes the point that, even if actual martyrs had become rare in
Europe during the High Middle Ages, through devotion and ascetical practices, "martyrs and
martyrdom coursed through the veins and strengthened the sinews of late medieval Christianity." Gregory, *Salvation at Stake*, 73. This emphasis on martyrdom helped keep the "price" of
Christianity high. In early modernity, the Reformation and the expansion of Christianity into
hostile environments, such as Japan, made literal martyrdom a possibility again.

147. Urdanoz, "La necesidad de la fe explícita para salvarse," 4:83.

be salvific. This starting point, however, degenerated into a question of how much of Christianity could be left unprofessed. Moreover, "optimism" was by no means predominant. Suárez's fellow Jesuits, Bellarmine and Peter Canisius, assessed the portion of the human race that would be lost more pessimistically.[148] Flemish Jesuit Leonardus Lessius (1554–1623) considered and rejected the idea of salvation in non-Christian religions on the grounds that it would have made the work of the apostles and the suffering of the martyrs unnecessary.[149] And the writings of Belgian theologian Michael Baius (1513–1589) were to prove a precursor to Jansenism. Our focus on Suárez should not obscure what Marenbon calls "the most striking development of the time," namely, "the reemergence of a very powerful, strict Augustinian position on all matters to do with salvation." In Protestantism, he says, this position was "all but universal."[150] We will now turn to its most famous Catholic instantiation.

The Jansenist Detour

The intellectual advances of the sixteenth and seventeenth century did not correspond to a more optimistic view of salvation. In 1622–1623, Milanese professor Francesco Collius published a five-volume study of major pagan figures, *De animabus Paganorum*, making use of the era's improved historical methods and concluding that, but for a handful of exceptions such as Melchizedek, Job, and the Sibyls, nearly all of them had been damned.[151] In 1640, Dutch bishop Cornelius Jansen's massive tome *Augustinus* appeared posthumously. The movement that would eventually be named for Jansen is notoriously difficult to categorize; from different angles it was either reactionary or radically anti-establishment, ultra-Catholic or crypto-Calvinist. On one level, the controversy it provoked was a conflict

148. Dulles, "The Population of Hell," 391.

149. Ilaria Morali points out that Lessius's thought was shaped by the religious pluralism in his native Netherlands, while Spanish and Roman theologians worked in uniformly Catholic environments. Ilaria Morali, "The Early Modern Period (1453–1650)," in *Catholic Engagement with World Religions*, ed. Karl J. Becker and Ilaria Morali (Maryknoll, NY: Orbis Books, 2010), 86–88.

150. Marenbon, *Pagans and Philosophers*, 293–94.

151. Capéran, *Le problème du salut des infidèles*, 1:286–95; Marenbon, *Pagans and Philosophers*, 295. This included Socrates, Plato, Aristotle, and Trajan. Collius seemed uninterested in pagans living in the recently discovered continents.

over "efficacious grace," on another, a quite particularly French political reaction against Cardinal Richelieu's sacralizing of the state.[152] Jansenism was characterized by a rigorously Augustinian view of salvation, and in the popular imagination the censure of several Jansenist writers is sometimes understood as a defeat for a strict medieval soteriology. But in their moralism and tendency to overlook the sacraments, the Jansenists were more modern than medieval.[153] Setting labels aside, if we carefully examine the theological substance of the Jansenist controversy, we will find that it affects our theme surprisingly little.

Arnauld. Nonetheless, if only to illustrate again the ways in which baptism of desire tended to get lost in the era, we cannot bypass the episode entirely. But it will be sufficient to examine only one of the most important works on the Jansenist side, Antoine Arnauld's (1612–1694) *The Necessity of Faith in Jesus Christ to Obtain Salvation*, as well as the magisterial interventions in the controversy ranging from 1653 to 1713. Arnauld's book, published posthumously in 1701, was written in response to another book, François de La Mothe Le Vayer's *De la vertu des payens* (1642). Le Vayer is sometimes portrayed as an early representative of seventeenth- and eighteenth-century French skepticism, which would come to include such figures as Montesquieu, Voltaire, and Diderot. How subversive he intended his work to be is a matter of debate.[154] Like Collius, Le Vayer's main concern was with the pagans of antiquity, though he also applied his arguments to the virtuous pagans of the New World. In fact, in Le Vayer's work we can see the first stages of an important development in the role that the pre-Columbian inhabitants of the New World would play in debates over salvation: their use, for polemical purposes, by Enlightenment deists. Le Vayer paints an idealized portrait of "a poor American" living a morally good life, adoring God the Creator and living

152. Ephraim Radner, "Early Modern Jansenism," in Lehner et al., *Oxford Handbook of Early Modern Theology*, 436–50.

153. Jansenist diffidence toward "the sensual side of baroque Catholicism" fueled the charge of "covert Calvinism." Dale K. Van Kley, "Catholic Conciliar Reform in an Age of Anti-Catholic Revolution," in *Religious Differences in France: Past and Present*, ed. Kathleen Perry Long (Kirksville, MO: Truman State University Press, 2006), 102–3.

154. For differing interpretations, see Jean-Michel Gros, "Bayle and the Question of the Salvation of the Infidels," in Frigo, Inexcusabiles, 295–99.

without idolatry.[155] If Thomas had known of the existence of such people, Le Vayer claims, he would no doubt have adjusted his theology accordingly.[156] Such a claim—basing one's conclusions on what Thomas *would* have said rather than what he actually said—left Le Vayer open to attack from Arnauld. *Le grand Arnauld*, as he was known to his contemporaries, was, like his fellow Jansenist Blaise Pascal (1623–1662), accomplished in mathematics, philosophy, and theology. Bergin describes him as "probably the ablest polemicist of the entire century."[157] The epitaph on his tomb, written by poet Nicolas Boileau, calls him "*Le plus savant mortel qui jamais ait écrit*"—the most learned mortal who ever wrote. Like some of Arnauld's opinions, the encomium is perhaps a touch exaggerated.

Arnauld's choice of opponent is both the strength and the weakness of his work. As Capéran notes, Le Vayer was a courtier, not a trained theologian, and his writing was often imprecise.[158] Consequently, Arnauld is not always addressing the strongest version of the positions he criticizes. His principal argument is against the proposition that pagans who have led morally good lives and "hated idolatry and polytheism" can attain heaven. Even his opponents acknowledge that faith in Christ is at least implicitly necessary, but Arnauld claims that their notion of implicit faith amounts to "the mere knowledge of a just and merciful God."[159] This is less than the faith of the Jews, who believed in a future Messiah. Arnauld points out that this is not Aquinas's understanding of implicit faith and that neither scripture nor the Fathers—whom he discusses at length—support such a view. Interestingly, John 3:5 and the necessity of

155. Capéran, *Le problème du salut des infidèles*, 1:320. Le Vayer's figure does not seem to be based on any great familiarity with the American peoples but is, rather, simply the transfer of his analysis of antiquity to their context. This is also the era in which the phrase "noble savage" appeared in English for the first time, in John Dryden's 1672 play *The Conquest of Granada*. Earl Miner, "The Wild Man Through the Looking Glass," in *The Wild Man Within: An Image in Western Thought from the Renaissance to Romanticism*, ed. Edward Dudley and Maximillian E. Novak (Pittsburgh: University of Pittsburgh Press, 1972), 106.

156. Capéran, *Le problème du salut des infidèles*, 1:321.

157. Joseph Bergin, *The Politics of Religion in Early Modern France* (New Haven, CT: Yale University Press, 2014), 187.

158. Capéran, *Le problème du salut des infidèles*, 1:327. Though he cites a variety of theological sources, Le Vayer does not always seem to grasp their significance. He begins by taking issue with Gregory of Rimini, hardly the ideal representative of the theological mainstream. François de La Mothe Le Vayer, *De la vertu des payens* (Paris: Augustin Courbe, 1647), 2–3.

159. Antoine Arnauld, *The Necessity of Faith in Jesus Christ to Obtain Salvation*, trans. Guido Stucco (Bloomington, IN: Xlibris Corporation, 2011), 27–28.

baptism do not fit prominently in Arnauld's discussion of scripture—further evidence of the age's diminishing sacramental sensibility.[160] Arnauld objects that, by reducing implicit faith to a mere natural knowledge of God, his opponents' religion is indistinguishable from Pelagianism or Deism.[161] The inadequacy of their position is demonstrated by the fact that many—deists and Muslims—believe in God while explicitly rejecting Jesus Christ.[162] Nor was the Greco-Roman notion of divinity compatible with Christianity.[163]

Arnauld's fundamental objection is that the reduction of implicit faith to mere ethical monotheism renders the entirety of the Christian story unnecessary. If a vague belief in God and being a good person were enough for salvation, why would the Jews have hoped for a Messiah? Why would Paul have carried the name of Jesus to the Gentiles if they already possessed salvation?[164] Why would the martyrs die for doctrines that were, in the end, superfluous?[165] And Arnauld goes on. He repeatedly returns to the virtue of humility—which led Christians to forgo the world's admiration, but was little celebrated in pagan literature—to show that Christianity's teachings are sometimes counter-intuitive. Yet those arguing for the salvation of the greats of antiquity do so precisely on the grounds of those luminaries' achievements.[166] We might admire Homer's verse or Aristotle's logic—but do we expect God to be so overawed? Jesus did not teach that such accomplishments brought one closer to heaven. Because the difference between Christian and pagan moral values is so massive, an essentially deistic understanding of salvation means moral as well as religious relativism. Why should Christians observe precepts more burdensome than those of the pagans? Why not settle for the minimum of not upsetting the laws of the state and public order?[167] In fact, why

160. Arnauld places more emphasis on Jesus' exclusive role as mediator, especially Jn 17:3, Jn 3:18, and Acts 4:12. Arnauld, 29–30, 36.

161. Arnauld, 42, 48.

162. Arnauld, 38.

163. He points especially to the absence of hope and contrition in pagan writings. Arnauld, 178–79, 235.

164. Arnauld, 39–40.

165. Arnauld, 49–50.

166. Arnauld, 256, 283. He repeats Bernard's charge against Abelard: "While endeavoring to make Plato a Christian, he proved himself a pagan." Arnauld, 287.

167. Arnauld, 268–70.

insist on moral obligations at all if dispensing from religious ones? If God could, through an extraordinary grace, dispense the obligation to believe in Jesus, could he not just as well, through an equally extraordinary grace, dispense the obligation of marital fidelity?[168] If God truly desires *all* to be saved, doesn't this include unrepentant adulterers?

Arnauld's artillery barrage is devastating for any notion of implicit faith unable to distinguish itself from Deism. At times, however, Arnauld himself ends up on equally indefensible terrain. His curt dismissal of baptism of desire is a case in point. This comes at the end of his analysis of the story of Cornelius. He argues, reasonably, that Cornelius makes a poor example of implicit faith because he almost certainly had some knowledge of the Messiah through his contact with the Jews.[169] Furthermore, the fact that he sends for Peter and undergoes baptism demonstrates that the centurion's good life and incipient faith were not enough for salvation. For people such as "catechumens and Cornelius," who are "conceived" but not yet "born," the "grace of faith is not sufficient to obtain the Kingdom of heaven [...] before they are incorporated into the church through participation in the sacraments."[170] He would thus seem to rule out baptism of desire—though without providing an argument beyond the analogy of conception and birth. He has indeed sniffed out what is perhaps the weakest piece of evidence used in the tradition to support baptism of desire, the story of Cornelius. But the doctrine hardly rests on that example alone, and Arnauld does not engage with any other evidence. Nor does he consider how his own observation that the yearning expressed in prayer is already the result of God's grace might affect a case such as Valentinian's.[171] He repeatedly cites Bellarmine and the Council of Trent—even those canons that mention baptism *in voto*—without acknowledging that both support the doctrine.[172] And he never really engages Aquinas's more robust version of implicit faith.

We need not catalogue all of Arnauld's excesses. However, it is important not to reduce him to a caricature. In some ways—his demythologizing of the ancients, for example—Arnauld is a decisively modern

168. Arnauld, 251.
169. Arnauld, 156–58.
170. Arnauld, 158.
171. Arnauld, 89–91.
172. Arnauld, 61.

figure.[173] Ironically, he mentions Native Americans more in *The Necessity of Faith in Jesus Christ* than does the "optimistic" Suárez. In any case, both Arnauld and his opponents are more concerned to discuss the pagans of antiquity than those of the Western Hemisphere.[174] His skirmishes with Le Vayer on this question, however, show the beginning of the shift in the way the discovery of the New World would come to affect theology centuries after the discovery itself. Vitoria and the theologians of the sixteenth century applied traditional theology to the new situation they encountered. In the polemics of Enlightenment deists, the specter of unbaptized masses would be turned against that same theology to argue that it should be replaced with something else. Baptism of desire would savor of medieval circumlocution to the deist, of excessive laxity to the Jansenist. Perhaps what is most interesting is what Jansenists, deists, and Baroque scholastics alike all failed to notice: In different ways, they had each begun to treat what had been central to the Fathers—the sacrament—as an afterthought.

Roman intervention. A glance at the magisterial censures issued over the course of the Jansenist controversy, between 1653 and 1713, shows that the dispute had less to do with the sacraments' relationship to salvation than with more abstract notions of grace. As far as the controversy involved the sacraments, it mainly had to do with confession, reflecting the shift in theological emphasis noted by Pinckaers toward law and obedience. The fundamental excess of Jansenist theology was its notion of grace and predestination, so strong that it ruled out any meaningful role for human free will. Such a notion comes at the expense of the universal salvific will of God as well as the possibility of refusing cooperation with God's grace. This seems to have been at issue in the papal constitution *Cum occasione* directed against Jansen himself in 1653, as well as in a later decree of the Holy Office in 1690. Both of these pronouncements take issue with the idea that Christ died only for the elect.[175] Likewise, a 1690 decree of

---

173. In this respect he is more like Montaigne than Erasmus; see Alberto Frigo, "Montaigne's Gods," in Frigo, Inexcusabiles, 16.

174. Arnauld treats the possibility of vast numbers of such pagans being saved as so obviously false that it serves as a *reductio ad absurdum* of his opponents' position. Arnauld, *The Necessity of Faith*, 47.

175. *Enchiridion symbolorum*, 2005–2006; 2304.

the Holy Office censures the proposition that non-Christians and heretics have not received sufficient grace from God.[176] But the Holy Office also upholds the ability of sinners to refuse God's grace.[177] As when Suárez made the same argument, these principles do not imply that any non-Christians are saved, merely that no one is lost because God has been too stingy with his grace.

In reality, the potential salvation of non-Christians was not really at issue in the Roman interventions, and the magisterium's vindication of human freedom rules out certain forms of universalism as surely as it rules out the double-predestination of Calvin. Moreover, throughout the course of the controversy Rome sought to maintain a balanced theological position by condemning a number of laxist positions in 1665, 1666, and 1679. Reflecting discussion of the necessity of an act of faith, the Holy Office condemns the proposition that "A man is not bound at any time at all in his life to utter an act of faith, hope, and charity," leaving undefined, however, what such an act would look like or whether ignorance or inability might excuse one from the "divine precepts" that give such an obligation its force.[178] Two of the condemnations are directed against permissive lines of thought found within the baroque scholastic school represented by Suárez and, more obviously, Ripalda; these insist that faith "in the broad sense" (*fides late*) is insufficient for justification, as is a generic faith in God that does not recognize a "Rewarder."[179] In the condemnation of both rigorists and laxists, moral questions form the heart of the decrees' concerns. No Church pronouncement from the controversy calls into question Trent's affirmation of the doctrine of baptism of desire or elaborates on it. As far as our question is concerned, the sound and fury of Jansenism had changed almost nothing.

176. *Enchiridion symbolorum*, 2305; cf. 2426–2429.

177. *Unigenitus* condemns the propositions: "All whom God wishes to save through Christ are infallibly saved" and "The desires of Christ always have their effect." *Enchiridion symbolorum*, 2430–2431. Leszek Kolakowski observes, "true Catholic doctrine—of the Thomists, the Jesuits, and the great doctors of the Church—teaches us that, as a result of the corruption of the will, grace may altogether fail to achieve its effect or achieve it only in part." Leszek Kolakowski, *God Owes Us Nothing: A Brief Remark on Pascal's Religion and on the Spirit of Jansenism* (Chicago: University of Chicago Press, 1995), loc. 327 of 4817, Kindle.

178. *Enchiridion symbolorum*, 2021.

179. *Enchiridion symbolorum*, 2122–23.

Summing up the significance of early modernity for the doctrine of baptism of desire, therefore, is not easy. On the one hand, the doctrine had been vindicated at Trent, enjoying broad support among the Council Fathers and receiving official validation in the conciliar decrees. After a thousand years of discussion, the case of the sincere catechumen dying before the Easter Vigil might no longer be considered quite so hard. But other cases had not gotten any easier. The boldest theological proposal of the era, Cajetan's attempt to apply the doctrine to unborn children and unbaptized infants, had met with a resounding thud, though it escaped official condemnation. A wide array of thinkers—from John Major to Francisco Suárez—recognized baptism of desire's relevance for those who had not yet heard the Gospel preached. Vitoria's principle that such people—though still culpable for original and personal sin—would not be punished for their ignorance won wide acceptance. So did Bellarmine's application of the logic of baptism of desire to the necessity of the Church. Both thinkers, however, recognized that salvation required more than release from a religious requirement, and the necessity of baptism for salvation continued to provide inspiration and impetus for the era's impressive missionary undertaking. Identifying what that "more" might be exercised the theologians of the post-Tridentine era, though their reduction of the question to the search for a minimum of doctrinal belief ended up exacerbating their difficulties. Part of the problem was that, while these thinkers used the *in re*/*in voto* distinction articulated by Aquinas, they set aside the sacrament as furnishing any relevant theological data. This shift made discussions more abstract and legalistic—emphasizing precept and obligation—though not always clearer. In this respect, little would change in the eighteenth century. The Enlightenment was dawning, but baptism of desire was fading into the shadows.

Chapter Five

The Long Nineteenth Century

In his book on the Second Vatican Council, historian John O'Malley applies the term "the Long Nineteenth Century"—used by historians since the 1990s to refer to the period between the French Revolution and World War I—to the Catholic Church before the 1960s.[1] In this chapter, I am suggesting that, as far as our topic is concerned, we are still living in a Long Nineteenth Century. In other words, the bloody upheaval of the French Revolution and its aftermath—politically, the collapse of Christendom; intellectually, the end of the Age of Faith—provoked a crisis in Catholic attitudes toward salvation and the necessity of the sacraments with which we are still struggling to come to terms. In the previous chapter, I challenged the idea that the geographical discoveries of the fifteenth and sixteenth centuries provoked a radical rethinking of Catholicism's teaching on salvation. Around the middle of the nineteenth century, however, something indeed began to change in the way theologians spoke about salvation such that, by the late twentieth century,

---

1. John W. O'Malley, *What Happened at Vatican II* (Cambridge, MA: Harvard University Press, 2008), 53–92; see also Joseph A. Carola, "The Academics, the Artist, and the Architect: Retrieving the Tradition in Nineteenth-Century Catholicism," *Logos: A Journal of Catholic Thought and Culture* 23, no. 1 (2020): 66–67.

theologian Richard McBrien could identify baptism of desire with the belief that "grace and revelation are universally available."[2]

Here we will try to come to grips with what those changes were and how they came about. The answer is not particularly neat. It involves a hodgepodge of social, intellectual, political, and religious factors, some of which can be considered genuine advances, others the result of decline and defensiveness. My use of the term "Long Nineteenth Century" is not meant to be taken too far; Catholicism, particularly at the Second Vatican Council, has come to terms with many aspects of this civilizational upheaval. But on the question of salvation and its relationship to the sacraments, the era's confusion and unease have yet to be overcome. In the first part of this chapter, we will see the roots of this unease in the religious attitudes of Enlightenment thinkers such as Rousseau and Kant, who severed the connection between liturgical acts and salvation in favor of a religion of universal ethics. Next, we will examine those changes in Catholic culture that, around 1850, produced a shift in attitudes about the relative number of those saved. The problems that emerge in this era—an exaggerated emphasis on invincible ignorance; difficulty explaining the reason for religious ritual; unease with the diminished role of Christianity in the West; ambivalence over the dogma *extra ecclesiam nulla salus*—would lead to tumult in the twentieth century. Radically different responses to Christendom's demise included, on the one extreme, the first serious opposition to baptism of desire since the Middle Ages (from Leonard Feeney of Boston) and, on the other extreme, interpretations of the doctrine that left out both baptism and desire. The tensions that produced these reactions were not stilled by the Second Vatican Council and continue to dog theology today. The era we are studying in this chapter, with all its ambiguities and anxieties, is our own.

Revolution and Reaction

Just as the Long Nineteenth Century did not end in 1900, neither did it begin in 1800. The dynamics that shaped how baptism of desire came to be addressed—or ignored—today have their beginning in the 1700s. The Enlightenment—from the scientific discoveries of Isaac Newton (1642–1727)

2. Richard P. McBrien, *Catholicism*, 2 vols. (Minneapolis: Winston Press, 1980), 2:752–53.

to the caustic anti-clericalism of Voltaire (1694–1778)—permanently reshaped the cultural dynamics in which Catholic theology was done. As a
result, by the 1850s Catholic apologists realized that they needed to strike
a different tone when discussing salvation. When this shift happened—
though not *why* it happened—is surprising clear. More than a change in
theology, what happened in the 1850s could be thought of as a change in
mood and attitude. The theological arguments meant to justify this shift
in the years that followed were somewhat cobbled together, and the less-
than-precise treatment of baptism of desire in twentieth century theology
is symptomatic of these dynamics.

Enlightenment Religion

As noted at the end of the previous chapter, the seventeenth and eighteenth centuries produced no revolutions in the Catholic theology.[3]
Other aspects of European intellectual life, however, underwent dramatic changes. Newton's formulation of the laws of motion and gravitation,
John Locke's (1632–1704) empiricism, and weariness from the bloody sec-
tarian wars fought in the wake of the Reformation combined to produce
an environment favorable to the idea of "natural religion"—that is, to a
religion based on the belief that God's will can be discovered by studying
the workings of the universe without recourse to revelation.[4] Aristotle's
physics crumbled before the new science, and his metaphysics became
collateral damage. René Descartes (1596–1650) used skepticism as a philosophical technique and introduced a dichotomy between body and soul
that had been foreign to Thomism. Luxury goods—such as coffee—from
abroad created a fascination with the exotic, clothing the lands discovered
in previous centuries with a glamor they had not enjoyed in the accounts

3. Alphonsus Liguori (1696–1787) provides an example of a direct, if brief, treatment of
baptism of desire from the era, which does not differ substantially from what we saw after
Trent. He mentions baptism *flaminis* alongside baptism of blood, defining it as perfect conversion to God though contrition (not attrition) and love of God above all things with either
explicit or implicit desire for baptism in water. Baptism of desire provides the remission of
sins, he says, though it does not impart baptismal character and does not take away all of the
punishment due to sin. Alphonsus Liguori, *Theologia Moralis: Editio Nova*, 4 vols., ed. Leonardi
Gaudé (Rome: Ex Typographia Vaticana, Rome, 1909), vol. 3, 6.2.1, 95–96, p. 75.

4. Stephen Gaukroger, "The Challenges of Empirical Understanding in Early Modern
Theology," in Lehner et al., *Oxford Handbook of Early Modern Theology*, 566–70.

of the first missionaries.[5] Nonetheless, European intellectual consciousness had been indelibly shaped by Christianity and continued to take
monotheism and Christian ethics for granted. The result of this particular
cultural milieu, especially among a certain class of northern European
intellectuals, was deism, belief in a God who set the universe in motion
but then remained distant.

The difficulties Enlightenment culture posed for Christian teaching
can be illustrated by three figures: Jean-Jacques Rousseau (1712–1778), Immanuel Kant (1724–1804), and Thomas Jefferson (1743–1826). Rousseau's
treatise on education *Emile* contains—between his opinions on everything
from breastfeeding to courtship—a celebrated attack on belief in the necessity of Christian faith for salvation. Rousseau calculates that "two-
thirds of mankind" are neither Jews, nor Muslims, nor Christians. He asks:

> Will they all go to hell for having been recluses? Even if it were
> true that the gospel has been proclaimed everywhere on earth, what
> would be gained by it? Surely on the eve of the day that the first
> missionary arrived in some country, someone died there who was
> not able to hear him [...] If there were only a single man in the
> whole universe who had never been preached to about Jesus Christ,
> the objection would be as strong for that single man as for a quarter
> of mankind.[6]

Rousseau's objection strikes not only at specific Christian doctrines, but
at revealed religion as such. He invents his own alternative religious vision, not only rejecting, but seeming to invert, the idea of original sin. It
is God who is in debt to his creatures, he claims, because he has endowed
them with desire for the good.[7] Rousseau's thought revolves around his
idealized state of nature and depends upon a limitless faith in his own
ability to arrive at religious truth without external aid.[8] As such, his religion amounts largely to self-assertion impervious to rational critique.
In the end, such self-absorption leaves no room—or need—for a savior.[9]

---

5. China, for example, was portrayed as "a well-ordered and highly moral nation of atheists." Gaukroger, 573.

6. Jean-Jacques Rousseau, *Emile*, trans. Allan Bloom (New York: Basic Books, 1979), 305.
Rousseau's argument is found within "The Creed of a Savoyard Priest" in Part IV of the work.

7. Rousseau, 282.

8. Rousseau, 305–7.

9. His self-regard becomes, in its own peculiar way, salvific when he declares in his ninth

Given his presuppositions, Rousseau can offer no insight into baptism of desire, but his work is worth highlighting because it shows how Christianity was put on the defensive by the Enlightenment. Rousseau's deism was the religion adopted by the French Revolution—his relics interred with pomp in the French *Panthéon* alongside Voltaire's—and his depiction of the alleged cruelty of Christian beliefs may have contributed to the bloodthirsty zeal with which the faith was persecuted by the revolutionaries. *Emile*, unsurprisingly, was strongly censured by the theological faculty of the Sorbonne, which focused not so much on Rousseau's assertions about the afterlife as on his rejection of the possibility of revelation.[10] In itself, Rousseau's theology did not have much staying power beyond the eighteenth century, though his critique of Christianity continues to exert a certain force.[11] His polemic in *Emile* introduces, but also reveals the limits of, what was to become a popular line of attack against traditional Christian belief—the sheer number of non-Christians. In the end, Rousseau admits his argument would be the same if the number of those damned for professing the wrong religion were one or one hundred billion. Invoking the specter of suffering masses is for rhetorical, not logical, effect.

Immanuel Kant—a substantially more rigorous thinker than Rousseau—would exert a more complex and lasting influence on theology. As Yong and Watkins put it, Kant's influence on liberal Protestantism is "difficult to overstate," while nineteenth century Catholic theologians saw him as a top opponent.[12] Early in the twentieth century, Kant's thought received a more sympathetic reception in Catholic circles thanks to Belgian Jesuit

Reverie, "I love myself too much to hate anybody." Carolina Armenteros, "The Anti-Theological Theology of Jean-Jacques Rousseau," in Lehner et al., *Oxford Handbook of Early Modern Theology*, 597.

10. *Determinatio Sacrae Facultatis Parisiensis Super Libro cui Titulus, Émile ou De L'Éducation* (Paris: Charles-Pierre Berton, 1776).

11. Armenteros describes Rousseau's theology being "absorbed—and dissolved" in Romanticism. Armenteros, "The Anti-Theological Theology of Jean-Jacques Rousseau," 600.

12. Peter Yong and Eric Watkins, "Kant's Philosophical and Theological Commitments," in Lehner et al., *Oxford Handbook of Early Modern Theology*, 606. They add, "the theological programs of Hegel and Schleiermacher would have been unthinkable apart from the critical revolution Kant initiated." For background on the theological terrain of early nineteenth century Catholicism and Kant's role in it, see the early chapters in Gerald A. McCool, *Nineteenth-Century Scholasticism: The Search for a Unitary Method* (New York: Fordham University Press, 1989).

Joseph Maréchal (1878–1944). Maréchal's synthesis of Kantian transcendentalism and Thomism—transcendental Thomism—greatly influenced later theologians, such as Karl Rahner.[13] Kant too proposed a religion fundamentally independent of revelation, asserting that his version of religion has no need for historical doctrines and "can be elicited from every human being, upon questioning, in its entirety, without any of it having ever been taught to him."[14] Only one aspect of Kant's thought, however, need detain us here—namely, his attitude toward ritual. For Kant, the only religious service that counts is the fulfillment of one's moral duties. Consequently, he asserts as an axiom "requiring no proof" that religious acts beyond ethical conduct are "mere religious delusion and counterfeit service of God."[15] While he allows that baptism might have some ceremonial value as an encouragement to good citizenship, he specifically rejects the rite's efficacy, calling the idea that the sacrament washes away sins "a delusion that openly betrayed its ties to an almost more than pagan superstition."[16] Neither can faith be considered necessary for salvation, for "true religion is not to be placed in the knowledge or the profession of what God does or has done for our salvation, but in what we must do to become worthy of it."[17] There is no room in the Prussian philosopher's vision for anything approaching mystical participation in divine life. His emphasis on duty and obedience to the law shows certain resonances with the Ockhamist strain of Christian ethics identified by Servais Pinckaers and discussed in the previous chapter, though he takes that emphasis to its extreme. Perhaps more than any other Enlightenment thinker, Kant demonstrates the loss of what Grillo calls the "classical" attitude toward religious ritual, in which the rite's necessity and effectiveness were presupposed.[18] In a Kantian world, worship becomes almost incomprehensible.

Kant's position is important because he frames it as the preservation of what is most pure and authentic in Christianity; he supposes himself

13. Gerald A. McCool, *The Neo-Thomists* (Milwaukee: Marquette University Press, 1994), 117–35, 160.

14. Immanuel Kant, *Religion within the Boundaries of Mere Reason and Other Writings*, trans. and ed. Allen Wood and George Di Giovanni (Cambridge: Cambridge University Press, 2019), 207.

15. Kant, 196.

16. Kant, 222.

17. Kant, 160.

18. Grillo, *Introduzione alla teologia liturgica*, 177–230.

to be on the cutting edge of a historical progression to an almost utopian future.[19] He does preserve, in modified form, certain Christian concepts such as original sin—putting him at odds with Rousseau, whom he criticizes—and he occasionally quotes a limited stock of Biblical passages to support what remains a fundamentally unbiblical natural religion.[20] Similarly, he leaves open the possibility of continuing to practice some sort of religious rites, but only insofar as these reinforce an all-consuming sense of moral duty.[21] Kant's "Christianity" seems almost designed to embody the belief anathematized by Trent that "the sacraments are not necessary for salvation, but that they are superfluous."[22]

The same basic conception of religion is illustrated colorfully by an odd literary production of the third president of the United States, Thomas Jefferson. The author of the Declaration of Independence produced his own version of the life of Jesus, as he describes it, by "cutting the texts out of the book [of the gospels] and arranging them on the pages of a blank book."[23] Kant would have been pleased with Jefferson's results, which omit all traces of the miraculous from the narrative and focus exclusively on Jesus' ethical teachings. The book ends with the Lord's burial and no trace of the Resurrection.[24] Jefferson claims the book as proof that "I am a REAL CHRISTIAN."[25] While it possesses no particular theological merit, the work illustrates the difficult dynamic for credal Christianity created by the Enlightenment. For more than a millennium Western culture and Christendom had been synonymous. Jefferson thought of himself as a Christian; his beliefs arose out of a Christian milieu and probably would not have been possible in any other. In the Western mind, therefore, it became possible to reject the Creed, more or less, in its entirety and still be a "Christian." Rousseau's objections to Christianity's teachings about the afterlife were not all that different from those raised by

19. Kant, *Religion within the Boundaries of Mere Reason*, 150–52, 181.

20. Kant, 54.

21. Kant, 203. Rousseau too allows that religious rituals could have a reassuring effect if attached to attractive doctrines in the service of prior moral duties. Rousseau, *Emile*, 308–10.

22. *Enchiridion symbolorum*, 1604.

23. Thomas Jefferson, *The Life and Morals of Jesus of Nazareth* (St. Louis: N.D. Thompson, 1902), 18.

24. Jefferson denied the divinity of Jesus. Jefferson, 12. Belief in judgment and the afterlife are retained because he thought these contributed to good morals. Jefferson, 17, 141.

25. Jefferson, 18.

second-century Platonists confronting Justin Martyr or by the Japanese bonzes debating Francis Xavier. Yet, their incompatibility with Christianity became more difficult to recognize because they were the product of Western thinkers. Such ideas, therefore, entered more easily and more subtly into circulation among Christians themselves.

The Apologists Maneuver

As the Sorbonne's condemnation of Rousseau indicates, the first Catholic thinkers to respond to what we today call the Enlightenment treated the movement as a threat. This attitude was true both of the Sorbonne's professional theologians and of popular preachers and apologists. The dominant figure of seventeenth- and eighteenth-century French Catholicism was the bishop, scholar, and celebrated orator Jacques-Benigne Bossuet (1627–1704).[26] Bossuet took a firm line against religious indifferentism, emphasizing faith in Christ as the only sure path to salvation, while avoiding the double-predestination of Jansenism. Apologists of the following century followed in Bossuet's footsteps, affirming the absolute necessity of the Gospel of Jesus Christ for salvation while refuting Rousseau.[27] The line of thought propounded by Rousseau, they saw, would lead to something like the cut-and-paste religion of Jefferson. The papal magisterium of the early nineteenth century likewise railed against religious indifferentism, defined as the opinion that "man can attain the eternal salvation of his soul by any profession of faith, provided his moral conduct conforms to the norms of right and good."[28]

26. One biographer compares Bossuet's place in French letters to that of Shakespeare in English. Ella K. Sanders, *Jacques Bénigne Bossuet: A Study* (New York: MacMillan, 1921), 1. In the nineteenth century, Henri-Dominique Lacordaire, who will be discussed below, spoke with reverence of Bossuet. Henri-Dominique Lacordaire, *Thoughts and Teachings of Lacordaire* (New York: Benziger Brothers, 1903), 331. Capéran, *Le problème du salut des infidèles*, 1:382–83.

27. For example, Deforis, *Préservatif pour les fidèles contre les sophisms et les impiétés des incrédules* (Paris: Desaint & Saillant, 1764). For discussion, see Capéran, *Le problème du salut des infidèles*, 1:423. Gottfried Hermann and Antonio Valsecchi also forcefully rejected the Enlightenment claim that one can be saved in any religion. Ilaria Morali, "The Travail of Ideas in the Three Centuries Preceding Vatican II (1650–1964)," in Becker and Morali, *Catholic Engagement with World Religions*, 103–4.

28. Gregory XVI, Encyclical Letter *Mirari vos* (August 15, 1832); *Enchiridion symbolorum*, 2730. *Mirari vos* is a problematic encyclical because of its condemnation of freedom of the press and its conception of Church-state relations, which does not sit well with Vatican II's *Dignitatis*

While theology between Bossuet and Gregory XVI remained constant, the social context in which the Church found herself could hardly have changed more dramatically. Bossuet had been the court preacher for Louis XIV. In 1793, Louis XVI went to the guillotine. The French Revolution resulted in the confiscation of Church property, the suppression of religious orders, and a *de facto* schism between clergy who swore loyalty to the new regime and those who refused. At around the same time, over papal protests, Emperor Joseph II imposed a number of religious "reforms" in the Hapsburg Empire, including the suppression of contemplative religious orders. In 1796, at the behest of the Republican government, Napoleon invaded and plundered Italy, taking Pope Pius VI prisoner in 1799 and shipping him to France, where he died in captivity. After establishing himself as ruler of France, Napoleon relaxed the Revolution's religious persecution but left no question that the Church would be subordinate to the state. It took the Corsican's defeat at Waterloo by the Protestant British for control of the papal states to return to another Napoleonic captive, Pope Pius VII. Revolution again broke out across Europe in 1848, leading to the overthrow of another French monarch, the establishment of another short-lived French Republic, and, soon enough, another Napoleon at the helm of another French Empire. The revolution of 1848, however, was accompanied by uprisings across Europe, including Rome, where the young Pope Pius IX fled the city in disguise. The Church, in other words, was on the defensive.

Lacordaire. The effect of the nineteenth century's destabilizing political changes on Catholic attitudes toward salvation has yet to be adequately explored by either theologians or historians. This is a real lacuna, because the 1850s witnessed a more significant shift in Catholic thinking about the number of those saved than the three centuries following the discovery of the New World. We will turn to Pius IX's role in this shift in the next section. First, however, our attention must remain in France, where attitudes were shaped by the very peculiar dynamics of French Catholicism. Among

---

Humanae. It seems to me that the parts of the encyclical dealing with the civil order presuppose the existence of a very particular type of Christian state; absent that presupposition, Gregory's arguments cannot hold up and are thus only of historical, not doctrinal, interest. The incompatibility of religious indifferentism with Christianity, however, does not rest on such historical presuppositions and is consonant with the ancient *regula fidei* and subsequent papal teaching.

the few scholars to appreciate the importance of this moment for the theology of salvation, Guillaume Cuchet draws attention to conferences delivered at Notre Dame in Paris by the Dominican Henri Lacordaire.[29]
Lacordaire was the most celebrated orator of the nineteenth century, as
Bossuet had been in the seventeenth. In 1851, Lacordaire directly challenged the view that only a very small number of people would be saved.
This view had been particularly strong in France thanks, in part, to Bossuet, as well as Jansenism and the reaction to religious indifferentism. Here,
however, we should stress that the rigorism against which Lacordaire and
other mid-nineteenth century preachers were reacting was not primarily
concerned with the necessity of baptism. The main question under dispute was the number of Catholics who would get into heaven; baptism
was assumed, and controversy centered on the exigencies of the moral life
and the practice of the sacrament of penance.[30] This rigorism demanded
of Christians not only perfect moral observance, but also perfect interior
motivation. Eighteenth-century preaching would later be criticized for
its paralyzing effect on Christian life; by focusing exclusively on the Gospel's most frightening dimensions—the narrowness of the gate—it made
spiritual progress seem hopeless.[31] A generation later, the Jesuit Auguste
Castelein (1840–1922) decried the lack of sobriety and balance in the era's
hellfire sermons.[32]

Lacordaire was among the first to challenge the eighteenth century's
rigorism, denying that Catholic doctrine taught "as an article of faith
that it is the smaller proportion of men who will be saved"—though it
did teach that some were lost.[33] The fact that, even into the early twen-

29. Guillaume Cuchet, "Une révolution théologique oubliée: Le triomphe de la thèse du
grand nombre des élus dans le discours catholique du XIXe siècle," *Revue d'histoire du XIXe
siècle*, 41 (2010): 131. See also Henry Bordeaux, "Le centenaire de la mort de Lacordaire," *Revue
des Deux Mondes (1829–1971)* (1961): 25–39.

30. See the valuable study of Jean-Louis Quantin, *Il rigorismo cristiano*, trans. G. Cavalli
(Milan: Jaca Book, 2002). The term "rigorist" came to be used to describe an anti-probabilism
stance toward penitential practice in the seventeenth and eighteenth centuries. Quantin, 12–20.
Quantin maintains that rigorism should be understood as a reaction against laxist tendencies
in casuistry and would have developed even without the influence of Jansenism. Quantin, 65.
His analysis of the drift of moral theology toward an Ockhamist fixation on law and obligation
agrees with that of Pinckaers. Quantin, 22.

31. Quantin, 14, 93, 124.

32. Cuchet, "Une révolution théologique oubliée," 147.

33. Lacordaire, *Thoughts and Teachings of Lacordaire*, 160–61, 245–58.

tieth century, proponents of the greater number of the elect position felt compelled to argue that the question could be freely debated shows how dominant the more restrictive view had been. In his seventy-first conference at Notre Dame, Lacordaire laid out an argument that the proportion of the saved was higher than of the damned.[34] The argument has the character of demographic analysis, and he speaks of the "admirable tricks" used by God to boost the number of the elect.[35] First, Lacordaire points out that one third of children die before reaching the age of reason; for the baptized, this means automatic admission to the kingdom of heaven.[36] Citing statistics from the *Annuaire du Bureau des longitudes* and adding in those who die between the ages of seven and fourteen, he estimates that half of the human race dies before reaching puberty, making them unlikely to have succumbed to mortal sin. He points out that even unbaptized children are spared damnation because, guilty of original sin alone, they "find in the asylum of limbo an existence which at least they do not regret."[37] Lacordaire also considers the somewhat sheltered existence of women—who make up half the survivors of childhood—a shield from sin; women, in his view, are at a statistical advantage for salvation because of the graces of virginity and motherhood. Adult men present the most challenging case for Lacordaire. But, because most of these are poor, the majority seems likely at least to avoid the self-indulgences that come from wealth. Even the wealthy, though at a disadvantage, can benefit from God's particular graces.

Lacordaire's analysis is intended to demonstrate that a substantial majority of Catholics are saved. It is not clear how he would answer the question of whether a majority of mankind is saved, though he does offer two considerations that apply to non-Catholic contexts.[38] First, he applies the concept of invincible ignorance to non-Catholic Christians. If simple believers growing up in Protestant or Orthodox countries profess erroneous beliefs, they do so only because they do not know any

34. Henri-Dominique Lacordaire, *Conférences de Notre-Dame de Paris*, vols. 1 and 4 (Paris: Sagnier et Bray, 1844–1851), 4:147–83.

35. Lacordaire, 4:174.

36. Under the old law, the faith of parents was sufficient; since the faith of adults is liable to waver, Lacordaire claims that baptism provides a more reliable help for salvation than was available before Christ. Lacordaire, 4:175.

37. Lacordaire, 4:252.

38. Lacordaire, 4:181–82.

better and despite their good will. Lacordaire's use of "invincible igno-rance" is consistent with the reasoning of Francisco de Vitoria, whose definitive analysis of the concept we saw in the previous chapter; it can excuse Christian believers from the sin of inadvertently professing her-esy, though it cannot provide Christian faith where it is lacking. As for non-Christians, Lacordaire believes it at least possible for them to find their way to salvation, though he does not appear to think that such extraordinary occurrences would be decisive in his statistical reckoning because he adds a second argument, namely that the Church may spread farther across the earth in the future.

As for those exceptional cases of non-Christians being saved, Lacor-daire alludes to a previous conference, which is of particular interest to us because it includes a reference to "the baptism of fire."[39] The confer-ence discusses the history of God's providential plan for humanity, a plan that culminates in Jesus Christ, the fullness of truth, toward whom all of God's other actions are directed. The orientation of all divine action to Catholic truth allows Lacordaire to oppose religious indifferentism; he contrasts God's providence with the confusion wrought by the devil and the false paths of polytheism, dualism, Judaism, Islam, and heresy. The truth, he grants, has not always been present in the world to the same degree, but God has always provided men of good will with sufficient in-struction for salvation. In places where explicit Christianity is not known, three conditions must be met if one is to attain salvation: First, one must practice the truth to the degree it is known; second, one must make prog-ress by embracing and practicing a truth greater than the one into which one was born; and, third, one must die loving God above all things.[40] If these conditions are met, one might very well arrive at explicit Christian faith through the ordinary means provided through the Church. Where that is not possible, Lacordaire says, one can be saved by an extraordinary infusion of grace and love at the hour of death. This infusion he calls the "baptism of fire."[41]

While it is sketched out only briefly, Lacordaire's appeal to baptism

39. The discussion comes from his fifth conference given at Notre Dame. Lacordaire, 1:97–114; cf. Lacordaire, *Thoughts and Teachings of Lacordaire*, 48–51.

40. Lacordaire, *Conférences de Notre-Dame de Paris*, 1:110.

41. Lacordaire, 1:113.

of desire has much to recommend it. Since he was challenging the conventional wisdom of his day, Lacordaire needed to ground his thinking in authoritative theological terminology. Baptism of desire achieved that aim. He applies the concept more broadly than to catechumens, but his second condition for receiving baptism of fire—progress toward a greater truth than that into which one was born—conveys a sense of desire for the fullness of Christian truth that is hardly trivial. His emphasis on progress toward the fulness of truth also avoids having to identify an artificial minimum of truth necessary for salvation. All three of his conditions make salvation possible for anyone, but their orientation toward the objective truth of Christianity means that one would always be better off with the helps provided by revelation and the sacraments. And even if his conditions are fulfilled, salvation still requires an extraordinary divine intervention. Moreover, by positing a baptism of desire only at the moment of death, Lacordaire avoids the mistake made by many medieval theologians of creating a pre-baptismal baptism. Lacordaire's formulation is just a sketch, and he does not explain how he arrived at it or how baptism of fire is related to the sacrament of baptism. But Lacordaire was more apologist than theologian, and it is unreasonable to expect a sermon to contain all the argumentation of a theological treatise. His insight into the question is among the most lucid we find in the whole of the Long Nineteenth Century.

Faber. Lacordaire undeniably struck a chord and was cited as an authority by another popular apologist credited by Cuchet with changing opinions about the proportion of the elect, the British Oratorian Frederick William Faber (1814–1863).[42] Faber's work—popular in England, France, and America—provides insight into the reasons behind the mid-nineteenth century shift away from rigorism. Faber was a spiritual writer who wanted Catholics to fight for the Lord with enthusiasm. Jansenist pessimism was an obstacle to the spirited discipleship Faber advocated because it made salvation seem impossibly distant, ironically leading to a kind of

---

42. Frederick William Faber, *The Creator and the Creature* (London: Thomas Richardson and Son, 1856), 348. Cuchet, "Une révolution théologique oubliée," 135–38. Cf. A. Michel, "Élus (Nombre des)," in *Dictionnaire de théologie Catholique*, vol. 4, ed. A. Vacant and E. Mangenot (Paris: Letouzey et Ané, 1911), 2350.

melancholy paralysis and secularization by default.[43] Faber's analysis of
the different positions taken by theologians about the number of the elect
is clear and accurate and continued to be quoted by scholars into the
twentieth century. Like Lacordaire, the Englishman aimed to show the
legitimacy of discussing the question because he knew his own position
to be, historically, in the minority.[44] His argument is fundamentally an
extension of the position taken by Suárez. While he engages in some numerical analysis along the lines of Lacordaire, the heart of Faber's case is
the effectiveness of the means of salvation God has made available in the
Church. Like Suárez, his argument centers on the effectiveness and wide
availability of the sacraments, especially baptism and confession. Early in
the book, he asks rhetorically,

> What is the Church but His way of rendering the blessings of His
> Incarnation omnipresent and everlasting? What is the Baptism of
> infants but a securing prematurely, and as it were against all reason,
> the eternal love of their unconscious souls? What is Confession, but
> mercy made common, justice almost eluded, the most made out of
> the least?[45]

In marked contrast to Jansenism, he argues that only the simplest of dispositions is required for confession to be salvific: "God puts the requisites
for absolution so low."[46] Later, arguing that "the action of the sacraments
is probably much greater than we have any notion of," he blames the
distinctly modern tendency to discount the supernatural—and therefore
sacramental grace—for pessimism about the number of the saved.[47]

As we saw with Suárez, the arguments Faber makes for the salvation
of a majority of those within the Church do not necessarily imply salvation for those outside of the Church. In fact, he explicitly declares this
question outside the scope of his argument; he regards fixation on the salvation of non-Catholics as leading to ingratitude for the gifts God makes
available within Catholicism and distracting from spiritual progress.[48]

---

43. Faber explicitly targets "Baius, Jansenius, and Quesnel." Faber, *The Creator and the
Creature*, 48, 391. He also criticizes a Kantian "mercantilist" ethos of commandment and obligation. Faber, 201–3.

44. Faber, 351–53.

45. Faber, 150; cf., 322–323.

46. Faber, 357.

47. Faber, 365–66.

48. "We will not advert, however distantly, to those outside the Church. People tempt

Thus, the implications of Faber's work for the salvation of non-Catholics are ambiguous. On the one hand, optimism about the salvation of Catholics is probably a prerequisite for any broader view of salvation outside of the Church; if Catholicism is of divine origin, it would be hard to maintain that one is more likely to be saved outside the Church than within. On the other hand, his optimism is based on the power of those means only available through the Church. The thrust of his work also tends to favor a vigorous evangelical and missionary outlook. Like Lacordaire, Faber was convinced that belief in the reality of hell is necessary for a balanced spirituality.[49]

Other factors. Why did the mid-1800s produced this shift in Catholic thinking on salvation? Both Faber and Lacordaire, as well as later scholars, point to rigorism's excesses, excesses that did not cohere with the pragmatic attitudes of a growing middle class.[50] The persecution the French Church underwent during the revolutionary period tended to freeze Gallican rigorism in place.[51] By the 1850s, the Church in France was experiencing a remarkable revival, and the sympathies of the younger clergy tended toward ultramontanism rather than Gallicanism.[52] Roman theology in the nineteenth century was driven by its own complex set of motivations, as we shall soon see, but Rome had never provided fertile soil for Jansenism. The new priests tended to associate Gallicanism and Jansenism with the disasters of the past several decades.

A number of other factors indirectly affected the way Westerners thought about themselves and their salvation. Universal male suffrage, adopted by France in 1848, and the sort of political rhetoric common to

---

themselves about them, and play tricks with their gift of faith, for which they ought to be thanking God their whole lives long. We have no business to concern ourselves with God's relations to others: however wistfully the ties of love may make us gaze upon that dark abyss." Faber, 338–39; cf. 36, 302, 388, 392–93.

49. Faber, 333. Lacordaire, *Conférences de Notre-Dame de Paris*, 4:183.

50. Eugène Julien seems to have been one of few scholars at the time to take note of the shift in mid-19th century soteriology and to recognize the larger social and political forces contributing to it. Eugène Julien, "La question sociale et le nombre des élus," *Revue du Clergé Français* 10, no. 60 (1897): 481–500. While he offers a number of interesting insights, his article suffers from the progressive hubris characteristic of the epoch—as when he claims, "We know the spirit of Jesus better" than did the preachers of the old regime—and a certain utopianism. Julien, 488, 499.

51. Quantin, *Il rigorismo cristiano*, 134–36.

52. Cuchet, "Une révolution théologique oubliée," 139.

democracies—appealing to rights rather than grace, to the will of the people (or at least the majority) rather than the will of God, and to common
citizenship across confessional divides—changed both the arguments and
the language heard in public discourse. Criminal justice, too, began to emphasize more nuanced punishments, and the French criminal code of 1832
made more general use of the principle of attenuating circumstances.[53]
Toward the end of the nineteenth century and the beginning of the twentieth, an emphasis on the determinative role of sociological factors—class,
upbringing, race—on human behavior at times seemed to crowd out any
role for free will, arriving at the fundamental error of Jansenism but from
the opposite direction. Some hint of this can already be perceived in Lacordaire's use of social categories to boost the demographics of the saved.
Indeed, the Dominican's fondness for statistics is one characteristic of the
period that persisted well into the twentieth century.[54] Numbers, however,
could be used to prove whatever one's presuppositions required. Lacordaire claims Catholicism's superiority by citing statistics showing that it
has the most followers among world religions. In the twentieth century
his fellow French Dominican, Yves Congar, would cite the small number
of Catholics in the world to argue for the existence of broad means of
salvation outside of the Church.[55] The same numbers could just as easily
support the contention that Bossuet and the rigorists had it right all along.
Not all of the arguments advanced by the nineteenth century apologists
stand up well to historical scrutiny. The effect of medical advances on infant mortality, women in the workplace, and the industrial revolution, for
example, spoil the conclusions Lacordaire draws based on age, gender, and
poverty. This is not to say that his overall conclusions were wrong, but we
should be alert to the need for a critical assessment of any received narrative of theological progress. The foundations of the Long Nineteenth
Century's theological constructions contain both stone and sand.

---

53. Cuchet, 142.

54. Morali notes this statistical obsession, reflected even in the preparation for Vatican I:
"Statistics, graphs, and similar considerations would for several decades continue to charac-
terize not only missionary publications but also reviews and dictionaries of theology." Morali,
"The Travail of Ideas," 111.

55. Henri-Dominique Lacordaire, *Jesus Christ: Conferences Delivered at Notre Dame in Paris*
(London: Chapman & Hall, 1869), 119; Yves Congar, *The Wide World My Parish: Salvation and
Its Problems*, trans. Donald Attwater (London: Darton, Longman & Todd, 1961), 8–9.

Perrone and the Pope

Lacordaire and Faber, though possessing keen theological minds, were apologists addressing popular audiences. Among the era's professional theologians, few carried more weight than the Jesuit Giovanni Perrone (1794–1876), who held the chair in dogmatic theology at the Roman College—today's Gregorian University—for the half century from 1824 until his death. Perrone is considered the patriarch of what historians refer to as the "Roman School" of nineteenth century theology. Though largely overlooked today, the theological curriculum written by Perrone, his *Praelectiones theologicae*, was "arguably the most influential pedagogical text in the Church between the French Revolution and the First Vatican Council."[56] Perrone's influence extended to other scholars—such as John Henry Newman, who sought him out when visiting Rome—and students who went on to become the most important theologians of the post-Vatican I generation.[57] Just as important was the Roman School's "nearly hegemonic" influence on the circle around Pope Pius IX.[58] This influence makes Perrone's theology of interest not only in its own right but also for the light it sheds on key parts of Pius's magisterium.

Joseph Carola locates Perrone's work within the larger Catholic project of intellectual and cultural rebuilding after the devastation of the French Revolution and Napoleonic Wars.[59] The Church's political struggles throughout the period, as well as the challenges posed by modern philosophy, put the question of ecclesiastical—particularly papal—authority at the center of Perrone's work; even when he was discussing salvation, the question of authority was never far in the background. Perrone's spirit, like that of Lacordaire and Faber, was apologetical.[60] Perrone identified Protestantism as the root cause of the intellectual, social, and political turmoil of his time and dedicated two apologetical works to

---

56. Charles Michael Shea, "Faith, Reason, and Ecclesiastical Authority in Giovanni Perrone's *Praelectiones theologicae*," *Gregorianum*, 95, no. 1 (2014): 161.

57. McCool, *Nineteenth-Century Scholasticism*, 81–83.

58. Charles Michael Shea, "*Ressourcement* in the Age of Migne: The Jesuit Theologians of the *Collegio Romano* and the Shape of Modern Catholic Thought," *Nova et Vetera* 15, no. 2 (2017): 608.

59. Carola, "The Academics, the Artist, and the Architect," 65–66.

60. McCool describes Perrone as "an enthusiastic apologist and controversial theologian" who was "neither a methodologist nor a speculative theologian." McCool, *Nineteenth-Century Scholasticism*, 136. He goes on, "Perrone made no secret of his lack of interest in all systems."

countering its influence.[61] At the same time, as we shall see, he took a nuanced view of Protestants as individual believers. Ironically, when Italian
revolutionaries overthrew the papal government of Rome in 1848, Perrone and the Jesuits of the Roman College took refuge in Wales. When
evaluating certain Roman theological formulations of the era, we should
not entirely discount the fact that the political position of the pope sometimes depended upon Protestant goodwill and English military success.

Non-Catholic Christians. Perrone's chapter on baptism in the *Praelectiones theologicae* sets the stage for questions surrounding baptism of desire.
He addresses the legitimacy of infant baptism and of godparents giving
answers on a child's behalf, practices cast into doubt by Rousseau and
some Protestants. Here, he makes a crucial move, echoed in Lacordaire,
with regard to the salvation of non-Catholic Christians. Those children
baptized in non-Catholic sects, he allows, are adopted into the one true
Church and continue to be part of the Church unless they actively turn
away from the truth.[62] Such children's upbringing within heretical sects
presents obstacles to their salvation, but Perrone recognizes that the children are not responsible for the errors they are taught. He does not think
it necessary in all cases for them to actually reach Catholic unity so long
as they move toward, not away from, the one true faith. Those presented
with heretical ideas, however, will sometimes need to reject what they are
being taught—or, at least, to doubt it—in order to seek what is truer and
more faithful; the action of grace can only lead toward the fulness of truth.
The sacrament of baptism, therefore, provides the basis for the salvation of
a significant number of Protestants and, presumably, Orthodox believers.

Necessity. In his next chapter, on the necessity of baptism, Perrone develops his presentation around the decrees of Trent, using the proposition,
"baptism is not optional, but is necessary for salvation," as his starting
point.[63] His discussion reveals some of the ambiguity left by Trent's de-

61. Giovanni Perrone, *Il Protestantesimo e la Regola di Fede* (Turin: Giancito Marietti, 1854);
Giovanni Perrone, *Catechismo intorno al protestantesimo ad uso del popolo* (Naples: Tipografia di
Giovanni di Majo, 1864).
62. Giovanni Perrone, *Tractatus de Baptismo*, in *Praelectiones theologicae quas in Collegio
Romano habebat Ioannes Perrone e Societate Jesu*, vol. 6 (Louvain: Vanlinthout et Vandenzande,
1841), 126–27, pp. 54–56.
63. Perrone, 134, p. 59.

crees, especially the Council's use of the language of promulgation to account for the salvation of unbaptized people before the coming of Christ. Perrone begins the chapter by introducing the distinction between necessity of means and necessity of precept. Baptism is necessary in both ways. For adults, it can be received either *in re* or *in voto*; for children, the possibility of a *votum* does not exist, making the sacrament the only means of salvation, except in the case of martyrdom. Perrone adds an important qualifying phrase to what he says about adults, "at least to those introduced to the Gospel."[64] On the question of when the promulgation of the Gospel can be said to occur, Perrone takes the position that it is relative both to nations—shortly after the Resurrection in Palestine, but in the sixteenth century in America—and to individuals. Therefore, all "negative infidels"—that is, those to whom the Gospel has not been promulgated—are held to the same standards as those who lived before Christ. Perrone discusses how Catholic doctrine applies to infants who die either with or without baptism, a theme to which he returns in greater detail when answering objections at the end the chapter.[65]

If Perrone's analysis of promulgation seems to open the possibility of alternative paths to salvation, what he says next about John 3:5 limits them.[66] The text's words apply in the most general sense—that is, to all people present and future: Everyone needs rebirth. He points to the universal consensus among orthodox theologians—quoting Ambrose and Gennadius—that baptism is of absolute necessity. He singles out for criticism the anti-Trinitarian theologian, Fausto Sozzini (1539–1604), whose teaching denied the doctrine of original sin and, therefore, the need for baptism, which became merely an aid to faith.[67] He ends by referring to Aquinas's treatment of the obligation to receive baptism in a way that preserves all the ambiguity of the question. No one, "at least in the new law," can obtain salvation without being incorporated into Christ, which cannot happen except through baptism either *in re* or *in voto*.[68]

Insight into Perrone's thinking can be gleaned from the "difficulties" he discusses at the end of the chapter, the equivalent of the *Summa*'s

64. Perrone, 133, p. 58.

65. Perrone, 135, pp. 59–60.

66. Perrone, 137–40, pp. 61–62.

67. On Fausto Sozzini, see Hugh Pope, "Socinianism," in *The Catholic Encyclopedia* (New York: Robert Appleton, 1912), http://www.newadvent.org/cathen/14113a.htm.

68. Perrone, *Tractatus de Baptismo*, 140, p. 62.

objections and replies. Against a Calvinist, figurative interpretation of
the sacrament, he defends baptism's necessity as a universal and perpetual
precept. Then he addresses the argument that several New Testament
figures—the Good Thief, the Apostles, and Mary—were not baptized.[69]
Here he quotes Augustine's exegesis of the story of the Good Thief from
De Baptismo. This allows him to include the classic conditions for baptism
of desire—the impossibility of water baptism and the absence of contempt for religion—in his answer. He next argues that the prevalence of
adult baptism in the early Church is not evidence of a weaker conviction
in the absolute necessity of baptism, and he introduces *De obitu Valentiniani.* The eulogy, he says, in no way diminishes the necessity of baptism,
because Ambrose presupposes Valentinian's desire for the sacrament.[70]

The unbaptized. The most interesting of the objections Perrone addresses
is that dedicated to the fate of unbaptized infants and of children who
die *in utero.*[71] Here he gives a fair hearing to Cajetan's proposal that parents' faith might obtain salvation for an unbaptized child. In the end,
he acknowledges that Cajetan's proposal was never formally condemned
but thinks that the poor reception it received means we must consider
the sense of the Church to be against it; he adds that if the prayer suggested by Cajetan were sufficient for the salvation of infants, the Church
would have officially prescribed it. Perrone explains these children's destiny, limbo, in Thomistic terms. He holds that human nature is not in
itself ordered to supernatural beatitude; only when someone's humanity
is elevated through baptism does one become capable of experiencing
supernatural happiness.[72] As we saw when examining Aquinas's views,
this means that unbaptized infants might enjoy a certain degree of happiness—perhaps even greater than what we can experience in this life—in
the afterlife. Infants who die without baptism, therefore, are in no way
punished for their failure to be baptized. Nor are they unfairly deprived
of anything they are owed, because the grace of supernatural beatitude is
an unearned gift, a "*beneficium indebitum.*"[73]

69. Perrone, 141–49, pp. 62–67.
70. Perrone, 157–65, pp. 72–75.
71. Perrone, 150–56, pp. 67–71.
72. Perrone, 135, p. 60.
73. Perrone, 154, p. 70.

An even more important part of Perrone's answer, however, is the argument that by providing baptism as the means of salvation for infants Christ has not constricted the path to salvation. Very few people held the true faith before the coming of Christ, he says, which means that very few infants could have been saved by the faith of their parents. With the Gospel now promulgated across the whole earth, many more infants, who would otherwise have been lost, are saved through baptism.[74] These comments also shed light on the ambiguities of Perrone's position regarding the salvation of negative infidels. According to Perrone, those living in such a state after the time of Christ are in no worse a position than those living before the time of Christ. But the state of those living before Christ was not enviable—since very few held the true faith, very few could have been saved. Perrone's comment about the promulgation of the Gospel across the whole earth also suggests—without saying so directly—that he would have considered the number of "invincibly ignorant" non-Christians to be relatively small by his own day.

These considerations help to clear up a confusion Sullivan expresses about Perrone's theology. Examining Perrone's use of the axiom *extra ecclesiam nulla salus*, Sullivan attributes to the Roman theologian the belief that "only those who died in a culpable state of heresy or unbelief [...] would be excluded from salvation," but then expresses perplexity when Perrone comments that it would be "absurd" to conclude that even "Jews and Moslems and idolaters" are saved.[75] The only explanation Sullivan can muster for the ostensible discrepancy is that Perrone was suffering from "ingrained and unexamined prejudice" against Jews and Muslims. The fault, however, lies with Sullivan for failing to realize, as Perrone did, that "invincible ignorance" means different things for Protestants and non-Christians. To be fair, Perrone does not always make this distinction clear himself; because of his theological preoccupations, when speaking of those outside the Church, often enough he simply has Protestants in mind. However, as his discussion of baptism indicates, when he does make the distinction, his logic leads him to conclude that non-Catholic

74. Perrone, 152, p. 68. While Perrone's reckoning may be true, it misses the heart of the difficulty. Cajetan could respond that, even though Christian revelation means that more people in total are saved than before, there seems to be a category of people *in principle* excluded from salvation in the Christian era who were not so under the Old Law.

75. Sullivan, *Salvation Outside the Church?* 111–12.

Christians are much closer to salvation than those who do not know Christ at all. A wider glance at Perrone's works confirms this conclusion. His *Catechismo intorno al protestantesimo ad uso del popolo* asks what invincible ignorance means. Perrone responds that it refers to those who are sure that their religion, "which is called Christian," is true and have never had serious cause to doubt it. He even believes it plausible that many Protestants, at least among simple people, find themselves in this condition. Then he goes on to say that it is necessary that such people know and believe at least the principal mysteries of faith, have hope and charity, and experience true sorrow for their sins. In some Protestant sects, he adds, these elements are missing, and salvation would be quite difficult in these.[76] Perrone's explanation shows that he recognizes that invincible ignorance can excuse the guilt of certain personal sins, but that it cannot supply other elements necessary for salvation, such as adherence to the principal mysteries of faith. What Perrone says here is consistent with his position that the baptized children of Protestants can enter heaven while unbaptized children cannot.

Even if he does not always specify whether he means Protestants or non-Christians when speaking about those outside the Church, Perrone recognizes that baptism is decisive for salvation. He is crystal clear when he denies that our natural virtues alone are adequate for salvation.[77] He adheres to the proposition that some kind of explicit faith in God who rewards and redeems is necessary to all people in all times, though—like Aquinas and Suárez—he recognizes that how much of the Christian creed must be explicitly professed varies with circumstances.[78] Perrone seems unimpressed by objections based on the large number of the damned. Responding to the objection that it is unfair to damn people for their invincible ignorance, he says that, though no one will be punished for the mere absence of belief, this does not mean that unbelievers will be saved. He specifies that those who are damned will be punished for their own sins, which include both personal sins and original sin.[79] Perrone

---

76. Perrone, *Catechismo intorno al protestantesimo ad uso del popolo*, 63–66. Perrone dismisses the possibility that a Catholic converting to Protestantism could plead invincible ignorance and considers it certain that Catholics who leave the Church and do not repent are damned.

77. Perrone, *Il Protestantesimo e la Regola di Fede*, 413.

78. Giovanni Perrone, *De Fide*, in *Praelectiones theologicae de virtutibus fidei, spei et caritatis*, 2nd ed. (Turin: Hyacinthi Marietti, 1867), 299, p. 75; 325, p. 80.

79. Perrone, *De Fide*, 316–18, pp. 78–79.

adds that God indeed desires that all be saved, but he also desires that they be saved in the way that he himself has established.

Pius IX. Perrone's understanding of invincible ignorance is important because the term enters into the papal magisterium during this period in an allocation of Pius IX, *Singulari quadam* (1854), and in two of the same pope's encyclicals, *Singulari quidem* (1856) and *Quanto conficiamur* (1863).[80] Since the theological issues are the same in all three documents, we will concentrate on the last of these here. Sullivan's analysis of *Quanto conficiamur* demonstrates that its language is practically identical to that of Perrone, who might plausibly have ghostwritten the document.[81] At the very least, the encyclical reflects his ideas. *Quanto conficiamur* is a lament over the present difficulties in which the Italian Church finds itself and a rallying cry to fight for the rights of the Roman pontiff. The root cause of the Church's troubles, according to the pope, is "the deadly virus of *unbelief* and *indifferentism*," which he defines as the "very grave error entrapping some Catholics who believe that it is possible to arrive at eternal salvation although living in error and alienated from the true faith and Catholic unity."[82] The references to "error" and "Catholic unity," as well as the encyclical's Italian context, suggest that Pius's main concern is not with the unevangelized, but, rather, with Catholics infected with liberal ideas. Later in the encyclical, he takes special aim at members of the Italian clergy who "oppose our civil rule and that of the Chair itself."[83] Read in the overall context of the encyclical, Pius's reference to "invincible ignorance" functions principally to warn such wayward clergy that they risk a fate worse than that of non-believers. The tone of the pope's words about the virtuous but inculpably ignorant is, however, surprisingly warm—so much so that, sandwiched between adamant condemnations of religious indifferentism, the effect is almost schizophrenic.

---

80. The key passages of *Singulari quadam* can be found in Joseph C. Fenton, *The Catholic Church and Salvation in Light of Recent Pronouncements by the Holy See* (Glasgow: Sands & Co., 1958), 42–56. The speech urges bishops vigorously to oppose the claim that salvation can be found in any religion. See also Pius IX, *Singulari quidem*, trans. Norman Desmarais, in *The Papal Encyclicals 1740–1878*, ed. Claudia Carlen (Ann Arbor, MI: Pierian Press, 1990), 7, p. 341.

81. Sullivan, *Salvation Outside the Church?* 116.

82. Pius IX, *Quanto conficiamur moerore*, trans. Marie Liguori Ewald, 3, 7, pp. 369–70, in Carlen, *The Papal Encyclicals*.

83. *Quanto conficiamur moerore*, 11, p. 371.

We know as well as you that those who suffer from invincible ignorance with regard to our most holy religion, by carefully keeping the
natural law and its precepts, which have been written by God in the
hearts of all, by being disposed to obey God and to lead a virtuous
and correct life, can, by the power of divine light and grace, attain
eternal life. For God, who sees, examines, and knows completely the
minds and souls, the thoughts and qualities of all, will not permit,
in his infinite goodness and mercy, anyone who is not guilty of a
voluntary fault to suffer eternal punishment.[84]

This statement is immediately followed by an affirmation of the *extra
ecclesiam* dogma that Fenton describes as more "forceful and explicit [...]
than in any other document, except perhaps the *Cantate Domino*" of the
Council of Florence.[85]

However, also well known is the Catholic dogma that no one can
be saved outside the Catholic Church and that those who obstinately oppose the authority of the definitions of the Church and
who stubbornly remain separated from the unity of this Church
and from the Roman pontiff [...] cannot obtain salvation.[86]

Sullivan observes wryly that "it is not immediately evident" how to reconcile the Holy Father's apparently contradictory statements.[87]

The fact that the pope does not feel the need to explain himself,
however, is itself an important datum. The pontiff assumes that his readers—the bishops of Italy—are already familiar with the relevant doctrine
and would understand that he is not proposing anything either more or
less restrictive than what he takes to be standard Catholic teaching, for
which Perrone would have been his main point of reference. As doctrine,
his formulations are inexact. Pius IX does not address whether invincible ignorance might apply differently to non-Christians or to baptized
non-Catholics, nor the difference between adults and children, because
such distinctions do not enter into the scope of the encyclical. His use of
invincible ignorance is polemical, to score a point against liberals in the

84. *Enchiridion symbolorum*, 2866.
85. Fenton, *The Catholic Church and Salvation*, 58–59.
86. *Enchiridion symbolorum*, 2867.
87. Sullivan, *Salvation Outside the Church?* 114.

Italian clergy. They ought to know better, he is charging, and are, therefore, worse than pagans.

Pius IX's formulations also show the effects of the Enlightenment charge that Christianity's view of the afterlife was unjust. In *Singulari quadam*, the pope had answered those who claimed that it was unfair to damn invincibly ignorant non-Catholics by declaring that such people "will never be charged with any guilt on this account."[88] As Perrone had argued and as Fenton points out in his analysis of the allocution, "non-appurtenance to the Catholic Church is by no means the only reason why men are deprived of the Beatific Vision."[89] They are excluded for both original and personal sin. The key phrase to resolve what would otherwise be a contradiction then is "on that account." Moreover, the theology of limbo then current suggested that only voluntary sins would be subject to positive punishment; original sin would deprive unbaptized children—also innocent of voluntary fault—only of the Beatific Vision. The nineteenth century produced some defenders of the idea that virtuous pagans might experience limbo as well, though there is no evidence that Pius IX embraced this belief.[90] In any case, we see that, even in papal writings, Enlightenment criticism resulted in a certain amount of apologetical maneuvering. While casting the invincibly ignorant in a positive light, Pius IX does not budge from traditional scholastic theology. Ignorance itself remains an obstacle to salvation, which must be removed by "divine light and grace." Like Aquinas, the pontiff sees the necessity of some sort of divine illumination if a virtuous person in invincible ignorance is to achieve salvation. Moreover, the conclusion Pius IX draws from his discussion of salvation is that the Church must assiduously seek the conversion of those outside it; he does not, in other words, think that salvation can be separated from belonging to the Catholic Church.[91]

88. Fenton, *The Catholic Church and Salvation*, 43.

89. Fenton, 46.

90. Capéran, *Le problème du salut des infidèles*, 1:478–79, 485–86. In 1794, Pope Pius VI had condemned the rejection of limbo by the Jansenist Synod of Pistoia as "false, rash and injurious," *Enchiridion symbolorum*, 2626. The teaching does not define limbo as Catholic doctrine but implies that it does not contradict Catholic doctrine.

91. In *Singulari quadam*, he urges "continual prayer to God that all nations everywhere may be converted to Christ," adding, "let us do all in our power to bring about the common salvation of men." Fenton, *The Catholic Church and Salvation*, 49. In *Quanto conficiamur* (9, p. 371) the pope underlines the importance of evangelization, urging Catholics to be charitable to those

Fenton captures Pius's thought when he says, "It would be worse than idle to imagine that one could work for the salvation of men without trying to influence them to enter and to stay within the Mystical Body of Jesus Christ."[92]

This conclusion is confirmed by the *Syllabus of Errors* published in 1864; indeed, the preparation of the *Syllabus* was the context in which *Quanto conficiamur* was written.[93] Among the "evil opinions and doctrines" condemned in that controversial document are these:

> 16. Men can find the way of eternal salvation and attain eternal salvation by the practice of any religion whatever.
>
> 17. At the very least, there must be good hope for the eternal salvation of all those who do not dwell in any way in the true Church of Christ.[94]

In *Singulari quadam*, Pius's language had likewise ruled out even "hope for the eternal salvation of those who have in no way entered into the true Church of Christ."[95] In a private letter to the ailing King Leopold I of Belgium, written in the summer of 1862, Pius IX, writing with personal warmth to a leader who had proven himself well-disposed to the Holy See, urged conversion on the grounds that the "most holy Catholic religion" is necessary to obtain eternal life.[96] While baptism was not at issue in the case of the Protestant, Leopold, these references do make it clear that Pius did not intend his references to invincible ignorance in *Singulari quadam* and *Quanto conficiamur* to weaken the necessity of Catholicism for salvation. Nonetheless, his concern with political questions—the temporal power of the papacy—sometimes came at the expense of theological coherence; the incongruity that resulted would ensure that, as his words rippled into the following century, their effect would not be quite what the pontiff intended.

---

outside the Church with a view to rescuing them from their errors and welcoming them back into the fold so that "they will gain eternal salvation." Here he probably has in mind former Catholics who have strayed. Nonetheless, salvation is identified with (re)entering the Church.

92. Fenton, *The Catholic Church and Salvation*, 53.

93. Giacomo Martina, *Pio IX (1851–1866)* (Rome: Editrice Pontificia Università Gregoriana, 1986), 320.

94. *Enchiridion symbolorum*, 2916–17.

95. Fenton, *The Catholic Church and Salvation*, 42.

96. Martina, *Pio IX (1851–1866)*, 553.

Twentieth Century Turmoil

Dustjacket versions of twentieth century Catholicism sometimes describe a period of stability—either of serene confidence or of complacent stagnation, depending on one's ideology—shattered by the Second Vatican Council, an event depicted either as rescuing the Church from its benighted past or plunging it into a whirlpool of relativism. More nuanced histories of the era might delve into the Liturgical Movement, the neo-Thomist revival, the condemnation of Modernism under Pius X, renewed debate over nature and grace, and the *nouvelle théologie* that arose in France and Germany in an attempt broaden the sources of theology beyond scholasticism. We cannot enter into these in detail, though we will touch on what the Liturgical Movement tells us about attitudes toward the necessity of the sacraments. One advantage of studying a topic such as baptism of desire, which is relevant to twentieth-century theological debates but does not easily fall into twentieth-century categories, is that it forces us to reject simplistic narratives. The pre-conciliar era was neither so tranquil nor so uniform as it is often depicted. With respect to the issues surrounding baptism of desire, perhaps the most important characteristic of the period between Pius IX and Pius XII was the prevalence of traditional-sounding terminology detached from its original meaning. Before entering into specific incidents in the twentieth century—the excommunication of Leonard Feeney and the debate at the start of the Liturgical Movement—we will examine a few themes present in a diffuse way throughout the period, beginning with the increasingly problematic use of the concept of invincible ignorance and preoccupation with the diminished place of institutional Christianity in the West.

Ignorance and Anxiety

Invincible ignorance. In Catholic moral theology, "invincible ignorance," as we have seen, excuses one from the guilt of failing to complete a duty of which one was faultlessly unaware. After Pius IX used the phrase in *Quanto conficiamur*, the term took on new life. If the author of the *Syllabus of Errors* had used the phrase, after all, who could dispute its orthodoxy? A summary of the *status questionis* from the 1950s describes invincible ignorance as providing "a comforting reassurance" that no one will be punished unjustly for religious ignorance.[97] The concept is given outsized prominence in two documents we will soon examine, the Holy Office's 1949 letter to the Archbishop of Boston and Vatican II's *Lumen Gentium*. Neither uses the term inaccurately, but the issue addressed by invincible ignorance—personal culpability for missed religious duties—is a relatively minor one. In fact, it somewhat distracts from the more fundamental—but more difficult—issues of original sin and the contact with Christ necessary for salvation.

The distortion of Catholic thought caused by overemphasizing invincible ignorance remains perceptible today. An example of this distortion came across my desk while I was preparing this chapter: an obituary for Swiss theologian Hans Küng in the *National Catholic Register*, a publication with little sympathy for Küng's theology. Its headline read, "Praying for Salvific Ignorance for the Clever Hans Küng."[98] The obituary's closing lines are framed as a prayer that "ignorance embrace the clever Father Küng, so that he may be admitted one day to the [beatific] vision." Setting aside whatever one thinks of Küng's theology and character, what is most alarming about the article is that it speaks of ignorance as if it were a *means* of salvation. The unfortunate implication is that it is "salvific ignorance"—and not truth—that sets us free. The language has an orthodox ring but is used in a way that almost perfectly inverts Christian redemption. The tendency to speak of invincible ignorance in this way was already present early in the twentieth century, prompting an exasperated Fenton to observe, "Invincible ignorance is by no means a sacrament, communicating goodness of life to those who are afflicted with it."[99] Sullivan's analysis of *Quanto conficiamur* makes a similar point; invincible ignorance, he says, is a "*condition* that must be fulfilled to avoid culpability, but is in no sense a *cause* of salvation."[100] But even describing invincible ignorance as a condition for salvation is too generous; for ignorance is

97. Francis S. Shea, "The Principles of Extra-Sacramental Justification in Relation to '*Extra ecclesiam nulla salus*,'" in *Proceedings of the Tenth Annual Convention* (New York: The Catholic Theological Society of America, 1955), 131.

98. Roger Landry, "Praying for Salvific Ignorance for the Clever Hans Küng," *National Catholic Register*, April 10, 2021, https://www.ncregister.com/commentaries/praying-for-father-hans-kueng.

99. Fenton, *The Catholic Church and Salvation*, 66.

100. Sullivan, *Salvation Outside the Church?* 115.

really an *obstacle*. Like concupiscence, it may not be the individual's fault, but it is still one of the doleful consequences of the Fall from which we require salvation; thus, the ancient Church described both baptism and salvation as "enlightenment." The fact that invincible ignorance would be invoked as it is in the obituary—by an author manifestly concerned with orthodoxy—shows how deeply its exaggerated version has penetrated Catholic thought. Why, after all, would we pray for Küng's ignorance instead of his conversion?

The obituary also illustrates just how broadly the concept of invincible ignorance has been stretched since Pius IX used it. Küng was a Catholic theologian of global stature, not a pre-Columbian Inca. But broadening the reach of invincible ignorance was a distinctive characteristic of mid-twentieth century theology.[101] The seeds of this line of thought are to be found in Perrone's reasonable contention that only an adequate announcement of the Gospel binds one to obey its precepts. It is exceedingly hard, however, to determine whether a presentation of the Gospel has been adequate or not; even adequate presentations of the Gospel can fail to achieve conversions. Not everyone who heard Jesus preach seems to have converted—was the Lord an inadequate evangelist? In *Singulari quadam*, Pius IX effectively admits the impossibility of determining where the line of invincible ignorance is drawn and discourages speculation on the question.[102] Such speculation almost inevitably turns theologians from apologists into defense attorneys. And such skilled lawyering raises more uncomfortable problems: One has to question the competence of a legislator who writes a law from which everyone is excused. If invincible ignorance is so diffuse, would it not be more honest simply to stop speaking of faith, baptism, or the Church as necessary for salvation? Moreover, if ignorance is so widespread as to render even theologians

---

101. Congar, for example, speaks of someone baptized as a child and "given years of religious instruction" before leaving the Church as an adolescent as "one of the non-evangelized too." Congar, *The Wide World My Parish*, 114. The near universal reach of invincible ignorance is the presupposition that allows Rahner to classify modern European atheists as Anonymous Christians; their ignorance is so profound that they believe the opposite of what they profess. Karl Rahner, "Atheism and Implicit Christianity," in *Theological Investigations*, vol. 9, trans. Graham Harrison (New York: Herder and Herder, 1972), 145–64; Karl Rahner, "Anonymous and Explicit Faith," in *Theological Investigations*, vol. 16, trans. David Morland (London: Darton, Longman & Todd, 1979), 54–56.

102. Fenton, *The Catholic Church and Salvation*, 43.

powerless to access the Good News, the human ability to participate in any meaningful way in our own salvation comes into question. Such a stance necessitates an extraordinarily dim view of human intellectual and spiritual capacities.

Billot and limbo. Such a flawed view of the human ability to make meaningful religious decisions doomed an intriguing proposal dealing with the fate of non-Christians offered by Cardinal Louis Billot early in the century.[103] Billot's thesis did not involve salvation, but limbo, considered at the time "a virtually revealed truth" about the destination of unbaptized children.[104] From time to time, certain thinkers—Dante in the Middle Ages, Claude Seyssel after the discovery of America—had suggested that some adults might end up in limbo as well. The Thomistic revival following Pope Leo XIII's publication of the encyclical *Aeterni Patris* in 1879, however, meant that such speculation faced a particularly intractable obstacle: the Angelic Doctor's treatment of the first moral act.[105] According to Thomas, a state of neutrality—even mere venial sin—is impossible after one reaches the age of reason because at that point one faces the obligation to order one's life to God. Failing to do so inevitably results in mortal sin. Billot's ingenious way around this problem is to argue that one reaches moral adulthood when one recognizes God and his law; in other words, those in invincible ignorance remain "moral infants" no matter their age. As such, they cannot be considered responsible for their sins.

Billot's thesis was attacked on a number of grounds. It seemed to consign the natural law to practical oblivion. The Dominican, Réginald Garrigou-Lagrange, maintained that non-culpable ignorance of God's existence was impossible. One theologian conceded that Billot's principles were sound but could not imagine that the category of moral infants was as widespread as the cardinal suggested, encompassing entire nations and the whole of pagan antiquity. History was rife with sophisticated

---

103. This account is based on Capéran's summary of Billot's thesis—developed in a series of articles published in Etudes between 1919 and 1923—and the controversy it provoked, *Le problème du salut des infidèles*, 1:512–31.

104. George J. Dyer, *Limbo: Unsettled Question* (New York: Sheed and Ward, 1964), 167.

105. Thomas Aquinas, *ST*, 1-2.89.6. Hector Scerri describes Billot as "ardently Thomistic," in "The Revival of Scholastic Sacramental Theology after the Publication of *Aeterni Patris*," *Irish Theological Quarterly* 77, no. 3 (2012): 277.

non-theists; it seemed a stretch to classify them all as moral toddlers. In this respect, Billot's thesis makes glaringly clear a problem inherent in the use of invincible ignorance as a bringer of salvation: The more expansive invincible ignorance is claimed to be, the more one must devalue the meaningfulness of conscious religious decision-making. Criticism of Billot parallels the critique by liberal theologians, Hans Küng and John Hick, of Rahner's thesis of the Anonymous Christian.[106] Billot's unfortunate framing of the question and its generally negative reception may have contributed to the diminishment of limbo's credibility among theologians in the latter half of the twentieth century.[107] The fundamental problem with Billot's thesis, however, was not the suggestion of adults in limbo *per se* but, rather, the lengths to which he had to go to fit that suggestion within a Thomistic framework.

Numbers. Driving Billot and other thinkers who attempted to improve the fate of non-Christians by minimizing the value of their conscious decisions was a growing preoccupation with the size of the world's non-Christian population. Even among those who acknowledged that numbers do not tell us much about who is saved or how, the invocation of demographic figures became an almost obligatory preamble to discussions of salvation and affected the direction theologians took.[108] Billot, for exam-

---

106. Hans Küng called Rahner's theory a "pseudo-orthodox stretching of the meaning of Christian concepts like 'Church' and 'salvation,'" in *On Being a Christian*, trans. Edward Quinn (Garden City, NY: Doubleday, 1976), 98. He goes on, "[I]n reality, they—Jews, Muslims, Hindus, Buddhists and all others, who know quite well that they are completely 'unanonymous'— remain outside. Nor have they any wish to be inside. And no theological sleight of hand will ever force them, against their will and against their desire, to become active or passive members of this Church [...] And it would be impossible to find anywhere in the world a sincere Jew, Muslim or atheist who would not regard the assertion that he is an 'anonymous Christian' as presumptuous." Likewise, Hick considered Rahner's concept paternalistic, granting "honorary status [...] unilaterally to people who have not expressed any desire for it." Alister E. McGrath, *Christian Theology* (Oxford: Blackwell, 2001), 548.

107. The International Theological Commission allows that, while limbo remains "a possible theological hypothesis," the concept is "problematic" and expresses the desire to surpass it "in view of a greater theological hope," in *The Hope of Salvation for Infants Who Die Without Being Baptized* (2007), http://www.vatican.va/roman_curia/congregations/cfaith/cti_documents/rc_con_cfaith_doc_20070419_un-baptised-infants_it.html, 95.

108. Surveying the post-war discussion, F.H. Drinkwater admits that, even though the "appeal to numbers is merely sentimental," "considerable stress is laid" on the issue, in "The 'Baptism Invisible' and its Extent," *The Downside Review* 71, no. 223 (1953): 28.

ple, rejected the traditional Thomistic thesis that Providence would arrange for a preacher, angel, or special inspiration to bring the Good News to righteous non-Christians because he thought the scope of the problem too large.[109] The nineteenth century's fascination with statistics had clearly carried over. However, the contrast between Lacordaire's use of such figures and that of twentieth century theologians is striking; for the nineteenth century preacher, the size and reach of Catholicism was a mark of its veracity. Mid-twentieth century theologians, on the other hand, emphasize Catholicism's shrinking market share.[110] The retreat of faith in Europe seems to be the unspoken source of this anxiety. This preoccupation explains why Rahner devotes more energy to arguing that atheists can be saved—and his atheists display a remarkable affinity for post-Enlightenment values—than he does to animists or unbaptized infants.

Viewed from an historical perspective, the driving force behind the twentieth century's shift in soteriological sensibilities is almost certainly anxiety over the collapse of Christendom, a more decisive factor than the discovery of the Americas in the fifteenth century. As the twentieth century progressed, it became increasingly clear that Christendom would not be returning. The papal states were not restored to the prisoner in the Vatican; *Action française* fizzled out; World War I swept aside what was left of the Catholic monarchies. Occasionally, the language used by theologians of the era suggests anxiety over Christianity's ostensible "defeat," as if God's plan might be thwarted if a certain quota of humanity were not saved.[111] Such rhetoric can be traced to the nineteenth century.

109. Capéran, *Le problème du salut des infidèles*, 1:518.

110. "[W]hat is the position of the Christian faith in the world, statistically speaking?" Congar asks, when "it is said a new Chinese is born every second of the day," in *The Wide World My Parish*, 93. He even compares Catholic and non-Catholic birthrates. Congar, 9. Karl Rahner notes the disheartening position of Christians who now find themselves in the minority, surrounded by non-believers, in "Anonymous Christians," in *Theological Investigations*, vol. 6, trans. Karl-H. Kruger and Boniface Kruger (London: Darton, Longman & Todd, 1984), 396. E. Hillman expresses this anxiety even more baldly: "in the foreseeable future, only a relatively small (and now progressively diminishing) segment of mankind can be counted among the Church's juridical members." Eugene Hillman, "'Anonymous Christianity' and the Missions," *The Downside Review* 85, no. 277 (1966): 370. He also frets that these Christians have not been distributed equally in terms of geography and race.

111. Karl Rahner, for example, claims "God can be victorious [...] even where the Church does not win the victory," in "Christianity and the Non-Christian Religions," in *Theological Investigations*, vol. 5, trans. Karl-H. Kruger (London: Darton, Longman & Todd, 1984), 134. Hans Urs von Balthasar at times speaks as if the damnation of anyone would represent God's

Noting that century's fascination with the percentage of the saved, John King finds the argument explicitly made that "the final divine triumph of Christ necessitates a large number of 'saved.'"[112] Such an assumption cannot long withstand scrutiny. Is a plurality enough for God to declare victory? A simple majority? Or must he achieve the absolute proportions of a North Korean election? The Gospel itself—with its narrow gates and mustard seeds—seems to steer away from such thinking. The conflation of "divine victory" with numerical dominance is the residue of a certain kind of "triumphalism"—exemplified by Lacordaire's over-confidence in numbers—hanging on after Christendom's collapse.[113]

In the end, the expectation of numerical victory had the effect of undermining a presupposition far more fundamental to the coherence of the Christian narrative of salvation. As we observed in the first chapter of this study, ancient Near Eastern and Greco-Roman worldviews assumed that the fate awaiting most people after death was, at best, melancholy and gray. This assumption made the possibility of salvation in Christ good news, allowing early Christians to see their baptism as akin to finding refuge on Noah's Ark (1 Peter 3:20–21). Ironically, the adoption of universal infant baptism in the Middle Ages made it plausible to think of salvation, in practice, as the starting position for most people. Even if Christian doctrine formally said otherwise, it was easy to assume that, barring rare misfortune, we start life saved and can only lose that salvation by breaking some divine precept. When early modern "globalization" and the erosion of Christianity in Europe removed the factors that had made this worldview plausible—when Christian initiation seemed once again not so universal—the result was a kind of cognitive dissonance. Popes continued to teach the traditional doctrine of salvation and to encourage

---

will being "frustrated by man's wickedness," in *Dare We Hope "That All Men Be Saved?,"* trans. David Kipp and Lothar Krauth (San Francisco: Ignatius Press, 1988), 184.

112. John J. King, *The Necessity of the Church for Salvation in Selected Theological Writings of the Past Century* (Washington, DC: The Catholic University of America Press, 1960), 95–96.

113. The long experience of Christendom also meant that Europeans in particular were accustomed to associate Christianity with their continent. The civilizational failure represented by the two World Wars understandably shook the confidence of Europeans in the goodness of their own cultures, even if the neo-pagan ideologies that plunged the world into those bloodbaths were the products of a post-Christian worldview and did not logically entail anything about the truth or falsehood of the Gospel. Nonetheless, at a visceral level, the moral catastrophe they represented had the effect of shaking the West's confidence in itself and made Christianity, in some sense, guilty by association.

missionary efforts to bring those who had not yet embraced Christianity to salvation.[114] But Christians *felt* uneasy and defensive. Especially when progress was being made in so many other areas—technology and medicine—it was hard to accept that Providence would allow the means of salvation to recede. Such a situation led to a certain diffidence with regard to these means. More than baptism, however, the era's ambivalence focused on the necessity of the Church for salvation.

Extra ecclesiam forsitan salus?

At several points in this study, we have seen the doctrine *extra ecclesiam nulla salus* appear in theology and in magisterial pronouncements. At some points in history—during the apostolic age or the missionary era of the sixteenth century—the more ancient doctrine of the necessity of baptism rose to the forefront of theological discussion, while at others—when heresy, schism, and disputes over papal authority loomed large—the *extra ecclesiam* formulation prevailed. The late nineteenth century fell squarely into this second category. Maruice Eminyan's influential mid-twentieth century summary of the issue points out that, since Vatican I, "theologians have generally preferred to consider the problem of salvation from an ecclesiological standpoint."[115] On the next page, he lists six authoritative principles that must guide any discussion of salvation without mentioning, or even hinting at, baptism. This nearly exclusive focus on ecclesiology did not bring clarity to the issue. If we take, for example, Robert Bellarmine's definition of the three characteristics that define membership in the Church—profession of the true faith, sacramental communion, and recognition of the authority of the Church's legitimate pastors—it is not obvious that each part plays the same role in salvation. To put the point in another way, much was made in the era over the distinction between necessity of means and necessity of precept. It is not, however, obvious that faith, baptism, and the recognition of papal jurisdiction all fall into the same category vis-à-vis this distinction. It seems plausible, for example, to consider faith and baptism to be means, but episcopal jurisdiction a

---

114. For example, Leo XIII, Encyclical Letter *Annum Sacrum* (May 25, 1899), 9; Benedict XV, Apostolic Letter *Maximum Illud* (November 30, 1919).

115. Maurice Eminyan, *The Theology of Salvation* (Boston: St. Paul Editions, 1960), 23.

matter of precept. After all, Cyprian's notion of papal authority was quite different from those of Boniface VIII or Pius IX. Moreover, both faith and, less directly, Church authority are implicitly present in baptism; by consigning the sacrament to the sidelines, twentieth century theologians lost a potentially fruitful source for understanding one of the most crucial and contentious concepts of the era, implicit faith.

The ecclesiological setting of the discussion also seemed to invite certain terminological imprecisions, such as the use of the general category "the others" to describe all non-Catholics.[116] King's extensive study of the issue finds wide use of the language of "soul" and "body" to explain how one could be invisibly part of the Church without membership in it.[117] The language had been used by Bellarmine and thus seemed orthodox, but, pushed too far, it tended to imply two churches—one spiritual, the other bodily—something Bellarmine sought to avoid. Speaking of ordinary and extraordinary paths to salvation posed other problems—if God needed to resort to extraordinary means, did that imply that his general plan had failed? And what was the relationship between ordinary and extraordinary means? The more careful theologians of the era tended to return to the concept of desire (*in voto*) as providing the only workable approach to the problem, but sometimes this was mixed together haphazardly with body-soul language without any attempt to resolve the tensions this created.[118]

The vagueness of such language, however, may have been part of its attraction. The polemical terrain in which the Church found itself asserting its doctrinal claims had shifted, and by the early twentieth century—in marked contrast to the era of Bossuet—a preacher was more likely to be heckled for giving a hellfire sermon than for sentimental indulgence. Then, as today, one is on much safer ground socially and rhetorically railing

116. Congar announces the theme of his book as "the salvation of 'the others,'" in *The Wide World My Parish*, ix, 1.

117. King, *Necessity of the Church for Salvation*, 14. The language of an "invisible" Church posed similar problems. Can someone belong to the invisible Church without desiring to belong to the visible Church? And if belonging to the invisible Church is good enough for salvation, then why desire to belong to the visible Church?

118. King credits Louis Capéran with demonstrating that the *in re/in voto* distinction made the soul/body distinction unnecessary. King, 129. At the same time, he criticizes Capéran's use of the extraordinary/ordinary distinction for failing to show how the two means relate to each other. King, 131.

against Jansenists than almost any other enemy.[119] Even proponents of the *extra ecclesiam* doctrine admit that it is decidedly not in sync with the tenor of the times. Since the doctrine could not be done away with, imprecise but comforting language about the "soul of the Church" and being a Christian "at heart" served the function of a rhetorical smoke screen. While the theologians of the era may not have been consciously obfuscating the difficulties involved, they had every reason to want to avoid the issue. Polemics have their own dynamics, and if a rhetorical dodge proves effective, it is likely to be repeated.[120] Unfortunately, rhetorical maneuvers do not always make for accurate theology.

An amusing passage from English Catholic writer Evelyn Waugh's 1945 novel *Brideshead Revisited* hints that some had begun to suspect sophism in the spiritualized language characteristic of the era. In the passage, Rex Mottram—a cunning but soulless businessman—is undergoing catechesis in order to marry into the Catholic Marchmain family. The priest charged with Mottram's instruction reports the results to Lady Marchmain: Rex has no interest in faith and sees Catholicism—like everything else he comes into contact with—as a means to his profit-seeking ends. As the priest tells it:

> "Yesterday I asked him whether Our Lord had more than one nature. He said, 'Just as many as you say, Father.'

119. The most important work of scholarship on the salvation of non-Catholics in the early twentieth century—and arguably to this day—was Capéran's *Le problème du salut des infidèles*. Capéran explicitly states that he is writing to correct the misleading impression left by a French literature dominated by Jansenist sympathizers who had reduced Catholic teaching to a caricature. Capéran, *Le problème du salut des infidèles*, 1:viii–ix. Capéran's is an extraordinary work of scholarship, but, because it is a reaction to Jansenism, it tends to overemphasize "optimistic" perspectives in history, particularly among the Fathers. As with so many dogmatic theologians of the era, Capéran underemphasizes the importance of religious ritual in the mindset of earlier ages and pays surprisingly little attention to baptism of desire, dedicating only a brief section to its medieval development. Capéran, 1:179–83.

120. Examples abound of blustery formulations that hide theological difficulties and ignore historical evidence. Henry Perreyve (1864) declares it "the teaching of all the theologians without exception" that the *extra ecclesiam* formula refers only to the "personal and voluntary crime" of knowingly resisting the true religion and Church authority. King, *Necessity of the Church for Salvation*, 11. Writing of "good people who are not Catholics," F. Verhelst (1919) opts for pathos over precision, declaring, "It is beyond doubt that God does not cruelly condemn these lost sheep." King, 149. The point here is not that the conclusions of these theologians are incorrect, but that the path they take to get there—ignoring mountains of historical opposition to their view and assuming their conclusions in their premises—makes it hard to distinguish theology from wishful thinking.

"Then again I asked him: 'Supposing the Pope looked up and saw a cloud and said "It's going to rain," would that be bound to happen?' 'Oh, yes, Father.' 'But supposing it didn't?' He thought a moment and said, 'I suppose it would be sort of raining spiritually, only we were too sinful to see it.'[121]

Mottram finds such spiritual language to his liking because, detached from reality, it can produce whatever result he wants—it can be spiritually raining regardless of the weather. Waugh was not the only thinker to realize that vague spiritualized language could be used to produce "whatever you say, Father." Just as the liberalizing trends of the mid-nineteenth century were a reaction against the previous century's rigorism, the airy excesses of the early twentieth century produced their own contrary reactions. Pius XII offered some cautions in the early 1950s. A more outlandish response came from the American Jesuit Leonard Feeney. Feeney's response briefly thrust baptism of desire into the center of theological controversy, a place it had not occupied since the Middle Ages.

The Feeney episode. Leonard Feeney (1897–1978) was a popular essayist, poet, one-time literary editor of *America* magazine, and a charismatic lecturer, once hailed by a Jesuit Provincial as "the greatest theologian we have in the United States by far."[122] In 1942, he began pastoral work at the St. Benedict Center, located just off the campus of Harvard University in Boston. The Center, which housed a bookstore and hosted social and educational events, had been founded two years earlier by laypeople. Feeney's ministry was astonishingly successful; in its decade of existence, the Center produced two hundred converts and a hundred religious and priestly vocations, among them Avery Dulles, a future cardinal and son of Secretary of State John Foster Dulles.[123] The St. Benedict Center advocated a robust Catholicism, in contrast to the relativism and materialism of modern American society, and its counter-cultural message resonated among young people even at Harvard, epicenter of WASP elitism. The decisive turning point for Feeney, however, came on the 6th and 9th of

---

121. Evelyn Waugh, *Brideshead Revisited* (New York: Little, Brown, 2012), 220–21, Kindle.

122. Gary Potter, *After the Boston Heresy Case* (Fitzwilliam, NH: Loreto Publications, 2013), ch. 1, Ebook.

123. Mark Silk, *Spiritual Politics: Religion and America Since World War II* (New York: Simon and Schuster, 1988), 73.

August, 1945, when the United States dropped atom bombs on the Japanese cities of Hiroshima and Nagasaki, bringing World War II to an end.
The St. Benedict Center community reacted with horror. They saw the
bombings as proof of the irremediable corruption of America's Protestant culture.[124] This, in turn, led to an implacable hostility toward those
currents of liberal Catholicism seeking accommodation with that culture.
At the root of this catastrophic cultural misdirection, as the Feeneyites
saw it, was the neglect, brewing over the course of the past century, of the
dogma *extra ecclesiam nulla salus.*

Feeney and his followers were convinced that only an infallible papal
pronouncement—a modern *Unam sanctam*—would be sufficient to correct the Church's course. Their rhetoric and actions became ever-more
provocative, leading to an increasingly hostile relationship with Harvard's
powerful authorities and Boston's Archbishop Richard Cushing.[125] While
Cushing had initially supported the St. Benedict Center, the archbishop
advocated an ecclesial direction diametrically opposed to that of Feeney.
As Patrick Carey puts it, Cushing was part of a generation of post-war
American bishops who "saw little or no inconsistency between his avid
patriotic Americanism and his Romanism."[126] Cushing urged Americans
to stop "fighting one another over doctrines concerning the next world"
so that they could "unite their forces to save what is worth saving in
this world."[127] Mark Massa's insightful article on the incident points out
that the condemnation of Fr. Feeney served a useful purpose for Catholics

124. According to the Center's founder, "We were never quite the same [...] after the
dropping of the atom bomb. It seemed to have shocked us awake [...] The scales fell from our
eyes, and we beheld clearly as actualities many things which we had dreaded might one day be
the outcome of our exclusively humanitarian society." Catherine Goddard Clarke, *The Loyolas
and The Cabots: The Story of the Crusade of Saint Benedict Center 1940–1950* (Richmond, NH:
St. Benedict Center, 1992), 45. Carey observes, "The Feeneyite critique of capitulation to American values, moreover, seems to me to be comparable to some American Catholic critiques of
the 1960's—in style if not in substance." Patrick Carey, "St. Benedict Center and No Salvation
Outside the Church, 1940–1950," *The Catholic Historical Review* 93, no. 3 (2007): 574.

125. Feeney's polemics took on a personal tone. He repeated the story that Harvard's President, James Bryan Conant, an important figure in the Manhattan Project, had once told a
dinner party that the United States should have dropped ten atomic bombs on Japan "to make
a more interesting experiment." Silk, *Spiritual Politics*, 74.

126. Carey, "St. Benedict Center," 562.

127. Mark Massa, "On the Uses of Heresy: Leonard Feeney, Mary Douglas, and the Notre
Dame Football Team," *Harvard Theological Review* 84, no. 3 (1991): 334–35. Cushing almost
certainly had the fight against communism in mind. Silk, *Spiritual Politics*, 86.

eager to prove themselves enthusiastic participants in the American mainstream by distancing themselves from perceptions of medieval intolerance. If Leonard Feeney had not existed, Massa concludes, "the North American Catholic community might have had to invent him."[128]

For their part, the Feeneyites seemed willing to play the role of foil, engaging in increasingly ugly behavior over the course of the conflict. In September 1947, a member of the St. Benedict Center and professor of philosophy at Boston College, Fakhri Maluf, published an article titled "Sentimental Theology" in the Center's newspaper *From the Housetops* in which the *extra ecclesiam* doctrine was invoked for the first time.[129] The article provoked controversy, but Boston's auxiliary bishop John Wright admitted that a discussion among the faculty at the archdiocesan seminary had failed to find anything doctrinally wrong in it.[130] At the same time, a number of members of the Center and Feeney himself provoked conflicts with the administration of Boston College and other Jesuits in the New England Province. In 1948, Feeney was ordered by his provincial to leave St. Benedict Center. He refused, claiming he could not in conscience break the promises he had made to the Center's members. This disobedience resulted in the suspension of Feeney's priestly faculties, the placing of the Center under interdict, and, eventually, Feeney's excommunication. As the conflict escalated, Boston College fired four professors associated with St. Benedict Center for their views, and Feeney's followers employed ever-more outrageous tactics, picketing churches on Good Friday and engaging in invective-filled preaching on Boston Common.

At the beginning of the conflict, Feeney and his followers had emphasized its doctrinal aspect, appealing to the Vatican in an attempt to

128. Massa, "On the Uses of Heresy," 329.

129. Maluf describes his interaction with a group of young Catholics who had never heard the *extra ecclesiam* doctrine and the shallow slogans that had replaced it: "'Salvation by sincerity,' 'Membership in the soul of the Church,' 'Don't judge,' 'Don't disturb the good faith of unbelievers,' 'It is not charitable to talk about hell or to suggest that anybody may go there,' and Isn't faith a gift? and 'How about baptism of desire?' and so on," quoted in Potter, *After the Boston Heresy Case*, ch. 4. Maluf's criticism is not that far from the conclusions reached by sociologist Will Herberg in his classic study *Protestant-Catholic-Jew: An Essay in American Religious Sociology* (Garden City, NY: Doubleday, 1955). Herberg found 1950s American religiosity to be good-natured, widespread, tolerant, and largely vacuous. "Of course, religious Americans speak of God and Christ, but what they seem to regard as really being redemptive is primarily religion, the 'positive' attitude of believing." Herberg, 282.

130. Potter, *After the Boston Heresy Case*, ch. 5.

elicit a definitive refutation of the liberal position. Rome's response, however, was a rebuke of the Feeneyites in the form of a letter from the Holy
Office to Archbishop Cushing dated August 8, 1949. When Feeney was
ordered to Rome to defend his views, he refused to go—the action that
in 1953 provoked of his excommunication. Eventually the St. Benedict
Center moved out of Boston, and the acrimony subsided. Feeney and
the main body of the group were reconciled to the Church, and, significantly, he was never required to recant any of his doctrinal positions.[131]
In fact, the doctrinal legacy of the sordid incident is less clear than it
might initially appear. The main substance of the doctrinal conflict was
expressed in an exchange of articles between Philip J. Donnelly, professor
of dogmatic theology at the Jesuit Seminary in Weston, Massachusetts,
and Raymond Karam, at the time a graduate student in philosophy at
Boston College.[132] Donnelly criticizes the contention that "salvation is
impossible for anyone who does not believe explicitly in the Catholic
Church." Citing the authority of the Council of Trent, he counters that
sanctifying grace and "a title to the Beatific Vision" are also conferred by
baptism of desire. In reality, his argument is a bit careless since he seems
to conflate baptism of desire with the absence of explicit belief, which is
hardly Trent's intention. If anything, this maneuver reinforced the charge,
made by Maluf in "Sentimental Theology," that the phrase "baptism of
desire" had become a slogan for religious indifferentism. Donnelly de-
flects, rather vaguely, the claim that Catholicism is no help to salvation,
but, as Patrick Carey notes, his article was "not calculated to bring peace
to the Boston Catholic community."[133] Instead Donnelly accuses his opponents of "a spirit of smug Protestant righteousness, of arrogating to
oneself the prerogative of judging others with the mercilessness of a Lutheran or Calvinistic God."

131. To complete the formal process of reconciliation, Feeney was required only to recite
one of the Church's approved professions of faith; he chose the Athanasian Creed. Potter, *After
the Boston Heresy Case*, ch. 10.

132. Karam's reply appeared in *From the Housetops* on April 15, 1949, and is mentioned in the
letter from the Holy Office. See Raymond Karam, "Reply to a Liberal," *From the Housetops* 3,
no. 3 (1949), repr. *Catholicism.org*, February 7, 2006, https://catholicism.org/author/cyrilkaram.

133. Carey, "St. Benedict Center," 564. Donnelly writes, "It is quite one thing to maintain
that Protestants or pagans are just as favorably situated with regard to salvation as Catholics,
and quite another to maintain that they are in bad faith and are to be spurned because they do
not submit to a distorted interpretation of Catholic doctrine," quoted in Karam, introduction
to "Reply to a Liberal."

Karam hit back with a lengthy article in *From the Housetops* entitled "Reply to a Liberal." Baptism of desire is a particular target of Karam's attack, though on closer examination his opposition to the concept is not as absolute as his rhetoric makes it seem.[134] In fact, Karam, who would be ordained a Maronite priest and found a breakaway community with other former members of the St. Benedict Center, later affirmed of his group, "The brothers hold firmly to the position that there is a Baptism of desire and Baptism of Blood."[135] The scorched earth nature of the debate precluded more nuanced discussion, however, which is unfortunate because some of the issues Karam raised were entirely legitimate. For example, he questioned the name given to the concept, suggesting that "baptism of purpose" or "will for baptism" would more accurately capture the Latin sense of *votum*. Feeney critic and editor of the *American Ecclesiastical Review*, Monsignor Joseph Clifford Fenton, had also seen the need to clarify the way the term *votum* was used in the tradition, distinguishing—in good scholastic fashion—between an "intention" and "velleity."[136] While not rejecting Trent's teaching, Karam takes aim at Donnelly's over-broad interpretation. Specifically, he objects to the propositions (1) that someone "*totally ignorant*" of the Catholic faith can receive baptism of desire; (2) that one can receive baptism of desire while knowing and refusing the Catholic faith; (3) that one can receive baptism of desire while explicitly refusing the sacrament of baptism. It is not clear to me whether Donnelly was, in fact, committed to the three above positions, though his loose

---

134. Karam deals with baptism in Part 3 of "Reply to a Liberal." Leonard Feeney himself took issue with baptism of desire—more categorically than had Karam—in a collection of talks, in *Bread of Life* (Fitzwilliam, NH: Loreto Publications), 2018. Because the book was first published in 1952, however, it was not at issue in the Holy Office's 1949 letter.

135. George B. Pepper, *The Boston Heresy Case in View of the Secularization of Religion: A Case Study in the Sociology of Religion* (Lewiston, NY: Edwin Mellen Press, 1988), 57. Karam's position that baptized babies, even those baptized by Protestants, will go to heaven is in line with the position advocated by Perrone. Karam, however, did not extend the saving effects of baptism to those who had begun to practice in heretical sects and insisted on the necessity of submission to the Roman pontiff for adults.

136. An intention is "an act of the will which is expressed by the statement that I am actually setting out to do a certain thing; a velleity, on the other hand, is an act of the will expressed in the declaration that I would like to do a thing." Fenton, *The Catholic Church and Salvation*, 39. An intention "necessarily affects all the rest of my plans and my conduct." Fenton gives the example of someone planning to take a trip to New York, who would not schedule engagements that conflicted with the trip (intention), versus someone who would like to visit New York someday but arranges no time to do so (velleity).

use of the term almost invites mischaracterizations. The first proposition does not reject baptism of desire, but only implicit desire, a concept about which the tradition is more ambivalent. The second and third propositions are, indeed, problematic, and nearly every advocate of baptism of desire before the twentieth century would be with Karam in rejecting them. He points out that the complete absence of a will to be baptized would make the sacrament invalid, and it makes little sense to argue that baptism of desire could be given against a person's will. Still, there does seem to be at least some gray area, which Karam does not acknowledge, between an explicit request for baptism and the explicit refusal of it.

He does, however, accept the classic case of baptism of desire for a catechumen dying unexpectedly.[137] To be saved, such a person would need to hold the Catholic faith, as well as to express an explicit desire for baptism and for membership in the Catholic Church. To these Karam adds an additional condition, namely, that such a person must make an act of perfect charity. Adding this condition seems to create a high bar, making baptism of desire rare even among catechumens, but Karam's stand is not as extreme as it might seem at first glance. The requirement for an act of perfect charity was standard fare in many turn-of-the-century articles on baptism of desire.[138] Karam attributes the condition to the Council of Trent. However, his reasoning reflects the Council's teaching on penance rather than on baptism, and there are enough differences between the two sacraments—penance presumes one already possesses Christian faith and can be repeated—that one should not automatically assume that what is said of the one applies to the other.[139] The Thomistic framework assumed by writers of the time reveals another difficulty with treating an act of perfect charity as a condition for baptism of desire. Charity is understood to be a specifically Christian virtue, a theological virtue infused along with

---

137. Feeney, on the other hand, gives an implausible interpretation of Ambrose's *De obitu Valentiniani* in order to avoid the issue, in *Bread of Life*, 116–17. According to Feeney, Ambrose "hoped Valentinian had been baptized by somebody, even though he (Ambrose) did not know who it was, and even though there was no official record of it."

138. For example, see William Fanning, "Baptism," in *The Catholic Encyclopedia*; E. Dublanchy, "Charité," in *Dictionnaire de théologie Catholique*, vol. 2, bk. 2, ed. A. Vacant and E. Mangenot (Paris: Letouzey et Ané, 1910), 2236–2252. Even *Suprema haec sacra* adds the condition that, in order to be salvific, one's desire to enter the Church must "be animated by perfect charity." *Enchiridion symbolorum*, 3872. Feeney dismisses such language as arbitrary and impossible to define, in *Bread of Life*, 118–19.

139. *Enchiridion symbolorum*, 1677.

faith and hope. Speaking of it as a condition for the reception of baptism of desire is, therefore, tautological.

Letter to the Archbishop of Boston. What, then, was the error of the St. Benedict Center? In response to the Center's appeal, the Holy Office sent a letter to the Archbishop of Boston—sometimes known by its Latin title *Suprema haec sacra*—dated August 8, 1949, and excerpts from the letter were published in the Boston archdiocesan newspaper. *Suprema haec sacra*, however, is somewhat cagey regarding the error of the Feeneyites. It states that "Reply to a Liberal" is "very far" from "the genuine teaching of the Catholic Church" but makes no attempt to identify erroneous propositions.[140] The letter says that the teaching that "outside the Church there is no salvation" is infallible, though it also insists that the dogma "must be understood in that sense in which the Church herself understands it"— though how the Church understood it at the midpoint of the twentieth century was hardly obvious.[141] Trent's canons mentioning the *votum* for baptism and penance, the letter asserts, mean that actual membership in the Church is not always necessary, but that one can be united to the Church by will and desire.[142] The next assertion is the crux of the dispute with the Feeneyites:

> However, this desire need not always be explicit, as it is in catechumens; but when a person suffers from invincible ignorance, God accepts also an implicit desire, so called because it is included in that good disposition of soul whereby a person wishes his will to be conformed to the will of God.[143]

This paragraph does not cite any particular authority for its description of implicit desire, though a few lines later it refers to Pius XII's 1943 encyclical on the Church, *Mystici Corporis Christi*, which had mentioned those who "are related to the Mystical Body of the Redeemer by a certain unconscious yearning and desire."[144] Pius XII's encyclical, however, had been written to reign in the nineteenth and twentieth century trends

---

140. *Enchiridion symbolorum*, 3873. This is followed by a lengthy condemnation of the St. Benedict Center's disrespect of lawful ecclesiastical authorities.
141. *Enchiridion symbolorum*, 3866.
142. *Enchiridion symbolorum*, 3869–3870: "eidem voto et desiderio adhaereat."
143. *Enchiridion symbolorum*, 3870.
144. Pius XII, Encyclical Letter *Mystici Corporis Christi* (June 19, 1943), 103.

in ecclesiology we saw earlier; it repudiates, for example, the idea of an invisible Church distinct from the visible, the possibility of belonging to the soul of the Church but not to its body, and any distinction between a "Church of charity" and the juridical Church.[145] Moreover, the section referred to in the letter to the Archbishop of Boston does not quite greenlight salvation through implicit desire; in fact, it is a call directed by the Holy Father at those outside the Church to enter the safe harbor of Catholicism. An unconscious longing for the Church without full incorporation, it warns, leaves one in an uncertain state.

The Holy Office's letter to the Archbishop of Boston concludes that the "wise words" of Pius XII's encyclical reprove both "those who exclude from eternal salvation all united to the Church only by implicit desire and those who falsely assert that men can be saved equally well in every religion."[146] It adds that not any kind of desire is adequate but only one "animated by perfect charity" and "supernatural faith." This language is not taken from the encyclical but, as noted above, had become such a standard part of twentieth century neo-scholastic discourse that Karam used it as well.

Were Feeney and his followers at the St. Benedict Center, therefore, guilty of heresy? The episode, after all, has come to be known as the "Boston Heresy Case." Still, the indefiniteness of the concept of "implicit desire" makes such a charge hard to prove. Moreover, it is not at all clear what doctrinal impact the Holy Office intended its letter to make. Only excerpts were published in 1949, and then only in the Boston archdiocesan newspaper the *Pilot*. Gary Potter, whose account of the affair is sympathetic to the St. Benedict Center, makes much of the fact that the letter never appeared in the *Acta Apostolicae Sedis*, in which the Holy See's official documents are published.[147] The full version appeared only in 1952 in the *American Ecclesiastical Review*, its publication provoked by the Feeneyites' increasingly disturbing antics. The letter is widely cited today because it was added to Denzinger's *Enchiridion symbolorum* in 1963 by then-editor Karl Rahner, who took its text from the *American Ecclesiastical Review*. In the end, as with any document issued by a Roman

145. *Mystici Corporis Christi*, 13, 22, 40, 57, 60, 62, 64–65.
146. *Enchiridion symbolorum*, 3872.
147. Potter, *After the Boston Heresy Case*, ch. 9.

congregation, the letter's authority depends ultimately on the sources it cites—in this case Trent and *Mystici Corporis*. Geertjan Zuijdwegt makes the case that *Suprema haec sacra* was meant to serve the secondary purpose of reinforcing the teaching of *Mystici Corporis* that the Mystical Body of Christ is to be identified with the Roman Catholic Church.[148] This was the explicit aim of the 1950 encyclical *Humani generis*, which criticized those who "reduce to a meaningless formula the necessity of belonging to the true Church in order to gain eternal salvation."[149] Feeney took *Humani generis* as a vindication of his position.[150] The encyclical did, in fact, identify as erroneous a number of positions that Feeney had also attacked for minimizing the role of the Church in salvation.[151] Zuijdwegt concludes that the Holy Office's letter "was not as theologically distinct from the Feeneyite position as has generally been taken for granted."[152] The offence for which Feeney was excommunicated was disobedience, not heresy; so doctrinal questions played a minimal role in his eventual reconciliation. A 1988 letter from the Judicial Vicar for the Diocese of Worcester, Massachusetts, where Feeney and his group relocated after leaving Boston, explained, "In our discussion with the Congregation [for the Doctrine of the Faith], it seemed rather clear that the proponents of a strict interpretation of the doctrine [*extra ecclesiam*] should be given the same latitude for teaching and discussion as those who would hold more liberal views."[153] Feeney's friend, Catholic publisher Frank Sheed, lamented, "He was condemned but not answered [...] Everyone would have been helped by a full-length discussion."[154]

The Feeney affair, then, demonstrates the existence of a certain amount of theological disarray on the question of salvation even before Vatican II. The response of Church authorities to the crisis was by

148. Geertjan Zuijdwegt, "Salvation and the Church: Feeney, Fenton and the Making of *Lumen Gentium*," *Louvain Studies* 37 (2013): 160.

149. Pius XII, Encyclical Letter *Humani Generis* (August 12, 1950), 27.

150. Potter, *After the Boston Heresy Case*, ch. 9; Carey, "St. Benedict Center," 569n36.

151. Pius XII, *Humani Generis*, 2, 4, 11, 14, 26–27, 43.

152. Zuijdwegt, "Salvation and the Church," 153.

153. Potter, *After the Boston Heresy Case*, Introduction.

154. Potter, *After the Boston Heresy Case*, ch. 9. Carey notes that, despite several insightful studies of the episode from a sociological perspective, its theological dimension has been relatively neglected. Carey, "St. Benedict Center," 574–75. "The issue of salvation [...] has been given little attention in the histories of American Catholicism, and one wonders why?"

no means sure-footed, either theologically or pastorally. Still, of all the theological points raised in the Holy Office's letter to the Archbishop of Boston, baptism of desire emerged as the most solid doctrinal point of reference, on which all but the most absolute interpretations of the doctrine *extra ecclesiam nulla salus* depend. Karam may not have liked the term, but even he ended up acknowledging some version of the doctrine. Looked at from the standpoint of the doctrine's broader history, however-er, one rather strange feature of the twentieth century discussion stands out. A variety of theological concepts are employed to understand what baptism of desire means for non-Catholics—necessity of precept and of means, membership in the Church, explicit and implicit desire, invincible ignorance, supernatural faith, perfect charity, obedience to the will of God—and yet one thing is almost always left out: Baptism.

Salvation Disappears

A telling feature of *Suprema haec sacra* is that, even though the letter recognizes that baptism is a necessary *means* of salvation, it primarily uses the language of command and obedience (precept) to describe this necessity.[155] The Holy Office recognizes that treating baptism as necessary solely by precept is inadequate, but it seems to lack the theological tools to talk about it in any other way. Pinckaers's analysis suggests why: an Ockhamist theological framework over-dependent on legal categories. This framework contributed to baptism of desire's paradoxical treatment in the late twentieth century: the doctrine was recognized as indispensable to "authorize" discussion of the salvation of non-Catholics, while, at the same time, the sacrament at its root was ignored.[156] The *lex orandi*, in other words, did not seriously factor into the discussion. For greater

---

155. "[I]n the first place, the Church teaches that in this matter there is a question of a most strict command [...] [A]mong the commandments of Christ, that one holds not the least place by which we are told to be incorporated by baptism into the Mystical Body of Christ, which is the Church." *Enchiridion symbolorum*, 3867.

156. E.g., Monika K. Hellwig, "Baptism of Desire," in *The Modern Catholic Encyclopedia*, ed. Michael Glazier and Monika K. Hellwig, A Michael Glazier Book (Collegeville, MN: Liturgical Press, 1994), 69; Baum, "Baptism of Desire," in Sacramentum Mundi, 144–46. This also meant ignoring the doctrine's history. Hellwig and Baum rely on such phrases as "Many theologians maintained ..." and "It was generally taught ..." to efface the tensions that made the doctrine the locus of passionate debate for centuries.

perspective on why this would be the case, it is worth briefly examining the issues brought to the surface by the early twentieth century's Liturgical Movement.

The Liturgical Movement. Today the Liturgical Movement is most associated with the reform of rites both before and after Vatican II, but Andrea Grillo points out that the movement's early thinkers, such as Odo Casel (1886–1948) and Romano Guardini (1885–1968), were driven by a deeper theological problem, what he calls "the liturgical question."[157] The liturgical question addresses not so much the individual liturgical rites as what sense religious ritual has to begin with. We already saw this question arise implicitly in nineteenth-century versions of "Christianity" claiming to have left religious ritual behind. For Kant, we may recall, worship has value only insofar as it illustrates our duty to obey the categorical imperative. Yet for most Christians before the nineteenth century religious ritual was so obviously necessary that it did not need to justify its utility by reference to ethical or doctrinal criteria. Casel and Guardini saw the need to render this classical sensibility comprehensible again in a modern context.

Guardini writes of the "playfulness" of liturgy to suggest the rite's refusal to conform to a utilitarian logic.[158] This sense of the rite not as a means to an extrinsic end, but as participation in the ultimately meaningful end itself makes its connection to salvation clearer than it is in a system based on obedience to commands.[159] Casel's theology centers on the category of mystery that he finds present in Ambrose and Leo the Great.

157. Grillo, *Introduzione alla teologia liturgica*, 77–101.

158. "Grave and earnest people, who make the knowledge of truth their whole aim, see moral problems in everything, and seek for a definite purpose everywhere, tend to experience a peculiar difficulty where the liturgy is concerned. They incline to regard it as being to a certain extent aimless, as superfluous pageantry [...] What is the use of it all? [...] Objects which have no purpose in the strict sense of the term have a meaning. This meaning is not realized by their extraneous effect or by the contribution which they make to the stability or the modification of another object, but their significance consists in being what they are. Measured by the strict sense of the word, they are purposeless, but still full of meaning." Romano Guardini, *The Spirit of the Liturgy*, trans. Ada Lane (New York: Sheed and Ward, 1935), 33–34, Kindle.

159. Guardini, *The Spirit of the Liturgy*, 37. The "liturgy must be chiefly regarded from the standpoint of salvation." Guardini, 48. "In the end, eternal life will be [the liturgy's] fulfillment. Will the people who do not understand the liturgy be pleased to find that the heavenly consummation is an eternal song of praise?" Guardini, 40.

Mystery, for him, means "three things and one": God; God's redemptive action in the life, death, and resurrection of Jesus; and our participation in that action through the sacraments.[160] At the heart of Casel's sense of mystery is the conviction that salvation cannot be reduced to a system of dogmatic propositions, moral precepts, or religious sentiments, though all of these things are necessary aspects of Christianity.[161] The utterly unique action of God in Jesus Christ is irreducible to anything else, but God enables us to participate in it—even though we are far removed in time from the earthly life of Jesus—through the mysteries. This participation is inseparable from what it means, in Christian terms, to be saved:

> Christ's salvation must be made real in us. This does not come about through a mere application, with our behaviour purely passive, through a 'justification' purely from 'faith', or by an application of the grace of Christ, where we have only to clear things out of the way in a negative fashion, to receive it. Rather, what is necessary is a living, active sharing in the redeeming deed of Christ; passive because the Lord makes it act upon us, active because we share in it by a deed of our own.[162]

As in Paul's theology of baptism (Rom. 6:3–5), salvation is inseparable from participation in the utterly unique event of the Paschal Mystery. The irreducibility of the liturgical symbol resists doctrinal or moral minimalism, and the open-endedness of mystery reflects the total dedication of oneself required for Christian salvation.[163]

Navatel. Casel and Guardini felt the need to turn to the Fathers for inspiration because several of the currents we have been tracking throughout this study—scholastic minimalism, Ockhamist moralism, and the end of Christendom—seem to have come together in the late nineteenth century to make the very existence of the Christian sacraments difficult to understand. This incomprehension is illustrated by Jesuit Jean-Joseph Navatel's article "L'apostolat liturgique et la piété personnelle," published

---

160. Odo Casel, *The Mystery of Christian Worship* (New York: Crossroad Publishing, 2016), 5–7.

161. Casel, 9.

162. Casel, 14.

163. Casel, 56.

in *Études* in 1913. Navatel's article was a response to one of the Liturgical Movement's early but lesser-known figures, the French Benedictine Maurice Festugière (1870–1950), who blamed the modern era's difficulty appreciating the liturgy on the "Protestant individualism" of Ignatius Loyola.[164] Navatel struck back, unfortunately, not by defending Ignatius but by belittling the liturgy.[165] His response is valuable for us because it makes explicit many of the assumptions implicit in the era's theology. For Navatel, the role of the liturgy within Catholicism is entirely secondary; belief—correct doctrine—is what is important. At most liturgy serves to illustrate and reinforce dogmas already understood.[166] For this reason, a well-prepared sermon is to be preferred to a sung Credo, even at Notre Dame. It is difficult to see how, in Navatel's way of thinking, the sacraments could exercise any genuine causal effect, as is required by Catholic doctrine. At most, the liturgy serves as a kind of visual aid for beliefs already held—and not always a particularly good visual aid, at that.[167]

Navatel constructs a dichotomy between personal and liturgical prayer and sees one's relationship with God developing more or less exclusively through personal prayer.[168] Liturgy is necessary, he says, for the fulfillment of public, formal duties. We can perceive here the void created by the disappearance of the ancient rites of the catechumenate, in which Christian formation was experienced as liturgical initiation. Navatel's thought is closer to Kant than Ambrose, yet we can also see that it picks up on—and brings to extreme conclusions—the intellectualism, minimalism, and emphasis on legal obedience present in scholasticism.[169]

164. Grillo, *Introduzione alla teologia liturgica*, 260–64.

165. To see Ignatian spirituality as conflicting with liturgical spirituality is misguided. Having been formed sacramentally is the prerequisite of the method of imaginative prayer Ignatius recommends in the *Spiritual Exercises*. Ignatius's emphasis on the use of the senses in prayer comes out of a prior conviction that the Incarnation is not just a compelling doctrine, but a reality to be experienced. Ignatius assumes that the person making the Exercises will naturally be participating daily in Mass and Vespers. Ignatius of Loyola, *The Spiritual Exercises of St. Ignatius*, trans. Louis J. Puhl (Chicago: Loyola University Press, 1951), 20, p. 9.

166. Jean-Joseph Navatel, "L'apostolat liturgique et la piété personnelle," *Études* 137, no. 4 (1913): 455–56.

167. Navatel, 452.

168. Navatel, 474.

169. A reductive tendency in sacramental theology also grew in connection with the Modernist controversy. Scerri, "The Revival of Scholastic Sacramental Theology," 280–81. Pius X's 1907 decree *Lamentabili* condemns the thesis "The sacraments are intended merely to recall to man's mind the ever-beneficent presence of the Creator." *Enchiridion symbolorum*, 3441.

The confluence of these tendencies also helps to explain the prevalence of the exceptionally spiritualized language used in the era to talk about the Church. The experience of salvation had disappeared. Catholic theologians still believed in salvation, of course, but it had become something ethereal, detached from the incarnational sensibilities of Catholic worship, something invisible rather than sacramental. And if worship is mere ceremony, then making salvation depend upon participating in any rite does seem arbitrary and unfair, like throwing someone in jail for forgetting to initial a box on a tax form.

This attitude toward religious worship puts into perspective the change in the way baptism of desire came to be treated in twentieth-century theology. Whereas the doctrine's patristic and medieval proponents understood it as an extension of the necessity of the rite, twentieth-century theologians took baptism of desire to mean that baptism was not *really* necessary for salvation. This explains why the conditions deemed essential for the doctrine's acceptance in medieval debates—expressed by the contrast between *contemptus religionis* and *articulus necessitatis*—disappear in twentieth century accounts of the concept. This shift should not be confused with theological progress because it represents the loss of a fundamental source for theology, the *lex orandi*, and is thus an impoverishment. Even Eminyan perceived the loss of theological cogency as discussion of salvation moved away from the sacraments and into ecclesiology. The sacramental language of *re* and *voto*, he notes, had been adopted by ecclesiology, but "the terminology failed to enjoy the same stability it enjoyed in its native field."[170] The inadequacy of Navatel's understanding of liturgical action would be recognized as the twentieth century progressed, and the insights of the Liturgical Movement formed the basis for Vatican II's constitution on the liturgy *Sacrosanctum Concilium*. But the minimizing tendency in scholasticism ran deep, and, by the century's end, the search for salvation in ever greater abstraction only increased.

---

170. Eminyan, *The Theology of Salvation*, 154. Counterexamples of authors who treat baptism of desire more carefully do exist in this period. Peter Gumpel proceeds with great precision in his discussion of how the concept might apply to the ever-agonizing question of infants who die before baptism in a series of articles from the 1950s, in Peter Gumpel, "Unbaptized Infants: May They Be Saved?" *The Downside Review* 72, no. 230 (1954): 342–458; Peter Gumpel, "Unbaptized Infants: A Further Report," *The Downside Review* 73, no. 234 (1955): 317–46.

The Rahnerian Turn and Vatican II

Given the pivotal role that baptism of desire played in the Holy Office's response to Leonard Feeney, it is perhaps surprising that the doctrine was not the subject of greater theological reflection at the time. The prevalence of attitudes like that expressed by Navatel, which treated sacramental and liturgical theology as marginal to serious questions, partially explains this neglect. A number of the era's most innovative theologians, to be sure, thematized the sacramental nature of Catholicism, notably Edward Schillebeeckx and Otto Semmelroth, who developed the theme of Church as sacrament. Unfortunately, they rely on the abstract idea of "sacrament" at the expense of the particular character of the Christian rites. As "the sacramental" becomes ever more nebulous, the connection between the sacraments and the utterly unique event of the Incarnation also weakens.[171] Diminished interest in baptism of desire can also be attributed to the emergence of a serious rival, a theory which claimed the more ancient doctrine in support while simultaneously rendering it obsolete—the theory of the Anonymous Christian.

The theory's author, German Jesuit Karl Rahner (1904–1984), widely considered the century's most influential Catholic theologian, introduced the idea prior to the start of the Second Vatican Council, making the essential case for the concept in a 1961 lecture in Eichstätt. The lecture reveals with particular clarity the Long Nineteenth Century trends to which Rahner's theory attempts to respond. Anxiety over the erosion of Christianity's role in the world sets its tone. Staggering numbers—"millions upon millions," including those living "a million years before Christ"—provoke anxiety about the Church's defeat.[172] Rahner approaches salvation as a moral question, the necessity of Christianity

---

171. Edward Schillebeeckx, *Christ the Sacrament of the Encounter with God* (New York: Sheed and Ward, 1963), 7. José Granados offers a nuanced critique of the use of the terminology of Church as "sacrament," in *Introduction to Sacramental Theology: Signs of Christ in the Flesh* (Washington, DC: The Catholic University of America Press, 2017), 357–372. Granados faults theologians such as Schillebeeckx, Semmelroth, and Rahner for privileging ecclesiology over sacramental theology. He credits Henri de Lubac with correcting this imbalance by emphasizing the origin of the Church in the celebration of the Eucharist. In any case, one must recognize that when describing the Church as sacrament and baptism as sacrament, the word is being used in very different ways.

172. Rahner, "Christianity and the Non-Christian Religions," 116, 123.

as a matter of "obligation."[173] His attitude rhymes with that of Navatel, with morals taking the place of dogma. Moral decisions are "supernaturally elevated" while "theoretical and ritualistic factors" are downgraded to a "very inadequate expression of what man actually accomplishes in practice."[174] In both cases, "interior union"—expressed more generically by Rahner as "the religious person" acting "really religiously"—come at the expense of the concrete sacraments.[175]

Rahner's thought, it must be stressed, is rich and complex, with both dazzling insights and astonishing lacunae. We can only hint at certain ideas in the background of our discussion—his theology of the *Realsymbol*, of grace, and of mystery—though the theory of Anonymous Christianity, along with its principal critiques, can be sketched out relatively briefly. Most important for us, however, will be to see how it absorbs—and eventually dissolves—the concept of baptism of desire.

Anonymous Christians

The method Rahner uses to develop his theory of Anonymous Christianity is deductive. As his starting point, he takes a principle, God's universal salvific will. While most Catholic theologians throughout the centuries would have affirmed some version of this principle, what it means for the salvation of any individual is not particularly clear.[176] At a minimum it rules out double-predestination, as we saw during the Jansenist controversies. But, as we also saw, acknowledging human free will entails rejecting the notion that grace inevitably achieves its end. It is hard to deny that actions and outcomes contrary to God's will do indeed come to pass—doing so would require us to affirm that God willed Auschwitz. Classic Catholic theology, therefore, has followed John Damascene in distinguishing between God's antecedent and consequent will.[177] On its own, then, the principle of God's universal salvific will has never provided

173. Rahner, 119–20.
174. Rahner, 124–25.
175. Rahner, 123–24.
176. Rahner admits that the "absolute universality of God's salvific will in regard to all men (who come to the use of reason)" has not been defined by the magisterium but says it can nonetheless "no longer be denied." Karl Rahner, "Salvation," in *Sacramentum Mundi: An Encyclopedia of Theology*, vol. 5, ed. K. Rahner et al. (London: Burns & Oates, 1970), 407.
177. Rahner acknowledges the necessity of this distinction. Rahner, 405.

theologians with sufficient evidence to determine how many people are actually saved or who they might be.

Rahner, however, needs the concept to do more. To be "serious," he insists, it must mean that everyone without exception must have a "real and historically concrete" possibility of salvation.[178] At first glance, this seems unobjectionable—who would describe God's will as trivial?—but Rahner has in mind more than what he says explicitly. In his later writings on atheism and Anonymous Christianity, it becomes clear that even access to explicit Christianity is unlikely to qualify as a "serious" possibility of salvation. On the contrary, it must be necessary for those who explicitly reject belief in God to be saved even if they have concrete access to the Christian message—even if they are surrounded by, or raised by, believers. Rahner hints that, in order for God's will to be serious, it must "attain its purpose."[179] He cannot claim this outright, however, without denying human freedom the ability to refuse God's grace—falling into Anonymous Jansenism—so he takes another tack. Not only must each person have a real and concrete possibility of salvation, but the possibility of achieving salvation must be always and everywhere present. This means that salvation cannot really depend on anything categorical and particular, such as sacraments or beliefs with any specific content. Rahner here is taking the baroque scholastic search for a minimum content of faith to its ultimate extreme and is forced to dismiss even Hebrews 11:6—"whoever would draw near to God must believe that he exists and that he rewards those who seek him"—as unhelpful.[180] In Rahner's system, it is possible for the explicit rejection of God to be an act of Anonymously Christian faith. In the end, subjective moral conscience is the only absolute.[181]

On the surface such a conclusion flatly contradicts Biblical revelation,

---

178. Rahner, "Anonymous Christians," 391. Rahner sometimes resorts to rhetorical sleights of hand, asking if one can believe that "the overwhelming mass of his brothers" is "unquestionably and in principle [...] condemned to eternal meaninglessness." A great number of theologians—Suárez comes to mind—believed that the numerical majority of the human race was lost but not that this happened "unquestionably and in principle."

179. Rahner, "Salvation," 407.

180. Rahner, "Atheism and Implicit Christianity," 152–53.

181. "Even if a man does not think of God [...] or even feels that he has to reject such a concept [...] he accepts God when he freely accepts himself in his own unlimited transcendence. He does this when he genuinely follows his conscience." Rahner, "Anonymous and Explicit Faith," 55; cf. Rahner, "Atheism and Implicit Christianity," 149. It is not clear, however, that Rahner manages to meet his own criterion of universality. By emphasizing salvation

though Rahner makes a vigorous effort to defend the orthodoxy of his
theory. Even the name "Anonymous Christianity" reflects his conviction
that salvation, to whomever it comes, can only come from Christ.[182] He
also takes seriously the belief, affirmed repeatedly by the tradition against
various incarnations of Pelagianism, that salvation cannot be gained
through human effort alone but must be a gift of grace. This doctrine
causes Rahner to reject the proposal that had emerged from the *nouvelle
théologie* that our natural desire for God, even in the absence of contact
with supernatural revelation, could be sufficient to orient our actions toward salvation.[183] Rahner saw the contradiction between such a claim
and the magisterial rejection of Pelagianism, so he introduces a new concept—the supernatural existential—to resolve the problem. He acknowledges the theoretical possibility of a merely natural orientation of human
life—which would aim toward something less than the beatific vision—
but he claims that God, in an act which is truly gratuitous, elevates this
natural orientation to a supernatural end always and immediately at the
first moment of human existence. This gives every human life a supernatural trajectory. If we consider what such a supernatural orientation means
within a Thomistic framework—Rahner's theory remains in important
respects indebted to such a framework—its relevance to the theory of the
Anonymous Christian becomes clear. Thomas had argued (against Augustine) that the virtuous acts of pagans were not sinful but in themselves
good. This goodness, however, was only relative, confined to this world
because it did not aim at union with Christ. Only once one had entered
into Christianity through baptism did such naturally good acts take on
a newer, higher orientation; they became part of a life directed by faith

---

through moral choices, he arguably makes the problem of the salvation of infants even more
intractable.

182. Rahner dedicates substantial space to defending his terminology, insisting on the
word "Christian" because the "individual who is justified, even though he is a non-Christian
is justified through the grace of Christ." Karl Rahner, "Observations on the Problem of the
'Anonymous Christian,'" in *Theological Investigations*, vol. 14, trans. David Bourke (London:
Darton, Longman & Todd, 1987), 280–83.

183. David Coffey explains the subtle difference between Rahner and Henri de Lubac on
the question: "The central point of [the *nouvelle théologie*] was that all human beings have by
nature a spiritual orientation to the one true God revealed in Jesus Christ. The single element
of this to which Rahner took exception was the phrase 'by nature.'" David Coffey, "The Whole
Rahner on the Supernatural Existential," *Theological Studies* 65, no. 1 (2004): 98.

toward supernatural beatitude. (Thomas used the technical term "merit" to describe this qualitative difference.) The supernatural existential allows Rahner to maintain this distinction in theory while eliminating its practical consequences. No human life ever has a merely natural orientation, so all of our actions are already oriented toward the beatific vision; the orientation of every human life is always, already Christian. Rahner can thus conclude: "a Christian is simply man as he is [...] The really ultimate thing is that he accepts himself just as he is."[184]

Critiques. Rahner does, then, attempt to preserve the language and much of the structure of the theological tradition, though, as in much early twentieth-century theology, one soon suspects that his use of traditional sounding terms—like "supernatural"—actually vacates them of meaning. His theology retains some of the most limiting features of scholasticism as well. Rahner reasons from axioms down. The forensic tools of scholasticism do, of course, have a role to play in helping us make sense of revelation, of the encounter with Jesus Christ. But they cannot replace the concreteness of that event. This problem becomes apparent in the first principle from which all of Rahner's deductions flow, the universality of God's salvific will. Any principle involving God's will, as we have seen, requires almost instant qualification in order to account for the presence of evil in the world. Moreover, it is not at all obvious what the final outcome of the encounter between divine benevolence and creaturely freedom will look like. Scripture offers the unruly vision of the Book of Revelation, a text which simply cannot fit within Rahner's deductive methodology. While the principle seems straightforward at first glance, much depends on how one defines its terms. Does the universality of God's will admit of gradations in rewards or punishments? Does it demand equal outcomes? Equal opportunities? Does it leave God the freedom to love Jacob and hate Esau (Rom 9:13)? How does such universality account for non-human beings, their fate and purpose—the medievals might have asked about angels, post-moderns about animals? Even more problematic for Rahner, is the notion of salvation itself. For the idea implies need of rescue. Rahner's "always and already" rhetoric implies the opposite. For him,

---

184. Karl Rahner, *Foundations of Christian Faith*, trans. William V. Dych (New York: Crossroad Publishing, 1987), 402.

in practice, we start our existence saved and can only (perhaps) lose this salvation through deliberate moral failing.[185]

Though usually stingy with scriptural references, Rahner offers a rare prooftext to bolster his foundational principle, the "classical text for the universal salvific will of God": 1 Timothy 2:1–6.[186] Read fully and in context, however, the text offers more difficulty than support for Anonymous Christianity, for in the same breath Paul affirms that God "desires all men to be saved" and that they "come to the knowledge of the truth." As Philip Towner puts it, expressing a strong exegetical consensus, "Paul emphasizes that salvation and adherence to the apostolic message are inseparable. God's will is that all people commit themselves in faith to the truth about Christ."[187] Luke Timothy Johnson adds that such universal language must be read in the context of Paul's defense of his mission to the Gentiles.[188] Such a mission only makes sense if (1) God wills that the Gentiles be saved, and (2) the Christian mission to them is necessary for the fulfillment of that will. The problem is that, in order to achieve universality, Rahner must separate salvation and knowledge of the truth. The abstraction to which he is forced to resort makes his theory hard to reconcile with other New Testament passages that present salvation as involving a choice between Christ and any other good.[189] In order

---

185. Rahner, 143.

186. Rahner, "Salvation," 406; Rahner, "Anonymous Christians," 391.

187. Philip H. Towner, *The Letters to Timothy and Titus: The New International Commentary on the New Testament* (Grand Rapids, MI: Eerdmans, 2006), 179. In the Pastoral Epistles, "'knowledge of the truth' is akin to a *terminus technicus* for accepting Christianity." Benjamin Fiore, *The Pastoral Epistles: First Timothy, Second Timothy, Titus*, ed. Daniel J. Harrington, Sacra Pagina Series 12 (Collegeville, MN: Liturgical Press, 2007), 59. "Salvation is from ignorance" as well as from sin.

188. "Salvation has a specific sociological referent: God wills all people to belong to the people God is forming in the world." Luke Timothy Johnson, *The First and Second Letters to Timothy*, The Anchor Bible 35A (New York: Doubleday, 2001), 191. The context of the passage is Paul urging prayers to be offered, especially "for kings and all who are in high positions, that we may lead a quiet and peaceable life" (v. 2). The passage assumes that the salvific will of God is accomplished through the evangelizing work of Paul and his fellow Christians. Good relations with authorities create conditions favorable for the accomplishment of this will. Fiore, *The Pastoral Epistles*, 57. While the passage does indeed affirm the universal salvific will of God, it does not support the idea that this will is accomplished apart from the Christian proclamation. Neither did the Fathers read the passage in a Rahnerian key. *Colossesi, 1–2 Tessalonicesi, 1–2 Timoteo, Tito, Filemone*, ed. Peter Gorday, La Bibbia Commentata Dai Padri, Nuovo Testamento 9 (Rome: Città Nuova, 2004), 215–18.

189. E.g., Mt 10:37–38, 16:25; Mk 8:34–35; Lk 9:23–24; cf. Jn 11:25, 14:6.

to apply the label "Christian" as universally as Rahner wishes, he must empty the concept of any specifically Christian content. His language of self-acceptance—identifying Christianity with "man as he is"—makes it hard to maintain that revelation adds much of anything to what is meant by salvation. One can accept one's own humanity and even make serious choices in conscience without one's life taking on a distinctly paschal character. This leads to one of the sharpest critiques directed against Rahner from Joseph Ratzinger: "Just to accept one's humanity as it is (or, even, 'in its ultimate unconditionality')—that is not redemption; it is damnation."[190] Rahner could reply that the human trajectory toward the beatific vision—and, thus, beyond human finitude—is always and already present thanks to the supernatural existential, though doing so creates another problem: We lose any input we might have in our life's direction. Ratzinger's ultimate critique of Rahner is that, by absorbing all of the particulars of Christianity into the universal, he empties the choices we make—which can only be particular—of any real meaning. Our conscious choices mean little if, even when I explicitly reject God, I nonetheless affirm him.[191] There is, in the ineluctable logic of Rahner's system, something of Dostoyevsky's Grand Inquisitor, who, out of compassion for humanity, relieves man of the awful burden of his freedom. Our confession is already written—no matter what we say.

To shore up the tenuous connection between the content of Christian revelation and salvation in his theory, Rahner insists that Anonymous Christianity has an intrinsic dynamism directing it toward explicit Christianity. But he does not develop the point or offer evidence for it, and it is not obvious that it is true.[192] Rahner's "always already" theology of salvation tends to remove the need for movement in any particular direction, as does his need to preserve the theory's universality. Rahner is

190. Joseph Ratzinger, *Principles of Catholic Theology*, trans. Mary Frances McCarthy (San Francisco: Ignatius Press, 1987), 166–67.

191. Rahner, *Foundations of Christian Faith*, 147. At times Rahner conflates making a choice rendered possible by God with the acceptance of God's will. Rahner, "Anonymous and Explicit Faith," 56.

192. Karl Rahner, "Anonymous Christianity and the Missionary Task of the Church," in *Theological Investigations*, vol. 12, trans. David Bourke (London: Darton, Longman & Todd, 1987), 171. The continued resistance of large parts of the world's population to Christianity and the growing rejection of Christianity in the West are strong empirical evidence against a trajectory toward explicit Christianity.

less willing to discard Christian morality than Christian belief.[193] Even
when attempting to distinguish Christianity from mere humanism, he
insists that one cannot discover God except in one's neighbor.[194] This
claim makes it hard for him to account for any act of love directed toward
God as such. Tellingly, in an attempt to justify prayer and worship, he
inadvertently equates these Christian religious practices with going on
walks and recreation. "Even the most radical protagonists of a secularized
form of responsibility for the world [...] sometimes go for walks, take
recreation, enjoy life, etc. Even a Christianity that is radically aware of
its responsibility for the world should still pray, still pursue theology, still
rejoice in God and his peace, thank God and praise him."[195] Even here,
however, his commitment to universalism forces him to fall back on the
subjective conscience as the ultimate arbiter of salvation. This naturally
occasions the charge of relativism that Rahner never fully answers. If
rejecting God in good faith can be a salvific act, are there any limits on
what actions can be supernaturally elevated? If one is acting out of sincere
love for the proletariat, can shooting kulaks be an Anonymous Christian's
baptism? And if the moral law does contain obligations to *neighbor* that
can never be transgressed, why can all of one's duties to *God* be set aside
if one is sincere? The problem of the practical contentlessness of Anonymous Christianity is at the heart of a devastating critique leveled against
the theory by Hans Urs von Balthasar in the form of an imaginary dialogue between a Rahnerian Christian and a well-intentioned commissar
sent to interrogate him. The dialogue ends with the Christian insisting
to the commissar, "You are with *us*!" and the commissar concluding that
Christianity is not even worth persecuting.[196]

193. Rahner, *Foundations of Christian Faith*, 98–99. Though he recognizes that reducing
Christianity to mere love of neighbor is unacceptable "horizontalism," his insistence that
Christianity can remain anonymous forces him to claim that love of God is always unconsciously present in love of neighbor, so that the first collapses into the second. Karl Rahner,
"The Church's Commission to Bring Salvation and the Humanization of the World," in *Theological Investigations*, vol. 14, trans. David Bourke (London: Darton, Longman & Todd, 1987),
295, 305.
194. Rahner, 307.
195. Rahner, 310.
196. Hans Urs von Balthasar, *Cordula ovverosia il caso serio*, trans. G. Viola (Brescia: Queriniana, 1974), 121–24.

Baptism of desire and Anonymous Christianity. While it is important to mention these lines of criticism, we cannot pursue them further here; instead, to see how Anonymous Christianity becomes, in a sense, the rival of baptism of desire, we must turn to the role the older doctrine plays in Rahner's theology. That role is, in fact, crucial. For, astute student of theology that he is, Rahner knows that those historical theories that came closest to yielding the universalistic results of Anonymous Christianity—such as the *apokatastasis* or Ripalda's broad faith—are unavoidably heterodox.[197] So he traces the genesis of his theory back to the most reliable source he can find—Ambrose of Milan.

> No truly theological demonstration of this thesis [Anonymous Christianity] can be supplied here from scripture or tradition. Such a demonstration would not be easy to make, because the optimism of universal salvation entailed in this thesis has only gradually become clear and asserted itself in the conscious faith of the Church. We can trace a course of development from the optimism concerning salvation for unbaptized catechumens in Ambrose, through the doctrine of the *baptismus flaminis* and the *votum ecclesiae* in the Middle Ages and at the Council of Trent, down to the explicit teaching in the writings of Pius XII to the effect that even a merely implicit *votum* for the Church and baptism can suffice.[198]

But is Rahner's theory in continuity with Ambrose's? In order to make it so, Rahner needs to reduce Ambrose's argument to an attitude—optimism—which implausibly stretches the Latin Doctor's thought. One discontinuity between Ambrose and Rahner deserves to be particularly underlined: the role of desire. A decisive argument in *De obitu Valentiniani* is its appeal to the late emperor's "poverty": Ambrose's argument that Valentinian's want drove him to ardent prayer for that which he did not yet possess—namely, baptism. This desire aligned his will with that of Christ and the Church. It also depended upon Valentinian realizing that he did not have what he desired. Rahner's always- and already-present salvation unwinds this thread of desire.

---

197. Rahner, "Salvation," 406; Perry, "Juan Martínez de Ripalda and Karl Rahner's Supernatural Existential," 443.

198. Rahner, "Observations on the Problem of the 'Anonymous Christian,'" 283.

Behind this disjunct is another profound divergence between the outlook of Ambrose and that of Rahner—namely, their understanding of the Christian sacraments. In a way, Rahner preserves the scholastic framework of salvation that developed around the sacraments, but he moves it. To see this, we need to return to the supernatural existential. The concept is essential for the theology of the Anonymous Christian, but, as one of Rahner's commentators admits, "It does not seem by any means clear what precisely this supernatural existential is."[199] The roots of the concept in revelation are, at best, thin, but Rahner needs it to avoid falling into Pelagianism. We already saw how the concept preserves some of the structure of Thomistic theology; here, we can go further and note its striking similarity to a difficult-to-define concept in sacramental theology—the baptismal character. Both represent a permanent spiritual change in the individual, who is habilitated to participate in the life of grace—in one case, through participation in Christian worship; in the other, through the elevation of one's moral actions to a supernatural plane. The parallels are not exact but are enough to see that, as far as salvation is concerned, the supernatural existential takes over a role once played by baptism. Among the most significant differences between the two concepts, however, is that the supernatural existential is automatic; unlike baptism, it does not involve the participation of one's will.[200]

One aspect of the medieval theory of baptism of desire is particularly important for Rahner—namely, the idea that it takes place before baptism.[201] This contention is found in the tradition, though, as I have argued, it is based on a weak interpretation of the story of Cornelius (Acts 10), first offered by Augustine and repeated unreflectively by later theologians. Even if one accepts the Cornelius story as an example of baptism of desire—and not as the preparatory action of the Holy Spirit—

---

199. Patrick Burke, *Reinterpreting Rahner: A Critical Study of His Major Themes* (New York: Fordham University Press, 2002), 70. Even Rahner's defenders concede the point. "It is regrettable therefore that Rahner has not provided a more careful and detailed account of the metaphysics of the supernatural existential which is such a vital element in his whole system." Gerald A. McCool, *A Rahner Reader* (New York: Crossroad, 1981), xxvi. Coffey agrees that the theory's "more fundamental weakness" was that Rahner "was unable to say what the supernatural existential *was*." Coffey, "The Whole Rahner on the Supernatural Existential," 97.

200. As Burke puts it, in light of the supernatural existential, "it is difficult to see how man remains in any real sense free." Burke, *Reinterpreting Rahner*, 71.

201. Rahner, "Anonymous Christianity," 166–67.

it is clearly meant to be exceptional. While, in some of Rahner's earlier writings, he treats pre-baptismal justification as a mere possibility, the logic of his position makes it an exceptionless norm, as becomes apparent in his later writings.[202] This, of course, raises the question of original sin. Rahner argues lucidly that we exist in a state conditioned by the guilt of others; this guilt is ours because we never exist apart from it, and so it forms part of our own exercise of freedom.[203] His language is not entirely traditional, but the content of his theology of original sin seems to fit within Catholic orthodoxy. Because of the supernatural existential, however, the guilt of original sin has no real bearing on one's salvation. Concupiscence remains, but this is not removed by baptism either. It is, therefore, hard to see how the sacrament makes any difference as far as original sin is concerned.

If we are honest, we must admit that the sacraments do not fit naturally within Rahner's theology. Or, rather, though he makes room for the *idea* of sacraments, the particular rites of Catholicism remain an awkward fit. In his liturgical and sacramental writing, Rahner shows a marked preference for speaking of the sacraments in general instead of specific rites.[204] For Rahner, sacraments serve the role of making "explicit and official" what is always and everywhere present.[205] In this respect, his

202. "Properly speaking, when we come to baptism we must already have faith, hope and love, in other words the state of justification [...] through such a baptism [an Anonymous Christian] may indeed be validly baptized, but not justified. In the case of adult baptism the justification is prior to the baptism itself." Rahner, "Anonymous Christianity," 172–73. Grace "apart from the sacrament" is "*always* and *everywhere* present." Rahner, "Atheism and Implicit Christianity," 161. Schillebeeckx, by contrast, understands pre-sacramental grace to be "an initial stage" of the bestowal of grace that does not anticipate "the effect of the future ecclesial act." Schillebeeckx, *Christ the Sacrament of the Encounter with God*, 143–44.

203. Rahner, *Foundations of Christian Faith*, 106–15. The "co-determination of the situation of every person by the guilt of others is something universal, permanent, and therefore also original. There are no islands for the individual person whose nature does not already bear the stamp of the guilt of others." Rahner, 109.

204. Karl Rahner, "On the Theology of Worship," in *Theological Investigations*, vol. 19, trans. Edward Quinn (New York: Crossroads, 1983), 141. He writes in *Foundations of Christian Faith*, 411, "From a methodological point of view it is highly questionable to consider the seven sacraments in isolation." Similarly, he is ill at ease with the material element of the sacrament, belaboring the obvious point that without the word there is no sacrament, but not fully acknowledging that without matter there is no sacrament either. Rahner, "The Word and the Eucharist," 267.

205. Rahner, *Foundations of Christian Faith*, 411. It is not clear what advantage there is in being "official."

sense of the sacrament is close to that of Navatel, for whom the liturgy was a container for doctrine; especially in Rahner's later writings, worship is instructive, a pointer toward the transcendent. He rejects the idea that something happens in Christian worship which does not happen elsewhere.[206] This means that baptism is never *really* necessary for salvation.[207]

Rahner's unease with the specificity of Christianity's rites has to do with the scandal of particularity, but it also arises from the content of those rites. For the Christian sacraments as they actually exist are poor expressions of Rahnerian theology. Baptism does not announce that we can feel peace in discovering that we were already saved; it begins with a request for faith, followed by an exorcism. Little in the ritual reflects the "always and already" Rahner so insists upon. If the fundamental truth of our existence is that salvation means accepting ourselves as we really are, baptism, with its imagery of death, rebirth, and conversion, is rather misleading. The rite might be made to fit within a Rahnerian worldview with a sufficiently clever eisegesis, but if a symbol requires a tortured explanation to make it speak the truth, then it is not a particularly good symbol. It is not much better with the stubborn corporality of the other sacraments—not the idea of corporality, but the specificity of Mediterranean agricultural products. The *lex orandi* is simply not congenial territory for Rahner's supernatural existential or the Anonymous Christianity that depends upon it.[208]

At this point the fundamental incompatibility of Anonymous Christianity with the doctrine of baptism of desire should be clear. The Rahnerian theory represents an alternative path to salvation, amounting, in

206. Rahner, 85; "On the Theology of Worship," 149.

207. The full extent of the downgrade suffered by the sacraments in Rahner's theory is reflected in the difficulty he finds in showing that infant baptism, "even if not absolutely necessary, is at least meaningful." Rahner, "On the Theology of Worship," 145.

208. Rahner, in "On the Theology of Worship," 148, effectively admits that the *lex orandi* is against him when he concedes that "there are many people even today who come to learn through worship itself, through its outward shape and through the natural way in which it is carried out, that God's grace becomes an event here in the midst of a world which they experience only as profane." His pastoral motivation for offering his alternative theory is no doubt sincere; he accurately notes that many modern people no longer participate in Christian worship. It is not clear, however, how his claim that "God is worshiped in spirit everywhere" and "not in ecclesial-liturgical ceremony" would motivate greater participation in the Church's sacramental life. Rahner, 148–49.

practical terms, to the denial that baptism is necessary for salvation. Despite all his talk of optimism, there is a profound pessimism at the heart of Rahner's theology. It is premised on the belief that the Christian mission has failed. God wanted all to be saved, but explicit Christianity and its sacraments were not up to the task. So, Rahner offers an alternative that preserves something of the intellectual framework that had grown up around Christian worship but reduces the rites themselves to mere ceremony. Quite naturally, it no longer makes sense to speak of desire for baptism leading to salvation. Of the convictions that guided Ambrose and Augustine, Thomas and Trent, Rahner's theory contains but a ghostly memory.

Vatican II

There can be little doubt that the pivotal event in twentieth-century Catholicism was the ecumenical council opened by Pope John XXIII in October 1962 and closed by Paul VI in December 1965. Interpreting that event, however, remains a matter of considerable dispute. Some argue for a "hermeneutic of continuity," emphasizing the Council's unity with the prior theological tradition; others underline what is original in the Council's approach, seeing it as opening up a new Christian era. A few reject the Council's legitimacy altogether.[209] As far as our topic is concerned, the choice between a hermeneutic of continuity or of rupture is less decisive than it may seem, for, as we have seen, the Long Nineteenth Century was already theologically unsettled. Vatican II does not treat baptism of desire directly, but the Council's documents touch issues that shape how the doctrine is conceived. Before turning to these documents, it is necessary to emphasize the complexity of the task involved. Reading the Council as a conflict between "progressives" and "conservatives" is

209. The only contemporary opposition to *any* concept of baptism of desire I have found is among such *sedevacantist* groups. The website of the Most Holy Family Monastery of Fillmore, NY, for example, contains numerous articles and YouTube videos attacking baptism of desire, https://vaticancatholic.com. The number of authorities these videos must oppose—Ambrose, the Council of Trent, Alphonsus Liguori—and the theological contortions to which they must resort is a testament to the doctrine's solidity. Other traditionalist groups, such as the Society of St. Pius X, have used their affirmation of baptism of desire to assert their orthodoxy against the Feeneyites, e.g., François Laisney, *Is Feeneyism Catholic? The Catholic Meaning of the Dogma "Outside the Catholic Church There Is No Salvation"* (Kansas City, MO: Angelus Press, 2001).

inadequate; sometimes its documents show tension between divergent theological tendencies that can both be considered "reformist"—like that between the liturgical theology of Casel and the philosophical approach of Rahner. As a recent commentator on Vatican II has pointed out, the accessible style with which the documents are written often masks the intricacy of the theological issues they confront.[210]

Historian John O'Malley, in fact, argues that Vatican II's method of communication—its style—is among its most significant innovations.[211] Vatican II is unusual among ecumenical councils because it was not convoked to address a clear theological crisis, like Arianism or the Reformation. However, the broader view of history that I have proposed in this chapter—studying the nineteenth and twentieth centuries together—does suggest that Vatican II was addressing a crisis—the same crisis addressed by Vatican I. Both councils were dealing with the collapse of Christendom and the uncertain place of the institutional Church in the new world order. Vatican I proposed a theological answer to an essentially political crisis—a ringing affirmation of papal authority to counter the loss of the papal states—but this answer was, at most, partial. The turmoil of the first half of the twentieth century—the unresolved Roman question, the two world wars—prevented the Church from articulating a more comprehensive response. Vatican II gives such a response, proposing a substantial role for the modern Church; the Council's pastoral constitution, *Gaudium et Spes*, offers a panorama of the present state of the world, as well as a "programmatic" section addressing problems the Council Fathers considered particularly urgent—marriage and family; social and political development; world peace. The Council wished the Church to continue occupying a place on the world stage, one no longer based on the pontiff's status as a European monarch, but, rather, on the Church's positive contribution to international discussion, ideals offered for the world's benefit.

A dialogical approach to the world necessitated an accessible style and a positive tone; the Council's documents, in the words of an influential

210. Thomas G. Guarino, *The Disputed Teachings of Vatican II: Continuity and Reversal in Catholic Doctrine* (Grand Rapids, MI: Eerdmans, 2018), 4.

211. O'Malley, *What Happened at Vatican II*, 11–12. He describes the Council as adopting the style of the panegyric. O'Malley, 47.

speech by Belgium's Cardinal Léon-Josef Suenens, needed to accent "what unites Catholics with others, not what separates them."[212] As with any approach, focusing on what unifies has both advantages and limitations; it facilitates the sort of dialogue the Council sought to foster, but it is not so well suited for addressing complex theological questions with precision. In fact, on certain issues touching on our topic, the Council deliberately chose not to address doctrinal disputes; for example, on the question of limbo and the state of unbaptized infants, conciliar theologians found themselves unable to come to an agreement and so decided to say nothing at all, leaving the issue just as difficult in 1966 as it had been in 1961—or, for that matter, for the previous nineteen centuries.[213] In certain instances, the Council did intend to make authoritative doctrinal statements—for example, by repudiating the claim that the Jewish people are collectively responsible for the death of Jesus in *Nostra Aetate.* Distinguishing between what is a doctrinally significant development and what is an invitation to further dialogue requires careful attention to the texts and knowledge of the theological tradition. While, for our topic, the most important conciliar texts to consider are *Lumen Gentium* and the Council's decree on missionary activity, *Ad Gentes,* a number of other documents provide clues for interpreting the Council's intentions. These include the Council's most controversial texts, *Nostra Aetate* and *Dignitatis Humanae.*

Dignitatis Humanae. We turn first to *Dignitatis Humanae,* Vatican II's declaration on religious liberty. As we saw when Alcuin rebuked Charlemagne for imposing forced baptisms, a certain respect for religious liberty is implicit in the Church's theology of baptism. Popes of the previous century had also insisted on the rights of Catholics to free religious expression. *Dignitatis Humanae* took a step forward—and generated controversy—by grounding the right to religious liberty not only in the truth of the faith professed, but in the dignity of the human person, thus providing a theological reason for the state to respect the religious liberty of both Catholics and non-Catholics. One of the document's architects,

212. Guarino, *The Disputed Teachings of Vatican II,* 26.
213. Giuseppe Alberigo and Joseph A. Komonchak, *History of Vatican II,* vol. 1, Announcing and Preparing Vatican Council II (Maryknoll, NY: Orbis, 1995), 241, 245, 310.

the American Jesuit John Courtney Murray, points out in his commentary on *Dignitatis Humanae*, "In no other conciliar document is it so explicitly stated that the intention of the Council is to 'develop' Catholic doctrine."[214] Indeed, the document could hardly be more explicit: "the council intends to develop the doctrine of recent popes on the inviolable rights of the human person and the constitutional order of society."[215] In the same paragraph, however, the Council Fathers identify equally explicitly what they do not intend to change: The Council "leaves untouched the traditional Catholic doctrine on the moral duty of men and societies toward the true religion and toward the one Church of Christ." The Council's explicit recognition of the possibility of doctrinal development means that this statement is not mere pious rhetoric about the eternal truth of the Catholic faith; it is the Council's explanation of how to interpret its intentions. Simply put, the Council does not understand itself to be changing Catholic doctrine on salvation. Murray agrees, "Once given by Christ to His true Church, the true religion remains the one way in which all men are bound to serve God and save themselves. Consequently, religious freedom is not a title to exemption from the obligation to 'observe all things whatsoever I have enjoined upon you.'"[216]

Nostra Aetate. This explicit declaration of intent gives us an authoritative key to interpret other documents that are potentially more ambiguous on the question of salvation. *Nostra Aetate* is one of these. As alluded to above, the document's most pressing aim was to repudiate anti-Semitism and to correct erroneous beliefs about collective Jewish guilt for the death of Christ.[217] *Nostra Aetate* also aims to foster peaceful relationships with other religions based on dialogue and mutual understanding. Thus, it has positive things to say about Hinduism, Buddhism, and Islam. It makes clear, however, that these words of respect and warmth do not alter Catholic teaching that Christ is the way, the truth, and the life. When the document claims, therefore, that the "Catholic Church rejects nothing that is true and holy in these religions," it deliberately sidesteps the question

214. John Courtney Murray, "Religious Freedom," in *The Documents of Vatican II*, ed. Walter M. Abbott (London: Geoffrey Chapman, 1967), 677n4.
215. Vatican Council II, *Dignitatis Humanae* (December 7, 1965), 1.
216. Murray, "Religious Freedom," 676n3.
217. Vatican Council II, *Nostra Aetate* (October 28, 1965), 4.

of salvation.[218] Nor does the declaration mention elements in other religions that are not good and holy, though we can hardly conclude that the omission means such elements no longer exist. The document aimed to promote "unity and love among men," not to offer a general theology of religion or of salvation.[219]

Lumen Gentium. Bearing more directly on our question, the dogmatic constitution *Lumen Gentium* ranks among the magisterium's most significant statements of ecclesiology. Affirming the necessity of the Church for salvation—though in decidedly tentative terms—the constitution's second chapter comments on the relationship of different categories of people to the Church; the chapter is organized as if moving outward in a series of concentric circles, with baptized Catholics at the center and non-believers in the most distant sphere.[220] While the document does not treat baptism of desire directly, its treatment of catechumens—who, interestingly, are placed closer to the center by the document's structure than non-Catholic Christians—certainly does nothing to undermine the concept.[221] The vocabulary used in these paragraphs shifts in subtle but important ways. Those who accept the "entire system" of Catholicism, "all the means of salvation given" to the Church, and live in obedience to the pope and bishops—those who meet Bellarmine's criteria for ecclesial membership—are "fully incorporated" (*plene ... incorporantur*). Both catechumens, who seek to be incorporated, and baptized, non-Catholic Christians are described as "joined" to the Church (*coniunguntur*). Non-Christians, however, are neither incorporated nor joined to the Church but "related in various ways" (*diversis rationibus ordinantur*).[222] This differentiated vocabulary allows the Council to acknowledge the significant differences between these groups without entering into the implications of those differences. It leaves open the question of what such differences mean for salvation.

218. *Nostra Aetate*, 2.
219. *Nostra Aetate*, 1.
220. Vatican Council II, *Lumen Gentium* (November 21, 1964), 14–16.
221. "Catechumens who, moved by the Holy Spirit, seek with explicit intention to be incorporated into the Church are by that very intention joined with her. With love and solicitude Mother Church already embraces them as her own." *Lumen Gentium*, 14.
222. *Lumen Gentium*, 14–16; cf. *AAS* 57 (1965) 5–71.

Among *Lumen Gentium*'s most quoted paragraphs regarding salvation is that dedicated to non-Christians. Unfortunately, as a recent study by Ralph Martin shows, the paragraph is also one of the document's most frequently misquoted or, rather, partially quoted.[223] After affirming the special role of the Jews in God's plan and the Savior's will that all men be saved (citing 1 Tim 2:4), the constitution states:

> Those also can attain to salvation who through no fault of their own do not know the Gospel of Christ or His Church, yet sincerely seek God and moved by grace strive by their deeds to do His will as it is known to them through the dictates of conscience. Nor does Divine Providence deny the helps necessary for salvation to those who, without blame on their part, have not yet arrived at an explicit knowledge of God and with His grace strive to live a good life.[224]

On their own, these sentences easily lend themselves to a Rahnerian reading. Unfortunately, they could also lend themselves to a Pelagian reading. Their mention of grace is perhaps intended to avoid this, but grace seems to play only a supporting role in a process defined mostly by good deeds and obedience to conscience, a decidedly moralistic emphasis.[225] As we have seen repeatedly when dealing with invincible ignorance—a concept strongly present in the paragraph—moral probity in itself cannot guarantee salvation. The decisive factors are the strikingly vague "helps necessary for salvation." What precisely are those helps? Baptism? The angel, preacher, or interior inspiration favored by Aquinas? The supernatural existential? The Council does not say. Consistent with its stated intentions in *Dignitatis Humanae*, the Council seems determined to maintain the theological status quo with regard to salvation, leaving the trickiest questions open.

Lumen Gentium, however, does not end with the two oft-repeated sentences quoted above. The paragraph continues:

---

223. Ralph Martin, *Will Many Be Saved? What Vatican II Actually Teaches and Its Implications for the New Evangelization* (Grand Rapids, MI: Eerdmans, 2012), 16; see also 229n27.

224. *Lumen Gentium*, 16.

225. Joseph Ratzinger mentions dissatisfaction emerging among the Council Fathers on this point after the passage of the Constitution, in "The Church and Man's Calling: Introductory Article and Chapter 1; The Dignity of the Human Person," in *Commentary on the Documents of Vatican II*, ed. Herbert Vorgrimler (New York: Herder and Herder, 1969), 5:161–63. The shift in wording in *Gaudium et Spes*, which we will see below, was intended to achieve a more balanced effect.

Whatever good or truth is found amongst [those blamelessly ignorant of the Gospel] is looked upon by the Church as a preparation
for the Gospel. She knows that it is given by Him who enlightens
all men so that they may finally have life. But often [*at saepius*] men,
deceived by the Evil One, have become vain in their reasonings
and have exchanged the truth of God for a lie, serving the creature
rather than the Creator. Or some there are who, living and dying in
this world without God, are exposed to final despair. Wherefore to
promote the glory of God and procure salvation of all of these, and
mindful of the command of the Lord, "Preach the Gospel to every
creature," the Church fosters the missions with care and attention.

The full paragraph renders *Lumen Gentium* far more interesting, though
decisively less optimistic. If anything, the text is closer to the "optimism"
of Suárez than of Rahner. Perhaps the most theologically substantive idea
in the paragraph is its reference to "preparation for the Gospel"; for this
suggests *how* the unevangelized might be connected to Jesus Christ and,
therefore, salvation. "Preparation for the Gospel" goes beyond the negative condition of not violating one's conscience and suggests a more
specific religious orientation than the vague language of the first two
sentences. In our analysis of Trent's decrees, I suggested that just such a
concept was necessary to connect those who lived before the "promulgation of the Gospel" to baptism of desire. The idea is not much developed by either Council, but its inclusion in *Lumen Gentium* does seem to
me an improvement over the legal framework popularized by medieval
thinkers, such as Bernard and Hugh, who implied that the requirements
for salvation simply changed each time God promulgated a new law code.
Instead, "preparation for the Gospel" more cogently maintains that salvation is always inseparable from participation in the Paschal Mystery, even
if people's way of relating to that Mystery varies based on circumstances.
Preparation is consistent with participation through desire.

The final sentences of *Lumen Gentium* 16 present a glaring problem
for any unliterally "optimistic" reading of the text. For the Council asserts that the conditions laid down for salvation in the first part of the
paragraph are "often" not met. Indeed, if we examine the Latin text, we
find that the translation "often" is too weak. The Latin word for often or
frequently (*saepe*) has been placed in the comparative (*saepius*), the most

natural translation of which would be "more often" or "more frequently."[226] Such a translation is supported by the logic of the paragraph itself
and its role in the document's structure. The paragraph that follows is
a call to evangelization. It begins by repeating the Great Commission
to make disciples and to baptize. The sentences introduced by *saepius*
establish a logical connection between the grim prospects for unbelievers—"living and dying [...] exposed to final despair"—and the motive
for mission. It must be stressed that *Lumen Gentium* understands the
motive for Christian mission to be helping non-believers attain salvation
through baptism and incorporation into the Church. In fact, *Lumen Gentium* 17 relativizes the significance of the non-Christian elements of truth
and goodness mentioned in the previous paragraph.

> By the proclamation of the Gospel [the Church] prepares her hear-
> ers to receive and profess the faith. She gives them the dispositions
> necessary for baptism, snatches them from the slavery of error and
> of idols and incorporates them in Christ so that through charity
> they may grow up into full maturity in Christ. Through her work,
> whatever good is in the minds and hearts of men, whatever good
> lies latent in the religious practices and cultures of diverse peoples,
> is not only saved from destruction but is also cleansed, raised up and
> perfected unto the glory of God, the confusion of the devil, and the
> happiness of man.[227]

Consistent with the fundamental presupposition undergirding the missionary thrust of the early Church, *Lumen Gentium* treats even those elements of good present in pre-Christian individuals and religions as need-
ing salvation. Moreover, in its claim that "All men are called to belong
to the new people of God," *Lumen Gentium* resists those theologies that
would see God's universal salvific will fulfilled apart from the Church.[228]

Ad Gentes. Any reading of *Lumen Gentium* that undermines the Church's
missionary activity is, therefore, contrary to the document's intentions.

226. Martin compares several translations in *Will Many Be Saved?* 224n7.
227. *Lumen Gentium*, 17.
228. *Lumen Gentium*, 13. Richard McBrien, for example, contradicts the Council, arguing
that "All men are called to the Kingdom; not all men are called to the Church." Richard P.
McBrien, *Do We Need the Church?* (London: Collins, 1969), 15.

The importance the Council placed upon this missionary effort is reinforced by a document dedicated specifically to that theme, *Ad Gentes*. At the same time, as observers then noted, such a document would not have been needed at all had missionary work not been perceived to be in some trouble as a result of contemporary theological trends.[229] From its first words, *Ad Gentes* makes it clear that the purpose of the Church's missionary effort is salvation.[230] The document joins 1 Timothy 2:45— God "wishes all men to be saved and to come to the knowledge of the truth"—with Acts 4:12—"neither is there salvation in any other." God's universal salvific will is the reason for missionary work.[231] The necessity of baptism is mentioned, though *Ad Gentes* merely repeats the cautious formulation of *Lumen Gentium*, 14, avoiding difficult cases. The way the document addresses the problem of those invincibly ignorant of the Gospel, however, is notably different than that found in *Lumen Gentium*. Instead of suggesting that their righteous deeds will lead them to salvation, *Ad Gentes* says that God alone knows how such people might "find the faith without which it is impossible to please [God]," a reference to Hebrews 11:6. *Gaudium et Spes* echoes the language of *Ad Gentes*, emphasizing the limits of what we can claim about the salvation of non-Christians.[232] Furthermore, just as *Ad Gentes* mentions the necessity of faith, *Gaudium et Spes* emphasizes that we are saved through the Paschal Mystery. These formulations condition *Lumen Gentium*'s words about conscience and good deeds.[233]

229. Wolfgang Seibel, "Die vierte Sitzungsperiode des Konzils," *Stimmen der Zeit* 177 (1966): 57. See also Suso Brechter, "Decree on the Church's Missionary Activity," in Vorgrimler, *Commentary on the Documents of Vatican II*, 4:122.

230. Vatican Council II, *Ad Gentes* (December 7, 1965), 1.

231. *Ad Gentes*, 7. "Article 7 names as motives for the missions the necessity of faith, baptism and membership in the Church for salvation." Brechter, "Decree on the Church's Missionary Activity," 121.

232. "For, since Christ died for all men, and since the ultimate vocation of man is in fact one, and divine, we ought to believe that the Holy Spirit in a manner known only to God offers to every man the possibility of being associated with this Paschal Mystery." Vatican Council II, *Gaudium et Spes* (December 7, 1965), 22. Ratzinger highlights the shift in emphasis between *Lumen Gentium*, 16 and *Gaudium et Spes*, 22, in "The Church and Man's Calling," 161–63. The earlier document "lays too much emphasis on man's activity," but *Gaudium et Spes* "decisively acknowledged that the way to salvation is God's affair and cannot be defined by us." Ratzinger, 162.

233. It is significant that *Lumen Gentium*, 16 provoked little debate. Martin, *Will Many Be Saved?* 11; cf. 224–25n9. Rahner, too, notes the absence of "debate or opposition," though in one of his least plausible conclusions, he takes this as an indication that his own interpretation

Taken together, all the factors mentioned in the documents of Vatican II hardly add up to a Rahnerian sea-change in Catholic teaching on salvation. The hard cases theologians grappled with before the Council remained just as difficult afterwards. Moreover—and, in my view, unfortunately—Vatican II's approach to the question of salvation generally relied upon the moral and juridical language—duty, obligation, culpability—that dominated the Long Nineteenth Century. The Council's embrace of the Liturgical Movement in *Sacrosanctum Concilium* potentially opened up other ways of conceiving of the problem grounded in the *lex orandi*, but the Council's liturgical insights did not strongly penetrate its other documents. None of this is a mark against Vatican II, since it was never the Council's intention to alter Catholic teaching on salvation. In substance, though in an unsystematic way, Vatican II's documents contain most of the traditional considerations that make the hard cases hard: the necessity of faith, baptism, and contact with the Paschal Mystery; God's universal salvific will; the universal mission of the Church; the limits of human knowledge; invincible ignorance and the moral law; the freedom of the individual; grace. *Lumen Gentium*'s reference to preparation for the Gospel is the only substantial hint at how all these considerations might be held together. The Council's strong missionary emphasis adds yet another factor that must be taken into consideration when updating the theology of baptism of desire—namely, that if such a theology were to undercut the motive for missionary work, it would have to be considered contrary to the Council's intent.[234]

A Very Long Century

Paul VI. Paul VI (1963–1978), the pope who promulgated Vatican II's decrees, considered the Council's missionary call to be its defining characteristic.[235] Even his choice to take the name of the great missionary apostle

---

of the texts was "self-evident." Rahner, "Church, Churches and Religions," in *Theological Investigations*, vol. 10, trans. David Bourke (London: Darton, Longman & Todd, 1984), 32. As O'Malley points out in *What Happened at Vatican II*, 6, perceived departures from previous teaching inevitably generated more debate.

234. As Brechter puts it, "No Council has ever so consciously emphasized and so insistently expounded on the Church's pastoral work of salvation and its worldwide missionary function as Vatican II." Brechter, "Decree on the Church's Missionary Activity," 87.

235. Paul VI celebrated Vatican II's tenth anniversary with an apostolic exhortation

testifies to this conviction. Francis Sullivan, a proponent of the Rahnerian interpretation of the Council, concedes that Pope Paul "had little sympathy for [the Rahnerian view] about the salvific role of non-Christian religions."[236] Pope Paul's encyclical *Ecclesiam Suam* highlights the necessity of baptism to escape "the unhappy state of original sin," to be "reborn to a supernatural life," and to attain eternal happiness.[237] This is, in sum, the ancient *regula fidei*. With respect to other religions, the pontiff highlights *Lumen Gentium*'s description of their positive elements as "preparation for the Gospel."[238] But, he is clear that it is only the Gospel that saves:

> The presentation of the Gospel message is not an optional contribution for the Church. It is the duty incumbent on her by the command of the Lord Jesus, so that people can believe and be saved. This message is indeed necessary. It is unique. It cannot be replaced. It does not permit either indifference, syncretism or accommodation. It is a question of people's salvation.[239]

Baptism, as we would expect, is indispensable: "There is no new humanity if there are not first of all new persons renewed by Baptism."[240] Outside of Christianity, Paul VI is convinced, man falls short of salvation. This does not, however, preclude a theology of salvation based on the desire for what can be found only in Christianity, as a striking image from *Evangelii Nuntiandi* implies:

> Our religion effectively establishes with God an authentic and living relationship which the other religions do not succeed in doing,

---

dedicated to evangelization, *Evangelii Nuntiandi* (December 8, 1975). The objectives of the Council, he says, "are definitively summed up in this single one: to make the Church of the twentieth century ever better fitted for proclaiming the Gospel to the people of the twentieth century." Elsewhere, he emphasizes that the Church's mission is the salvation of souls. Paul VI, Encyclical Letter *Ecclesiam Suam* (August 6, 1964), 1.

236. Sullivan, *Salvation Outside the Church?* 189.

237. Paul VI, *Ecclesiam Suam*, 39. The encyclical also warns against a "naïve optimism" that places too much faith on human abilities and against "the illusion that man is naturally good and self-sufficient, and needs only the ability to express himself as he pleases." *Ecclesiam Suam*, 59. Insisting on the "difference between the Christian and the worldly life," the pope turns to the Pauline theology of Rom 6:3–4, to which he adds, "Justification is produced in us by our sharing in the Paschal Mystery, particularly in Baptism, which is truly a rebirth." *Ecclesiam Suam*, 60.

238. Paul VI, *Evangelii Nuntiandi*, 53.

239. *Evangelii Nuntiandi*, 5.

240. *Evangelii Nuntiandi*, 18.

even though they have, as it were, their arms stretched out towards heaven.[241]

The image of beseeching hands calls to mind an equally striking image from earlier in this study—Ambrose's description of the Emperor Valentinian as a beggar. Taken together, these images suggest that of all the salvific elements found outside of Christianity, the most decisive is desire for what is within. This image contrasts with the Rahnerian sense of salvation already attained.

Just as the publication of *Ad Gentes* reflected the Council's perception that the need for missions required reinforcing, so too the fact that Paul VI felt the need to dedicate *Evangelii Nuntiandi* to evangelization shows that the hoped-for renewal had not taken place. It is impossible to escape the conclusion that the twentieth-century trend toward ever more generic expressions of the Christian idea of salvation, coupled with the Rahnerian interpretation of the Council, contributed to this result. Protests from missionaries in the field, who believed that their work was being undercut by theologians, multiplied.[242] Rather than confront the problem of missionary motivation after the Council, however, Rahner denied it: "But in fact the real motivation of the mission has become still clearer."[243] Yet, Rahner's own attempts to articulate that motivation

241. *Evangelii Nuntiandi*, 53. The Holy Father seems to be drawing on the theology of Jean Daniélou, who grants the possibility of salvation for those formally adhering to other religions, but puts greater stress on the uniqueness of the Incarnation, an event "continued among us in the sacraments of the Church." Jean Daniélou, "The Transcendence of Christianity" in *Introduction to the Great Religions*, trans. Albert J. La Mothe (Notre Dame, IN: Fides Publishers, 1964), 134. Daniélou describes other religious traditions as man's search for God, whereas revelation is "no longer a question of man's search for God, *but of God's quest for man.*" Jean Daniélou, "Christianity and the Non-Christian Religions," in *Introduction to the Great Religions*, 17. Joseph Ratzinger hints at a similar theology of desire in *Jesus of Nazareth: From the Baptism in the Jordan to the Transfiguration*, trans. Adrian J. Walker (New York: Doubleday, 2007), 90–92. The longing expressed in the beatitude "Blessed are those who hunger and thirst for righteousness" (Mt 5:6), he thinks, hints at a path to salvation for the unevangelized.

242. Lawrence Nemer, "Salvation and Mission in Contemporary Catholic Thought," in *Early Proceedings of the Association of Professors of Mission*, vol. 2, *1962–1974*, ed. Robert A. Danielson and David E. Fenrick (Wilmore, KY: First Fruits Press, 2015), 290–91.

243. Karl Rahner, "Salvation of the Non-Evangelized," in Sacramentum Mundi: *An Encyclopedia of Theology*, vol. 4, ed. K. Rahner et al. (London: Burns & Oates, 1969), 79. Rahner is clearly on the defensive. "Hence it would be foolish to think that the recognition of 'implicit Christianity' must diminish the significance of the mission, baptism, etc. On the contrary, it releases energies for the service of the mission, since it banishes panic." Rahner, 81. The decisive

fell flat.[244] It is true, even in a later work, he repeats a claim made parenthetically in his pre-conciliar articulation of Anonymous Christianity that being evangelized improves one's position with regard to salvation, but he does not explain why.[245] This lacuna is unfortunate because such an explanation might have provided a way to reconcile Rahner's theory with the doctrine of baptism of desire, as well as a reason for the missions. It is not obvious, however, how such a claim fits within Rahner's larger theory, and his followers, by and large, do not seem to have pursued the question.[246] Fundamentally, Rahner ends up falling back on the duty to preach the Gospel.[247]

John Paul II. Indeed, on this most important question, theology seems stuck in a Long Nineteenth Century traffic jam. Sullivan correctly points out that John Paul II was more effusive in his praise of other religions than either Paul VI or Vatican II.[248] At the same time, the pontificate of

---

question, however, is not whether missionaries should proceed in a state of panic, but whether they would be better off pursuing religiously neutral goals instead of evangelization.

244. Even in those works ostensibly dedicated to the Christian mission, Rahner devotes more energy to the argument that atheists can be saved than to why evangelization is necessary. Rahner, "Anonymous Christianity," 177. The fact that the final word in his chapter on Christian life and the sacraments is that such a life can be lived even by non-Christians can hardly have inspired much missionary enthusiasm. Rahner, *Foundations of Christian Faith*, 430.

245. An explicit Christian, "other things being equal, [has] a still greater chance of salvation than someone who is merely an anonymous Christian." Rahner, "Christianity and the Non-Christian Religions," 132. "It is obvious that mission improves the situation in which salvation can be achieved and the opportunity of salvation for the individual." Rahner, "Anonymous Christianity," 177.

246. Hillman follows the dominant logic of the theory in the opposite direction. Hillman, "'Anonymous Christianity' and the Missions," 374.

247. Rahner's followers continue gamely to offer reasons other than salvation for continuing in the missions, from giving glory to God to improving the plight of the materially less fortunate to identifying the good present in other religions. See, for example, John Fuellenbach, "The Church in the Context of the Kingdom of God," in *The Convergence of Theology: A Festschrift Honoring Gerald O'Collins, S.J.*, ed. Daniel Kendall and Stephen T. Davis (Mahwah, NJ: Paulist Press, 2001), 221–37; John Sivalon, *God's Mission and Postmodern Culture: The Gift of Uncertainty* (Maryknoll, NY: Orbis, 2012). The fundamental problem with these suggestions is that the goods they propose can be achieved without Christianity's religious trappings.

248. Sullivan, *Salvation Outside the Church?* 196. Nonetheless, for John Paul II, the value of other religions comes from their orientation toward Christ. John Paul II, Encyclical Letter *Redemptor Hominis* (March 4, 1979), 18. Desire, therefore, is the decisive factor that allows for his positive evaluation, a point reinforced by his reference to the soul's restlessness before finding Christ in Augustine's *Confessions*.

John Paul II was marked by the growing suspicion that late-twentieth-century theology was undercutting the Church's missionary activity. In 1990—twenty-five years after the promulgation of *Gaudium et Spes* and *Ad Gentes*—the pontiff felt the need to issue an encyclical, *Redemptoris Missio*, defending the very legitimacy of the Church's missionary mandate.[249] Several high profile doctrinal notifications from the Congregation for the Doctrine of the Faith over the next decade and a half, along with the declaration *Dominus Iesus* in 2000, manifested concern that, in the work of many theologians, optimism about the possibility of salvation outside of the Church had come at the expense of compromising the confession of Jesus Christ as humanity's sole savior and redeemer.[250] Though John Paul II recognized the fundamental tension posed by late twentieth century theology—the need to hold together the "possibility of salvation in Christ for all mankind and the necessity of the Church for salvation"—he was not able to resolve it.[251] *Redemptoris Missio* struggles to give an account of how and why the Church's missionary effort is necessary for the salvation of those to whom it is directed and ends up falling back on the missionary's obligation.[252] The pope frames this obligation in inspiring terms but cannot escape the rather grim logic of the dilemma. For the Christian, proclaiming the Gospel may allow one to escape punishment for disobedience—which one would also have avoided through the lighter yoke of invincible ignorance—but its benefits for those who receive the message are less clear. For them, the proclamation of the Gospel does not really bring eternal life since that could have been theirs if the missionaries had left them alone. It may mean new benefits

249. John Paul II, Encyclical Letter *Redemptoris Missio* (December 7, 1990), 2. On the necessity of baptism, see 47.

250. Congregation for the Doctrine of the Faith, Declaration *Dominus Iesus* (August 6, 2000), 5, 10, 11, 13. *Dominus Iesus* draws heavily from *Redemptoris Missio*. The theologians whose work on religious pluralism proved problematic were Jesuits Jacque Dupuis (2001) and Roger Haight (2004); a notification on the work of Jon Sobrino (2006), though dealing with questions raised by liberation theology, was fundamentally about the unique role of Jesus Christ. See "Congregazione per la Dottrina della Fede: Lista completa dei documenti," https://www .vatican.va/roman_curia/congregations/cfaith/doc_doc_index_it.htm.

251. John Paul II, *Redemptoris Missio*, 9. For non-Christians, he seems to favor the possibility, postulated by certain medieval thinkers, of an interior illumination, "a grace which, while having a mysterious relationship to the Church, does not make them formally part of the Church but enlightens them in a way which is accommodated to their spiritual and material situation." *Redemptoris Missio*, 10.

252. *Redemptoris Missio*, 4, 11.

that come from being a part of the earthly Church, but these are offset by new obligations. Often many of the benefits the Church offers—a sense of community, for example—can be more easily found elsewhere. The dilemma is extremely grave, and it should not surprise us that, in the absence of a convincing answer to it, once-Christian parts of the world have responded with creeping religious indifference, the suspicion that the Christian religion does not matter all that much anymore.[253]

While many have commented upon the phenomenon of religious indifferentism, the sacramental dimension of the problem tends to be overlooked. Yet, it seems to me that the modern tendency to treat baptism—the rite synonymous with awe-inspiring transformation in the early Church—as a formality lies near the root of the problem. In this chapter I have suggested how I believe we arrived at this point: The anxieties, moralism, and abstraction of the Long Nineteenth Century left little room for a theology rooted in the *lex orandi*. Of course, a sober assessment of the evidence must recognize substantial advances made over the past two centuries of theology as well. The Jansenist-tinged pessimism of the seventeenth and eighteenth centuries, opposed by the apologists Lacordaire and Faber, had suffocated the hope of rebirth expressed in baptism; even the era's emphasis on invincible ignorance served as a corrective to prosecutorial attitudes toward non-Christians. The shock of the nineteenth century—the intellectual attack of the Enlightenment and the brutality of the French Revolution—shook Christianity on many levels. Vatican II was able to address some aspects of this shock, but it did not address them all. On the question of salvation, the Council maintained the Long Nineteenth Century status quo.

But this status quo is not adequate. It has purchased optimism about

---

253. This ambivalence is visible in the landmark study of Christian Smith, *Soul Searching: The Religious and Spiritual Lives of American Teenagers*, with Melina Lundquist Denton (New York: Oxford University Press, 2005). Smith famously concluded that "the de facto dominant religion among contemporary U.S. teenagers is what we might well call 'Moralistic Therapeutic Deism,'" which is defined by a God who is neither too involved nor too demanding and the optimistic assumption that "Good people go to heaven when they die." Smith, 163–65. More recent surveys have shown increasing disaffiliation from religion even in the United States, long the most religiously observant of industrialized nations. Jeffrey M. Jones, "U.S. Church Membership Falls Below Majority for First Time," March 29, 2021, https://news.gallup.com/poll/341963/church-membership-falls-below-majority-first-time.aspx. See also, Stephen Bullivant, *Mass Exodus: Catholic Disaffiliation in Britain and America since Vatican II* (Oxford: Oxford University Press, 2019).

the salvation of the world at the cost of pessimism about Christianity's relevance to that enterprise. Even baptism of desire seems to have fallen out of fashion, dissolved into the supernatural existential and the most generic of moral imperatives. If we are honest, it is hard to distinguish certain twentieth-century formulations of the doctrine from an admission that baptism is not *really* necessary for salvation. Yet the structure of Catholicism dictates that, when the necessity of the Christian sacraments disappears, the necessity of Christ himself will not be far behind.

At the same time, our analysis has shown that the Long Nineteenth Century was not a complete defeat for baptism of desire. In the strange affair of Father Feeney, the doctrine emerged again to provide authoritative grounds to address the most difficult aspects of Christian teaching on salvation. And, while the tensions that made this problem so difficult in the twentieth century continued to exist under the two popes elected in the twenty-first, Benedict XVI and Francis, the former's encyclical dedicated to the theme of Christian salvation, *Spe Salvi* (2007), hints at the need to return to the *lex orandi*. Benedict begins the section "Eternal life—what is it?" by examining the rite of baptism.

> In the search for an answer, I would like to begin with the classical form of the dialogue with which the rite of Baptism expressed the reception of an infant into the community of believers and the infant's rebirth in Christ. First of all the priest asked what name the parents had chosen for the child, and then he continued with the question: "What do you ask of the Church?" Answer: "Faith". "And what does faith give you?" "Eternal life". According to this dialogue, the parents were seeking access to the faith for their child, communion with believers, because they saw in faith the key to "eternal life". Today as in the past, this is what being baptized, becoming Christians, is all about.[254]

The earliest Christians, in their own way, looked for answers in the same place. And so, it seems to me, in light of all this history, baptism of desire is worth a fresh look. In my concluding chapter, therefore, I will attempt not just to summarize the journey we have traveled, but also to indicate where the theory needs polishing if it is to offer light in a new century.

254. Benedict XVI, Encyclical Letter *Spe Salvi* (November 30, 2007), 10.

Conclusion

Water, Blood, and Desire

Is baptism a good thing?

For the early Church, the answer was an obvious *yes*. References to the rite in Paul's writing testify to a powerful experience of conversion and personal identification with the death and resurrection of Jesus.[1] The New Testament treats the rite as intrinsic to the process of salvation.[2] Not even Jesus skips baptism, and early Christians seemed disinclined to accept substitutions for it.[3] What baptism offered could not be found elsewhere and could by no means by taken for granted. The people of the ancient world, quite naturally, dreaded death, and ancient religions offered them little solace. The Hebrew Bible is ambivalent about the continuation of life after death, though, after the Babylonian exile, the idea of a final separation of the righteous from sinners became more widespread. Judgment, however, was not necessarily a comforting prospect for those who realized that they, too, had taken part in the world's unrighteousness. Escape from death's all-consuming jaws required a power greater than our own, a savior. Jesus Christ proclaimed salvation—freedom from sin

1. Cf. Rom 6:3–4; 1 Cor 12:13; Col 2:12; cf. Mk 10:38–39; Lk 12:50.
2. Cf. Mk 16:16; Jn 3:5; Acts 2:38.
3. Cf. Acts 19:3–5.

and access to everlasting life—for those who would follow him. But what he meant by following him went beyond obeying his moral teachings. The discipleship Jesus offered involved losing one's own life and sharing in his death—a kind of total identification so beyond the range of human experience and capacities that it was hard even to put into words.[4] Jesus' resurrection confirmed his power over death, yet it still left the insurmountable problem of how to participate in the saving event that had opened the door to new life, how to die with Jesus, go down into the tomb with him, and be reborn. It was not a matter simply of dying. Of all the uncountable billions of human deaths, only one had been salvific. The announcement of the death and resurrection of Jesus could be experienced as good news by those hearing it only because, from its earliest moments, the apostolic proclamation was accompanied by the belief that this saving event could be accessed, that one could participate in it, making the Lord's death and resurrection one's own through a rite that Jesus had made his own—through baptism. The faith and the sacrament were inseparable; the one without the other was no longer good news.

But even good news did not mean there were no longer hard cases. We saw in our first chapter that the early Church encountered situations in which it seemed that baptism's reach should stretch a little farther; in the earliest Christian communities, new converts most likely remembered relatives and friends who had died before the arrival of the apostles, loved ones whose outlook, hopes, and dispositions were not that far from their own; catechumens sometimes died unexpectedly before their baptism; babies, too, died before birth or so soon afterwards that it was impossible to administer the sacrament. Later, during the persecution of the North African Church and the theological confusion that resulted, Cyprian encountered cases in which (he thought) the rite had been inadvertently omitted. Two features of the early Church's groping for a solution for these hard cases stand out as different from our modern mindset. The first was the absence of any sense of entitlement to salvation. We do not start life saved, and we do not deserve salvation. Eventually, this conviction—implicit in the *regula fidei* and the Church's baptismal practice—led to the articulation of the doctrine of original sin. The basis of this doctrine was not primarily Augustine's interpretation of the book of

4. Mt 10:38–39, 16:24–25; Mk 8:34–35; Lk 9:23–24; Jn 12:25; cf. Mk 10:38–39.

Genesis, which came later, but an assumption so basic that the story of Christianity would collapse without it—each of us needs a savior.

The second feature of the early Church's response to cases in the borderlands of salvation was the inchoate but perceptible conviction that baptism still had to be the solution to the problem. In other words, early Christians looked for a sacramental solution. The Corinthians attempted a sort of baptism on behalf of the dead; the *Shepherd of Hermas* described posthumous baptisms performed by the apostles; mythic approaches in the early Middle Ages pictured saints temporarily resuscitating the deceased to baptize them. These "solutions" do not quite stand up to scrutiny, but they tell us something important about the faith of the early Church. Just as there were no substitutes for Jesus—mankind's one savior and redeemer—so too the Church felt bound to the means of salvation instituted by him. In the High Middle Ages, when Hugh of St. Victor articulated the scholastic principle that God's grace is not limited by the sacraments, he pointed out in the same breath that *our* claims and actions are limited by what God has revealed. Baptism, a divinely instituted mystery, was not the sort of thing for which one was free to invent substitutes. A number of patristic thinkers, probably the majority, took this to mean that, with the sole exception of martyrs, those who died without the waters of baptism were not saved. This doctrine was nuanced only slightly by Gregory Nazianzen's observation that being *unrewarded* does not necessarily imply being *punished*, an instinct that would find later expression in the theology of limbo.

Yet a certain amount of evidence also suggested that, even if the need for baptism did not exactly admit exceptions, something more needed to be said. The salvation of the holy men and women of the Old Testament, of John the Baptist, of Simeon and Anna, and—the example that was to prove decisive in the Middle Ages—of the Good Thief at least required explanation. And no one disputed the martyrs' baptism of blood. This evidence was in the background in 392, when Ambrose of Milan, speaking after the unexpected death of the catechumen Valentinian, concluded that the Lord would surely grant Valentinian's sincere prayer for baptism. At around the same time, Augustine's analysis of the story of the Good Thief led him to theorize the possibility of salvation for someone in a similar situation prevented from receiving the sacrament not by disdain or carelessness but by circumstances beyond his control. Not all were in agreement, and Augustine himself waffled on the example of the Good Thief, but the hypothesis of a baptism of desire to complement baptism of water and of blood was born. The hypothesis was not much discussed over the next several centuries—at least as far as our records show—though the social and liturgical changes that did occur between the death of Augustine and the rise of scholasticism ensured that, when theologians took up baptism of desire as a topic of debate again in the twelfth century, the context in which the sacrament was practiced would be notably different. Europe had adopted Christianity during that time. Infant baptism was practiced almost universally, and the rite had shrunk to fit its tiny recipients. Baptism of desire was vigorously debated, but, with very few actual catechumens around, it was largely an academic question.

The topic gained theological prominence in the twelfth-century cathedral school of Laon. Not only did that school's great master, Anselm, for the first time employ the scholastic *res/sacramentum* distinction to support the theory, he also offered a vision of salvation history held together by desire. Whatever was salvific in the Old Testament or in pagan antiquity, in Anselm's view, was so because of its relation to the Paschal Mystery, because it expressed a yet inarticulate desire for that union with Christ which alone is salvific. The essential elements for a theory of baptism of desire capable of addressing all the hard cases we have examined were put in place by the Laon masters. Unfortunately, the era also saw the development of another framework for explaining how it had been possible to be saved through circumcision in one era and baptism in the next: The law had simply changed. This legal framework was used by defenders of baptism of desire such as Hugh of St. Victor and Bernard of Clairvaux, but it had the disadvantage of making the means of salvation seem essentially arbitrary. The *res/sacramentum* distinction, too, was both a blessing and a curse since it provided scholastic thinkers with a general sacramental theory that could easily accommodate baptism of desire but, if pushed too far, tended to make the connection between participation in the rite and its effect seem artificial.

Another problematic aspect of the medieval treatment of baptism of desire related to the *res/sacramentum* distinction is the interpretation given to the conversion of Cornelius in Acts 10. Because Acts 10:44

speaks of the Holy Spirit falling on all those of Cornelius's household who hear Peter's preaching before being baptized, Augustine had read the passage as supporting the idea that one could receive the effects of baptism before baptism. In the Middle Ages, other theologians repeated this interpretation. This reading, however, led to a distortion in the way baptism of desire was conceived. The earlier interpretation of the story of Cornelius offered by Irenaeus is more cogent. The angel appearing to Cornelius (Acts 10:3–8), the dream of Peter (Acts 10:9–23), and the out-pouring of the Spirit (Acts 10:44–46) all lead to the narrative's crescendo, Peter's declaration that baptism should be extended to the Gentiles (Acts 10:47–48).[1] For the apostolic Church, granting baptism to the Gentiles was both controversial and, arguably, its most momentous decision. The Holy Spirit's actions before the baptism of Cornelius's household are meant to authorize and justify that baptism, not to replace it. The effect of the Holy Spirit's descent is speaking in tongues, a dramatic gift but not really the essence of baptism. All of the events prior to the actual baptism of Cornelius, in other words, are preparatory. There is no hint within the narrative itself that they are meant to replace the sacrament; in fact, were they to do so, it would undermine Peter's declaration and command. If the Gentiles could receive the effects of baptism without the sacrament, then there would be no need to extend the rite to them.

Aside from requiring an implausible interpretation of the text itself, citing Cornelius as an example of baptism of desire presents another, equally serious, problem: It contradicts the *lex orandi*. The non-repeat-ability of baptism is firmly established in the Church's practice. If bap-tism of desire can be received before the sacrament, a note of falsehood enters the celebration. It becomes almost the simulation of a sacrament; what is really happening in the rite no longer lines up with what seems to be happening in the rite. A number of medieval theologians recog-nized this problem and struggled to come up with ways around it. Scotus,

---

1. Johannes Munck calls the outpouring of the Holy Spirit "an irrefutable sign of God's acceptance of the Gentiles," which was "necessary for the baptism of the first Gentiles," in *The Acts of the Apostles: A New Translation with Introduction and Commentary*, The Anchor Bible 31 (New York: Doubleday, 1967), 95–96. Chrysostom and Cyril of Jerusalem had seen proof of the absolute necessity of water baptism in the story. *Atti degli Apostoli*, ed. Francis Martin, Evan Smith, Gianluca Gilara, and Ilaria Maggiulli, La Bibbia Commentata Dai Padri: Nuovo Testamento 5 (Rome: Città Nuova, 2009), 210.

representing an influential line of thought, treated the sacrament from the point of view of obligation; one may have received the grace of baptism already, but, if one did not then obey the commandment to be baptized, one sinned and squandered that grace. One was damned just the same as one would have been without baptism of desire. Other theologians, following Peter Lombard and Thomas Aquinas, posited benefits the sacrament might offer that a pre-baptismal baptism of desire did not. The theology that resulted, however, was among the weakest to emerge in the doctrine's history. The only real reason for these claims—that the sacrament offered greater grace, say, or shortened purgatory—was the need to justify the conviction that one still had to receive the sacrament. Looking at the problem from the perspective of sacramental and liturgical theology more generally, the move to posit a pre-baptismal baptism of desire seems to be symptomatic of an overly spiritualized sense of the *res* as something absolutely separable from the *sacramentum*. This seems to me inadequate, like positing the existence of a human soul without relation to a human body. The answer that Scotus was forced to give, moreover, creates an even more insidious problem because it turns the sacrament from a means of salvation into a legal obligation with penalty attached. If baptism is necessary because we will be punished for not receiving it, then the sacrament begins to seem no longer such a good thing.

The hypothesis of a baptism of desire occurring *before* baptism, therefore, strikes me as one aspect of the theological tradition that should be corrected. And correction is readily available, for also present in the tradition—from Ambrose to Lacordaire—is the identification of baptism of desire with death. To be in keeping with the *lex orandi*, in my opinion, baptism of desire can be conceived of only as something granted in the moment of death. Such a conception results in a more coherent theology in other ways. A more plausible biblical exemplar of baptism of desire than Cornelius is the Good Thief, who quite literally participates in the death of Jesus. In fact, the relationship between baptism and death is not accidental (Rom 6:3). The predominant contemporary practice of baptism by affusion instead of immersion makes the descent into the tomb implied by the sacrament less obvious but no less essential. Here, we can offer a word of credit to one of baptism of desire's most intractable opponents, Gennadius of Massilia, whose theology drew out the parallels between the act of martyrdom—baptism of blood—and the rite of baptism. These are important on more than a metaphorical level, and identifying baptism of desire with the moment of death brings it closer to both of the other two modes of baptism. In baptism of desire, one's desire for union with the Paschal Mystery transforms physical death into a moment of rebirth. This approach also helps us to avoid over-spiritualizing baptism of desire because, by involving the physical act of death, it maintains the importance of the corporeal. It allows us to discard the *ad hoc* reasoning involved in justifying the continued necessity of the sacrament after one has already received its effect.

Despite these corrections to the medieval theology of baptism of desire, we should not discount the medieval achievement when it came to the eventual acceptance of the doctrine. It is also worth highlighting those conditions medieval theologians saw as essential to baptism of desire, conditions needed so that the doctrine does not simply dissolve into the negation of the necessity of baptism. Those conditions were typically expressed by the Augustinian phrases *contemptus religionis* and *articulus necessitatis*, and they underscored the fact that the reason one did not arrive at the font was relevant to salvation. The circumstances preventing one's baptism had to come from outside of oneself; one could not refuse the sacrament or treat it as something unimportant and claim baptism of desire. One's desire had to be real; not even being a catechumen was a guarantee of salvation because sometimes catechumens procrastinated for less than virtuous reasons. One actually had to desire the sacrament. This is not to say that medieval thinkers did not consider cases in which one did not have enough knowledge to be able to articulate an explicit request for water baptism. They most certainly did, and the greatest of the medievals, Thomas Aquinas, offered an account of implicit desire which to this day remains the best starting point for considering the problem of baptism of desire and non-Christians.

The consensus in favor of baptism of desire reached by the end of the Middle Ages, by and large, seems to have convinced posterity. The doctrine's most important validation came in the decrees of the Council of Trent. Theologians, beginning with John Major, responded to the European geographical discoveries of the fifteenth and sixteenth centuries by speculating that baptism of desire might provide a path to salvation for some of those living in unevangelized territories, though no real consensus emerged on the question. In the baroque era, focus shifted to the question of the minimum of faith necessary for salvation instead of baptism specifically. The era also saw a drift toward treating the question with the categories of moral theology, a trend which would accelerate in the nineteenth century. The nineteenth century, in fact, witnessed a remarkable change in Catholic attitudes toward salvation, with theologians more willing than in past centuries to posit a larger number of the saved. Their arguments mostly focused on the number of Christians saved, so baptism of desire played only a minor role in this shift. Influenced by tendencies in both scholasticism and Enlightenment religion, discussion of salvation moved almost exclusively into the fields of ecclesiology and of morals. The salvation of non-Christians became a major topic of concern in the twentieth century, and the term baptism of desire was sometimes used so broadly as to amount simply to a denial of the doctrine—the necessity of baptism—that had given rise to the idea in the first place. This produced divergent reactions. On the one hand, the first serious opposition to the concept since the Middle Ages arose from the Feeneyites of Boston and earned a swift rebuke from the Holy Office. On the other, Karl Rahner's theory of the Anonymous Christian proposed a more universally available path to salvation than that found in the sacraments, rendering baptism of desire obsolete.

So, is baptism still a good thing? Theories such as Rahner's make it seem, fundamentally, more of an indifferent thing, and we can now understand how we arrived at this point. Seen primarily from the vantage point of legal obligation, the necessity of baptism for salvation appears to be an arbitrary imposition, easily waved aside for the invincibly ignorant. Within such a framework, the Lord's command to baptize seems to make salvation less rather than more accessible by tying it to a specific, even if quite simple, religious ritual. Such a conclusion adds a certain ambivalence to the Christian proclamation itself; so, before proceeding to attempt a response to those hard questions that remain—the possibility of implicit desire, the significance of baptism of desire for non-Christians, infants dying before baptism—we need to identify a stronger basis than arbitrary divine command for the conviction that baptism is necessary for salvation.

We can begin with the observation that whatever difficulties exist with respect to our salvation, they come from us, not from God. This has always been the case; the breathless proclamations of certain twentieth-century theologians to have rediscovered the universal salvific will of God should be taken with a tablespoon of salt. God's salvific will has never been the problem. The sacraments are intended to help us to overcome problems on the human side of the God-man relationship that stand in the way of our salvation. Among the most significant of these problems, which would have been as obvious to the first recipients of the Gospel message as it is opaque to us who have inherited twenty centuries of Christian history, is that, on our own, we do not even know what salvation is. Our brief survey of ancient conceptions of the afterlife at the beginning of this work reminded us that the Christian idea of salvation has never been universal and cannot be taken for granted. For how to articulate the nature of salvation we can start with the *lex orandi*, which proclaims salvation as communion with God. Here, again, the impediments that prevent us from achieving that union do not result from any lack of will or goodness on God's part. But the very goodness and infinity of God's love is also the greatest obstacle to such union because, insofar as our own love is indecisive, misdirected, or partial, we remain in a state of disunion with the divine. We are, in fact, so far from the divine that entering into communion with God requires a total loss—the death symbolized by baptism, from which we rise newly capable of communion. Again, not just any death makes such transformation possible, but Christ's alone, so the very specificity of the sacrament is part of its meaning.

Here a few dimensions emerge from the celebration of baptism that will allow us to see the sacrament as a help—an essential help—to salvation, rather than a hurdle. The prospect of aligning ourselves—primarily our wills, of course, but also our intellects and even our bodies—with God is, to say the least, daunting. When salvation is understood as communion with God, however, doing so is not the sort of thing that can be separated from redemption. Popular depictions of heaven often treat it as something detached from the person, like a piece of particularly prime real estate. If we think of heaven as being like an extremely pleasant place—Tahiti without sunburn or mosquitos—then there is no reason God could not put anyone there. A hitman and a saint can equally enjoy Tahiti. But if heaven is essentially union with God, then salvation is something dependent no longer entirely on God's generosity but also on who we are. It is something that requires our own participation to be what it is. Here we can see why the Pauline understanding of baptism as participation in the Paschal Mystery is so crucial. We can also see how the *res/sacramentum* distinction, if leaned on too hard, distorts what happens in the sacramental encounter; it lends itself to thinking about what is received in the sacrament as fundamentally detached from the rite itself, as if the latter were simply the packaging for a gift. A new iPhone works just the same whether it comes in gold wrapping paper, a paper bag, or no packaging at all. Such a gift will also work regardless of the character of its recipient—whether given to a drug dealer or a social worker, an iPhone is still an iPhone. Salvation, however, is not this kind of gift, and the specificity of the rite cannot be considered packaging. Instead, the particular materiality of the sacraments is a participation in the particularity of the Incarnation. This connection between the sacraments and the Incarnation was readily perceived by patristic thinkers such as Ambrose and Leo the Great. Its erosion helps to explain the trajectory of twentieth-century theology; the disregard for the unique role of the sacraments in salvation shown by the branch of Neo-Scholasticism represented by Navatel was, by the century's end, followed by theologies calling into question the uniqueness of Jesus himself.[2]

If we recognize that, by its nature, salvation requires our participation and remember Paul's baptismal theology, which explains the sacrament as participation in the Paschal Mystery, then it becomes possible to see baptism anew as more than a legal requirement testing our obedience, but rather a necessary help to salvation. The Liturgical Movement and the Second Vatican Council also embrace a theology of liturgical participation. This perspective allows us to say a bit more about how baptism helps us to achieve salvation. We can get a sense of the help the sacraments provide by recalling the difficulties both baroque scholastics and modern theologians ran into when treating salvation from a non-sacramental perspective. One such problem was the difficulty identifying a minimum of explicit beliefs necessary for salvation. Agreement on such a minimal

2. See, for example, John Hick and Paul F. Knitter, *The Myth of Christian Uniqueness: Toward a Pluralistic Theology of Religions* (Maryknoll, NY: Orbis Books, 1987).

creed could never be achieved, and the approach had the highly unsatisfactory side effect of making most of Christian revelation seem superfluous, or—within the nominalist legal framework—merely an obligation.
Rahner's stress on atheism highlighted another problem: No minimum
of belief can ever be low enough to achieve universality. In fact, searching
for a minimum is simply the wrong approach to the problem. Salvation
is not an offer of partial truth; at the same time, in this lifetime, even the
wisest of Christian believers never have a complete grasp of the fullness
of truth. Christian sacramental initiation responds to this dilemma with
the open-endedness of a rite, the symbols of which cannot be reduced to
a list of propositions. There is a propositional element to baptism—the
profession of the Creed—but the logic of the rite itself implies that the
Creed is just the beginning; the patristic approach to theology through
mystagogy expresses the same dynamic. The world itself cannot contain
all the books needed to express the faith, but a Christian is never called to
a minimum of faith. Thus, the word of entry into Christianity is an action.
At the same time, liturgical rites do possess definite content. They are not
empty containers, and they are not compatible with every belief. When
we turn to the subject of implicit faith shortly, this point should be kept
in mind so as not to equate implicit with generic faith.

Another way in which the sacrament of baptism is a help for salvation
has to do with our exercise of freedom. The choice that Christ demands
of us—to love God with all our heart, mind, and soul; to take up the
cross; to lose one's life to save it—is hard even to conceptualize, let alone
to embrace. Sometimes the lofty expressions used to talk about such a
decision—words like "radically," "absolutely," "the depth of one's being"—
remove it from the plane of reality, turning discipleship into pious rhetoric. The loftier the intention, the more removed it can become from the
reality of concrete decisions that define any human life. The concreteness
of the sacrament places the choice to enter into Christianity in the realm
of genuinely human decisions. In other words, the choice to be baptized
allows us to make a decision to identify ourselves with the death and
resurrection of Jesus (or to refuse to do so) in a way that is truly human.
Here it is not coincidental that theologians have so consistently insisted
on the freedom necessary for baptism. Again, the symbolic open-endedness of the rite is important, for it means that, though such a decision

is concretely accessible, its scope is unlimited. The yes to Christ is total. Body and soul, nature and grace, natural and supernatural, conscious and unconscious—it is the nature of a sacrament to bring all of these elements together. No part of our existence is left out of baptism. The completeness of the baptismal commitment is best seen in total immersion, even if today this is less frequently practiced. Nonetheless, recognizing the "total immersion" of the human person demanded by the rite is essential to any theology of the sacrament. The rite of baptism makes giving away one's life—dying with Christ—accessible to human freedom.

These observations, if far from exhaustive, can at least begin to suggest a way to think about baptism as a means, a help, to salvation and, therefore, a good thing. This, in turn, puts into correct context the Church's constant affirmation—from the New Testament to the present *Catechism*—that baptism is necessary for salvation. As we saw when analyzing 1 Timothy 2:4, God "desires all men to be saved and to come to the knowledge of the truth" because these two things—salvation and knowledge of the truth—are not separate realities but one; so too salvation cannot be separated from baptism because the rite is participation in salvation. Certain currents of scholastic theology and its successors have undoubtedly drifted away from this sacramental understanding of salvation and ended up treating baptism as a formality. This drift—accelerated by socio-cultural factors set in motion by the Enlightenment and French Revolution—explains how baptism of desire could get lost in the theology of the late twentieth century even as that theology acknowledged its dependence on the doctrine. The "optimism" of twentieth-century theology, however, leaves too much out, like the mirage of a desert spring that looks like water but is only sand and air. The instinct of the early Church to emphasize the ritual was not wrong, for the ritual says and does what nothing else can. In speaking of *baptism* of water, blood, and desire, the theological tradition was not merely exercising poetic license but affirming the sacrament as a divine and necessary help for salvation. But what do these conclusions mean for the most pressing questions we face today, such as the eternal destiny of non-Christians or unbaptized infants? At a minimum, I think they mean that the sacrament itself, the *lex orandi*, provides us with the starting point from which to search for answers.

What desire is necessary for baptism of desire?

The answer to this question is elusive because of its simplicity: The desire necessary to receive baptism of desire is the desire necessary to receive the sacrament of baptism. Such an answer may seem unsatisfactory to those wanting a formula grounded in a specific metaphysics or anthropology. Here we should refer to what was said above; by linking salvation to the sacraments, God has made salvation accessible through a concrete human decision, not a theory about decision-making. The fact that our decisions do not always fit neatly within our theories, however, means that, when speaking of baptism of desire, we will have to accept a degree of uncertainty in all of our conclusions. This is not to say that we will have to rely on such amorphous concepts as optimism or pessimism—casts of mind that bear no particular relationship to what is true and what is false. As Terry Eagleton puts it with characteristic wit, "There may be many good reasons for believing that a situation will turn out well, but to expect that it will do so because you are an optimist is not one of them."[3] Instead, we will be able to speak of *grounds for belief.* Having a basis for our beliefs helps us to avoid succumbing to wishful thinking. Just because we find a conclusion agreeable, after all, does not mean that it is true. Plenty of phenomena in the world God created are less than agreeable; yet they still exist. Too much twentieth-century theology reasons deductively from the principle of God's goodness down to whatever conclusions one finds good, a procedure akin to arguing that a truly benevolent creator could not possibly have made a world with bedbugs. Since bedbugs seem incompatible with God's mercy, they cannot really exist. Yet their bites still itch.

Epistemological caution was among the more salubrious contributions to the medieval debate to emerge from baptism of desire's critics, such as Master Simon. When it comes to matters of salvation, we cannot make claims that go beyond what has been revealed to us; the self-correction seen in the documents of Vatican II, the shift in the language used to talk about the salvation of non-Christians from *Lumen Gentium* to *Gaudium et Spes* and *Ad Gentes*, shows the recognition of the need for such caution. We cannot know with certainty the eternal fate of most people and are

---

3. Terry Eagleton, *Hope Without Optimism* (New Haven, CT: Yale University Press, 2017), 1.

likely to be surprised by at least a few of the companions we find wherever we end up in the afterlife. This does not mean that we can or should say nothing about salvation. If we were to let our lack of absolute certainty about what happens in eternity prevent us from saying anything about the topic, then we would effectively eliminate one of Christianity's most central teachings as a force capable of shaping our actions. Jesus clearly intended for his disciples to consider the effect of their actions and non-actions on the judgment they would face after death. What we are searching for is not absolute certainty, but "actionable probability"—that is, a degree of certainty necessary to guide our actions. Quite happily, theologians will not be delivering judgment on the last day, but before that time Christians need to make decisions about everything from whether catechumens should be buried in holy ground to how much energy to expend on explicit evangelization. Just as God has made our participation in salvation possible through the sacraments, so too the sacraments—understood within the totality of revelation—enable us to reason about salvation.

Let us return then to the decision to be baptized. People do not make decisions in the same way. Some are more rational, others more emotional; some more inclined to stability, others to novelty. We are, to varying degrees, susceptible to the opinions of others. Not all our religious decisions fall neatly into moral categories; they are also influenced by our aesthetic perceptions, our interpersonal relationships, our social standing. Our decisions are based on a whole range of factors, each of which we weigh in a manner uniquely our own. The decision to receive the sacrament of baptism does not require absolute certainty, perfect motives, or perfect charity. It does require, however, that the desire one has to be baptized overcome both inertia and the pull of other internal forces urging one to remain unbaptized. The distinction used by Feeney's critic, Monsignor Joseph Clifford Fenton, between an intention, which shapes one's plans, and a velleity, which is merely a wish, is helpful here, because the sacrament of baptism requires a desire strong enough to lead to a concrete and specific action.[4] Nor should we forget that this action—baptism—implies much more than the one-time participation in a liturgical rite; that rite itself requires commitment to a particular way of life. It does not require that one has achieved Christian perfection already but, rather,

4. Fenton, *The Catholic Church and Salvation*, 39.

that one's desire is resolute enough to enter into such an undertaking. As the Fathers realized, not every catechumen is willing to make such a commitment, so being a catechumen is no guarantee of receiving baptism of desire, particularly if one is still beholden to something—a relationship, a lifestyle, the opinion of others, a particular sin, another religion—that is holding one back from baptism. The desire necessary for baptism of desire cannot be less than what is required to receive the sacrament. What prevents one's reception of the sacrament must be circumstances beyond one's control, not factors in one's own decision-making process. To illustrate the point with a concrete case, we could imagine a man who has expressed interest in Christianity but is practicing polygamy and is, therefore, prevented from receiving the sacrament. His desire for the sacrament is not strong enough to lead to the concrete actions necessary to receive it, to commit to marriage with only one wife and to make acceptable arrangements for the well-being of his other wives. If such a man were to die unexpectedly, we would not have grounds to believe that he would receive baptism of desire. The case would be different if he were in the process of arranging for his secondary wives to live in different circumstances, a process which might naturally take some time. If he were taking such actions, then we have strong grounds for believing he would receive baptism of desire. What was within his power to do in order to receive the sacrament, he was doing.

But just as the desire necessary for baptism of desire cannot be less than what is required to receive the sacrament without amounting to a denial of the sacrament's necessity, so too I do not see reason to believe that it needs to be more. The driving factor behind the accumulation of additional requirements for baptism of desire—perfect charity, for example—was the same as that behind the attempt to identify benefits of water baptism that made it obligatory even if one had already received a pre-baptismal baptism of desire. If water baptism were not in some way better or more accessible than baptism of desire, it seemed to be either merely ornamental or necessary only to fulfill a command and avoid punishment. Such problems disappear, however, when we abandon the hypothesis of a baptism of desire occurring before baptism rather than only at death. One does not need to make baptism of desire any harder to receive than the sacrament because it can no longer be in competition with the sacrament. The intention to receive baptism is all that baptism of desire requires. This understanding of the doctrine allowed its earliest proponents, such as Ambrose, to continue strongly to affirm the necessity of baptism for salvation without contradiction. Baptism of desire was a corollary of the earlier belief. The Tridentine decrees that provide support for the doctrine are also written in this way; the sacraments or the desire *for them* (*aut eorum voto*) is necessary for salvation.[5] Baptism of desire can never be understood to create an alternative to baptism.

Implicit desire and non-Christians

If catechumens dying unexpectedly before the scheduled date of their baptism were the only hard cases we had to deal with, this study might have been considerably shorter. It may not be possible to define all of the elements that go into a salvific desire for baptism when the rite is impossible, but the *lex orandi* provides us with the general guidance that the desire necessary to receive the sacrament is sufficient. This answer means that a degree of uncertainty will always exist over whether some-one has received baptism of desire; the only certain proof of such a desire is whether one goes through with the rite or not. Still, we can have very solid grounds for believing that someone like Valentinian is saved. The factors Ambrose mentions in his eulogy—actions Valentinian took testi-fying to his loyalty to Christianity and the sincerity of his conversion—provide us with a high degree of confidence in his salvation. The Church's practice of providing burial rites for catechumens indicates that our con-fidence in such cases, even if not mathematical certainty, is enough to guide our actions. We have "actionable probability," in some cases verging on practical certainty. The situation changes when we move away from explicit Christian profession for the simple reason that we have fewer grounds for believing that someone had a genuine desire for baptism.

When someone knew of baptism and chose not to receive it, our grounds for believing that they could receive baptism of desire are nec-essarily weak. We would not be justified in making any practical decision based on such a probability, even if we labeled it a "hope." The suggestion that someone who explicitly *refused* the sacrament could receive baptism

---

5. *Enchiridion symbolorum*, 1604.

of desire is not cogent. A baptism carried out against the will of the person receiving it is neither salvific nor even valid, and we have no grounds for imagining that forced baptisms of desire exist. The concept itself is oxymoronic. We can have good or bad reasons for the decisions we make, including the decision to refuse the sacrament, but they are still our decisions. When we are dealing with people who had no knowledge of the sacrament at all, however, evaluating the possibility of baptism of desire becomes more speculative. In such cases, we are forced to rely on the concept of implicit desire. The concept is not easy to grasp and has been much misused, but we have no other choice.[6] Still, a perhaps surprising number of theologians across the centuries have accepted the possibility of some form of implicit desire. The plausibility of such hypotheses has varied greatly, but, as I have indicated before, I think that Aquinas's development of the concept is robust enough to withstand scrutiny.

Aquinas, we should recall, pointed out that there is no such thing as an *entirely* implicit desire, but that what is implicit must be objectively present in something (or combination of things) that one desires explicitly. Moreover, if one accepts that what is salvific in the Old Testament is so because it expresses a desire for baptism, then we already have a number of examples of implicit desire from revelation. But the concept is so slippery that we must be scrupulous to avoid misunderstandings. To say that baptism is necessary for salvation means that what is necessary is not some partial approximation of the rite or a single dimension of its symbolism, but baptism. Implicit desire cannot, therefore, mean desiring something *less* than baptism. To do so would mean to desire something less than full participation in what is meant by salvation. Immersion in the Paschal Mystery—sharing in the death and resurrection of Jesus—is not the sort of thing that can be done partially. If one's desire is for something less than salvation, then one is not really participating in God's salvific will; and if God grants one's desire, then one is not saved.[7] Thus, the object of

6. Avery Dulles, for example, criticizes the term "implicit faith" as "vague and ambiguous" in "Who Can Be Saved?" in *Church and Society*, 530. Implicit desire is a slightly different—and better—concept because desire implies movement toward something not yet fully attained, a connotation less apparent when speaking of implicit faith.

7. This observation could provide alternative grounds for a thesis such as Billot's that some adults might experience a kind of limbo, a state of existence which falls short of the highest happiness but still reflects their good desires.

implicit desire must be the same as that of explicit desire, which is one reason I believe the language of baptism of desire should be preserved even if one is speaking about salvation in a non-Christian context. To speak of anything else is to fall into the trap of inventing an alternative to baptism. The same reason suggests the flaw in the baroque scholastic search for a minimum of faith necessary for salvation; such a minimum can never be sufficient. Whatever beliefs one starts with, one's desire must always be directed toward the fullness of faith and salvation. As Paul VI put it, the Christian message is necessary, unique, and irreplaceable. Speaking of the concrete sacrament—itself part of that message—helps us to remain honest and to resist the temptation to flee into generalities. The irreplaceability of the sacrament also reveals another aspect of implicit desire that must always, to some degree, be present. Implicit desire must contain at least some element of thirst, of restlessness, of dissatisfaction, a desire for more than what one has. It must contain something of the desire for the conversion that baptism entails. Ambrose's eulogy of Valentinian emphasizes this quality—the emperor's poverty—which made him implore the Lord for what he did not have. Simeon could not go in peace until his eyes had seen the Lord.

Just as implicit does not mean *partial* with regard to the object of desire, so too it cannot mean a *weaker* desire. Thus, speaking of what is required of non-Christians as "openness" to grace seems to me misleading and inadequate. Openness to baptism is not enough to receive the sacrament in a Christian context, because mere passivity means something less than participation. Passive openness, therefore, falls short of salvation. What was said above about the need for a desire strong enough to lead to a concrete action holds in all cases; even an implicit desire must be strong enough that—with wholly external obstacles removed—it would lead to the action of baptism. The "test" of desire present in the *lex orandi* is whether one's desire for baptism is strong enough to overcome other inclinations holding one back from the sacrament. The same holds true for an implicit desire. Like explicit converts, those who do not know about Christianity have attachments and desires, both explicit and implicit, that work against their desire for baptism. Unless their implicit desire for baptism is stronger than all those other contrary drives, it is not enough to lead to baptism of desire. Here we must also be careful to avoid what I think of as "hypothetical desire," an idea that might be expressed by the thought, "If circumstances were different, I would desire something else." Whatever the circumstances are, I am what I am. The hypothetical "me" who desires something else might indeed be saved, but this does not do the actually existing me any good. Implicit desire would have to be expressed by the thought, "If circumstances were different, I would be able to realize the desire that I now have but am unable to articulate adequately." An implicit desire must actually exist.

Setting aside these pretenders—partial, weak, or hypothetical desire—we can now review what emerged in chapter three about what implicit desire actually is. We can begin with Thomas's observation that an implicit desire requires some explicit desire in which to inhere. Implicit desire means doing (or desiring to do) one thing (A), which necessarily implies another (B). Because the concept relies on the objective relationship of A to B, it is not necessary for one to request B explicitly in order to desire it. One may not even have any particularly definite awareness of what B is. Aquinas provides an example from the *lex orandi*. Baptism is oriented toward the fullness of Christian life; receiving baptism, therefore, implies a desire for confirmation and communion, regardless of whether one articulates it or even knows that these two other sacraments exist. When Lacordaire and Perrone argued that baptized Protestant children would be saved, they were using this line of reasoning, relying on the objective relationship between baptism and the Catholic Church. Their reasoning seems to me to be a sound extension of Aquinas's doctrine.

Nonetheless, sometimes, even if we do A, it is possible for us to act incoherently by rejecting B. People act this way all the time, for example, by not living out the promises they make in baptism. By rejecting B, they distort A, dissolving its objective meaning. Making such a mistake is more common if one does not have a clear sense of what B is or of the relationship between A and B. As a practical matter, when a desire becomes explicit it almost always becomes more reliable. If a desire does not grow in strength once its object is in view, this is a strong indication of the absence of implicit desire for that object. We should here repeat that implicit desire is not to be confused with generic desire; the more generic a desire is, the less likely it is to lead to a specific—or any—action. If one desires "to practice a religion," this does not amount to an implicit desire for baptism, because such a desire could be equally fulfilled in Sufism, Unitarianism, or Mormonism. In fact, such a general desire seems likely to impede the sort of committed decision that baptism and Christian discipleship require; experience teaches that this kind of generic desire quite often leads to practicing no religion at all. Several generic desires in combination, however, might point to a more specific object. Here we quickly run up against the limits of what can be deduced and calculated with human abilities; no supercomputer could satisfactorily calculate whether the implicit desires of someone who has never heard the Gospel add up to the desire for baptism. God alone is capable of such a reckoning.

At this point, one might naturally feel the frustration inherent in the concept of implicit desire. We cannot say that it involves believing X and doing Y because, if we were to do so, we would have invented an alternative to baptism. Because implicit desire must necessarily remain inarticulate, we might be tempted either to reject the concept altogether or to settle for just such an alternative. To shore up the plausibility of the concept, I will offer two examples to show how implicit desire works, the first rather mundane. Let us say that, doing a bit of tourism in South Dakota's Black Hills, I decide I want to go to the charming little town of Hill City. The main road to get to Hill City from the nearest airport is US-16, but, never having been to the area before, I do not know this. There are, of course, other ways of getting to Hill City (overland hiking, parachuting), but a variety of unarticulated desires—to arrive safely and in a reasonable amount of time—necessarily preclude these. So even before I turn on the ignition in my rental vehicle and plug Hill City into the GPS, I implicitly desire to take US-16. And note that in this scenario, even before I know the name of the highway, I am already taking what actions I can to drive on it. If I die of a heart attack before the GPS can do its work, then I will die with an implicit desire to take US-16. Of course, US-16 is hardly the road to heaven, and the sort of implicit desires leading to baptism are infinitely more complex, so much so that we can never finally define them. Another, somewhat more elevated example, however, comes close to what such a phenomenon might look like. A parishioner once scheduled an appointment with me, wishing to talk about a number of spiritual issues in her life. We had a conversation, and I cast about offering observations and various bits of advice, and, at a certain point, her eyes lit up, and she interrupted, "That's it! That's what I came here to hear." I don't remember what the advice was, but her reaction seems to me to provide an example of someone with a desire that is only partially known and articulated but nonetheless is capable of generating real action. It was enough to cause her to make the appointment with me in the first place. The identity of that desire, however, became recognizable only after the fact.

The same can also be said of the concrete examples of implicit desire we find in revelation, beginning with the history of the people of Israel. In these cases, we see the "preparation for the Gospel" at work. On the surface, what God required of his people for salvation might seem to have changed rather randomly. The robust sense of implicit desire I am suggesting saves us from having to understand these changes as arbitrary or from having to reduce them to an inevitably airy abstraction. Instead, God's revelation to Israel, everything in the Law and the Prophets, should be understood as salvific insofar as it leads to participation in a single ultimately important event—the Paschal Mystery of Jesus Christ. In itself, circumcision does not save; insofar as it implies desire for baptism, it does. The value of all pre-Christian revelation is entirely relative to Jesus Christ; this makes its relationship to salvation less certain than the revelation of Christ himself. Consider belief in the Messiah. The scriptures suggest that many faithful Jews before the time of Jesus desired the coming of a savior, a desire fulfilled in the Incarnation. Since the rite of baptism did not exist at the time, a desire for it could only have been implicit in the desire to embrace the Messiah, who, when he became known, instituted baptism. The patristic typological reading of the Old Testament, which saw baptism everywhere from Noah's Ark to the crossing of the Red Sea, while rather distant from modern exegetical sensibilities, has an immense theological value because it represents the early Church's assertion of the sacrament's implicit presence before New Testament revelation. All of this indicates that even an implicit desire which, on the surface, seems rather remote from its object can be salvific. "Proof" of the adequacy of such implicit desire comes in the example of Simeon, capable of recognizing the Savior without further explanation at his appearance (Lk 2:25–35). Of course, Simeon had received extraordinary grace from the Holy Spirit, and the New Testament also shows that hoping for a Messiah did not in itself always lead to faith in Jesus.

The Pharisees also believed in the Messiah, but their hope for a particular kind of Messiah—perhaps one more politically adept than Jesus—became an impediment to their redemption, which caused them to reject the Savior. Thus even "belief in the Messiah" is not quite equal to desire for baptism and requires other sensibilities and desires, which are impossible ever fully to define, to be salvific. The presence of implicit desire is always uncertain.

With respect to salvation, the value of whatever is found in belief systems and practices outside of Christianity is entirely relative to faith in Christ and cannot avoid this uncertainty. The same element, belief in the Messiah, could be for one person a genuine preparation for accepting Jesus Christ, while, for another, an impediment to salvation. The concept of divinity one receives outside of Christianity might nurture or hinder an implicit desire for baptism. Believing in a God to whom one can direct prayer would generally seem to be a help to seeking more from him, and we saw the value Ambrose put on Valentinian's prayer for baptism. On the other hand, dissatisfaction with the religion of one's birth sometimes contributes to conversions to Christianity, so those implicitly desiring baptism might be found among either the pious or the rebellious. Both stances also include potential obstacles to implicit desire. The way the divinity is depicted in non-Christian religions might prevent one from hoping for the sort of relationship with God that Christianity offers. Attachment to other religions is often a significant reason people do not receive baptism when it is available, so the sophistication of another religious tradition and whatever admirable qualities it possesses, even parallels and resonances with Christianity, provide no firm ground to believe particular non-Christians will be saved. We are not dealing with linear mathematics; contentment with ninety-five percent of the truth is infinitely distant from desiring one hundred percent of it. We would do well to remember Romano Guardini's sage observation, repeated by Daniélou, that Buddha is both the precursor of Christ and his final enemy.[8]

Similar considerations mean that a purely ethical approach to the salvation of non-Christians is inadequate. Baum's account of a prototypical candidate for baptism of desire in *Sacramentum Mundi* reads like the description of an ethical superman, but the classic scriptural example of

---

8. Daniélou, "Christianity and the Non-Christian Religions," 22–23.

baptism of desire, the Good Thief, would have made a poor Anonymous Christian.[9] He does not seem to have been particularly obedient to his conscience, and, by his own admission, his conduct was reprehensible enough to merit death. A well-lived life may reveal a desire to please God, or it may simply indicate a good-natured desire to get along with others or to contribute to some secular goal, none of which equals a desire for participation in the Paschal Mystery. Those content with socially acceptable lives without seeking much beyond do not possess a drive toward baptism. At the same time, attachments to sinful behaviors often prevent people from receiving the sacrament even when they feel some attraction to it, and a life lived according to the natural law can at least remove these obstacles.

What I am arguing means that we have grounds for believing that implicit desire for baptism is possible even in situations where Christianity is not known, but it also seems unlikely to be common. The surest evidence we can have of the existence of implicit desire for Christianity is a positive reception of the faith when it is presented—Simeon's reaction, if not necessarily so dramatic. The response of previously unevangelized people to missionaries has sometimes been quite positive almost from the beginning; Francis Xavier, for example, found some Japanese people inclined to conversion after relatively brief instruction. Reflecting on such evidence might have helped the great missionary saint give a more positive response than he was able to muster to the Japanese catechumens distressed by the thought that their ancestors were in hell. As we will discuss a bit more when examining the implications of baptism of desire for infants, our desires do not spring out of nowhere but are influenced by our family, friends, culture, and a host of other factors. Particularly in a tradition-bound society, individuals' desires will, in large part, reflect the desires of their ancestors. Xavier might have answered his catechumens that their own enthusiasm for baptism itself provides grounds for believing that an implicit desire for the sacrament may have been present among their ancestors. Passed on in subtle ways, this desire may have been a genuine preparation for the Gospel. Such an answer is far from promising certainty, which we do not have, but it is more substantive than declaring vaguely that Christianity is an optimistic religion. It also

9. Baum, "Baptism of Desire," 146.

acknowledges that the catechumens themselves are in a much better position with regard to salvation than were their ancestors; the arrival of the
Gospel is good news for their salvation.

The same realism that makes this answer credible also demands honestly acknowledging that "more often" (*saepius*) unevangelized people
have not responded so favorably to the Gospel and, when they have, it
has only been after a lengthy process of conversion. Implicit desire for
baptism does not seem particularly widespread. The role of missionaries
in channeling, correcting, and soliciting the desire for participation in the
fullness of truth is almost always necessary before the jumble of positive
and negative instincts that guide every human life amount to an actionable desire for immersion in the Paschal Mystery. Revelation, after all, is
meant to help us to salvation. Even if our more ample reflection on baptism of desire allows us to modify one of Francis Xavier's more unsettling
teachings, it does not mean that the Apostle to the Indies was mistaken
in the urgency he felt for evangelization. The motive for such urgency
remains salvation. If an implicit desire for baptism already exists, missionaries will find themselves welcome and can rejoice in helping to bring to
fulfillment the deepest longings of future saints. At the same time, unarticulated and vaguely understood desires are difficult to maintain; hu-
manly, it is simply hard to want something which one has never seen. It
is even harder to want something consistently and with enough resolve to
overcome all of the contrary claims the world makes on our loyalties. The
arrival of the Gospel, therefore, always improves one's ability to realize
whatever desires for the Christian life might prepare someone to ask for
faith in baptism.[10] For many, the difference indubitably means salvation.

Can babies receive baptism of desire?

When the Holy Office responded to the appeal of Leonard Feeney and
his followers in the 1940s, its answer relied on baptism of desire because
of the authoritative support the doctrine enjoyed within the tradition.
The letter's assertion that implicit desire for the sacrament could result

10. We should acknowledge but, for the purposes of developing a general theory, can set
aside exceptional cases involving missionary malpractice, such as the behavior of the conquistadors condemned by Las Casas. Such cases do not diminish the necessity of the Christian
mission any more than cases of medical malpractice diminish the need for health care.

in the salvation even of those not yet fully incorporated into the Church also finds support in the tradition, though such support is less firm. When it comes to the question of whether baptism of desire can save unbaptized infants, however, the clear majority of theologians throughout the ages have responded in the negative. The reason is simply that, due to their limited cognitive development, it is hard to see how babies could have any meaningful desire, implicit or explicit, for baptism. However, the tradition is not quite unanimous on this point, and I have argued throughout this study that the approach taken by scholastic theology to the question of salvation has not always adequately taken the *lex orandi* into account. On this question, in fact, I believe the *lex orandi* provides evidence strong enough to overturn the majority opinion.

As I have argued above, an adequate theology of baptism of desire must take the sacrament of baptism as its starting point. The basic structure and practice of the rite is a fundamental element of Christian revelation to which our theology must conform. I have argued on this basis that the essential answer to the question of what kind of desire is necessary for salvation is the desire necessary for baptism. The celebration of the sacrament should guide how we conceptualize implicit desire; doing so serves as a guarantee that our theology does not presume to invent an alternative to the sacrament or to deny its necessity. Moreover, the Church's practice has consistently affirmed the absolute urgency of baptism for infants, an urgency so great that, in danger of death, the *Code of Canon Law* even permits the baptism of infants against the will of their parents.[11] Still, the same practice also provides a decisive piece of evidence for the minority position that infants can benefit from baptism of desire. The evidence is hiding in plain sight: We baptize infants.

If the desire necessary for baptism of desire is what is necessary to receive the sacrament, and we baptize infants, then the *lex orandi* suggests that infants can in some way possess this desire. Certainly, it seems to me that—despite the weight of the tradition—the burden of proof should shift to those giving a negative answer to the above question. This does not mean that this observation alone resolves the difficulties raised by

11. Canon 868 §2. For a summary of the discussion that went into the formulation of this controversial canon, see Kevin T. Hart, "Baptism," in *New Commentary on the Code of Canon Law*, ed. John P. Beal, James A. Coriden, and Thomas J. Green (Mahwah, NJ: Paulist Press, 2000), 1056–1057.

the theological majority. The question of how infants can, in any meaningful way, desire baptism still needs to be answered. But the *lex orandi*
suggests that we should look harder for an answer. The natural law does
not help. No evidence of any inherent desire for baptism exists, and the
doctrine of original sin is unassailable. As Augustine recognized, the fact
of baptism's existence and necessity implies that we are not automatically
headed toward salvation. On the contrary, without a course correction, we
are headed toward Babel and the Flood.

Instead of the natural law, then, we should look for a solution in the
rite itself, where the consent of the child is supplied by parents and godparents. Again, I believe that the *lex orandi* suggests that the burden of
proof should fall on those who argue that this consent is insufficient for
baptism of desire because it is sufficient for the sacrament. In fact, in
chapter two we saw an ancient assertion of the belief that the intention
of Christian parents to baptize a child who died unexpectedly is sufficient for salvation—the fifth century epitaph of little Theudosius found
in southern Gaul. Cajetan's argument picks up on the same basic insight, and, in his extremely thorough mid-twentieth century survey of the
problem, Jesuit Peter Gumpel defends the plausibility of a solution along
the lines proposed by Cajetan.[12] The current *Roman Missal* adds further
plausibility to such a solution by providing a funeral rite for a child who
died *before* baptism, the instruction for which refers to "a child whom the
parents wished to be baptized."[13]

To defuse the objection of the majority position against this solution,
an observation made in a 1980 instruction issued by the Congregation for
the Doctrine of the Faith, *Pastoralis actio*, defending the practice of infant
baptism, is suggestive. In response to the argument that parents should

12. Gumpel, "Unbaptized Infants: May They Be Saved?" 362, 390, 443; "Unbaptized Infants:
A Further Report," 317–18.

13. *The Roman Missal*, 3rd Typical Edition (Totowa, NJ: Catholic Book Publishing Corporation, 2011), 1224. The instruction adds that "proper care is to be taken that the doctrine of the
necessity of Baptism is not to be obscured in the minds of the faithful." The *Order of Christian
Funerals* also includes several options for prayers for a child who died before baptism. *The Rites
of the Catholic Church: Study Edition*, vol. 1, Pueblo Book (Collegeville, MN: Liturgical Press,
1990), 909–1118. Further adaptation of these rites for situations in which it is not possible to
celebrate a funeral can be found in the *Order for the Naming and Commendation of an Infant
Who Died before Birth* (St. Louis, MO: Archdiocese of St. Louis Office of Sacred Worship,
2013). In some cases, this rite has been adapted for use with mothers who have repented of
their abortion.

refrain from baptizing their children because doing so is an imposition upon their children's freedom, the Congregation observes, "Such an attitude is simply an illusion: there is no such thing as pure human freedom, immune from being influenced in any way."[14] The assumption that, in order for a decision to be free or to be truly "my own," it must be detached from the will of others is, as the Congregation says, illusory. We are the product of our families and cultures; these do not merely influence the decisions that we make, but they make us who we are.

In discussions of salvation, one occasionally finds the observation that most people adopt the religion of their family or of the culture into which they are born; sometimes this fact is used to imply that our choice of religion should not exercise a decisive role on our salvation. This argument does not hold up, however, because, even if my decisions are heavily influenced by my upbringing, it does not follow that they are any less my decisions. My religious decisions are, at least in part, the product of my upbringing because *I* am the product of my upbringing. There exists no "I" to be saved apart from those countless relationships that make me who I am. This observation is even more valid when it comes to children. Especially before adolescence, the opinions, tastes, preferences, and desires of children mirror those of their parents and other significant adults in their lives. Civil law recognizes this anthropological reality by giving parents the right to express consent for their children. In a way that is difficult to define precisely and is subject to variation from person to person, the desires of a child's parents really are the desires of that child. Cramer makes this point brilliantly in his analysis of early medieval liturgical texts, which begin to reflect the practice of universal infant baptism; these prayers reveal "the ability of the adult community to see itself in the child, and conversely to see in itself the qualities of childhood."[15] When parents and godparents answer for a child in baptism, they are, in a real sense, expressing the child's will.

I hold, therefore, that we have strong grounds to believe that, if parents intend to baptize their child but that child dies before they are able to so, then that child will be saved through baptism of desire. This

---

14. Congregation for the Doctrine of the Faith, Instruction *Pastoralis actio* (October 20, 1980), 22.

15. Cramer, *Baptism and Change*, 134.

includes children dying *in utero*. Parents need not express their intention verbally, but it is implicit in their own practice of the Christian faith. It is quite clear, for example, that parents who have had all their children baptized and lose a child to a miscarriage possess the desire to baptize the child who is lost. The same would hold even if the mother miscarried without yet knowing that she was pregnant because, as we saw in the previous section, implicit desire is an objective concept. In such an instance, in my opinion, a pastor would be as justified asserting the child's salvation as Ambrose was asserting Valentinian's. The same degree of certainty does not exist with parents who are neglectful of religious practice. For example, we have to admit honestly that, if a couple does not practice their faith and does not have any of their children baptized, our grounds for believing that a miscarried child would receive baptism of desire are thin. Gumpel makes the valuable observation that the single category of "unbaptized infants" is not particularly useful because, like the adults whose lives they reflect, infants are not all the same.[16] Part of the difficulty theologians have had dealing with this issue may have been the result of the category error of imagining that all unbaptized infants can be lumped together and will share the same fate. We should be clear here that God's desire for the salvation of infants—and, for that matter, adults—is not in dispute, regardless of the particularities of their individual circumstances; nor is the desire of the Church, which by her nature seeks to incorporate all of humanity into the Body of Christ. But to *participate* in salvation, an active human response to this desire is necessary. And the response that people give to God is as varied as are people themselves; infants too reflect such human diversity.

In general, then, while the grounds for believing that the not-yet-baptized children of Christian parents can be saved through baptism of desire are secure, the salvation of other categories of infants depends upon the same uncertain variables that factor into implicit desire. By definition, an implicit desire for baptism includes the implicit intention to practice the Christian faith with all its attendant duties; these duties would include the baptism of children, so that, say, a mother's own implicit desire for baptism seems likely to extend to her children. I should also add that, while the desire of parents can in real ways be considered the desire of

16. Gumpel, "Unbaptized Infants: May They Be Saved?" 345.

their child, this is not an iron-clad rule. Obvious cases exist in which parents act contrary to the interests of their child; in civil law, the state sometimes intervenes to remove a child from an abusive parent. Similarly, in the case of abortion, the will of the mother is turned against that of the child in the most elemental way possible. Could someone else represent the child's will in that case? For sacramental baptism, after all, parents are not *always* the decision-makers. Sometimes grandparents, siblings, neighbors, or adoptive families exercise a more decisive role in the up-bringing of a child. In rare cases—say, an orphan in danger of death—a nurse might baptize a baby and could genuinely be said to represent the child's will for no other reason than that she was physically present and cared about the baby's well-being. Some groups have dedicated them-selves to praying especially for the victims of abortion, and it may be possible, particularly in cases where a biological mother's love has failed, that these prayers create some real bond of spiritual maternity.[17] But we cannot know. As with adults, our grounds for believing that salvation is likely in the case of unbaptized infants become more tenuous the farther we move away from Christ and the sacraments. As a result, we must live with uncertainty.

In the end, baptism of desire cannot abolish the uncertainty that results from salvation entering into the rough-edged reality of human existence. It does not reduce salvation to clear-cut, soothingly abstract principles. It does not diminish the desperate need of every human person for a savior or obscure the identity of that savior. Instead, adhering closely to the rite handed on by the apostles, it gives us a certain practical way of thinking about the cases that will arise on salvation's rough edges. Uncertainty, after all, can paralyze us. It can paralyze either through pessimism or through

---

17. The late American Archbishop Fulton Sheen composed a prayer, now widely distributed in pro-life circles, for the "spiritual adoption" of children in danger of abortion. Tucker Cordani, "Spiritual Adoption, Sheen-Style," *National Catholic Register*, July 10, 2007, https://www.ncregister.com/features/spiritual-adoption-sheen-style. Though the prayer asks for the child's life to be saved rather than for the salvation of an unbaptized child, the idea of "spiritual adoption" might have broader implications. The newsletter of the Sacred Heart Guardian Society, an organization dedicated to the dignified burial of discarded human embryos, raises the possibility that baptism of desire could offer some hope for the salvation of such individuals. Andrew Jaspers, "What is the eternal destination for deceased embryos?" *Tiny Sparks*, no. 2, Fall 2018, https://sacredheartguardians.org/wp-content/uploads/2018/08/2018-August-Tiny-Sparks.pdf; "Can Frozen Embryos be Baptized? Part 2," *Tiny Sparks*, no. 4, Fall 2019, https://sacredheartguardians.org/wp-content/uploads/2019/09/Tiny-Sparks-2019-Fall.pdf.

optimism, through despair or presumption—taking away either the hope that our actions matter or faith in the necessity of acting. And the really astonishing thing about Christian faith in the sacraments is that it holds that our actions *do* matter, that we can make a decision to participate in the saving act of God himself, and that the communion that results is salvation. It is no coincidence, therefore, that the first articulation of the doctrine of baptism of desire came not from speculation about Platonic forms, but in a moment of pastoral crisis. Baptism of desire has always been connected to our ability to make decisions, so the comfort and the caution that it offers is not absolute, but practical.

Baptism of desire cannot offer absolute certainty where revelation leaves matters uncertain. It maintains the tensions present in the Gospel itself that make the Christian message more than just—*pace* Monty Python—an inclination to always look on the bright side. But the doctrine does allow our decisions, even in hard cases, to be guided by Christian teaching on salvation. With respect to catechumens, the doctrine provides good grounds for believing in the salvation of those whose unexpected death alone prevents their baptism. In practical terms, this gives us reassurance that a thorough and effective process of Christian formation can be pursued where there is no particular danger of death. When it comes to non-Christians, the fragility of implicit desire means that, excepting special cases mentioned in revelation, we do not have grounds for confidence. It is possible that any given non-Christian will find salvation, but the evidence we have suggests that this is unlikely and probably uncommon. In other words, precisely because God wishes for all to be saved, we have no grounds for diminishing or reducing our missionary efforts. On the contrary, the proclamation of the Gospel makes it possible to fix one's desire on what is always the necessary object for salvation—the Incarnate Lord—making salvation more attainable on a human level. Christianity responds to how we humans make the decisions that direct our lives and actions. The faith was not revealed, after all, because God needed the publicity, but for our human benefit, to help us creatures bring our wayward desires into communion with his. In the hardest of hard cases, children dying before baptism, the doctrine provides grounds for a confident response to Christian parents who have lost a child. For non-Christians, such grounds do not exist; as a practical matter, this means little, because non-Christians will presumably turn to their own beliefs to make sense of their misfortune and grief. The doctrine, it seems to me, does not preclude our prayers in such cases, even for those we do not know, though we must, like Valentinian, pray from our poverty.

By definition, baptism of desire never provides reason to neglect baptism. It allows us to continue to proclaim the necessity of baptism for salvation—and to mean it—without claiming that anyone is, in principle, excluded. The doctrine's compatibility with Christian sacramental practice and the Church's age-old missionary drive is, I believe, one of its primary advantages over its twentieth-century rivals. Baptism of desire, as I have developed the concept here, is a more sober doctrine than what was, perhaps, the theological mainstream in the late twentieth century. Here, I have been willing to trade in optimism for well-grounded belief, and I believe that any mature theology should do the same. Baptism of desire does not alter, relax, or diminish what the Church has always proclaimed is necessary for salvation. When the people of Jerusalem, some two thousand years ago, turned to Peter, moved by his proclamation of the death and resurrection of Jesus Christ, and asked what was needed for redemption, the Apostle replied, "Repent, and be baptized every one of you" (Acts 2:38).

At the end of this study, I have no better answer.

Bibliography

Unless quoting from translations within sources, Biblical citations are from:

The Holy Bible Revised Standard Version Second Catholic Edition. San Francisco: Ignatius Press, 2006.

Unless otherwise noted, papal and conciliar documents are taken from vatican.va.

Primary Sources

Alan of Lille. *De fide catholica contra haereticos sui temporis.* PL 210:305–428. Edited by J.-P. Migne. Paris 1855.

Ambrose. *Opere esegetiche VIII/I: Commento al Salmo CXVIII (Lettere I–XI).* Translated by Luigi F. Pizzolato. Vol. 9 of *Opera Omnia di Sant'Ambrogio.* Rome: Città Nuova, 1987.

———. *Opere esegetiche II/II: De Abraham.* Translated by Franco Gori. Vol. 2, bk. 2, of *Opera Omnia di Sant'Ambrogio.* Rome: Città Nuova, 1984.

———. *De apologia prophetae David ad Theodosium Augustum.* In *Opere esegetiche V: De apologia prophetae David ad Theodosium Augustum, Apologia David Altera,* translated by Filippo Lucidi, 53–141. Vol. 5 of *Opera Omnia di Sant'Ambrogio.* Rome: Città Nuova, 1981.

———. *De obitu Valentiniani.* In *Discorsi e Lettere I: Le Orazioni Funebri,* edited by Gabriele Banterle, 162–209. Vol. 18 of *Opera Omnia di Sant'Ambrogio.* Rome: Città Nuova, 1985.

———. *Opere esegetiche IX/II: Expositionis Evangelii Secundum Lucam.* Translated by Giovanni Coppa. Vol. 12 of *Opera Omnia di Sant'Ambrogio.* Rome: Città Nuova, 1978.

———. *Saint Ambrose: Letters.* Translated by Mary Melchior Beyenka. The Fathers of the Church 26. Washington, DC: The Catholic University of America Press, 1967.

_____. *The Mysteries*. In *Theological and Dogmatic Works*, translated by Roy J. Deferrari, 1–28. The Fathers of the Church 44. Washington, DC: The Catholic University of America Press, 1963.

_____. *On Abraham*. Translated by Theodosia Tomkinson. Etna, CA: Center for Traditionalist Orthodox Studies, 2000.

_____. *On Emperor Valentinian*. In *Funeral Orations by Saint Gregory Nazianzen and Saint Ambrose*, translated by Roy J. Deferrari, 263–302. The Fathers of the Church 22. Washington, DC: The Catholic University of America Press, 1988.

_____. *The Sacraments*. In Deferrari, *Theological and Dogmatic Works*, 261–328.

Ambrosiaster. *In Epistulas ad Corinthios*. Edited by Heinrich Joseph Vogels. CSEL 81. Vienna: Hoelder-Pichler-Tempsky, 1968.

Anselm of Laon. *Liber pancrisis* and "Sentences d'authenticité probable." In *Problèmes d'histoire littéraire: L'école d'Anselme de Laon et de Guillaume de Champeaux*, 32–121. Vol. 5 of *Psychologie et Morale aux XIIe et XIIIe siècles*, edited by Odon Lottin. Gembloux: J. Duculot, 1959.

_____. *Sententie divine pagine*. In *Anselms von Laon Systematische Sentenzen*. Edited by Franz P. Bliemetzrieder. Münster: Aschendorffscehn Verlagsbuch-handlung, 1919.

Atti degli Apostoli. Edited by Francis Martin and Evan Smith. Italian edition edited by Gianluca Pilara and Ilaria Maggiulli. La Bibbia commentata dai Padri, Nuovo Testamento 5. Rome: Città Nuova, 2009.

Arnauld, Antoine. *The Necessity of Faith in Jesus Christ to Obtain Salvation*. Translated by Guido Stucco. Bloomington, IN: Xlibris Corporation, 2011.

Augustine. *The Augustine Catechism: The Enchiridion on Faith, Hope, and Charity*. Edited by Boniface Ramsey. Translated by Bruce Harbert. Hyde Park, NY: New City Press, 1999.

_____. *Baptism*. In *The Donatist Controversy I*, translated by Maureen Tilley and Boniface Ramsey. Part 1, vol. 21 of *The Works of Saint Augustine: A Translation for the 21st Century*. Hyde Park, NY: New City Press, 2019.

_____. *The City of God (1–10)*. Translated by William Babcock. Part 1, vol. 6 of *The Works of Saint Augustine: A Translation for the 21st Century*. Hyde Park, NY: New City Press, 2012.

_____. *The City of God (11–22)*. Translated by William Babcock. Part 2, vol. 7 of *The Works of Saint Augustine: A Translation for the 21st Century*. Hyde Park, NY: New City Press, 2013.

_____. *Confessions*. Translated by Henry Chadwick. Oxford: Oxford University Press, 1992.

_____. *De Baptismo Contra Donatistas*. In *Polemica con i Donatisti*. Translated by Antonio Lombardi. Vol. 15, bk. 1, of *Opere di Sant'Agostino* (*Nuova Biblioteca Agostiniana*). Rome: Città Nuova, 1998.

_____. *Eighty-Three Different Questions*. Translated by David L. Mosher.

The Fathers of the Church 70. Washington, DC: The Catholic University of America Press, 1982.

——. *Saint Augustine Letters II (83–130)*. Translated by Wilfrid Parsons. The Fathers of the Church 18. Washington, DC: The Catholic University of America Press, 1967.

——. *Homilies on the Gospel of John 1–40*. Edited by Allan D. Fitzgerald. Translated by Edmund Hill. Part 3, vol. 12 of *The Works of Saint Augustine: A Translation for the 21st Century*. Hyde Park, NY: New City Press, 2009.

——. *The Nature and Origin of the Soul*. In *Answer to the Pelagians I*, edited by John E. Rotelle, translated by Roland J. Teske, 449–542. Part 1, vol. 23 of *The Works of Saint Augustine: A Translation for the 21st Century*. Hyde Park, NY: New City Press, 2018.

——. *The Punishment and Forgiveness of Sins and the Baptism of Little Ones*. In Rotelle, *Answer to the Pelagians I*, 17–132.

——. *Questioni sull'Ettateuco: Questioni sul Levitico*. http://www.augustinus.it/italiano/questioni_ettateuco/index2.htm.

——. *Revisions*. Edited by Roland J. Teske. Translated by Boniface Ramsey. Part 1, vol. 2 of *The Works of Saint Augustine: A Translation for the 21st Century*. Hyde Park, NY: New City Press, 2010.

——. "Sermo 294." In *Discorsi V*, translated by Marcella Recchia, 280–309. Vol. 33 of *Opere di Sant'Agostino*. Rome: Città Nuova, 1986.

Basil. "Protreptic on Holy Baptism." In *Baptism: Ancient Liturgies and Patristic Texts*, edited by André Hamman, translated by Thomas Halton, 75–87. New York: Alba House, 1967.

——. "Regole Brevi." In *Opere Ascetiche di Basilio di Cesarea*, edited by Umberto Neri, translated by Maria Benedetta Artioli, 331–511. Turin: Unione Tipografico-Editrice Torinese, 1980.

Bede. *In Lucae Evangelium Expositio*. Edited by D. Hurst. CCL 120. Turnhout: Brepols, 1960.

Bellarmine, Robert. *De amissione gratiae et statu peccati*. In *De Controversiis Christianae Fidei*. Vol. 4, bk. 1, of *Roberti Cardinalis Bellarmini Opera Omnia*. Naples: J. Giuliano, 1858.

——. *De Baptismo et Confirmatione*. In *De Controversiis Christianae Fidei*. Vol. 3 of *Roberti Cardinalis Bellarmini Opera Omnia*. Naples: J. Giuliano, 1858.

——. *De Ecclesia militante*. In *De Controversiis Christianae Fidei*. Vol. 2 of *Roberti Cardinalis Bellarmini Opera Omnia*. Naples: J. Giuliano, 1857.

——. *De gratia et libero arbitrio*. In *De Controversiis Christianae Fidei*. Vol. 4, bk. 1.

——. *De Sacramentis in genere*. In *De Controversiis Christianae Fidei*. Vol. 3.

Benedict XV. *Maximum Illud*. Apostolic Letter. November 30, 1919.

Benedict XVI. *Spe Salvi*. Encyclical Letter. November 30, 2007.

Bernard of Clairvaux. *Letter 77 to Master Hugh of Saint Victor*. Translated by Hugh
    Feiss. In *Bernardus Magister*, edited by John R. Sommerfeldt, 360–78. Spencer,
    MA: Cistercian Publications, 1992.

Bonizo of Sutri. *Liber de Vita Christiana*. Edited by Ernst Perels. Berlin: Weid-
    mannsche Buchhandlung, 1930.

Cajetan (Thomas de Vio). *Commentarii*. In vol. 12 of *Thomae Aquinatis Opera
    Omnia*. Rome: Typographia Polyglotta S.C. de Propaganda Fide, 1906.

Catechism of the Catholic Church. Vatican City: Libreria Editrice Vaticana, 1993.

Catechism of the Council of Trent. Translated by J. Donovan. New York: Catholic
    Publishing Society, 1829.

Colossesi, 1–2 Tessalonicesi, 1–2 Timoteo, Tito, Filemone. Edited by Peter Gorday.
    La Bibbia commentata dai Padri, Nuovo Testamento 9. Rome: Città Nuova,
    2004.

*Concilii Tridentini actorum, pars altera: acta post sessionem tertiam usque ad Concili-
    um Bononiam translatum*. Edited by S. Ehses. Vol. 5 of *Concilium Tridentinum:
    Diariorum, Actorum, Epistularum, Tractatuum*. Freiburg im Breisgau:
    B. Herder, 1911.

Congregation for the Doctrine of the Faith. "Congregazione per la Dottrina della
    Fede: Lista completa dei documenti." https://www.vatican.va/roman_curia/
    congregations/cfaith/doc_doc_index_it.htm.

————. *Dominus Iesus*. Declaration. August 6, 2000.

————. *Pastoralis actio*. Instruction. October 20, 1980.

Cyprian of Carthage. "Letter 64." In *Saint Cyprian: Letters (1–81)*, translated by
    Rose Bernard Donna, 216–19. Washington, DC: The Catholic University of
    America Press, 1981.

————. "Letter 69." In Donna, *Saint Cyprian: Letters (1–81)*, 244–57.

————. "Letter 73." In Donna, *Saint Cyprian: Letters (1–81)*, 268–85.

————. "The Unity of the Catholic Church." In *Saint Cyprian: Treatises*, trans-
    lated by Roy J. Deferrari, 95–121. Washington, DC: The Catholic University of
    America Press, 1981.

Cyril of Jerusalem. "Lenten Lectures (*Catecheses*)." In *The Works of Saint Cyril of
    Jerusalem*, vol. 1, translated by Leo P. McCauley and Anthony A. Stephenson,
    69–252. The Fathers of the Church 61. Washington, DC: The Catholic Uni-
    versity of America Press, 1969.

Dante Alighieri. *Inferno*. Translated by Robert Hollander and Jean Hollander.
    New York: Doubleday, 2000.

————. *Paradiso*. Translated by Robert Hollander and Jean Hollander. New
    York: Doubleday, 2007.

Deforis. *Préservatif pour les fideles contre les sophisms et les impiétés des incrédules*.
    Paris: Desaint & Saillant, 1764.

Determinatio Sacrae Facultatis Parisiensis Super Libro cui Titulus, Émile ou De L'éducation. Paris: Charles-Pierre Berton, 1776.

The Didache: Text, Translation, Analysis, and Commentary. Edited and translated by Aaron Milavec. A Michael Glazier Book. Collegeville, MN: Liturgical Press, 2003.

"*Epitaphe* de Theudosius." In *Le baptême des enfants dans la tradition de l'église*, edited by J.C. Didier, 125. Tournai: Desclée, 1959.

Enchiridion symbolorum definitionum et declarationum de rebus fidei et morum. Edited by Heinrich Denzinger and Peter Hünermann. Latin-English 43rd ed. San Francisco: Ignatius Press, 2012.

Faber, Frederick William. *The Creator and the Creature*. London: Thomas Richardson and Son, 1856.

Gennadius. *Liber de ecclesiasticis dogmatibus*. PL 58:979–1000. Edited by J.-P. Migne. Paris, 1862.

Gregory IX. *Decretales*. Rome: In Aedibus Populi Romani, 1584.

Gregory XVI. *Mirari vos*. Encyclical Letter. August 15, 1832.

Gregory Nazianzen. "Oration 7: Panegyric on his Brother S. Caesarius." In *S. Cyril of Jerusalem, S. Gregory Nazianzen*, edited by Philip Schaff and Henry Wace, translated by Charles Gordon Browne and James Edward Swallow, 229–38. Nicene and Post-Nicene Fathers of the Christian Church, 2nd ser., vol. 7. Grand Rapids, MI: Eerdmans, 1989.

———. "Oration 18: On the Death of his Father." In Schaff and Wace, *S. Cyril of Jerusalem, S. Gregory Nazianzen*, 254–69.

———. "Oration 39: Oration on the Holy Lights." In Schaff and Wace, *S. Cyril of Jerusalem, S. Gregory Nazianzen*, 352–59.

———. "Oration 40: The Oration on Holy Baptism." In Schaff and Wace, *S. Cyril of Jerusalem, S. Gregory Nazianzen*, 360–77.

Gregory of Nyssa. "The Great Catechism." In *Gregory of Nyssa: Dogmatic Treatises, Etc.*, edited by Philip Schaff and Henry Wace, translated by W. Moore, 471–509. Nicene and Post-Nicene Fathers of the Christian Church, 2nd ser., vol. 5. Grand Rapids, MI: Eerdmans, 1988.

———. "On Infants' Early Deaths." In Schaff and Wace, *Gregory of Nyssa: Dogmatic Treatises, Etc.*, 372–81.

———. "On the Soul and the Resurrection." In Schaff and Wace, *Gregory of Nyssa: Dogmatic Treatises, Etc.*, 428–68.

Hermas. "The Pastor." Translated by F. Crombie. In *Fathers of the Second Century*, 3–58. The Ante-Nicene Fathers 2. Grand Rapids, MI: Eerdmans, 1986.

———. *Il Pastore*. Edited and translated by Maria Beatrice Durante Mangoni. Bologna: Dehoniane Bologna, 2003.

Hugh of St. Victor. *On the Sacraments of the Christian Faith*. Edited by

J. Saint-George. Translated by Roy J. Deferrari. Cambridge, MA: The Mediaeval Academy of America, 1951.

Ignatius of Loyola. *The Spiritual Exercises of St. Ignatius*. Translated by Louis J.
Puhl. Chicago: Loyola University Press, 1951.

International Theological Commission. *The Hope of Salvation for Infants Who
Die Without Being Baptized*. 2007. http://www.vatican.va/roman_curia/
congregations/cfaith/cti_documents/rc_con_cfaith_doc_20070419_
un-baptised-infants_it.html.

Irenaeus. *Against Heresies*. Edited by Alexander Roberts and James Donaldson,
translated by Alexander Roberts and W.H. Rambaut. Nicene and Post-
Nicene Fathers of the Christian Church vol. 5 and 9. Edinburgh: T&T Clark,
1868–1869.

———. *On the Apostolic Preaching*. Translated by John Behr. Crestwood, NY:
St. Vladimir's Seminary Press, 1997.

Isidore. *De Ecclesiasticis officiis*. Edited by Christopher M. Lawson. CCL 113.
Turnhout: Brepols, 1989.

Ivo of Chartres. *Panormia*. PL 161:1037–1343. Edited by J.-P. Migne. Paris 1889.

Jefferson, Thomas. *The Life and Morals of Jesus of Nazareth*. St. Louis: N.D.
Thompson Publishing, 1902.

Jerome. "Letter 57." In *Select Letters of St. Jerome*, translated by F.A. Wright, 338–71.
Loeb Classical Library 262. Cambridge, MA: Harvard University Press, 1991.

John Chrysostom. *Commentary on Saint John the Apostle and Evangelist: Homilies
1–47*. Translated by Thomas Aquinas Goggin. Washington, DC: The Catholic
University of America Press, 2000.

———. "On Acts of the Apostles Homily 21." In *Saint Chrysostom: Homilies on
the Acts of the Apostles and the Epistle to the Romans*, edited by Philip Schaff,
134–41. Nicene and Post-Nicene Fathers, 1st ser., vol. 11. Grand Rapids, MI:
Eerdmans, 1989.

———. "On Colossians Homily 8." In *Saint Chrysostom: Homilies on Galatians,
Ephesians, Philippians, Colossians, Thessalonians, Timothy, Titus, and Philemon*,
edited by Philip Schaff, 293–300. Nicene and Post-Nicene Fathers, 1st ser.,
vol. 13. Grand Rapids, MI: Eerdmans, 1988.

———. "On First Corinthians Homily 12." In *Saint Chrysostom: Homilies on
First and Second Corinthians*, edited by Philip Schaff, 64–72. Nicene and Post-
Nicene Fathers, 1st ser., vol. 12. Grand Rapids, MI: Eerdmans, 1989.

———. "On Thessalonians Homily 6." In Schaff, *Saint Chrysostom: Homilies on
Galatians, Ephesians, Philippians, Colossians, Thessalonians, Timothy, Titus, and
Philemon*, 348–52.

John Damascene. *An Exact Exposition of the Orthodox Faith*. In *Saint John of Damascus Writings*, translated by Frederic H. Chase Jr. Fathers of the Church 37.
Washington, DC: The Catholic University of American Press, 1958.

John Duns Scotus. *Ordinatio IV, dist. 1–7.* Vol. 11 of *Opera Omnia*, edited by
B. Hechich, B. Huculak, J. Percan, S. Ruiz de Loizaga, W. Salamon, and
G. Pica. Vatican City: Typis Vaticanis, 2008.

————. *Reportata Parisiensia IV.* In *Opera Theologica*, edited by Giovanni Lauriola. Vol. 2, bk. 2, of *Opera Omnia: Editio minor*. Alberobello: Editrice AGA,
1999.

John Paul II. *Redemptor Hominis.* Encyclical Letter. March 4, 1979.

————. *Reconciliatio et Paenitentia.* Post-Synodal Apostolic Exhortation.
December 2, 1984.

————. *Redemptoris Missio.* Encyclical Letter. December 7, 1990.

Justin Martyr. "Dialogue with Trypho." In *Saint Justin Martyr*, edited and translated by Thomas B. Falls, 147–366. New York: Christian Heritage, 1948.

————. "The First Apology." In Falls, *Saint Justin Martyr*, 33–111.

————. "The Second Apology of Justin to the Roman Senate on Behalf of the
Christians." In Falls, *Saint Justin Martyr*, 119–35.

Kant, Immanuel. *Religion within the Boundaries of Mere Reason and Other
Writings.* Translated and edited by Allen Wood and George Di Giovanni.
Cambridge: Cambridge University Press, 2019.

Lacordaire, Henri-Dominique. *Conférences de Notre-Dame de Paris.* Vols. 1 and 4.
Paris: Sagnier et Bray, 1844–1851.

————. *Jesus Christ: Conferences Delivered at Notre Dame in Paris.* London:
Chapman & Hall, 1869.

————. *Thoughts and Teachings of Lacordaire.* New York: Benziger Brothers, 1903.

La Mothe Le Vayer, François de. *De la vertu des payens.* Paris: Augustin Courbe,
1647.

Las Casas, Bartolomé de. *A Short Account of the Destruction of the Indies.* Translated
by Nigel Griffin. Penguin Classics, 2004. Kindle.

Leo I. *Pope Leo I: Sermons.* Translated by Jane Patricia Freeland. The Fathers of the
Church 93. Washington, DC: The Catholic University of America Press, 1996.

Leo XIII. *Annum Sacrum.* Encyclical Letter. May 25, 1899.

Liguori, Alphonsus. *Theologia Moralis: Editio Nova.* 4 vols. Edited by Leonardi
Gaudé. Rome: Ex Typographia Vaticana, 1905–1909.

The Liturgy of the Hours. Vol. 3. New York: Catholic Book Publishing, 1975.

Luca. Edited by Arthur A. Just Jr. Italian edition edited by Sara Petri and Giovanna Taponecco. La Bibbia commentata dai Padri, Nuovo Testamento 3. Rome:
Città Nuova, 2006.

Major, John. *Quartus sententiarum.* Paris: Poncet le Preux, 1509.

Nicholas I. *Epistola XCVII: Responsa Nicolai ad Consulta Bulgarorum.* PL 119:
978–1016. Edited by J.-P. Migne. Paris 1880.

Order for the Naming and Commendation of an Infant Who Died before Birth.
St. Louis: Archdiocese of St. Louis Office of Sacred Worship, 2013.

Les Ordines Romani du Haut Moyen Age. Edited by Michel Andrieu. Vol. 2,
 Les Texts (*Ordines I–XIII*). Louvain: Spicilegium Sacrum Lovaniense, 1971.

Origen. *Commentary on the Epistle to the Romans, Books 1–5.* Translated by Thomas
 P. Scheck. The Fathers of the Church 103. Washington, DC: The Catholic
 University of America Press, 2001.

———. "An Exhortation to Martyrdom." In *Origen: An Exhortation to Martyrdom, Prayer and Selected Works*, edited and translated by Rowan A. Greer,
 41–79. New York: Paulist Press, 1979.

———. *On First Principles.* 2 vols. Edited and translated by John Behr. Oxford:
 Oxford University Press, 2017.

———. "On Prayer." In Greer, *Origen*, 81–170.

Otto of Fresing. *The Two Cities: A Chronicle of Universal History to the Year 1146
 A.D.* Translated by Charles Christopher Mierow. New York: Columbia University Press, 2002.

Paul VI. *Ecclesiam Suam.* Encyclical Letter. August 6, 1964.

———. *Evangelii Nuntiandi.* Apostolic Exhortation. December 8, 1975.

Perrone, Giovanni. *Tractatus de Baptismo.* In *Praelectiones theologicae quas in Collegio Rom. habebat Ioannes Perrone e Societate Jesu.* Vol. 6. Louvain: Vanlinthout
 et Vandenzande, 1841.

———. *Il Protestantesimo e la Regola di Fede.* Turin: Giancito Marietti, 1854.

———. *Catechismo intorno al protestantesimo ad uso del popolo.* Naples: Tipografia
 di Giovanni di Majo, 1864.

———. *De Fide.* In *Praelectiones theologicae de virtutibus fidei, spei et caritatis.*
 2nd ed. Turin: Hyacinthi Marietti, 1867.

Peter Abelard. *Commentary on the Epistle to the Romans.* Translated by Steven R.
 Cartwright. The Fathers of the Church Mediaeval Continuation 12. Washington, DC: The Catholic University of America Press, 2011.

———. "Letter 7." In *The Letter Collection of Peter Abelard and Heloise*, edited by
 David Luscombe, translated by Betty Radice and revised by David Luscombe,
 260–351. Oxford: Oxford University Press, 2013.

———. *Theologia Christiana.* In *Theologia Christiana, Theologia Scholarium,
 Accedunt Capitula haeresum Petri Abaelardi*, edited by E.M. Buytaert. Vol. 2 of
 Petri Abaelardi Opera Theologica. CCCM 12. Turnhout: Brepols, 1969.

———. *Yes and No.* Translated by Priscilla Throop. Charlotte, VT: MedievalMS,
 2008.

Peter Lombard. *The Sentences.* Bk. 4, *On the Doctrine of Signs.* Translated by Giulio
 Silano. Toronto: Pontifical Institute of Mediaeval Studies, 2010.

Peter of Tarentaise. *In IV Librum Sententiarum Commentaria.* Vol. 4. Edited by
 J.-B. de Marinis. Toulouse: Arnaldum Colomerium, 1651. Reprinted, Ridgewood, NJ: Gregg Press, 1964.

Pius IX. *Quanto conficiamur moerore.* Translated by Marie Liguori Ewald. In

The Papal Encyclicals, 1740–1878, 369–73. Vol. 1 of *The Papal Encyclicals*, edited by Claudia Carlen. Ann Arbor, MI: Pierian Press, 1990.

_____. *Singulari quidem.* Translated by Norman Desmarais. In *The Papal Encyclicals, 1740–1878*, 339–46. In Carlen, *The Papal Encyclicals.*

Pius XII. *Mystici Corporis Christi.* Encyclical Letter. June 19, 1943.

_____. *Humani Generis.* Encyclical Letter. August 12, 1950.

Plato. *Phaedrus.* Translated by Alexander Nehamas and Paul Woodruff. In *Complete Works*, edited by John M. Cooper, 506–56. Indianapolis, IN: Hackett Publishing Co., 1997.

_____. *Republic.* Translated by G.M.A. Grube and revised by C.D.C. Reeve. In Cooper, *Complete Works*, 971–1223.

The Rites of the Catholic Church: Study Edition. Vol. 1. Pueblo Book. Collegeville, MN: Liturgical Press, 1990.

Rituale Romanum: Editio Princeps (1614). Edited by Manlio Sodi and Juan Javier Flores Arcas. Vatican City: Libreria Editrice Vaticana, 2004.

The Roman Missal. 3rd Typical Edition. Totowa, NJ: Catholic Book Publishing Corporation, 2011.

Rousseau, Jean-Jacques. *Emile.* Translated by Allan Bloom. New York: Basic Books, 1979.

Sacramentarium Gelasianum. Edited by Leo Cunibert Mohlberg, Leo Eizenhöffer, and Peter Siffrin. Rome: Casa Editrice Herder, 1960.

School of Laon. "Sentences," "Recueils systematiques," and "Sententiae Atrebatenses." In *Problèmes d'histoire littéraire: L'école d'Anselme de Laon et de Guillaume de Champeaux*, 229–447. Vol. 5 of Lottin, *Psychologie et Morale aux XIIe et XIIIe siècles.*

Simon. *Tractatus Magistri Simonis de sacramentis* and *Tractatus de septem sacramentis ecclesie.* In *Maître Simon et son groupe De sacramentis*, edited by Henri Weisweiler. Louvain: Spicilegium Sacrum Lovaniense, 1937.

Soto, Domingo de. *De natura et gratia.* Paris: Apud Ioannem Foucher, 1549.

Suárez, Francisco. *De Deo Uno et Trino.* Vol. 1 of *Opera Omnia R.P. Francisci Suárez, s.j.* Paris: Ludovicum Vivès, 1856.

_____. *De Fide Theologica.* In *De Virtutibus Theologicis.* Vol. 12 of *Opera Omnia R.P. Francisci Suárez, s.j.* Paris: Ludovicum Vivès, 1858.

_____. *Commentaria ac Disputationes in Tertiam Partem D Thomae.* Vol. 20 of *Opera Omnia R.P. Francisci Suárez, s.j.* Paris: Ludovicum Vivès, 1866.

Tertullian. "Concerning Baptism." In *Tertullian's Treatises, Concerning Prayer, Concerning Baptism*, translated by Alexander Souter, 44–72. Leopold Classic Library. London: Society for Promoting Christian Knowledge, 1919.

_____. "On Repentance." Translated by S. Thelwall. In *Latin Christianity: Its Founder, Tertullian*, edited by Alexander Roberts, James Donaldson, and

A. Cleveland Coxe, 657–668. The Ante-Nicene Fathers 3. Grand Rapids, MI: Eerdmans, 1989.

Theodore of Mopsuestia. "In Ep. Ad Timotheum I." In *I. Thessalonians–Philemon, Appendices, Indices*. Vol. 2 of *In Epistolas B. Pauli Commentarii*, edited by H.B. Swete. Cambridge: Cambridge University Press, 1882.

Thomas Aquinas. *Commentary on the Sentences*. Aquinas Institute. https://aquinas .cc/la/en/~Sent.I.

———. *Commentary on the Sentences, Book IV, Distinctions 1–13*. Translated by Beth Mortensen. Green Bay, Wis.: Aquinas Institute, 2018.

———. *On Evil*. Edited by Brian Davies. Translated by Richard Regan. New York: Oxford University Press, 2003.

———. *Quaestiones disputatae de veritate*. Translated by Robert W. Mulligan, James V. McGlynn, and Robert W. Schmidt. Edited by J. Kenny. 1952–1954. https://isidore.co/aquinas/QDdeVer.htm.

———. *Summa contra Gentiles*. https://isidore.co/aquinas/ContraGentiles4 .htm#56.

———. *Summa contra Gentiles 3:I*. Translated by Vernon J. Bourke. Notre Dame, IN: University of Notre Dame Press, 1975.

———. *Summa theologica*. Translated by Fathers of the English Dominican Province. New York: Benziger Brothers, 1947.

———. *Thomas Aquinas's Quodlibetal Questions*. Translated by Turner Nevitt and Brian Davies. New York: Oxford University Press, 2020. Apple Books.

Tirechani. *Tirechani collectanea de sancto Patricio*. Translated by Ludwig Bieler. Royal Irish Academy, 2011. https://www.confessio.ie/more/tirechan_english#.

"A Treatise on Re-Baptism by an Anonymous Writer." In *Fathers of the Third Century: Hippolytus, Cyprian, Caius, Novatian, Appendix*, edited by Alexander Roberts, James Donaldson, and A. Cleveland Coxe, 665–78. The Ante-Nicene Fathers 5. Grand Rapids, MI: Eerdmans, 1986.

Vatican Council II. *Lumen Gentium*. November 21, 1964.

———. *Nostra Aetate*. October 28, 1965.

———. *Ad Gentes*. December 7, 1965.

———. *Dignitatis Humanae*. December 7, 1965.

———. *Gaudium et Spes*. December 7, 1965.

Vitoria, Francisco de. *De Indis*. Translated by John Pawley Bate. Appendix A in *The Spanish Origin of International Law: Francisco de Vitoria and his Law of Nations*, by James Brown Scott, i–xlvi. Oxford: Clarendon Press, 1934.

———. *Summa sacramentorum Ecclesiae*. Rome: Apud Iulium Accoltum, in platea Peregrini, 1567.

William of Champeaux. *Sentences*. In *Problèmes d'histoire littéraire: L'école d'Anselme de Laon et de Guillaume de Champeaux*, 189–227. Vol. 5 of Lottin, *Psychologie et Morale aux XIIe et XIIIe siècles*.

William of Ockham. *Quaestiones in Librum Quartum Sententiarum.* Vol. 7 of *Opera Theologica,* edited by Rega Wood, Gedeon Gál, and Romualdo Green. St. Bonaventure, NY: The Franciscan Institute of St. Bonaventure University, 1984.

Xavier, Francis. *The Letters and Instructions of Francis Xavier.* Translated and edited by M. Joseph Costelloe. St. Louis, MO: The Institute of Jesuit Sources, 1992.

Secondary Sources

Adams, Marilyn McCord. "Ockham on Will, Nature, and Morality." In *The Cambridge Companion to Ockham,* edited by Paul Vincent Spade, 245–72. New York: Cambridge University Press, 1999.

Alszeghy, Zoltán, and Maurizio Flick. "Il Decreto Tridentino sul peccato originale." *Gregorianum* 52, no. 4 (1971): 595–637.

Alberigo, Giuseppe, and Joseph A. Komonchak. *History of Vatican II.* Vol. 1, Announcing and Preparing Vatican Council II. Maryknoll, NY: Orbis, 1995.

Armenteros, Carolina. "The Anti-Theological Theology of Jean-Jacques Rousseau." In *The Oxford Handbook of Early Modern Theology, 1600–1800,* edited by Ulrich L. Lehner, Richard A. Muller, and A.G. Roeber, 594–600. New York: Oxford University Press, 2016.

Ayres, Lewis, and Thomas Humphries. "Augustine and the West to AD 650." In *The Oxford Handbook of Sacramental Theology,* edited by Hans Boersma and Matthew Levering, 156–69. Oxford: Oxford University Press, 2015.

Baghos, Mario. "Reconsidering *Apokatastasis* in St Gregory of Nyssa's *On the Soul and Resurrection* and the *Catechetical Oration.*" *Phronema* 27, no. 2 (2012): 125–62.

Balthasar, Hans Urs von. *Cordula ovverosia il caso serio.* Translated by G. Viola. Brescia: Queriniana, 1974.

———. *Dare We Hope "That All Men Be Saved?"* Translated by David Kipp and Lothar Krauth. San Francisco: Ignatius Press, 1988.

Barbaglio, Giuseppe. *La Prima Lettera ai Corinzi.* Bologna: Dehoniane, 2005.

Bauer, Emmanuel J. "Francisco Suarez (1548–1617): Scholasticism after Humanism." In *Philosophers of the Renaissance,* edited by Paul Richard Blum, 236–55. Washington, DC: The Catholic University of America Press, 2010.

Baum, Gregory. "Baptism of Desire." In Sacramentum Mundi: *An Encyclopedia of Theology,* vol. 1, edited by Karl Rahner, Juan Alfaro, Alberto Bellini, et al., 144–46. London: Burns & Oates, 1968.

Baun, Jane. "The Fate of Babies Dying Before Baptism in Byzantium." In *The Church and Childhood,* edited by Diana Wood, 115–25. Studies in Church History 31. Oxford: Blackwell, 1994.

Beiting, Christopher. "The Idea of Limbo in Thomas Aquinas." *The Thomist* 62, no. 2 (1998): 217–44.

———. "The Idea of Limbo in Alexander of Hales and Bonaventure." *Franciscan Studies* 75 (1999): 3–56.

Bergin, Joseph. *The Politics of Religion in Early Modern France*. New Haven, CT: Yale University Press, 2014.

Beuchot, Maurice. "El primer planteamiento teológico-jurídico sobre la conquista de América: JOHN MAIR." *Ciencia Tomista* 103, no. 2 (1976): 213–30.

Bobertz, Charles A. *The Gospel of Mark: A Liturgical Reading*. Grand Rapids, MI: Baker Academic, 2016. Ebook.

Bordeaux, Henry. "Le centenaire de la mort de Lacordaire." *Revue des Deux Mondes (1829–1971)* (1961): 25–39.

Borobio, Dionisio. *Sacramentos en general: Bautismo y Confirmación en la Escuela de Salamanca: Fco. Vitoria, Melchor Cano, Domingo Soto*. Salamanca: Publicaciones Universidad Pontificia, 2007.

Brechter, Suso. "Decree on the Church's Missionary Activity." In *Commentary on the Documents of Vatican II*, vol. 4, Herbert Vorgrimler, editor, 87–181. New York: Herder and Herder, 1969.

Bright, Pamela. "Donatist Bishops." In Fitzgerald, *Augustine through the Ages*, Allan D. Fitzgerald, editor, 281–84. Grand Rapids, MI: Eerdmans, 2009.

Brundage, James A. *Medieval Canon Law*. London: Routledge, 1995.

Bullivant, Stephen. *Mass Exodus: Catholic Disaffiliation in Britain and America since Vatican II*. Oxford: Oxford University Press, 2019.

Burke, Patrick. *Reinterpreting Rahner: A Critical Study of His Major Themes*. New York: Fordham University Press, 2002.

Byer, Glenn C.J. *Charlemagne and Baptism: A Study of Responses to the Circular Letter of 811/812*. Lanham, MD: International Scholars Publications, 1999.

Capéran, Louis. *Le problème du salut des infidèles*. 2 vols. Toulouse: Grand Séminaire, 1934.

Cardia, Giulio. *La posizione del De Lugo nella dottrina della universale necessità e possibilità della fede*. Cagliari: F. Tois, 1941.

Carey, Patrick. "St. Benedict Center and No Salvation Outside the Church, 1940–1953." *The Catholic Historical Review* 93, no. 3 (2007): 553–75.

Carola, Joseph A. "The Academics, the Artist, and the Architect: Retrieving the Tradition in Nineteenth-Century Catholicism." *Logos: A Journal of Catholic Thought and Culture* 23, no. 1 (2020): 65–93.

Casel, Odo. *The Mystery of Christian Worship*. New York: Crossroad Publishing, 2016.

Cavallera, Ferdinand. "Le décret du Concile de Trente sur les sacrements en général (VIIe session)." *Bulletin de Littérature Ecclésiastique* 6, no. 6 (1914): 361–425.

Certeau, Michel de. *The Writing of History.* Translated by Tom Conley. New York: Columbia University Press, 1988.

Chojnacki, Marek. *Il battesimo e l'eucaristia: fonti rituali della vita Cristiana secondo San Bernardo di Chiaravalle.* Rome: Pontificia Università Gregoriana, 2002.

Clarke, Catherine Goddard. *The Loyolas and The Cabots: The Story of the Crusade of Saint Benedict Center 1940–1950.* Richmond, NH: St. Benedict Center, 1992.

Coffey, David. "The Whole Rahner on the Supernatural Existential." *Theological Studies* 65, no. 1 (2004): 95–118.

Colish, Marcia L. "Another Look at the School of Laon." *Archives d'histoire doctrinale et littéraire du Moyen Age* 53 (1986): 7–22.

_____. *Peter Lombard.* 2 vols. Leiden: Brill, 1994.

_____. "The Virtuous Pagan: Dante and the Christian Tradition." In *The Fathers and Beyond: Church Fathers between Ancient and Medieval Thought,* 1–40. Aldershot: Ashgate, 2008.

_____. *Faith, Fiction & Force in Medieval Baptismal Debates.* Washington, DC: The Catholic University of America Press, 2014.

Congar, Yves. *The Wide World My Parish: Salvation and Its Problems.* Translated by Donald Attwater. London: Darton, Longman & Todd, 1961.

Cordani, Tucker. "Spiritual Adoption, Sheen-Style." *National Catholic Register,* July 10, 2007. https://www.ncregister.com/features/spiritual-adoption -sheen-style.

Cramer, Peter. *Baptism and Change in the Early Middle Ages, c. 200 – c. 1150.* Cambridge: Cambridge University Press, 2002.

Cross, Richard. *Duns Scotus.* New York: Oxford University Press, 1999.

Crouzel, Henri. *Origen: The Life and Thought of the First Great Theologian.* Translated by A. S. Worrall. San Francisco: Harper & Row, 1989.

Cuchet, Guillaume. "Une révolution théologique oubliée: Le triomphe de la thèse du grand nombre des élus dans le discours catholique du XIXe siècle." *Revue d'histoire du XIXe siècle* 41 (2010): 131–48.

Daley, Brian E. *The Hope of the Early Church: A Handbook of Patristic Eschatology.* Grand Rapids, MI: Baker Academic, 2010.

Daniélou, Jean. "Christianity and the Non-Christian Religions." In *Introduction to the Great Religions,* 7–28. Translated by Albert J. La Mothe. Notre Dame, IN: Fides Publishers, 1964.

_____. "The Transcendence of Christianity." In *Introduction to the Great Religions,* 133–142.

Dauphinais, Michael. "Christ and the Metaphysics of Baptism in the *Summa theologiae* and the *Commentary on John.*" In *Rediscovering Aquinas and the Sacraments,* edited by Matthew Levering and Michael Dauphinais. Chicago: Hillenbrand Books, 2009. Kindle.

Dauphinais, Michael, and Matthew Levering. *Knowing the Love of Christ.* Notre Dame, IN: University of Notre Dame Press, 2002.

Davies, Jon. *Death, Burial and Rebirth in the Religions of Antiquity.* London: Routledge, 1999.

Deller, William S. "The First Rite of Passage: Baptism in Medieval Memory." *Journal of Family History* 36, no. 1 (2011): 3–14.

De Roten, Philippe. *Baptême et mystagogie enquête sur l'initiation chrétienne selon S. Jean Chrysostome.* Münster: Aschendorf, 2005.

DiNoia, J. A. "Implicit Faith, General Revelation and the State of Non-Christians." *The Thomist* 47, no. 2 (1983): 209–41.

Doval, Alexis J. *Cyril of Jerusalem, Mystagogue: The Authorship of the Mystagogic Catecheses.* Washington, DC: The Catholic University of America Press, 2001.

Doyle, John P. "Francisco Suárez: On Preaching the Gospel to People Like the American Indians." *Fordham International Law Journal* 15, no. 4 (1991): 879–951.

Diekman, Godfrey. "Some Observations on the Teaching of Trent Concerning Baptism." In *Lutherans and Catholics in Dialogue II: One Baptism for the Remission of Sins,* edited by Paul C. Empie and William W. Baum, 61–70. New York: U.S.A. National Committee of the Lutheran World Federation; Washington, DC: Bishops' Commission for Ecumenical Affairs, 1967.

Drinkwater, F. H. "The 'Baptism Invisible' and its Extent." *The Downside Review* 71, no. 223 (1953): 25–42.

Driscoll, Jeremy. "Uncovering the Dynamic *Lex Orandi—Lex Credendi* in the Baptismal Theology of Irenaeus." *Pro Ecclesia* 12, no. 2 (2003): 213–25.

Driscoll, Michael S. "The Conversion of the Nations." In *The Oxford History of Christian Worship,* edited by Geoffrey Wainwright and Karen B. Westerfield Tucker, 175–215. New York: Oxford University Press, 2006.

Drummond, Richard H. "Christian Theology and the History of Religions." *Journal of Ecumenical Studies* 12, no. 3 (1975): 389–405.

Dublanchy, E. "Charité." In *Dictionnaire de théologie Catholique,* vol. 2, bk. 2, edited by A. Vacant and E. Mangenot, 2217–2266. Paris: Letouzey et Ané, 1910.

Dulles, Avery. "The Population of Hell." In *The Church and Society: The Laurence J. McGinley Lectures, 1988–2007,* 387–400. New York: Fordham University Press, 2008.

———. "Who Can Be Saved?" In *Church and Society,* 522–34.

Dupont, Anthony, and Matthew A. Gaumer. "*Gratia Dei, Gratia Sacramenti*: Grace in Augustine of Hippo's Anti-Donatist Writing." *Ephemerides Theologicae Lovanienses* 86, no. 4 (2010): 307–29.

Duval, André. *Des Sacrements au Concile de Trente.* Paris: Cerf, 1985.

Dyer, George J. *Limbo: Unsettled Question.* New York: Sheed and Ward, 1964.

Eagleton, Terry. *Hope Without Optimism*. New Haven, CT: Yale University Press, 2017.

Elliott, John H. *1 Peter: A New Translation with Introduction and Commentary*. The Anchor Bible 37B. New York: Doubleday, 2000.

Eminyan, Maurice. *The Theology of Salvation*. Boston: St. Paul Editions, 1960.

Fanning, William. "Baptism." In *The Catholic Encyclopedia*. New York: Robert Appleton, 1907. http://www.newadvent.org/cathen/02258b.htm.

Feeney, Leonard. *Bread of Life*. Fitzwilliam, NH: Loreto Publications, 2018.

Feiss, Hugh. "*Bernardus Scholasticus*: The Correspondence of Bernard of Clairvaux and Hugh of Saint Victor on Baptism." In Sommerfeldt, *Bernardus Magister*, 349–78.

Fenton, Joseph C. *The Catholic Church and Salvation in Light of Recent Pronouncements by the Holy See*. Glasgow: Sands & Co., 1958.

Ferguson, Everett. *Baptism in the Early Church: History, Theology, and Liturgy in the First Five Centuries*. Grand Rapids, MI: Eerdmans, 2009.

————. "Exhortations to Baptism in the Cappadocians." In *Studia Patristica*, vol. 32, edited by Elizabeth A. Livingstone, 121–29. Leuven: Peeters, 1997.

————. "Inscriptions and the Origin of Infant Baptism." *The Journal of Theological Studies* 30, no. 1 (1979): 37–46.

Fernández, Benito Méndez. *El problema de la salvacion de los "infieles" en Francisco de Vitoria*. Rome: Pontificia Universitate Gregoriana, 1993.

Fink, David C. "John Mair's Doctrine of Justification within the Context of the Early 16th Century." In *A Companion to the Theology of John Mair*, edited by John T. Slotemaker and Jeffrey C. Witt, 223–40. Leiden: Brill, 2015.

Fiore, Benjamin. *The Pastoral Epistles: First Timothy, Second Timothy, Titus*. Sacra Pagina Series 12, edited by Daniel J. Harrington. Collegeville, MN: Liturgical Press, 2007.

Fitzmyer, Joseph A. *First Corinthians*. The Anchor Yale Bible 32. New Haven, CT: Yale University Press, 2008.

Fletcher, Richard. *The Conversion of Europe: From Paganism to Christianity, 371–1386 AD*. London: Fontana Press, 1998.

Fransen, P. "The Sacramental Character at the Council of Trent (Wording en strekking van de canon over het merkteken te Trente)." *Bijdragen* 32, no. 1 (1971): 2–34.

Frigo, Alberto, ed. Inexcusabiles: *Salvation and the Virtues of the Pagans in the Early Modern Period*. Cham: Springer, 2020.

————. Introduction to Frigo, Inexcusabiles, 1–12.

————. "Montaigne's Gods." In Frigo, Inexcusabiles, 15–32.

Fuellenbach, John. "The Church in the Context of the Kingdom of God." In *The Convergence of Theology: A Festschrift Honoring Gerald O'Collins, S.J.*, edited by Daniel Kendall and Stephen T. Davis, 221–37. Mahwah, NJ: Paulist Press, 2001.

Gál, Gedeon. "Gregory of Rimini." In *New Catholic Encyclopedia*, vol. 6, 797. Washington, DC: The Catholic University of America Press, 1967.

Gaukroger, Stephen. "The Challenges of Empirical Understanding in Early Modern Theology." In Lehner et al., *Oxford Handbook of Early Modern Theology*, 564–76.

Gavigan, John J. "Fulgentius of Ruspe on Baptism." *Traditio* 5 (1947): 313–22.

Gill, Joseph. *The Council of Florence*. New York: Cambridge University Press, 1959.

Gillman, Neil. "Death and Afterlife, Judaic Doctrines of." In *The Encyclopaedia of Judaism*, vol. 1, edited by Jacob Neusner, Alan J. Avery-Peck, William Scott Green, 196–212. Leiden: Brill, 2000.

Giraud, Cédric. *Per verba magistri: Anselme de Laon et son école au XII* siècle. Turnhout: Brepols, 2010.

Girolimon, Michael T. "Hugh of St Victor's *De sacramentis Christianae fidei*: The Sacraments of Salvation." *Journal of Religious History* 18, no. 2 (1994): 127–38.

Granados, José. *Introduction to Sacramental Theology: Signs of Christ in the Flesh*. Translated by Michael J. Miller. Washington, DC: Catholic University of America Press, 2017.

Gregory, Brad S. *Salvation at Stake: Christian Martyrdom in Early Modern Europe*. Cambridge, MA: Harvard University Press, 1999.

Grellard, Christophe. *De la certitude volontaire: Débats nominalistes sur la foi à la fin du Moyen Âge*. Paris: Publications de la Sorbonne, 2014.

Grillo, Andrea. *Introduzione alla teologia liturgica: Approccio teorico alla liturgia e ai sacramenti cristiani*. Padua: Edizioni Messaggero Padova, 2011.

Gros, Jean-Michel. "Bayle and the Question of the Salvation of the Infidels." In Frigo, Inexcusabiles, 127–44.

Grossi, Vittorino. "Regula Fidei." In *Nuovo Dizionario Patristico e di Antichità Cristiane*, vol. 3, edited by Angelo Di Berardino, 4491–93. Genova: Marietti 1820, 2008.

―――――. *I sacramenti nei Padri della Chiesa: l'iter semiologico, storico, teologico*. Rome: Istituto Patristico Augustinianum, 2009.

Grundeken, Mark. *Community Building in the Shepherd of Hermas: A Critical Study of Some Key Aspects*. Leiden: Brill, 2015.

Guardini, Romano. *The Spirit of the Liturgy*. Translated by Ada Lane. New York: Sheed and Ward, 1935. Kindle.

Guarino, Thomas G. *The Disputed Teachings of Vatican II: Continuity and Reversal in Catholic Doctrine*. Grand Rapids, MI: Eerdmans, 2018.

Gumpel, Peter. "Unbaptized Infants: May They Be Saved?" *The Downside Review* 72, no. 230 (1954): 342–458.

_____. "Unbaptized Infants: A Further Report." *The Downside Review* 73, no. 234 (1955): 317–46.

Haar, Christoph P. "A Juridicized Language for the Salvation of Souls: Jesuit Ethics." In *Jesuit Philosophy on the Eve of Modernity*, edited by Cristiano Casalini, 193–212. Leiden: Brill, 2019.

Hardon, John. *History and Theology of Grace*. Ypsilanti, MI: Veritas Press, 2002.

Harent, S. "Infidèles (Salut des)." In *Dictionnaire du Théologie Catholique*, vol. 7, bk. 2, edited by A. Vacant, E. Mangenot, and E. Amann, 1726–1930. Paris: Letouzey et Ané, 1923.

Harkins, Franklin T. "The Early Aquinas on the Question of Universal Salvation, or How a Knight May Choose Not to Ride His Horse." *New Blackfriars* 95, no. 1056 (2014): 208–17.

Harmless, William. "Baptism." In Fitzgerald, *Augustine through the Ages*, 84–91.

Harmon, Thomas P. "The Sacramental Consummation of the Moral Life According to St. Thomas Aquinas." *New Blackfriars* 91, no. 1034 (2010): 465–80.

Hart, David Bentley. *That All Shall Be Saved: Heaven, Hell, and Universal Salvation*. New Haven, CT: Yale University Press, 2019.

Hart, Kevin T. "Baptism." In *New Commentary on the Code of Canon Law*, edited by John P. Beal, James A. Coriden, and Thomas J. Green, 1033–1064. Mahwah, NJ: Paulist Press, 2000.

Hartman, Lars. "Obligatory Baptism—but Why? On Baptism in the *Didache* and in the *Shepherd* of Hermas." *Svensk exegetisk årsbok* 59 (1994): 127–43.

Healy, Mary. *The Gospel of Mark*. Grand Rapids, MI: Baker Academic, 2008.

Hellwig, Monika K. "Baptism of Desire." In *The Modern Catholic Encyclopedia*, edited by Michael Glazier and Monika K. Hellwig, 69. A Michael Glazier Book. Collegeville, MN: Liturgical Press, 1994.

Herberg, Will. *Protestant-Catholic-Jew: An Essay in American Religious Sociology*. Garden City, NY: Doubleday, 1955.

Hick, John, and Paul F. Knitter. *The Myth of Christian Uniqueness: Toward a Pluralistic Theology of Religions*. Maryknoll, NY: Orbis Books, 1987.

Hillman, Eugene. "'Anonymous Christianity' and the Missions." *The Downside Review* 85, no. 277 (1966): 361–79.

Hörger, Paulus. "Concilii Tridentini: de necessitate baptismi doctrina in decreto de iustificatione (Sess. VI)." *Antonianum* 17, no. 3 (1942): 193–222; 17, no. 4 (1942): 269–302.

Hsia, Ronnie Po-Chia. "Theological Developments in the Non-European World, 1500–1800." In Lehner et al., *Oxford Handbook of Early Modern Theology*, 11–24.

Hull, Michael F. *Baptism on Account of the Dead (1 Cor 15:29)*. Atlanta, GA: Society of Biblical Literature, 2005.

Jaspers, Andrew. "What is the eternal destination for deceased embryos?" *Tiny*

Sparks, no. 2, Fall 2018. https://sacredheartguardians.org/wp-content/uploads/2018/08/2018-August-Tiny-Sparks.pdf.

————. "Can Frozen Embryos be Baptized? Part 2." *Tiny Sparks*, no. 4, Fall 2019. https://sacredheartguardians.org/wp-content/uploads/2019/09/Tiny-Sparks-2019-Fall.pdf.

Jedin, Hubert. *A History of the Council of Trent*. Translated by Ernest Graf. Vol. 2, *The First Sessions at Trent, 1545–47*. Edinburgh: Thomas Nelson and Sons, 1961.

Jensen, Robin M. "'With Pomp, Apparatus, Novelty, and Avarice': Alternative Baptismal Practices in Roman Africa." In *Studia Patristica*, vol. 45, edited by J. Baun, A. Cameron, M. Edwards, and M. Vinzent, 77–83. Leuven: Peeters, 2010.

Johnson, Luke Timothy. *The First and Second Letters to Timothy*. The Anchor Bible 35A. New York: Doubleday, 2001.

Jones, Jeffrey M. "U.S. Church Membership Falls Below Majority for First Time." *Gallup*, March 29, 2021. https://news.gallup.com/poll/341963/church-membership-falls-below-majority-first-time.aspx.

Julien, Eugène. "La question sociale et le nombre des élus." *Revue du Clergé Français* 10, no. 60 (1897): 481–500.

Karam, Raymond. "Reply to a Liberal." *From the Housetops* 3, no. 3 (1949). Reprinted, *Catholicism.org*. February 7, 2006. St. Benedict Center, NH: Slaves of the Immaculate Heart of Mary. https://catholicism.org/author/cyrilkaram.

Keefe, Susan A. *Water and the Word: Baptism and the Education of the Clergy in the Carolingian Empire*. 2 vols. Notre Dame, IN: University of Notre Dame Press, 2002.

Keith, Graham. "Justin Martyr and Religious Exclusivism." *Tyndale Bulletin* 43, no. 1 (1992): 57–80.

Kelly, Thomas A. *Sancti Ambrosii Liber de Consolatione Valentiniani: A Text with a Translation, Introduction and Commentary*. Washington, DC: The Catholic University of America Press, 1940.

Kemeny, Paul C. "Peter Abelard: An Examination of His Doctrine of Original Sin." *Journal of Religious History* 16, no. 4 (1991): 374–86.

King, John J. *The Necessity of the Church for Salvation in Selected Theological Writings of the Past Century*. Washington, DC: The Catholic University of America Press, 1960.

King, Peter. "Ockham's Ethical Theory." In Spade, *The Cambridge Companion to Ockham*, 227–44.

King, Ronald F. "The Origin and Evolution of a Sacramental Formula: *Sacramentum tantum, res et sacramentum, res tantum*." *The Thomist* 31, no. 1 (1967): 21–82.

Kolakowski, Leszek. *God Owes Us Nothing: A Brief Remark on Pascal's Religion and on the Spirit of Jansenism*. Chicago: University of Chicago Press, 1995. Kindle.

Küng, Hans. *On Being a Christian*. Translated by Edward Quinn. Garden City, NY: Doubleday, 1976.

Lafaye, Jacques. *Quetzalcóatl and Guadalupe: The Formation of Mexican National Consciousness, 1531–1813*. Translated by Benjamin Keen. Chicago: University of Chicago Press, 1976.

Laisney, François. *Is Feeneyism Catholic? The Catholic Meaning of the Dogma "Outside the Catholic Church There Is No Salvation."* Kansas City, MO: Angelus Press, 2001.

Lamberigts, Mathijs. "Pelagius and Pelagians." In *The Oxford Handbook of Early Christian Studies*, edited by Susan Ashbrook Harvey and David G. Hunter, 258–78. New York: Oxford University Press, 2008.

Landgraf, Artur M. *Dogmengeschichte der Frühscholastik*. Part 3, vol. 1, *Die Lehre von den Sakramenten*. Regensburg: Verlag Friedrich Pustet, 1954.

Landry, Roger. "Praying for Salvific Ignorance for the Clever Hans Küng." *National Catholic Register*. April 10, 2021. https://www.ncregister.com/commentaries/praying-for-father-hans-kueng.

Lauchert, Friedrich. "Albert (Pigghe) Pighius." In *Catholic Encyclopedia*. New York: Encyclopedia Press, 1913. https://en.wikisource.org/wiki/Catholic_Encyclopedia_(1913)/Albert_(Pigghe)_Pighius.

Laurent, M.H. "La causalité sacramentaire d'après le commentaire de Cajetan sur les *Sentences*." *Revue des sciences philosophiques et théologiques* 20, no. 1 (1931): 77–81.

Leal, J. "Tertulliano." In *Letteratura Patristica*, edited by Angelo Di Bernardino, Giorgio Fedalto, and Manlio Simonetti, 1156–162. Cinisello Balsamo: Edizioni San Paolo, 2007.

Levering, Matthew. *Paul in the Summa theologiae*. Washington, DC: The Catholic University of America Press, 2014.

Lewis, Charlton T., and Charles Short. *A Latin Dictionary*. Oxford: Clarendon Press, 1879. Perseus Digital Library. http://www.perseus.tufts.edu/hopper/text?doc=Perseus:text:1999.04.0059.

Lienhard, Joseph T. *The Bible, the Church, and Authority: The Canon of the Christian Bible in History and Theology*. A Michael Glazier Book. Collegeville, MN: Liturgical Press, 1995.

Lookadoo, Jonathon. *The Shepherd of Hermas: A Literary, Historical, and Theological Handbook*. London: T&T Clark, 2021.

Lottin, Odon, ed. *Problèmes d'histoire littéraire: L'école d'Anselme de Laon et de Guillaume de Champeaux*. Vol. 5 of Lottin, *Psychologie et Morale aux XIIe et XIIIe siècles*.

Lynch, Joseph H. *Godparents and Kinship in Early Medieval Europe*. Princeton, NJ: Princeton University Press, 1986.

Manzi, Franco, ed. *Prima lettera ai Corinzi: Introduzione, traduzione e commento.* Cinisello Balsamo: Edizioni San Paolo, 2013.

Marenbon, John. *Pagans and Philosophers.* Princeton, NJ: Princeton University Press, 2015.

Markus, Robert A. "Donatus, Donatism." In Fitzgerald, *Augustine through the Ages,* 284–87.

Marschler, Thomas. "Providence, Predestination, and Grace in Early Modern Catholic Theology." In Lehner et al., *Oxford Handbook of Early Modern Theology,* 89–103.

Martin, Craig. *Subverting Aristotle: Religion, History, and Philosophy in Early Modern Science.* Baltimore: Johns Hopkins University Press, 2014.

Martin, Ralph. *Will Many Be Saved? What Vatican II Actually Teaches and Its Implications for the New Evangelization.* Grand Rapids, MI: Eerdmans, 2012.

Martina, Giacomo. *Pio IX (1851–1866).* Rome: Editrice Pontificia Università Gregoriana, 1986.

Massa, Mark. "On the Uses of Heresy: Leonard Feeney, Mary Douglas, and the Notre Dame Football Team." *Harvard Theological Review* 84, no. 3 (1991): 325–41.

McBrien, Richard P. *Do We Need the Church?* London: Collins, 1969.

———. *Catholicism.* 2 vols. Minneapolis, MN: Winston Press, 1980.

McClymond, Michael J. *The Devil's Redemption: A New History and Interpretation of Christian Universalism.* Grand Rapids, MI: Baker Academic, 2018.

McCool, Gerald A. *A Rahner Reader.* New York: Crossroad, 1981.

———. *Nineteenth-Century Scholasticism: The Search for a Unitary Method.* New York: Fordham University Press, 1989.

———. *The Neo-Thomists.* Milwaukee, Wis.: Marquette University Press, 1994.

McGonigle, Thomas D. "The Significance of Albert the Great's View of Sacrament within Medieval Sacramental Theology." *The Thomist* 44, no. 4 (1980): 560–83.

McGrath, Alister E. *Christian Theology.* Oxford: Blackwell, 2001.

McLeod, Frederick G. "The Christological Ramifications of Theodore of Mopsuestia's Understanding of Baptism and the Eucharist." *Journal of Early Christian Studies* 10, no. 1 (2002): 37–75.

McLynn, Neil B. *Ambrose of Milan: Church and Court in a Christian Capital.* Berkeley: University of California Press, 1994.

Meens, Rob. *Penance in Medieval Europe 600–1200.* Cambridge: Cambridge University Press, 2014.

Mews, Constant J. "The Council of Sens (1141): Abelard, Bernard, and the Fear of Social Upheaval." *Speculum* 77, no. 2 (2002): 342–82.

Michel, A. "Élus (Nombre des)." In *Dictionnaire de théologie Catholique,* vol. 4, edited by A. Vacant and E. Mangenot, 2350–378. Paris: Letouzey et Ané, 1911.

Miner, Earl. "The Wild Man Through the Looking Glass." In *The Wild Man Within: An Image in Western Thought from the Renaissance to Romanticism*, edited by Edward Dudley and Maximillian E. Novak, 87–114. Pittsburgh, PA: University of Pittsburgh Press, 1972.

Mitchell, Nathan. "Christian Initiation: Decline and Dismemberment." *Worship* 48, no. 8 (1974): 458–79.

Montague, George T. *First Corinthians*. Grand Rapids, MI: Baker Academic, 2011.

Morali, Ilaria. "*Gratia* ed *infidelitas*: nella Teologia di Francisco de Toledo e Francisco Suarez al tempo delle grandi missioni gesuitiche." *Studia missionalia* 55 (2006): 99–150.

———. "The Early Modern Period (1453–1650)." In Becker and Morali, *Catholic Engagement with World Religions*, 69–90.

———. "The Travail of Ideas in the Three Centuries Preceding Vatican II (1650–1964)." In Becker and Morali, *Catholic Engagement with World Religions*, 91–121.

Moreschini, Claudio. "Il battesimo come fondamento dell'istruzione del cristiano in Gregorio Nazianzeno." In *Sacerdozio battesimale e formazione teologica nella catechesi e nella testimonianza di vita dei padri*, edited by Sergio Felici, 73–82. Biblioteca di scienze religiose 99. Rome: Libreria Ateneo Salesiano, 1992.

Moriarty, Michael. "The Problem of the Pagans and the Number of the Elect." In Frigo, Inexcusabiles, 67–80.

Morison, Samuel E. *Admiral of the Ocean Sea: A Life of Christopher Columbus*. Boston: Northeastern University Press, 1983.

Most Holy Family Monastery. *VaticanCatholic.com*. Fillmore, NY https://vatican catholic.com

Munck, Johannes. *The Acts of the Apostles: A New Translation with Introduction and Commentary*. The Anchor Bible 31. New York: Doubleday, 1967.

Murray, A. Victor. *Abelard & St Bernard: A Study in Twelfth Century 'Modernism.'* Manchester: Manchester University Press, 1967.

Murray, John Courtney. "Religious Freedom." In *The Documents of Vatican II*, edited by Walter M. Abbott, 672–96. London: Geoffrey Chapman, 1967.

Navatel, Jean-Joseph. "L'apostolat liturgique et la piété personnelle." *Études* 137, no. 4 (1913): 449–76.

Nemer, Lawrence. "Salvation and Mission in Contemporary Catholic Thought." In *Early Proceedings of the Association of Professors of Mission*, vol. 2, *1962–1974*, edited by Robert A. Danielson and David E. Fenrick, 290–320. Wilmore, KY: First Fruits Press, 2015.

Nutt, Roger W. *General Principles of Sacramental Theology*. Washington, DC: The Catholic University of America Press, 2017.

O'Connor, Michael. "The Meritorious Human Life of Jesus: Renaissance

Humanist Tendencies in the Thomism of Cardinal Cajetan." *New Blackfriars* 81, no. 952 (2000): 285–96.

O'Malley, John W. *What Happened at Vatican II.* Cambridge, MA: Harvard University Press, 2008.

———. *Trent: What Happened at the Council.* Cambridge, MA: Harvard University Press, 2013.

Osborne, Thomas M. "Unbelief and Sin in Thomas Aquinas and the Thomistic Tradition." *Nova et Vetera* 8, no. 3 (2010): 613–26.

Osiek, Carolyn. *Shepherd of Hermas: A Commentary.* Minneapolis, MN: Fortress Press, 1999.

Ottolini, Enzo V. *Fede e Sacramenti nella VII sessione del Concilio di Trento.* Rome: Pontificia Università Gregoriana, 1981.

———. "L'istituzione dei sacramenti nella VII sessione del Concilio di Trento." *Rivista Liturgica* 81 (1994): 60–117.

Pasini, Cesare. *Ambrogio di Milano: Azione e pensiero di un vescovo.* Cinisello Balsamo: Edizioni San Paolo, 1997.

Pepper, George B. *The Boston Heresy Case in View of the Secularization of Religion: A Case Study in the Sociology of Religion.* Lewiston, NY: Edwin Mellen Press, 1988.

Perry, John F. "Juan Martínez de Ripalda and Karl Rahner's Supernatural Existential." *Theological Studies* 59, no. 3 (1998): 442–56.

Pinckaers, Servais. *The Sources of Christian Ethics.* Translated by Mary Thomas Noble. Washington, DC: The Catholic University of America Press, 1995.

Podolak, Pietro. *Introduzione a Tertulliano.* Brescia: Morcelliana, 2006.

Pope, Hugh. "Socinianism." In *The Catholic Encyclopedia.* http://www.newadvent.org/cathen/14113a.htm.

Potter, Gary. *After the Boston Heresy Case.* Fitzwilliam, NH: Loreto Publications, 2013. Ebook.

Pricoco, Salvatore. "Gennadio di Marsiglia." In *Nuovo dizionario patristico e di antichità cristiane*, vol. 2, edited by Angelo Di Bernardino. Genova: Marietti 1820, 2007, 2075–76.

Quantin, Jean-Louis. *Il rigorismo cristiano.* Translated G. Cavalli. Milan: Jaca Book, 2002.

Radner, Ephraim. "Early Modern Jansenism." In Lehner et al., *Oxford Handbook of Early Modern Theology*, 436–50.

Rahner, Karl. "Salvation of the Non-Evangelized." In Sacramentum Mundi: *An Encyclopedia of Theology*, vol. 4, edited by Karl Rahner, Juan Alfaro, Alberto Bellini, et al., 79–81. London: Burns & Oates, 1969.

———. "Salvation." In Sacramentum Mundi: *An Encyclopedia of Theology*, vol. 5, edited by Karl Rahner, Juan Alfaro, Alberto Bellini, et al., 405–38. London: Burns & Oates, 1970.

_____. "Atheism and Implicit Christianity." In *Theological Investigations*, vol. 9, translated by Graham Harrison, 145–64. New York: Herder and Herder, 1972.

_____. "Anonymous and Explicit Faith." In *Theological Investigations*, vol. 16, translated by David Morland, 52–59. London: Darton, Longman & Todd, 1979.

_____. "On the Theology of Worship." In *Theological Investigations*, vol. 19, translated by Edward Quinn, 141–49. New York: Crossroads, 1983.

_____. "Anonymous Christians." In *Theological Investigations*, vol. 6, translated by Karl-H. Kruger and Boniface Kruger, 390–98. London: Darton, Longman & Todd, 1984.

_____. "Christianity and the Non-Christian Religions." In *Theological Investigations*, vol. 5, translated Karl-H. Kruger, 115–34. London: Darton, Longman & Todd, 1984.

_____. "Church, Churches and Religions." In *Theological Investigations*, vol. 10, translated by David Bourke, 30–49. London: Darton, Longman & Todd, 1984.

_____. "Anonymous Christianity and the Missionary Task of the Church." In *Theological Investigations*, vol. 12, translated by David Bourke, 161–78. London: Darton, Longman & Todd, 1987.

_____. "The Church's Commission to Bring Salvation and the Humanization of the World." In *Theological Investigations*, vol. 14, translated by David Bourke, 295–313. London: Darton, Longman & Todd, 1987.

_____. *Foundations of Christian Faith.* Translated by William V. Dych. New York: Crossroad Publishing, 1987.

_____. "Observations on the Problem of the 'Anonymous Christian.'" In *Theological Investigations*, vol. 14, 280–94.

Ramage, Matthew. "*Extra Ecclesiam Nulla Salus* and the Substance of Catholic Doctrine: Towards a Realization of Benedict XVI's 'Hermeneutic of Reform.'" *Nova et Vetera* 14, no. 1 (2016): 295–330.

Raphael, Simcha Paull. *Jewish Views of the Afterlife.* Lanham, MD: Rowman & Littlefield, 2019.

Ratzinger, Joseph. "The Church and Man's Calling: Introductory Article and Chapter 1; The Dignity of the Human Person." In Vorgrimler, *Commentary on the Documents of Vatican II*, vol. 5, 115–63.

_____. *Principles of Catholic Theology.* Translated by Mary Frances McCarthy. San Francisco: Ignatius Press, 1987.

_____. *Jesus of Nazareth: From the Baptism in the Jordan to the Transfiguration.* Translated by Adrian J. Walker. New York: Doubleday, 2007.

Rordorf, Willy. "Baptism according to the *Didache*." In *The* Didache *in Modern Research*, edited by Jonathan A. Draper, 212–22. Leiden: Brill, 1996.

Rosemann, Philipp W. *Peter Lombard.* New York: Oxford University Press, 2004. Kindle.

_____. *The Story of a Great Medieval Book Peter Lombard's* Sentences. Toronto: University of Toronto Press, 2007.

Rossi, Giovanni. *L'opinione di Andrea Vega sulla necessità della fede per la giustificazione*. Rome: Scuola Tipografica Pio X, 1942.

Rusch, W.G. "Baptism of Desire in Ambrose and Augustine." In *Studia patristica*, vol. 15, edited by Elizabeth A. Livingstone, 374–78. Berlin: Akademie, 1984.

Russell, David Syme. *Between the Testaments*. Philadelphia: Fortress Press, 1975.

Sachs, John R. "Current Eschatology: Universal Salvation and the Problem of Hell." *Theological Studies* 52 (1991): 227–54.

_____. "Apocatastasis in Patristic Theology." *Theological Studies* 54 (1993): 617–40.

Salomon, David A. *An Introduction to the 'Glossa Ordinaria' as Medieval Hypertext*. Cardiff: University of Wales Press, 2012.

Sanders, Ella K. *Jacques Bénigne Bossuet: A Study*. New York: MacMillan, 1921.

Scerri, Hector. "The Revival of Scholastic Sacramental Theology after the Publication of *Aeterni Patris*." *Irish Theological Quarterly* 77, no. 3 (2012): 265–85.

Schillebeeckx, Edward. *Christ the Sacrament of the Encounter with God*. New York: Sheed and Ward, 1963.

Schmemann, Alexander. *Of Water & the Spirit: A Liturgical Study of Baptism*. Crestwood, NY: St. Vladimir's Seminary Press, 1974.

Schurhammer, Georg. *Francis Xavier*. Vol. 4. Translated by M. Joseph Costelloe. Rome: The Jesuit Historical Institute, 1982.

Scott, James Brown. *The Spanish Origin of International Law: Francisco de Vitoria and his Law of Nations*. Oxford: Clarendon Press, 1934.

Seibel, Wolfgang. "Die vierte Sitzungsperiode des Konzils." *Stimmen der Zeit* 177 (1966): 45–63.

Senior, Donald P. "1 Peter." In *1 Peter, Jude and 2 Peter*, edited by Daniel J. Harrington, 1–173. Sacra Pagina Series 15. Collegeville, MN: Liturgical Press, 2003.

Sesboüé, Bernard. *"Fuori Dalla Chiesa Nessuna Salvezza": Storia di una formula e problemi di interpretazione*. Cinisello Balsamo: Edizioni San Paolo, 2009.

Shea, Charles Michael. "Faith, Reason, and Ecclesiastical Authority in Giovanni Perrone's *Praelectiones theologicae*." *Gregorianum* 95, no. 1 (2014): 159–77.

_____. "*Ressourcement* in the Age of Migne: The Jesuit Theologians of the *Collegio Romano* and the Shape of Modern Catholic Thought." *Nova et Vetera* 15, no. 2 (2017): 579–613.

Shea, Francis S. "The Principles of Extra-Sacramental Justification in Relation to '*Extra ecclesiam nulla salus*.'" In *Proceedings of the Tenth Annual Convention*, 125–51. New York: The Catholic Theological Society of America, 1955.

Sivalon, John C. *God's Mission and Postmodern Culture: The Gift of Uncertainty*. Maryknoll, NY: Orbis, 2012.

Silk, Mark. *Spiritual Politics: Religion and America Since World War II*. New York: Simon and Schuster, 1988.

Smith, Christian. *Soul Searching: The Religious and Spiritual Lives of American Teenagers*. With Melinda Lundquist Denton. New York: Oxford University Press, 2005.

Smith, Shawn C. "Was Justin Martyr an Inclusivist?" *Stone-Campbell Journal* 10 (2007): 193–211.

Sparks, Adam. "Was Justin Martyr a Proto-Inclusivist?" *Journal of Ecumenical Studies* 43, no. 4 (2008): 495–510.

Spinks, Bryan D. *Early and Medieval Rituals and Theologies of Baptism*. Farnham: Ashgate, 2006.

Stark, Rodney. *The Rise of Christianity*. San Francisco: Harper Collins, 1997.

Stogre, Michael. *That the World May Believe: The Development of Papal Social Thought on Aboriginal Rights*. Sherbrooke: Éditions Paulines, 1992.

Stump, Eleonore. *Aquinas*. London: Routledge, 2003.

Sullivan, Francis A. *Salvation Outside the Church? Tracing the History of the Catholic Response*. New York: Paulist Press, 1992.

Taylor, Nicholas H. "Baptism for the Dead (1 Cor 15:29)?" *Neotestamentica* 36, no. 1/2 (2002): 111–20.

Tirimanna, Vimal. "*Logos*: A Bridge-Builder for Interreligious Dialogue?" *Studies in Interreligious Dialogue* 19, no. 2 (2009): 195–214.

Torrell, Jean-Pierre. "Saint Thomas et les non-chrétiens." *Revue thomiste* 106, no. 1/2 (2006): 17–49.

Towner, Philip H. *The Letters to Timothy and Titus: The New International Commentary on the New Testament*. Grand Rapids, MI: Eerdmans, 2006.

Trémolières, François. "The Virtue of the Pagans and the Salvation of the Infidels in the Works of Fénelon." In Frigo, Inexcusabiles, 145–58.

Trigg, Jonathan D. *Baptism in the Theology of Martin Luther*. Leiden: Brill, 1994.

Trumbower, Jeffrey A. *Rescue for the Dead: The Posthumous Salvation of Non-Christians in Early Christianity*. New York: Oxford University Press, 2001.

Umberg, J.B. "Kajetans Lehre von der Kinderersatztaufe auf dem Trienter Konzil." *Zeitschrift für katholische Theologie* 39, no. 3 (1915): 452–64.

Urdanoz, Teofilo. "La necesidad de la fe explícita para salvarse según los teólogos de la Escuela Salmantina." *Ciencia Tomista* 59, no. 4 (1940): 398–414; 59, no. 5/6 (1940): 529–53; 60, no. 2 (1941): 109–34; 61, no. 4 (1941): 83–107.

Van Kley, Dale K. "Catholic Conciliar Reform in an Age of Anti-Catholic Revolution." In *Religious Differences in France: Past and Present*, edited by Kathleen Perry Long, 91–140. Kirksville, MO: Truman State University Press, 2006.

Verbaal, Wim. "The Council of Sens Reconsidered: Masters, Monks, or Judges?" *Church History* 74, no. 3 (2005): 460–93.

Vives, Josep. "Los Padres de la Iglesia ante las religiones no cristianas." *Estudios Eclesiásticos* 79 (1995): 289–316.

Vogel, Cyrille. *Medieval Liturgy: An Introduction to the Sources.* Translated by William G. Storey and Niels K. Rasmussen. Washington, DC: Pastoral Press, 1986.

Walsh, Liam G. "Sacraments." In *The Theology of Thomas Aquinas*, edited by Rik van Nieuwenhove and Joseph Wawrykow, 326–64. Notre Dame, IN: University of Notre Dame Press, 2005.

Waugh, Evelyn. *Brideshead Revisited.* New York: Little, Brown, 2012. Kindle.

Weed, Jennifer Hart. "Thomas Aquinas and the Baptism of Desire." *Res Philosophica* 96, no. 1 (2019): 77–89.

Weingart, Richard E. "Peter Abailard's Contribution to Medieval Sacramentology." *Recherches de théologie ancienne et médiévale* 34 (1967): 159–78.

Weisheipl, J. A. "Cajetan (Tommaso de Vio)." In *New Catholic Encyclopedia*, vol. 2, 1053–55. Washington, DC: The Catholic University of America Press, 1967.

White, Joel R. "'Baptized on Account of the Dead': The Meaning of 1 Corinthians 15:29 in its Context." *Journal of Biblical Literature* 116, no. 3 (1997): 487–99.

Wicks, Jared. Introduction to *Cajetan Responds: A Reader in Reformation Controversy.* Edited by Jared Wicks. Washington, DC: The Catholic University of America Press, 1978.

Williams, George Huntston. "The Sacramental Presuppositions of Anselm's *Cur Deus Homo.*" *Church History* 26, no. 3 (1957): 245–74.

Winslow, D. F. "Orthodox Baptism—A Problem for Gregory of Nazianzus." In *Studia Patristica*, vol. 14, edited by Elizabeth A. Livingstone, 371–74. Berlin: Akademie, 1976.

Yarnold, Edward. *The Awe-Inspiring Rites of Initiation: The Origins of the R.C.I.A.* Edinburgh: T&T Clark, 1994.

Yates, Arthur S. *Why Baptize Infants? A Study of the Biblical, Traditional and Theological Evidence.* Norwich: The Canterbury Press, 1993.

Yong, Peter, and Eric Watkins. "Kant's Philosophical and Theological Commitments." In Lehner et al., *Oxford Handbook of Early Modern Theology*, 601–7.

Zuijdwegt, Geertjan. "Salvation and the Church: Feeney, Fenton and the Making of *Lumen Gentium.*" *Louvain Studies* 37 (2013): 147–78.

Index

Abelard. *See* Peter Abelard

afterlife: Gehenna, 12–13; pre-Christian views, 11–13, 43, 285; Sheol, 11–13. *See also* beatific vision; hell; limbo; purgatory

Alan of Lille. *See fluminis, flaminis, sanguinis*

Alcuin of York, 116–17, 317

Alvarez, Diego, 238

Amalarius of Metz, 114

Ambrose: on baptism, sin, and faith, 66–70; *uoluntas* and *petitio*, 72–73; Valentinian's death and, 63–65. *See also* Ambrose, works

Ambrose, works: *On Abraham*, 66–67, 69; *De obitu Valentiniani*, 70–74; *The Mysteries*, 68; *The Sacraments*, 68, 69

Ambrosiaster, 134

Anonymous Christianity: baptism of desire and, 311–15; context, 303–4; critiques of, 307–10; Justin Martyr and, 19–23; theory of, 304–7

Anselm of Canterbury, 114–15

Anselm of Laon: *Liber pancrisis*, 130; *Sententie divine pagine*, 126–29. *See also* school of Laon

apokatastasis, 43–60, 311

Aquinas. *See* Thomas Aquinas

Arbogast, 63–64, 72. *See also* Ambrose

Arnauld, Antoine, 194, 246–50

articulus necessitatis: Augustine's formulation of, 82–83; in medieval theology, 129, 132, 150, 167, 184; twentieth-century disappearance, 302. *See also contemptus religionis*

Augustine of Hippo: *articulus necessitatis*, 82–83; conditions for salvation, 82, 96; *contemptus religionis*, 82–83, 94; Cyril of Jerusalem and, 87; *ex opere operato*, 78; experience of baptism, 94; familiarity with *De obitu Valentiniani*, 79n38; on the Good Thief, 81–85, 89, 91–94; original sin, 86–89; position on baptism of desire, 77–78, 94–97; principles of baptism of desire, 83–84; response to Cyprian of Carthage, 79, 81–85, 92; response to Vincent Victor, 92–93. *See also* Augustine of Hippo, works

Augustine of Hippo, works: *The City of God*, 80, 96, 115; *De baptismo contra Donatistas*, 78–85, 93–94, 96, 121, 129; *De peccatorum meritis et remissione, et de baptismo parvulorum*, 86–89; *Eighty-Three Different Questions*, 93;

Augustine of Hippo, works: (*cont.*)
  On the Nature and Origin of the Soul,
  92; *Retractationes,* 93, 129
authority, ecclesiastical, 269, 286–287

Baghos, Mario, 48
Baius, Michael, 245
Balthasar, Hans Urs von, 310
Bañez, Domingo, 233n118, 238, 239n132
baptism: apostles', 31–32, 41, 164–65;
  Gregory Nazianzen's five types,
  56–57; invisible, 82; Jesus's, 56; John
  Damascene's eight types, 105–6;
  objective and subjective dimensions
  of, 79–81, 83–84; politics and, 115–17,
  232; preparation required of converts,
  207–8; *quamprimum,* 110, 112, 117; seal
  of, 17–18, 52, 79, 169–70; unrepeatable,
  156, 160, 176, 335. *See also* baptism,
  necessity of; baptism, precursors of;
  baptism of desire; blood, baptism
  of; character; faith; fire, baptism of;
  fluminis, flaminis, sanguinis; infant
  baptism; posthumous baptism; rebaptism; rite of baptism; tears, baptism of
baptism, necessity of: in Aquinas's
  works, 163–64, 171, 174–75; Council of
  Trent, 226, 230; denied by Anonymous Christianity, 314–15; in early
  modernity, 192; Giovanni Perrone's
  discussion of, 270–72; grounding for,
  338–42; as legal obligation, 124, 338;
  in the Middle Ages, 112; in the patristic era, 61, 106–7; in the twentieth
  century, 323, 325
baptism, precursors of: ablutions of the
  Law, 105; baptism of Moses, 39n100,
  41, 56, 91, 105; circumcision, 67, 68,
  126–27, 130, 137, 139, 141, 202–3; Gentile practices, 76, 139, 141, 146; healing
  at the pool of Bethsaida, 76; Old

Testament precedents, 27–28, 75–76,
  105, 167, 351; Old Testament rituals,
  96–97. *See also* John the Baptist
baptism, ritual. *See* rite of baptism
baptism of desire: Aquinas's conception of, 160–183; Augustine's
  principles of, 83–84; before baptism
  vs. at moment of death, 186, 221–22,
  335–36, 345; birth of the doctrine,
  63–65; defined, 1–2; the doctrine's
  history, summary of, 331–38; in early
  modernity, 189–90, 252; introduction,
  1–7; limits, 100, 186; in the Long
  Nineteenth Century, 253–55, 279,
  329–30; patristic doctrine summarized, 106–9; patristic precursors,
  8–9, 61–62; scholasticism and, 122–25,
  187–88; waning interest in, 183, 187,
  230–31. *See also articulus necessitatis; baptism; baptismus flaminis;
  contemptus religionis;* Cornelius (Acts
  10); Good Thief, the (Luke 23); hard
  cases; *sacramentum/res* distinction
baptism of desire, terminology: baptism of charity, 85; baptism of repen-
  tence (*poenitentiae*), 167; *in re/in voto*
  distinction, 224, 236, 252, 271, 287n118;
  in voto, 210, 212, 223–24, 226–28, 240,
  249. *See also baptismus flaminis*
baptismus flaminis: early modern usage,
  189, 203, 204; *ex opere operantis* and,
  234–35; medieval usage, 171–72, 184,
  185–86; superseded by *in voto* at
  Council of Trent, 223. *See also fluminis, flaminis, sanguinis*
Basil the Great, 53–55
Baum, Gregory, 4, 352
beatific vision: supernatural existential
  and, 306–7, 309; unbaptized children
  and, 161, 197, 209, 216, 277
Bede, the Venerable, 119–21

belief. *See* faith

Bellarmine, Robert: baptism of desire and ecclesiology, 235–36; necessity of precept and of means, 233–35. *See also* Suárez, Francisco

Benedict XVI (pope), 309, 330

Bergin, Joseph, 247

Bernard of Clairvaux: *Letter 77 to Hugh of St. Victor*, 138–42. *See also* invincible ignorance

Beuchot, Maurice, 202

Bible: 1 Corinthians 15, 13–15, 17, 18, 47, 235; 1 Timothy 2, 308, 323, 342; Acts 2:38, 1, 10, 331n2, 361; Galatians 3:27, 217–18; John 3:5, 8, 10, 24, 39, 41, 53, 67, 87n60, 98, 119n26, 132, 133, 139, 143, 150, 153, 172, 179, 185, 247, 271, 331n2; Mark 10:38–39, 1, 10, 244n146, 331n1, 332n4; Mark 16:16, 10, 11n5, 203, 331n2; Romans 6:3–5, 120, 300; Romans 10:10, 82, 83, 120, 149. *See also* Cornelius (Acts 10); Good Thief, the (Luke 23); Lazarus (Luke 16); Nicodemus, Christ's conversation with (John 3:5); Simeon (Luke 2)

Billot, Louis (cardinal), 282–84

blood, baptism of: baptism in water and, 46, 52–53; character and, 169, 177; *ex opere operato* and, 234; faith and, 142, 144; the Good Thief and, 40, 82, 120; Holy Innocents and, 175n213, 212; John the Baptist and, 106; precedent for baptism of desire, 32, 40, 74, 244; reception of *res* without *sacramentum*, 152–53; sacramental obligation and, 185; type or mode of baptism, 40, 56–57, 67n5, 105, 119, 150, 167–68. *See also* baptism; *fluminis, flaminis, sanguinis*

Bonaventure, 160–61

Bonizo of Sutri, 121, 129

Bossuet, Jacques-Benigne, 260, 261

Boston Heresy Case. *See* Feeney episode, the

Cajetan (Thomas de Vio): baptism of desire, unbaptized and unborn children, 210–12; commentary on Aquinas's *Summa theologiae*, 209–10; discussed by Council of Trent, 213–14. *See also* Perrone, Giovanni

Canisius, Peter, 245

Cano, Melchor, 201, 233n118, 236, 238

Capéran, Louis, 6, 241, 244, 247, 288n119

Cappadocians, 42. *See also* Basil the Great; Gregory Nazianzen; Gregory of Nyssa

Carey, Patrick, 290, 292

Carola, Joseph, 269

Carolingian Age: baptismal policies, 113, 116–17, 118–19; forced baptisms, 116–17

Casel, Odo, 299–300

catechumens: baptism of desire and, 70, 147, 201–2, 208, 294, 345; Church membership, 236; Corinthian solution and, 14n14, 15; deceased, salvation of, 33–34, 40, 41–42, 98, 130–31, 135; delaying baptism, 33, 52–53, 54, 57–59, 337; explicit faith and, 242; faith, 141–42, 154, 218–19; funerary inscriptions and, 30; implicit desire and, 179; *lex orandi* and, 353; *Lumen Gentium* and, 319; unsaved, 102, 121, 168, 235. *See also* Ambrose

Catharism, 158

Cavallera, Ferdinand, 227

character: Aquinas's treatment of, 168–70; effect of baptism, 166; grace and, 160, 170, 312; indelible seal and, 169; as mark of Christ the king, 150; supernatural existential and, 312

Charlemagne. *See* Carolingian Age

Christ: baptism of, 165, 229n110; fullness of revelation, 95–96; merits of, sole remedy for original sin, 217–18, 229. *See also* Paschal Mystery, participation in

Church: ecclesiological focus since Vatican I, 286–87; membership, characteristics that define, 235–36; membership *in voto*, 240; necessity of, 95, 99n100, 189, 236, 319; soul/body, invisible/visible, 236, 287, 291, 296. *See also extra ecclesiam nulla salus;* Vatican II

circumcision. *See* baptism, precursors of

Colish, Marcia, 77–78, 119, 121, 122, 135, 136, 138, 148, 160, 183, 185, 187

Collius, Francesco, 245, 246

confession (penance), sacrament of: Jansenist controversy, 250; means of salvation, 266; perfect charity and, 294; rigorism and, 262. *See also* tears, baptism of

Congar, Yves, 268, 281n101, 284n110

contemptus religionis: Augustine's formulation of, 82–83, 94; in medieval theology, 129, 132, 150, 152–53, 158, 166, 167, 172, 184; in modern theology, 272, 302. *See also articulus necessitatis*

contrition, 152, 158, 166, 226n101, 234–35, 255n3

conversion: baptism and, 33, 99; facilitated by catechesis, 207; of heart, 85; perfect, required for baptism *flaminis*, 234–35; for salvation, 81–82, 83, 95

Corinthians, 13–15. *See also* baptism; Bible; Paul; *Shepherd* of Hermas

Cornelius (Acts 10): Augustine's use of, 82, 83, 91–92, 108; baptism of the Holy Spirit and, 41; baptism's

necessity and, 53, 98, 108, 130, 184; Basil's treatment of, 54; Council of Trent and, 221; implicit faith and, 249; Irenaeus's interpretation, 27, 335; medieval scholastics and, 121, 129, 130, 134, 137, 150, 171; natural reason and, 182; reception of *res* before *sacramentum*, 129, 153, 168, 176; weak interpretation, 312

council. *See* Florence, Council of; Trent, Council of; Vatican II

Cramer, Peter, 102, 154, 195, 357

Crouzel, Henri, 44

Cuchet, Guillaume, 262, 265

Cushing, Richard (archbishop). *See* Feeney episode, the

Cyprian of Carthage: about, 34–35; Augustine's response to, 79, 81–85, 92; on baptism, 38–40; *extra ecclesiam nulla salus*, 35–38. *See also On Rebaptism* (Anonymous)

Cyril of Jerusalem: Augustine and, 87; *Catechetical Lectures*, 52–53

Daley, Brian, 54–55, 60, 99

Daniélou, Jean, 326n241, 352

Dante Alighieri, 161, 192, 194, 282

dead, the. *See* afterlife; catechumens; non-Christians; righteous dead (Old Testament); unbaptized infants

deism, 243, 248, 249, 256, 257

De Roten, Philippe, 98

desire: act of perfect charity, 294–95, 296, 345; *aut eius/eorum voto*, 221, 226, 287, 346; human will and, 96, 179; knowledge and, 28, 96–97, 179; partial, weak, or hypothetical, 348–49; quality of, 72–73; for water baptism necessary for baptism of desire, 343–46. *See also* baptism of desire;

implicit desire; intention; *votum;* will, human

determinism, 48

Didache, 18–19

Diekman, Godfrey, 226

disciplina arcani, 69

divine law, 111, 143, 202

Donatist controversy, 78–81

Donnelly, Philip J. *See* Feeney episode, the

Driscoll, Jeremy, 26

Drummond, Richard H., 24

Dulles, Avery, 237, 289, 347n6

Duval, André, 225

Eagleton, Terry, 343

ecclesiology. *See* Church

elect, number of the, 283–86. *See also* Faber, Frederick William; Lacordaire, Henri; Suárez, Francisco

Eminyan, Maurice, 286, 302

Enlightenment, the, 250, 254–60, 277

Eucharist: implicit desire and, 177–78; *lex orandi* and, 88n64; medieval accentuation of, 114–15; participation in, 25; *sacramentum/res* distinction, 128; Trent's decree on, 215. *See also* sacraments

evangelization: early medieval missions, 116; early modern missions, 190–91; undercut by twentieth-century theology, 326–29. *See also* Anonymous Christianity; Las Casas, Bartolomé de; Vitoria, Francisco de; Xavier, Francis

ex opere operato, 78, 204, 212, 234, 239

extra ecclesiam nulla salus, 35, 124, 235–36, 273, 286–88, 290. *See also* Feeney episode, the

Faber, Frederick William, 265–67

faith: act of, sufficient for salvation, 243; alone, 215, 216, 226, 234; baptism and, 100–101, 106, 166, 226; condition for baptism of desire, 158, 294, 296; evolution of concept of, 154–55, 218–19; *fides late* insufficient for justification, 251; minimum of, 240–45; salvation and, 142, 144–46, 258. *See also* faith, explicit; faith, implicit

faith, explicit, 182, 199, 207, 240–42, 274

faith, implicit: Hugh's understanding of, 146–47; not general belief, 243; pagans, non-Christians and, 246–48; primitive revelation as basis for, 239. *See also* Thomas Aquinas

Feeney, Leonard. *See* Feeney episode, the

Feeney episode, the: context, 289–92; doctrinal conflict, 292–95; *Suprema haec sacra,* 295–98. *See also extra ecclesiam nulla salus*

Fenton, Joseph Clifford, 276, 277, 278, 280, 293, 344

Ferguson, Everett, 8, 16, 29–30, 59n171, 101

fire, baptism of, 46, 49, 57, 67n5, 264–65

Fitzmyer, Joseph, 14

Fletcher, Richard, 117

Florence, Council of, 189–90, 210, 276

fluminis, flaminis, sanguinis: Alan of Lille's triad, 158, 160, 167; Aquinas's defense of, 171–72; *flaminis, sanguinis, et aquae,* 204, 210

freedom, 120, 251, 305, 317–18, 324, 341–42, 357

French Revolution, 253, 257, 261, 269, 329, 342. *See also* Enlightenment, the

Fulgentius of Ruspe, 101

funerary inscriptions, 29–30. *See also* Theudosius

Garrigou–Lagrange, Réginald, 282

Gehenna, 12–13. *See also* afterlife; hell

Gelasianum Vetus, 113

Gennadius of Massilia: *Liber de eccle-siasticis dogmatibus*, 103, 135; opposition to baptism of desire, 65, 102–3, 223n94, 235, 336; parallel between martyrdom and rite of baptism, 107, 168, 336–37; scholasticism and, 121, 135, 139, 151, 153, 168. *See also* blood, baptism of

Gilbert of Poitiers, 149

Girolimon, Michael, 142, 143, 144, 147

Gnosticism, 25, 30

Good Thief, the (Luke 23): Ambrose's exegesis, 73n25; Augustine's interpretation, 65, 81–85, 89, 90, 91–94, 108, 129, 134, 152, 333–34; ethical approach to salvation and, 352–53; intention and, 99–101; as martyr, 40, 82, 92–93, 120–21, 152; participation in Jesus's death, 336; Romans 10:10 and, 82, 120; salvation without water baptism, 81–82, 99–100, 133, 149, 152–53, 272

grace: character and, 160, 170, 312; effect of baptism, 166; not conferred by baptism of desire, 204; as theological focus, 154–55

Gratian, 121

Gregory, Brad, 200, 231–32

Gregory I, the Great (pope), 102

Gregory IX (pope), 158–59

Gregory Nazianzen: against baptism of desire, 58, 72, 106; classes of the unbaptized, 59; introduction, 55; *Oration 39*, 56–57, 119; *Oration 40*, 57–61; types of baptism, 56–57, 67n5, 105. *See also* Cappadocians

Gregory of Nyssa: *On Infants' Early Deaths*, 49–51; *On the Soul and the Resurrection*, 47–49. *See also* apoka-tastasis

Gregory XVI (pope), 260n28, 261

Grellard, Christophe, 218, 226

Grillo, Andrea, 118n20, 258, 299, ix

Grossi, Vittorino, 79–80

Guardini, Romano, 299–300, 352

Gumpel, Peter, 302n170, 356, 358

hard cases: baptism of desire as approach to, 1–7, 215, 228; created by necessity of baptism, 8–9; scholasticism and, 111; unbaptized priest (Innocent II), 158–59. *See also* catechumens; Corinthians; non-Christians; unbaptized infants

Harmless, William, 94, 99

hell: eternity of, 21–22, 43, 45, 51, 55, 61; non-Christians and, 198, 205, 256, 353; punishment and, 60, 88, 161n167, 210; unbaptized infants and, 50, 86. *See also* afterlife; elect, number of the

heretics: baptism by, 37, 79; reception of baptism, 82; salvation of, 79, 273

Hermas. *See Shepherd* of Hermas

Hick, John, 283

Hugh of St. Victor: *De Sacramentis*, 142–48; effect of geographical knowledge on soteriology, 124–25; treatment of faith, 144–47. *See also* faith, implicit; legal framework

Ignatius of Loyola, 301

ignorance, invincible. *See* invincible ignorance

implicit desire: Ambrose's theology and, 75–76; Aquinas's concept of, 177–83; infants and, 354–59; non-Christians and, 346–54; orientation toward baptism, 229, 347–48

implicit error, 178

Incarnation: Incarnational logic, 15, 43; sacraments and, 173–74

infant baptism: Aquinas's defense of, 166, 175; faith and, 83–84; Giovanni Perrone on, 270; Gregory Nazianzen on, 59; medieval meaning of, 195; medieval shift, 112–15; original sin and, 37, 88; *Pastoralis actio*, 356–57. *See also* funerary inscriptions; unbaptized infants

Innocent II (pope). *See* hard cases

intention: the Good Thief and, 99–101; velleity vs., 293, 344. *See also* Ambrose; desire

invincible ignorance: Bernard of Clairvaux's application of, 139–40; Billot's "moral infants" thesis and, 282–83; Francisco de Vitoria's analysis, 204–7; Giovanni Perrone's understanding of, 273–74; not a patristic concept, 98n96, 124; original sin and, 206; Pius IX on, 275–78; twentieth-century theology and, 279–86, 320. *See also* limbo

Irenaeus: on desire, 28; *Against Heresies*, 25–29; *regula fidei*, 26

Isidore of Seville, 105n11, 119

Ivo of Chartres, 121

Jansenism: about, 245–46; Roman intervention, 250–51. *See also* Arnauld, Antoine

Jedin, Hubert, 216, 219, 220

Jefferson, Thomas, 259–60

Jerome, 99

John Chrysostom, 97–99

John Damascene: *An Exact Exposition of the Orthodox Faith*, 105–6; antecedent and consequent will, 105; *The Fount of Knowledge*, 104–5; types of baptism, 105–6

John Duns Scotus, 185–87

John Paul II (pope), 327–28

Johnson, Luke Timothy, 308

John the Baptist: baptism by, 32, 56, 106, 167, 235n123; baptism of, 106; salvation of, 91, 137, 147–48, 179, 212, 333. *See also* non-Christians

Judas, 51

justification: Council of Trent's decree on, 219–25; pre-baptismal, 155–56, 313; process inseparable from sacraments, 219–20

Justin Martyr: *Dialogue with Trypho*, 23; *First Apology*, 20–22; Rahner and, 19–20, 24; *Second Apology*, 23. *See also* Anonymous Christianity; non-Christians

Kant, Immanuel: parallel with Ockhamist ethics, 230–31; religious ritual, attitude toward, 257–59

Karam, Raymond. *See* Feeney episode, the

Keefe, Susan, 117

Keith, Graham, 23, 24

King, John J., 285, 287

King, Ronald F., 128

Küng, Hans, 280–81, 283

Lacordaire, Henri: context, 261–62; non-Christians and baptism of desire/fire, 264–65; number of the elect, 262–64, 284, 285. *See also* elect, number of the

La Mothe Le Vayer, François de, 246–47

Landgraf, Artur Michael, 123, 129

Laon, school of. *See* school of Laon

Las Casas, Bartolomé de, 197–98

law. *See* divine law; natural law; New Law; Old Law

Lazarus (Luke 16), 98

legal framework, 123, 139–40, 202, 321, 334, 341. *See also* Bernard of Clairvaux; Hugh of St. Victor; Major, John

Leo I, the Great (pope), 101

Leo XIII (pope), 209, 282

Lessius, Leonardus, 245

lex orandi: corollary with *lex credendi*, 208; need to return to, 330; prebaptismal baptism irreconcilable with, 186; study's emphasis on, 6; twentieth-century theology's distance from, 298, 302; the unbaptized and, 159; unbaptized infants and, 355–56

Liguori, Alphonsus, 255n3

limbo: adults and, 161, 194, 197, 282–83; in early modernity, 197; in medieval tradition, 132, 134, 137, 160–61, 194, 209; in the nineteenth century, 263, 272, 277; patristic precursors, 59, 67, 88; virtuous pagans and, 277. *See also* Sheol

"Little Theudosius." *See* Theudosius

Liturgical Movement: modern minimization of liturgy, 300–302; sense of religious ritual, 299–300

Lugo, Juan De (cardinal), 239–40

Luther, Martin, 209, 214, 215, 231

Major, John, 202–3

Maluf, Fakhri. *See* Feeney episode, the

Maréchal, Joseph, 258

Marenbon, John, 146, 192–93, 232, 245

Martin, Ralph, 320

martyrdom. *See* blood, baptism of; Good Thief, the (Luke 23); rite of baptism

Massa, Mark, 290–91

McBrien, Richard, 254

McLeod, Frederick, 100

Medina, Bartolomé de, 238

mission. *See* evangelization; Vatican II

Mitchell, Nathan, 114, 123, 154

Montague, George T., 15

Moreschini, Claudio, 55

Murray, John Courtney, 318

mystery. *See* Liturgical Movement; Paschal Mystery, participation in

Napoleon, 261, 269

natural law: first moral act, 238–40, 282; remedies of, 127; sacraments of, 143, 202; salvation and, 199, 229, 276, 353, 356

Navatel, Jean-Joseph, 300–302. *See also* Liturgical Movement

necessity of means. *See* necessity of precept

necessity of precept: context, 123; distinction between necessity of means and, 233–35, 271, 286; inadequacy, 298

New Law, 202–3, 226, 228. *See also* necessity of precept

Nicholas I (pope), 118

Nicodemus, Christ's conversation with (John 3:5), 139, 141, 150

nominalism, 202, 218, 226, 230–31, 234, 341

non-Christians: atheists, 20, 35, 196n14, 256n5, 281n101, 284, 327n244; Gentiles, 22, 27, 28–29, 134, 179–82, 228, 308, 335. *See also* Anonymous Christianity; evangelization; invincible ignorance; Lacordaire, Henri; Old Testament; pagans; "promulgation of the Gospel"; religions, non-Christian; universalism

Ockham. *See* William of Ockham

Old Law: observances and salvation,

139–40, 228–29, 351; sacraments, 96–97, 162, 179–80, 228. *See also* baptism, precursors of; New Law

Old Testament. *See* baptism, precursors of; Old Law; righteous dead (Old Testament)

O'Malley, John, 253, 316

On Rebaptism (Anonymous), 40–42

Origen: baptism of fire and of blood, 46–47; *extra ecclesiam nulla salus,* 35n89; *On First Principles,* 44–45; Gregory Nazianzen and, 60

original sin: Augustine's articulation of, 86–89; Council of Trent's decree on, 216–18; doctrine anticipated by Cyprian of Carthage, 37; Enlightenment attitudes toward, 256, 259; infants and, 89–90, 277; invincible ignorance and, 206; need for a savior and, 87; in Peter Abelard's theology, 136–37; supernatural existential and, 313; the unevangelized and, 203

Osiek, Carolyn, 17

Otto of Freising, 149

pagans: Augustine's critique, 96, 115; Justin Martyr on, 20–24; of modernity, 246–47; salvation of, 75, 191–96, 245, 246–47; Valentinian's rejection of paganism, 75. *See also* faith, implicit

Paschal Mystery, participation in, 32, 80, 95, 155, 157, 190, 229, 231, 300, 321, 323, 340

Patrick (saint), 118

Paul (apostle), 9–10, 13–15, 300. *See also* Bible

Paul VI (pope): *Ecclesiam Suam,* 324–25; *Evangelii Nuntiandi,* 325–26

Pelagianism, 85–89, 92, 216, 243n144, 248, 306, 312

penance: medieval shift in penitential disciplines, 114; pre-baptismal, 70–71, 123. *See also* confession (penance), sacrament of

Perrone, Giovanni: background, 269–70; *extra ecclesiam nulla salus* and invincible ignorance, 273–74, 281; fate of unbaptized and unborn children, 272–73; necessity of baptism, 270–72; non-Catholic Christians and salvation, 270. *See also* Pius IX (pope)

Peter Abelard: *Commentary on the Epistle to the Romans,* 137–38; on original sin, 136–37; *Sic et Non,* 134–35; *Theologia Christiana,* 135–36

Peter Chrysologus, 101

Peter Comestor, 158

Peter Lombard: baptism and justification, 155–56; *sacramentum/res* distinction, 152–53; *Sentences,* 151–57. *See also* *sacramentum/res* distinction

Peter of Poitiers, 158

Peter of Tarentaise, 183–84

Peter the Chanter, 158

Pinckaers, Servais, 230–31, 237, 250, 258, 298

Pius IX (pope): on invincible ignorance, 275–78, 279; *Quanto conficiamur,* 275–76, 278, 279; *Singulari quadam,* 275, 277, 278, 280; *Singulari quidem,* 275; *Syllabus of Errors,* 278

Pius XII (pope): *Humani generis,* 297; *Mystici Corporis Christi,* 295–96, 297

Plato. *See* Platonism

Platonism: *apokatastasis* and, 43, 45, 47, 48, 51; comparison to Christianity, 21–22, 23; post-mortem punishment, 21; reincarnation, 89. *See also* pagans

posthumous baptism. *See* Corinthians; *Shepherd* of Hermas

Potter, Gary, 296

precept, necessity of. *See* necessity of precept

predestination, 6, 137–38, 223, 241, 250–51, 260, 304

"promulgation of the Gospel," 224–25, 271, 273

propositum, 99, 224n97

Protestantism, 214, 269–70, 273–74. *See also* Luther, Martin

Pullen, Robert (cardinal), 148–49

punishment: fire and, 60–61; ignorance as, 90; limbo and, 131–32; of non-Christians, 199; as non-salvific baptism, 105–6; Platonism and, 21, 43; pre-baptismal justification and, 155–56; temporal, remitted (partially) by baptism of desire, 155, 168, 184; of unbelief, eliminated by invincible ignorance, 206. *See also* hell; limbo

purgatory, 45, 51, 176, 177, 235, 336

Rahner, Karl, 200, 258, 284. *See also* Anonymous Christianity

Raphael, Simcha Paull, 11

Ratzinger, Joseph. *See* Benedict XVI (pope)

rebaptism. *See* Cyprian of Carthage; Donatist controversy; *On Rebaptism* (Anonymous)

Reformation, Protestant, 214

regula fidei, 26, 51, 55

religions, non-Christian: implicit desire and, 75, 351–52; *Nostra Aetate* and, 318–19; patristic views on, 19; Paul VI on, 325; salvation, 49n133, 96, 106, 198, 278; "the seeds of the truth," 22–23. *See also* non-Christians

repentance: baptism of, 158n160, 167–68, 235n123; post-baptismal, 105. *See also* tears, baptism of

res sacramenti. *See* sacramentum/res distinction

righteous dead (Old Testament), 27–29, 31, 95–96. *See also* baptism, precursors of; Old Law

rigorism, 262, 265, 267

Ripalda, Juan Martínez de, 238, 243n144, 251, 311

rite of baptism: commitment required, 344–45; core of Christian proclamation, 106; irreducible importance of, 232; martyrdom and, 102, 168; participation in salvation, 342; ritual minimalism, 112–15, 208, 232; Thomistic notion of congruence and, 165. *See also Didache*; *lex orandi*; sacraments

ritual. *See* Kant, Immanuel; Liturgical Movement; rite of baptism

Robert of Melun, 148–49

Roland of Bologna, 148

Roman Missal, The, 356

Rousseau, Jean Jacques, 256–57

Sachs, John R., 60

sacraments: Anonymous Christianity and, 313–15; God not bound by, 147, 149, 150–51, 155, 157, 164–65; institution of, 147, 156–57; marginalization in discussions of salvation, 231–32; necessity of, 163–65, 172–75, 192, 202, 226; validity and fruitfulness, 78–79. *See also* baptism; baptism, necessity of; baptism, precursors of; confession (penance), sacrament of; Eucharist; *lex orandi*

sacramentum. *See* sacramentum/res distinction

sacramentum/res distinction: medieval usage of framework, 131, 148, 150, 151–54, 184; reception of *res* without *sacramentum* and vice versa, 165–67, 168, 185–86; *res* as faith necessary for baptism, 128–29, 132; *res* as forgiveness, remission of guilt, 152, 155; *res* as "ultimate effect of baptism," 169. *See also* Cornelius (Acts 10)

Salamanca, School of, 201, 233n118; response to baptismal controversy, 207–9. *See also* Vitoria, Francisco de

salvation: of baptized infants, 83–84, 98–99; conditions for, 82, 264–65; effect of geographical knowledge on soteriology, 124–25, 191–93; gratuitousness of, 89; necessity of Catholicism for, 278; non-Catholic Christians and, 270, 271; soteriological shifts, 267–68, 284–85, 326; suffering and, 93–94, 167, 185. *See also* Anonymous Christianity; *articulus necessitatis;* baptism, necessity of; baptism of desire; Church; *contemptus religionis;* elect, number of the; non-Christians; Paschal Mystery, participation in; sacraments; unbaptized infants

Schillebeeckx, Edward, 200, 303, 313n202

schism: baptism and schismatics, 39, 79–80; Church membership and schismatics, 236; *extra ecclesiam nulla salus* and, 35–36, 286; Great Western Schism, 189

Schmemann, Alexander, 155, 157

scholasticism, medieval: baptism of desire and, 122–25, 187–88; interest in theological conundrums, 111. *See also sacramentum/res* distinction; Thomas Aquinas

scholasticism, post-Tridentine. *See* Suárez, Francisco

school of Laon: about, 126;

groundwork for theory of limbo, 88; on pre-Christian rites, 229; unattributable sentences, 132–33. *See also* Anselm of Laon; William of Champeaux

Schurhammer, Georg, 198–99, 200, 201

Semmelroth, Otto, 303

Senior, Donald, 12–13

Sententiae divinitatis (Anonymous), 149

Seripando, Girolomo, 213, 224, 229

Sesboüé, Bernard, 6, 10n4, 12, 19n29, 35n90

Sheol, 11–13. *See also* afterlife; limbo

Shepherd of Hermas, 15–18, 74

Simeon (Luke 2), 28, 333, 348, 351, 353

Simon, Master, 150

Simon the Magician (Acts 8), 91, 99

sin: in Ambrose's theology, 67–68; first moral act and, 282; personal, 195; post-baptismal, 29, 32, 40; of schism, 79; of unbelief, 205. *See also* original sin

Smalley, Beryl, 126

solipsism, 80

Soto, Domingo de, 201–2

Sozzini, Fausto, 271

St. Benedict Center. *See* Feeney episode, the

Suárez, Francisco: first moral act, 238–40; flaws in his theology, 243–45; minimum necessary faith, 240–43; number of the elect, 237–38, 241. *See also* Bellarmine, Robert; elect, number of the

Sullivan, Francis, 6, 35–36, 37, 124, 191–92, 273, 275, 276, 280, 325, 327

Summa sententiarum (Anonymous), 148

supernatural existential. *See* Anonymous Christianity

Tatian, 19

Taylor, Nicholas H., 14

tears, baptism of, 57, 107, 119

Tertullian: *De baptismo*, 30–32; *De paenitentia*, 32–34

Theodore of Mopsuestia, 99–101

Theudosius, 103–4, 211, 356

Thomas Aquinas: baptism of desire vs. baptism, 176–77; effects, recipients, and modes of baptism, 165–68; implicit desire and explicit faith, 177–83; intrinsic relationship of *flaminis* to *fluminis*, 171–72; introduction, 160–62; necessity, categories of, 163–65, 172–75; sacramental character, 168–70. *See also* Billot, Louis (cardinal); Thomas Aquinas, works

Thomas Aquinas, works: *Commentary on the Sentences*, 162–70; *De veritate*, 181–83; *Summa theologiae*, 170–81

Tírechán. *See* Patrick (saint)

Towner, Philip H., 308

Trent, Council of: on baptism of desire, 221–24, 226–27; on Cajetan's proposal, 213–14; faith, concept of, 218–19; introduction and evaluation, 214–15, 227–29; on justification, 219–25; on original sin, 216–19; on sacraments, 225–27

Umberg, J.B., 213

unbaptized infants: Augustinian position on, 51n140, 86–89, 92, 95, 134, 153–54; baptism of desire and, 141, 354–59; incapable of negligence, 130–31. *See also* Cajetan (Thomas de Vio); Gregory Nazianzen; Gregory of Nyssa; implicit desire; infant baptism; limbo; Perrone, Giovanni

unborn children, 359. *See also* Cajetan (Thomas de Vio); Perrone, Giovanni

unevangelized, the. *See* non-Christians

universalism: *apokatastasis* and, 42–43, 45, 47; rejection of, 55, 95, 174n210, 251

universal salvific will, 53, 95, 250, 275, 304–5, 307–8, 320, 323. *See also* Anonymous Christianity

Urdanoz, Teofilo, 244

Valentinian II (emperor), 63–64. *See also* Ambrose

Valladares, Marcos de, 238, 239n133

Vatican II: *Ad Gentes*, 322–23; *Dignitatis Humanae*, 317–18; introduction, 315–17; *Lumen Gentium*, 280, 319–22; *Nostra Aetate*, 318–19; *Sacrosanctum Concilium*, 302, 324

Vega, Andrés, 207, 233n118, 238, 242

Vincent Victor, 92–93

virtue: differentiation in eternal destinies and, 50; insufficiency for salvation, 71, 83, 89, 274

Vitoria, Francisco de: invincible ignorance, analysis in *De Indis*, 203–7; School of Salamanca and, 201–2; *Summa sacramentorum Ecclesiae*, 204

Vives, Josep, 19

votum, 222n86, 240–41, 271, 293, 295. *See also* desire

water, baptism of. *See* baptism; baptism, necessity of; baptism, precursors of; *fluminis, flaminis, sanguinis;* rite of baptism

Watkins, Eric, 257

Waugh, Evelyn, 288–89

will, free, 48, 52, 220, 223, 250, 268, 304. *See also* freedom; will, human

will, God's: antecedent and consequent will, 105, 304; Incarnation and, 165;

natural religion and, 255. *See also* universal salvific will

will, human: defect of, 84; desire and, 96, 179; in Pelagianism, 86; power and limits, 80; to receive baptism or confess Christ, 84. *See also* will, free

William of Champeaux, 131

William of Ockham: Ockhamist ethics, 187, 230, 258; Ockhamist influence on paradoxical treatment of baptism of desire, 298; parallel with Kant's moral approach, 230–31

Williams, George, 114–15

Xavier, Francis, 198–201, 353, 354

Yates, Arthur, 154–55

Yong, Peter, 257

Zuijdwegt, Geertjan, 297

Baptism of Desire and Christian Salvation was designed
in Adobe Caslon and composed by Reflective Book
Design of Durham, North Carolina.